# Human-Machine Interface

**Scrivener Publishing**
100 Cummings Center, Suite 541J
Beverly, MA 01915-6106

*Publishers at Scrivener*
Martin Scrivener (martin@scrivenerpublishing.com)
Phillip Carmical (pcarmical@scrivenerpublishing.com)

# Human-Machine Interface

## Making Healthcare Digital

Edited by

### Rishabha Malviya
*Department of Pharmacy, School of Medical and Allied Sciences,
Galgotias University, Noida, India*

### Sonali Sundram
*Department of Pharmacy, School of Medical and Allied Sciences,
Galgotias University, Noida, India*

### Bhupendra Prajapati
*Department of Pharmaceutics, Shree S.K.Patel College of Pharmaceutical
Education and Research, Ganpat University, Gujarat, India*

and

### Sudarshan Kumar Singh
*Department of Pharmaceutical Science, Chiang Mai University,
Chiang Mai, Thailand*

Scrivener
Publishing

**Wiley Global Headquarters**

111 River Street, Hoboken, NJ 07030, USA

For details of our global editorial offices, customer services, and more information about Wiley products visit us at www.wiley.com.

*Library of Congress Cataloging-in-Publication Data*

ISBN 978-1-394-19991-4

Cover image: Pixabay.Com
Cover design by Russell Richardson

Set in size of 11pt and Minion Pro by Manila Typesetting Company, Makati, Philippines

Printed in the USA

10  9  8  7  6  5  4  3  2  1

# Dedication

*This book is dedicated to all those wonderful readers who are working in healthcare and put their effort into improved patient care.*

# Contents

**8  Human-Machine Interaction in Leveraging the Concept**
**of Telemedicine**                                            **211**
*Dipa K. Israni and Nandita S. Chawla*

# Foreword

It gives me immense pleasure to write the foreword for this book edited by Dr. Rishabha Malviya. Dr. Malviya is a highly dedicated and enthusiastic individual who works tirelessly to achieve his goals. His commitment to his work is unparalleled, and he is truly one of the most exceptional people I have had the pleasure of meeting.

As for the book's topic, Human-Machine Interface (HMI) is a hot trend in the medical field. Developers are always exploring ways to enhance the technologies that play a crucial role in daily life. In the context of a hospital, HMI holds immense significance as it enables devices to function better and enhance the experience of both healthcare professionals and patients. The implementation of HMI in a clinical setup offers a range of advantages. The development of dynamic human-machine interfaces and user interfaces has significantly benefited the healthcare sector. As new and innovative techniques for patient care emerge, HMI will continue to evolve, offering even more benefits for healthcare professionals and patients alike.

As a comprehensive resource, this book empowers readers to utilize their skills and expertise to advance healthcare through HMI. The book delves into a variety of HMI tools and related strategies that can be used to evaluate, design, regulate, and upgrade healthcare delivery systems and processes. Finally, it offers a comprehensive overview of the state-of-the-art applications of computational intelligence in the healthcare sector, providing insights into how these technologies can be utilized to improve patient care and outcomes. I fully believe that this book will be a helpful reference for healthcare professionals, academicians, students, and computer engineers who work on, or want to learn about, medical systems.

**Mr. Dhruv Galgotia**
*CEO, Galgotias University, Greater Noida, India*

# Preface

With increasing healthcare expenditures and greater demand for afford-able, user-friendly medical devices, Human-Machine Interface (HMI) has emerged as an essential trend in product development. HMI systems offer the controls necessary for a user to operate a device or instrument. When done correctly, they facilitate simple, dependable accessibility and stream-line technological operations. HMI systems are vital in the medical sector and can accelerate recovery, improve clinical monitoring, and even save lives.

Most medical procedures are improved by HMI systems, from calling an ambulance to ensuring that a patient receives adequate treatment. This book describes biomedical technologies in the context of advanced HMI, with a focus on direct brain-computer connection. This book describes several HMI tools and related techniques for analyzing, creating, con-trolling, and upgrading healthcare delivery systems, and provides details regarding how advancements in technology, particularly HMI, ensure eth-ical and fair use in patient care.

Written by renowned authors from various regions, this book starts an introduction to basics of the human-machine interface and moves on to a second chapter that deals with how HMI can improve healthcare prac-tices. A third chapter explains the connection between patient safety and security using HMI, and a fourth discusses how HMI improves the qual-ity of patient care. Chapter 5 explores the most advanced application of the technology in the form of robotics for healthcare, while the sixth and seventh chapters investigate the latest research in the development of med-ical devices that use HMI. Chapter 8 provides current information about the robust technology framework that enables telemedicine. Chapter 9 discusses the hot topic, the "environment-friendly hospital." This chapter gives a better understanding of how to improve the environment of hospi-tals and therefore make future healthcare places and spaces more respon-sive to patient needs.

The second half of the book explores and investigates how the most recent advancement of this technology can improve patient care. Chapter 10 explains HMI's emergence as a highly successful means of treating mental health issues, depression, Alzheimer's disease, dementia, and paralysis by repairing human cognitive or sensory-motor functions. The next chapter deals with the privacy of patients and the security of their information, specifically with the adoption of electronic records in the healthcare industry, while Chapter 12 explores the latest progress made in combating COVID-19 with advanced medical devices. Chapter 13 outlines how pharmaceutical manufacturing has entered a new level of productivity and quality assurance thanks to HMI. The next chapter discusses how the brain-computer interface is used for communication, while Chapter 15 focuses on important regulatory perspectives about the implementation of HMI. The book concludes with two chapters that address record and supply chain management.

Potential readers of the book include practitioners and researchers interested in applying the ideas of human-computer interaction. Our thanks go to all the authors for their great contributions to this book's success. We also want to express our regards to the prestigious Wiley and Scrivener Publishing for their continuous kind support and guidance.

**Editors**
August 2023

# Acknowledgement

Firstly, we would like to express our gratitude toward the superpower that enables us to complete this work.

We are also grateful for our friends who always encourage and motivate us to start this work. A special word of gratitude to the management of Galgotias University, who believe in us and give us the opportunity so we can serve our nation through our education.

We are eternally grateful to our families for their continuous support and encouragement that made it possible to complete this task. They all kept us going beyond all the ups and downs.

Many thanks to all contributors, without their participation, this task cannot be completed. At last, we would like to thank, our publisher whose constant support and guidance assisted us in making the best possible book.

# Part I

# ADVANCED PATIENT CARE WITH HMI

# Introduction to Human-Machine Interface

Shama Mujawar[1]*, Aarohi Deshpande[1], Aarohi Gherkar[1],
Samson Eugin Simon[2] and Bhupendra Prajapati[3]

*[1]MIT School of Bioengineering Sciences and Research, MIT-Art,
Design and Technology University, Loni Kalbhor, Pune, India
[2]Department of Hematology, University of Tennessee Health Science Centre,
Memphis, Tennessee, USA
[3]Department of Pharmaceutics and Pharmaceutical Technology Shree S.K.,
Patel College of Pharmaceutical Education and Research, Ganpat University,
Gujarat, India*

## Abstract

Human-machine interface or HMI is quite omnipresent today due to its innumerable advantages in various fields from basic everyday vending machines to massive and complex industrial operations. Its only goal is to make machines more user-friendly and automatic so that they may be operated with a single-button press as opposed to having it done manually. It is incredibly helpful in some of the most significant healthcare and life sciences areas by allowing lucid and coherent communication between a human and a machine. By providing efficient patient monitoring systems and keeping track of some of the crucial factors like blood pressure, oxygen levels, ECG monitors, etc. They can aid in speeding up the recovery of patients. Another regular execution of HMI in medical systems is the display monitors in hospitals, interfaces of medical equipment, touch screen devices, etc. portraying the accurate levels of a patient's daily health status. One of the main advantages of HMI is its potential to bridge the communication gaps even when physicians could not treat patients during pandemics like COVID. It has provided us with systems that can interconnect monitors in hospitals, which feed into a single or wide range of computers to consistently be updated about a patient's doses, medicine timings, treatment plan, etc. The capability of software or hardware to be able to transmit appropriate information to an end user in an uncomplicated way is what makes HMI more personalized and handier to the entire population.

*Corresponding author*: shamamujawar@gmail.com; ORCID ID: 0000-0003-3828-4662

Rishabha Malviya, Sonali Sundram, Bhupendra Prajapati and Sudarshan Kumar Singh (eds.)
Human-Machine Interface: Making Healthcare Digital, (3–24) © 2024 Scrivener Publishing LLC

In this chapter, we have introduced HMI along with its origins and history and highlighted some of its most significant uses in various industries. Applications from areas, such as medicine, manufacturing, automation and processing, biomedical engineering, robotic surgery, etc., have also been highlighted, illuminating the function that HMIs and AI play and demonstrate how they have been a consistent support in a multitude of fields.

*Keywords*: Human-machine interface, Covid-19, SCADA, healthcare, biomedical

## 1.1   Introduction

Man has long desired a more transparent and cordial relationship with machines. In the beginning, was the push button, and with the push button were the lights and the switches. After that, hardwired gadgets turned into electronic panels, and the integrated circuit came into existence. The advancement in electronics has paved the way for operators to communicate with machines seamlessly, be it to monitor the machine data or send the data to operate the machines. From push buttons to PCs, text-based to graphical, CRT to LCD, the shape and role of what has come to be called "visualization" has changed dramatically over a few short years. Human-machine interface also sometimes referred to computer–human interface, man–machine interface, or human–computer interface [1], from an industrialist's perspective can be defined as an "eye" through which an operator views and controls the machine or a whole plant's worth of machinery or equipment. It is a part of the supervisory control and data acquisition (SCADA) system. SCADA is a generic term for any computerized system that can acquire data, process it, and apply operational controls over great distances, such as a pipeline system or a power transmission and distribution network [2]. HMIs are designed for better usability by specific users to achieve their specific goals. The design of an HMI depends on the application for which it has to be used [2]. It is and rather should be customized according to the operators of certain management that use interfaces to control their systems (Table 1.1).

A typical HMI consists of two components: hardware and software components. The hardware part of HMI has a processor (can be 16- or 32-bit), data storage, an input, and display unit, a membrane switch (works to open and close the electronic circuit), a rubber keypad, several types of pushbuttons (illuminated, double, door opening/closing) and switches, such as emergency stop, keylock, and ID switches, lever switches, illuminated

**Table 1.1** HMI and SCADA.

| HMI | SCADA |
|---|---|
| 1. Human-machine interface<br>2. Is the hardware and software through which operators can monitor and control equipment in an industrial environment<br>3. Includes touchscreen, buttons, etc. | 1. Supervisory control and data acquisition<br>2. Used to monitor and control on a larger scale such as an industrial plant, oil and gas pipelines, electrical substations, etc.<br>3. Include several other systems (PLCs, RTUs, sensors, and HMI) |

selector switches, universal switches, etc. [3–5]. The HMI software has two main types: supervisory level and machine level. The supervisory level is more commonly used for control room environments, whereas the machine level uses multiple machine-level devices embedded within the production facility [6]. Another major component that works with HMIs is the PLCs or programmable logic controllers. The main purpose of using these is to monitor and control processes and automate systems. In order to manage any task that may be readily carried out once understood by the user, the HMI systems feature a graphical interface that consists of a variety of images, buttons, clicks, videos, gifs, and animations [7]. These interfaces, which are built into large machineries like factories, multinational corporations, and industries, make it convenient to operate equipment on a daily basis without having to pay attention to them constantly. They also allow users to communicate instructions via the PLC (for example, Touchscreen). In addition to sending out orders, they also collect and transmit feedback data from the PLC which is displayed on the screen [8].

Some of the most desirable advantages provided by HMIs include the conversion of hardware into software and the facilitation of human-machine interaction. To begin with, HMI increases User Satisfaction. Any industry (manufacturing, automotive, processing, etc.) that deals with the exchange of information between a human and a machine can benefit from having an HMI because it makes systems simpler and easier to understand, making them much easier to use and ramping up user satisfaction with the tasks they are given to complete. It also makes operations easier by digitizing several functions that can be used to track, control, and assist other systems. Second of all, HMIs are customizable. Every industry has very different needs and priorities in terms of process control and monitoring.

HMIs can represent different equipment shapes and functions which differ from industry to industry. For example, a manufacturing plant may have huge vessels, such as bioreactors, whereas a packaging plant may be more compact with robotic assembly lines. Taking into consideration these differences, an HMI can be customized to suit the needs. Third, HMIs are convenient and safe. With HMIs, one does not need to go to the equipment to start or stop them. It can be controlled remotely. This makes it convenient and safe for the operators. For example, consider a pump in a plant that is located in a hazardous area such as a crude oil refinery, which must be operated and troubleshooted remotely. HMI can provide the necessary functions. Lastly, HMIs are cost effective. By eliminating a lot of the manual work (documentation and keeping a track record) done in various industries, HMIs reduce the amount of manual intervention that is required to analyze and store information, especially in a batch process. This is beneficial to a firm financially as it helps reduce labor costs by automating the systems that do not require any external resources to intercede in their processes. Since the information is stored on a cloud, the storage cost is reduced and promotes a paper-free environment.

HMIs are ubiquitous in today's era. They can be found in almost every industry, including food processing, pharmaceutical industry, medical industry, automobile industry, Household applications, Smart technology, etc. This chapter has discussed some of the applications of HMI in various industries, including pharmaceutical, in brief, and also the potential of HMI lying in the biological field.

## 1.2   Types of HMI

HMIs can be broadly categorized into three basic types: the pushbutton replacer, the data handler, and the overseer [9].

### 1.2.1   The Pushbutton Replacer

The main purpose of the pushbutton replacer is to act as a control function for switches, ON/OFF buttons, LEDs, or any other mechanical device in the overall architecture. This has reduced manufacturing functions by combining all the different tasks for each button into a central spot. The visual representation of all these devices is displayed on the screen, which also performs the same function, making the integration of the devices more likely.

### 1.2.2   The Data Handler

This type of HMI is better suited for applications that require constant feedback from the system as well as monitoring. It involves functions such as recipes, data training, data logging, and alarm handling/logging. These are often equipped with large memories.

### 1.2.3   The Overseer

This type of HMI is involved in and highly beneficial for applications concerning SCADA and/or manufacturing execution system (MES). MES is dynamic software that is used to track, monitor, and document the manufacturing process of any good right from its raw material to the final product [10]. It provides data in real-time, something that majorly differentiates it from an ERP or Enterprise resource planning, which generates a generic report over a long period [11]. The overseer has several ethernet ports and usually requires a window for its operation.

## 1.3   Transformation of HMI

We consider HMIs as a system that facilitates simpler communication between machines and people. Up until now, the operator had to continuously monitor the process and rely on push buttons or specific commands for each action. However, this has drastically altered as a result of technical improvements, increased networking, and bandwidth, providing it an advantage in the modern era [12]. HMI was referred to as man–machine interface (MMI) in view of the fact that it had very confined boundaries for development in processing capabilities for machines, complex processes, and the inability of machines to understand operations and sophisticated applications of MMI in various fields. The HMIs that were being used in the earlier times can be termed as a 'first generation HMI'. The first-generation HMIs came into existence due to the appropriate use of electricity for signaling purposes [13]. The use of the human-machine interface was initiated with dial panels, wired buttons, alphanumeric operators, operator terminals, and other basic components that a computer consists of. Now the prime drawback of these systems was figured out to be the importance of humans looking over every process carried out in these systems. They were not developed to be intelligent enough for administering the whole process; operators had to be present for any machine breakdowns, starting, and terminating these processes which became more subjective to human errors.

Companies went into loss as a result of the laborers' miscalculations that were not fixed in time [13]. The lack of knowledge that HMIs could be used on a wide scale for carrying out a number of processes is what was pulling back machines from communicating with humans to solve bigger problems. As these MMIs were a basic fix to controlling other machines, only basic operations were carried out which used to provide a basic interface for those operations, which users could visualize by screens [14]. This provoked the need for better interfacing systems that can monitor a range of other systems connected to it and provide a general overview of processes existing in machines.

Times started to change when buttons were substituted by electronic terminals was the word given by 'Marco H. Wishart' (business manager at Rockwell automation) due to its cost-effectiveness [14]. Not only did bandwidth and networking play a big role but also connecting and integrating the internet to ethernet caused a major shift in how HMI's were being used [13]. Internet connections made the use of mobile phones, computers, and laptops much more easier and entertaining which created opportunities for mass-scale visualization techniques to be implemented for better usage of available machines. This widens the scope for screening and visualization in machines that could be controlled by humans who did not necessarily have to be in the same area. Depending on the type of operation we wish to conduct, visualization platforms can be customized which talks about the up-scaling of machines and their appropriate usage.

The recasting of HMI set in when systems using older versions of microprocessors and control systems slowed down as new technological advances emerged such as inbuilt networks, better speed of operation, enhanced microprocessor optimization, and rational use of computing. One main reason for the late development of HMI can be the level of complexity of systems it had to handle back then which was near to nothing fancy compared to what we control under machines now [13]. HMI's these days have been constructed in a way that they are able to withstand any kind of abnormalities during their usage. Resistance towards high temperatures, high pressures, vapor, pH levels, etc. is making machines and displaying interfaces more advanced according to the activities performed in them. Reading and monitoring processes inside a machine became easier with sensors, buttons, and easy-to-use touchscreens integrated onto machine surfaces. Alarm sensing and threat monitoring became simplified just by viewing information displayed on the interfaces thereby reducing unnecessary damage to heavy equipment and machinery. Specialized machines are designed to be tolerant towards hazardous chemicals that are used in pharmaceutical or large chemical factories.

Furthermore, Industrial HMI's have become massive considering that HMI's can keep surveillance of the control systems according to the environment, and command specifications and drive the whole process by themselves upon understanding any crisis.

Capacitive and multi-touch-resistant screens enabled workers to utilize interactive tools in touchscreens using various icons, 3D touches, and logic controllers [15]. Application and website interfaces are a more live example of how a man can develop nothing without them. We collect, store, sort, analyze, integrate, interrelate, and conclude all kinds of data from the internet on a daily basis. It is an example of how we depend on the information we see on the interface of these systems to give a final reading on our part. There are a number of ways to spreading information on a huge scale; the Internet being the prime source, we rely on data available here which would've only been possible due to interfacing and the advancement of being able to share data.

Majority of HMI's today are touch screen devices, colorful display systems, and user-friendly interfaces which can be smoothly operated by humans which is another milestone achieved by drastically improving technology. This increased support of advancements in all fields has led to the various applications of HMI in almost every field which was not a privilege we had in the past due to lack of knowledge and advancements. The foremost reason for such wide-scale dependency on human-machine interfaces is seen even more with the COVID-19 pandemic where humans couldn't help but rely on technology for a number of reasons. More emphasis on the mentioned topic is done below.

## 1.4    Importance and COVID Relevance With HMI

Since the COVID-19 pandemic has left a significant mark on the whole world, correlating dependency on smartphones, tablets, computers, or any other gadgets has shot up exceedingly. Interfaces and machine dependency were one of the ways in which information about COVID and other related news was spread out on a larger scale for awareness purposes. Official websites and applications used these HMI to reach out to people for awareness, donations, funds, campaigns, etc. which played a major role in combating the pandemic. HMIs helped not only in one country but on a global scale which majorly focused on networking, and connections and helped hospitals, doctors, and the common man to stay in touch with the latest and updated news.

Following this period, not only companies but people in every sector felt the need for better interfacing tools in their professional lives [15]. People all around the world found touchscreens more appealing to work with on a daily basis, which consisted of a wide number of features such as easy to maintain and use, touch resolution, multi-touch resistivity, accessibility, faster response time, high display resolution (4K-Ultra HD), interactive, durability, the ease with which they can be designed (depending on the application whether it has to be vertical on a wall or flat on a table for planning designs or similar work), continuity to be evolved, etc. Digi-Key enables the showcase of all the information stored and control mechanisms in a single area. By doing this, the danger of subjecting the user to possibly hazardous cultures and conditions involving nanobots, handling equipment, and organic and chemical threats are diminished. The potential to showcase precise information about errors has also been incorporated. The HMI can identify the interruption; pinpoint its exact coordinates, offering comprehensive instructions on how to fix it instead of going to have to rely on the markers to notify the user of a breakdown.

Due to these capabilities, touchscreens being a main spot for interfacing activities, started to come into use more often than before.

During the pandemic, medical attention was of utmost importance. Medicine was in great demand for all countries and not being able to communicate physically stood out to be a problem bigger than expected during Covid times. HMIs have contributed to combating this pandemic across the whole world substantially. Connecting doctors across seas for medical assistance would've never been unattainable without networking and the capacity of HMI to provide persistent support throughout the two most crucial years. Treating patients in such a huge number physically was impractical but HMIs have helped a ton in connecting people in need to doctors and hospitals. Hospitals were at full capacity after a point and HMI gave us a solution of being able to treat ourselves at home, quarantined, resulting in safer and better outcomes for patients. There is a need to design HMIs in a way that they can smoothly run with medical kits, personal protective equipment (PPEs), biohazard suits, gloves, anti-contamination gear, etc. [15]. HMI needs to be redesigned with COVID-19 in mind so that doctors may use it to monitor patients who are infected with the virus. HMIs are currently challenging to manufacture and not adequately accustomed to the huge population. It is possible that there's a need for an HMI featuring a more adaptive design that can be instantly constructed in bulk to fulfill existing and anticipated requirements given the growing manufacturing of non-invasive ventilation and Emergency department beds by several suppliers, including Ford, Motors, Philips, etc. [15].

Furthermore, a useful example of HMI is the recently installed food ordering systems in restaurants. A contact-free, safer, and precautionary measure taken after these tough times involves ordering food through apps and placing it on sanitized systems in the restaurant with no contact whatsoever with staff present there. This also reduced the overall workforce that used to work in the restaurant making it more hygienic for people.

Another aspect of HMI interconnecting with humans is the usage of various platforms for education. The education domain has vastly gotten a hold of teaching through online mode all over the world in the past two years. Platforms that we all often used for educational purposes show how human-machine interfaces are gradually encroaching on various industries. Instead, the continued usage of online tools for purposes such as office meetings, and family gatherings also shows how significantly HMIs have become popular. The ease with which online tuitions, meetings, connecting people, and medical practices were conducted shows another milestone man might've been able to achieve with the help of HMI's.

## 1.5  Applications

HMIs are widely used in several fields including biological, industrial, manufacturing, processing, and automotive. We have listed down a handful of important applications of HMI in various sectors of life (Figure 1.1).

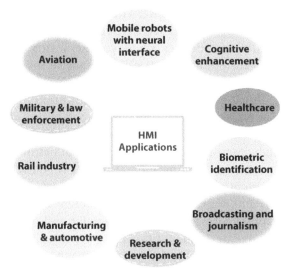

**Figure 1.1** Applications of HMI in different industries.

## 1.5.1   Biological Applications

### 1.5.1.1   HMI Signal Detection and Procurement Method

Using various signal harvesting techniques, the various physiological signals in the HMI technology are recorded. These primarily fall under the categories of invasive, semi-invasive, and non-invasive procedures. Invasive approaches use a medical procedure termed a craniotomy to install electrodes deep within the brain and record signals from the cerebral cortex region of the brain. The implants are placed using a semi-invasive method and located just outside the brain's gray matter, but underneath the cranium membrane. Because the mucoperiosteal flap does not need to be mirrored from its position and does not cut off the blood supply to tissues, less invasive techniques allow for quick recovery and minimally painful surgery [16]. By performing specific tasks, such as target-oriented motions of the limbs/extremities, ECoG can be employed to survey brain functioning and associated brain conditions. Particularly in patients with chronic epilepsy disorders, ECoG plays a crucial role in the assessment of neurophysiological illness [16].

### 1.5.1.2   Healthcare and Rehabilitation

HMI has been the main spot playing an important role in different domains, such as neurosurgery, medical diagnosis, rehabilitation, neurosciences, neuroimaging, etc. The HMI-based mobile healthcare devices with efficient and accurate results are extensively implemented for medical diagnostics whenever measuring hyperglycemia, heart rate, hypertension, as well as other extensive diseases related to the well-being of a patient [16]. One such example of HMI Technology used to enable direct brain-computer communication for severely disabled people is discussed in [17]. The brain–computer interface (BCI) establishes a direct connection to pathways between the brain and the external world, by not relying on the usual output pathways of the central nervous system, such as peripheral nerves or muscles [17]. This creates a great potential to help individuals with speech impairment in communication and augmentative environmental control, disabilities involving the spinal cord by Neural Prosthetics and making new customized sources of entertainment through virtual reality and advanced control systems [17].

### 1.5.1.3   Magnetoencephalography

It is a non-invasive technique wherein mechanical signals are recorded from the inference of electrical waves emerging from the brain's activity during different events brain activity mapping is used to research numerous diseases, including schizophrenia, early-onset dementia, and Parkinson's diseases, alcoholism, and developmental problems, psychosis, as well as language and memory processes and sensory processing [16].

### 1.5.1.4   Flexible Hybrid Electronics (FHE)

An FHE is an electronic device that can be stretched and is sufficiently flexible to be worn [18]. It is a cohesive system with numerous functional chip components, compliant membranes, and a combination of soft functional materials that makes it possible. HMIs have recently been employed in non-invasive, extremely sensitive wearable FHBs to enable the collection of physiological data (EMG, EOG, and EEG) for the treatment of patients [18].

### 1.5.1.5   Robotic-Assisted Surgeries

Robot-assisted surgeries are the new trend as more and more hospitals are turning toward them to provide more sophisticated treatments with minimum risk of complications. It provides surgeons with an enhanced view of the real-time, high-resolution, magnified images with 3D capabilities. HMI's makes it possible by acting as a channel allowing the flow of information between the user and the device. The type of HMI, such as force sensing/reflecting devices, tactile instruments, graphical HMI with or without virtual reality facilities, and natural language interfaces, depends on the system's input parameters [19–21]. For instance, the HMI for the 2008-proposed telerobotic surgery system neuroArm makes use of two force-feedback hand controllers based on visual data from a stereoscopic viewing device and two liquid crystal displays [21]. FAce MOUSe is another example of an HMI illustration that was introduced in 2003 for managing the location of the laparoscope and enabling endoscopic surgeons to conduct solo operations [21]. A telerobotic surgical system's HMI is in charge of receiving system commands and disseminating optical, acoustic, and haptic input. The requirements for performance, attractiveness, and led screens have shaped the creation of the neuroArm GUI. Webcam feeds have been given the highest priority based on their frequency of utilization and usefulness in order to successfully deliver the surgeon all of the vital visual data [21]. A terminal that the human operator uses to operate, oversees, and gathers data from a robotics system can also be utilized to develop the system. An arm pole, pendant interface, spin key, or visual display unit can serve as this type of human-machine interface [22].

### 1.5.1.6   *Flexible Microstructural Pressure Sensors*

Flexible microstructural pressure sensors (FMPSs), in particular, have drawn a lot of interest due to their adjustable shape, compact size, and excellent sensitivity. For FMPSs to enhance sensitivity and response time, microstructures are crucial. The FMPSs offer excellent application opportunities in the sectors of medicine, social connection, electronic equipment, etc. in depth a variety of microstructures (such as wave, pillar, and pyramid shapes) that have been intricately constructed to drastically improve the sensing capability of FMPSs has been introduced recently [23].

### 1.5.1.7   *Biomedical Applications*

The HMI for telemonitoring exoskeleton technology is created to accommodate crisis situations and those with different medical impairments and related illnesses to stand up, walk, move around, and carry out daily specific anatomical movements. They have been seen to assist in military activities, such as disaster management. With the aid of these mobile robots and exoskeleton systems, a person with a physical impairment or afflicted by any congenital defect can still have their operating potential boosted. Exoskeletons and robotic systems with GUI control systems are employed expressly to raise a patient's safety standards by helping and supporting them in possible hazards like explosive device tracking and destruction chores to improve the load-carrying capacity. It minimizes the level of discomfort in the individual carrying the equipment [24].

With the use of sophisticated human-machine interface (HMI) technologies, adaptation hypotheses and methods can be investigated in great depth. The HMI proposed solution consists of:

1. Interface for medical equipment
2. Controls for vital equipment
3. Membrane keypads for infrastructure and medical gear
4. Complete sealed panels [22]

### 1.5.1.8   CB-HMI

Highly skilled human-machine interfaces that have the ability to perceive and understand biological signals are indeed necessary. With this in mind, we created a multimodal cryptographic biohuman–machine interface (CB-HMI) that converts human touch-based inputs into encrypted biological processes, biomechanical, and biometric parameters. To simultaneously measure the user's heart rate, blood oxygen level, and fingerprint minute pattern, CB-HMI has a hardware sensor and related algorithms. By modernizing the typical virtual objects with the CB-HMI, interactive solutions for medication usage and driving safety were created. The primary objective of CB-HMI through several levels of bio perception was to achieve profound awareness of patients' behavioral and physiological states and demands. Electrochemical sensors coated with hydrogel were employed to achieve the same [24]. Nowadays, owing to broad networking and the availability of data related to HMI, psychological investigations on the brain and other essential organs are possible [22] which helps us understand the complexity of the human body and untangle the problems associated with them.

### 1.5.1.9   HMI in Medical Devices

With the introduction of newer, more sophisticated HMI-embedded medical equipment; disease diagnosis has become considerably quicker and more effective. The accurate and understandable representation of medical information (such as MRI or X-ray data) on medical diagnostic equipment has also improved treatments (www.eao.com). To administer a shock to individuals who are experiencing cardiac arrest, a medical instrument called an automated external defibrillator (AED) is an example. The voice instructions provided by the HMI in this device are intended to enable anyone utilizing it to revive the patient. It essentially functions as a portable, lightweight version of the clinical defibrillators used in hospitals to administer an electrical shock. The electrocardiogram (ECG) patches used in the majority of AEDs evaluate the cardiac rhythm by being applied to specific body parts [25]. It determines whether or not a shock is necessary based on that.

## 1.5.2   Industrial Applications

HMIs are employed by line service providers, executives, and directors across the business for integrating massive models into informative information. HMIs are being used, for instance, to inspect if the equipment is functioning effectively. Virtually actual data about tank levels, pressures and seismic assessments, motors and valve performance, and other aspects are given significant context by simple visual displays. Nevertheless, supervisors and executives can now accomplish much more than supervise procedures thanks to the increased features of today's HMIs [26].

### 1.5.2.1    Metal Industries

An HMI may make it simple to regulate the speed and technique of slicing and bending metal in the fabrication of metals. Xie *et al.,* 2021 have employed HMI and DNN to regulate the mechanical qualities of steel online and to direct the manufacturing of steel plates with certain mechanical properties.

### 1.5.2.2    Video Game Industry

This includes several remote rendering applications. It refers to the process of rendering a specific industrial GUI on a robust 3D accelerated server machine, capturing, and encrypting the displayed program to a video, and simultaneously broadcasting the finished product to a receiving consumer. The client could be a computing device, a touchpad system installed on a device, a computer in a command center, or even a cell phone. The client's work is limited to showing an encrypted live stream and obtaining data from the user (such as touch signals) in order to feed it again to the processing servers [27]. Due to the availability of games that were remotely created on the internet, the video lives telecasting-based approach has gradually received much interest. A variety of for-profit internet gaming organizations are presently offering their products relying upon remote rendering systems [27].

### 1.5.2.3    Aerospace and Defense

In the military and aerospace fields, where technologies like geographic information systems/topographic maps, cross-domain guard information security systems, and deployed methodologies for defense and aerospace applications are often used, human-machine interface (HMI) plays a critical role. Through these technologies, the technical procedures and machines used to serve the ideal representatives are best defined [22].

### 1.5.2.4    Water Purification Plant HMI Based on Multi-Agent Systems (MAS) [28]

Multi-agent systems are structures consisting of several autonomous agents, each focusing on solving a specific task by considering multiple inputs [29]. These have a tremendous potential to solve complex problems by breaking them into smaller separate errands. It is not only used in computer networks but also in various modeling complex systems and smart grids [29]. One such example has been proposed in [29] that is designed to supervise the filtration stage of a water purification plant. The main purpose of using this type of advanced HMI was to make a more collaborative system that can work with multiple agents to overcome the projection and integration problems faced by distributed architectures. The design for this system in a water treatment plant was simulated, validated, and implemented by using the unified modeling language (UML) and Petri nets (PN) [28].

### 1.5.2.5    Virtual and Haptic Interfaces

The touch-sensitive GUI is used to manage operations in the haptic interface (human engagement with digital reality). To regulate and balance primary and secondary driving operations effectively, the auditory interaction offers a variety of voice entries using natural language processing (NLP) voice recognition software. The visual interface gives the driver reviews via virtual server projections or monitor shows, basically telling them to offer supplementary information to the automobile monitoring system [29].

### 1.5.2.6    Space Crafts

One of the most crucial components of every space trip is the crew seating arrangement in the spacecraft. The seating arrangement in spacecraft is a perfect illustration of the majority of contemporary HMI systems, which show the crew's technical and clinical trends in both regular and crises. One of the main concerns of the HMI systems in space applications is for the pilot to be able to access the control and display panels despite rotational and linear accelerations of the seats and roller, pitching, and vertical movements. There are two other essential components to the HMI-based automatic monitoring technologies used in spacecraft. Initially, it should be simple to operate and free of extraneous information that could confound the crew. Furthermore, there should be no uncertainty as it may cause imprecise navigation. The majority of interactions between operators at the ground control station and the unmanned aircraft vehicles (UAV) are supported by next-generation HMI systems, which carry out all transmission, command, and signal conditioning automatically. The adaptive human interface and interactions offer three-tier processes of detecting, judging, and remodeling for anything from intelligent transportation systems to guidance systems, safety procedures, and mission systems [29].

### 1.5.2.7   Car Wash System

Automatic car washing stations are common in developed countries. It is a structure of several electronic pieces of electronic hardware that deliver car cleaning and maintenance services. They use cleaning supplies, such as water, detergents, several sprayers, scrubbing rollers and brushes, and a dryer system. They promote the more economical use of water and provide a convenient and faster method of maintaining vehicles. HMIs can be beneficial in applications, such as these to further ease the communication between the user and the machine. It can offer customized services such as rinsing, drying a wet vehicle, or cleaning it thoroughly, etc. Mumtaz *et al.* [30] propose an HMI-based automatic car servicing system using the (HMI) weintek 8071IP along with the software easy builder version 6.03 visual monitoring and control.

### 1.5.2.8   Pharmaceutical Processing and Industries

HMIs are frequently utilized in pharmaceutical operations and medication production in the pharmaceutical industry. They are essential to the plant's operation and control procedures. They are mostly utilized in clean room applications for coating tablets, loading or unloading liquids (chemicals), etc., as well as simple viewing of several parameters like temperature, pressure, speed, and quantity of raw materials present in each stage of a bioreactor reaction, etc. [31].

## 1.6   Challenges

Despite the fact that HMIs have numerous advantages and little to no drawbacks, every rose has its thorn. Here are some of the drawbacks of HMI. First off, HMIs might be a security risk. An HMI is fundamentally an IOT device that may be connected to the internet, even though they provide the maximum level of security for a control system. Any gadget with internet access runs the danger of being compromised. If a system is not secured properly with multiple layers of verifications and passwords, there is a possibility of hackers breaking into the system remotely to access confidential information. They also require skilled labor during construction. HMIs require specialized professionals to implement them appropriately within a particular industry because of how complex their architecture and design can become. Poorly designed interfaces can cause errors and have a negative influence on worker safety, product quality, and performance. Third, their initial investment is quite high. Although HMIs can result in significant long-term cost savings, they are still an additional piece of hardware and software that raises the price of system setup.

Last, but not the least, the effectiveness of an HMI is entirely dependent on its design. This includes technical, financial, and communication-oriented factors (www.eao.com). For medical applications, the design process is done taking into consideration the opinions of several physicians, medical professionals, surgeons, and patients as well.

## 1.7   Conclusion and Future Prospects

Due to recent developments in a range of materials, adaptive systems, microelectronics, and modern networks, this topic has advanced significantly over the past ten years. The speed at which HMI has advanced recently raises questions about the impact it has had on several facets of technology. We have gained knowledge about how HMIs were created, as well as how important that progress meant to us since we began integrating HMIs into all of our routine tasks. Even though HMI has had its risks with some of the steps outlined in the parts mentioned before this section in our chapter, artificial intelligence would not revert to developing virtual reality in all spheres of life. Because we are accustomed to staying in our comfort zones, going outside for even a short period might make it seem as though there is nothing else to do or that the willpower to achieve a certain goal has died down. Is HMI a result of our inability to step beyond our comfort zones? Have we created HMI with the intention of making it more pleasant for us to complete tasks without having to look elsewhere? Humans now get a peek of how powerful and valuable technology can be. Future applications for HMI could be in practically any industry, from self-driving automobiles to regular household microwaves. Human-machine interaction (HMI) has greatly facilitated human-machine communication. To heat food in our microwave for 30 seconds, for instance, we do not need to sit down and write a program for those instructions; instead, we may simply hit a button. This study shows how the development of HMI has been revolutionary in practically every aspect of life.

HMI predominantly focuses on the varieties of artificial devices that, as technology is infused into them, might make it easier for people to manage their lives. With the aid of an intuitive HMI, the constant technological developments will serve as the foundation for the creation of new AI systems, which will be presented to us on a silver platter. Since artificial intelligence was responsible for the development of robots, virtual assistants, and chatbots, it is reasonable to assume that AI will soon produce ever more sophisticated robotic engines that will work with and on people. This continuous development will open chances of incorporating HMI into furthermore professions and daily tasks over the years.

By combining historical and present-day data, they offer a variety of fresh opportunities to increase production effectiveness and product quality [32]. Many of these developments might help to pave the way for the emergence of a new era of virtual reality and virtual therapy [33]. Modern machines are living proof that HMI has been successful in enabling straightforward interaction between machines and humans over the years. Despite the fact that technology has brought us much closer together online, it has undoubtedly begun to initiate the end of face-to-face interactions. The question is, will this herald the death of human interaction since we all appear to be wholly dependent on HMI for just about any objective? Or will people still opt to be physically sociable enough to communicate? We have to decide whether to submit to these sophisticated AI systems or create a society where all segments may live in peace.

## References

1. iotWorm, & byiotWorm, Introduction to human-machine interface (HMI) technology, IoT Worm, 2016, July 30, Retrieved November 16, 2022, from https://iotworm.com/introduction-human-machine-interface-hmi-technology/.
2. Human-Machine Interface Design, Human factors in control room design, pp. 51–68, 2017.
3. Admin., What are the components of a human-machine interface?, Nelson Miller, 2016, August 30, Retrieved November 16, 2022, from https://nelson-miller.com/what-are-the-components-of-a-human-machine-interface/.
4. What is HMI: Stone Teshnogies. STONE TFT LCD module touch screen display, 2022, April 9, Retrieved November 16, 2022, from https://www.stoneitech.com/what-is-hmi/#:~:text=HMI%20Interface%20HMI%20interface%20common%20sense&text=2.,%2C%20data%20storage%20unit%2C%20etc.

5. HMI functions, Human-Machine Interfaces (HMI - HMIC - HMIS - HMIA) from EAO, Retrieved November 16, 2022, from https://eao.com/north-america/en_us/products-and-solutions/hmi-components/hmi-functions/.

6. Human-machine interface, Human-Machine Interface - an overview | ScienceDirect Topics, Retrieved November 16, 2022, from https://www.sciencedirect.com/topics/engineering/human-machine-interface.

7. Kirill Yusov CPOCPO in Jelvix with 8+ years in software development, What are human-machine interface systems and how do they work?, Jelvix, 2022, July 5, Retrieved October 17, 2022, from https://jelvix.com/blog/human-machine-interface.

8. Correspondent, HMI software: A primary component in the Industrial Space, The Daily Guardian, 2022, July 19, Retrieved November 18, 2022, from https://thedailyguardian.com/hmi-software-a-primary-component-in-the-industrial-space/.

9. Anaheim Automation - your source for Stepper Motor, brushless DC Motor, DC motor, and planetary gearbox products, Anaheim Automation - Your source for Stepper Motor, Brushless DC Motor, DC Motor, and Planetary Gearbox Products, Retrieved November 16, 2022, from https://www.anaheim-automation.com/.

10. What is an MES (manufacturing execution system)?, SAP insights. SAP, Retrieved November 16, 2022, from https://www.sap.com/insights/what-is-mes-manufacturing-execution-system.html#:~:text=A%20manufacturing%20execution%20system%2C%20or,raw%20materials%20to%20finished%20products.

11. 3 major differences between an MES and ERP system, Pyramid Solutions, 2022, November 14, Retrieved November 16, 2022, from https://pyramidsolutions.com/intelligent-manufacturing/blog-im/3-differences-between-mes-and-erp/.

12. Human-machine interface (HMI) and its importance in industrial automation, ManufacturingTomorrow, Retrieved November 16, 2022, from https://www.manufacturingtomorrow.com/article/2022/01/human-machine-interface-hmi-and-its-importance-in-industrial-automation/18191.

13. Papcun, P., Kajáti, E., Koziorek, J., Human-machine interface in concept of industry 4.0, in: *2018 World Symposium on Digital Intelligence for Systems and Machines (DISA)*, 2018, August, IEEE, pp. 289–296.

14. Human-machine interface (HMI) and its importance in industrial automation, ManufacturingTomorrow, Retrieved November 16, 2022, from https://www.manufacturingtomorrow.com/article/2022/01/human-machine-interface-hmi-and-its-importance-in-industrial-automation/18191.

15. The impact COVID-19 will have on HMIS, Industrial Equipment News, 2020, May 1, Retrieved October 20, 2022, from https://www.ien.com/automation/article/21131160/the-impact-covid19-will-have-on-hmis.

16. Singh, H.P. and Kumar, P., Developments in the human-machine interface technologies and their applications: A review. *J. Med. Eng. Technol.*, 45, 7, 552–573, 2021.

17. Andreoni, G., Parini, S., Maggi, L., Piccini, L., Panfili, G., Torricelli, A., Human-machine interface for healthcare and rehabilitation, in: *Advanced Computational Intelligence Paradigms in Healthcare-2*, pp. 131–150, Springer, Berlin, Heidelberg, 2007.

18. Herbert, R., Kim, J.H., Kim, Y.S., Lee, H.M., Yeo, W.H., Soft material-enabled, flexible hybrid electronics for medicine, healthcare, and human-machine interfaces. *Materials*, 11, 2, 187, 2018.

19. Bennett, P.A., Advances in the design and deployment of human-machine interfaces, in: *Proceedings of First IEEE International Conference on Engineering of Complex Computer Systems*. ICECCS'95, 1995, November, IEEE, pp. 68–69.

20. Tzafestas, S.G., Supervisory and distributed control in automation, in: *Human and Nature Minding Automation*, pp. 83–108, Springer, Dordrecht, 2010.

21. Greer, A.D., Newhook, P.M., Sutherland, G.R., Human-machine interface for robotic surgery and stereotaxy. *IEEE/ASME Trans. Mechatron.*, 3, 13, 355–361, 2008.

22. Theautomization, Human-machine interface example in industry, The Automization, 2020, May 20, Retrieved November 18, 2022, from https://theautomization.com/human-machine-interface-example/.

23. He, F., You, X., Wang, W., Bai, T., Xue, G., Ye, M., Recent progress in flexible microstructural pressure sensors toward human-machine interaction and healthcare applications. *Small Methods*, 5, 3, 2001041, 2021.

24. Lin, S., Zhu, J., Yu, W., Wang, B., Sabet, K.A., Zhao, Y., Emaminejad, S., A touch-based multimodal and cryptographic bio-human-machine interface. *Proc. Natl. Acad. Sci.*, 119, 15, e2201937119, 2022.

25. Clinical Defibrillators and automated external defibrillators (aeds), Xilinx, Retrieved November 16, 2022, from https://www.xilinx.com/applications/medical/clinical-defibrillators-automated-external-defibrillators.html.

26. HMI - the interface between process and operators, AVEVA, Retrieved October 29, 2022, from https://www.aveva.com/en/solutions/operations/hmi/.

27. Perez, P.G., Beer, W., Dorninger, B., Remote rendering of industrial HMI applications, in: *2013 11th IEEE International Conference on Industrial Informatics (INDIN)*, 2013, July, IEEE, pp. 276–281.

28. Mendoza, E., Andramuño, J., Núñez, J., Córdova, L., Human-machine interface (HMI) based on a multi-agent system in a water purification plant. *J. Phys.: Conf. Ser.*, 2090, 1, 012122, 2021, November, IOP Publishing.

29. Dorri, A., Kanhere, S.S., Jurdak, R., Multi-agent systems: A survey. *IEEE Access*, 6, 28573–28593, 2018.

30. Mumtaz, F., Saeed, A., Nabeel, M., Ahmed, S., Autonomous car washing station based on PLC and HMI control, IET Digital Library, 2021, January 1, Retrieved November 16, 2022, from https://digital-library.theiet.org/content/conferences/10.1049/icp.2022.0322.
31. Innovative HMI and visualization systems for pharmaceutical processing, Retrieved November 16, 2022, from https://www.mtl-inst.com/images/uploads/AN9042_Gecma_pharma_process_181016.pdf.
32. HMI - the interface between process and operators, AVEVA, Retrieved October 29, 2022, from https://www.aveva.com/en/solutions/operations/hmi/.
33. Human-machine interface - mechanical sensors, biosensors and beyond, Frontiers, Retrieved October 29, 2022, from https://www.frontiersin.org/research-topics/33664/human-machine-interface—mechanical-sensors-biosensors-and-beyond.

# 2

# Improving Healthcare Practice by Using HMI Interface

Vaibhav Verma[1], Vivek Dave[1]* and Pranay Wal[2]

*1Department of Pharmacy, School of Health Sciences,
Central University of South Bihar, Gaya, India*
*2Department of Pharmacy, Pranveer Singh Institute of Technology, Kanpur,
Uttar Pradesh, India*

## Abstract

Healthcare is the fundamental assurity of people's well-being, and unavailability of medical personnel will have a wide-ranging impact on healthcare. As the population ages, the issues with complex and costly medical care and hospital treatment becomes increasingly obvious. The expenditure of educating doctors is exorbitant, medical talent is unusual, and medical staff funding is minimal. Second, those patients who are unable to communicate with their doctors because of some disability or their body organs not working properly, with the help of this system, this problem can be minimized. This system allows to easily interact with their physicians, healthcare staffs. This system utilizes image processing and machine vision technology as well as a digital camera and software, to create the interface system. HMI refers to human-machine interface, which is the study of people, machine, and their interactions. HMI is the two-way method of sharing information through various sign and actions between the human and the machine. A detailed understanding of the operational and functional requirements is the first step in designing an HMI system for medical diagnostic equipment. The human-machine interface with head control has several applications. This Interface technology is based on the creation of a new miniature system for the discreet monitoring of biological signals utilizing wearable or embedded sensors incorporated in advanced HMI to be employed in the performance of healthcare jobs. The true purpose and application is to enable communication for severely handicapped persons with the hope of expanding the possibilities given by this technology in rehabilitation and healthcare field in the future. This chapter's objective is to discuss in detail about

*Corresponding author*: vivekdave1984@gmail; https://orcid.org/0000-0001-7337-6365

Rishabha Malviya, Sonali Sundram, Bhupendra Prajapati and Sudarshan Kumar Singh (eds.)
Human-Machine Interface: Making Healthcare Digital, (25–58) © 2024 Scrivener Publishing LLC

HMI system, how it works as well as its application and future role in improving healthcare practice.

*Keywords*: Fundamental, human-machine interface (HMI), healthcare, interface, advanced, rehabilitation, application

## 2.1   Background of Human-Machine Interaction

HMI stands for "human-machine interaction," which describes how people and machines interact and communicate [1]. AI-based devices, robotics, computer–human interaction, and robot-human interaction are all subfields of the multidisciplinary field of HMI. HMI is frequently used in the healthcare industry and practices settings to improve productivity, quality, and process security. HMI is a common component of current medical, transportation, and entertainment systems [2].

## 2.2   Introduction

### 2.2.1   Healthcare Practice

The enhancement and strengthening of health through the treatment, diagnosis, rehabilitation or cure and prevention of disease, illness, injury, and other mental and physical disabilities in people is identified as healthcare. Health professionals and allied health workers provide healthcare to the patient. So, as per the above definition, we conclude that healthcare practice is an act of caring for an unhealthy person by well-trained health professionals with the help of mainly medically suited standard technical equipment, chemicals, and biological things [3].

### 2.2.2   Human-Machine Interface System in Healthcare

In the disciplines of medical and health care fields, the interface based on human-machine is extremely unique and broad. Due to their surveillance and comparative functions, medical monitoring gadgets and devices demand much more in this field and give patients health information very accurately and made easy to understand by medical staff along with some more benefits like this device working rapidly and operating part being simple and user friendly. As a result, the human-machine interaction planning, conception, and development and design of the medical monitoring system display is crucial. Overseas medical device innovations are currently

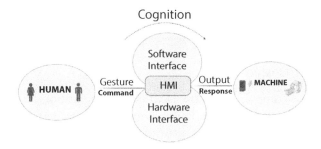

**Figure 2.1** Basic design of HMI.

based on graphical interfaces, whereas domestic innovations are mostly based on following and adopting overseas technology and modeling.

Therefore, when it comes to designing as well as developing home medical devices, comfort and humanization are fundamental aspects of the design that is considered while creating and establishing a harmonious interaction between the users and machines. For a better understanding, the basic design of HMI is illustrated in Figure 2.1.

So from the above lines, we observed that HMI in healthcare means "a phenomenon where the hardware or software are being used by a healthcare professional to communicate with a patient to diagnosis and treat their problems." In further proceedings, we discuss how HMI can be used to help people with major impairments and disabilities, as well as for those who face difficulties during communication. Also, messages and directives can be expressed utilizing electrophysiological occurrences associated with the user's intention. It may also enhance the quality of life for those whose engagement with the outside world is extremely limited [4].

## 2.3    Evolution of HMI Design

### 2.3.1    HMI Design 1.0

In the 1980s, we needed a programmable display unit, or HMI for short, along with some basic programming software to create a graphical user interface for machines and equipment. Before the creation as well as the development of software specifically for HMI screen design, this creating and building required advanced computer knowledge, coding and programming abilities along with a technical skillset. The creation and proper maintenance of HMI required a lot of time and money (we can relate to this stage as 1.0 HMI Design). The volume of labor necessary to produce and sustain HMI screens was decreased by the introduction of HMI design software.

### 2.3.2   HMI Design 2.0

There are dual components to the HMI design application-based software in HMI Design 2.0. These two main components are a graphical one that uses graphics to make the screen display and a functional one for programming screen functions. Screen tags, which are specialized commands, had to be set up for the operational component. Both the design and the operation might still be improved, and some technical knowledge was still needed to configure and customize these screen tags.

### 2.3.3   HMI Design 3.0

The Windows operating system provided a wealth of opportunities in the 1990s. As more companies and businesses began using Windows software, HMI design began to combine and unite the graphical and operational modules, allowing you to program your operations by simply altering the lengths or characteristics of a visual and graphical component. While elements such as placing objects and feature modification continued to remain unchanged for many years and time necessity for HMI design did not decrease, a specialist in HMI design, like tag and label settings, become useless and Screen creation become considerably easier.

### 2.3.4   HMI Design 4.0

Through the elimination of pointless steps and the reuse of previously created resources, HMI design time has recently been significantly decreased with the commencement of a variety of new HMI design approaches and ideas. The design process is made simpler, operators are more effective, and operations are more productive in HMI Design 4.0 [5]. The progression of HMI design through multiple phases is shown in Table 2.1.

## 2.4   Anatomy of Human Brain

The brain is ranked amongst the most advanced, complex, intricate organ in the human body and is composed of about 100 billion neurons divided into distinct sections. Taste, sensation, aroma, auditory, and visual are the five senses which are used by the brain to gather information from the

**Table 2.1** HMI design evolution.

| Phase | HMI design 1.0 | HMI design 2.0 | HMI design 3.0 | HMI design 4.0 |
|---|---|---|---|---|
| Parts | Program | Locate Manually | Place Manually | Automatic |
| Change Screen | Program | Manually Design | Manual Design | Automatic |
| Graphical Design | Program | Basic Graphics | Function with Parts | Pre-configured |
| Operational Design | Program | Function with Tags | Function with parts | Pre-configured |
| Automated Design | Program | Not Supported | Program with Scripts | Without Scripts |

outside world. It gives instructions to the body on how to respond appropriately in various situations. The brain regulates our feelings, perceptions, and reactions to our surroundings through voice, facial gestures, leg motions as well as other conscious and unconscious physical movements. Voice, sensation, motor coordination, and other specific biological activities are carried out by various brain regions. The anatomy of the brain is depicted in Figure 2.2. The brain is divided into 52 distinct sections along with the cerebrum, cerebellum, and brainstem, the brain's three major structural components. Right and left cerebral hemispheres make up the cerebrum. There are four lobes or divisions in each hemisphere: the frontal, parietal, temporal, and occipital lobes. Each of these four lobes controls particular functions. The cerebrum notably regulates touch, hearing, and sight senses as well as acquisition, rational thinking, sensations, memorization, judgment, and speech in the limb. The hindbrain region of the human brain is responsible for balancing the anatomy of humans through mobility, supervision, creating the proper body alignment, and coordinating muscle movements to execute various body movements correctly. The brainstem connects the cerebrum and cerebellum to the spinal cord and is in control of many involuntary motions such as the inhale–exhale process, eye motion, digesting, vomiting, sniffling, wheezing, and coughing, as well as controlling body temperature and heart rate. The brain can quickly

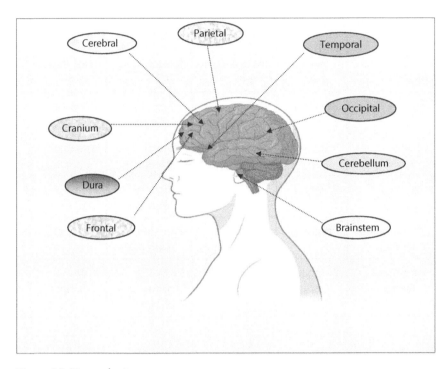

**Figure 2.2** Human brain structure.

increase its level of alertness to process signals with high priority is another crucial function. The brain has the power to shift and modify the connections between neurons and redirect impulses via other neural pathways in the event of any damage or issues. This is commonly referred to as brain or neuroplasticity, one of the important factors in the recovery of brain function. It is interpreted as the ability of the central nervous system (CNS) to adapt to modifications in its structure and operations. Specific brain functions can be restored using various mechanisms, including unmasking, sprouting, and super-sensitivity to denervation. Brain plasticity is understood to be one of the nervous system's fundamental qualities that is crucial in enabling long-lasting functional changes. Neurochemical receptor and neuro-structural changes in various regions of the brain with varying functional properties can all be part of the brain's working mechanism. The brain's neuroplasticity enables various bionic and auxiliary devices, especially sensory substitution tools to adapt to a variety of settings while performing a variety of tasks depending on skilled activities. Tools for sensory substitution are primarily based on how brain plasticity works [6–8].

## 2.5 Signal Associated With Brain

The brain produces various signal types with unique characteristics. HMI enables explicit machine and computer control using the bioelectrical impulses produced by biological events taking place in the body's living cells. There are many different applications for these signals. Evoked signals, spontaneous signals, and hybrid signals are the three fundamental categories of control signals, which are displayed in Figure 2.3 [9].

### 2.5.1 Evoked Signals

Evoked signals (ESs) also termed evoked potential (EPs), are electrical signals emitted by specific components of the nervous system, most notably the brain, in response to an external influence commonly referred to as stimulus. Evoked signals include P300, auditory-visual (hearing) potentials, steady-state (constant mode) evoked potentials, visual event potentials, and steady-state visual event potentials [10]. Approximately 300 milliseconds after the subsequent visual or auditory stimulus, P300 gives the peak amplitude. AVP signals are produced and released in the cortical area after the effect of sound frequencies leads it to generate a potential difference for the same frequency. Visually evoked potentials (VEPs) or

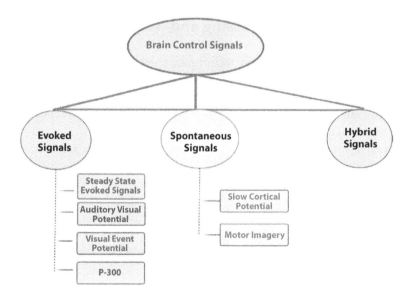

**Figure 2.3** Classification of BCI control signals.

SSVEPs are produced as a result of visual stimuli and are picked up by the cerebral cortex [11].

### 2.5.2   Spontaneous Signals

Voluntarily produced signals by the subject in the absence of any outside stimulus. Slow cortical potential (SCP) and motor imagery (MI) are two significantly diverse types of spontaneous (random) signals [12]. MI results from the subject's motor intentions through the states of motor imagery to produce electroencephalography (EEG) signals in a specific region of the motor cortex [13]. Slow-cortical potentials (SCPs) are electrical signals emanating from the brain that often originated in an activity-related manner for a few seconds and recorded at frequencies below 1 Hz. Between 0.05 and 10 seconds after voltage fluctuations on the cerebral cortical region, SCP appeared [14].

### 2.5.3   Hybrid Signals

To overcome the challenges of utilizing just one type of mental control signal, hybrid signals mix any two or more evoked and spontaneous signal types [15].

## 2.6   HMI Signal Processing and Acquisition Methods

The various signal acquisition techniques used in HMI technology are used to capture the various physiological signals. The signal processing and acquisition mechanism of HMI is shown in Figure 2.4. Invasives, semi-invasives, and non-invasive methodologies are the main categories for these signal acquisition [16].

Invasive methods during a craniotomy, electrodes are inserted deep inside the brain by way of a tiny hole or gap in the skull to capture signals from the cerebral cortex region. In a semi-invasive methodology, the implants are placed just below the skin of the scalp but ultimately outside of the brain's grey matter. Transgingival implant therapy is a highly critical mildly invasive surgery accustomed to placing an implant in the brain tissues [17, 18]. This technique allows for a quick surgical procedure with minimal pain because the mucoperiosteal flap does not need to be reflected from its position and the blood supply to the tissues is not interrupted [19]. Three different electrode electrochemical types— foramen ovale, subdural strip, and stereotactically (precise positioning

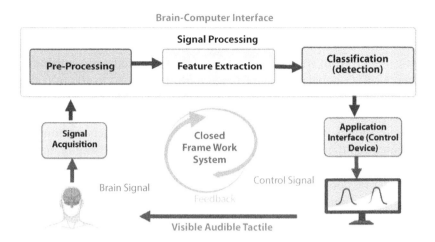

**Figure 2.4** Mechanism of HMI signal processing and acquisition.

in three-dimensional space) implanted depth electrodes—have been inserted into the brain cortex's delicate tissues area of the brain to explore memory disorders. This is yet another non-BCI surgical insertion method that is intrusive. When performing a few specific important tasks, such as a target-specific, goal-oriented movements of the limbs, electrocorticography (ECoG) can be employed to assess brain working and associated brain disorders. Particularly in patients suffering from chronic epilepsy disorders, ECoG plays a noticeable role in the detection of neurophysiological abnormalities. The simple placement of the electrodes over the scalp's skin or skeletal muscles constitutes a noninvasive technique. Conductive gel is widely utilized to increase the electrode's conduction and contact area with the skin surface. By utilizing near-infrared light that can reasonably well penetrate and enter biological tissue. It is achievable and possible to monitor as well as quantify brain activity in human beings noninvasively by using an intact skull. Optic spectroscopy is the term used for this. Each method produces bio-signals with a unique quality because active electrodes come with filters, but they are the comparatively more effective noninvasive choice for capturing high-quality biosignals than others. High spatial and temporal resolution using the invasive method produces better results. However, invasive techniques are more difficult, expensive and very time-taking to perform than noninvasive ones. Regardless of the method used to acquire the signal, the majority of bioelectrical signals have less amplitudes and frequencies. Consequently, extraction of features and information amplification are vital for all bioelectrical signals in order to be employed in a variety of applications [77, 78].

The EEG signals are very weak and it takes about 50,000 functioning cortical neurons to engage in real-time activity to produce calculable signals [79]. EEG signals can range in strength from 1 mV to 100 mV, along with all kinds of noises [80]. EEG is divided into several frequency categories ranging from 0.5 to 50 Hertz. Due to a variety of subsequent unfavorable movements of the skin, eye motion (blink phenomenon), muscular movement, and auditory interferences during the processing of specific, signal information, EEG signal acquisition is challenging [81]. These signals must be boosted by roughly a thousand times and conditions to get rid of various noises coming from different components. Using a modular BCI hardware unit, the EEG signals through the human brain are captured (in other word-recorded). It comprises electrodes, either active electrodes or passive electrodes, coupled to an electronic circuit unit. A differential amplifier is included in the electronic circuit module to first amplify brains to the desired output voltage before filtering them. Low band pass and high-frequency selective filters are used to filter out various unwanted noise components from signals. After performing peak wave detection and band pass filtering, additional amplification is required before analyzing through an analog-to-digital converter. Utilizing computer software, signal decoding converts input signals into the voltage output form, a very needful procedure to control actuator operations [82].

The five types of brain waves that make up EEG signals have frequencies that range from delta (0.5–4 Hz), theta (4–8 Hz), alpha (8–14 Hz), beta (14–30 Hz), and gamma (30 Hz and higher) 0 are produced in certain regions of the brain depending on the individual's mental state [86]. Eye closure causes alpha waves, which may then be altered by subsequent eye movements. Alpha waves are more often employed than delta and beta waves for a variety of purposes, despite the fact that they may be freely regulated and used for motor control by persons who are paralyzed. Signal conditioning is necessary because of the alpha waves' very small frequencies, which span from 40 to 180 V [83, 84].

Bipolar electrodes are applied to the skeletal muscles as part of the EMG signal-capturing procedure to record electrical impulses with low amplitudes. For the most part, surface electrodes and needle electrodes are introduced to record the EMG signals from the bellies of the muscles as they are contracting and relaxing [85]. A differential amplifier performs pre-amplification after signal capture. The boosted signal is then transferred for band-pass filtering utilizing high-pass and low-pass filters. After filtering out the unfavorable noises, rectifiers rectify the signals, and then an analog-to-digital converter performs the analog-to-digital conversion. The microcontroller receives the digital signals in the final stage and uses them to control the actuating processes of the device. Various human prosthetic devices are typically controlled by EMGs. The average EMG ratio using current technologies is close to 70%, but using various sets of algorithms, the accuracy of signal identification can reach up to 99.8% [20].

During multiple and numerous eye motions in distinct ways, electrooculogram (EOG) signals are detected. Because of the electrical potential (EP) difference between the eye's cornea and retina, EOG signals are produced with a quite low voltage output which is between 0.40 and 1.00 mV. Patch electrodes are often used to detect and capture EOG signals, and pre- and post-amplification are two stages of the amplification process. Numerous band pass filters made for electronic circuit boards are used to filter the signal's noise before sending them to the Arduino board (microcontroller smart hardware device having software or IDE) to match its impedance (perceived loudness). The signals are transferred to the transmitter, encoder, and finally, the receiver to control the device's motor actuation after being converted from analog to digital. Although EOG signals are still being used, they have a distinct pattern, as well as a recognizable signal form, and they can be applied to monitor various HMI-based systems [21, 22].

Clinicians use electrocardiogram (ECG) signals to identify disorders of the heart. In the method for retrieving ECG methodology and records, noninvasive electrodes, often constructed of silver chloride substance are employed to capture the heart's electrical activity through the electrochemical reaction resulting in an ion exchange process between the electrode substance and the skin. An electrolyte, such as electrode gel or skin, is considered necessary to transfer and exchange ions between an electrode that attracts cation and an electrode that accepts anion. The degree and extent of chemical equilibrium between an electrode and an electrolyte impacts and regulate the rate and extent of ion exchange [23]. The ECG signal is produced in millivolts with a wide variety of sounds due to unwanted and unfavorable electrode movements, skin wetness, i.e., moisture variation, temperature fluctuation, gel leakage conditions, etc. These noises must always be eliminated through analog filtering and signal amplification, which is typically accomplished in two instances because amplification in one instance can amplify undesirable noises and result in a low signal to noise ratio. High signal-to-noise ratio values are made and generated by second-stage amplification, combined with the required amplitude of the signal for an analog-to-digital converter operation [24, 25].

## 2.7   Human-Machine Interface–Based Healthcare System

### 2.7.1   Healthcare Practice System

#### 2.7.1.1   Healthcare Practice

Medical practice or healthcare practice is a lawful organized corporate entity in which one or more doctors work alone or in partnership, such as associates, partners, founders, owners, members, shareholders, or employees [30]. Figure 2.5 showed the components involved in the betterment of health car. Healthcare seeks to improve people's total health by preventing, recognizing, treating, minimizing, or curing disease, illnesses, injuries, and other physical, as well as mental disabilities. Healthcare is provided by health professionals and various allied health areas. Dental treatment, pharmacy, prenatal care, nursing, ophthalmology, audiologist, psychotherapy, occupational therapists, physical rehabilitation, and athletic training are all examples of healthcare. It encompasses and involves working in public health services, such as primary healthcare, secondary healthcare, and tertiary healthcare [26].

**Figure 2.5** Components involved healthcare practice.

## 2.7.1.2    Current State of Healthcare Provision

People's health is the certainty of a prosperous life and better future. Moreover, we can see that people are more attentive to their own health, hence the market for domestic health assessments is expanding. The utilization of medical rehabilitative tools has risen significantly over the last couple of years. Among them, magnetic stimulation rehabilitative medical devices are getting extreme popularity, and it is presently the most extensively utilized. Electrical stimulation rehabilitative medical equipment is the second type of medical technology and the usage of medical robots is eventually expanded. This development suggests that there will be more electrical stimulation rehabilitative medical devices developed in the upcoming days [27, 30]. The features of a machine-based healthcare system are shown in Figure 2.6.

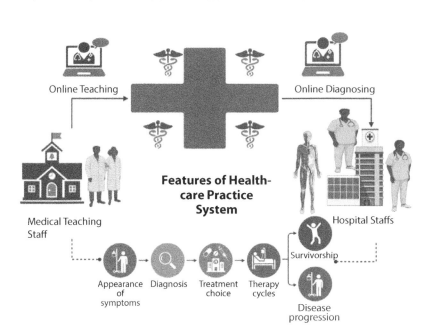

**Figure 2.6** Features of machine-based healthcare practice system.

### 2.7.1.3   Concerns With Domestic Healthcare

The distribution of welfare systems has not indeed achieved an optimal level, and there are currently some inconsistencies in the medical- and heath-associated field, which is critical to people's livelihoods. The economy and society are still in a period of tremendous change and development. For instance, the healthcare practice is imperfect because there are insufficient medical resources, and resources are distributed unevenly [28, 31].

## 2.7.2   Medical Education System

Medical education involves both the basic training to become a doctor and subsequent training (internship). It is an education pertaining to the activity of practicing medicine (e.g., residency, fellowship, and continuing medical education) [29, 32].

### 2.7.2.1   Traditional and Modern Way of Providing Medical Education

Traditional teaching environments for physiology and medicine include schools and hospitals, and the teaching subjects are generally handled by a team of instructors and pupils with similar academic interests. Everyone is aware that everyone's health is connected, and everyone should be able to learn about healthcare at any time, anywhere, and despite their age in order to further promote universal healthcare in a better way. Online educational learning has earned a huge amount of attention, and this enhances the development of the Internet, as well as innovative thinking of the domestic educational system. Network education has many benefits, including the ability to learn at any time and from any location, low teaching costs, a variety of course offerings and retrospective teaching content, that can only partially address the issues associated with teaching [4, 33].

## 2.8   Working Model of HMI

Predictive HMI models can illustrate how clients and users engage with electronic-digital health proposals at the level of specific human cognitive ability. Empirically developed predictive HMI models have been used for more than 50 years to ensure the privacy and usefulness of new info and data management (physical and digital) for use in the context of industrial and commercial applications that typically span from avionics to power plant station control systems [37]. The first desktop computers' designs were influenced by these models, which brought about advancements like the desktop computer mouse with windows-based graphical user interfaces. The "classic" HMI model, also known as the "model human processor," merged models of the interactions (inputs and outputs) between people and computers with various elements of human cognitive systems. Depending on the environment or the type of tasks being examined, there are now numerous distinctive types of HMI models for the prediction that can be applied [34].

The Fitts law is applied for pointing a cursor and the Hick-Hyman law is applied as well as utilized for pursuing an ordered array, both as an example of the cognitive procedure and technique entailed in using a computer to achieve and accomplish the assigned task. The goals operator's methodologies and selection rules (GOMS) is an elevated model that is utilized to express these technique and perspectives [35].

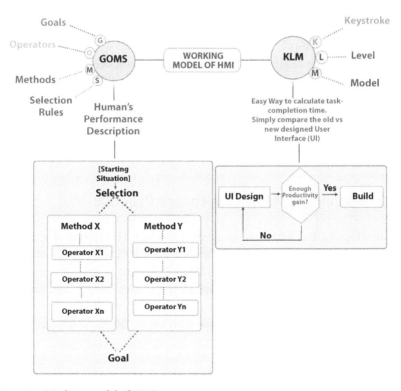

**Figure 2.7** Working model of HMI.

The keystroke-level model (precisely called KLM), a more particular sort of GOMS model, is employed and utilized to create activities that simulate an experienced user's interactions with the interface. Additionally, recently updated touch interfaces are KLM. Despite the fact that everyone performs at a different pace, these models provide a good sense of the matching and comparative effort which is needed to complete a task. These models generally strive to reduce the amount of time usually essential to accomplish tasks by removing superfluous clicks and making UI components and elements simple to use. Simplifying designs and boosting efficiency in the healthcare industry are also likely to reduce mistakes that could endanger patients, such as selecting the wrong item from an excessively long menu or clicking quickly through a protracted screen [36–38, 76]. The working model of HMI is displayed in Figure 2.7.

## 2.9    Challenges and Limitations of HMI Design

- Design is a common issue with HMIs. Because the engineers involved in the design process are not the end users, problems frequently occur, leading to complicated displays and functionality.
- Although HMI software systems have long been thought to be antiviruses, their capacity to connect to the internet puts them at risk of hacking.
- The end user may have been assumed by the designers to be fully knowledgeable about the system and aware of all the necessary steps to use it [34, 74, 75].

## 2.10    Role of HMI in Healthcare Practice

An interface called a human-machine interface (HMI) enables users to control machines, systems, or instruments. Some HMI systems transform data into understandable visuals. HMI systems are crucial in the medical sector and can hasten to heal, enhance patient monitoring, and even save lives.

Here we discuss the role of HMI systems in the medical field.

## 2.10.1    Simple to Clean

Maintaining a clean, sterile environment is crucial in medicine. HMI systems are frequently handled and touched, which makes them the ideal breeding ground for germs. Fortunately, HMIs are created with a surface that is simple to clean and anti-microbial materials, removing the possibility of infection. The HMI products are created with many years of engineering expertise to safeguard against blood, gel, and other types of liquids and bacteria, keeping patients safe and extending the product's lifespan.

## 2.10.2    High Chemical Tolerance

Chemicals and strong solutions are frequently used to treat patients. Repeated exposure to such chemicals can cause many home systems to malfunction. Dependable, long-lasting HMI solutions made especially for professionals who work with medical equipment. Our HMI systems can be controlled with the touch of a finger, a stylus, or a latex glove to increase efficiency.

## 2.10.3    Transportable and Light

Accessible medical devices are becoming more and more important as the market for home medical diagnostics expands. The portability and simplicity of use of HMI systems are arguably some of their best qualities. The thin, light, and ergonomic HMI was created to improve user experience. Every system, regardless of function, is created with simple, universal, and understandable symbols for effective use. This helps medical professionals and increases the independence of patients who use medical equipment at home.

## 2.10.4    Enhancing Communication

HMI systems can significantly enhance communication in medical settings using a variety of techniques. Medical staff can communicate more quickly and effectively to make sure patients receive the care they require. Additionally, HMI systems enable "paperless offices," which help to minimize clutter and concentrate on what matters most: the health and well-being of the patient [4, 39].

In short, we depicted the below points of HMI's role in healthcare via above (Figure 2.8).

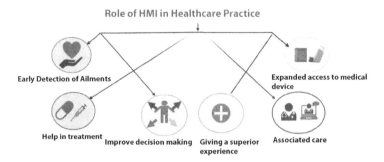

**Figure 2.8** HMI role in healthcare.

- easy detection of ailments,
- improve decision making,
- help in treatment,
- expanded access to medical devices,
- associated care,
- giving a superior experience.

## 2.11   Application of HMI Technology in Medical Fields

### 2.11.1   Medical and Rehabilitative Engineering Using HMI

HMI technology is currently having a considerable impact on the domains of neuroscience, neurology, psychotherapy, medical diagnostics, and quality improvement. Sensors-based HMI is essential for preserving and saving lives, whether it is a crucial, as well as critical life-sustaining system or monitoring the breathing factors during renal patient dialysis. Stretchers-based, self-contained life-supporting systems are used for trauma and transportation that offers urgent care while a patient is being transported in order to save lives in vehicle accidents and other traumas that happen in remote locations without access to complete hospital facilities [40]. Employing HMI-based mobile healthcare devices for diagnostic purposes while examining a person's blood pressure, blood sugar, hypertension, or other health-related parameter is a widespread way of practice. The eventual cardiovascular outcome can be calculated by employing and utilizing HMI-based home measurements that precisely track isolated and sequestered systolic, diastolic, and pulse pressure. In order to support and aid patients in their everyday activities at a vital time after joint replacement surgery procedures, a smart and very novel home monitoring system has been designed and developed [41]. The devices associated with the HMI working mechanism have been displayed in Figure 2.9. It uses sensor technology to monitor the home's overall environment developing a smart home, where HMI gives technology solutions for daily job facilitation and mobility help, is another approach to give the elderly and disabled a comfortable and straightforward way of life. Existing HMI technology can be combined with EMG and EEG biosignals to operate prosthetic devices that are part of sophisticated mechanical drives with several levels of flexibility. Depending on the user's intentions, these implant devices provide impartial controls for all conceivable manipulations using either brain signals (EMGs) or EMGs produced by muscle twitches, contractions and relaxations. In order to identify and treat a broad range of intracranial and extracranial vascular illnesses, a range of Biometrics, electrical, magnetism, and metabolic neuroimaging technologies are selected and employed for structural (anatomic) and physiological imaging throughout motor, perceptive and cognitive-perceptual operations. BCI can now be used to create sensory substitution systems that restore the missing sensations of hearing, sight, and touch to persons with impaired sensory modalities [42]. The automated humanoid robot ARMAR (Anthropomorphic

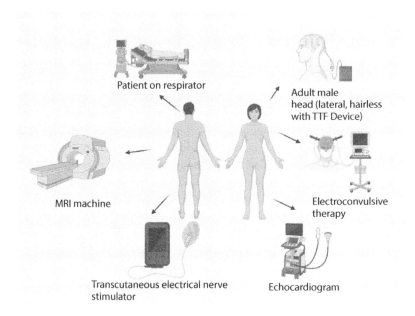

**Figure 2.9** Devices associated with HMI working mechanism.

Multi-Arm Robot), which seems to have two identical humanoid arms and end effectors with 20 degrees of freedom and executes tasks in sync with humans, and other assistive technologies, such as EEG control-based wheelchairs are excellent examples of HMI. Other metabolic neuroimaging techniques namely functional magnetic resonance imaging positron emission tomography and functional near-infrared spectroscopy briefly denoted by fMRI, PET, and fNIRS, respectively, could also be employed to diagnose medical disorders by employing biosignals. A type of MRI scanning method called functional magnetic resonance imaging measures the metabolic activity of the brain by observing variations in blood flow to determine the hemodynamic response. Additionally, it is employed for the diagnosis and management of a variety of diseases and brain disorders that cannot be identified using any further MRI methods [43]. PET is a radiological technology that is used to examine human tissues in certain conditions. Neurology, cardiology, and oncology are currently the three main fields of application for PET. During a PET scan, a radionuclide, a small quantity of radioactive material, is administered into the patient's blood. This radioactive substance emits positrons, which are then tracked by specialized equipment using emerged gamma rays. Infrared light is projected into the brain using the fNIR technology, which then tracks changes in reflected light and detects shifts in different wavelengths [44, 45]. Based on both scattering and absorption characteristics, function maps of brain activities are created in form. However, due to its poor temporal resolution, fNIR is not widely used by researchers. Near-infrared spectroscopy (in short-NIRS) is employed in vital care to track the oxygenation of the local brain tissues. SPECT, which stands for single-photon emission computed tomography, employs a designed and developed gamma camera to create 3D pictures of the inside organs or tissues being researched after administering radioactive material into the patient's bloodstream. A phenomenon known as "biomagnetism" occurs when magnetic fields are created as a result of electrical currents induced by various body parts and the magnetic characteristics of the substances that make up the body. The two different kinds of biomagnetic signals, magnetocardiography (MCG) and the magnetoencephalogram (MEG), are produced by the physiological behavior of the heart and the brain respectively. By assessing the electrical characteristics of the living tissues, bio-inductance and impedance signals are frequently used methods for monitoring and analyzing the state of one's physical health. To evaluate the make-up of the human anatomy and the assessment of various body organs, various strategies are employed with bioelectrical-impedance signals relying on the frequently used algorithms in medical assessment [46]. Because of the significant advancements in biocompatible materials' imperceptibility, stretchability, and self-healing capabilities, many biocompatible and flexible technological devices can now be interconnected closely with human body parts. The various anatomical studies are evaluated by surgeons using HMI-based 3D design models, as well as 2D displays. Contemporary supplemented reality and virtual reality tools allow surgeons to precisely diagnose patients' anatomical conditions and administer precise care. In contemporary healthcare and rehabilitation engineering, HMI is proving to be a bridge between people and medical diagnostic tools [47].

## 2.11.2    Controls for Robotic Surgery and Human Prosthetics

It is possible to control the movements of artificial limbs by integrating many touchscreen sensors and 3D accelerating sensor systems with BCI systems, which offer real-time messaging and methods of communication built on EEG pattern detection and character recognition. Due to some limitations and challenges in pattern identification and character recognition in EEG signals, BCI can now only reliably facilitate chosen few critical physical actions. Using surface-exterior EMG signals to operate a bionic hand with more liberty level is problematic because there are not many isolated controls and repeatable separate controls. The implanted electrode method produces superior outcomes for enhancing control with prosthetic limbs [48]. This was initially implemented on animals and after that on humans with the use of minimally invasive surgery procedures. This approach allowed the volunteer to operate two degrees of freedom with the bionic arm intuitively and simultaneously, which was unachievable with surface EMG controls [49]. The surgical technique known as targeted muscle reinnervation (TMR) is used to give advanced prosthetic hands inherent control. This procedure enervates new muscle goals that are no longer functional by using the remaining nerves from the amputated limb. The advanced prosthetic hands receive tactile feedback so they can reclaim their sensory abilities to perceive force, temperature, vibrations, etc. Another methodology for controlling the movements of a prosthetic, bionic hand is the recording of data from a healthy participant in the manner of a sequence of data defined and framed, each of which contains sets of varied postures by a genuine hand and the corresponding EMG data [50]. This technique makes advantage of forearm muscle EMG potentials produced throughout hand and finger motions. A data form equipped with tiny electromagnetic detectors for the appropriate movements and postures is used to record the data frames leveraging a 3D navigation system. The data gloved loaded with tiny electromagnetic detectors for the appropriate motions and stances is used to capture the data frames utilizing a 3D tracking and electromagnetic-based magnetic system. It acknowledges the variety of hand forms, boosting the agility of the bionic arm and the efficiency of practical tasks carried out by a disabled person using the prosthetic hand [51, 52]. The most modern prosthetic hands to date include excellent control mechanisms, high levels of usefulness, and unique mechanical design aspects. The Be bionic hand, Bebionic hand v2, the iLimb and iLimb pulse, the Southampton hand, the Michelangelo hand, the Mero hand and Vincent's hand are some of the very biggest technologically superior humanoid prosthetic hands made to date. Very new and unique functional and operational control methods and tactics have been designed, developed, and established by researchers to operate immensely sensitive prosthetic hands. Patients must endure time-consuming exercise procedures in order to understand how flexible prosthetic hands should be handled, necessitating the development of new and improved HMI-based instruction, training and learning techniques. As a result, training amputees with virtual reality simulators is a recent development. According to a different study, users require extensive training before they can accurately control an EEG-based prosthetic arm with BCI. A biomechatronic multi-finger prosthetic hand was made possible by the creation of a multi-force sensitivity resistor interface. Each finger is equipped with force and torque detectors to guarantee stability while grabbing various things. EMG-based pattern recognition offers a significantly higher rate of success (over 90%) for a variety of motion types. Just a prosthetic hand with more degrees of freedom, thus offers better controls [53]. Surface EMG has several drawbacks, including inherent noise, insufficient electrode positioning as well as displacement, fatigue, sweating, and gel performance. Measurements of inertial and surface EMG work together to significantly reduce the number of sensors required to create prosthetic hands with improved performance characteristics and multi-DOF functionality. Using the BCI interface, surgical procedures can be made safer and more effective overall by reducing human error. To enhance teleoperation robotic laser surgery, a brain-controlled augmented reality (BcAR) system based on BCI technology has been created [54]. It advocates training-based, real-time feedback self-regulation of mental state while performing surgery. The task load index is a tool provided by NASA's human performance research group to gauge workload following task completion. The evaluation assesses the surgeons' subjective cognitive load in accordance with the initial, single, and dual tasks carried out throughout the medical procedures. The list is owing six sub-dimensions:

logical demands, behavioral demands, bodily demands, own efficiency, irritation, and effort. When performing difficult surgical procedures, BCI linked up computerized task load monitoring with EEG offers the surgeon a channel for goal-oriented conversation without interfering with their work or placing any more demands on them outside of surgery. This makes it easier to accomplish surgical duties, especially in robotic surgery, while holding the entire focus [55]. Further advancements in HMI technology will enable the development of prosthetic limbs with greater levels of freedom and superior control that replicate the capabilities and working properties of legitimate human body parts-functions that are currently either impossible or extremely difficult to perform with outgoing HMI technique [56, 57].

### 2.11.3    Sensory Replacement Mechanism

The basic idea behind the sensory replacement mechanism is to change the stimuli and impulses from one sense medium, such as touch, into stimuli from some other sensory medium, like vision or any type. A sensory replacement system can be broken down into three separate parts, including a sensor, an electronic coupler, and a stimulator. An electronic coupler system, which is in charge of coordinating the activation of a stimulator, can interpret signals from a specific sort of energy that can be converted into signals by a sensor. The ability of the brain(CNS) to function with sensory substitution and replacement tools is referred to as "sensory substitution," and it enables the learner to have a fresh view of the environment [58]. Blind people and subjects may perceive simple objects, even shifting, moving ones, and have additional sensations like depth estimation and analysis, magnification, perspective parallax, etc. using simply a tactile vision sensory substitution (in short, TVSS) setup. Blind individuals with TVSS set-up can recognize simple geometric shapes after learning certain specific strategies. When using auditory substitution devices, people with hearing loss can hear effectively. The proposed framework of the retina is utilized as a prototype for the rough simplistic model of audible substitution. It is integrated with the cochlea's inverse linear architecture and model to improve the sensory replacement process [59]. This system utilizes headphones, a head-mounted camera, and a computer in a sequential configuration to capture visual scenes and transform them into audio impulses. An electronic device known as a cochlear implant, which is medically inserted into the cochlea and transforms sound into electrical impulses, can help patients who are severely deaf and have sensor neuronal deafness regain some hearing. Bilateral vestibular hypofunction makes walking in poor light and on the uneven ground difficult due to movement problems and unstable motion. High levels of stability and efficient brain and body synchronization are provided by vestibular sensory replacement [60]. The bilateral substitution system models are combined with touch, visibility, and reflexes systems that indicate characteristic motion properties and minimize or eliminate the magnitudes of deficient aspects. The key criteria of consumers of sensory replacement devices are lightness, compactness, less power consumption, and simplicity of use with elevated personalized functional settings combining high flexibility. In complex virtual reality sensory systems, tactile pin matrices are utilized to demonstrate body contact with the virtualized world in a nonvisual means. With the use of HMI technologies, people who are blind, deaf, or mute due to diseases that emerged after birth or birth defects may be able to partially or completely restore their ability to see, hear, and speak [61].

### 2.11.4    Wheelchairs and Moving Robots Along With Neurological Interface

An individual who is handicapped is always relying on others to complete daily tasks, even in the most difficult or urgent circumstances. Using prosthetics and assistive devices, technology assists these people and allows them to function independently [62]. Due to the fact that eye movements are required to generate EOG signals, which are then used to operate and drive the wheelchair, EOG-operated wheelchairs are becoming more and more common in society, especially among physically challenged persons. MATLAB/SIMULINK software is interfaced with a biosignal booster and amplifier (like g.USBampRESEARCH) to process the EOG signals produced and formed using distinct eye gestures (in different directions and at numerous stages) in an asynchronous wheelchair. A moving robot based on EEG has a high potential to assist disabled people with routine life tasks. In 2004, a proposal for the first neurologically robotic system was made [63]. EEG-SSVEP signal instructions are utilized to monitor multiple operations of motorized wheelchairs via a fuzzy inference technique method to assist people with motor limitations. Smart wheelchairs or telepresence mobile robots could be moved with merely dual output protocols and commands of brain motar imagery (MI) signals and a dual low transmission frequency network of BCI along with an intelligent adaptive user interface (in short, iAUI) [64]. Six orientation and speed control movements of a motorized wheelchair were controlled by six EMG signals produced by left and right eye closures, three-jaw clinched motions, solo jaw clinched, dual jaw clinched, and continuously jaw clinched or eye blinking movements The goal of the HMI for mobile healthcare gadgets, exoskeleton digital equipment and devices is to allow injured patients and those with a range of physical limitations and illnesses to rise, move, and engage in other bodily activities. People with complex medical conditions or physical limitations may be able to work more effectively thanks to these robotic systems and exoskeleton systems [65, 66]. By helping people in risky circumstances like hazardous detection and disposal of jobs, exoskeletons and robotic systems with HMI controllers are specifically employed to raise a person's level of safety. To boost weight-bearing capacity and lessen tiredness in the equipped individual, it is also employed in security uses or during disaster risk management operations [67].

### 2.11.5    Cognitive Improvement

Cognitive ability is the capacity of a human's mind and body to judge, calculate, and carries out any activity using mental motor function. Currently, a human's brain abilities can be improved by both medications and mindfulness. By encouraging executive function and enhancing brain structure, exercising mindfulness meditation helps to improve brain functions [68]. Medications, supplements, and other compounds known as serotonergic drugs claim to enhance cognitive function. The three main types of these drugs are piracetam, modafinil and methylphenidate. Methylphenidate, a manufactured stimulant, is used to treat severe sleep diseases like narcolepsy and insomnia as well as other deficit disorders, such obsessive-compulsive disorder by stimulating the central nervous system [69]. Patients with narcolepsy or extreme sleepiness are treated with modafinil. It is additionally used to lessen weariness and increase attentiveness The chemical piracetam is used to enhance remembering and other brain processes in people. Despite being used to treat conditions like dizziness, seizures, learning disabilities, and sickle cell anemia, piracetam has yet to receive legal status as a nutritional supplement in the eyes of the US Food and Drug Administration (in short, FDA). In addition to these three classes of drugs used to improve cognition, other drugs like oxiracetam, acetylcholine precursor chemicals, choline alfoscerates, citicoline, acetyl-carnitines, lecithins are presently being used to treat a wide range of illness and diseases induced by the different kinds of neurological diseases. Several medications, notably galantamine, donepezil and rivastigmine have received FDA approval and acceptance to enhance cognitive function and treat conditions including Alzheimer's and other dementia-related problems. Pilot efficiency is also improved by the usage of donepezil. Additionally, army applications and boosting helicopter simulator skills are both being tested using modafinil [70]. Additionally, it has been noted that consuming sugary beverages can make someone's Hmi performance worse. Professors and students at colleges and universities across the globe utilize a variety of cognitive-enhancing medications to boost their academic results. However, using pharmaceuticals and stimulant chemicals to enhance cognition increases the risk of adverse effects, which is still a controversial and nebulous

**Table 2.2** Information about various HMI-based medical devices.

| Medical devices | Brief knowledge | Uses | Application |
|---|---|---|---|
| MRI Machine | A large tube with strong magnets inside of it to look at organ and structure inside your body | Spinal cord and Brain imaging test | Cerebral vessel aneurysms disorders of the inner ear and eyes |
| TTF device | Noninvasive method based device | Treatment of brain tumor | Applied adults with glioblastoma |
| Echocardiogram | A test that give image of your heart by using sound waves | Diagnose heart associated problems | Assessment of myocardial perfusion |
| Electroconvulsive Therapy | Procedure whereby the brain is electrically stimulated while under general anesthesia | To treat mental illness | Deep depression mania, Catatonia |
| Transcutaneous Electrical Nerve Stimulator | Small, Battery-operated device, Low-voltage electric currents are applied during therapy | Muscle relaxation and Pain relief | Elicit segmental analgesia, Extrasegmental analgesia, Peripheral nerve blockade |

subject [71, 72]. While HMI technology interacts with brain neurons by utilizing brain microchip interfacing and on-chip electromechanical technologies to enhance memory and some additional sensory stimuli with cognitive processes, this also offers the possibility of enhancing and boosting and maximizing the natural brain's exercise abilities up to thousands of times. For a range of attributes, including the treatment of many brain diseases and illnesses, medically implantable cranium chips are used and employed to trigger brain sensory neurons. Utilizing circuits built on electrolyte oxide metal oxide semiconductor field effect transistor, in short EOS-FET, several aspects of brain functioning are analyzed. The first phase of a more recent HMI technology that has the ability to revolutionize healthcare is the direct incorporation of biosensors based on nanotechnology and microtechnology with the human body. In the upcoming years, it may be capable of immediately raising a person's cognitive ability to a very significant level using HMI technologies [4, 73]. The brief information mainly uses and applications of various HMI-based medical devices is shown in Table 2.2.

## 2.12    Conclusion and Future Perspective

Management for healthcare and rehabilitative services, human prosthetics and robotic surgery, bioengineering, automobile technology and other fields have all found major applications of HMI techniques. The HMI is the sole method that enables actual human regulation and control of machine functions. A person can complete any activity through machines by using the HMI. Recent research has examined a number of methods for finely controlling mechanical prosthetic devices, especially prosthetic hands. Before it can perform as an authentic human hand, it needs to be much improved. HMI technologies have increased performance levels and improved functional ability to handle several activities at once, hence boosting human potential. It can enhance one's capacity for thinking critically in a variety of challenging parameters, as well as configurations with varying constraints. Given how reliant and dependent today's medical fields are on machines, the world will be in the future of accurately managing and efficiently handling them, so there will be importance as well as a need to enhance HMI for greater versatility and high efficiency. Given the HMI technologies' current successes, the future is undoubtedly very bright. HMI technologies would be crucial in creating better and safer working environments for people to collaborate with machines in almost every aspect of life.

# References

1. Johansen, G., Human-machine interaction, in: *Control Systems, Robotics and Automatics*, vol. 21, p. 132, 2009.

2. Ke, Q., Liu, J., Bennamoun, M., An, S., Sohel, F., Boussaid, F., Computer vision or human-machine interaction: Background of human-machine interaction, in: *Computer for Assistive Healthcare*, M. Leo, and M.G. Farinella, (Eds.), p. 128, Elsevier, Cambridge, Massachuetts, 2018.

3. Jacobs, M. and Mynatt, E.D., Design principles for supporting patient-centered journeys, in: *Designing Healthcare That Works*, pp. 19–35, 2018.

4. Li, X. and Xu, Y., Role of human-computer interaction healthcare system in the teaching of physiology and medicine. *Comput. Intell. Neurosci.*, 1–12, 2022.

5. Greenfield, D., Understanding HMI's evolution toward easier design, Automation World, pp. 1–3, 2018.

6. Singh, H.P. and Kumar, P., Developments in the human-machine interface technologies and their applications: A review. *J. Med. Eng. Technol.*, 1–23, 2021.

7. Ramadan, R.A. and Vasilakos, A.V., Brain computer interface: Controls signals review. *Neurocomputing*, 223, 26–44, 2017.

8. Golub, M.D., Chase, S.M., Batista, A.P., Brain-computer interfaces for dissecting cognitive processes underlying sensorimotor control. *Curr. Opin. Neurobiol.*, 37, 53–58, 2016.

9. Amiri, S., Fazel-Rezai, R., Asadpour, V., A review of hybrid brain-computer interface systems. *Adv. Hum. Comput. Interact.*, 1–8, 2013.

10. Chumerin, N., Manyakov, N.V., Vliet, M.V., Pre-processing and decoding steady-state visual evokedpotentials for brain-computer interfaces, in: *Digital Image and Signal Processing for Measurement Systems*, pp. 1–33, Denmark River Publishers, Denmark, 2012.

11. Nakanishi, M., Wang, Y., Wang, Y.-T., A high-speed brain speller using steady-state visual evoked potentials. *Int. J. Neural Syst.*, 24, 6, 1–18, 2014.

12. Kubler, A., Neumann, N., Kaiser, J., Brain-computer communication: Self-regulation of slow cortical potentials for verbal communication. *Arch. Phys. Med. Rehabil.*, 82, 1533–1539, 2001.

13. Padfield, N., Zabalza, J., Zhao, H., EEG-based brain-computer interfaces using motor-imagery: Techniques and challenges. *Sensors*, 19, 6, 1423, 2019.

14. Zhang, W., Tan, C., Sun, F., A review of EEG-based brain-computer interface systems design. *Brain Sci. Adv.*, 4, 2, 156–167, 2018.

15. Li, Z., Yuan, Y., Luo, L., Hybrid brain/muscle signals powered wearable walking exoskeleton enhancing, motor ability in climbing stairs activity. *IEEE Trans. Med. Robot. Bionics*, 1, 4, 218–227, 2019.

16. Prashant, P., Joshi, A., Gandhi, V., Brain computer interface: A review. *5th Nirma University International Conference on Engineering (NUiCONE)*, Ahmedabad, pp. 1–6, 2015.

17. Yadav, M.K., Verma, U., Parikh, H., Minimally invasive transgingival implant therapy: A literature review. *Natl. J. Maxillofac. Surg.*, 9, 2, 117, 2018.

18. Cauvery, N.K., Lingaraju, G., Anupama, H., Brain-computer interface and its types- A study. *Int. J. Eng. Adv. Technol.*, 3, 739–745, 2012.

19. Kassiri, J.J., Pugh, J., Carline, S., Depth electrodes in pediatric epilepsy surgery. *Can. J. Neurol. Sci., Le Journal Canadien des Sciences Neurologiques*, 40, 48–55, 2013.

20. Gohel, V. and Mehendale, N., Review on electromyography signal acquisition and processing. *Biophys. Rev.*, 12, 6, 1361–1367, 2020.

21. Kavitha, C. and Nagappan, G., Sensing and processing of EOG signals to control human-machine interface system. *Int. J. Sci. Eng. Technol.*, 5, 1330–1336, 2015.

22. Guo, X., Pei, W., Wang, Y. *et al.*, A human-machine interface based on single channel EOG and patchable sensor. *Biomed. Signal Process. Control*, 30, 98–105, 2016.

23. Salinet, J.L. and Silva, O.L., Chapter 2-ECG signal acquisition systems, in: *Developments and Applications for ECG Signal Processing*, J.P.V. Madeiro, P.C. Cortez, J.M.S.M. Filho, A.R.A. Brayner (Eds.), pp. 29–51, Elsevier, Amsterdam, Netherlands, 2019.

24. Macfarlane, P.W., Oosterom, A.V., Pahlm, O., *Comprehensive electrocardiology*, p. 1, Springer Science & Business Media, Verlag, London, 2010.

25. Gao, Z., Wu, J., Zhou, J., Design of ECG signal acquisition and processing system. *International Conference on Biomedical Engineering and Biotechnology*, Macau, Macao, May, pp. 28–30. p. 762–764, 2012.

26. Pere, P. and Guasch, D., A human–computer interaction approach for healthcare. *Univers. Access Inf. Soc.*, 17, 1–3, 2018.

27. Iglehart, K.J., *Meeting the Demand for Primary Care: Nurse Practitioners Answer the Call*, October, 2014.

28. Stephanidis, C., *The universal access handbook*, CRC Press, Boca Raton, FL, 2009.

29. Roe, P., Towards and inclusive future: Impact and wider potential of information and communication technology, COST. Brussels, 2007.

30. Hutsaliuk, O.M. and Navolokina, A.S., Research on the economic interaction of the labor market and human resources in the healthcare sector in Ukraine. *Econ. Innov.*, 22, 74, 37–51, 2020.

31. Suresh, K. and Chellappan, C., Robust spontaneous human behaviour prediction system in healthcare. *Int. Res. J. Pharm.*, 8, 11, 172–178, 2017.

32. Kimberly, S. and Mustapha, M., Human computer interaction trends in healthcare: An update. *Proceedings of the International Symposium on Human Factors & Ergonomics in Health Care*, vol. 7(1), pp. 88–91, 2018.

33. Su, H., Lallo, A.D., Murphy, R.R., Taylor, R.H., Garibaldi, B.T., Krieger, A., Physical human-robot, interaction for clinical care in infectious environments. *Nat. Mach. Intell.*, 3, 3, 184–186, 2021.

34. Borycki, E., Kushniruk., A., Nohr, C., Takeda, H., Kuwata, S., Carvalho, C., Usability methods for ensuring health information technology safety: Evidence-based approaches. Contribution of the IMIA working group health informatics for patient safety. *Yearb. Med. Inform.*, 8, 20–27, 2013.

35. Rice, A. and Lartigue, J., Touch-level model (TLM). *2014 Presented at: ACM SE '14: Proceedings of the 2014 ACM Southeast Regional Conference*, Kennesaw Georgia, pp. 1–6, 2014.

36. Marcilly, R., Peute, L., Beuscart-Zephir, M., From usability engineering to evidence-based usability in health IT. *Stud. Health Technol. Inform.*, 222, 126–138, 2016.

37. Hick, W.E., On the rate of gain of information. *Q. J. Exp. Psychol.*, 4, 1, 11–26, 2018.

38. Paton, C., Kushniruk, A.W., Borycki, E.M., English, M., Wareen, J., Improving the usability and safety of digital health systems: The role of predictive human-computer interaction modelling. *J. Med. Internet Res.*, 23, 5, 1–8, 2021.

39. Secinaro, S., Calandra, D., Secinaro, A., Muthurangu, V., Biancone, P., The role of artificial intelligence in healthcare: A structured literature review. *BMC Med. Inf. Decis. Making*, 21, 125, 2021.

40. Sandberg, F., Holmer, M., Olde, B., Monitoring respiration using the pressure sensors in a dialysis machine. *Physiol. Meas.*, 40, 2, 1–13, 2019.

41. Niiranen, T., Rissanen, H., Johansson, J., Overall cardiovascular prognosis of isolated systolic hypertension, isolated diastolic hypertension and pulse pressure defined with home measurements: The finn-home study. *J. Hypertens.*, 32, 3, 518–524, 2014.

42. Grant, S., Blom, A.W., Craddock, I., Home health monitoring around the time of surgery: Qualitative study of patients' experiences before and after joint replacement. *BMJ Open*, 9, 12, 1–10, 2019.

43. Li, R., Lu, B., McDonald Maier, K.D., Cognitive assisted living ambient system: A survey. *Digital Commun. Networks*, 1, 4, 229–252, 2015.

44. Ruhunage, I., Perera, C.J., Nisal, K., EMG signal controlled transhumerai prosthetic with EEG-SSVEP based approach for hand open/close. *IEEE International Conference on Systems, Man, and Cybernetics (SMC)*, Banff, AB, Canada, pp. 3169–3174, 2017.

45. Zhang, X., Li, R., Li, H., Novel approach for electromyography-controlled prostheses based on facial action. *Med. Biol. Eng. Comput.*, 58, 2685–2698, 2020.

46. Wang, G., Li, L., Xing, S., Intelligent HMI in orthopedic navigation, in: *Intelligent Orthopaedics, Advances in Experimental Medicine and Biology*, vol. 1093, G. Zheng, W. Tian, X. Zhuang, (Eds.), pp. 207–224, Springer, Singapore, 2018.

47. Zhang, X., Chen, G., Liao, H., High-quality see-through surgical guidance system using enhanced 3-D autostereoscopic augmented reality. *IEEE Trans. Biomed. Eng.*, 64, 8, 1815–1825, 2017.

48. Zhang, X., Li, R., Li, Y., Research on brain control prosthetic hand. *11th International Conference on Ubiquitous Robots and Ambient Intelligence*, Kuala Lumpur, pp. 554–557, 2014.
49. Cheesborough, J.E., Smith, L.H., Kuiken, T.A., Targeted muscle reinnervation and advanced prosthetic arms. *Semin. Plast. Surg.*, 29, 1, 62–72, 2015.
50. Osborn, L.E., Iskarous, M.M., Thakor, N.V., Chapter 22-sensing and control for prosthetic hands in clinical and research applications, in: *Wearable robotics*, J. Rosen, and P.W. Ferguson, (Eds.), pp. 445–468, Elsevier, Amsterdam, Netherlands, 2022.
51. Su, Y., Fisher, M.H., Wolczowski, A., Towards an EMG-controlled prosthetic hand using a 3-D electromagnetic positioning system. *IEEE Trans. Instrum. Meas.*, 56, 178–186, 2017.
52. Ting, Z., Wang, X.Q., Jiang, L., Biomechatronic design and control of an anthropomorphic artificial hand for prosthetic applications. *Robotica*, 34, 10, 2291–2308, 2015.
53. Manfredo, A., Matteo, C., Henning, M., Deep learning with convolutional neural networks applied to electromyography data: A resource for the classification of movements for prosthetic hands. *Front. Neurorob.*, 10, 9, 2016.
54. Wang, N., Lao, K., Zhang, X., Design and myoelectric control of an anthropomorphic prosthetic hand. *J. Bionic Eng.*, 14, 1, 47–59, 2017.
55. Brunner, I., Skouen, J.S., Hofstad, H., Virtual reality training for upper extremity in subacute stroke (VIRTUES), a multicenter RCT. *Neurology*, 89, 24, 2413–2421, 2017.
56. Perry, B.N., Armiger, R.S., Yu, K.E., Virtual integration environment as an advanced prosthetic limb training platform. *Front. Neurol.*, 9, 785, 2018.
57. Bright, D., Nair, A., Salvekar, D., EEG-based brain controlled prosthetic arm. *Conference on Advances in Signal Processing (CASP)*, pp. 479–483, 2016.
58. Kristjansson, A., Johannesson, O., Mitrut, O., Designing sensory-substitution devices: Principles, pitfalls and potential. *Restor. Neurol. Neurosci.*, 34, 5, 769–787, 2016.
59. Paterson, M., Molyneux, neuroplasticity, and technologies of sensory substitution, in: *The Senses and the History of Philosophy*, B. Glenney, and J.F. Silva, (Eds.), pp. 340–352, Routledge, Oxfordshire, England, UK, 2019.
60. Egilmez, O.K. and Kalcioglu, M.T., Cochlear implant: Indications, contraindications and complications. *Scr. Sci. Med.*, 47, 4, 9–28, 2015.
61. Tyler, M., Danilov, Y., Bach-y-Rita, P., Closing an open-loop control system: Vestibular substitution through the tongue. *J. Integr. Neurosci.*, 2, 159–164, 2003.
62. Collinger, J.L., Foldes, S., Bruns, T.M., Neuroprosthetic technology for individuals with spinal cord injury. *J. Spinal Cord Med.*, 36, 4, 258–272, 2013.
63. Noor, N.M.M. and Ahmad, S., Analysis of different EOG based eye movement strength levels for wheelchair control. *Int. J. Biomed. Eng. Technol.*, 11, 2, 175–196, 2013.

64. Turnip, A., Soetraprawata, D., Turnip, M., EEG based brain-controlled wheelchair with four different stimuli frequencies. *Internetworking Indones. J.*, 8, 65–69, 2016.

65. Geng, T., Gan, J.Q., Hu, H., A self-paced online BCI for mobile robot control. *Int. J. Adv. Mechatron. Syst.*, 2, 1/2, 28–35, 2010.

66. Wei, L. and Hu, H., A hybrid human-machine interface for hands-free control of an intelligent wheelchair. *Int. J. Mechatron. Autom.*, 1, 2, 97–111, 2011.

67. Strausser, K.A. and Kazerooni, H., The development and testing of a human-machine interface for a mobile medical exoskeleton. *IEEE/RSJ International Conference on Intelligent Robots and Systems*, San Francisco, C.A., pp. 4911–4916, 2011.

68. Crescentini, C., Fabbro, F., Tomasino, B., Editorial special topic: Enhancing brain and cognition through meditation. *J. Cognit. Enhancement*, 1, 2, 81–83, 2017.

69. Wilms, W. and Karczewska, M.W., Nootropic drugs: Methylphenidate, modafinil and piracetam - population use trends, occurrence in the environment, ecotoxicity and removal methods - a review. *Chemosphere*, 233, 771–785, 2019.

70. Malykh, A.G. and Sadaie, M.R., Piracetam and piracetam like drugs. *Drugs*, SpringerLink, 70, 287–312, 2010.

71. Colucci, L., Bosco, M., Ziello, A.R., Rea, R., Amenta, F., Fasanaro, A.M., Effectiveness of nootropic drugs with cholinergic activity in treatment of cognitive deficit: A review. *J. Exp. Pharmacol.*, 4, 163–172, 2012.

72. Dan-Dan, L., Ya-Hon, Z., Wei, Z., Zhao, P., Meta-analysis of randomized controlled trials on the efficacy and safety of donepezil, galantamine, rivastigmine, and memantine for the treatment of Alzheimer's disease. *Front. Neurosci.*, 13, 472, 2019.

73. Meng, J., Mundahl, J., Streitz, T., Maile, K., Gulachek, N., He, J., He, B., Effects of soft drinks on resting state EEG and brain-computer interface performance. *IEEE Access*, 5, 18756–18764, 2017.

74. Kushniruk, A., Nohr, C., Borycki, E., Human factors for more usable and safer health information technology: Where are we now and where do we go from here? *Yearb. Med. Inform.*, 10, 120–125, 2016.

75. Kushniruk, A. and Patel, V., Cognitive and usability engineering methods for the evaluation of clinical information systems. *J. Biomed. Inform.*, 37, 1, 56–76, 2004.

76. Cox, A.L. and Peebles, D., Cognitive modelling in HCI research, in: *Research Method for Human-Computer Interaction*, P. Cairns and A.L. Cox (Eds.), pp. 72–85, 2008.

77. Tsoukaki, M., Kalpidis, C.D.R., Sakellari, D., Tsalikis, L., Mikrogiorgis, G., Konstantinidis, A., Clinical, radiographic,microbiological, and immunological outcomes of flapped vs. flapless dental implants: A prospective randomized controlled clinical trial. *Clin. Oral Implants Res.*, 24, 9, 969–76, 2013.

78. Ball, T., Kern, M., Mutschler, I., Signal quality of simultaneously recorded invasive and non-invasive EEG. *NeuroImage*, 46, 3, 708–716, 2009.

79. Okada, Y., Neurogenesis of evoked magnetic fields, in: *Biomagnetism: An Interdisciplinary Approach*, J.S. Williamson, (Ed.), pp. 399–408, Springer, Berlin/Heidelberg, Germany, 1983.

80. Ramadan, R.A., Refat, S., Elshahed, M.A., Basics of brain computer interface, in: *Brain-computer interfaces: Current Trends and Applications*, A. Hassanien, and A. Azar, (Eds.), p. 74, Springer, Berlin/Heidelberg, Germany, 2015.

81. Fouad, M.M., Amin, K.M., El-Bendary, N., Brain computer interface: A review, in: *Brain computer interfaces*, vol. 74, A. Hassanien, and A. Azar, (Eds.), p. 330, Springer International Publishing, Switzerland, 2014.

82. Rao, K.T., Lakshmi, M.R., Prasad, T.V., An explorationon brain computer interface and its recent trends. *Int. J. Adv. Res. Artif. Intell.*, 1, 8, 1, New York, 2012.

83. Ramadan, R.A. and Vasilakos, A.V., Brain computer interface: Control signals review. *Neurocomputing*, 223, 26–44, 2017.

84. Rohan, H., Brain computer interface controlling devices utilizing the alpha brain waves. *Int. J. Sci. Technol. Res.*, 4, 281–285, 2015.

85. Merlo, A., Farina, D., Merletti, R., A fast and reliable technique for muscle activity detection from surface EMG signals. *IEEE Trans. Biomed. Eng.*, 50, 3, 316–323, 2003.

86. Campisi, P. and Rocca, D.L., Brain waves for automatic biometric-based user recognition. *IEEE Trans. Inf. Forensics Secur.*, 9, 5, 782–800, 2014.

# 3

# Human-Machine Interface and Patient Safety

**Arun Kumar Singh and Rishabha Malviya***

*Department of Pharmacy, School of Medical and Allied Sciences, Galgotias University, Greater Noida, India*

## Abstract

Medical errors may be reduced by using health information technology (HIT), which promises to modernize the healthcare system and improve efficiency. Even if HIT systems, like electronic health records (EHRs) or personal health records (PHRs), are correctly built and tested, they may unwittingly add new sorts of mistakes known as technology-induced errors, according to the literature. Errors of this kind may occur due to the complicated interactions between healthcare providers, patients, and the HIT systems now in use, and they may not be readily apparent until they are put in place. Here, we offer a methodology for preventing technology-induced mistakes from spreading across the healthcare system and making sure technologies are implemented in a safe and effective way. A tiered approach to system design and testing, including usability testing methodologies and clinical simulations, has been proposed in order to achieve this goal. The study discusses a novel way to assuring healthcare system safety that incorporates numerous methodologies.

*Keywords*: Patient safety, double human interface, color coding, software, anesthesia, medical device, human-machine interface, healthcare

## 3.1 Introduction

Almost everyone might benefit from today's therapeutic methods. More potent and effective treatments for a broader range of ailments are becoming accessible as the healthcare sector continues its complicated and

*Corresponding author*: rishabhamalviya19@gmail.com

Rishabha Malviya, Sonali Sundram, Bhupendra Prajapati and Sudarshan Kumar Singh (eds.)
*Human-Machine Interface: Making Healthcare Digital*, (59–88) © 2024 Scrivener Publishing LLC

sophisticated evolution [1]. Many patients are hurt or killed as a consequence of therapy not going as anticipated for a number of causes [2–6]. Given the unexpected nature of the situation and other external considerations, the human and financial implications of this treatment-related harm are substantial. Treatment-related adverse events account for 44,000 to 98,000 annual deaths in the United States. The annual cost of non-fatal injuries is estimated to be in the millions or perhaps the billions of dollars [7, 8], and the death rate is estimated to be much higher based on more current information. The strength of anesthetics used, the huge number of drugs delivered during anesthesia, and the broad range of anesthetics used across the globe all make anesthesia a particularly dangerous time for medication administration errors to occur [2, 3, 9]. Parenteral injection and infusion devices are seldom used in anesthesia due to a lack of technical safety assessments, such as the computerized order input systems used in other medical settings. Diseases associated with industrial civilization, such as cardiovascular disease, cancer, and cerebrovascular illness, are contributing to an increase in the global need for surgical treatments. As a result, more people are likely to be harmed by the treatments [10, 11]. Current estimates place the number of surgeries performed annually worldwide at seven per person [1, 10], with 50 million of them taking place in the United States. New and potentially fatal mechanisms for medicines to backfire have emerged as medicine has progressed [1, 12]. Evidence like this suggests that healthcare safety regulations have not kept pace with the rapid development of new technologies. Anesthesiologists have always been very concerned with patient safety [13, 14], but the development of modern healthcare technology has provided new opportunities to further this goal. Despite advancements in technology, many aspects of intravenous anesthesia have stayed unaltered and remain error-prone. A variety of interesting methods for enhancing patient safety, including one that draws on the work of our own team and addresses the prevalence and nature of intravenous anesthetic medication distribution errors, will be presented in the following sections.

## 3.2   Detecting Anesthesia-Related Drug Administration Errors and Predicting Their Impact

Approaching low-incidence events, such as those that occur less than 1% of the time, raises methodological problems. This kind of incidence is more likely to be recorded than non-harmful ones, despite the fact that it is infrequent [15]. As a first step, this estimate cannot be used to establish that a specific safety action had a direct impact on rates, but it is critical in determining whether or not they did. It is a bad idea to base rare phenomenon rates on clinical perceptions. When a patient is harmed as a result of a pharmaceutical error, no one doctor will notice. Thus, a practitioner who has never made a pharmaceutical error that resulted in patient damage may have an optimistic bias and underestimate the true prevalence of medication error [16]. The incidence of pharmaceutical errors might be overestimated if a clinician has had a few negative experiences with medication blunders [17, 18]. Even if the reality of the phenomenon lies somewhere in the between of these two extremes, huge amounts of data must be collected in order to accurately assess its frequency. Although there are several statistical techniques for establishing how big a denominator (sample size) is required to achieve a valid estimate of any specific low-incidence event, even guesstimates sometimes need data gathering from hundreds of cases, which might hinder such investigations. It is also difficult to discover significant differences across key subgroups of interest even in big studies due to difficulties in obtaining enough statistical significance.

### 3.2.1  Methodological Difficulties in Studying Rare, Dangerous Phenomena

Heart valve or artery rupture is a rare but potentially catastrophic consequence of central venous catheters (CVCs). Perforation rates are reported to be anything from 1 in 100,000 to 1 in 10,000 [19–31]. In a study of 1,000 consecutive CVC patients, perforations occurred in the right atrium from a triple-lumen CVC and in the pulmonary artery from a PAC [32]. For instance, it has been shown that PACs are associated with a higher risk of perforations compared to CVCs.

This is equivalent to a perforation rate of around 0.2% (with a 95% confidence interval of 0.02–0.7%). The high sample size and prospective nature of this data collection suggest that this estimate of perforation incidence is more accurate and has a narrower confidence range than many previously reported estimates. More research is needed to further reduce the confidence interval, however. If the perforation rate of 0.2% is correct, then 10,000 patients would be needed for a 95% confidence range of 0.1% to 0.3%. For such a long-term research, just collecting the necessary data would take years in our labs. Despite data suggesting differences, a study of 1,000 patients was unable to assess the probability of CVC perforation in separate CVC subgroups. It is true that perforation of conventional CVCs is more common, but the processes by which this occurs in PACs are unique [33–36].

Perforation by a PAC was not statistically distinguished from perforation by other study CVCs (1 in 1000 patients, or 0.1%, 95 CI 0.003–0.6%) in this 1000-patient trial (1 in 223 patients, or 0.4%, 95% CI 0.01–2.5%) [32]. It is possible that even in a somewhat big study, no occurrences of the event under inquiry will be uncovered since rare events have small numerators. The upper 95% CI for a zero numerator may be estimated by dividing the number of observations by the total number of observations. A 95% upper limit of confidence on the number of patients with vascular perforation is roughly 3/1000 or about 0.3%.

Many studies [9, 37–45] have used questionnaires and interviews instead of actual patient data to estimate the number of patients who were injured due to anesthetic drug administration errors. However, although these studies might help pinpoint immediate areas of concern, they cannot be utilized to determine how often medication administration errors occur overall. When designing strategies to increase safety over the long run, it is essential to use consistent base rates and denominators. A precise estimate still requires careful methodological consideration, even when denominator data are readily accessible and extensive study is undertaken. Retrospective studies overestimate the frequency with which medication errors occur during delivery. Approximately 0.01% and 0.08% per case were found in retrospective event monitoring investigations including 113 and 64 thousand anesthetic patients, respectively [46, 47]. In subsequent studies, the error rate for anesthetic drugs was determined to be between 0.11% and 0.16% [48–51]. Approximately one-tenth of their former size. Due to their inclusion in a broader strategy to event monitoring rather than a dedicated investigation of this specific issue, drug errors in anesthesia may be underreported. We published a medicine administration error estimate using a denominator and data collected specifically for the study of drug administration errors based on prospective event data in 2001 [52]. We called our system "facilitated incident monitoring" since we handed out incident forms whenever anesthetic was administered, and the great majority of them reported that no events had happened. If an incident form is not included in the anesthetic file, a designated staff member will investigate. There are now fewer issues when reporting events thanks to these improvements [53]. Those who report events will remain anonymous and may be given additional safety measures if an incident study is seen as a quality assurance exercise. The largest estimate of this sort to date comes from a study of 10,806 anesthetics, which found that a medication distribution mistake happened once in every 133 occurrences of anesthetics (or 0.75%). IV administration accounted for 83% of all mistakes, with bolus injections being responsible for 63% and infusion administration making up the other 20%. Evidence like this highlights the significance of IV administration in causing damage to people under anesthesia. Medical treatment was administered intravenously rather than by epidural injection (IV). The majority (59%) of all drug administration errors occurred due to the inappropriate dosage or medication being used. Sixty-nine percent of all intravenous bolus substitution errors (11 of 16) and 75% of all infusion substitution errors (75%) included drugs from different classes, posing a greater risk of injury to the patient. This worries me a lot.

## 3.2.2   Consequences of Errors

Nobody was hurt or lost their life because of a medication mix-up within the time frame of this investigation. One of the patients was the only one who did not know this. Previous studies [54, 55] have shown that only a tiny minority of pharmacological mistakes really cause patients damage. In light of the study's finding that one of the 81 errors had serious consequences (awareness). New Zealand's anesthesiologists perform over a thousand anesthetics annually [56]. Anesthesiologists are human, and they make mistakes. If there is one drug administration error for every 133 anesthetics, then they will make seven medication administration errors every year. Over the course of a 30-year career, more than 200 mistakes have been committed in the pharmaceutical industry. If just 1% of an anesthesiologist's mistakes cause serious harm to patients, that doctor may anticipate to damage two people throughout the course of their career.

Later studies [52, 57–60] all use the same kind of assisted event reporting techniques. There are several notable similarities between these research. Three of the five studies looked at the rate of errors made during the delivery of medicines, and found that it was between 0.61% and 0.75%. These two errors were shown to be the most common and second most common in four of the five trials, and the most common and second most common in all three experiments in the fifth research. According to one research [57], infusion pump problems were the root cause of unexpected pharmacological effects in 14 of 29 instances. Mistakes are most often attributed to factors like distraction, inattention, output pressure, and an inability to check, according to all five studies (Table 3.1). Extra training for those who make drug errors is probably not helpful since just one research found that lack of knowledge was the third most prevalent cause of medication mistakes. The factors listed in Table 3.1 may lead some to conclude that human

**Table 3.1** Estimates of drug administration error in anesthesia using dedicated, prospective incident reporting.

| Year of report | Country of study | Response rate | Number of anesthetics studied | Number of drug errors reported | Error rate per anesthetic (%) | Top three error types (%) | Top three contributing factors (if reported) |
|---|---|---|---|---|---|---|---|
| 2001 | New Zealand | 72% | 10,806 | 81 | 1/133 (0.75 %) | 1. Incorrect dose (32 %) 2. Substitution (27 %) 3. Omission (18 %) | 1. Failure to check 2. Distraction 3. Inattention |
| 2003 | United States | 90% | 6709 | 41 | 1/163 (0.61 %) | 1. Incorrect dose (43 %) 2. Substitution (17 %) 3. Insertion (drug not intended) (9 %) | |
| 2009 | South Africa | 53% | 30,412 | 66 | 1/450 (0.22 %) | 1. Substitution (60 %) 2. Incorrect dose (23 %) 3. Repetition/incorrect route (13 %) | |
| 2012 | United states | 83% | 10574 | 35 | 1/302 (0.33 %) | 1. Incorrect dose (37 %) 2. Substitution (25 %) 3. Omission (19 %) | 1. Distraction 2. Production pressure 3. Misread label |
| 2013 | China | 68% | 24,380 | 179 | 1/137 (0.73 %) | 1. Omission (27 %) 2. Incorrect dose (23 %) 3. Substitution (20 %) | 1. Haste 2. Inattention 3. Inadequate knowledge |

error is to blame for incident rates, but I contend that they instead indicate an environment that sets an unreasonable premium on employee effort in order to guarantee sufficient safety. To ensure that patient safety does not entirely depend on the clinician being invincible and never falling to distraction or inattention, it is vital to include human nature into the process of developing a workplace that better supports job activities, including patient safety. Drug ampoule misidentification is responsible for 37% of medication delivery mistakes [58], as shown in Table 3.1. Why, for example, are ampoules used in the pharmaceutical industry so badly made? This will be discussed further on in the review. Despite many advancements in anesthetic technology, these studies show that drug distribution errors remain a serious issue.

### 3.2.3   Lessons From Other Industries

There has been a lot of emphasis on reducing workplace injuries and mishaps via various preventative measures. A pioneer in the subject of industrial safety in the United States, Herbert Heinrich began researching workplace accidents in the 1920s. A former inspector for the Travelers Insurance Company, Heinrich published the seminal work "Industrial Accident Prevention—A Scientific Approach" in 1931. There will be 29 minor injuries and 300 near-misses for every major injury, according to Heinrich's 300-29-1 ratio, which is discussed in detail here. A. Heinrich Insights gained from these instances may lead to the early detection and elimination of weak points. "Safety begins with safe equipment, safe machinery, safe processes, and a safe atmosphere," Heinrich says in the fourth edition of his book [61]. Studies of near misses, in addition to accident investigations, have shown to be a more relevant and extensive data source for determining the chance of harm in the past and the present [62]. Although the ratio of near-misses to actual injuries varies widely among sectors, the collection and analysis of such data may help address the problem of requiring unusually large numbers in studies that focus purely on errors. As may be illustrated in Table 3.1, certain estimates [63, 64] imply that medical accidents occur 3300 times more frequently than real errors. It is now feasible to report anesthesia incidents utilizing web-based approaches. Contextual information crucial to understanding the reported events may be lacking [65–67], and reporting rates may be insufficient, both of which reduce the usefulness or representativeness of the data. Every tactic has both advantages and disadvantages, although many have been handed down through conventional wisdom in similar fields. Approaches that rely on theory to anticipate problems may be advantageous, while methods that rely on facts to address problems after they have already occurred can be as useful. Constant monitoring may result in long-term savings, but it is time-consuming and not always feasible. Clinical monitoring, the continuous gathering of data by appropriately qualified personnel, is one method of data collection that may be compromised [68–72]. Clinical surveillance provides the advantage of collecting data on both treatment outcomes and patient adherence; nevertheless, there are still issues with statistical power [73]. Accordingly, a combination of methods should be used to provide the maximum level of safety [74]. Data from electronic medical records and charts, administrative data, and morbidity and mortality statistics may also be utilized to assess quality and safety. I will examine a couple of them in additional depth later in the chapter.

### 3.2.4   The Double-Human Interface

Anesthesia and the commercial setting are fundamentally different because of the two-human interface, which defines the way humans and technology interact. Interaction between humans and technology is a prevalent issue in human factors and ergonomics discipline. When dealing with the medicine administration and monitoring equipment, the anesthesiologist (A) in Figure 3.1 uses a double-ended, symbolically designated arrow (x). But in a traditional human/technological system, the anesthetized patient (y) is a vital individual. There are many factors that might affect the behavior of the anesthetic system that are within the purview of the anesthesiologist's responsibility in terms of maintaining patient biotechnological stability (Figure 3.1).

The initial effect of the biotechnological system's nature is complexity. As a complex system is difficult or impossible to predict adequately based on knowledge of the system's components, it is conceivable to characterize it as such. Under normal conditions, the physiological compartments of the human body are capable of sustaining homeostasis (the state of equilibrium). A number of normally self-regulating subsystems in an anesthetized patient have been stopped, modified, or taken over by anesthetic technology. Paralysis of the muscles around the lung by anesthetic medications results in breathing via a ventilator, which might lead to unanticipated system behavior. As a result of these and many other factors, even the most modern machines are less reliable and need more constant monitoring than the physiological systems inside human bodies. This results in a highly complex and potentially unpredictable bio-technological system that may diverge from the planned path of action and reach an unanticipated state (System 2 in Figure 3.2). The patient's health might be adversely

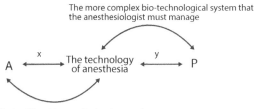

**Figure 3.1** A biotechnological system in which the anesthesiologist and the anesthetic technology are linked by a second person, the patient, is shown in this conceptual diagram of anesthesia's double-human interface. The bottom bracket indicates the scope of the conventional human/technology system, which is normally investigated by ergonomics and human factors.

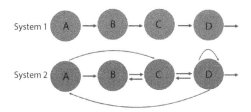

**Figure 3.2** Those systems that are neither linear nor simple are called nonlinear systems. System 1's subsystems and operational states interact in a linear fashion, resulting in a predictable and deterministic flow of operations. Because of the complex, non-linear causal interaction between subsystems in a system like an anesthetized patient, it is hard to forecast which path would lead to completion or how long the process will take.

affected by both the treatment and the pathology. While the patient is undergoing surgery or therapy, this is particularly true. It might be difficult to determine at any one moment what stage a biotechnological system is at. Trying to identify a patient in crisis when the sole certainty is that there is a problem, but physicians do not know what that issue is may be difficult. When it comes to human/technology interactions, industrial settings tend to think in terms of simple, predictable interactions between humans and machines [75, 76]. Healthcare's safety culture is not as well established as it should be [77, 78] as a consequence of this.

### 3.2.5   The Culture of Denial and Effort

Patient safety is compromised to some degree by the cult of individual physicians that has developed in modern healthcare. Doctors used to be urged to be more cautious or new safety standards would be introduced to try to cut down on medical blunders [79, 80]. People-centered safety refers to a focus on the person rather than the wider system or work environment in which they are supposed to operate. Taking a more human-centered approach means attributing all errors to human frailty and negligence [81]. Therefore, we think that paying more attention or following safety regulations may help reduce the possibility of mistakes. I have coined the term "denial and effort" to reflect the widespread belief among doctors that they can protect themselves and their patients without any additional safeguards. Safety culture in aviation, the antithesis of healthcare's denial and effort, has stymied the development of safety measures in the field and persists despite the inherent complexity of medical care [82].

### 3.2.6  Poor Labeling

Because of the potential risk of mislabeled ampoules and syringes, they have long been a subject of worry in the field of anesthesia. There is a prevalent misconception that eliminating workplaces with a high incidence of human mistake is essential, making it hard to increase patient safety. In the January 1981 issue of *Anaesthesia*, one reader argued that "quite convincing grounds" supported the idea that all ampoules should look the same. It was emphasized in the declaration that this approach would encourage people to read the inscription [83]. These "legitimate reasons" were already debunked by 1981 research [2, 3, 84–86] in the disciplines of psychology, industrial accident prevention, and human factors. One must "constantly retrain oneself to understand the sentences" if one is to inject properly, as stated in a 1996 editorial published in the journal *Anaesthesia*. Sometimes it is preferable to study what being read than to read what we anticipate [87]. The British Medical Journal [88] states, "Doctors must study medicine labels, not moan about them." One lesson to be learned from this tale is that physicians are a rare breed, capable of overcoming their flaws by the force of their will alone. For decades [6, 89, 90] this notion has been advocated, yet drug distribution issues persist. Undoubtedly, the great majority of physicians are committed professionals who want to provide excellent care to their patients. Since there will always be the possibility of iatrogenic injury so long as humans are involved, effort alone can never be enough.

## 3.3   Systematic Approaches to Improve Patient Safety During Anesthesia

Anesthetic medicine distribution processes are prone to human error and depend mainly on hand-checking rather than automated controls because of their intrinsic peculiarities [91, 92]. Improved patient safety may be achieved via the use of the systems approach. Instead than concentrating just on the individual, this method focuses on removing dangerous components of equipment, procedures, work environments, and organizations in order to improve safety. To improve patient safety, our team has been developing intravenous drug delivery methods in anesthesia since 1996 [93]. The new system's architecture incorporates lessons learned from other safety-critical industries, such as nuclear power generation [85, 94–97], empirical event reporting, psychological variables driving human error, and safe system design principles [52].

### 3.3.1   Design Principles

The updated system components and rules are summarized in Table 3.2 of this report. The anesthesiologist is not put in a worse situation than when using just standard methods since each module may be utilized alone or in combination with others. The new setup is meant to be assembled piece by piece. The new system's physical architecture makes use of pharmaceutical tray organization and aseptic process to boost efficiency. A tangible record of the anesthetic's advancement may be created in the form of a tray by including a prompt zone, a zone for currently used syringes, and a zone for previously administered ampoules of medication. Used syringe needles may be safely kept in the tray has raised "in use" area. The majority of commonly used drugs are now offered in pre-filled syringes, which both expedite the dosing process and eliminate the margin for error that comes with human intervention. All pharmaceutical labels use color-coding based on pharmacological class per international and Joint Commission color code requirements for anesthetic labels [98–100]. The same technology is used for computer screens and the storage spaces on medical carts. Nomogram labels for infusion pumps eliminate the need for time-consuming and prone-to-error dosage calculations by clearly displaying the patient's weight and the recommended amount. By scanning the barcode on the syringe label with a barcode reader and then listening to an audio recording

**Table 3.2** Features of a new multimodal system designed to improve safety during anesthesia.

| Physical Aspects | Operational rules |
|---|---|
| 1. Preparation of an anesthetic workspace and aseptic approach is made easier with the use of customized medication trays. | 1. Ampoules are arranged correctly at the beginning of the case. |
| 2. Most widely used anesthesia medicines in pre-filled syringe form. | 2. For reconciliation, all empty ampoules and syringes were kept. |
| 3. Color-coded anesthetic labels in accordance with the international standard for anesthetic labels on large, readable medicine labels. | 3. Labeling all syringes is an absolute need. |
| 4. Automatic aural and visual verification of the chosen medication before to each administration is provided by a barcode scanner connected to a computer. The verification is recorded throughout the delivery of the medicine. | 4. Cross-checking of computerized voice is heard throughout each anesthesia. |
| 5. A visual and auditory alert will be shown on the screen if an antibiotic is not administered within 15 minutes of the start of anesthesia. | 5. Before each dose of medication is administered, the medicine label is checked. |
| 6. The worldwide standard for anesthetic medication labeling is followed in the design of the medicine trolley drawers, which include color coding. | |
| 7. Nomograms on drug infusion labels show weight and dosage, doing away with the necessity for dose calculations. | |
| Anesthetic records may be automatically compiled on the screen in real time and can be printed off. | |

of the drug name, it is able to conduct an auditory cross-check of each medication [101, 102]. We chose this particular warning tone because it stands out among the others often used in the operating room, allowing anesthesiologists to do the drug identification cross-check without having to look at a screen. Once the cross-check is finished, the medicine administration event is entered into the electronic anesthetic record. If an antibiotic is not given 15 minutes before the start of anesthesia, an audio and visual warning will be sent.

## 3.3.2  Evidence of Safety Gains

For clinical viability, anesthesiologists put the innovative gadget through its paces on a human-patient simulator with excellent realism [103]. At the same time that we were implementing the new system at one institution, we were collecting assisted incident reports at the other two. By analyzing data from 74,478 anesthetics, we were able to determine that the new approach significantly decreased medication mistakes by 35% (p = 0.002). Approximately 183,852 drug administrations (0.032%) were messed up, however just 268 medication administrations (0.049%) were messed up using the previous method [104]. The new method significantly cut down on omission errors and dose problems. Additionally, we found supporting data on the efficiency of drug class-specific color-coding. As opposed to the 47 errors detected when using conventional methods, only five occurred while using the novel method of replacement (with the identical denominators as before, p 14 0.01) When compared to prior methods, which had 11, p = 0.05 indicates that the new methodology had no significant negative consequences due to these errors. Two patients were conscious during the treatment, and one patient had an allergic response to neostigmine, which had been given to them instead of the neuromuscular blocking medicine they were supposed to receive (one after receiving a neuromuscular blocking drug prior to induction and the other after the propofol infusion was accidentally shut off). After anesthesia, four patients stayed longer than expected in the postoperative care unit (three due to overdosing on a neuromuscular blocking drug and one due to a substitution error).

It was shown that the new method resulted in lower error rates after studying 1075 cases, however the auditory crosscheck was equally useful. On average, anesthesiologists made six errors for every one hundred medicines given, compared to nine errors on average (p = 0.004) when they did not scan the drug barcode and activate the audio alert beforehand. Our results show the need of taking a systematic approach to decreasing anesthetic drug distribution mistakes, as opposed to depending only on manual methods, by equipping anesthesiologists with appropriate automation, enhanced prompts, and checks.

### 3.3.3   Consistent Color-Coding

A color-coding standard for anesthetic medicines has never before been shown to reduce interclass drug substitution errors [98, 99, 104], and this study is the first to prove that this is the case [105]. Interclass substitution mistakes, such as neostigmine and nitroglycerine being substituted for rocuronium, have been reported in incident reports. This is especially encouraging in view of the possible dangers associated with such substitutions. Although color coding has been used in healthcare for decades to reduce errors, there has been a lot of debate over its appropriateness and how it should be used in anesthesia [106–109]. The color coding of anesthetic drugs was a worry in some circumstances, while in others, respondents expressed concern about the lack of different colors or combinations of colors to adequately identify all anesthetic medications. In most Western countries, anesthetic labeling has been established, however, drug companies continue to disregard color code requirements when creating packaging and labels for pharmaceutical ampoules. In most cases, the information that the physician requires is put in the smallest type feasible on the label of the drug container [110, 111].

When I first brought this up more than a decade ago, I mentioned that the ampoule labels themselves may employ color coding in accordance with the international user-applied labeling standard [108]. There is no reason why labels on ampoules and syringes could not be the same color to increase ergonomics. Current rules and regulations state that all medication delivery lines must be prominently labeled and color-coded [112]. There are various measures that may be taken besides color labeling to reduce the likelihood of medication errors. The chemotherapy medication vincristine, for instance, might be fatal if injected into the spine [82, 113]. Connections that prohibit intravenous connectors from being used with intrathecal medication delivery lines have been developed. Mistakes with intrathecal lines are unusual compared to those with intravenous and epidural lines [52]. Because cross-connections are so much more prevalent than intrathecal faults, it makes sense to try to eliminate them wherever possible by utilizing connectors that are physically separate from one another.

### 3.3.4    The Codonics Label System

In accordance with worldwide and Joint Commission color guidelines, many recent articles [114, 115] explore the usage of anesthetic labels with barcodes and medication class-specific coloring. Through this method, labels for individual syringes are generated using digitally scanned images of ampoules containing medication. A voice recording of the drug's name is played when the syringe is injected. Two of these files report on the underlying mechanics of the labeling system. Based on observations of 277 operations [115], the new label system shows no evidence of effectiveness in avoiding adverse medication events and patient damage. Reducing the risk that errors will be repeated in the future depends on pinpointing their origins. Although the Codonics label system has not been researched in terms of the reduction of drug administration errors, it is expected that color-coded labels and an auditory cross-check of medicine identification would give equivalent safety gains as described above in these specific aspects.

## 3.4    The Triumph of Software

Additional software on a device increases its functionality, but also increases its learning curve. With all its programs, a computer is much more complicated to use than a microwave. By utilizing a highly specialized computer for each activity or application (the so-called knowledge appliance) with a straightforward and easy-to-understand user interface [116, 117], the issue of complicated software may be mitigated. In place of a central computer used by the organization to host a wide variety of programs (the current personal computer approach). The ease with which we may now produce information appliances is perhaps best shown by the first generation of mobile phones. As "smart" features like e-mail access, apps, and the ability to play games, take photos, and record video become more commonly accessible, mobile phones are quickly taking on the role of general-purpose computers. To ignore the necessity to "upgrade" to newer software in today's digitally sophisticated society is to seem like a Luddite. Due to their decreased speed in comparison to older versions, even the newest and fastest computer processors are unable to keep up with today's feature-heavy software [118]. But the vast majority of software's potential is still unrealized.

The number of transistors on a computer chip has a tendency to double every 18–24 months, and this exponential regularity has become a standard against which manufacturers measure their own market competitiveness [119]. Moore's Law characterizes this pattern. Many software companies employ an argument similar to Moore's Law when explaining why their products have more and more lines of code. For example, commercial aircraft manufacturers must produce planes that are both more affordable and more competitively designed by making them lighter and more feature-rich than their predecessors. Despite its high cost, software is the most practical means of achieving this objective [120, 121].

A single line of code might cost anything from $25 to $100 to create [122]. Due to the extensive validation procedures needed to erase any mistakes or malfunctions, the price per line for a safety-critical system, such as an airplane, nuclear power plant, or weapons system, is often several times higher. Each new line of code increases the time and effort required to do formal validation [123]. The software used in the space shuttle flight control system is among the safest in use today, but it is also one of the most expensive at roughly $1000 per line owing to rigorous validation. Experts now believe there are at least 50 bugs in this program. Even if most commercial software is not mission-critical, it is still hard to evaluate the code's reliability with any degree of certainty due to the vast amount of code (at least with current methods). There are 45 million lines of code in Microsoft Office 2013 [124]. Even if all of this software were rigorously tested, there would still be around 20,000 problems, according to estimates. Although Microsoft Office 2013 has undergone thorough testing, many additional vulnerabilities are anticipated to be introduced due to the software's complexity.

When compared to mechanical systems, software has several advantages, including more flexibility in configuration and the potential for improvement, as well as reduced costs and shorter manufacturing times. However, it is difficult to develop software that is both error-free and totally secure due to the lack of physical limits on the ways in which software may go wrong. The system's intricacy means that even seasoned experts may be baffled by its actions. Your computer may behave normally again after a restart or a software reinstallation if you experience any strange behavior. It is possible that software is the weakest link in the system if a catastrophic software failure or "crash" can be traced back to a single fault in the code. Any of the on-board power generators might go into fail-safe mode after 248 days of continuous operation due to a software vulnerability in Boeing's $200 million Dreamliner passenger aircraft, leading to a catastrophic loss of control of the aircraft in flight. Every three months, each Boeing aircraft is given a complete checkup and inspection [125].

### 3.4.1   Software in Hospitals

Integration of software into hospitals and healthcare is necessary, yet it requires prudence owing to software's potential benefits. Healthcare software has a hard time since it is typically created by committees of technical people without enough involvement with the intended consumers [126, 127]. If the product is completely novel and will not cause any disruption to users' routines, or if the users are relatively inexperienced and can be taught the ropes of the new application, then this approach may be suitable. Since hospital software is designed to be used by trained professionals, who follow strict protocols that have been developed over time for good reason, this issue does not arise. Healthcare is a challenging field to work in because of the wide range of patient demands and the varying degrees of expertise among professionals [75]. Both patients and doctors are not just commodities to be shuffled about. However, this industrial way of thinking still provides the bulk of the technical expertise needed to create the vast majority of today's computer programs. Reasons for using an industrial model in healthcare administration sometimes include the pursuit of greater efficiency and lower operating costs [128]. Despite this, medical IT fails often because of the complexity of healthcare. Healthcare software controllability and dependability concerns will need more attention as the number of medical devices controlled by software grows [129–132]. Examples of such devices include artificial neural networks for clinical diagnosis and virtual reality headsets.

### 3.4.2    Software in Anesthesia

As state-of-the-art surgical suites invest in more cutting-edge equipment, it stands to reason that anesthetic software will be used more often. A growing trend in several hospitals is the use of fully computerized anesthetic equipment, which is being hailed as "state of the art" by its supporters. In order to replace mechanical control layers, developers have created novel software, which includes electronic representations of spinning rotameters [133]. After multiple power failures and "software faults" with these high-tech automated anesthetic systems, it has been normal custom in some hospitals to maintain an Ambubag or other manual ventilation equipment on the back of the machine. If the anesthesiologist's biotech system were to have a software failure, its reliability would be significantly reduced (Figure 3.1).

Additional anesthetic devices that need a great deal of software include syringe pumps and Target Controlled Infusion (TCI) systems [134, 135]. As closed-loop infusion systems become more commonplace, infusion pumps are expected to need more than 100,000 lines of code. Even though these computerized pumps are used in a vast majority of operating rooms throughout the globe every day, there are certain adverse events associated with their usage [136–138]. Over 11,000 complaints of infusion pump-related adverse events, including those that result in patient harm or death, are submitted annually to the FDA [139]. There were very few problems that could be attributed to pump failure. Most complaints are related to users not understanding the pump's default settings or being bothered by "annoying" or otherwise ineffective warning messages. As with earlier attempts to provide anesthetic drugs, making more efforts will not solve the difficulties at hand makes it clear that the present state of pump interfaces is inadequate, and that further work is needed to create displays and programming sequences that are more intuitive. It is vital to standardize, for example, the displays and medication libraries of different brands and types.

After analyzing the user interfaces of infusion pumps, researchers discovered a "virtuality" issue [139]. One characteristic of software is its inability to prevent a large variety of "impossible" or "nonsensical" failure situations. However, physical systems cannot have their components ordered in a limitless number of ways, and therefore prevents an infinite number of meaningless and destructive states from forming [140]. For example, 1000 overdoses were given when infusion pumps were adjusted wrongly owing to a misunderstanding of grams vs. milligrams [141]. The optimal answer to this issue is to impose functions that simplify and confine user interaction sequences, as this precludes configurations that are useless or destructive in some manner. Pump designers should have a better understanding of their products' actual use to avoid unintended consequences. This is a perfect use for devices like drug infusion pumps.

### 3.4.3    The Alarm Problem

While a plane's cockpit and an anesthesiologist's office could not be more different, comparisons between the two are occasionally made when talking about safety cultures in their respective fields. A major distinction is that the many tools and systems utilized in an operating room are not coordinated with one another. The majority of today's medical equipment are made by a plethora of companies that only seldom work together. The alert problem [128, 142] is one of the most egregious integration issues. Any time the anesthetic machines, infusion pumps, or other equipment in the operating room detect a deviation from the expected operational parameters, an alert will sound. There are several issues that patients have that the anesthesiologist either ignores or dismisses as unimportant. Captain Chesley "Sully" Sullenberger, a renowned pilot, was recently interviewed by Dr. Robert Wachter for his review The Digital Doctor [128]. Avoiding alarm fatigue, which occurs when operators ignore or disable alarms, requires a warning system free of false positives. When designing aviation systems, engineers and pilots must reach consensus on what data should be sent to the pilot and what data should not be [143]. After the permitted alarms are put into a strict hierarchy, some alarms are simply named "advisories" or "cautions" and exhibited in color-coded text on a screen without an audible warning since they are not time-critical events and may be dealt with when the pilot has the time. As an added convenience, an on-screen checklist for each occurrence is available to pilots, outlining both the default and recommended responses. A stall warning may take several forms, such as a red light blinking, a red message popping up on the screen, an audible alert being given, or even the control column shaking. If one engine fails in a multi-engine aircraft, a warning will be sent rather than a top-level alert since the situation is not considered to be urgent [128]. When in the "cockpit" of an anesthetic machine, a lack of prioritization, filtering, or synchronization of warnings results in a cacophony of beeps and tones, sometimes drowning out vital information since they all look and sound the same.

## 3.5    Environments that Audit Themselves

Several components of current operating room equipment, such as infusion pumps [128, 141, 144], continually record data on how they are utilized, giving a picture of clinical activity. With the use of Radiofrequency Identification (RFID) sensors and transmitters located in important regions of the operating room, automatic data gathering may be increased and enhanced [145]. Using radio frequency identification (RFID) sensors and other wirelessly linked devices, one may create a "network of things" in the OR [146, 147]; a high-tech environment that can constantly monitor and audit itself. The results of a self-audit may be put to a variety of purposes. An example of a solution to the current alarm problem would be the implementation of a universal computer system capable of linking and managing all surgical equipment, which could then provide hierarchical management over warnings and alarms in order to rationalize and priorities them, much like an airplane cockpit. Through a display in the anesthesiologist's workspace, real-time analysis of data streaming from the network of sensors might potentially help in the identification of subtle and occasionally not-so-subtle signals of patient danger (with or without an auditory signal). One approach in which a system based on an infusion pump may detect an overdose of an infusion running at 10 times the average rate would be to monitor the dosage and compare it to the patient's body weight. Wachter's perceptive analysis of patient data may have applications outside the emergency room [128].

## 3.6    New Risks and Dangers

It is important to proceed with care while trying to fix technical issues by introducing new, cutting-edge technology. Nonetheless, this does not justify halting advancements in medical technology, which would be neither desired nor feasible [148]. We need improved technology, not worse; technology that takes into consideration the complexity of the double-human

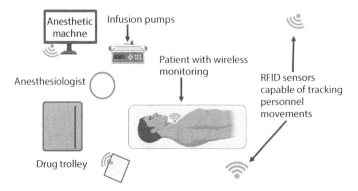

**Figure 3.3** An unbiased look at a self-assessing operating room. Medical devices like infusion pumps and anesthesia monitors might be connected to a network of things using radio frequency identification (RFID) readers positioned strategically around the room. Potentially life-threatening abnormalities, such as an infusion pump distributing a drug dose that is beyond the projected range for a patient's weight, might be seen by this network, which may have access to patient information and monitor staff mobility and operating room usage. It is possible that alarm fatigue might be avoided if networks were able to coordinate gadgets in the same way a plane's cockpit does.

interface and the patients' ever-changing requirements. We must continually be on the lookout for new threats and hazards, since every technological advancement comes with the prospect of both benefits and drawbacks. It is possible that current RFID tags cause electromagnetic interference that "crashes" existing medication infusion pumps [149, 150]. This is especially problematic since just turning the pump off and on again may not address the issue. When used in a commercial setting, radio frequency identification (RFID) technology has the potential to cause clinically significant interference with implanted pacemakers [151]. Since the software in the pumps may be automatically updated by the manufacturer in real time, some experts consider wireless communication between infusion pumps and a hospital's Wi-Fi network to be a crucial safety element [141]. Wi-Fi-enabled pumps can accomplish this; however, hackers might potentially exploit this feature to remotely administer a deadly quantity of the patient's medicine [152].

Self-assessing operating room is shown in Figure 3.3.

## 3.7   Conclusion

When it was first created more than a century ago, anesthesia was heralded as a game-changing improvement in the protection of surgical patients.

Several facets of intravenous anesthesia have not altered much in decades and are still prone to mistake, despite recent technical developments. A patient-centered approach is no longer adequate for ensuring patient safety during modern anesthetic treatments. Human factors ideas, such as improved workplace organization, cueing, checking, and color coding, may help minimize medication administration errors in anesthesia, according to the available evidence.

Patient safety may be improved by applying lessons learned from the aviation sector to the integration of technology in the operating room. It is clear that robots and humans have quite distinct abilities. Data entry, event tracking, and information verification are all activities that may benefit from being computerized and hence automated. While we may have trouble with the everyday, we are masters at seeing around corners and surmounting challenges. The safest possible anesthetic administration depends on a partnership between the anesthesiologist and the operating room's infrastructure, and this partnership must take into account the respective strengths of each. By keeping in mind that individuals are neither robots nor super humans, anesthetic technology may be more useful to anesthesiologists.

# References

1. Gawande, A., *The checklist manifesto – how to get things right*, Metropolitan Books, New York, 2009.
2. Institute of Medicine, *To err is human – building a safer health system*, National Academy Press, Washington, 2000.
3. Department of Health, *An organisation with a memory – report of an expert group on learning from adverse events in the NHS*, Stationery Office, London, 2000.
4. Bates, D.W., Frequency, consequences and prevention of adverse drug events. *J. Qual. Clin. Pract.*, 19, 13–7, 1999.
5. Merry, A.F. and McCall Smith, A., *Errors, medicine and the law*, Cambridge University Press, Cambridge, 2001.
6. Webster, C.S., The iatrogenic-harm cost equation and new technology. *Anaesthesia*, 60, 843–6, 2005.
7. Andel, C., Davidow, S.L., Hollander, M., Moreno, D.A., The economics of healthcare quality and medical errors. *J. Healthcare Finance*, 39, 39–50, 2012.
8. James, J.T., A new, evidence-based estimate of patient harms associated with hospital care. *J. Patient Saf.*, 9, 122–8, 2013.
9. Wheeler, S.J. and Wheeler, D.W., Medication errors in anaesthesia and critical care. *Anaesthesia*, 60, 257–73, 2005.

10. Weiser, T.G., Regenbogen, S.E., Thompson, K.D., Haynes, A.B., Lipsitz, S.R., Berry, W.R. *et al.*, An estimation of the global volume of surgery: A modelling strategy based on available data. *Lancet*, 372, 139–44, 2008.

11. Gawande, A.A., Thomas, E.J., Zinner, M.J., Brennan, T.A., The incidence and nature of surgical adverse events in Colorado and Utah in 1992. *Surgery*, 126, 66–75, 1999.

12. Webster, C.S., The nuclear power industry as an alternative analogy for safety in anaesthesia and a novel approach for the conceptualization of safety goals. *Anaesthesia*, 60, 1115–22, 2005.

13. Bagshaw, R.J., Systems theory and the anaesthetist. *Acta Anaesthesiol. Scand.*, 24, 379–92, 1980.

14. Cooper, J.B. and Gaba, D., No myth – anesthesia is a model for addressing patient safety. *Anesthesiology*, 97, 1335–7, 2002.

15. Altman, D.G. and Bland, J.M., Absence of evidence is not evidence of absence. *Br. Med. J.*, 311, 485, 1995.

16. Webster, C.S. and Grieve, D.J., Attitudes to error and patient safety. *Prometheus*, 23, 253–63, 2005.

17. Bach, L.A. and Sharpe, K., Sample size for clinical and biological research. *Aust. N. Z. J. Med.*, 19, 64–8, 1989.

18. Hanley, J.A. and Lippmann-Hand, A., If nothing goes wrong is everything all right? Interpreting zero numerators. *JAMA*, 249, 1743–5, 1983.

19. Rutherford, J.S., Merry, A.F., Occleshaw, C.J., Depth of central venous catheterization: An audit of practice in a cardiac surgical unit. *Anaesth. Intensive Care*, 22, 267–71, 1994.

20. Sitzmann, J.V., The technique of managing central venous lines. *J. Crit. Illn.*, 1, 50–5, 1986.

21. Pellegrini, R.V., Marcelli, G., Di Marco, R.F., Bekoe, S., Grant, K., Marrangoni, A.G., Swan-Ganz catheter induced pulmonary hemorrhage. *J. Cardiovasc. Surg. (Torino)*, 28, 646–9, 1987.

22. Karnauchow, P.N., Cardiac tamponade from central venous catheterization. *Can. Med. Assoc. J.*, 135, 1145–7, 1986.

23. Ellis, L.M., Vogel, S.B., Copeland, E.M., Central venous catheter vascular erosions – diagnosis and clinical course. *Ann. Surg.*, 209, 475–8, 1989.

24. Merry, A.F., Webster, C.S., Van Cotthem, I.C., Holland, R.L., Beca, J.S., Middleton, N.G., A prospective randomized clinical assessment of a new pigtail central venous catheter in comparison with standard alternatives. *Anaesth. Intensive Care*, 27, 639–45, 1999.

25. Mukau, L., Talamini, M.A., Sitzmann, J.V., Risk factors for central venous catheter-related vascular erosions. *J. Parenter. Enteral Nutr.*, 15, 513–6, 1991.

26. Fraser, R.S., Catheter-induced pulmonary artery perforation: Pathologic and pathogenic features. *Hum. Pathol.*, 18, 1246–51, 1987.

27. Shah, K.B., Rao, T.L.K., Laughlin, S., El-Etr, A.A., A review of pulmonary artery catheterization in 6,245 patients. *Anesthesiology*, 61, 271–5, 1984.

28. Sirivella, S., Gielchinsky, I., Parsonnet, V., Management of catheterinduced pulmonary artery perforation: A rare complication in cardiovascular operations. *Ann. Thorac. Surg.*, 72, 2056–9, 2001.

29. Sekkal, S., Cornu, E., Christidès, C., Laskar, M., Serhal, C., Ghossein, Y. *et al.*, Swan-Ganz catheter induced pulmonary artery perforation during cardiac surgery concerning two cases. *J. Cardiovasc. Surg.*, 37, 313–7, 1996.

30. Choh, J.H., Khazei, A.H., Ihm, H.J., Thatcher, W.C., Batty, P.R., Catheter induced pulmonary arterial perforation during open heart surgery. *J. Cardiovasc. Surg.*, 35, 61–4, 1994.

31. Malbezin, S., Gauss, T., Smith, I., Bruneau, B., Mangalsuren, N., Diallo, T. *et al.*, A review of 5434 percutaneous pediatric central venous catheters inserted by anesthesiologists. *Paediatr. Anaesth.*, 23, 974–9, 2013.

32. Webster, C.S., Merry, A.F., Emmens, D.J., Van Cotthem, I.C., Holland, R.L., Middleton, N.G., A prospective clinical audit of central venous catheter use and complications in 1000 consecutive patients. *Anaesth. Intensive Care*, 31, 80–6, 2003.

33. Cohen, J.A., Blackshear, R.H., Gravenstein, N., Woeste, J., Increased pulmonary artery perforating potential of pulmonary artery catheters during hypothermia. *J. Cardiothorac. Vasc. Anesth.*, 5, 234–6, 1991.

34. Chernow, B., Pulmonary artery flotation catheters: A statement by the American College of Chest Physicians and the American Thoracic Society [editorial]. *Chest*, 111, 261–2, 1997.

35. Barash, P.G., Nardi, D., Hammond, G., Walker-Smith, G., Capuano, D., Laks, H. *et al.*, Catheter-induced pulmonary artery perforation:mechanisms, management, and modifications. *J. Thorac. Cardiovasc. Surg.*, 82, 5–12, 1981.

36. Polderman, K.H. and Girbes, A.R.J., Central venous catheter use – part 1: mechanical complications. *Intensive Care Med.*, 28, 1–17, 2002.

37. Cooper, J.B., Newbower, R.S., Long, C.D., McPeek, B., Preventable anesthesia mishaps – a study of human factors. *Anesthesiology*, 49, 399–406, 1978.

38. Utting, J.E., Gray, T.C., Shelley, F.C., Human misadventure in anaesthesia. *Can. Anaesth. Soc. J.*, 26, 472–8, 1979.

39. Cooper, J.B., Newbower, R.S., Kitz, R.J., An analysis of major errors and equipment failures in anesthesia management –considerations for prevention and detection. *Anesthesiology*, 60, 34–42, 1984.

40. Chopra, V., Bovill, J.G., Spierdijk, J., Koornneef, F., Reported significant observations during anaesthesia – a prospective analysis over an 18-month period. *Br. J. Anaesth.*, 68, 13–7, 1992.

41. Currie, M., Mackay, P., Morgan, C., Runciman, W.B., Russell, W.J., Sellen, A. *et al.*, The "wrong drug" problem in anaesthesia – an analysis of 2000 incident reports. *Anaesth. Intensive Care*, 21, 596–601, 1993.

42. Short, T.G., O'Regan, A., Jayasuriya, J.P., Rowbottom, M., Buckley, T.A., Oh, T.E., Improvements in anaesthetic care resulting from a critical incident reporting programme. *Anaesthesia*, 51, 615–21, 1996.

43. Sinclair, M., Simmons, S., Cyna, A., Incidents in obstetric anaesthesia and analgesia – an analysis of 5000 AIMS reports. *Anaesth. Intensive Care*, 27, 275–81, 1999.

44. Orser, B.A., Chen, R.J.B., Yee, D.A., Medication errors in anestheticpractice: A survey of 687 practitioners. *Can. J. Anaesth.*, 48, 139–46, 2001.

45. Abeysekera, A., Bergman, I.J., Kluger, M.T., Short, T.G., Drug error in anaesthetic practice – a review of 896 reports from the Australian Incident Monitoring Study database. *Anaesthesia*, 60, 220–7, 2005.

46. Sakaguchi, Y., Tokuda, K., Yamaguchi, K., Irita, K., Incidence of anesthesia-related medication errors over a 15-year period in a university hospital. *Fukuoka Igaku Zasshi*, 99, 58–66, 2008.

47. Chopra, V., Bovill, J.G., Spierdijk, J., Accidents, near accidents and complications during anaesthesia. *Anaesthesia*, 45, 3–6, 1990.

48. Craig, J. and Wilson, M.E., A survey of anaesthetic misadventures. *Anaesthesia*, 36, 933–6, 1981.

49. Kumar, V., Barcellos, W.A., Mehta, M.P., Carter, J.G., An analysis of critical incidents in a teaching department for quality assurance – a survey of mishaps during anaesthesia. *Anaesthesia*, 43, 879–83, 1988.

50. Short, T.G., O'Regan, A., Lew, J., Oh, T.E., Critical incident reporting in an anaesthetic department quality assurance programme. *Anaesthesia*, 48, 3–7, 1993.

51. Fasting, S. and Gisvold, S.E., Adverse drug errors in anesthesia, and the impact of coloured syringe labels. *Can. J. Anaesth.*, 47, 1060–7, 2000.

52. Webster, C.S., Merry, A.F., Larsson, L., McGrath, K.A., Weller, J., The frequency and nature of drug administration error during anaesthesia. *Anaesth. Intensive Care*, 29, 494–500, 2001.

53. Morag, I., Gopher, D., Spillinger, A., Auerbach-Shpak, Y., Laufer, N., Lavy, Y. *et al.*, Human factors-focused reporting system for improving care quality and safety in hospital wards. *Hum. Factors*, 54, 195–213, 2012.

54. Runciman, B., Merry, A., McCall Smith, A., Improving patients' safety by gathering information – anonymous reporting has an important role. *Br. Med. J.*, 323, 298, 2001.

55. Bates, D.W., Medication errors – how common are they and what can be done to prevent them. *Drug Saf.*, 15, 303–10, 1996.

56. Merry, A.F. and Peck, D.J., Anaesthetists, errors in drug administration and the law. *N. Z. Med. J.*, 108, 185–7, 1995.

57. Bowdle, A., Kruger, C., Grieve, R., Emmens, D., Merry, A., Anesthesia drug administration error in a university hospital. *Anesthesiology*, 99, A1358, 2003.

58. Llewellyn, R.L., Gordon, P.C., Wheatcroft, D., Lines, D., Reed, A., Butt, A.D. *et al.*, Drug administration error – a prospective survey fromthree South African teaching hospitals. *Anaesth. Intensive Care*, 37, 93–8, 2009.

59. Zhang, Y., Dong, Y.J., Webster, C.S., Ding, X.D., Liu, X.Y., Chen, W.M. *et al.*, The frequency and nature of drug administration error during anaesthesia in a Chinese hospital. *Acta Anaesthesiol. Scand.*, 57, 158–64, 2013.

60. Cooper, L., DiGiovanni, N., Schultz, L., Taylor, A.M., Nossaman, B., Influences observed on incidence and reporting of medication errors in anesthesia. *Can. J. Anaesth.*, 59, 562–70, 2012.

61. Heinrich, H.W., *Industrial accident prevention – a scientific approach*, 4th ed, McGraw-Hill, New York, 1959.

62. Barach, P. and Small, S.D., Reporting and preventing medical mishaps –lessons from non-medical near miss reporting systems. *Br. Med. J.*, 320, 759–63, 2000.

63. Mason, K.P., Green, S.M., Piacevoli, Q., International Sedation Task Force, Adverse event reporting tool to standardize the reporting and tracking of adverse events during procedural sedation: A consenses document from the World SIVA International Sedation Task Force. *Br. J. Anaesth.*, 108, 13–20, 2012.

64. WebAIRS., Anaesthetic incident reporting system, Australasian and New Zealand College of Anaesthetists (ANZCA), Demonstration page: http://www.anztadc.net/Demo/IncidentTabbed.aspx. Accessed 18 Feb 2016

65. Shojania, K.G., The frustrating case of incident-reporting systems. *Qual. Saf. Healthcare*, 17, 400–2, 2008.

66. Kringos, D.S., Sunol, R., Wagner, C., Mannion, R., Michel, P., Klazinga, N.S. *et al.*, The influence of context on the effectiveness of hospital quality improvement strategies: A review of systematic reviews. *BMC Health Serv. Res.*, 15, 277, 2015.

67. Sittig, D.F. and Singh, H., A new sociotechnical model for studying health information technology in complex adapative healthcare systems. *Qual. Saf. Healthcare*, 19, i68–74, 2010.

68. Boyd, M., A method for prioritizing interventions following root cause analysis (RCA) – lessons from philosophy. *J. Eval. Clin. Pract.*, 21, 461–9, 2015.

69. Jeffs, L., Berta, W., Lingard, L., Baker, G.R., Learning from near misses: From quick fixes to closing off the Swiss-cheese holes. *BMJ Qual. Saf.*, 21, 287–94, 2012.

70. Thomas, E.J. and Petersen, L.A., Measuring errors and adverse events in healthcare. *J. Gen. Intern. Med.*, 18, 61–7, 2003.

71. Reason, J., Understanding adverse events: Human factors. *Qual. Healthcare*, 4, 80–9, 1995.

72. Keers, R.N., Williams, S.D., Cooke, J., Walsh, T., Ashcroft, D.M., Impactof interventions designed to reduce medication administration errors in hospitals: A systematic review. *Drug Saf.*, 37, 317–32, 2014.

73. Thomas, E.J., The future of measuring patient safety: Prospective clinical surveillance. *BMJ Qual. Saf.*, 24, 244–5, 2015.

74. Vincent, C., Burnett, S., Carthey, J., Safety measurement and monitoring in healthcare: A framework to guide clinical teams and healthcare organisations in maintaining safety. *BMJ Qual. Saf.*, 23, 670–7, 2014.

75. Webster, C.S., Anderson, B.J., Stabile, M.J., Merry, A.F., Improving the safety of pediatric sedation – human error, technology and clinical microsystems, in: *Pediatric Sedation Outside of the Operating Room: A Multispecialty International Collaboration*, K.P. Mason (Ed.), pp. 587–612, Springer Science, New York, 2015.

76. Webster, C.S., Why anaesthetising a patient is more prone to failure than flying a plane. *Anaesthesia*, 57, 819–20, 2002.

77. Weaver, S.J., Lubomksi, L.H., Wilson, R.F., Pfoh, E.R., Martinez, K.A., Dy, S.M., Promoting a culture of safety as a patient safety strategy: A systematic review. *Ann. Intern. Med.*, 158, 369–74, 2013.

78. Pronovost, P. and Vohr, E., *Safe patients, smart hospitals*, Hudson Street Press, London, 2010.

79. Webster, C.S., Human psychology applies to doctors too. *Anaesthesia*, 55, 929–30, 2000.

80. Anderson, D.J. and Webster, C.S., A systems approach to the reduction of medication error on the hospital ward. *J. Adv. Nurs.*, 35, 34–41, 2001.

81. Reason, J., Human error – models and management. *Br. Med. J.*, 320, 768–70, 2000.

82. Webster, C.S., Doctors must implement new safety systems, not whinge about them. *Anaesthesia*, 57, 1231–2, 2002.

83. Nott, M.R., The labelling of ampoules. *Anaesthesia*, 36, 223–4, 1981.

84. Reason, J., *Human error*, Cambridge University Press, New York, 1990.

85. Sagan, S.D., *The limits of safety – organizations, accidents, and nuclear weapons*, Princeton University Press, Princeton, 1993.

86. Reason, J., The contribution of latent human failures to the breakdown of complex systems. *Philos. Trans. R. Soc. Lond. B*, 327, 475–84, 1990.

87. Nunn, D.S. and Baird, W.L.M., Ampoule labelling [editorial]. *Anaesthesia*, 51, 1–2, 1996.

88. Wildsmith, J.A.W., Doctors must read drug labels, not whinge about them. *Br. Med. J.*, 324, 170, 2002.

89. Norman, D.A., *The psychology of everyday things*, Basic Books, New York, 1998.

90. Rasmussen, J., Pejtersen, A.M., Goodstein, L.P., *Cognitive systems engineering*, Wiley, New York, 1994.

91. Merry, A.F., Webster, C.S., Mathew, D.J., A new, safety-oriented, integrated drug administration and automated anesthesia record system. *Anesth. Analg.*, 93, 385–90, 2001.

92. Spath, P.L., *Error reduction in healthcare – a systems approach to improving patient care*, Jossey-Bass, San Francisco, 2000.

93. Merry, A.F. and Webster, C.S., Anaesthetists and drug administration error— Towards an irreducible minimum, in: *Australasian Anaesthesia*, J. Keneally

and M. Jones (Eds.), pp. 53–61, Australian and New Zealand College of Anaesthetists, Melbourne, 1996.

94. Perrow, C., *Normal accidents – living with high risk technologies*, Basic Books, New York, 1984.

95. Chiles, J.R., *Inviting disaster – lessons from the edge of technology*, Harper Collins Publishers, New York, 2001.

96. Takano, K. and Reason, J., Psychological biases affecting human cognitive performance in dynamic operational environments. *J. Nucl. Sci. Technol.*, 36, 1041–51, 1999.

97. Pronovost, P.J. and Hudson, D.W., Improving healthcare quality through organisational peer-to-peer assessment: Lessons from the nuclear power industry. *BMJ Qual. Saf.*, 21, 872–5, 2012.

98. Anonymous, Anaesthetic and respiratory equipment – userapplied labels for syringes containing drugs used during anaesthesia – colours, design and performance (ISO 26825:2008), International Organization for Standardization, 2008, Available from: http://www.iso.org. Accessed 18 Feb 2016.

99. Jelacic, S., Bowdle, A., Nair, B.G., Kusulos, D., Bower, L., Togashi, K., A system for anesthesia drug administration using barcode technology: The Codonics Safe Label System and Smart Anesthesia Manager. *Anesth. Analg.*, 121, 410–21, 2015.

100. Merry, A.F., Webster, C.S., Connell, H., A new infusion syringe label system designed to reduce task complexity during drug preparation. *Anaesthesia*, 62, 486–91, 2007.

101. Li, B., Parmentier, F.B.R., Zhang, M., Behavioral distraction by auditory deviance is mediated by the sound's informational value. *Exp. Psychol.*, 60, 260–8, 2013.

102. Merry, A.F., Webster, C.S., Hannam, J., Mitchell, S.J., Edwards, K., Jardim, A. *et al.*, Multimodal system designed to reduce errors in recording and administration of drugs in anaesthesia: A prospective randomised clinical evaluation. *BMJ*, 343, d5543, 2011.

103. Merry, A.F., Webster, C.S., Weller, J., Henderson, S., Robinson, B., Evaluation in an anaesthetic simulator of a prototype of a new drug administration system designed to reduce error. *Anaesthesia*, 57, 256–63, 2002.

104. Webster, C.S., Larsson, L., Frampton, C.M., Weller, J., McKenzie, A., Cumin, D. *et al.*, Clinical assessment of a new anaesthetic drug administration system: A prospective, controlled, longitudinal incident monitoring study. *Anaesthesia*, 65, 490–9, 2010.

105. Hunter, D.T. and Sumsion, E.G., A color code system in blood banking. *Transfusion*, 7, 451–2, 1967.

106. Webster, C.S., Manufacturers' obligations to colour-code prefilled syringes correctly. *Anaesthesia*, 68, 783–4, 2013.

107. Merry, A.F. and Webster, C.S., Labelling and drug administration error. *Anaesthesia*, 51, 987–8, 1996.

108. Webster, C.S., Mathew, D.J., Merry, A.F., Effective labelling is difficult, but safety really does matter. *Anaesthesia*, 57, 201–2, 2002.

109. Smellie, G.D., Lees, N.W., Smith, E.M., Drug recognition by nurses and anaesthetists. *Anaesthesia*, 37, 206–8, 1982.

110. Webster, C.S. and Anderson, D.J., A practical guide to the implementation of an effective incident reporting scheme to reduce medication error on the hospital ward. *Int. J. Nurs. Pract.*, 8, 176–83, 2002.

111. James, R.H. and Rabey, P.G., Illegibility of drug ampoule labels. *Br. Med. J.*, 307, 658–9, 1993.

112. Merry, A.F., Shipp, D.H., Lowinger, J.S., The contribution of labelling to safe medication administration in anaesthetic practice. *Best Pract. Res. Clin. Anaesthesiol.*, 25, 145–59, 2011.

113. Lanigan, C.J., Safer epidural and spinal connectors. *Anaesthesia*, 57, 567–71, 2002.

114. Ang, S.B.L., Hing, W.C., Tun, S.Y., Park, T., Experience with the use of the Codonics Safe Label System to improve labelling compliance of anaesthesia drugs. *Anaesth Intensive Care*, 42, 500–6, 2014.

115. Nanji, K.C., Patel, A., Shaikh, S., Seger, D.L., Bates, D.W., Evaluation of perioperative medication errors and adverse drug events. *Anesthesiology*, 124, 25–34, 2016.

116. Norman, D.A., *The invisible computer*, MIT Press, Cambridge, 1999.

117. Bergman, E., *Information appliances and beyond*, Morgan Kaufmann, San Francisco, 2000.

118. Negroponte, N., Hack out the useless extras – bloated software is swamping hard-won advances in computing power. *New Sci.*, 182, 26, 2004.

119. Moore's Law, https://en.wikipedia.org/wiki/Moore%27s_law.Accessed 18 Feb 2016.

120. Wiener, L.R., *Digital woes – why we should not depend on software*, Addison-Wesley, New York, 1993.

121. Campbell-Kelly, M. and Aspray-Kelly, W., *Computer – a history of the information machine*, Basic Books, New York, 1996.

122. Leveson, N.G., *Safeware – system safety and computers*, Addison-Wesley, New York, 1995.

123. Patton, R., *Software testing*, Sams Publishing, Indianapolis, 2000.

124. Information is Beautiful, http://www.informationisbeautiful.net/visualizations/million-lines-of-code/. Accessed 18 Feb 2016.

125. Neumann, P.G., *Computer related risks*, Addison-Wesley, New York, 1995.

126. Gibbs, S., US aviation authority: Boeing 787 bug could cause 'loss of control', The Guardian, United Kingdom, 2015, http://www.theguardian.com/business/2015/may/01/us-aviation-authority-boeing-787-dreamliner-bug-could-cause-loss-of-control. Accessed 18 Feb 2016.

127. Goodin, D., Boeing 787 Dreamliners contain a potentially catastrophic software bug, ARS Technica, Netherlands, 2015, http://arstechnica.com/information-technology/2015/05/boeing-787-dreamlinerscontain-a-potentially-catastrophic-software-bug/. Accessed 18 Feb 2016.

128. Wachter, R.M., *The digital doctor: Hope, hype, and harm at the dawn of medicine's computer age*, McGraw-Hill, USA, 2015.

129. Baxt, W.G., Application of artificial neural networks to clinical medicine. *Lancet*, 346, 1135–8, 1995.

130. McCloy, R. and Stone, R., Virtual reality in surgery. *Br. Med. J.*, 323, 912–5, 2001.

131. Buckingham, R.A. and Buckingham, R.O., Robots in operating theatres. *Br. Med. J.*, 311, 1479–82, 1995.

132. Catchpole, K., Perkins, C., Bresee, C., Solnik, M.J., Sherman, B., Fritch, J. *et al.*, Safety, efficiency and learning curves in robotic surgery: A human factors analysis. *Surg. Endosc.*, 30, 9, 3749–61, 2015.

133. Langford, R., All in the name of progress. *Anaesthesia*, 57, 313, 2002.

134. United States Food and Drug Administration, http://www.fda.gov/MedicalDevices/ProductsandMedicalProcedures/GeneralHospitalDevicesandSupplies/InfusionPumps/ucm202511.htm. Accessed 18 Feb 2016.

135. Liu, N. and Rinehart, J., Closed-loop propofol administration: Routine care or a research tool? What impact in the future? *Anesth. Analg.*, 122, 4–6, 2016.

136. Absalom, A.R., Glen, J.I., Zwart, G.J., Schnider, T.W., Struys, M.M., Target-controlled infusion: A mature technology. *Anesth. Analg.*, 122, 70–8, 2016.

137. Schnider, T.W., Minto, C.F., Struys, M.M., Absalom, A.R., The safety of target-controlled infusions. *Anesth. Analg.*, 122, 79–85, 2016.

138. Ohashi, K., Dalleur, O., Dykes, P.C., Bates, D.W., Benefits and risks of using smart pumps to reduce medication error rates – a systematicreview. *Drug Saf.*, 37, 1011–20, 2014.

139. Schraagen, J.M. and Verhoeven, F., Methods for studying medical devices technology and practitioner cognitition – the case of user-interface issues with infusion pumps. *J. Biomed. Inform.*, 46, 181–95, 2013.

140. Manrique-Rodriguez, S., Sanchez-Galindo, A., Fernandez-Llamazares, C.M., Lopez-Herce, J., Garcia-Lopez, I., Carrillo-Alvarez, A. *et al.*, Developing a drug library for smart pumps in a pediatric intensive care unit. *Artif. Intell. Med.*, 54, 155–61, 2012.

141. Mansfield, J. and Jarrett, S., Using smart pumps to understand and evaluate clinician practice patterns to ensure patient safety. *Hosp. Pharm.*, 48, 942–50, 2013.

142. Woods, D.D., The alarm problem and directed attention in dynamic fault management. *Ergonomics*, 38, 2371–93, 1995.

143. Rayo, M.F. and Moffatt-Bruce, S.D., Alarm system management: Evidence-based guidance encouraging direct measurement of informativeness to improve alarm response. *BMJ Qual. Saf.*, 24, 282–6, 2015.

144. Catlin, A.C., Malloy, W.X., Arthur, K.J., Gaston, C., Young, J., Fernando, S. *et al.*, Comparative analytics of infusion pump data across multiple hospital systems. *Am. J. Health Syst. Pharm.*, 72, 317–24, 2015.

145. Houliston, B.R., Parry, D.T., Merry, A.F., TADAA: Towards automated detection of anaesthetic activity. *Methods Inf. Med.*, 5, 464–71, 2011.

146. Agarwal, S., Joshi, A., Finin, T., Yesha, Y., Ganous, T., A pervasive computing system for the operating room of the future. *Mob. Netw. Appl.*, 12, 215–28, 2007.

147. Reicher, J., Reicher, D., Reicher, M., Use of radio frequency identification (RFID) tags in bedside monitoring of endotracheal tube position. *J. Clin. Monit. Comput.*, 21, 155–8, 2007.

148. Webster, C.S., Resistance is futile – the future and post-humanity. *Prometheus*, 24, 341–8, 2006.

149. Houliston, B., Parry, D., Webster, C.S., Merry, A.F., Interference with the operation of medical devices resulting from the use of radio frequency identification technology. *N. Z. Med. J.*, 122, 9–16, 2009.

150. van der Togt, R., van Lieshout, E.J., Hensbroek, R., Beinat, E., Binnekade, J.M., Bakker, P.J.M., Electromagnetic interferance from radio frequency identification inducing potentially hazardous incidents in critical care medical equipment. *JAMA*, 299, 2884–90, 2008.

151. Seidman, S.J., Brockman, R., Lewis, B.M., Guag, J., Shein, M.J., Clement, W.J. *et al.*, *In vitro* tests reveal sample radiofrequency identification readers inducing clinically significant electromagnetic interference to implantable pacemakers and implantable cardioverter-defibrillators. *Heart Rhythm.*, 7, 99–107, 2010.

152. Armstrong, D., Hospital drug pump can be hacked through network, FDA Warns, http://www.bloomberg.com/news/articles/2015-07-31/hospital-drug-pump-can-be-hacked-on-wireless-network-fda-warns. Accessed 18.

# 4

# Human-Machine Interface Improving Quality of Patient Care

Rishav Sharma and Rishabha Malviya*

*Department of Pharmacy, School of Medical and Allied Sciences, Galgotias University, Greater Noida, Uttar Pradesh, India*

## Abstract

Care for patients needs doctors and nurses to communicate well with one other. There is a growing need for a two-way communication not just within the team but also with the medical equipment used to track and manage patients' conditions. Most HCIs include some kind of visual or aural display, and they have been the source of well-documented worries despite much testing. Remarkably few interfaces look at the benefits of multimodal communication despite abundant research that proves the brain's sensitivity to multimodal inputs. One of the most promising cutting-edge technical disciplines nowadays is medicine, thanks to the explosion of recent scientific knowledge and technological innovation in the field. As allowing users to automate their lives (by controlling everyday chores with just their minds) and even enjoy themselves, brain–computer interface (BCI) technology has broadened the definition of rehabilitation beyond its traditional medical context (hands-free gaming). This chapter examines the current state of the art in HMI design as it pertains to the field of biomedical engineering, with a focus on its potential for facilitating direct brain–computer interface. This strategy relies on the creation of a revolutionary miniaturized system for the covert detection of a biological signal via the use of sensors incorporated into an advanced HMI. This chapter explains current research that may have future relevance in human–computer interface design (HMI). The development of a low-cost mechanism for improving medical communication would have far-reaching effects on patient care and the expanding medical technology industry.

*Corresponding author*: rishabhamalviya19@gmail.com; rishabha.malviya@galgotiasuniversity.edu.in

Rishabha Malviya, Sonali Sundram, Bhupendra Prajapati and Sudarshan Kumar Singh (eds.)
Human-Machine Interface: Making Healthcare Digital, (89–114) © 2024 Scrivener Publishing LLC

*Keywords*: Human-machine interface, auditory alarms, brain–computer interface, amplitude envelope

## 4.1   Introduction

The great majority of individuals who seek medical attention today get the advantages of this modern system. More potent and effective therapies for a broader range of illnesses are becoming accessible all the time thanks to the ever-increasing sophistication and complexity of healthcare technology [1]. Despite these positives, it is important to remember that many patients do suffer injuries or even die as a direct consequence of medical treatment [2–6]. The human and monetary costs of treatment-related injury are high, and they are often made worse by emergency situations and other environmental elements that create an accident-waiting-to-happen scenario. There are a shocking number of avoidable fatalities in the United States that are believed to be treatment-related [2]. This number ranges from 44,000 to 98,000. When the price of diminished quality of life due to non-fatal injuries is included in, the yearly cost of such damage is in the tens of billions of dollars [7, 8]. There has been a steady rise in the expectations placed on doctors and other medical professionals as a consequence of the complexity of medico-technical gadgets and systems. Communication between the device and its operator is crucial for managing the apparatus's technical operations. There is a risk that this conversation may divert the staff's focus away from the patient. In addition, medical professionals, as nontechnical users, often have little familiarity with complicated technical systems. As a result, there is always the possibility that the medical personnel will not fully understand how to use the technology properly. This deficiency has the potential to worsen the quality and dependability of a process, as well as raise the likelihood of mistake. Man–machine interaction problems lead to subpar results for the whole system, which includes the doctor, the patient, and the equipment [9]. As a result, the accessibility among these complex systems and, by extension, the efficacy with which they operate in terms of patient care, depends critically on the layout of the man–machine interface between medical staff and technical equipment. Human-machine interfaces (HMIs) are often used in healthcare cyber-physical systems (CPS) as a means of user monitoring and control. The Integrated Healthcare Environment [10] (ICE) is an example of an interconnected infrastructure that facilitates the coordinated use of many pieces of medical technology and software for the sake of a common clinical goal. Users of ICE systems may monitor and manage all of the devices that are wired into the system from one convenient HMI. To ensure efficient and secure user–system interaction, the HMI may additionally contain safety interlocks and other intelligences (like a centralized smart alarm system, for example). It is a common misconception that human-machine interaction may be improved by putting all of the design effort into the user interface. Instead, it is important to have a holistic perspective of the complete man–machine system present in the intensive care unit. The objective is to develop a transparent technological system that is part of the intensive care setting by integrating various kinds of data, optimizing the flow and display of data, and designing consistent and easily learned interaction sequences [11]. Integration of patient care, which may involve operating rooms, critical care units, and regular wards, highlights the need of this coordination. When applied, system ergonomics approaches provide for a holistic understanding of the man–machine system as a whole. Smaller devices and sensors have been possible because of advances in semiconductor integration technology, opening the door to new fields of use such wearable sensors [12–15]. Measurement of electrical activity in the heart (ECG) [16, 17]. Many diagnostic procedures, including surface electromyography (sEMG) [18], electromyography (EMG) [19, 20], electroencephalography (EEG) [21], and others, depending on the non-invasive collecting of electrical data from electrodes attached to the skin. These sensors have widespread use in medical settings, where they aid in the detection and classification of diseases, as well as the continuous tracking of patient health. Cardiotoxicity [22] and angina pectoris [23] may be diagnosed using ECG sensors, while schizophrenia [24] can be diagnosed with EEG sensors. Electromyography (EMG) sensors, for example, monitor electrical impulses of muscle movements and have applications outside medical diagnosis [25, 26] not just in robotics and aerial vehicles [18, 27, 28], but also in #HMI (human-machine interface) applications. Although many different wearable EMG sensors have been created, they all have significant drawbacks when used in HMI applications, including their size, the need for cables to connect them to other devices, the need for an external power source, etc. These restrictions apply to any wearable sensor, not only EMG sensors. Researchers have developed a variety of all-in-one sensors using NFC and wirelessly to deal with these problems [17, 29, 30]. Standardization and post-processing of data are required to remedy signal variance [31–33] since signal variance might be caused by differences in muscle mass and the EMG signal at different sensor attachment locations. Thus, for a more genuine HMI application, it is crucial to think about all-in-one technologies that can work safely and independently in terms of information processing without a connection to an external system.

## 4.2   An Advanced Framework for Human-Machine Interaction

AHMI is more complicated systems that enable a high degree of interaction, shifting toward this new definition of the interface notion. HMI is a general word defining a system that permits the construction of a low grade man–machine interaction, such as mouse and keyboard. Supporting (Ambient Intelligence) applications via the optimization and development of the communication process is an essential and extremely fascinating issue. AHMI may pave the way for the development of an automated, adaptable system that ensures people are fully incorporated into their environments and are in harmony with it via attuning (mutual tuning). When the system is attuned to its environment, it can better understand and respond to the user's emotional state, allowing it to provide more personalized and satisfying service. As an example, take a speech recognition system that is often used to issue instructions or compose phrases; this system may be trained to recognize emotional changes in the speaker's voice as they complete various activities. Also, the computer may utilize a person's facial expression to better understand what they require during a video call, allowing for more effective communication. One of the most intriguing features of the AHMI is the ability to monitor and recognize a person's psycho-physiological condition, which may then be used to enhance both communication and the performance of tasks via interaction between humans and machines. It suggests that a high-level interface including the detection of subjects' state, with the monitoring of biomarkers, plays a a vital role necessary to produce meaningful adaptability to human needs. When a person is aware that a computer may comprehend him and work together to complete a job, this is a new scenario outlining AHMI exploitation [34].

### 4.2.1   A Simulated Workplace Safety and Health Program

The ERTRAG system must cater to the unique requirements and demands of healthcare apprentices if it is to effectively assist them in mastering ergonomic motion sequences. Consequently, the initial part of the process is to do a detailed requirement analysis. Movement tracking and analysis, as well as an appropriate platform for instruction and feedback, are all integral parts of the system's technological implementation.

## 4.3   Human–Computer Interaction (HCI)

The field of research known as human–computer interaction (HCI), often referred to as human-machine interaction (HMI), examines how humans interact with computers and other machines (Figure 4.1). The purpose of this chapter is to offer an overview of HCI subjects covered in papers presented at and published in special issues of the International Conference on Cognitive Info Communications (CogInfoCom). This survey was generated by utilizing the following Boolean expression to search two search engines for appropriate papers that appeared during the specified time limit. (human–computer interaction), "human-machine interaction," "brain–computer interface," "eye track," "gaze tracking," "gesture control," and "eye tracking" are all synonyms for the same concept. The years 2012 to 2020 were selected for this literature assessment since papers presented at the field's conference series and included in the special issue will be available in the main databases up to 2021 Q1. Through the implementation of state-of-the-art HCI-based support systems in the area of CogInfoCom [35], people with cognitive diseases and associated restrictions may have a better quality of life. The brain–computer interface (BCI) is an excellent example of this kind of complicated system since it enhances multimodal communication between the brain and the computer (Figure 4.2). The performance of the controller of a mobile robot was accomplished using a low-cost brain–computer interface (BCI), and its efficacy was evaluated in a real-world setting using human participants [36]. Development and research may be used to enhance already existing technology, such as brainwave-controlled wheelchairs for a person with mobility problems.

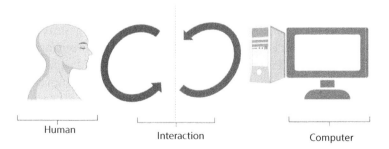

Human               Interaction                      Computer

**Figure 4.1** Diagrammatic representation of a common human–computer interaction at a high level (HCI).

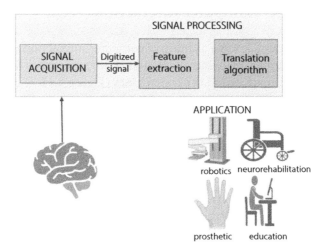

**Figure 4.2** Block diagram of a common brain–computer interaction at a high level (BCI).

A BCI-based neurorehabilitation system, with such an emphasis on the monitoring and manipulation of mu- beta occurrence desynchronization (ERD) and event-related synchronization, may enhance the quality of life of patients with severe disability (ERS). Moreover, the uncovered facts may be effectively exploited in robotics while executing the actual motion of a robot leg or an arm.

BCI systems may seem like a type of educational support system and play a vital role in boosting learning efficacy by checking up on attention as a fundamental cognitive activity [37, 38]. The mode of communication used to command the computer has a profound impact on how people engage with it. Some mouse and keyboard actions could be prompted or replaced by gesture- or eye-tracking-based systems. Assessing the standard mouse and its functionality to that of the low-cost hand gesture detection and processing device Leap Motion, [39] followed the movement of a computer mouse pointer (Figure 4.3a). Although data acquired with the gesture control indicated less accurate and uncertain mouse cursor movement, the relevance of these data may become clear when employing a gesture control system to perform a task that demands less precise movement. The low-priced gesture controllers featured in [39] are not the only gadgets of their kind on the market. The major emphasis of the research is on the Myo armband's (Figure 4.3b) auxiliary function for the visually handicapped. This investigation leads us to conclude that more improvements to the calibration methodology are required for more efficient operation and that the

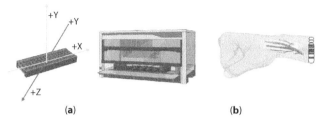

**Figure 4.3** (a) Leap motion controller (b) Myo armband.

device is only partly suited for conducting continuous search operations at present [40].

## 4.4    Multimodal Processing

To build a coherent worldview, our brains integrate information from several sensory channels (i.e., cross-modal inputs). Examining the differences between the brain responses to single- and multiple-sensory stimuli is one technique to officially record and investigate this integration. The amount of processing occurring at the cellular level may be inferred from the degree to which neurons' membrane potentials shift in response to inputs. An action potential (AP) is produced whenever the membrane potential is greater than a critical value. A stimulus' ability to evoke a certain neural response is positively associated with the neuron's firing rate and the frequency of its APs. Determination of the brain's response to cross-modal stimuli (e.g., audiovisual) with the responses to its unimodal components (e.g., auditory and visual) could be useful for understanding the complexity of multimodal integration [41]. Although a cell's reaction to a multimodal stimulus is greater than its response to the same stimulus presented in a single modality, we call it a multisensory neuron [42]. The effectiveness of unimodal stimuli is inversely proportional to the effectiveness of multisensory augmentation [43]. To detect an approaching cat, for instance, one may use both peripheral vision (a weak visual indication) and the sound of approaching footfall (a weak auditory cue). These single-sensory clues are not very compelling on their own, but when combined with a multi-sensory stimulus, they become more interesting. At the level of individual neurons, this behavior manifests as a cross-modal response that is substantially bigger than the sum of the replies to each of the unimodal signals [42–44]. The opposite applies to unimodal signals, which elicit robust reactions on their own. If a dog is barking and racing toward you, you may not need to see the dog to know what is going on; the sound alone (a powerful auditory signal) is enough to get your attention. This strikes at the level of individual neurons when many potent unimodal stimuli are combined. They are likely to have a sub-additive response, in which the cross-modal response is less than the reaction to each unimodal signal [42–44]. The idea of inverse performance [42] describes this relationship between multisensory augmentation and unimodal efficacy. This may prove useful in the implementation of a multi-modal alert system in a healthcare setting, where some members of the medical team might benefit from them but others might not because keeping independent warning signals should be as faint as feasible (while still being detectable) to avoid sensory overload from several systems running simultaneously.

## 4.5   Integrated Multimodality at a Lower Order (Stimulus Orientation)

Multimodal signal enhancement is useful in sound identification. Orienting and localizing stimuli are two functions that the superior response to specific stimuli excels at (SC). The SC, situated roughly in the center of the brain, is hypothesized to have a role in the integration of data from many sensory modalities and the development of spatially-motivated behavior. Consolidation of inputs from sensory information systems (e.g., visual, auditory, somatosensory) [41, 45], projections to motor regions [46], and availability of multisensory neurons [47] make the SC a remarkable platform to display multimodal processing at the neuronal level. Cats [43, 48], rats [49], ferrets [50], and primates [51] are just some of the numerous animals that exhibit multisensory enhancement in the SC, which shortens the amount of time needed to respond to changes in stimulus direction and localization. In humans, the SC continues to mediate multisensory spatial integration [52], which helps generate responses more quickly. Beyond its function in orienting attention toward stimuli, the SC may also contribute to the formation of early social abilities, such as facial imitation in newborns [53].

## 4.6   Higher-Order Multimodal Integration (Perceptual Binding)

Multimodal processing at a lower level may provide light on the brain mechanisms underlying multimodal processing. Higher-order multimodal integration, on the other hand, is essential to our interpretation of the complex stimuli we encounter on a daily basis and may teach us important lessons about how to improve multimodal interfaces. Perceptional binding, such as watching a speaker's lip movements, has been underappreciated for a long time despite its obvious importance in what was formerly thought to be an aural process alone, specifically, verbal communication. For example, sight and listening to the spoken sounds that are created (for example, hearing) [54]. The well-known McGurk effect [20] explains the effect of semantic limitations on the visual processing of speech. When the visual is removed, sounds of speech are reproduced correctly, but when the visual is present, an intermediate (e.g., "doze") is observed between the lip movements and audible speech (when the lips pronounce "bows" but the speech created is "goes"). Recent investigations of primate brains have connected the superior temporal sulcus (STS) to audiovisual integration in response to face and voice sounds [55, 56]. The superior temporal sulcus (STS) has been hypothesized to be the human brain's major location for high-level acoustic-visual processing [57–59]. Functional magnetic resonance imaging (fMRI) studies have demonstrated that the STS is multimodal by showing an increase in the blood oxygenated level-dependent signaling in response to temporally synchronized auditory stimuli, as compared to audio-only or visual-only stimuli [60]. According to the McGurk effect, there must be a causal connection between STS and AV integration. In a separate experiment [61], participants were subjected to McGurk and control stimuli before and after undergoing transcranial magnetic stimulation (TMS) guided by functional magnetic resonance imaging (fMRI).

## 4.7   Gains in Performance From Multisensory Stimulation

Multisensory stimulation, as shown by fundamental studies, modifies neuronal and perceptual responses. Concerning the advantages of multimodal presentations in human-machine interfaces, this raises interesting considerations. While a comprehensive evaluation does require probable interface testing, prior studies investigating broad enhancements to multimodal presentations provide helpful pointers. One example is that hearing has better temporal resolution than vision [62]. When compared to only audio or just a visual interface, an audiovisual interface has a superior temporal and spatial resolution. When used in conjunction with visual search tasks, audio cues (both spatially correlated and non-spatial) may increase target saliency [63] and speed up target recognition [64–66]. Multisensory stimulation has the potential to boost the efficiency of not just a few but all of the senses. When motion stimuli are presented visually and tactilely, for example, the detection time decreases, and the detection rate increases [67]. Graphical user interfaces (GUIs) may benefit from these types of impacts, particularly when designed with people with impairments in mind. Scanning input is a visual job in which users with motor impairments (such as those who cannot use a mouse) locate a desired destination by visually scanning things arranged in a grid. Adding sound to the scanning process has been shown to boost motivation and user engagement [68]. Additionally, Multimodal displays in typical GUI operations (like drag and drop) may decrease the impression of mental labor without detracting from performance [69, 70].

## 4.8    Amplitude Envelope and Alarm Design

A review of the literature on multimodal processing reveals the advantages of including many modes of presentation in the design of human-machine interfaces (HMI). However, designers think about how to effectively arrange data across modalities to facilitate seamless integration. As used here, "envelope" will refer to the amplitude envelope of the amplitude profile (or "shape") of a sound as it evolves in time. Figure 4.1's right panel depicts the flat envelope of a sound, which has a sharp cutoff and does not reveal anything about the materials (metal vs. wood) used to make the noise. On the other hand, impact noises that produce a percussive noise are long, decaying offsets, such as those produced when a hollow object is hit; providing listeners with information about the materials at play in an impact event [71]. However, alarm systems that employ melodious alarm tones with sounds that have flat envelopes are mandated by the International Electrotechnical Commission (IEC) and are widely recognized as problematic [72, 73]. Due to the difficulty in synthesizing musically exciting sounds [74], musicians have long been fascinated by compromises between the envelopes and other tone characteristics [75]. Psychologists, on the other hand, have traditionally focused on studying and adjusting discrete variables like stimulus presentation time, frequency, and intensity. With the development of the current human-machine interface (HMI) [76], these characteristics are more accessible for precise control and modification. Clarifying the significance of certain fundamental acoustic features, such as onset [77, 78], has benefited from this meticulous attention to readily manipulated factors. Since the start plays such a crucial role in identifying musical timbres [79], eliminating it completely makes previously identifiable instruments indistinguishable [80]. Reduced sensitivity to tone start may also be predictive of reading difficulties [81].

## 4.9 Recent Trends in Alarm Tone Design for Medical Devices

The preference for flat tones in investigations of auditory perception [82] is consistent with the usage of flatter tones in auditory interfaces. Researchers assume that this is due to the fact that its temporal structure can be easily and reliably established with a small number of factors [76], allowing for a great deal of sway over experimental outcomes. When compared to genuine sounds, however, stimuli that lack such temporal variation may be processed utilizing a distinct set of neural circuits [83]. This presents problems for both theoretical and practical work since it makes it difficult to generalize results from lab experiments to real-world situations.

For instance, when applied to sounds with natural forms, the ideas generated from a vast body of literature on visual integration based on flat tones fall short. However, when sounds include natural decay, visual cues may have a massive effect on auditory judgments of time [84–86]. Multiple trials using flat tones have demonstrated that visual cues did not affect auditory estimates of length, therefore these findings are at odds with one another. Whenever thinking about human issues in relation to auditory interfaces, the usage of flat tones also presents difficulties in practical situations. For instance, the usage of flat tones, which are aesthetically less pleasant than percussive tones, might decrease the value of a product [87]. They are also substantially more unpleasant than a comparable sequence of percussive tones [88]. These findings provide light on why medical professionals [89], who hear hundreds of alerts during a workday [90], have complained about the present generation of alarms (which relies mainly on flat tones). Some present alarms have such prevalent issues that their creators have publicly apologized for them in academic journals [91].

## 4.10 Percussive Tone Integration in Multimodal User Interfaces

More visual information facilitates the association of percussive sound envelopes with shared objects [92] and the assessment of duration [86] and event unity [93]. These results have big consequences for the development of user-dependent audible alerts memorizing and reacting to correlations between specific sound sequences in predetermined patterns. This is fascinating in light of the well-documented issues with learning [72, 73], retention [73, 94], and confusion [73, 95] that many conventional methods are known to cause. An envelope is a method for greater audiovisual integration, less pain, more aesthetically pleasing designs, and more positive user experiences using human-machine interfaces, all of which are important as the industry moves toward a more in-depth exploration of multimodal alarms for medical equipment (HMI). The development of multimodal alarm systems is viewed as a promising topic for future research due to the well-documented perceptual "gains" of stimulation in multiple modalities (Section 2) as well as the advantages of redundant systems in vital indicators capable of connecting to the essential problem of patient health. Medical alarm design may benefit greatly from these guidelines, but they apply to any human-machine interaction. There is a significant challenge in creating audible alarms for medical devices, considering Market Canada's projection that the sector is worth $6.7 billion (or $336 billion) yearly [96], the business is suffering. As a result of the high volume of patients in hospitals, hundreds of alerts are sent off daily, highlighting the significance of the tools utilized by such systems [97].

## 4.11   Software in Hospitals

Due to various software's potential, it will surely be used in hospital environments like hospitals. However, due to the dangers and challenges already identified, its implementation must continue with precaution. Computerized solutions to healthcare software issues are frequently developed by committees of technical specialists without sufficient input from the end users. If the product is unique enough that it does not interfere with users' established workflows, or if the users are sufficiently unsophisticated that they can be taught how to use the new software, then this strategy may be appropriate. However, none of these statements holds when it comes to the introduction of software systems into hospitals, where the intended users are often highly trained professionals who have developed and adhere to extremely particular procedures for a variety of reasons. The healthcare industry is notoriously difficult to navigate because of the wide range of practitioner expertise and the much more diverse patient requirements [98]. Despite the fact that patients are not car bodies and doctors are not assembly line workers, many software solutions are developed using the same kinds of technical knowledge that are common in the automotive industry. Hospital administration is drawn to the industrial model because it has a track record of success in improving efficiency and reducing costs via the use of computerized technologies. Unfortunately, the complexity of healthcare is frequently too much for computerized systems to handle, leading to failed systems [99]. The increasing prevalence of hospital-wide patient information systems and digital health records, as well as the increasing prevalence of software-controlled medical equipment, which include cutting-edge applications like diagnostic methods by deep neural networks and the utilization of virtual reality and robotics in surgery [100–103], raise significant concerns about the controllability and reliability of software in healthcare.

## 4.12    Brain–Machine Interface (BCI) Outfit

Detecting electrodes, BCI transducers, a control interface, and a controller for an output device are the standard components of a BCI system. Some BCI devices may have a human-machine interface (HMI) or a control panel. Through the use of electrodes to establish a connection with the brain, researchers are able to transform brain impulses into electrical signals. Both the neural activity in the brain and the surface activity on the scalp may be used to capture signals that originate in the brain. The 'feature generator' and 'feature translator' are components of the BCI transducer. Additionally, an "artifact processor" may be used by certain transducers to filter unwanted noise out of the amplified electrical signal at the electrodes. The neuro-mechanism is created by the "feature generator," which uses boosted brain impulses to create them. The 'feature translator' subsequently converts this neuro-mechanism into a logical control signal. The "interface controller" sends signals to the "device controller" [104, 105] so that the user may interact with the device, which might be anything from a robotic arm or wheelchair to a mobile robot.

## 4.13    BCI Sensors and Techniques

Several techniques have been developed to measure brain activity (SPECT), including electroencephalography (EEG), electrocorticography (ECoG), electromyography (EMG), magneto-encephalography (MEG), functional magnetic resonance imaging (fMRI), near-infrared spectroscopy (NIRS), positron emission tomography (PEC), and single photon emission computed tomography (SPECT) [106–108]. Depending on the technology, BCIs may use either invasive or non-invasive sensors. Sensors are surgically inserted in invasive systems to monitor mental processes. On the other hand, sensors for non-invasive systems may be attached to the skin or hair of the head without the need for any kind of surgery [109, 110].

### 4.13.1    EEG

Electroencephalography is a noninvasive method for examining brain activity. Various methods of detecting brain activity use electrodes placed on the scalp. This form of BCI interfacing has become the industry standard because of its low-stress nature [111]. When attaching electrodes to the scalp, we can pick up electrical impulses that can subsequently be amplified and sent to an A/D converter for processing. ADC (analog to digital converter) output digital signal may be modified as needed. EEG is less expensive and takes less time to develop than competing technologies. The method's main drawback is that it can only gather useful information if the researcher already knows where the Area of Interest (AOI) is within the chosen brain region. It features a component that can read the brain's electrical activity and interpret it. Obtaining reliable brain activity measurements requires attaching electrodes to the scalp, which may be done using an EEG cap [112].

### 4.13.2    ECoG

An invasive procedure, electrocorticography examines the brain directly. For this method to work, sensors must be surgically implanted into the brain. Monkeys and rats are among the test subjects for this technique. According to studies, similar sensors have also been implanted in people. The most common use of electrocorticography mapping is in studying animal brain anatomy. When compared to other methods, setting up this one takes hardly any time at all. The primary issue with ECoG is its lack of resources [113].

### 4.13.3    ECG

While recording the heart's electrical activity, electrocardiography does not cause any harm to the patient. The objective of this method is to quantify cardiac activity, and it does so by attaching sensors to the chest of a human or animal subject. Electrocardiogram (ECG) electrodes are used to approximate the heart's rhythm in this method. The biggest drawback of this method is that it can only be used for the heart. Particularly trained professionals in the medical area should apply this method. An electrocardiogram can show how strong the heart's electrical impulses are if the sensory stimulus is strong, but an electrocardiogram can only tell you so much (ECG). ECG readings would thereafter exhibit low-amplitude peaks [114].

### 4.13.4    EMG

Electromyography is a non-invasive procedure in which sensors are positioned on the body's muscles. Similarly, electrical impulses from skeletal muscles may be measured using electromyography. When an abnormal movement of the muscles (such as a biceps pump) occurs, EMG can provide you with honest feedback on what is going on. In comparison to EEG, the speed of reaction using this approach is much greater. Electromyography (EMG) is a method for detecting electrical impulses from the muscles to determine the brain's intentions. When the muscle's pumping force is weak, the corresponding brain electrical output will have a weak amplitude [115].

### 4.13.5    MEG

Magneto encephalography utilizes magnetic fields induced by the brain's electrical activity to record brain activity in a non-invasive manner. Many studies are being conducted to keep tabs on this, particularly in the field of neurofeedback. This technique calls for equipment to capture weak brain impulses while shielding them from more powerful magnetic fields in the surrounding environment [107, 116].

### 4.13.6    FMRI

Blood flow is used in functional magnetic resonance imaging to non-invasively gather data on brain activity. It is possible to use fMRI to identify brain signals when there is a change in hemodynamic behavior. In this technique, high-resolution photos are captured of various body areas to evaluate blood circulation. Recent research has integrated electroencephalography (EEG) and functional magnetic resonance imaging (fMRI) to better understand brain activity [117].

## 4.14    New Generation Advanced Human-Machine Interface

An intelligent system will be completed within a short future, and it will make it possible for anybody, even those with permanent neurological problems, to control a broad variety of electro-mechanical gadgets. The ultimate goal of the research being conducted in this area is to optimize the whole "from intention to action" chain (Figure 4.4), making it possible for each person to administer and use their control system in line with their specific strengths, weaknesses, aspirations, and limitations (such as most often done activities, prioritization of tasks to complete, etc.). Users will no longer be constrained by the machine's formal communication protocols because of the complexity of their interactions with the system. Intelligent "declarative" interaction is a need for the system. The machine must be able to read the user's mind in this situation.  Recent understanding of human communication is most constrained by our inability to describe the integration of data from the five senses (hearing, seeing, touching, and smelling) with the vast reservoir of experience and information associated with social interactions and the wider environment. It is challenging to think of a scenario in which a unified understanding of people's motives could be gleaned without some kind of merging of these perspectives. Individual channel inputs may provide only vague or conflicting information. Disambiguation is not guaranteed by a simple linear combination of all inputs; sometimes the user does not offer all the information needed to grasp the goal, and sometimes the various channels appear to bring

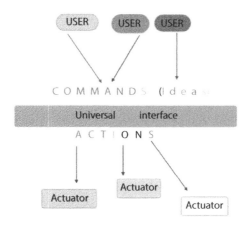

**Figure 4.4** Conceptual model of the "intention to action" paradigm.

contradicting contributions. Comprehension is a dynamic process, as shown by current knowledge of how people understand the goals of others (involving both signal-driven and interpretation-driven processes). Even in areas where they have been mostly ignored or treated extremely poorly, such as in current voice identification and natural language processing, active processes are integral to all parts [118].

These ambitious goals need a variety of strategies in the area of applied technologies:

1. User interface design: Any physiological indication that could allow the user to "message" an intention could be collected and interpreted with the use of wearable sensors and microelectronics technology. It is the first stage in gathering as much data as possible; having a larger pool of distinct instructions at your disposal will help you interface with your navigable devices more quickly.

2. Human-machine interface design: The "universal interface," or "brain" of the system, is a self-aware processing unit that can understand and carry out any request made by the user. The device in question should be able to identify its "master" and adjust its interpretation of the incoming signals to best suit the person using it. A software interface that is constantly aware of its "master's" demands might be created using prediction and learning methods. The communication protocols toward "end actuators" to execute the desired action must be standardized and harmonized for the system to be truly functional and simply distributable worldwide (such as household appliances, electronic wheel chairs, and personal communicators).

## 4.15    Conclusion

The goal of this chapter is to discuss the most up-to-date findings and theories when it comes to cutting-edge advanced human-machine interaction. The potential for direct machine-to-brain connection, bypassing any disruption to "conventional" communication channels and opening up whole new avenues of human-machine interaction, is one of the most fascinating aims of the study. By translating the user's electrophysiological events into text, a brain–computer interface may help those with severe impairments communicate intention. Current BCI systems are sluggish and inaccurate; however, advancements in algorithm development and electrical hardware are aimed at fixing these issues. Modules, such as electrodes for sensing, data collecting, processing, feature extraction and categorization, pattern recognition, and interface control, are all essential parts of a brain–computer interface system. The findings of a rigorous and comparative analysis of the current most recent technology of essential methods and sensors used in BCI systems are presented in this work. This chapter provides an in-depth summary of the relevant methods by analyzing their functionality and exploring their possible applications. There are several BCI-based medical treatments. These are based on ECOG, EEG, MEG, EMG, and fMRI.

# References

1. Gawande, A., *The checklist manifesto: How to get things right*, Picador, New York City, 2009.
2. Kohn, L.T., Corrigan, J.M., Donaldson, M.S., Institute of Medicine, *To err is human: Building a safer health system*, Washington (DC): National Academies Press (US), 2000.
3. Eva, K.W., Regher, G., *Department of Health: An organisation with a memory: Report of an expert group on learning from adverse events in the NHS*, DH, London, 2000.
4. Bates, D.W., Frequency, consequences and prevention of adverse drug events. *J. Qual. Clin. Pract.*, *19*, 1, 13–17, 1999.
5. Merry, A. and Smith, A.M., *Errors, medicine and the law*, Cambridge University Press, United Kingdom, 2001.
6. Webster, C.S., The iatrogenic-harm cost equation and new technology. *Anaesthesia*, *60*, 9, 843–846, 2005.
7. Andel, C., Davidow, S.L., Hollander, M., Moreno, D.A., The economics of healthcare quality and medical errors. *J. Healthcare Finance*, *39*, 1, 39, 2012.
8. James, J.T., A new, evidence-based estimate of patient harms associated with hospital care. *J. Patient Saf.*, *9*, 3, 122–128, 2013.
9. Thull, B., Popp, H.J., Rau, G., Man-machine interaction in critical care settings. *IEEE Eng. Med. Biol. Mag.*, *12*, 4, 42–49, 1993.
10. Goldman, J.M., Medical devices and medical systems-essential safety requirements for equipment comprising the patient-centric integrated clinical environment (ice)-part 1: General requirements and conceptual model. ASTM International, 2008.
11. Jungk, A., Thull, B., Hoeft, A., Rau, G., Ergonomic evaluation of an ecological interface and a profilogram display for hemodynamic monitoring. *J. Clin. Monit. Comput.*, 15, 469–479, 1999.

12. Agarwal, K., Hwang, S., Bartnik, A., Buchele, N., Mishra, A., Cho, J.H., Small-scale biological and artificial multidimensional sensors for 3D sensing. *Small*, *14*, 35, 1801145, 2018.

13. Nan, K., Kang, S.D., Li, K., Yu, K.J., Zhu, F., Wang, J., Dunn, A.C., Zhou, C., Xie, Z., Agne, M.T., Wang, H., Compliant and stretchable thermoelectric coils for energy harvesting in miniature flexible devices. *Sci. Adv.*, *4*, 11, 5849, 2018.

14. Kim, J., Gutruf, P., Chiarelli, A.M., Heo, S.Y., Cho, K., Xie, Z., Banks, A., Han, S., Jang, K.I., Lee, J.W., Lee, K.T., Miniaturized battery-free wireless systems for wearable pulse oximetry. *Adv. Funct. Mater.*, *27*, 1, 1604373, 2017.

15. Lü, X., Qi, L., Hu, H., Li, X., Bai, G., Chen, J., Bao, W., Ultra-sensitive flexible tactile sensor based on graphene film. *Micromachines*, *10*, 11, 730, 2019.

16. Koo, J.H., Jeong, S., Shim, H.J., Son, D., Kim, J., Kim, D.C., Choi, S., Hong, J.I., Kim, D.H., Wearable electrocardiogram monitor using carbon nanotube electronics and color-tunable organic light-emitting diodes. *ACS Nano*, *11*, 10, 10032–10041, 2017.

17. Jang, K.I., Li, K., Chung, H.U., Xu, S., Jung, H.N., Yang, Y., Kwak, J.W., Jung, H.H., Song, J., Yang, C., Wang, A., Self-assembled three dimensional network designs for soft electronics. *Nat. Commun.*, *8*, 1, 1–10, 2017.

18. Jeong, J.W., Yeo, W.H., Akhtar, A., Norton, J.J., Kwack, Y.J., Li, S., Jung, S.Y., Su, Y., Lee, W., Xia, J., Cheng, H., Materials and optimized designs for human-machine interfaces via epidermal electronics. *Adv. Mater.*, *25*, 47, 6839–6846, 2013.

19. Roland, T., Wimberger, K., Amsuess, S., Russold, M.F., Baumgartner, W., An insulated flexible sensor for stable electromyography detection: Application to prosthesis control. *Sensors*, *19*, 4, 961, 2019.

20. Kim, N., Lim, T., Song, K., Yang, S., Lee, J., Stretchable multichannel electromyography sensor array covering large area for controlling home electronics with distinguishable signals from multiple muscles. *ACS Appl. Mater. Interfaces*, *8*, 32, 21070–21076, 2016.

21. Casson, A.J., Wearable EEG and beyond. *Biomed. Eng. Lett.*, *9*, 1, 53–71, 2019.

22. Vallès, E., Bazan, V., Marchlinski, F.E., ECG criteria to identify epicardial ventricular tachycardia in nonischemic cardiomyopathy. *Circ.: Arrhythm. Electrophysiol.*, *3*, 1, 63–71, 2010.

23. Gorgels, A.P., Vos, M.A., Mulleneers, R., de Zwaan, C., Bär, F.W., Wellens, H.J., Value of the electrocardiogram in diagnosing the number of severely narrowed coronary arteries in rest angina pectoris. *Am. J. Cardiol.*, *72*, 14, 999–1003, 1993.

24. Boutros, N.N., Arfken, C., Galderisi, S., Warrick, J., Pratt, G., Iacono, W., The status of spectral EEG abnormality as a diagnostic test for schizophrenia. *Schizophr. Res.*, *99*, 1–3, 225–237, 2008.

25. Al-Jumaily, A. and Olivares, R.A., Electromyogram (EMG) driven system based virtual reality for prosthetic and rehabilitation devices, in: *Proceedings*

of the 11th International Conference on Information Integration and Web-Based Applications & Services, pp. 582–586, ACM, Malaysia, 2009.

26. Mulas, M., Folgheraiter, M., Gini, G., An EMG-controlled exoskeleton for hand rehabilitation, in: 9th International Conference on Rehabilitation Robotics, pp. 371–374, IEE Explore, Chicago, IL, USA, 2005.

27. Kiguchi, K. and Hayashi, Y., An EMG-based control for an upper-limb power-assist exoskeleton robot. IEEE Trans. Syst. Man Cybern., Part B (Cybern.), 42, 4, 1064–1071, 2012.

28. Rangwani, R. and Park, H., Vibration induced proprioceptive modulation in surface-EMG based control of a robotic arm, in: 2019 9th International IEEE/EMBS Conference on Neural Engineering (NER), pp. 1105–1108, IEEE, San Francisco, CA, USA, 2019.

29. Kim, J., Banks, A., Cheng, H., Xie, Z., Xu, S., Jang, K.I., Lee, J.W., Liu, Z., Gutruf, P., Huang, X., Wei, P., Epidermal electronics with advanced capabilities in near-field communication. Small, 11, 8, 906–912, 2015.

30. Xu, G., Cheng, C., Liu, Z., Yuan, W., Wu, X., Lu, Y., Low, S.S., Liu, J., Zhu, L., Ji, D., Li, S., Battery-free and wireless epidermal electrochemical system with all-printed stretchable electrode array for multiplexed in situ sweat analysis. Adv. Mater. Technol., 4, 7, 1800658, 2019.

31. Geist, D.R., Brown, R.S., Lepla, K., Chandler, J., Practical application of elec-tromyogram radiotelemetry: The suitability of applying laboratory-acquired calibration data to field data. N. Am. J. Fish. Manage., 22, 2, 474–479, 2002.

32. Fleischer, C. and Hommel, G., Calibration of an EMG-based body model with six muscles to control a leg exoskeleton, in: Proceedings 2007 IEEE International Conference on Robotics and Automation, pp. 2514–2519, 2007.

33. Yousefi, J. and Hamilton-Wright, A., Characterizing EMG data using machine-learning tools. Comput. Biol. Med., 51, 1–13, 2014.

34. Greene, J.O., Message production: Advances in communication theory, Routledge, Taylor and Francis Group, 2013.

35. Izsó, L., The significance of cognitive infocommunications in developing assistive technologies for people with non-standard cognitive characteris-tics: CogInfoCom for people with non-standard cognitive characteristics, in: 2015 6th IEEE International Conference on Cognitive Infocommunications (CogInfoCom), pp. 77–82, 2015.

36. Katona, J., Ujbanyi, T., Sziladi, G., Kovari, A., Speed control of Festo Robotino mobile robot using NeuroSky MindWave EEG headset based brain-computer interface, in: 2016 7th IEEE International Conference on Cognitive Infocommunications (CogInfoCom), pp. 000251–000256, 2016.

37. Katona, J. and Kovari, A., Examining the learning efficiency by a brain-computer interface system. Acta Polytech. Hung., 15, 3, 251–280, 2018.

38. Katona, J. and Kovari, A., The evaluation of bci and pebl-based attention tests. Acta Polytech. Hung., 15, 3, 225–249, 2018.

39. Sziladi, G., Ujbanyi, T., Katona, J., Kovari, A., The analysis of hand ges-ture based cursor position control during solves an IT related task, in:

*2017 8th IEEE International Conference on Cognitive Infocommunications (CogInfoCom)*, pp. 000413–000418, IEE, Debrecen, Hungar, 2017.

40. Csapo, A.B., Nagy, H., Kristjánsson, Á., Wersényi, G., Evaluation of human-Myo gesture control capabilities in continuous search and select operations, in: *2016 7th IEEE International Conference on Cognitive Infocommunications (CogInfoCom)*, pp. 000415–00042, IEE, Wroclaw, Poland, 2016.

41. Meredith, M.A. and Stein, B.E., Interactions among converging sensory inputs in the superior colliculus. *Science, 221*, 4608, 389–391, 1983.

42. Stein, B.E., Stanford, T.R., Ramachandran, R., Perrault, T.J., Rowland, B.A., Challenges in quantifying multisensory integration: Alternative criteria, models, and inverse effectiveness. *Exp. Brain Res., 198*, 2, 113–126, 2009.

43. Stein, B.E. and Meredith, M.A., *The merging of the senses*, The MIT Press, US, 1993.

44. Stein, B.E. and Stanford, T.R., Multisensory integration: Current issues from the perspective of the single neuron. *Nat. Rev. Neurosci., 9*, 4, 255–266, 2008.

45. Meredith, M.A. and Stein, B.E., Visual, auditory, and somatosensory convergence on cells in superior colliculus results in multisensory integration. *J. Neurophysiol., 56*, 3, 640–662, 1986.

46. May, P.J., The mammalian superior colliculus: Laminar structure and connections. *Prog. Brain Res., 151*, 321–378, 2006.

47. King, A.J., The superior colliculus. *Curr. Biol., 14*, 9, 335–338, 2004.

48. Wallace, M.T., Meredith, M.A., Stein, B.E., Multisensory integration in the superior colliculus of the alert cat. *J. Neurophysiol., 80*, 2, 1006–1010, 1998.

49. Hirokawa, J., Sadakane, O., Sakata, S., Bosch, M., Sakurai, Y., Yamamori, T., Multisensory information facilitates reaction speed by enlarging activity difference between superior colliculus hemispheres in rats. *PLoS One, 6*, 9, 25283, 2011.

50. Hammond-Kenny, A., Bajo, V.M., King, A.J., Nodal, F.R., Behavioural benefits of multisensory processing in ferrets. *Eur. J. Neurosci., 45*, 2, 278–289, 2017.

51. Sparks, D.L., Translation of sensory signals into commands for control of saccadic eye movements: Role of primate superior colliculus. *Physiol. Rev., 66*, 1, 118–171, 1986.

52. Leo, F., Bertini, C., Di Pellegrino, G., Làdavas, E., Multisensory integration for orienting responses in humans requires the activation of the superior colliculus. *Exp. Brain Res., 186*, 1, 67–77, 2008.

53. Pitti, A., Kuniyoshi, Y., Quoy, M., Gaussier, P., Development of the multimodal integration in the superior colliculus and its link to neonates facial preference, in: *Advances in Cognitive Neurodynamics (IV)*, pp. 543–546, Springer Dordrecht, Switzerland, 2015.

54. Ross, L.A., Saint-Amour, D., Leavitt, V.M., Javitt, D.C., Foxe, J.J., Do you see what I am saying? Exploring visual enhancement of speech comprehension in noisy environments. *Cereb. Cortex, 17*, 5, 1147–1153, 2007.

55. McGurk, H. and MacDonald, J., Hearing lips and seeing voices. *Nature, 264*, 5588, 746–748, 1976.

56. Ghazanfar, A.A., The multisensory roles for auditory cortex in primate vocal communication. *Hear. Res., 258*, 1-2, 113–120, 2009.

57. Venezia, J.H., Vaden Jr., K.I., Rong, F., Maddox, D., Saberi, K., Hickok, G., Auditory, visual and audiovisual speech processing streams in superior temporal sulcus. *Front. Hum. Neurosci., 11*, 174, 2017.

58. Beauchamp, M.S., Lee, K.E., Argall, B.D., Martin, A., Integration of auditory and visual information about objects in superior temporal sulcus. *Neuron, 41*, 5, 809–823, 2004.

59. Hein, G. and Knight, R.T., Superior temporal sulcus—It's my area: Or is it? *J. Cogn. Neurosci., 20*, 12, 2125–2136, 2008.

60. Noesselt, T., Rieger, J.W., Schoenfeld, M.A., Kanowski, M., Hinrichs, H., Heinze, H.J., Driver, J., Audiovisual temporal correspondence modulates human multisensory superior temporal sulcus plus primary sensory cortices. *J. Neurosci., 27*, 42, 11431–11441, 2007.

61. Beauchamp, M.S., Nath, A.R., Pasalar, S., fMRI-Guided transcranial magnetic stimulation reveals that the superior temporal sulcus is a cortical locus of the McGurk effect. *J. Neurosci., 30*, 7, 2414–2417, 2010.

62. Walker, J.T. and Scott, K.J., Auditory–visual conflicts in the perceived duration of lights, tones, and gaps. *J. Exp. Psychol.: Hum. Percept. Perform., 7*, 6, 1327, 1981.

63. Iordanescu, L., Grabowecky, M., Franconeri, S., Theeuwes, J., Suzuki, S., Characteristic sounds make you look at target objects more quickly. *Atten. Percept. Psychophys., 72*, 7, 1736–1741, 2010.

64. Vroomen, J. and Gelder, B.D., Sound enhances visual perception: Cross-modal effects of auditory organization on vision. *J. Exp. Psychol.: Hum. Percept. Perform., 26*, 5, 1583, 2000.

65. Van der Burg, E., Olivers, C.N., Bronkhorst, A.W., Theeuwes, J., Pip and pop: Nonspatial auditory signals improve spatial visual search. *J. Exp. Psychol.: Hum. Percept. Perform., 34*, 5, 1053, 2008.

66. Perrott, D.R., Sadralodabai, T., Saberi, K., Strybel, T.Z., Aurally aided visual search in the central visual field: Effects of visual load and visual enhancement of the target. *Hum. Factors, 33*, 4, 389–400, 1991.

67. Ushioda, H. and Wada, Y., Multisensory integration between visual and tactile motion information: Evidence from redundant-signals effects on reaction time. *Proceedings of Fechner Day*, vol. 23, 2007.

68. Brewster, S.A., Raty, V.P., Kortekangas, A., Enhancing scanning input with non-speech sounds, in: *Proceedings of the Second Annual ACM Conference on Assistive Technologies*, pp. 10–14, 1996.

69. Vitense, H.S., Jacko, J.A., Emery, V.K., Multimodal feedback: An assessment of performance and mental workload. *Ergonomics, 46*, 1–3, 68–87, 2003.

70. Brewster, S.A., Sonically-enhanced drag and drop, in: *International Conference on Auditory Display*, pp. 1–7, BCS Learning & Development Ltd., Swindon, United Kingdom, 1998.

71. Lutfi, R.A., Auditory detection of hollowness. *J. Acoust. Soc. Am., 110*, 2, 1010–1019, 2001.

72. Wee, A.N. and Sanderson, P.M., Are melodic medical equipment alarms easily learned? *Anesth. Analg., 106*, 2, 501–508, 2008.

73. Sanderson, P.M., Wee, A., Lacherez, P., Learnability and discriminability of melodic medical equipment alarms. *Anaesthesia, 61*, 2, 142–147, 2006.

74. Risset, J.C. and Wessel, D.L., Exploration of timbre by analysis and synthesis, in: *The Psychology of Music*, pp. 113–169, 1999.

75. Gaver, W.W., What in the world do we hear?: An ecological approach to auditory event perception. *Ecol. Psychol., 5*, 1, 1–29, 1993.

76. Sreetharan, S. and Schutz, M., Improving human–computer interface design through application of basic research on audiovisual integration and amplitude envelope. *Multimodal Technol. Interact., 3*, 1, 4, 2019.

77. Gordon, J.W., The perceptual attack time of musical tones. *J. Acoust. Soc. Am., 82*, 1, 88–105, 1987.

78. Strong, W. and Clark Jr., M., Perturbations of synthetic orchestral wind-instrument tones. *J. Acoust. Soc. Am., 41*, 2, 277–285, 1967.

79. Skarratt, P.A., Cole, G.G., Gellatly, A.R., Prioritization of looming and receding objects: Equal slopes, different intercepts. *Atten. Percept. Psychophys., 71*, 4, 964–970, 2009.

80. Saldanha, E.L. and Corso, J.F., Timbre cues and the identification of musical instruments. *J. Acoust. Soc. Am., 36*, 11, 2021–2026, 1964.

81. Goswami, U., A temporal sampling framework for developmental dyslexia. *Trends Cogn. Sci., 15*, 1, 3–10, 2011.

82. Schutz, M. and Vaisberg, J.M., Surveying the temporal structure of sounds used in Music Perception. *Music Percept.: Interdiscip. J., 31*, 3, 288–296, 2012.

83. Vallet, G.T., Shore, D.I., Schutz, M., Exploring the role of the amplitude envelope in duration estimation. *Perception, 43*, 7, 616–630, 2014.

84. Schutz, M. and Kubovy, M., Causality and cross-modal integration. *J. Exp. Psychol.: Hum. Percept. Perform., 35*, 6, 1791, 2009.

85. Armontrout, J.A., Schiutz, M., Kubovy, M., Visual determinants of a cross-modal illusion. *Atten. Percept. Psychophys., 71*, 7, 1618–1627, 2009.

86. Schutz, M.R., *Crossmodal integration: The search for unity*, 2009.

87. Sreetharan, S., Schlesinger, J.J., Schutz, M., Decaying amplitude envelopes reduce alarm annoyance: Exploring new approaches to improving auditory interfaces. *Appl. Ergon., 96*, 103432, 2021.

88. Sreetharan, S., Schlesinger, J.J., Schutz, M., Designing effective auditory interfaces: Exploring the role of amplitude envelope. *Proceedings of the ICMPC15/ESCOM10*, Graz, Austria, pp. 23–28, 2018.

89. Rayo, M.F. and Moffatt-Bruce, S.D., Alarm system management: Evidence-based guidance encouraging direct measurement of informativeness to improve alarm response. *BMJ Qual. Saf.*, *24*, 4, 282–286, 2015.

90. Sreetharan, S. and Schutz, M., Improving human–computer interface design through application of basic research on audiovisual integration and amplitude envelope. *Multimodal Technol. Interact.*, *3*, 1, 4, 2019.

91. Block Jr., F.E., For if the trumpet gives an uncertain sound, who shall prepare himself to the battle?"(I Corinthians 14: 8, KJV). *Anesth. Analg.*, *106*, 2, 357–359, 2008.

92. Schutz, M., Stefanucci, J.K., Sarah, H.B., Roth, A., Name that percussive tune: Associative memory and amplitude envelope. *Q. J. Exp. Psychol.*, *70*, 7, 1323–1343, 2017.

93. Grassi, M. and Casco, C., Audiovisual bounce-inducing effect: When sound congruence affects grouping in vision. *Atten. Percept. Psychophys.*, *72*, 2, 378–386, 2010.

94. Edworthy, J. and Hellier, E., Alarms and human behaviour: Implications for medical alarms. *BJA: Br. J. Anaesth.*, *97*, 1, 12–17, 2006.

95. Gillard, J. and Schutz, M., Composing alarms: Considering the musical aspects of auditory alarm design. *Neurocase*, *22*, 6, 566–576, 2016.

96. Markan, S. and Verma, Y., Indian medical device sector: Insights from patent filing trends. *BMJ Innov.*, *3*, 3, 167–175, 2017.

97. Sreetharan, S. and Schutz, M., Improving human–computer interface design through application of basic research on audiovisual integration and amplitude envelope. *Multimodal Technol. Interact.*, *3*, 1, 4, 2019.

98. Webster, C.S., Anderson, B.J., Stabile, M.J., Merry, A.F., Improving the safety of pediatric sedation: Human error, technology, and clinical microsystems, in: *Pediatric Sedation Outside of the Operating Room*, pp. 587–612, 2015.

99. Wachter, R.M., *The digital doctor: Hope, hype, and harm at the dawn of medicine's computer age*, McGraw-Hill, USA, 2015.

100. Baxt, W.G., Application of artificial neural networks to clinical medicine. *Lancet*, *346*, 8983, 1135–1138, 1995.

101. McCloy, R. and Stone, R., Science, medicine, and the future. Virtual reality in surgery. *BMJ*, *323*, 7318, 912–915, 2001.

102. Buckingham, R.A. and Buckingham, R.O., Robots in operating theatres. *BMJ*, *311*, 7018, 1479–1482, 1995.

103. Catchpole, K., Perkins, C., Bresee, C., Solnik, M.J., Sherman, B., Fritch, J., Gross, B., Jagannathan, S., Hakami-Majd, N., Avenido, R., Anger, J.T., Safety, efficiency and learning curves in robotic surgery: A human factors analysis. *Surg. Endosc.*, *30*, 9, 3749–3761, 2016.

104. Mason, S.G. and Birch, G.E., A general framework for brain-computer interface design. *IEEE Trans. Neural Syst. Rehabil. Eng.*, *11*, 1, 70–85, 2003.

105. Bashashati, A., Fatourechi, M., Ward, R.K., Birch, G.E., A survey of signal processing algorithms in brain–computer interfaces based on electrical brain signals. *J. Neural Eng.*, *4*, 2, 32, 2007.

106. Graimann, B., Allison, B., Pfurtscheller, G., Brain–computer interfaces: A gentle introduction, in: *Brain-Computer Interfaces*, pp. 1–27, Springer, Switzerland, 2009.

107. Wolpaw, J.R., Birbaumer, N., Heetderks, W.J., McFarland, D.J., Peckham, P.H., Schalk, G., Donchin, E., Quatrano, L.A., Robinson, C.J., Vaughan, T.M., Brain-computer interface technology: A review of the first international meeting. *IEEE Trans. Rehabil. Eng.*, 8, 2, 164–173, 2000.

108. Lebedev, M.A. and Nicolelis, M.A., Brain–machine interfaces: Past, present and future. *Trends Neurosci.*, 29, 9, 536–546, 2006.

109. Vidal, J.J., Real-time detection of brain events in EEG. *Proc. IEEE*, 65, 5, 633–641, 1977.

110. Becedas, J., Brain–machine interfaces: Basis and advances. *IEEE Trans. Syst. Man Cybern. Part C (Appl. Rev.)*, 42, 6, 825–836, 2012.

111. Nicolas-Alonso, L.F. and Gomez-Gil, J., Brain computer: A review. *Sensors*, 12, 2, 1211–1279, 2012.

112. Bogue, R., Brain-computer interfaces: Control by thought. *Ind. Rob.: Int. J.*, 37, 2, 126–132, 2010.

113. Schalk, G. and Leuthardt, E.C., Brain-computer interfaces using electrocorticographic signals. *IEEE Rev. Biomed. Eng.*, 4, 140–154, 2011.

114. Maruyama, T., Makikawa, M., Shiozawa, N., Fujiwara, Y., ECG measurement using capacitive coupling electrodes for man-machine emotional communication, in: *2007 IEEE/ICME International Conference on Complex Medical Engineering*, pp. 378–383, IEEE, Beijing, China, 2007.

115. Florimond, V., Basics of surface electromyography applied to psychophysiology. *Thought Technology Ltd, Doc Number MAR900*, 2008.

116. Ferraioli, F., Formisano, A., Martone, R., Romagnuolo, N., Criteria for the optimal design of magneto-encephalography measurement system. *IEEE Trans. Magn.*, 42, 4, 1155–1158, 2006.

117. Weiskopf, N., Mathiak, K., Bock, S.W., Scharnowski, F., Veit, R., Grodd, W., Goebel, R., Birbaumer, N., Principles of a brain-computer interface (BCI) based on real-time functional magnetic resonance imaging (fMRI). *IEEE Trans. Biomed. Eng.*, 51, 6, 966–970, 2004.

118. Andreoni, G., Parini, S., Maggi, L., Piccini, L., Panfili, G., Torricelli, A., Human-machine interface for healthcare and rehabilitation, in: *Advanced Computational Intelligence Paradigms in Healthcare-2*, pp. 131–150, 2007.

# 5

# Smart Patient Engagement through Robotics

**Rakhi Mohan[1]\*, A. Arun Prakash[1], Uma Devi N.[2], Anjali Sharma S.[1], Aiswarya Babu N.[1] and Thennarasi P.[3]**

*[1]Department of Management, Kristu Jayanti College, Bengaluru, India*
*[2]BSMED, Bharathiar University, Coimbatore, India*
*[3]Department of Management, Sri Krishna College of Technology, Tamil Nadu, India*

## Abstract

Health has become the priority post the wave of COVID-19. We are looking at the systems around us to get better healthcare, like various forms of hospitals, clinics, dispensaries, and primary healthcare centers, which provide service at the affordable and affirmative lead. We have witnessed more significant evidence through research and feedback that higher patient engagement can lead to better health benefits and quick recovery. Although we know patient engagement is an essential criterion for the progress of health and wellness, time spent on patients is less when compared with time spent on systems and monitors for documentation and filing. There is a common belief that technology has turned out to be a blockade, not a facilitator, for the patient to communicate with the physician. It is so factual that patients need to see, hear, and, most importantly, be empowered. But there are better moments of truth where humans can be any relatives, nurses, or caretakers to the patient; even those people cannot be involved to provide enough care and support. This study will try to help hospitals and other forms of health institutions to identify the areas like substituting robots in documentation, file creation, and data storing and mining, patients who do not have a relative or a caretaker, places where even nurses or caretakers hesitates to do certain intimate support to the patient. These are places where we can substitute robots; a human-machine interface can be created with the perception of the patients and assess adding economic value to the hospitals. This study will take responses from patients who hail service from top hospitals in metro cities and factors that can be considered for implementing robotics from patients, caretakers or relatives,

*\*Corresponding author*: rakhi@kristujayanti.com

Rishabha Malviya, Sonali Sundram, Bhupendra Prajapati and Sudarshan Kumar Singh (eds.)
*Human-Machine Interface: Making Healthcare Digital*, (115–160) © 2024 Scrivener Publishing LLC

doctors, nurses, and hospital management. The study will lead us to the will the robotics be the better technology enabler for sophisticated and complex patient engagement.

*Keywords*: Automation, robotics, patient engagement, data science, human–machine interface, perception of patients and health institutions

## 5.1   Introduction

### 5.1.1   Robotics in Healthcare

Robots in the field of medicine and healthcare transmuting [1]; however, the transplantations, diagnosis, surgeries are accomplished, rationalization of supply delivery and fumigation, and enabling providers to focus on engaging with care for patients. Robots have gradually turned inexpensive, shrewder, more bendable, and at ease to instruct. This facilitates the robots to penetrate the latest businesses and brood fresh use cases at large gauge, containing hospitals and healthcare. With cumulative enhancements in technology, machines are finding a new definition as actually exemplified artificial intelligence (AI) agents. Hospital administration robotic engineering dashboard brings you the collection of big data and evidence on robotics and engineering involved in healthcare. The rate of companies hiring for robotics roles dropped in August compared to last year.

Chart 5.1 shows the percentage of robots recruitment over from August 2021 to August 2022.

Emphasis on the necessity of robotics or automation in the field of healthcare, laterally with their supplementary benefits in improving the quality of healthcare, and this could save the costs that could lead way to deliver services considerably at the lower cost [2]. With this, the future of healthcare. The knowledge regarding robots is spread by the beginning of the 1950s. Robots, as we think, are unreal human beings that can almost substitute every job done by an actual human. Recently, robots got wide acceptance everywhere. It can be seen everywhere, from science fiction to your local hospital, where it is changing the face of healthcare. Robots are having a huge impact on the medical field. Most of the robots resemble R2D2 from star wars. Moreover, robots are now humanoids that can equally compete with real humans. Especially in the medical field, it has become more common and comfortable to use these kinds of robots to relieve medical personnel from routine jobs that take away their time from effective patient engagement. The usage of robots in the medical field is

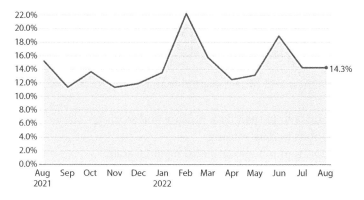

**Chart 5.1**  Chart showing the percentage of robots recruitment.

safer and even less costly for patients. It can even perform minute surgeries and transfer dangerous substances, which a human doctor may not be able to do perfectly.

The intervention of new technologies like 5G, AI, and augmented reality has greatly influenced the medical sector. It is evident that in 2021, the global medical robotics market was valued at $16.1 billion. It is now expected to grow at a rate of 17.4% by 2030. The major reason behind this growth is the unending demand for the usage of robotics in minimally invasive surgeries like neurologic, orthopedic, and laparoscopic procedures. Robots in the medical field can be classified into different categories according to the classification of hospital jobs.

The classification of hospital jobs is front-end and back-end operations, whereas the front end deal with patient engagement and back end deal with documentation and data handling. Robotics can be involved in both front and back end of the hospital management. List of robots based on the tasks are listed below;

Patient Engagement Tasks (Front End):

- Robotics in nursing, patient handling, and support;
- Robotics in patient reception;
- Robotics in ambulance services;
- Robotics in serving (food and medicine);
- Robotics in surgery and surgical assistance;
- Robotics in cleaning, moping, spraying, disinfecting;
- Robotics in physiotherapy, radiology, lab diagnostics and rehabilitation;
- Robotics in telepresence;

- Robotics in hospital kitchen and pantry management;
- Robotics in outdoor medicine delivery;
- Robotics in home healthcare.

Documentation and other hospital management tasks (back end):

- Robotics in patient data feeding and storing,
- Robotics in data mining,
- Robotics in job allocation to hospital staff,
- Robotics in payroll management (ERP),
- Robotics in medicine and medical equipment logistics,
- Robotics in medical wastes/residual management.

### 5.1.2   Patient Engagement Tasks (Front End)

#### 5.1.2.1   Robotics in Nursing, Patient Handling, and Support

Manually handling patients is one of the toughest jobs and a major challenge that can lead to musculoskeletal burdens among healthcare workers. The conventional way of doing things can be replaced by advanced technologies and innovations that help healthcare workers to adopt any technology according to their physical capacity. The use of robotics in nursing can be a big game changer that the nurses and healthcare workers will be able to get physical relief by getting the support of collaborative robots, which can assist them in manual patient handling. As per the reports, most nurses and healthcare workers are exerting much physical pressure on patients with kinetic and muscle disorders, especially for the movement of their body parts. There are two types of movements that can be classified as highly asymmetric postures and actions associated with divergent extremes in the lower limb and the spine muscle commotion, where the nurses are forced to give complete physical pressure to make movements easy for patients. Numerous studies show that with the usage of collaborative robots, nurses and caregivers have to exert very little pressure on the movement of patients with kinetic and muscle disorders. In other words, the physical pressure on nurses, healthcare workers, and caregivers has been reduced significantly because of the use of collaborative robots.

The healthcare system and society are largely dependent on the sociodemographic changes which is taking place and which are having a higher impact worldwide. As per studies, the life expectancy of people has increased due to a gradual decline in the birth rates. This gradually resulted in an increase in the number of old aged people, especially people older than 65 years. Here is the point of time when we realize the significant role of nurses and healthcare workers. If the old age population increases drastically because of the increased life expectancy due to technological advancement and other factors, it will surely be a great question of concern for the nurses, as well as healthcare workers regarding proper patient care. There should be a right balance in the patient-to-caregiver ratio, and in the worst case, many countries face tragic imbalances in this ratio. As per studies, the number of old aged people, especially people older than 80 years, is likely to increase from 143 million in 2020 to 426 million in 2050. This increase in the number of aged people will gradually result in the increased demand and requirement for nurses, healthcare workers, and caregivers. Hence, we can expect a global shortage in the number of nurses, healthcare workers, and caregivers. This will finally result in a dire impact on the healthcare sector, and there is a chance of occupational stress among nurses and caregivers.

The upcoming demand for healthcare workers and nurses put forward the need for efficient technology to reduce the occupational stress of the class of people. It can certainly reduce not only mental stress but can contribute largely to the kinematic activities, muscle activities, and kinetic activities during manual patient handling. The feasibility of using a light-weight telemanipulation or telepresence robot can provide physical and mental relief by assisting and integrating with nurses whilst repositioning a patient from one position to another in a care bed.

There is a greater need to identify and adopt robotics technology in order to contribute toward a healthy aging nursing and healthcare workforce and to meet the demand in the future.

### 5.1.2.2   Robotics in Patient Reception

The usage of human robots to interact is becoming vital nowadays. The main purposes of such robots are to give information to the public who are using the services. The robots in the healthcare sector need to be more friendly and polite in interacting with patients and bystanders who visit regularly.

Receptionist robots are intended to perform tasks like communication with the patients or bystanders like a human receptionist, even though they cannot perform as perfectly as human receptionist do, such as complex discussions or some physical tasks. The receptionist robots can help in checking the appointments with the doctor and guide the patients rightly toward the medical staff.

The receptionist robots can recognize human speech and they can easily register the patient details and can fix appointments as well as check the appointments. In addition to this feature, face recognition is another major feature of receptionist robots in the medical field. Once it is registered, it can automatically identify the patient and make an appointment with the medical staff. The Receptionist robot work with the help of a medical server system that enables to retrieve, update and register the patient details.

Additionally, some more features are also incorporated with the health-care receptionist robots such as motion sensor to have different expressional parts and functions as we found that friendliness and attention are most important for receptionist robots.

### 5.1.2.3    Robotics in Ambulance Services

The transformations in the medical field are drastic due to the recent technological advancement which not only answers the question of economy of scale and cost, but also it has increased the survival rates.

Technological innovations are helping the patients in case of any emergency, even before they reach the hospital through a connected ambulance. It enables the medical staff to get the details of the patient even before they reach the hospital and they can make the necessary arrangements. The advanced connectivity facilities and technologies are changing even the face of ambulance services. Because of the availability of better connectivity, high resolution video calling is possible between the ambulance service and the hospital that it makes possible to the hospital staffs to get a better idea of the patient's situation. This not only enables the medical staff to arrange required facilities but also they can remotely diagnose the current situation of the patient and also prescribes immediate treatment for the same.

### 5.1.2.4    Robotics in Serving (Food and Medicine)

Following are the major utilities of robots in the area of serving food and medicine:

- It facilitates the transportation of dishes and vessels between the kitchen/pantry area and the ward and then empty trays back to the kitchen.
- These robots can manage the trash cans, trolleys and full and empty containers.

- It facilitates the transportation of clothes/linens (clean and dirty).
- It facilitates the transportation and delivery of cleaning carts/trolleys and turn-on cart-washing systems.
- It facilitates transportation and delivery of sterile supplies.
- It facilitates the transportation of hospital medications and other supplies between different sections (laboratories, wards, pharmacies, theaters).

### 5.1.2.5   Robotics in Surgery and Surgical Assistance

The use of mechanical arms that are enabled either with a camera or with a surgical instrument and which is operated by a surgeon is the most distinctive application of robotics in surgical assistance [3].

These surgical robots are enabled with special features which can assist in operations, and they can even execute complex processes with greater precision and better control. These robots are minimally invasive and can serve as a better option for open surgeries that are riskier and need better care. Biopsies and the removal of cancerous tumors and bypass surgeries are all examples of robot-assisted treatments which are in common.

These surgical robots are enabled with a high-resolution 3D vision system and several tiny motion devices to carry out the surgeries more efficiently than a human hand. The surgeon will have complete control over the robot which allows them to conduct the process more accurately [4].

There are several advantages for robot-assisted surgical procedures. The patients are able to get the benefits directly and indirectly.

The advantages include:

- Quick and easy recovery.
- Less recovery time.
- Better surgeon dexterity and range of motion.
- Lower chance of infection.
- Lesser blood transfusions and blood loss
- High-definition image of the surgical field which enables in accurate conduct of surgeries.
- Less time to be spent in hospitals
- Lower level of discomfort

### 5.1.2.6   Robotics in Cleaning, Moping, Spraying and Disinfecting

Recently robots are very commonly used for cleaning and disinfecting the hospital spaces. These robots are widely used in spraying antiseptic and disinfectant on the floors and common spaces to reduce the further spread of infectious diseases and ensure the floors and common places are free from germs and viruses.

These robots can be remotely controlled in order to avoid hazardous contact with disinfectant chemicals or spray. These mobile robots can vacate a patient's room wisely while a supervisor will be monitoring the process from a distance it in real-time from a distance.

The cleaning and disinfecting robots basically include:

- Real-time heat maps tracking system is used for efficient cleaning.
- Location and identification of scrubbers and cleaning materials.
- Tracking system is enabled in desktop and mobile phones.

### 5.1.2.7   Robotics in Physiotherapy, Radiology, Lab Diagnostics and Rehabilitation (Exoskeletons)

Robotic technology is now being widely used in the areas of physiotherapy, radiology, and laboratory diagnostics and also for rehabilitation purposes, which is commonly known as exoskeletons [5]. These type of robots can detect electrical impulses in the human body via sensors that is being attached to the skin and can respond using moving their joints. These robots are anticipated to help people to resolve and recover from lower body issues, including paralysis and strokes with the application of physiotherapy. This technology enables to improve the interconnection with other healthcare technologies and gadgets. All healthcare workers will have an additional opportunity to take part in the development and usage of exoskeletons in various hospital settings.

### 5.1.2.8   Robotics in Tele-Presence

Tele-presence or tele-care systems allow the healthcare workers especially doctors to monitor the patients who are unable to meet the doctor in hospital and who are at home treatment. These tele-presence robots can monitor and track the patient's condition regularly and can generate reports immediately and inform the doctor at the same time. This help the doctors to diagnose the problems very early and they can rate of recovery is high.

The tele-presence robots works with the help of sensors fixed in the live environment and collect data on geriatric behaviours to offer appropriate assistance as and when needed. The major population who will get benefitted from these tele-presence robots are those who are suffering from severe age-related troubles, those who are severely ill and especially those with physical disabilities.

### 5.1.2.9    Robotics in Hospital Kitchen and Pantry Management

One of the vital area where we need to exert extra care in hospital is the kitchen and pantry area where patients needed to be served hygienic food. Robotic technology can play a vital part in the management of kitchenette and dining pantry. This helps to serve superior quality food as per the clean and hygienic criterions. Different types of automated machines and robots are playing vital role starting from cooking till serving the food to the patients.

### 5.1.2.10    Robotics in Outdoor Medicine Delivery

The scope of robotics in outdoor medicine delivery is now the new way of delivering medicines to the people, especially it was recognized during the pandemic situation. These types of robots are beneficial in transferring/carrying medicines/drugs and all forms of body fluid samples to/from the hospitals. Previously mentioned are capable of both land transport as well as air transport with a remote to control them. Example: Drone delivery system.

### 5.1.2.11    Robotics in Home Healthcare

Recently, in advanced countries, robots are being used for home healthcare. These robots provide in-house assistance especially for older people with disabilities.

The major tasks of these robots include monitoring the user health with the help of wearable devices, to support beneficial diet plan and to create a tele-alarm for the proper timings of food and health check-up [6]. Reminders are being enabled in these robots to remind the user about food timings, exercise timings, and other essential time schedules. It also helps to contact a care giver as and when required. The other major tasks of these robots are autonomous navigation, removing and changing bed sheets, interacting with people, in-built microwave to re-heat food and to deliver food to the desired location.

### 5.1.3 Documentation and Other Hospital Management Tasks (Back End)

#### 5.1.3.1 Robotics in Patient Data Feeding and Storing

Need for robotics in patient data feeding and storing:

- Access issues- there were lot of problems related to accessing the database of patients. All patient documents were paper-based and stored in filing cabinets in individual departments.
- Storage issues- As the hospitals followed paper-based system, it caused significant storage issues.
- The support and permission from the management to access the data was very limited and restricted. Administrative support was very limited for file retrieval and data collection.
- Persistent duplication of data between departmental records and medical charts were a major issue.
- Manual data acquisition system was followed for reporting, auditing and research.

Advantages of using robotics in data feeding and storing:

- Fewer burdens on human resource.
- Better data storage facility.
- Better and fast accessibility and retrieval of data.
- These robotics systems are more fast and secured.
- Several software can be incorporated with these robots to keep an electronic patient record.

#### 5.1.3.2 Robotics in Data Mining

The upcoming trend in the digital era is the trust and increasing confidence in machine learning techniques to improve almost all areas of life. Machine learning techniques can be widely employed in the hospital management system where a continuous storing of medical data from various sources becomes a vital facilitator for Artificial Intelligence/Machine learning-aided treatments and diagnosis. AI/ML is now capable of helping out doctors to fetch better patient outcomes with an early diagnosis.

Healthcare sector is now witnessing the wide usage of AI-aided operational procedures in the form of automatic documentation, automatic appointment scheduler and even virtual assistance for patients.

### 5.1.3.3  Robotics in Job Allocation to Hospital Staffs

Robotics technology is now being widely used in managing human resource as well. These types of robots are specially designed to allocate jobs for hospital staffs according to the need. These robots learn from human workers and they can support humans in the form of assigning and scheduling tasks.

These robots are enabled with a continual beck of exigent instant decision making capacity which helps in deciding the allocation of nurses to patients, patients to bed and even techniques to surgeries [7]. These types of robots can dynamically respond to the situations as it is well programmed.

### 5.1.3.4  Robotics in Payroll Management

Payroll management is a highly complex task in the area of human resource management. Robotic process automation (RPA) is becoming the new normal for almost all the hospital administrative systems. It is so beneficial because it is highly relevant and it is very easy to implement. It can reduce the time consumed for various HR tasks associated with payroll management. As these systems are implemented, there are less chance of mistakes and errors compared to manual system.

A mounting number of hospitals are now shifting to robotics technology to perform HR related tasks that require a set of control procedures and also it requires a systematic review of available data.

As major tasks are being performed by the robots, the other teams can lend their attention on tasks demanding higher-priority. These robots also enable the HR/Payroll function to be more easy and perfect by escalating exactness, timeliness and compliance.

Advantages of robotics in payroll management:

- Efficient Data Collection
- Quicker Data Access
- Error-free Data Validation
- Enhanced Task Handling

### 5.1.3.5   Robotics in Medicine and Medical Equipment Logistics

Robotics in equipment logistics is one of the emerging applications of robotics in hospital management. As we transport huge number of materials in hospitals each day, like medicine and allied supplies, samples from laboratories, food and linen, medical equipments, etc, it is the appropriate area for implementing the robotics technology.

### 5.1.3.6   Robotics in Medical Waste Residual Management

Hospital waste management is another vital area where extreme care is required as it involves hazardous and infectious process as the healthcare staffs are exposed to be in contact with medical and bio-hazardous waste materials. These bio-medical wastes collected from hospitals needed to be disposed within 24 hours and also we need to ensure that it is disposed regularly and safely to maintain a clean and hygienic hospital environment for the patients as well as staffs.

Robotic technology has a wider scope in this area where trash can be stored in smart bins which are enabled with infrared sensors for identifying the waste level detection in the bin. Then the waste can be transferred to a safer and less populated area where it can be safely disposed.

## 5.2   Theoretical Framework

Theoretical framework of the study depicts the interconnections and cross intervening variables and moderator. Patient demographics and hospital demographics can intervene in the patient perceptions and behaviors and hospitals feasibility factors for robotics implementation that could lead to successful implementation.

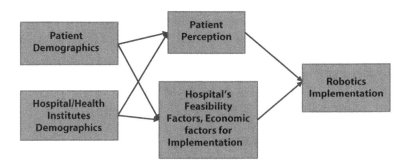

**Figure 5.1** Framework for robotics intelligence & implementation.

## 5.3    Objectives

- To understand the perception factors of patients that can help hospitals with the implementation decisions of robotics.
- To recognize the difficulties faced by caretakers, nurses, and relatives of patients, where we can bring on robotics to develop a support system.
- To assess the feasibility factors of hospitals and management to implement robotics to improve service quality.

## 5.4    Research Methodology

The whole paper works on the basic descriptive research mode. The demographics of patients and doctors are considered to do the rudimentary analysis followed by low-level to high-level statistical tools to resolve the hypothesis.

## 5.5    Primary and Secondary Data

A questionnaire was used to collect the data from patients and detailed interview schedules with the doctors, nurses, and staff. The secondary data is required for measuring the size and hospital demographics on the implementation of robotics in the various phases of patient engagement and substituting nurse and staff jobs inside and outside the purview of hospitals.

## 5.6    Factors for Consideration

### 5.6.1    Patient Demographics

Age, Gender, Availability of Bystanders, Residential Location, Marital Status, Income, Profession, Disability Status, Height, weight, BMI, Medical history details (BP, Diabetic, Surgery).

### 5.6.2    Hospital/Health Institutes Demographics

Year of existence, specialty, size of the hospital, approximate revenue per year, laboratories, operation theatres, radiology and scanning, the average number of inpatients and outpatients, pharmacy, nurses and doctors employed, no. of housekeeping and helpers, ambulance.

### 5.6.3    Patient Perception Factors

Level of education and knowledge factors, social and family, Economic status, and cultural factors, patient's attitude, behavioral factors.

### 5.6.4    Hospital's Feasibility Factors and Hospital's Economic Factors for Implementation

Location, Marketability of service, competition, financial stability, level of technology advancements, resources required, return on investment.

## 5.7    Robotics Implementation

Patient Engagement Tasks (Front End):

- Level of acceptance toward robotics in nursing, patient handling, and support
- Robotics in patient reception
- Robotics in ambulance services
- Robotics in serving (food and medicine)
- Robotics in surgery and surgical assistance
- Robotics in cleaning, moping, spraying, disinfecting
- Robotics in physiotherapy, radiology, lab diagnostics, and rehabilitation
- Robotics in telepresence
- Robotics in hospital kitchen and pantry management
- Robotics in outdoor medicine delivery
- Robotics in home healthcare

Documentation and other hospital Management Tasks (Back end):

- Robotics in patient data feeding and storing
- Robotics in data mining
- Robotics in job allocation to Hospital Staff
- Robotics in payroll management (ERP)
- Robotics in medicine and medical equipment Logistics
- Robotics in medical wastes/residual management

## 5.8    Tools for Analysis

- To understand the patient perception based on the demographics, we assess based on the cross tab and t-test.
- Factor Analysis and model fit summary is used to support the implementation factors of robotics based on the hospital demographics and feasibility factors.
- Regression is adapted to know the level of robotics implementation in hospitals with the measure of feasibility factors of hospital and perception levels of patients.

## 5.9    Analysis of Patient's Perception

The patient's perception takes a major change after the involvement of robotics which combines virtual reality, augmented reality, task automation & machine learning. But the patients, are they ready to take up the participation of robots in providing certain services and engage them during difficult times?

(1) Degree of Performance (questioning the patients to understand the degree to which the patients trusts that involving robots will be advantageous in the accomplishment of certain activities)

(2) Degree of Effort (questioning the doctors, nurses, and staff to estimate the degree of comfort related to the usage of robotics in the back-end jobs of hospitals)

(3) Degree of Social influence (questioning the caretakers, relatives and friends of patients to understand the degree to which robotics has a significant role in improving patient's health)

(4) Degree of affordability (to identify the degree to which the patient trusts that the benefits of the robotics are worth the costs involved)

## 5.10    Review of Literature

A research like this requires a wider areas of search and multidisciplinary approach has to be followed to scrutinize the factors. Acceptance to a robotic service and patient's recognition toward it is not an easy study.

There are lot of complex and unidentifiable factors that can affect the answer to the study. Also, it requires a greater level of observation and analytical ability to understand the patient's realization on robots involvement in patient care and support. Our study has started the from the base article of Health IT and the Human Interface, where he threw more insights on the human-machine interface in upgrading the healthcare sector globally. He also emphasized the patients has to get more attention and engagement by doctors and nurses for which their other time killing activity of theirs has to be replaced with robots.

A methodical analysis on the usability of robotic and automation technology and VR- virtual reality devices in neuro-motor reintegration: patients' and healthcare professionals' perspective Francesco Zanatta, Anna Giardini, Antonia Pierobon, Marco D'Addario, and Patrizia Steca. The backdrop of the study is application of virtual reality (VR) and robotic devices in neuro-motor rehabilitation. It has provided hopeful evidence in terms of efficacy so far. Usability evaluations of these technologies have been conducted comprehensively, but no overviews on this topic have been reported yet. The results of this study with VR devices were apparent and are having a virtuous benefit as a tool for endorsing patients' intimate and customized engagement and motivation during the treatment, as well as giving support and strong potential for tailored rehabilitation sessions. On the difference, they suffered from the effect of erudition and were judged as possibly requiring more physical and cerebral effort. Robotics execution and operation received positive feedback along with high satisfaction and perceived safety throughout the treatment. Robot-assisted rehabilitation was considered useful as it supported increased treatment intensity and contributed to improved patients' physical independence and psychosocial well-being. Technical and design-related issues may limit the applicability making the treatment difficult and physically straining. Moreover, cerebral and interaction deficits were remarked as expected barriers.

Then to compose the study deeper, we were focusing more on understanding the different types of robots for which we went through the paper "Robotics Utilization for Healthcare Digitization in Global COVID-19 Management" by Zeashan Hameed Khan, Afifa Siddique, and Chang Won Lee. As per the study, the demand of robotics was increasing year on year.

Table 5.1 shows the percentage increase in robots usage in the healthcare sector from 2018 to 2022.

Chart 5.2 is the graphical representation of the percentage increase in robots usage in the healthcare sector from 2018 to 2022.

Table 5.2 shows the different types of robots used in the healthcare sector with its specifications.

**Table 5.1** Percentage increase in robots usage in healthcare.

|  | 2018 | 2019 | 2020 | 2021 | 2022 |
|---|---|---|---|---|---|
| Logistics | 3.7 | 5.7 | 8.9 | 14.1 | 22.5 |
| Medical Robotics | 2.8 | 3.7 | 5 | 6.7 | 9.1 |
| Field Robotics | 1 | 1.1 | 1.2 | 1.3 | 1.4 |
| Defense | 1 | 1.2 | 1.3 | 1.5 | 1.7 |

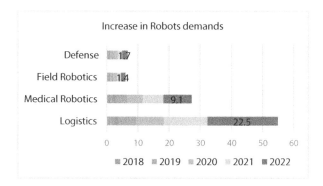

**Chart 5.2** Chart showing the percentage increase in robots usage in healthcare.

When we were looking at Robots and AI to give physicians more time with patients, NHS review calls for staff training, with 90% of jobs soon to require digital skills, says report and this article is more than three years old.

## 5.11    Hospitals Considered for the Study (Through Indirect Sources)

- Fortis Escorts Hospital
- Indra prastha Apollo Hospital
- Global Hospital
- MGM Healthcare
- Artemis Hospital
- BLK Super Specialty Hospital
- Kokilaben Dhirubhai Ambani Hospital
- Apollo Hospitals

**Table 5.2** Table showing the types of robots used in healthcare.

| Classifications of robots | Anatomy involved in operations | Applications in clinic/hospitals | Position of robots involved | Measure and specifications | Engined by | Source of power |
|---|---|---|---|---|---|---|
| Exterior big robot | Any | Surgery in general | Outside patient's body | Bulky robot, having many robotic hands | External | Electrical or pneumatic |
| Miniscule in vivo robot: endoscopic | Gastrointestinal track, Knee arthroscopy and others. | Surgery, Diagnosis and/or biopsy | Inside patient's body through incisions or natural tracks. | Incisions between 0.5 cm and 5 cm. | Internal/External propulsion | Battery or tethered |
| Miniature in vivo robot: laparoscopic | Abdominal cavity or thoracic cavity | Surgery assistant for vision/task/biopsy | Inside patient's body through incisions. | Small slits (usually 0.5–1.5 cm) | External propulsion | Tethered |
| Nano robots | Research ongoing | Tumour cancer, etc, Under research | Inside patient's body through natural holes or incisions. | From 0.1 to 10 μm atomic and molecular components. Nanobots will steer through usual biological motion ways, hence could be customized as body cells, and manufactured externally. | Internal Self-propelling under research | Battery - magnetic fields, etc. Under research |

## 5.12    Analysis and Interpretation

### 5.12.1    Crosstabulation

From Table 5.3, while drawing the Interpretation for the level of acceptance to the Implementation of Robotics versus the patient age has resulted in the following cross up 56 years to 75 years age group the great acceptance for the implementation of robotics. The same age group category has got more acceptance for the robots as assistance or the companions to the senior citizens. The work of cleaning and mopping patients with the age group of 56 to 75 has got the greater level of acceptance the instruction for the patience above the diet plan acceptance of robots in understanding

**Table 5.3** The crosstab of patient's age and factors considered for the level of acceptance of robotics.

| | | Level of acceptance to the implementation of robotics by patient | | | | | |
| --- | --- | --- | --- | --- | --- | --- | --- |
| | | Strongly disagree | Disagree | Neutral | Agree | Strongly agree | Total |
| Patient Age | 36-55 | 1 | 1 | 1 | 11 | 6 | 20 |
| | 56-75 | 5 | 11 | 6 | 10 | 14 | 46 |
| | 76-95 | 4 | 5 | 7 | 7 | 8 | 31 |
| Total | | 10 | 17 | 14 | 28 | 28 | 97 |
| | | Level of acceptance to robots as the assistant or companions | | | | | |
| | | Strongly disagree | Disagree | Neutral | Agree | Strongly agree | Total |
| Patient Age | 36-55 | 1 | 5 | 1 | 7 | 6 | 20 |
| | 56-75 | 4 | 16 | 5 | 6 | 15 | 46 |
| | 76-95 | 2 | 11 | 5 | 6 | 7 | 31 |
| Total | | 7 | 32 | 11 | 19 | 28 | 97 |

(*Continued*)

**Table 5.3** The crosstab of patient's age and factors considered for the level of acceptance of robotics. (*Continued*)

| | | Level of acceptance to robots for the work of cleaning and moping | | | | |
|---|---|---|---|---|---|---|
| | | Disagree | Neutral | Agree | Strongly agree | Total |
| Patient Age | 36-55 | 1 | 12 | 4 | 3 | 20 |
| | 56-75 | 1 | 31 | 9 | 5 | 46 |
| | 76-95 | 0 | 22 | 4 | 5 | 31 |
| Total | | 2 | 65 | 17 | 13 | 97 |

| | | Level of acceptance to instruct the patients about the diet plan | | | | | |
|---|---|---|---|---|---|---|---|
| | | Strongly disagree | Disagree | Neutral | Agree | Strongly agree | Total |
| Patient Age | 36-55 | 0 | 1 | 0 | 6 | 13 | 20 |
| | 56-75 | 2 | 2 | 5 | 17 | 20 | 46 |
| | 76-95 | 1 | 3 | 5 | 11 | 11 | 31 |
| Total | | 3 | 6 | 10 | 34 | 44 | 97 |

| | | Level of acceptance to robots for the work of intimate support | | | | | |
|---|---|---|---|---|---|---|---|
| | | Strongly disagree | Disagree | Neutral | Agree | Strongly agree | Total |
| Patient Age | 36-55 | 1 | 1 | 1 | 10 | 7 | 20 |
| | 56-75 | 4 | 12 | 6 | 7 | 17 | 46 |
| | 76-95 | 2 | 7 | 6 | 6 | 10 | 31 |
| Total | | 7 | 20 | 13 | 23 | 34 | 97 |

(*Continued*)

**Table 5.3** The crosstab of patient's age and factors considered for the level of acceptance of robotics. (*Continued*)

| | | Level of acceptance to robots toward understanding the communication | | | | | |
|---|---|---|---|---|---|---|---|
| | | Strongly disagree | Disagree | Neutral | Agree | Strongly agree | Total |
| Patient Age | 36-55 | 1 | 6 | 0 | 5 | 8 | 20 |
| | 56-75 | 4 | 4 | 11 | 17 | 10 | 46 |
| | 76-95 | 0 | 0 | 11 | 14 | 6 | 31 |
| Total | | 5 | 10 | 22 | 36 | 24 | 97 |

| | | Level of acceptance to robots toward understanding the communication | | | | | |
|---|---|---|---|---|---|---|---|
| | | Strongly disagree | Disagree | Neutral | Agree | Strongly agree | Total |
| Patient Age | 36-55 | 1 | 6 | 0 | 5 | 8 | 20 |
| | 56-75 | 4 | 4 | 11 | 17 | 10 | 46 |
| | 76-95 | 0 | 0 | 11 | 14 | 6 | 31 |
| Total | | 5 | 10 | 22 | 36 | 24 | 97 |

| | | Level of acceptance that elderly person should have control over robots | | | | Total |
|---|---|---|---|---|---|---|
| | | Disagree | Neutral | Agree | Strongly agree | |
| Patient Age | 36-55 | 2 | 0 | 9 | 9 | **20** |
| | 56-75 | 4 | 2 | 21 | 19 | **46** |
| | 76-95 | 2 | 3 | 15 | 11 | **31** |
| Total | | 8 | 5 | 45 | 39 | **97** |

(*Continued*)

**Table 5.3** The crosstab of patient's age and factors considered for the level of acceptance of robotics. (*Continued*)

| | | Level of acceptance toward robot should have entertainment function | | | | Total |
|---|---|---|---|---|---|---|
| | | Disagree | Neutral | Agree | Strongly agree | |
| Patient Age | 36-55 | 2 | 0 | 9 | 9 | 20 |
| | 56-75 | 7 | 4 | 19 | 16 | 46 |
| | 76-95 | 3 | 5 | 14 | 9 | 31 |
| Total | | 12 | 9 | 42 | 34 | 97 |

| | | Level of acceptance toward robot should detect the owners mood | | | | | Total |
|---|---|---|---|---|---|---|---|
| | | Strongly disagree | Disagree | Neutral | Agree | Strongly agree | |
| Patient Age | 36-55 | 1 | 2 | 0 | 8 | 9 | 20 |
| | 56-75 | 6 | 3 | 2 | 18 | 17 | 46 |
| | 76-95 | 2 | 2 | 3 | 14 | 10 | 31 |
| Total | | 9 | 7 | 5 | 40 | 36 | 97 |

| | | Level of acceptance that robot could encourage the elderly to engage | | | | | Total |
|---|---|---|---|---|---|---|---|
| | | Strongly disagree | Disagree | Neutral | Agree | Strongly agree | |
| Patient Age | 36-55 | 1 | 1 | 1 | 10 | 7 | 20 |
| | 56-75 | 4 | 12 | 6 | 7 | 17 | 46 |
| | 76-95 | 2 | 7 | 6 | 6 | 10 | 31 |
| Total | | 7 | 20 | 13 | 23 | 34 | 97 |

(*Continued*)

**Table 5.3** The crosstab of patient's age and factors considered for the level of acceptance of robotics. (*Continued*)

| | | Level of acceptance of the robot to turn on and turn off regular | | | | | |
| --- | --- | --- | --- | --- | --- | --- | --- |
| | | Strongly disagree | Disagree | Neutral | Agree | Strongly agree | Total |
| Patient Age | 36-55 | 1 | 1 | 1 | 10 | 7 | 20 |
| | 56-75 | 4 | 12 | 6 | 7 | 17 | 46 |
| | 76-95 | 2 | 7 | 6 | 6 | 10 | 31 |
| Total | | 7 | 20 | 13 | 23 | 34 | 97 |

the mutual communication how the elderly persons can gain control over the robots acceptance toward all your entertainment functions. The robot should able to detect the Honours move and should actively engage with seniors nursing the patience handling and providing a support ambulance services surgical and surgery assistance.

## 5.12.2 Regression and Model Fit

From Tables 5.4, 5.5 and 5.6, the model fit summary clearly depicts the level of acceptance of implementation of robotics that has got stationary

**Table 5.4** The crosstab of patient's age and factors considered for the level of acceptance of robotics.

| | | Robotics in Nursing patient handling and support | | | | |
| --- | --- | --- | --- | --- | --- | --- |
| | | Disagree | Neutral | Agree | Strongly agree | Total |
| Patient Age | 36-55 | 2 | 0 | 9 | 9 | 20 |
| | 56-75 | 6 | 4 | 20 | 16 | 46 |
| | 76-95 | 2 | 4 | 17 | 8 | 31 |
| Total | | 10 | 8 | 46 | 33 | 97 |

(*Continued*)

**Table 5.4** The crosstab of patient's age and factors considered for the level of acceptance of robotics. (*Continued*)

| | | Robotics in patient reception | | | | | |
|---|---|---|---|---|---|---|---|
| | | Strongly disagree | Disagree | Neutral | Agree | Strongly agree | Total |
| Patient Age | 36-55 | 0 | 6 | 12 | 2 | 0 | 20 |
| | 56-75 | 3 | 16 | 20 | 7 | 0 | 46 |
| | 76-95 | 2 | 11 | 11 | 4 | 3 | 31 |
| Total | | 5 | 33 | 43 | 13 | 3 | 97 |

| | | Robotics in Ambulance services | | |
|---|---|---|---|---|
| | | Agree | Strongly agree | Total |
| Patient Age | 36-55 | 7 | 13 | 20 |
| | 56-75 | 16 | 30 | 46 |
| | 76-95 | 13 | 18 | 31 |
| Total | | 36 | 61 | 97 |

| | | Robotics in serving Food and Medicine | | |
|---|---|---|---|---|
| | | Agree | Strongly agree | Total |
| Patient Age | 36-55 | 6 | 14 | 20 |
| | 56-75 | 17 | 29 | 46 |
| | 76-95 | 10 | 21 | 31 |
| Total | | 33 | 64 | 97 |

| | | Robotics in surgery and surgical assistance | | |
|---|---|---|---|---|
| | | Agree | Strongly agree | Total |
| Patient Age | 36-55 | 9 | 11 | 20 |
| | 56-75 | 13 | 33 | 46 |
| | 76-95 | 13 | 18 | 31 |
| Total | | 35 | 62 | 97 |

R square value as 0.813 which is more than 80 percentage. That supports the factors considered for the study, starting from patient involvement in robotics and hospitals, doctors, nurses, and staff acceptance toward the primary and secondary tasks of hospital management are highly commanding. Even if there is a change in the percentile value they are square and the stationery are square value remains constant that provides for the support to the list of factors considered in the study.

**Table 5.5** The model fit summary.

| Fit statistic | Mean | Minimum | Maximum | Percentile | | |
| --- | --- | --- | --- | --- | --- | --- |
| | | | | 5 | 10 | 25 |
| Stationary R-squared | 0.813 | 0.813 | 0.813 | 0.813 | 0.813 | 0.813 |
| R-squared | 0.813 | 0.813 | 0.813 | 0.813 | 0.813 | 0.813 |
| RMSE | 0.618 | 0.618 | 0.618 | 0.618 | 0.618 | 0.618 |
| MAPE | 14.703 | 14.703 | 14.703 | 14.703 | 14.703 | 14.703 |
| Max APE | 294.437 | 294.437 | 294.437 | 294.437 | 294.437 | 294.437 |
| MAE | 0.310 | 0.310 | 0.310 | 0.310 | 0.310 | 0.310 |
| Max AE | 2.944 | 2.944 | 2.944 | 2.944 | 2.944 | 2.944 |
| Normalized BIC | -0.396 | -0.396 | -0.396 | -0.396 | -0.396 | -0.396 |

**Table 5.6** The model fit summary.

| Model | Number of predictors | Model fit statistics Stationary R-squared | Ljung-Box Q(18) Statistics | DF | Sig. |
| --- | --- | --- | --- | --- | --- |
| Level of acceptance to the implementation of robotics by patient – Model _ 1 | 11 | 0.813 | 32.760 | 18 | 0.018 |

### 5.12.3   Factor Analysis

On the careful observation of the mean values considered for the factor analysis, the following statements have got the highest mean value starting from robotics involved in serving food and medicine robotics involved in surgery and surgical assistance robotics involved in cleaning mopping spraying and disinfecting robotics involved in hospital kitchen and pantry management robotics in patience data feeding and storing data mining robotics in job allocation to the hospital staffs payroll management ERP medicine and medical equipment logistics residual and waste management. The standard deviation value has not seen considerable deviations in payroll management, medicine and medical equipment logistics, medical and waste residual management, customizable information management system, task need assessment, checking the physiological parameters like a blood pressure, heart rate, etc., accompanying doctors, nurses and supporting staffs in everyday activities and observing the patience change in behavior and detecting their mood swings, these statements have not seen a considerable rise in the deviation value, which supports these factors are primarily considered for the output of the study. Table 5.7 depicts the basic descriptive statistic values like mean and deviation. The mean value of each factor which is more than 4 is considered to be highly accepted intervening variables in assessing the patient's perception and hospital's feasibility factors for robotics implementation. Some of the highlighted and accepted variables with 4.7 mean are Robotics in data mining, Robotics in payroll management ERP, Robotics in medicine and medical equipment logistics etc. Table 5.8 has a clear representation of extraction values of the statements that are considered for the study that can be factored into four categories. Table 5.9 illustrates the factor analysis table with the four-factor conversion. All the statements are categorized and classified into 4 main factors. The rotated component matrix represents the four main factors classified where the robotics need higher order replacement. Components/factors are named as follows, Robotics cleaning and Pantry, Robotic Lab assistance, Robotics in HR Planning, and Robotics in ERP. Table 5.10 depicts the involvement of robotics in assisting patients. The statements have been categorized into four factors. The majority of the statements fall under these four factors. The factors are named as follows Patient handling, patient support, patient healthcare, and patient data handling. Table 5.11 shows the regression values of the factors that are considered for the study. The majority of the factors have a significant value of more than 0.05, where we accept the null hypothesis that all these independent factors don't have huge differences from the dependent factor. The level of acceptance of robots toward understanding communication has the biggest impact factor. Table 5.12 describes the basic descriptive values of

**Table 5.7** Inception of robotics and factors to be considered through mean value.

| Statements | Mean | Std. dev. | Analysis N |
|---|---|---|---|
| Robotics in nursing patient handling and support | 3.70 | 1.059 | 10 |
| Robotics in patient reception | 2.90 | 0.994 | 10 |
| Robotics in ambulance services | 4.60 | 0.516 | 10 |
| Robotics in serving food and medicine | 4.70 | 0.483 | 10 |
| Robotics in surgery and surgical assistance | 4.80 | 0.422 | 10 |
| Robotics in cleaning moping spraying disinfecting | 4.70 | 0.483 | 10 |
| Robotics in physiotherapy, radiology, lab diagnostics and rehabilitation | 2.30 | 0.483 | 10 |
| Robotics in telepresence | 2.30 | 0.483 | 10 |
| Robotics in hospital kitchen and pantry management | 4.40 | 0.516 | 10 |
| Robotics in outdoor medicine delivery | 4.30 | 0.483 | 10 |
| Robotics in home healthcare | 4.40 | 0.516 | 10 |
| Robotics in patient data feeding and storing | 4.80 | 0.422 | 10 |
| Robotics in data mining | 4.70 | 0.483 | 10 |
| Robotics in job allocation to hospital staffs | 4.40 | 0.516 | 10 |
| Robotics in payroll management ERP | 4.70 | 0.483 | 10 |
| Robotics in medicine and medical equipment logistics | 4.70 | 0.483 | 10 |
| Robotics in medical wastes residual management | 4.30 | 0.483 | 10 |
| Involvement of robotics in storing, mining and retrieving of patient data | 4.70 | 0.483 | 10 |

*(Continued)*

**Table 5.7** Inception of robotics and factors to be considered through mean value. (*Continued*)

| Statements | Mean | Std. dev. | Analysis N |
|---|---|---|---|
| Robot should be used to track the patients appointments | 4.30 | 0.483 | 10 |
| Robot should be customisable based on the task needs | 4.70 | 0.483 | 10 |
| Measurement of certain physiological diagnosis like low and high blood pressure, fluctuating heart rate, etc | 4.30 | 0.483 | 10 |
| Robot should accompany the doctors staffs nurses in everyday act | 4.70 | 0.483 | 10 |
| Robots has to be involved in identifying the changes in the behavior of the patients to detect the mood volatiles | 4.30 | 0.483 | 10 |

robotic assistive and supportive factors at the hospital. The following factors have the level of acceptance toward robots with user mood recognition (facial expression), the level of acceptance of robot acting as a full-time companion (watching TV, preparing meals), the level of acceptance that robot that could reassure the aged people to keep in touch with their near and dear. Table 5.13 shows the factors that have got the highest mean value. The factors are the level of acceptance of the robot to turn on and turn off regularly and continual tracking Involvement of robotics in storing, mining, and retrieving patient data Robot should be used to track the patient's appointments, Robot should be customizable based on the task needs, Measurement of certain physiological diagnosis like low and high blood pressure, fluctuating heart rate, etc.

The extraction values for robotics involved in the ambulance services, robotics in telepresence are the only two factors which has got less than 0.6, whereas all the other extraction numbers are very much ahead of 0.6 which is very good sign for the improvization of factor analysis. The rotated component matrix has divided the statements into four different categories. In category one the list of factors that are involved are robots involved in cleaning, moping, spraying and disinfecting, robots involved in kitchen and pantry management in hospital, robotics involved in home healthcare, robotics involved in data mining, robotics involved in job allocation to the hospital staffs payroll management and logistics of medicine and medical equipment followed by task

**Table 5.8** Extraction values of robotic assistance factors at hospital.

| Statements | Initial | Extraction |
|---|---|---|
| Robotics in nursing patient handling and support | 1.000 | 0.646 |
| Robotics in patient reception | 1.000 | 0.803 |
| Robotics in ambulance services | 1.000 | 0.554 |
| Robotics in serving food and medicine | 1.000 | 0.766 |
| Robotics in surgery and surgical assistance | 1.000 | 0.913 |
| Robotics in cleaning moping spraying disinfecting | 1.000 | 0.983 |
| Robotics in physiotherapy, radiology, lab diagnostics and rehabilitation | 1.000 | 0.781 |
| Robotics in telepresence | 1.000 | 0.283 |
| Robotics in hospital kitchen and pantry management | 1.000 | 0.923 |
| Robotics in outdoor medicine delivery | 1.000 | 0.967 |
| Robotics in home healthcare | 1.000 | 0.923 |
| Robotics in patient data feeding and storing | 1.000 | 0.913 |
| Robotics in data mining | 1.000 | 0.983 |
| Robotics in job allocation to hospital staffs | 1.000 | 0.923 |
| Robotics in payroll management ERP | 1.000 | 0.983 |
| Robotics in medicine and medical equipment logistics | 1.000 | 0.983 |
| Robotics in medical wastes residual management | 1.000 | 0.967 |
| Involvement of robotics in storing, mining and retrieving of patient data | 1.000 | 0.983 |
| Robot should be used to track the patients appointments | 1.000 | 0.967 |
| Robot should be customisable based on the task needs | 1.000 | 0.983 |
| Measurement of certain physiological diagnosis like low and high blood pressure, fluctuating heart rate, etc | 1.000 | 0.967 |
| Robot should accompany the doctors staffs nurses in everyday act | 1.000 | 0.983 |
| Robots has to be involved in identifying the changes in the behavior of the patients to detect the mood volatiles | 1.000 | 0.967 |

**Table 5.9** Four factor conversion of robotic assistance factors at hospital.

| Statements | Component | | | |
|---|---|---|---|---|
| | 1 | 2 | 3 | 4 |
| Robotics in nursing patient handling and support | 0.306 | −0.155 | 0.645 | 0.337 |
| Robotics in patient reception | −0.195 | 0.304 | 0.380 | 0.727 |
| Robotics in ambulance services | −0.539 | 0.183 | 0.235 | −0.418 |
| Robotics in serving food and medicine | 0.200 | 0.519 | −0.607 | −0.298 |
| Robotics in surgery and surgical assistance | 0.284 | 0.365 | 0.822 | 0.154 |
| Robotics in cleaning moping spraying disinfecting | 0.942 | −0.289 | −0.098 | 0.049 |
| Robotics in physiotherapy, radiology, lab diagnostics and rehabilitation | −0.306 | −0.531 | −0.042 | 0.636 |
| Robotics in telepresence | −0.163 | −0.452 | 0.127 | 0.189 |
| Robotics in hospital kitchen and pantry management | 0.734 | 0.242 | 0.533 | −0.205 |
| Robotics in outdoor medicine delivery | 0.218 | 0.948 | 0.065 | 0.131 |
| Robotics in home healthcare | 0.734 | 0.242 | 0.533 | −0.205 |
| Robotics in patient data feeding and storing | 0.284 | 0.365 | −0.822 | 0.154 |
| Robotics in data mining | 0.942 | −0.289 | −0.098 | 0.049 |
| Robotics in job allocation to hospital staffs | 0.734 | 0.242 | 0.533 | −0.205 |
| Robotics in payroll management ERP | 0.942 | −0.289 | −0.098 | 0.049 |
| Robotics in medicine and medical equipment logistics | 0.942 | −0.289 | −0.098 | 0.049 |
| Robotics in medical wastes residual management | 0.218 | 0.948 | 0.065 | 0.131 |
| Involvement of robotics in storing, mining and retrieving of patient data | 0.942 | −0.289 | −0.098 | 0.049 |
| Robot should be used to track the patients appointments | 0.218 | 0.948 | 0.065 | 0.131 |

(*Continued*)

**Table 5.9**  Four factor conversion of robotic assistance factors at hospital. (*Continued*)

| Statements | Component | | | |
|---|---|---|---|---|
| | 1 | 2 | 3 | 4 |
| Robot should be customisable based on the task needs | 0.942 | −0.289 | −0.098 | 0.049 |
| Measurement of certain physiological diagnosis like low and high blood pressure, fluctuating heart rate, etc | 0.218 | 0.948 | 0.065 | 0.131 |
| Robot should accompany the doctors staffs nurses in everyday act | 0.942 | −0.289 | −0.098 | 0.049 |
| Robots has to be involved in identifying the changes in the behaviour of the patients to detect the mood volatiles | 0.218 | 0.948 | 0.065 | 0.131 |

**Table 5.10**  Comparison of robotic assistance factors at hospital.

| Statements | Component | | | |
|---|---|---|---|---|
| | 1 | 2 | 3 | 4 |
| Robotics in nursing patient handling and support | 0.035 | -0.024 | 0.196 | 0.208 |
| Robotics in patient reception | -0.022 | 0.047 | 0.115 | 0.448 |
| Robotics in ambulance services | -0.061 | 0.029 | 0.071 | -0.258 |
| Robotics in serving food and medicine | 0.023 | 0.081 | -0.184 | -0.184 |
| Robotics in surgery and surgical assistance | 0.032 | 0.057 | -0.250 | 0.095 |
| Robotics in cleaning moping spraying disinfecting | 0.107 | -0.045 | -0.030 | 0.030 |
| Robotics in physiotherapy, radiology, lab diagnostics and rehabilitation | -0.035 | -0.083 | -0.013 | 0.392 |
| Robotics in telepresence | -0.019 | -0.070 | 0.038 | 0.117 |

(*Continued*)

**Table 5.10** Comparison of robotic assistance factors at hospital. (*Continued*)

| Statements | Component | | | |
| --- | --- | --- | --- | --- |
| | 1 | 2 | 3 | 4 |
| Robotics in hospital kitchen and pantry management | 0.083 | 0.038 | 0.162 | -0.127 |
| Robotics in outdoor medicine delivery | 0.025 | 0.148 | 0.020 | 0.081 |
| Robotics in home healthcare | 0.083 | 0.038 | 0.162 | -0.127 |
| Robotics in patient data feeding and storing | 0.032 | 0.057 | -0.250 | 0.095 |
| Robotics in data mining | 0.107 | -0.045 | -0.030 | 0.030 |
| Robotics in job allocation to hospital staffs | 0.083 | 0.038 | 0.162 | -0.127 |
| Robotics in payroll management ERP | 0.107 | -0.045 | -0.030 | 0.030 |
| Robotics in medicine and medical equipment logistics | 0.107 | -0.045 | -0.030 | 0.030 |
| Robotics in medical wastes residual management | 0.025 | 0.148 | 0.020 | 0.081 |
| Involvement of robotics in storing, mining and retrieving of patient data | 0.107 | -0.045 | -0.030 | 0.030 |
| Robot should be used to track the patients appointments | 0.025 | 0.148 | 0.020 | 0.081 |
| Robot should be customisable based on the task needs | 0.107 | -0.045 | -0.030 | 0.030 |
| Measurement of certain physiological diagnosis like low and high blood pressure, fluctuating heart rate, etc | 0.025 | 0.148 | 0.020 | 0.081 |
| Robot should accompany the doctors staffs nurses in everyday act | 0.107 | -0.045 | -0.030 | 0.030 |
| Robots has to be involved in identifying the changes in the behaviour of the patients to detect the mood volatiles | 0.025 | 0.148 | 0.020 | 0.081 |

need assessment doctors and staffs everyday work schedule management. In category 2 robotics in serving food and medicine, robotics in outdoor medicine delivery, robotics in tracking the patience appointments, robotics in measuring the physiological parameters like blood pressure, heart rate and robotics involved in detection of mood and patients changing body behaviours. In category 3 robotics in patient handling and support system, robotics in surgery and surgical assistance. The last category starts from robotics in patient reception, robotics in physiotherapy, radiology, lab Diagnostics, and rehabilitation.

## 5.12.4   Regression Analysis

**Table 5.11**  Impact of robotic assistance factors at hospital using regression analysis. (*Continued*)

| Model | Unstandardized coefficients | | Standardized coefficients | | |
|---|---|---|---|---|---|
| | B | Std. error | Beta | t | Sig. |
| Level of acceptance to robots for the work of cleaning and moping | 0.010 | 0.138 | -0.005 | -0.070 | 0.944 |
| Level of acceptance to instruct the patients about the diet plan | 0.018 | 0.078 | -0.014 | -0.236 | 0.814 |
| Level of acceptance to robots toward understanding the communication | 0.187 | 0.069 | 0.155 | 2.717 | 0.008 |
| Level of acceptance that elderly person should have control over environment | 0.060 | 0.224 | -0.039 | -0.268 | 0.789 |

(*Continued*)

**Table 5.11** Impact of robotic assistance factors at hospital using regression analysis. (*Continued*)

| Model | Unstandardized coefficients | | Standardized coefficients | t | Sig. |
|---|---|---|---|---|---|
| | B | Std. error | Beta | | |
| Level of acceptance toward robot should have entertainment functions | 0.090 | 0.150 | 0.065 | 0.599 | 0.551 |
| Level of acceptance toward robot should detect the owners mood | 0.005 | 0.078 | -0.004 | -0.062 | 0.951 |
| Level of acceptance robot should accompany the owner in everyday | 0.091 | 0.111 | -0.069 | -0.827 | 0.411 |
| Level of acceptance of the robot to turn on and turn off regular | 0.573 | 0.085 | 0.572 | 6.711 | 0.000 |

## 5.12.5    Descriptive Statistics

**Table 5.12** Basic descriptives values of robotic assistive and supportive factors at hospital

| Particulars | Level of acceptance that elderly individuals should have command on the robot | Level of acceptance toward robots with in-built entertainment functions (e.g., games, auto reading, kindles, music player etc) | Level of acceptance toward robots with user mood recognition (facial expression) | Level of acceptance robot acting as a full time companion (watching TV, preparing meals) | Level of acceptance that robot that could reassure the aged people to keep in touch with their near and dear |
|---|---|---|---|---|---|
| Mean | 4.185567 | 4.185567 | 4.185567 | 4.185567 | 3.587629 |
| Standard error | 0.088334 | 0.088334 | 0.088334 | 0.088334 | 0.136501 |
| Standard deviation | 0.869984 | 0.869984 | 0.869984 | 0.869984 | 1.344375 |
| Sample variance | 0.756873 | 0.756873 | 0.756873 | 0.756873 | 1.807345 |
| Kurtosis | 0.961556 | 0.961556 | 0.961556 | 0.961556 | -1.13259 |
| Skewness | -1.14796 | -1.14796 | -1.14796 | -1.14796 | -0.46642 |

**Table 5.13** Basic descriptives values of robotic assistive and supportive factors at hospital.

| Level of acceptance of the robot to turn on and turn off regularly and continual tracking | Involvement of robotics in storing, mining and retrieving of patient data | Robot should be used to track the patients appointments | Robot should be customisable based on the task needs | Measurement of certain physiological diagnosis like low and high blood pressure, fluctuating heart rate, etc |
|---|---|---|---|---|
| 3.587629 | 4.649485 | 4.680412 | 4.649485 | 4.680412 |
| 0.136501 | 0.048697 | 0.047593 | 0.048697 | 0.047593 |
| 1.344375 | 0.47961 | 0.468739 | 0.47961 | 0.468739 |
| 1.807345 | 0.230026 | 0.219716 | 0.230026 | 0.219716 |
| -1.13259 | -1.62891 | -1.41178 | -1.62891 | -1.41178 |
| -0.46642 | -0.63648 | -0.78598 | -0.63648 | -0.78598 |

**Table 5.14** Basic descriptives values of robotic assistive and supportive factors at hospital.

| Particulars | Robotics in nursing, patient handling and support | Robotics in patient reception | Robotics in ambulance services | Robotics in serving (food and medicine) | Robotics in surgery and surgical assistance | Robotics in cleaning, moping, spraying, disinfecting |
|---|---|---|---|---|---|---|
| Mean | 4.051546 | 2.752577 | 4.628866 | 4.659794 | 4.639175 | 4.649485 |
| Standard error | 0.093117 | 0.087969 | 0.049307 | 0.048355 | 0.049014 | 0.048697 |
| Standard deviation | 0.917096 | 0.866397 | 0.485618 | 0.47624 | 0.482735 | 0.47961 |
| Sample variance | 0.841065 | 0.750644 | 0.235825 | 0.226804 | 0.233033 | 0.230026 |
| Kurtosis | 0.252624 | 0.169295 | -1.74271 | -1.56318 | -1.68863 | -1.62891 |
| Skewness | -0.93075 | 0.310048 | -0.5419 | -0.68519 | -0.58875 | -0.63648 |

Table 5.15 Basic descriptives values of robotic assistive and supportive factors at hospital.

| Robotics in physiotherapy, radiology, lab diagnostics and rehabilitation | Robotics in telepresence | Robotics in hospital kitchen and pantry management | Robotics in outdoor medicine delivery | Robotics in medical wastes/residual management |
|---|---|---|---|---|
| 2.443299 | 2.453608 | 4.474227 | 4.680412 | 4.680412 |
| 0.094942 | 0.095 | 0.050963 | 0.047593 | 0.047593 |
| 0.93507 | 0.935644 | 0.501929 | 0.468739 | 0.468739 |
| 0.874356 | 0.87543 | 0.251933 | 0.219716 | 0.219716 |
| -0.85296 | -0.85756 | -2.03133 | -1.41178 | -1.41178 |
| 0.011979 | -0.01842 | 0.104859 | -0.78598 | -0.78598 |

**Table 5.16** Basic descriptives values of robotic assistive and supportive factors at hospital.

| Particulars | Robotics in home health-care. | Robotics in patient data feeding and storing | Robotics in data mining | Robotics in job allocation to Hospital Staffs | Robotics in payroll management (ERP) | Robotics in medicine and medical equipment logistics |
|---|---|---|---|---|---|---|
| Mean | 4.474227 | 4.639175 | 4.649485 | 4.474227 | 4.649485 | 4.649485 |
| Standard error | 0.050963 | 0.049014 | 0.048697 | 0.050963 | 0.048697 | 0.048697 |
| Standard deviation | 0.501929 | 0.482735 | 0.47961 | 0.501929 | 0.47961 | 0.47961 |
| Sample variance | 0.251933 | 0.233033 | 0.230026 | 0.251933 | 0.230026 | 0.230026 |
| Kurtosis | -2.03133 | -1.68863 | -1.62891 | -2.03133 | -1.62891 | -1.62891 |
| Skewness | 0.104859 | -0.58875 | -0.63648 | 0.104859 | -0.63648 | -0.63648 |

## 5.13    Conclusion

Robotic technology is being adopted by the healthcare sector regionally and globally recently. The scope of robotic technology is can be used widely in the different areas such as surgery, tele-medicine, pharmacy, equipment logistics, bio-waste disposal, rehabilitation, etc. As the technology keeps on advancing, the cost to implement keeps on reducing and which helps the healthcare institutions to embrace the technology in wider areas. As we all know, robotic technology helps in reducing duplication of tasks, brings more accuracy and speed, it consistently reduces the work load of medical staffs, it can provide remote assistance, and thereby reduce costs to maximum extend.

It is worth it for the healthcare sector to look for the enormous potential and long-term benefits of robotic technology, which ensures the first mover advantage of innovative technology and thereby capture the market share. The innovative practices adopted today will surely generate profits tomorrow.

In this study, we presented a broad outline of the application and acceptability of robotics in medical and allied areas. The classifications of robots mentioned in the study are done based on different departments in the hospitals where robotics application can be implemented without failure. It ranges from cleaning robots to highly sophisticated surgical robots.

The scope of application of robotics in the area of healthcare sector is never ending. As the technological advancement takes place, the application of robotics may keep on changing according to the need. There are more areas which is crucial to be explored deeply in the robotics application related to healthcare sector. Tables 5.14, 5.15, and 5.16 depicts the basic descriptive values of robotic assistive and supportive factors at the hospital. Robotics in serving (food and medicine), Robotics in surgery and surgical assistance, Robotics in cleaning, moping, spraying, disinfecting, Robotics in nursing, patient handling, and support. Robotics in outdoor medicine delivery, Robotics in medical wastes/residual management.

## References

1. Riek, L.D., *A study paper within the Cornell University studies paper on health-care robotics.* Communications of the ACM, Volume 60, Issue 11, 2017.
2. Ashrafian, H., *A unique amendment of the turing take a look at for synthetic intelligence and robotics in healthcare.* https://onlinelibrary.wiley.com/doi/abs/10.1002/rcs.157., 2019, Vol. 10.1.2, 2019.
3. Guix, M., Mestre, R., Patiño, T. and De Corato, M., *Biohybrid soft robots with self-stimulating skeletons.* 53, Vol. 6, Issue 53, 2021.

4. Singh, R., Raja, S. Convergence in information and communication technology: strategic and regulatory considerations (English). Washington, D.C.: World Bank Group. 2023.
5. Intel. 2021. *Robotics in Healthcare: The Future of Robots in Medicine.* January 2021.
6. Kar, S., *Robotics in Healthcare.* 1, pp. 78-83, Noida : International Conference on Power Energy - IEEE, 02 03, Vol. 10, 2020.
7. Majidi, C., *Soft Robotics: A Perspective--Current Trends and Prospects for the Future.* Corpus ID: 109319815, *Materials Science*, Vol. 1, pp. 5-11, 2014.

# Annexure

Questionnaire:
Patient Name:
Patient Age:

| 18-35 | 36-55 | 56-75 | 76-95 | 95 and above |
|---|---|---|---|---|

Patient Profession:

| Self-employed | Business | Professional | Salaried | Others |
|---|---|---|---|---|

Patient Income (Annual):

| 300000-600000 | 600000-900000 | 900000-1200000 | 1200000-1500000 | 1500000 and above |
|---|---|---|---|---|

Marital Status:

| Married | Unmarried | Widow | Widower | Divorced |
|---|---|---|---|---|

Underwent any Surgery:

| Yes | No |
|---|---|

Kind of surgery:

| General surgery | |
|---|---|
| C-section | |

| | |
|---|---|
| Organ replacement | |
| Joint replacement | |
| Full hysterectomy | |
| Heart surgeries | |
| Bariatric surgeries including the gastric bypass | |
| Neuro surgery | |
| Orthopaedic Surgery | |
| Vascular Surgery | |
| Urologic Surgery | |
| Trauma Surgery | |
| Plastic & Reconstructive Surgery | |
| Head & Neck Surgery | |
| Others: | |

Total no. of days expected to be admitted in hospital:

| 0-5 days | 06-10 days | 11-15 days | 16-20 days | 20 days and more |
|---|---|---|---|---|

Availability of Bystanders:

| Yes | No |
|---|---|

Type of Bystanders:

| Relative | Non-relative |
|---|---|

Age of the Bystanders:

| 18-30 | 31-40 | 41-50 | 51-60 | 60 and above |
|---|---|---|---|---|

Condition of bed-ridden:

| Yes | No |
|---|---|

Level of acceptance to the implementation of robotics:

| Very High | High | Neutral | Low | Very Low |
|---|---|---|---|---|

Level of acceptance to robots as the assistant or companions to take care of them

| Very High | High | Neutral | Low | Very Low |
|---|---|---|---|---|

Level of acceptance to robots as the assistant or companions to take care of them

| Very High | High | Neutral | Low | Very Low |
|---|---|---|---|---|

Level of acceptance to robots for the work of cleaning and moping

| Very High | High | Neutral | Low | Very Low |
|---|---|---|---|---|

Level of acceptance to instruct the patients about the diet plans

| Very High | High | Neutral | Low | Very Low |
|---|---|---|---|---|

Level of acceptance to robots for the work of intimate support

| Very High | High | Neutral | Low | Very Low |
|---|---|---|---|---|

Level of acceptance to robots toward understanding the communication done by patients regarding the difficulties

| Very High | High | Neutral | Low | Very Low |
|---|---|---|---|---|

Level of acceptance to robots for the work of intimate support

| Very High | High | Neutral | Low | Very Low |
|---|---|---|---|---|

Level of acceptance that elderly individuals should have command on the robot

| Very High | High | Neutral | Low | Very Low |
|-----------|------|---------|-----|----------|

Level of acceptance toward robots with in-built entertainment functions (e.g., games, auto reading, kindles, music player etc)

| Very High | High | Neutral | Low | Very Low |
|-----------|------|---------|-----|----------|

Level of acceptance toward robots with user mood recognition (facial expression)

| Very High | High | Neutral | Low | Very Low |
|-----------|------|---------|-----|----------|

Level of acceptance robot acting as a full time companion (watching TV, preparing meals)

| Very High | High | Neutral | Low | Very Low |
|-----------|------|---------|-----|----------|

Level of acceptance that robot that could reassure the aged people to keep in touch with their near and dear

| Very High | High | Neutral | Low | Very Low |
|-----------|------|---------|-----|----------|

Level of acceptance of the robot to turn on and turn off regularly and continual tracking

| Very High | High | Neutral | Low | Very Low |
|-----------|------|---------|-----|----------|

| S. no. | Factors | Very high | High | Neutral | Low | Very low |
|--------|---------|-----------|------|---------|-----|----------|
| 1 | Robotics in nursing, patient handling and support | | | | | |

| S. no. | Factors | Very high | High | Neutral | Low | Very low |
|---|---|---|---|---|---|---|
| 2 | Robotics in patient reception | | | | | |
| 3 | Robotics in ambulance services | | | | | |
| 4 | Robotics in serving (food and medicine) | | | | | |
| 5 | Robotics in surgery and surgical assistance | | | | | |
| 6 | Robotics in cleaning, moping, spraying, disinfecting | | | | | |
| 7 | Robotics in physiotherapy, radiology, lab diagnostics and rehabilitation | | | | | |
| 8 | Robotics in telepresence | | | | | |
| 9 | Robotics in hospital kitchen and pantry management | | | | | |
| 10 | Robotics in outdoor medicine delivery | | | | | |
| 11 | Robotics in home healthcare | | | | | |

| S. no. | Factors | Very high | High | Neutral | Low | Very low |
|---|---|---|---|---|---|---|
| 1 | Robotics in patient data feeding and storing | | | | | |
| 2 | Robotics in data mining | | | | | |

| S. no. | Factors | Very high | High | Neutral | Low | Very low |
|---|---|---|---|---|---|---|
| 3 | Robotics in job allocation to Hospital Staffs | | | | | |
| 4 | Robotics in payroll management (ERP) | | | | | |
| 5 | Robotics in medicine and medical equipment logistics | | | | | |
| 6 | Robotics in medical wastes/ residual management | | | | | |
| 7 | Involvement of robotics in storing, mining and retrieving of patient data | | | | | |
| 8 | Robot should be used to track the patients appointments | | | | | |
| 9 | Robot should be customisable based on the task needs | | | | | |
| 10 | Measurement of certain physiological diagnosis like low and high blood pressure, fluctuating heart rate, etc | | | | | |
| 11 | Robot should accompany the doctors/staffs/nurses in everyday activities | | | | | |
| 12 | Robots has to be involved in identifying the changes in the behaviour of the patients to detect the mood volatiles | | | | | |

# 6

# Accelerating Development of Medical Devices Using Human-Machine Interface

Dipanjan Karati[1], Swarupananda Mukherjee[2*], Souvik Roy[2]
and Bhupendra G. Prajapati[3]

[1]*Department of Pharmaceutical Technology, School of Pharmacy,
Techno India University, Kolkata, West Bengal, India*
[2]*Department of Pharmaceutical Technology, NSHM Knowledge Campus, Kolkata –
Group of Institutions, B.L. Saha Road, Kolkata, West Bengal, India*
[3]*Shree S K Patel College of Pharmaceutical Education and Research,
Ganpat University, Mahesana, Gujarat, India*

## Abstract

A human-machine interface (HMI) is all the hardware and software components that allow a human user and a machine to engage in an interactive system to complete a specific task. HMI technologies can be referred to as a particular type of information technology because they include all equipment used to transfer and present data and commands inside a human-machine system. The direction of HMI technologies can be divided into input, output, and bidirectional. An HMI system's role is to make a technology's use evident to the user. A well-designed HMI conforms to the user's conception of the work to be completed. The usability of the HMI system, which also includes how simple it is to learn, is used to evaluate it. The HMI must be user-friendly, simple to see and recognize, and clear in its response to the operator in therapeutic diagnostic equipment applications. It must display important and comprehensive visual data. The patient must, moreover, feel secure, and at ease. The operational and functional requirements must be well defined before an HMI arrangement for medical analytical equipment can be designed. With less human input and greater efficiency, HMI technology offers real-time regulator permission and the capacity to manage several processes simultaneously. Health monitoring, medical diagnosis, the creation of prosthetic and assistive devices, the automobile and aerospace industries, robotic controls,

*Corresponding author*: swarupananda.mukherjee@nshm.com;
swarup_mukherjee@rediffmail.com; ORCID ID: https://orcid.org/0000-0002-6511-3116

Rishabha Malviya, Sonali Sundram, Bhupendra Prajapati and Sudarshan Kumar Singh (eds.)
Human-Machine Interface: Making Healthcare Digital, (161–182) © 2024 Scrivener Publishing LLC

and many more disciplines can all benefit from increased control access provided by HMI technology.

*Keywords*: Human-machine interface, medical devices, brain–computer interfaces, robotic surgery, Internet-of-Things (IoT) technologies

## 6.1    Introduction

The "first, do not harm" concept, which represents a mostly human-based perception of accountability, has been the foundation for much of medicine. But as neoteric surgery and operating chambers have advanced, the idea that therapeutic blunders are, by definition, unintentional human errors (HEs) have become obsolete [1, 2]. Incorporating sophisticated automated and robotic surgical systems (RAS) into the healthcare infrastructure has produced what Hollnagel [3]. refers to as combined "cognitive systems" and later re-discusses. The technical skill and familiarity of healthcare professionals with semi- and fully-automated systems, as well as HEs caused by groupwork and communication collapse (such as more time consumption to take decision, an absence of surgical efficiency, imperfect time regulation, etc.), should all be considered to confirm the security and superiority of surgical process. The assumption that medical devices (MD) innovation will easily defeat HEs [4, 5] results in shifting the liability burden to MDs. However, this is far from how surgical practice works because systems themselves cannot stop HEs and, worse, encourage errors. To mitigate intraoperative adverse events, HFE aims to bring a systems-founded approach that integrates human behaviors with machine interface. This approach offers acumen into human-machine interaction. This article aims to describe the practical distractions that can occur during surgical procedures, identify HF techniques that have been used to reduce intraoperative danger and inaccuracy-prone procedures, and improve the human-machine interface (HMI).

Significant advancements in exoneration, artificial intelligence (AI) (particularly in the application of sophisticated algorithms for the analysis and interpretation of human cognition), and HMIs have created a new evolutionary path for the creation of intelligent mobility aids [6]. Conventional wheelchairs cannot be used by people who have lost their lower limbs due to an accident or have diseases like quadriplegia or stroke that cause paralysis [7]. Researchers worldwide are working to create medical gadgets, and rehabilitation aids for physically challenged people, so they can go about their everyday lives with little or no help from carers, nurses, etc. [8]. Therefore, they are helping these patients feel better about themselves and be more functional, with the ultimate goal of raising their quality of life. Researchers have used bio signals captured by electroencephalography (EEG), electromyography (EMG), electrooculography (EOG), and other devices to develop intelligent, responsive, and real-time rehabilitative control systems [9, 10]. Eye motion control-based structures have recently drawn a lot of attention since, even in the population with the most severe physical disabilities, such as people with quadriplegia, eye movements are still fully functional. This is because the eye is these systems' primary source of direction [11]. An exclusive eyeball movement-oriented procedure for monitoring a wheelchair is thus presented, which will upsurge patient relief while also advancing the adoption of independent mobile rehabilitation expertise, such as intelligent wheelchairs and walkers. Scheming a self-governing system with little to no manual assistance is the primary goal to provide wheelchair users with a sense of competence, confidence, and freedom. Consequently, the method currently offered ought to be simple for a paralyzed person with a significant lower limb handicap. In addition, the system included voice-activated technologies [12]. The system is affordable, simple to operate, expandable, and comfortable for users.

HMI controls communication and interaction between people and machines. Robotics, artificial intelligence, human–computer interface, and human–robot interaction are all subfields of the multidisciplinary study of HMI. HMI is frequently used in industrial settings to improve productivity, quality, and safety. Nowadays, the medical system makes extensive use of HMI. Intelligent designs with neural interfaces are rapidly developing due to the world's rapid modernization in the twenty-first century, particularly in medical engineering. The capacity to monitor multiple machines simultaneously and accurately in real-time for various technological applications has dramatically improved over the past few decades thanks to the development of newer HMI interface systems [13, 14]. The worth of HMI is extensively acknowledged in terms of reliable human efforts and nuclear surety manifested by applying uplifted instrumentation and monitoring structures [15]. HMI can control devices and computers expressly by means of the bioelectrical motions generated by biochemical responses in the live tissues of the human anatomy [16].

The purpose of an HMI system is to make a technology's use evident to the user. A well-designed HMI fits the user's mental picture of the work they will accomplish. The usability of the HMI system, which considers how simple it is to learn, is what counts. The HMI for medical diagnostic equipment applications must be user-friendly, simple to view and discern, and explicit in its response to the operator. It must display critical and in-depth visual data. Additionally, the patient must feel secure and at ease. When a patient is a user, the interface must be straightforward, simple to use, uncomplicated, and free of jargon. There should be no opportunity for misinterpretation, inaccuracy, or confusion. Additionally, it will need to be portable and have a tiny form factor that a patient may use at home. Additionally, it must be trustworthy and robust, providing accurate readings throughout its lifespan. Manufacturers of medical devices and diagnostic tools prefer to collaborate with a skilled HMI systems associate who can address ergonomic issues, operational and functional requirements, information display and presentation, and regulatory issues involving the FDA, CE, ISO, and other notified bodies [17].

## 6.2   HMI Machineries

The HMI is all the hardware and software mechanisms used in interactive systems to exchange data and commands between a human user and a machine to carry out a specific task [18]. Figure 6.1 illustrates the schematic layout of the HMI. As a particular type of information technology, HMI technologies are all tools used to transmit and present data and commands within a human-machine system. HMI technologies can

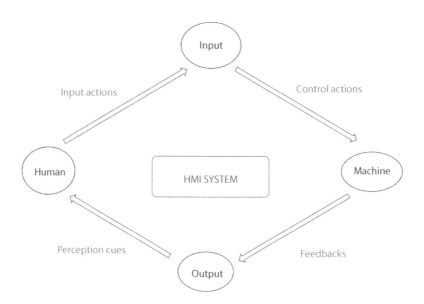

**Figure 6.1** Schematic layout of the HMI.

be refuted into three groups grounded on their direction: input, output, or bidirectional.

The last ten years have seen noteworthy advancements in HMI technology due to shifting operational and corporate requirements. Evolutionary HMI is becoming more prevalent at the moment. More progressive HMI examples possess advanced operating, good quality screen HMIs. These rationalized interfaces are creating more prospects for equipment interaction and analysis.

An HMI device for an X-ray machine goes to have one of a more helpful, kind necessity than an MRI or a puppy scanner. The features of a selected utility will drive the various design considerations. For instance, patient and operator protection can be the dominant element with an X-ray system; simultaneously, the affected person's consolation can be more crucial within the interface layout for an MRI gadget. An MRI will require a coloration monitor; an X-ray device may also use a black-and-white display. A diagnostic gadget or a surgical laser device should need foot-pedal control, even as a tool designed for affected person use in the domestic would typically be handheld. All of the valuable factors want to be depicted and addressed early inside the HMI gadget design system [19].

## 6.3    Brain–Computer Interface and HMI

Medical science advancements have given impaired persons more freedom to use their willpower. The majority of these disabled individuals struggle greatly to communicate through physical means. The capacity to interact directly with a user's brain has been elicited by cognitive neuroscience, and brain computing technology advances. You can accomplish this by utilizing the brain–computer interfaces (BCI) technology, which enables direct brain-to-physical device communication. The use of sensors can control the physical methods corresponding to numerous mental tiredness [20]. Using BCI, handlers forego their motor activity to produce neuronal impulses that may be utilized to operate robots and different communication gadget. At the moment, electrodes on a brain-machine interface record the brain's bioelectric activity. Many people worldwide have mobility issues and cannot do activities necessary for their everyday lives [21]. BCI comes in two varieties: Medical scanning equipment or sensors installed on the scalp that detects brain signals are classified as non-invasive or invasive, depending on how deeply they are implanted into the brain cortex and how high-quality their signals are. Comparatively speaking, this approach is the least intrusive and safest [22]. Thus, automated recognition systems are present; however, it is promised to provide a different interface that can be used to speak with autonomous systems. Many real-time tasks have been set as goals for BCI. It is a natural method of enabling communication between a paralyzed individual and the outside world [23].

Some BCI systems could come with HMI or control screens. Electrodes translate brain inputs into electrical signals. The scalp, the brain's surface, or neuronal activity can produce brain signals [24]. The BCI transducer comprises "feature generator" and "feature translator." An "artifact processor" may be used by some transducers to eliminate artifacts from the electrical signal that has been amplified from electrodes. The neuro-mechanism is created by the "feature generator" using the boosted brain signals. Using a "feature translator," this neuromechanism is converted into a logical control signal. The "device controller" engages a device, such as a robotic arm, wheelchair, mobile robot, etc., to carry out the device control signals that the "interface controller" has physically sent [25].

## 6.4   HMI for a Mobile Medical Exoskeleton

People with mobility impairments can now walk thanks to recent breakthroughs in exoskeleton robotics again. Using an HMI, the operator instructs the exoskeleton to move in the preferred manner. The handlers can now stand up, move about, and sit down without assistance.

Over 250,000 Americans suffer from spinal cord injuries that impair their quality of life, and 11,000 additional injuries occur yearly [26]. Patients with spinal cord injuries are more prone to numerous secondary wounds that develop due to pressure points or decreased blood supply. These wounds include fractures, breathing issues, osteoporosis, bed sores, and spasticity [27]. But a gadget that enables patients to stand up and walk helps reduce these secondary injuries. A robotic device called a lower-extremity exoskeleton can allow people with spinal cord injuries more mobility. A torso framework worn as a backpack and holds the electronics and batteries connects the two legs of such a contraption. The straps used to attach the exoskeleton legs to the user's limbs are made to exert as little pressure as possible on their skin. The user can direct the exoskeleton to the desired condition using HMI. One of the issues for lower extremity exoskeletons is figuring out a straightforward, trustworthy, and secure way for users to transmit their desired movements to the robot. Existing HMIs use human-initiated leg motion, additional motions, or brain impulses to direct the anticipated gesture. Across numerous HMIs, like the one employed by the Human Universal Load Carrier (HULC) exoskeleton, the person initiates the move, and the robot subsequently offers aid and support. However, because the user needs to initiate the motion independently, such as by taking a step, this is inappropriate for individuals with spinal cord injuries [28]. Additional movements are undesirable because they restrict the user's capacity to comprehend and operate while completing other assignments, like serving a keyboard or moving the tongue or arm in a particular way [29]. Argo Medical Technologies' ReWalk uses a keypad and rear motions to demonstrate moves [30]. Although more natural than other motions, these back motions create a swing in equilibrium and could impair the user's steadiness.

The HMI provides users having brainstem impairments with a dependable, secure, and simple way to operate eLEGS. The exoskeleton's sensors are the only ones used by the interface. By beginning the swing phase as soon as the heel lifts off the ground, the HMI delivers a more natural gait at a frequency similar to that of a non-disabled person using the exoskeleton. All five individuals were able to rapidly pick up how to operate the HMI with eLEGS, which suggests that the HMI is simple to learn.

## 6.5   Human Artificial Limb and Robotic Surgical Treatment by HMI

The latest technological brain regulation-oriented BCI arrangements are built to govern the movements of prosthetic hands by fusing with miscellaneous 3D acceleration software that give real-time transmission strategies founded on EEG pattern recognition. Because of the difficulties and restrictions in pattern confession and feature extraction in EEG readings, merely rare fundamental body movements are currently effectively facilitated by BCI [31]. For deficiency of synchronized multi-DOF control capability and the scarcity of independent controls and repeatability, using surface Electromyography (EMG) readings to operate a simulated hand with greater enfranchisement is challenging. The implanted electrode approach yields superior outcomes for gaining better control with prosthetic hands. Minimally invasive surgery techniques were initially adopted on animals and eventually on humans. The volunteer was able to control two degrees of freedom intuitively and simultaneously with the prosthetic hand using this way, which was not achievable with surface EMG controls [32]. The surgical technique known as targeted muscle reinnervation (TMR)

provides advanced prosthetic hands' innate controls. This procedure rein-
nervates new muscle targets that have lost their functioning by transferring
the remaining nerves from the severed limb [33]. The advanced prosthetic
hands get tactile feedback to regain their sensory abilities to perceive force,
temperature, vibrations, etc [34]. The recorded data from a healthy being
in the form of a sequence of data lists, each of which embraces groups of
numerous postures by a real hand and the accompanying EMG data, is an
innovative alternative way for using EMG signalling produced by the forearm muscle throughout hand movements to regulate the manipulations
of prosthetic hands. A data glove having tiny electromagnetic sensors for
the necessary movements and postures records the data frames using a 3D
electromagnetic positioning system. Additionally, it has various benefits
for controlling robotic and artificial hands, including improved precision
and faster signal processing. It recognizes a greater variety of hand forms,
enhancing a disabled person's ability to use a prosthetic hand with greater
dexterity and effectiveness [35]. The most flourished prosthetic hands created to date offer improved control systems, great functionality, and unique
mechanical design features [36–39]. Researchers have created new operational control approaches and tactics to manage highly dexterous artificial
hands [40, 41]. Patients must go through laborious exercise procedures to
master the command strategy of dextrous prosthetic hands, necessitating
new and improved HMI-based practicum methodologies. Consequently,
training amputees with virtual reality simulators is a relatively new method
[42, 43]. Another study revealed that the user needs substantial training to
manipulate an EEG-based prosthetic limb when using BCI accurately [44].
Developing a multi-force-sensitive resistor interface led to the creation of a
biomechatronic multi-finger prosthetic hand. Each finger is equipped with
force and torque sensors to ensure stability while holding various items
[45]. For numerous motion modes, EMG-founded pattern determination
has a noble achievement proportion (greater than 90%). Consequently, it
gives a prosthetic hand more freedom and superior control [46]. Surface
EMG has several drawbacks, including intrinsic noise, erroneous electrode
displacement, fatigue, sweating, and poor gel efficacy [47, 48]. Surface
EMG and inertial measurements work together to greatly minimize the
number of sensors required to accomplish multi-DOF capability and
improve the performance of prosthetic hands [49]. Using the BCI interface, surgical procedures can be made safer and more effective by reducing
human error. A brain-controlled augmented reality (BcAR) system based
on BCI technology has been created to enhance teleoperation robotic laser
surgery. It demonstrates how to control one's mental state while performing surgery using real-time feedback and training [50]. The NASA human

performance investigate square delivers a duty index to quantify workload following task completion. Based on the baseline, single, and dual works performed throughout the surgical operations, the questionnaire evaluates the subjective cognitive burden on the physicians. The index is grounded on six subscales (Figure 6.2) [51]. To diminish the complication and preserve entire focus while governing surgical works, exactly in robotic operation, BCI interfaced mechanized work load recognition with EEG affords a target-specific communication medium for the physician without producing any trouble and without creating any supplementary burden in any method apart from surgery on them throughout the perplexing operational process [52, 53]. With additional advancements in HMI process, prosthetic bibcock with advanced sophistication and improved regulation can be established that imitates the particular functionality and principle of performing of real physiological parts those are either immensely composite to carry out or not feasible in complete with existing HMI procedures.

EMG peaks are deliberated as the pre-eminent emergence of HMI as the electrical action of the signal is commenced by the human muscular system with EMG conductors and utmost convenient in the therapeutic field. With relation to the standard conductor, which is managed throughout the brain activity, these electrodes supply the galvanic signals created by muscle cells. The muscles' force and their activation level affect the EMG signal [54, 55] (Figure 6.3). It is of dyad categories; peripheral and intramuscular EMG [56]. Today, the most practical way to learn about muscles is non-invasive.

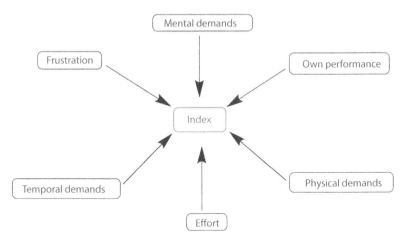

**Figure 6.2** Six subscales of index.

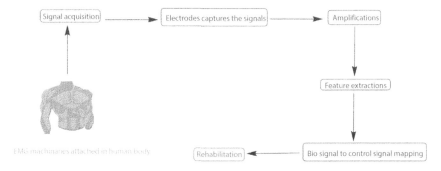

**Figure 6.3** EMG signals affected by the muscles' force and their activation level.

## 6.6 Cognitive Enhancement by HMI

The ability to judge, figure out, and perform any activity by means of CNS (central nervous system) motor skills is known as cognitive ability, a measure of an individual's anatomical competence. Currently, both medication and meditation can improve a person's cognitive function. The intelligence is enhanced by encouraging cerebral processing and enhancing brain structure through mindfulness meditation [57]. Nootropics are the names for medications, dietary supplements, and other substances that promise to enhance brain performance. These medicines primarily fall into one of three categories: piracetam, modafinil, and methylphenidate [58]. Methylphenidate is essentially a synthetic stimulant medicine that stimulates the central nervous system to treat attention deficit hyperactivity disorder (ADHD), narcolepsy, and other chronic sleep problems [59]. Patients with narcolepsy or excessive sleepiness can be treated with modafinil. It is also employed to lessen weariness and heighten attention [60]. Humans can use the compound piracetam to enhance their memory and other mental abilities. In addition to treating these conditions, this medication is also used to treat vertigo, seizure, and anaemia. However, the USFDA has not still granted piracetam permissible grade as a safe medication [61]. Beyond these three categories of drugs that improve cerebral function, another category of medications, such as phospholipase A2, oxiracetam, and acetylcholine congeners are presently utilized to treat a variety of illnesses brought on by a variety of brain disorders [62]. Several medications, including donepezil, galantamine, and rivastigmine, have received FDA approval to improve cognitive function and treat conditions including Alzheimer's disease and other dementia-related issues [63, 64]. Additionally, the use of donepezil helps pilots perform better [65].

Similarly, Modafinil is being studied for military use and enhancing performance in helicopter simulators [66]. Additionally, it has been noted that drinking soft beverages with added sugar can make someone perform worse on the BCI [67]. College students and academics worldwide use cognitive enhancement medicines to increase academic performance [68]. However, the potential side effects of drug and stimulant consumption are still up for discussion and unclear [69]. HMI technology, on the other hand, offers a way to arouse and increase the brain's natural purposeful capability numerous times by enhancing sensory modalities' memory and other cognitive functions using on-chip micro-electromechanical systems and brain chip interfaces by interacting with neurons [70, 71]. To activate the brain nerves for various objectives, such as treating various brain diseases and illnesses, surgically implantable cranial chips are employed [72]. Several aspects of brain functioning are investigated using chips based on electrolyte-oxide-metal-oxide-semiconductor field-effect transistors [73]. An early stage of more recent HMI technology, which has the potential to revolutionize the game, is the direct merging of biosensors based on nano- and micro-technology with the human body. In the upcoming years, HMI technology may make it feasible to instantaneously raise a person's cognitive ability to a very high degree.

## 6.7    Soft Electronics for the Skin Using HMI

Future trends will undoubtedly favor HMI systems with flexible and wearable components over large, stiff electronic equipment. It is crucial to create efficient methods for creating material microstructures on flexible sensors and electric devices with outstanding mechanical flexibility and stretchability in order to accomplish efficient, intuitive, and seamless manipulation of high-performance wearable HMI systems. The fundamental component of wearable HMIs is the real-time capture of human physiology and environmental information using precise and adaptable sensors [74, 75]. Table 6.1 describes the active components/construction techniques of several patterns of yieldable sensors and their useful HMI inflections.

Wearing soft electronics against the flexible, curved, and dynamic human skin offers comfort. Biological skin has a poor modulus of 140–160 kPa, also is smooth, elastic, and twistable. [76, 77] Soft electronics must make strong connection with the skin and share the same mechanical characteristics as the skin. To put it another way, limp skin-mountable anodic would be elastic and flexible to adapt to the skin's deformation and

**Table 6.1** Stretchy sensors and their uses [96].

| Active constituents | Sensor categories | HMI applications |
| --- | --- | --- |
| Carbon nanotubes (CNT) | Piezoresistive pressure sensor | Machine hands regulated by human limb postures |
| Fluorinated ethylene propylene | Piezoelectric sensor | Feedback control |
| Ag nanowires, carbon fabric | Piezoresistive pressure sensor | Virtual reality |
| polyester (PET), silicone | Triboelectric sensor | Two-factor authentication |
| Kapton film | Triboelectric sensor | Gesture control, augmented reality |

handle local stresses from daily activities. On the other hand, traditional electronics are incompatible with this use because they are constructed of heavy, fragile materials. Thus, lenient, elastic, and stretchy electronics have recently been designed to interface with skin for applications like health governing, and HMIs [78–80]. These devices offer benefits like high-quality data collecting, no skin discomfort, and accessible Internet of Things (IoT) technology integration [81].

Health monitoring technologies must now more than ever fulfil the expectations of the worldwide population due to rising healthcare spending and usage, notably in recent decades [82]. The rise in IoT-connected devices has stimulated the creation of portable and wearable technology [83, 84]. Most commercially available wearable health monitoring gadgets come in rigid designs, including smartwatches. Air cavities may be present at the device-skin interface, which is not always electrically stable [85]. The device-skin interface is significantly improved by soft skin-mountable electronics, which also have the advantages of deformability, imperceptibility, and comfortability over stiff counterparts.

HMI-based mobile machine control facilitates remote operation and raises the standard of living. For robot navigation, gentle pressure sensor-based HMIs have also been created in addition to Tribo-electronic generators (TENGs) [86–88]. Another major method for controlling mobile machinery is electrooculography (EOG), which measures the electrical potentials produced by eye movement. Subjects have controlled wheelchairs and drones by employing device learning calculations to categorize

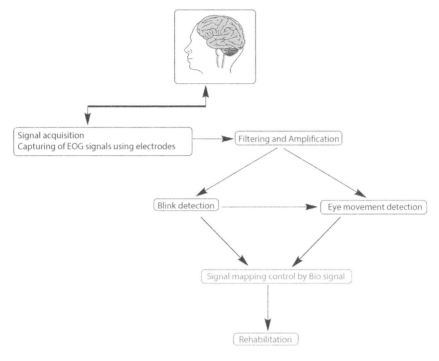

**Figure 6.4** EOG signal.

the EP indications gained from the petit sensors [89–91]. As seen in Figure 6.4, recording the EOG signal involves inserting a pair of conductors above and beneath the eye to track both straight and perpendicular eye rotation. The HMI system's ability to track the user's eye movement allows wheelchair control. The basis for EOG is the metering of modification in the corner retinal potential difference (0.4-1 mV) between the positive poles of the cornea and the opposing poles of the retina [92–95].

## 6.8    Safety Considerations

Safety issues play a crucial role in the design of HMI systems. Human mistakes cause most accidents in high-risk environments. Any HMI must have a clear presentation of alarms and the capability to report issues. Additionally, emergency stop switches, also known as E-Stops, guarantee the security of people and medical equipment and offer a reliable, constant, failsafe control response. E-Stops are different from ordinary stop switches (which mainly provide a limited system-stopping function) because they provide "fool proof" equipment shutdown. This is achieved via a sophisticated switch design, which calls for a twist, pull, or key to free electrical contacts and enable equipment restart.

## 6.9   Conclusion

The HMI systems have been recognized to improve the health service considerably. Since biocompatible materials have undergone significant advancements, many expandable and bioactive electronic instruments can readily integrate with human body limb. These materials also have essential attributes like imperceptibility and self-healing properties. The various pharmacological studies are evaluated by surgeons using HMI-oriented 3D models and 2D monitor. Current virtual reality tools give surgeons the ability to diagnose patients' physiological conditions and administer exact care properly. HMI demonstrates a bridge between people and medical technology in the current healthcare system. A meticulous design approach that considers all technical, ergonomic, and communication requirements are necessary for the HMI system's efficacy and, consequently, for the effectiveness of its use. Working with an experienced HMIS supplier for medical device applications can help guarantee that the system complies with all regulations and is easy for doctors, technicians, and patients to use. By improving functional capacity to manage several activities at once and raising performance rates, HMI technologies have expanded human potential. It can improve cognitive ability to handle many difficult scenarios with variable characteristics. Because machines will be so crucial to the future, it will be necessary to develop HMI for greater flexibility and efficiency to gain better management of these devices.

## References

1. Reason, J., Human error: Models and management. *BMJ*, 320, 7237, 768–77, 2000.
2. Kurmann, A., Tschan, F., Semmer, N.K., Seelandt, J., Candinas, D., Beldi, G., Human factors in the operating room - The surgeon's view. *Trends Anaesth. Crit. Care*, 2, 5, 224–227, 2012.
3. Hollnagel, E., Human factors/ergonomics as a systems discipline? "The human use of human beings" revisited. *Appl. Ergon.*, 45, 1, 40–44, 2014.

4. D'Addessi, A., Bongiovanni, L.F., Volpe, A., Bassi, P., Human factors in surgery: From Three Mile Island to the operating room. *Urol. Int.*, 83, 3, 249–257, 2009.

5. Kohn, L.T., *To err is human: Building a safer health system*, M.S. D (Ed.), National Academies Press, Washington DC, 2000.

6. Champaty, B., Jose, J., Pal, K., Thirugnanam, A., Development of EOG based human-machine interface control system for motorized wheelchair, in: *Proceedings of the 2014 Annual International Conference on Emerging Research Areas: Magnetics, Machines and Drives (AICERA/iCMMD)*, Kottayam, India, pp. 1–7, 2014.

7. Simpson, R.C., Smart wheelchairs: A literature review. *J. Rehabil. Res. Dev.*, 42, 423, 2005.

8. Parikh, S.P., Grassi, V., Jr., Kumar, V., Okamoto, J., Jr., Integrating human inputs with autonomous behaviours on an intelligent wheelchair platform. *IEEE Intell. Syst.*, 22, 33–41, 2007.

9. Valbuena, D., Cyriacks, M., Friman, O., Volosyak, I., Graser, A., Brain-computer interface for high-level control of rehabilitation robotic systems, in: *Proceedings of the 2007 IEEE 10th International Conference on Rehabilitation Robotics*, Noordwijk, The Netherlands, pp. 619–625, 2007.

10. Choi, K., Sato, M., Koike, Y., A new, human-cantered wheelchair system controlled by the EMG signal, in: *Proceedings of the 2006 IEEE International Joint Conference on Neural Network Proceedings*, Vancouver, BC, Canada, pp. 4664–4671, 2006.

11. Viswanathan, P., Zambalde, E.P., Foley, G., Graham, J.L., Wang, R.H., Adhikari, B. *et al.*, Intelligent wheelchair control strategies for older adults with cognitive impairment: User attitudes, needs, and preferences. *Auton. Robots*, 41, 539–554, 2017.

12. Hou, T.K., Arduino based voice-controlled wheelchair. *J. Phys. Conf. Ser.*, 1432, 012064, 2020.

13. Wanluk, N., Visitsattapongse, S., Juhong, A. *et al.*, Smart wheelchair based on eye tracking. *9th Biomedical Engineering International Conference (BMEiCON)*, Laung Prabang, Laos, pp. 1–4, 2016.

14. M.M. Lech, T.D. Hill, A.L. Arvidson *et al.*, Quality management system with human-machine interface for industrial automation. United States Patent US 6,539,271 B2, 2003 March 25.

15. Kim, I.S., Human reliability analysis in the man machine interface design review. *Ann. Nucl. Energy*, 28, 11, 1069–1081, 2001.

16. Varela, D.T., Penaloza, F.G., Rodelas, C.J.V., Characterized bioelectric signals by means of neural networks and wavelets to remotely control a human-machine interface. *Sensors*, 19, 8, 1923, 2019.

17. Singh, H.P. and Kumar, P., Developments in the human-machine interface technologies and their applications: A review. *J. Med. Eng. Technol.*, 552–573, 2021, https://doi.org/10.1080/03091902.2021.1936237.

18. Iannessi, A., Marcy, P.Y., Clatz, O., Bertrand, A.S., Sugimoto, M., A review of existing and potential computer user interfaces for modern radiology. *Insights Imaging*, 9, 4, 599–609, 2018.

19. Innocente, C., Ulrich, L., Moos, S., Vezzetti, E., Augmented reality: Mapping methods and tools for enhancing the human role in healthcare HMI. *Appl. Sci.*, 12, 4295, 2022.

20. Gandhi, V., Prasad, G., Coyle, D., Behera, L., McGinnity, T.M., EEG based mobile robot control through an adaptive brain-robot interface. *IEEE Trans. Syst. Cybern.*, 44, 9, 1278–1285, 2014.

21. Barbosa, A.O.G., Achanccaray, D.R., Meggiolaro, M.A., Activation of a mobile robot through a brain computer interface. *IEEE International Conference on Robotics and Automation*, pp. 3–8, 2010.

22. Millan, J.R., Renkens, F., Mourino, J., Non-invasive brain-actuated control of a mobile robot by human EEG. *IEEE Trans. Biomed. Eng.*, 51, 6, 1026–1033, 2004.

23. Diez, P.F., Torres Muller, S.M., Mut, V.A., Laciar, E., Avila, E., Bastos-Filho, T.F., Sarcinelli-Filho, M., Commanding a robotic wheelchair with a high-frequency steady-state visual evoked potential based brain computer interface. *Med. Eng. Phys.*, 35, 1155–1164, 2013.

24. Bashashati, M., Fatourechi, R.K., Ward, R.K. *et al.*, Topical review: A survey of signal processing algorithms in brain–computer interfaces based on electrical brain signals. *J. Neural Eng.*, 4, 2, R32–R57, 2007.

25. Mason, S.G. and Birch, G.E., A general framework for brain–computer interface design. *IEEE Trans. Neural Syst. Rehabil. Eng.*, 11, 1, 70–85, 2003.

26. Spinal cord injury facts and statistics, March 2002, The University of Alabama National Spinal Cord Injury Statistical Centre.

27. Walter, J.S. *et al.*, A database of self-reported secondary medical problems among VA spinal cord injury patients: Its role in clinical care and management. *J. Rehabil. Res. Dev.*, 39, 1, 53–61, 2002.

28. Amundson, K., Control and energetics of human exoskeleton, Ph.D. Thesis. University of California, Berkeley, USA, 2007.

29. Vaidyanathan, R., Chung, B., Gupta, L., Kook, H., Kota, S., West, J., Tongue-movement communication and control concept for hands-free human-machine interfaces. *IEEE Trans. Syst. Man Cybern.—Part A: Syst. Hum.*, 37, 4, 533–546, 2007.

30. Argo Medical Technologies, "Products." Welcome to Rewalk.com. 2010, Web. 14 July 2011.

31. Zhang, X., Li, R., Li, Y., Research on brain control prosthetic hand. *11th International Conference on Ubiquitous Robots and Ambient Intelligence*, Kuala Lumpur, pp. 554–557, 2014.

32. Merrill, D., Lockhart, J., Troyk, P.R. *et al.*, Development of an implantable myoelectric sensor for advanced prosthesis control. *Artif. Organs*, 35, 249–252, 2011.

33. Cheesborough, J.E., Smith, L.H., Kuiken, T.A. *et al.*, Targeted muscle reinnervation and advanced prosthetic arms. *Semin. Plast. Surg.*, 29, 1, 62–72, 2015.

34. Osborn, L.E., Iskarous, M.M., Thakor, N.V. *et al.*, Chapter 22 – Sensing and control for prosthetic hands in clinical and research applications, in: *Wearable Robotics*, J. Rosen and P.W. Ferguson (Eds.), pp. 445–468, Elsevier, London, United Kingdom, 2020.

35. Su, Y., Fisher, M.H., Wolczowski, A. *et al.*, Towards an EMG-controlled prosthetic hand using a 3-D electromagnetic positioning system. *IEEE Trans. Instrum. Meas.*, 56, 178–186, 2017.

36. Belter, J.T., Segil, J.L., Dollar, A.M. *et al.*, Mechanical design and performance specifications of anthropomorphic prosthetic hands: A review. *J. Rehabil. Res. Dev.*, 50, 5, 599–618, 2013.

37. Kyberd, P.J. and Chappell, P.H., The Southampton hand: An intelligent myoelectric prosthesis. *J. Rehabil. Res. Dev.*, 31, 4, 326–334, 1994.

38. Liu, H., Xu, K., Siciliano, B. *et al.*, The MERO hand: A mechanically robust anthropomorphic prosthetic hand using novel compliant rolling contact joint. *IEEE/ASME International Conference on Advanced Intelligent Mechatronics (AIM)*, Hong Kong, China, pp. 126–132, 2019.

39. Ting, Z., Wang, X.Q., Jiang, L. *et al.*, Biomechatronic design and control of an anthropomorphic artificial hand for prosthetic applications. *Robotica*, 34, 10, 2291–2308, 2015.

40. Manfredo, A., Matteo, C., Henning, M. *et al.*, Deep learning with convolutional neural networks applied to electromyography data: A resource for the classification of movements for prosthetic hands. *Front. Neurorob.*, 10, 9, 2016.

41. Wang, N., Lao, K., Zhang, X., Design and myoelectric control of an anthropomorphic prosthetic hand. *J. Bionic Eng.*, 14, 1, 47–59, 2017.

42. Brunner, I., Skouen, J.S., Hofstad, H., Virtual reality training for upper extremity in subacute stroke (VIRTUES): A multicentre RCT. *Neurology*, 89, 24, 2413–2421, 2017.

43. Perry, B.N., Armiger, R.S., Yu, K.E. *et al.*, Virtual integration environment as an advanced prosthetic limb training platform. *Front. Neurol.*, 9, 785, 2018.

44. Bright, D., Nair, A., Salvekar, D. *et al.*, EEG-based brain controlled prosthetic arm. *Conference on Advances in Signal Processing (CASP)*, Pune, pp. 479–483, 2016.

45. Andrecioli, R. and Engeberg, E., Adaptive sliding manifold slope via grasped object stiffness detection with a prosthetic hand. *Mechatronics*, 23, 8, 1171–1179, 2013.

46. Wang, Y., Liu, H., Leng, D. *et al.*, New advances in EMG control methods of anthropomorphic prosthetic hand. *Sci. China Technol. Sci.*, 60, 12, 1978–1979, 2017.

47. Reaz, M., Hussain, M., Mohd-Yasin, F., Techniques of EMG signal analysis: Detection, processing, classification and application. *Biol. Proced*, 8, 11–35, 2006.

48. Jiang, N., Dosen, S., Muller, K. *et al.*, Myoelectric control of artificial limbs— Is there a need to change focus? [In the Spotlight]. *IEEE Signal Process. Mag.*, 29, 152, 2012.

49. Krasoulis, A., Kyranou, I., Erden, M.S. *et al.*, Improved prosthetic hand control with concurrent use of myoelectric and inertial measurements. *J. Neuroeng. Rehabil.*, 14, 71, 2017.

50. Olivieri, E., Barresi, G., Leonardo, S.M., BCI-based user training in surgical robotics. *Conference Proceedings: 37th Annual International Conference of the IEEE Engineering in Medicine and Biology Society*, Milano, Italy, pp. 4918–4921, 2015.

51. Hart, S.G. and Staveland, L.E., *Development of nasa-tlx (task load index): Results of empirical and theoretical research, human mental workload*, P.A. Hancock and N. Meshkati (Eds.), vol. 52, pp. 139–183, North-Holland, Amsterdam, 1988.

52. Gallagher, A.G., Satava, R.M., Osullivan, G.C., Attentional capacity: An essential aspect of surgeon performance. *Ann. Surg.*, 261, 3, e60–e61, 2015.

53. Zander, T., Shetty, K., Lorenz, R. *et al.*, Automated task load detection with electroencephalography: Towards passive brain–computer interfacing in robotic surgery. *J. Med. Robot. Res.*, 02, 01, 1750003, 2017.

54. Farina, D., Jiang, N., Rehbaum, H. *et al.*, The extraction of neural information from the surface EMG for the control of upper-limb prostheses: Emerging avenues and challenges. *IEEE Trans. Neural Syst. Rehabil. Eng.*, 22, 797–809, 2014.

55. Merletti, R. and Farina, D., *Surface electromyography: Physiology, engineering, and applications*, Wiley, Hoboken (NJ), 2016.

56. Farina, D. and Negro, F., Accessing the neural drive to muscle and translation to neurorehabilitation technologies. *IEEE Rev. Biomed. Eng.*, 5, 3–14, 2012.

57. Crescentini, C., Fabbro, F., Tomasino, B., Editorial special topic: Enhancing brain and cognition through meditation. *J. Cogn. Enhanc.*, 1, 2, 81–83, 2017.

58. Wilms, W., Wozniak-Karczewska, M., Corvini, P.F.-X. *et al.*, Nootropic drugs: Methylphenidate, modafinil and piracetam – Population use trends, occurrence in the environment, ecotoxicity and removal methods – A review. *Chemosphere*, 233, 771–785, 2019.

59. Morton, W.A. and Stockton, G.G., Methylphenidate abuse and psychiatric side effects. *Prim. Care Companion J. Clin. Psychiatry*, 2, 5, 159–164, 2000.

60. Kim, D., Practical use and risk of modafinil, a novel waking drug. *Environ. Health Toxicol.*, 27, e2012007, 2012.

61. Malykh, A.G. and Sadaie, M.R., Piracetam and piracetam-like drugs. *Drugs*, 70, 287–312, 2010.

62. Colucci, L., Bosco, M., Rosario Ziello, A. *et al.*, Effectiveness of nootropic drugs with cholinergic activity in treatment of cognitive deficit: A review. *J. Exp. Pharmacol.*, 4, 163–172, 2012.

63. Dan-Dan, L., Ya-Hon, Z., Wei, Z. *et al.*, Meta-analysis of randomized controlled trials on the efficacy and safety of donepezil, galantamine, rivastigmine, and memantine for the treatment of Alzheimer's disease. *Front. Neurosci.*, 13, 472, 2019.

64. Santoro, A., Siviero, P., Minicuci, N. *et al.*, Effects of donepezil, galantamine and rivastigmine in 938 Italian patients with Alzheimer's disease: A prospective, observational study. *CNS Drugs*, 24, 2, 163–176, 2010.

65. Yesavage, J.A., Mumenthaler, M.S., Taylor, J.L. *et al.*, Donepezil and flight simulator performance: Effects on retention of complex skills. *Neurology*, 59, 1, 123–123, 2002.

66. Caldwell, J.A., Caldwell, J.L., Smyth, N.K. *et al.*, A double-blind, placebo-controlled investigation of the efficacy of modafinil for sustaining the alertness and performance of aviators: A helicopter simulator study. *Psychopharmacology*, 150, 272–282, 2000.

67. Meng, J., Mundahl, J.H., Streitz, T.D. *et al.*, Effects of soft drinks on resting state EEG and brain–computer interface performance. *IEEE Access*, 5, 18756–18764, 2017.

68. Teter, C.J., McCabe, S.E., Lagrange, K. *et al.*, Illicit use of specific prescription stimulants among college students: Prevalence, motives, and routes of administration. *Pharmacotherapy*, 26, 1501–1510, 2006.

69. Sattler, S., Forlini, C., Racine, E. *et al.*, Impact of contextual factors and substance characteristics on perspectives toward cognitive enhancement. *PLoS One*, 8, 8, e71452, 2013.

70. Vassanelli, S., Brain-chip interfaces: The present and the future. *Proc. Comput. Sci.*, 7, 61–64, 2011.

71. Indiveri, G., Barranco, B.L., Legenstein, R. *et al.*, Integration of nanoscale memristor synapses in neuromorphic computing architectures. *Nanotechnology*, 24, 38, 1–13, 2013.

72. V. John and D.S. Kondziolka, Device for multicentric brain modulation, repair and interface. U.S. Patent No. 2008/0154331 A1, June 26, 2008.

73. Vassanelli, S., Mahmud, M., Girardi, S. *et al.*, On the way to large-scale and high-resolution brain-chip interfacing. *Cognit. Comput.*, 4, 1, 71–81, 2012.

74. Gong, S., Schwalb, W., Wang, Y., Chen, Y., Tang, Y., Si, J., Shirinzadeh, B., Cheng, W.A., wearable and highly sensitive pressure sensor with ultrathin gold nanowires. *Nat. Commun.*, 5, 1, 1–8, 2014.

75. Lou, Z., Wang, L., Shen, G., Recent advances in smart wearable sensing systems. *Adv. Mater. Technol.*, 3, 1800444, 2018.

76. Kim, D.H., Lu, N., Huang, Y., Rogers, J.A., Materials for stretchable electronics in bioinspired and bio integrated devices. *MRS Bull.*, 37, 3, 226–35, 2012.

77. Arumugam, V., Naresh, M.D., Sanjeevi, R., Effect of strain rate on the fracture behaviour of skin. *J. Biosci.*, 19, 307, 1994.

78. Lee, Y.H., Kweon, O.Y., Kim, H., Yoo, J.H., Han, S.G., Oh, J.H., Recent advances in organic sensors for health self-monitoring systems. *J. Mater. Chem. C*, 6, 8569, 2018.

79. Ma, Z., Li, S., Wang, H., Cheng, W., Li, Y., Pan, L., Shi, Y., Advanced electronic skin devices for healthcare applications. *J. Mater. Chem. B*, 7, 173, 2019.

80. Wang, J., Lin, M.F., Park, S., Lee, P.S., Deformable conductors for human-machine interface. *Mater. Today*, 21, 508–526, 2018.

81. Wang, C., Wang, C., Huang, Z., Xu, S., Materials and structures toward soft electronics. *Adv. Mater.*, 30, 1801368, 2018.

82. Martin, A.B., Hartman, M., Washington, B., Catlin, A., National Health Expenditure Accounts Team, National health spending: Faster growth in 2015 as coverage expands and utilization increases. *Health Aff.*, 36, 1, 166–76, 2017.

83. Feng, S., Caire, R., Cortazar, B., Turan, M., Wong, A., Ozcan, A., Immunochromatographic diagnostic test analysis using Google Glass. *ACS Nano*, 8, 3, 3069–79, 2014.

84. Wile, D.J., Ranawaya, R., Kiss, Z.H., Smart watch accelerometery for analysis and diagnosis of tremor. *J. Neurosci. Methods*, 230, 1–4, 2014.

85. Tian, L., Zimmerman, B., Akhtar, A., Yu, K.J., Moore, M., Wu, J. *et al.*, Large-area MRI-compatible epidermal electronic interfaces for prosthetic control and cognitive monitoring. *Nat. Biomed. Eng.*, 3, 194, 2019.

86. Jung, S., Kim, J.H., Kim, J., Choi, S., Lee, J. *et al.*, Reverse-micelle-induced porous pressure-sensitive rubber for wearable human-machine interfaces. *Adv. Mater.*, 26, 4825, 2014.

87. Tao, J., Bao, R., Wang, X., Peng, Y., Li, J. *et al.*, Self-powered tactile sensor array systems based on the triboelectric effect. *Adv. Funct. Mater.*, 29, 1806379, 2019.

88. Shi, Q. and Lee, C., Self-powered bio-inspired spider-net-coding interface using single-electrode triboelectric nanogenerator. *Adv. Sci.*, 6, 1900617, 2019.

89. Ameri, S.K., Kim, M., Kuang, I.A., Perera, W.K., Alshiekh, M., Jeong, H., Topcu, U., Akinwande, D., Lu, N., Imperceptible electrooculography graphene sensor system for human–robot interface. *NPJ 2D Mater. Appl.*, 2, 1, 1–7, 2018.

90. Mishra, S., Norton, J.J.S., Lee, Y., Lee, D.S., Agee, N., Chen, Y. *et al.*, Soft, wireless periocular wearable electronics for real-time detection of eye vergence in a virtual reality toward mobile eye therapies. *Biosens. Bioelectron.*, 91, 796, 2017.

91. Jeong, J.W., Yeo, W.H., Akhtar, A., Norton, J.J.S., Kwack, Y.J. *et al.*, Materials and optimized designs for human-machine interfaces via epidermal electronics. *Adv. Mater.*, 25, 6839, 2013.

92. Simao, M., Mendes, N., Gibaru, O. *et al.*, A review on electromyography decoding and pattern recognition for human-machine interaction. *IEEE Access*, 7, 39564–39582, 2019.

93. Liu, J. and Zhou, P., A novel myoelectric pattern recognition strategy for hand function restoration after incomplete cervical spinal cord injury. *IEEE Trans. Neural Syst. Rehabil. Eng.*, 21, 96–103, 2013.
94. Yulianto, E. and Indrato, T.B., The design of electrical wheelchairs with electromyography signal controller for people with paralysis. *Electr. Electron. Eng.*, 8, 1–9, 2018.
95. Xia, W., Zhou, Y., Yang, X. *et al.*, Toward portable hybrid surface electromyography/a-mode ultrasound sensing for human-machine interface. *IEEE Sens. J.*, 19, 5219–5228, 2019.
96. Yin, R., Wang, D., Zhao, S., Lou, Z., Shen, G., Wearable sensors-enabled human–machine interaction systems: From design to application. *Adv. Funct. Mater.*, 31, 2008936, 2021.

# 7

# The Role of a Human-Machine Interaction (HMI) System on the Medical Devices

Zahra Alidousti Shahraki[1*] and Mohsen Aghabozorgi Nafchi[2]

[1]Department of Computer Engineering, University of Isfahan, Isfahan, Iran
[2]Department of Computer Science and Engineering, Shiraz University, Shiraz, Iran

## Abstract

Today, with the expansion of the population, an increase in various diseases can be seen this phenomenon grows the risk of contracting unknown diseases in the world. Therefore, in recent years, more attention has been paid to the development of new methods for the diagnosis and treatment of patients, which can be referred to efforts made to develop new medicines and diagnostic tools. With using these tools and new technologies, such as artificial intelligence, patients' data with great accuracy are collected and analyzed; a huge transformation in the field of treatment is tacked place. The design of intelligent medical devices has a high impact on the faster recognition and treatment of patients. On the other hand, making a relationship between patients and medical devices can have a positive effect on the treatment of patients. Patients who can feel relaxed and comfortable during the treatment will put more effort into their own treatment. A smart medical device, which has a friendly user interface with the patient, has a positive role in the treatment of patients. Patient experience is a part of user experience that describes the interaction between patients and medical devices. In the concept of patient experiences, the experience of illness and also the way of healthcare are examined. So, the role of human-machine interaction (HMI) systems should not be ignored in the field of treatment. In the field of treatment, HMI refers to facilitating communication between humans and machines. So, the goal of the designing system based on HMI is important to encourage patients to seek treatment and give them hope for life during their treatment period according to their age conditions. For example, the patient's age is an important criterion that should be considered in the design of a human–computer interaction system. Also, the gender of patients plays a role in communicating between patients and medical devices. On other hand, the role

*Corresponding author: zahra_alidousti@yahoo.com

Rishabha Malviya, Sonali Sundram, Bhupendra Prajapati and Sudarshan Kumar Singh (eds.)
Human-Machine Interface: Making Healthcare Digital, (183–210) © 2024 Scrivener Publishing LLC

of artificial intelligence in designing human–computer interaction systems cannot be ignored. This type of system can prevent disease by checking the patient's condition, predicting the patient's condition during the treatment period based on the patient's personality, and also can decide using decision-making systems. Also, recommender systems can use intelligent medical devices to treat patients according to the predictions made. Accurate diagnosis of medical devices according to the physical and mental conditions of the patient is an important point that affects HMI systems. Actually, an HMI system should be able to identify patients' mental states by using powerful sensors and facial image processing in order to be a user-friendly interface for the medical system. In this chapter, various factors and their solutions that can play a role in the design of an HMI system are examined.

*Keywords*: Human-machine interaction (HMI), machine learning, intelligent hospital, patient experience, cognitive science, emotional intelligence, blockchain, virtual reality

## 7.1   Introduction

The development of technology and the increasing of communication channels leads to make a relationship between people who were able to communicate with each other in different parts of the world using social media applications on different platforms. Making conversations through computers was a big experience in the modern age. Maybe one day nobody thought that technology would progress so much that computers could have conversations with humans, understand each other's messages and respond. This process is called human–computer interaction, which was known in 1975 by Carlisle [1]. The interaction between computers and humans has a significant impact on different parts of human life. Designing intelligent systems that can understand the physical condition of humans can help humans in situations of need. One of the tasks that can solve an important part of human needs in the interaction between humans and machines is medicine.

A correct understanding of human behavior using HCI systems can help for controlling their diseases. In other words, people can be exposed to physical and mental injuries due to geographical conditions, lifestyle, gender, medical records, and other factors. Managing people's physical and mental health is an important issue that HCI systems should be able to do with high quality. If a person suffers from physical or mental damage due to some factors, the HCI system will intelligently prevent further damage to the person by warning and prescribing medicine.

Also, designing a user interface in operating rooms can help doctors in performing the patient's operation accurately. Performing medical operations with high precision, accurately identifying the devices required for the patient during surgery, and accurately identifying the drugs needed by the patient with a correct understanding of the patient's physical and mental conditions, etc. using intelligent systems can help the doctor to treat the patient in less time. So, it can be a turning point in designing an intelligent human–computer interaction system for diagnosis the of medical equipment.

There are various challenges in designing human–computer interaction systems in this field. Studying and examining existing challenges help to design an intelligent system with high accuracy and less error in diagnosis. In this chapter, we examine the role of HCI systems in the interaction between computers and humans. In each section, new solutions are provided by examining the various effects of this system on humans. The challenge in this chapter is the introduction of high-quality human–computer interaction systems in the design of medical equipment. These systems help to improve human health in the field of treatment and improve the quality of human life.

## 7.2    Machine Learning for HCI Systems

Recognizing the movements and gestures of people, especially patients, using machine learning algorithms is an important issue that must be addressed. Accurate recognition of people's location and time and their gesture movement using machine learning is investigated [2]. If this algorithm is implemented on the data related to patients, it can have positive results. By understanding the patient's movement and the path and type of movement, medical devices can diagnose the deterioration of the disease and warn if necessary. Also, by using speech recognition algorithms and voice signal processing, they can predict and recognize the patient's condition from its sound. Always comparing healthy people and sick people based on their sound can be characteristic. People who are sick say words in a sad and uncomfortable manner or have a low tone of voice when they speak, while healthy people usually say words more cheerfully. Diagnosing patients' voices using signal processing algorithms can help an HCI system to establish better communication with patients. If the HCI system detects the patient's condition by establishing a friendly relationship and feeling sympathy with the patient, it can help in raising the morale of the patient.

This position can be effective in special conditions such as operating rooms and increase life expectancy and morale in patients.

An HCI system can make many changes in treatment systems and medical equipment that worked traditionally [3]. Establishing communication between doctor and patient, communication between pharmacist and patient at the time of drug delivery, and any communication in medical centers using HCI systems can have advantages. For example, a doctor or a pharmacist is uncomfortable or ill-tempered due to their daily problems and directly or indirectly transmits this behavior to the patient. This feeling has a negative effect on the patient who needs to create a positive mood. Modern ways of communicating using the HCI system prevent the transmission of negative emotions. These systems diagnose the patient's needs with data that has been trained in advance and create an energetic and positive situation for the patient. Of course, we cannot deny the positive effects of face-to-face communication between doctor and patient, but today, with the expansion of communication methods, the disadvantages of traditional methods can be covered with the advantages of new methods.

When the benefits of the HCI system's role in the relationship between people in therapeutic issues are deeply examined, a concept of psychology and psychotherapy is discovered in these HCI systems. When these systems are designed based on deep learning, they can measure the patient's states, the health conditions, and provide behavior based on the patient's existing conditions. So that the patient is associated with conditions such as stress, fear, negative feelings. An intelligent HCI system shows a positive relationship according to the patient's condition.

In Figure 7.1, an intelligent hospital is shown; all of its medical equipment using a human–computer interaction system creates a connection between the medical equipment online. It is also shown that patients can be treated using virtual communication. The design of this hospital can help to reduce treatment costs, save time for patients, and treatment staff.

HCI system in the hospital bed can help the patient to be comfortable during the treatment period [4]. The design of a user interface helps the patient to change the position on the hospital bed easily without the help of the nurse. This system can be set up in different departments of the hospital to create welfare for patients. Patients' need for an HCI system with a user interface in using the hospital toilet, bathrooms, elevator, tank of MRI machines, etc. plays an effective role. Nowadays, medical equipment can create a great revolution in the medical engineering industry with an HCI system based on machine learning. Also, for the safety of modern medical equipment using HCI systems, cryptographic algorithms can be used in the design of systems. Encryption algorithms play an effective role

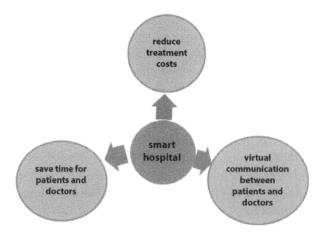

**Figure 7.1** Benefits of making an intelligent hospital.

in preventing medical device hacking and harm to patients. In the future sections, various cryptographic algorithms and the impact of blockchain in the protection of HCI systems in the design of medical devices will be discussed.

## 7.3    Patient Experience

Patient experience is a concept of positive and negative experiences that a patient has had during the course of treatment. Paying attention to the patient's experience in matters related to health and patient care causes more care to be taken in the care of patients in medical centers and hospitals. Patients with positive feedback about their treatment experience create more encouragement to use treatment services in the treatment center. Also, recording negative feedback by a patient for a treatment center creates a negative score in the service provided by the treatment center. As the concept of user experience is used in the use of applications and software sites, the patient experience is used in the use of programs related to providing services to patients. The combination of user experience and patient experience can help to design a treatment application to serve patients from the time of admission, duration of treatment, preparation of medicine, and discharge of the patient.

One of the issues that patients face during the treatment period in the hospital is the feeling of safety in the hospital. This feeling increases their quality of life during the treatment period and after. Also, according to the survey conducted [5], the feeling of security after discharge from the hospital is one of the things that patients, especially the elderly, need. According to the World Health Organization (WHO), providing health services to people should include the efficiency for people, to be effective and integrated, patient-centered in medical devices, and also be equitable. Designing medical systems that can establish communication between patients and the treatment center after discharge creates a pleasant feeling and increases the feeling of freshness in patients. The elderly are more exposed to illness and injury due to the history of numerous insurances they have, so it is more practical to take care of them through online medical systems. According to the history of various diseases, these systems can control the conditions of patients in real-time, and report the symptoms to the health center in case of danger. Examining the mental states of the patient during the treatment in the hospital and after discharge shows the effectiveness of the human–computer systems for the patients.

The results of a survey among elderly patients (older than 65 years), who were admitted to the hospital, show that high-quality special care for the elderly creates a long-term relationship between the patient and the special care center [6]. Establishing this relationship creates motivation for patients during the treatment period. It also makes the patients for performing the necessary care well, follow the medical orders for treatment, taking the medicine more carefully during the treatment period. Taking care of patients after discharge is one of the most important points in completing their treatment [7]. Human–computer interaction systems can play this role well for patients. Taking care of patients (especially the disabled, the elderly, and those who need special treatment) using online medical equipment can complete their treatment more accurately. Creating a feeling of vitality and life expectancy in patients is more effective than taking medicine.

Therefore, the patient communication system for medical equipment can play a good role in treatment. This system reminds the patient to take medicine by warning the patient. Also, according to the patient's condition, the HCI system announces the instructions needed to perform daily activities for physical and mental treatment (such as exercising, daily care, etc.).

Designing a communication system with patients can have a positive effect on their treatment process after being discharged from the hospital. In Mahmud et al. [8], it is examined the popularity of messaging systems. Each messenger has certain popularity in each specific geographical situation. WhatsApp is one of the popular messengers that are more user-friendly than Telegram and other messengers [8]. It seems that the reason for the popularity of WhatsApp compared to other mobile messaging applications is the ease of communication with the audience. Users in WhatsApp groups can easily access each other and make face-to-face group call. This application is more convenient for elderly people who have difficulty communicating with programs and digital devices. A patient communication system should be more convenient for users, especially the elderly. Creating a face-to-face relationship with patients, through online chat or profile pictures, can convey people's feelings well. Also, communicating with patients through voice chats can create a feeling of sympathy and hope for life during the treatment period for patients. Through the HCI system, which is connected to medical devices, patients can transfer their treatment conditions to the treatment staff if needed. This connection allows patients to be under care around the clock. This round-the-clock care creates a sense of security in them and the result of their treatment will be positive.

The rehabilitation training control system helps people who go through the recovery period to regain their ability by performing finger sports exercises [9]. This system, which is based on human–computer interaction, can communicate with users using voice recognition. The elderly who pass their discharge period and need to use the rehabilitation system can establish a good relationship with this system. The design of this system can be used for fingerprint recognition as well as face recognition. Recognizing the face of the elderly when they need help is sad and depressing. This system can meet the needs of the elderly by recognizing facial expressions.

The age of the users and their gender is one of things that the user interface specialist should consider in the design of human-based systems. This system has a different design according to its conditions. A human–computer interaction system for patients should be designed in such a way that it takes into account the mental and physical conditions of the patients according to their geographical conditions, age, gender, and interest in using communication systems with the doctor. The level of literacy and awareness of the people compared to the use of human-based software plays an important role in improving their quality. Also, physically and mentally disabled people should be able to use systems that meet their needs in using medical services. Due to their physical and mental conditions, these people do not have the ability to learn to use medical tools. Therefore, a user-friendly system can provide more convenient services for these people.

A user-friendly system should be able to use options that are attractive to the patient at the time of patient registration. According to his condition, the patient should be able to communicate well with the human-based medical equipment and develop a feeling of sympathy for the patient. According to cognitive science, these systems can learn about the patient's decisions at different times and help the patient. This communication can play a significant role in energizing the patient and raising the patient's morale.

## 7.4  Cognitive Science

Human cognition is a subset of cognitive science concepts that deal with the correct understanding of human thoughts. Human cognition using intelligent methods helps to design human-based systems. So it is possible to interact better with humans [10]. Humans have a lot of mental complexity and can have different thoughts at different times according to certain circumstances that arise. If a human-based intelligent system can access the level of people's thoughts by using the concepts of cognitive science and decision-making, a big step can be taken in knowing humans intelligently. The design of human interaction systems based on cognitive science can understand human needs in any situation. They can help humans in making decisions. Designing medical systems based on cognitive science helps patients in different situations when they need to take medicine or have physical and mental problems. These systems understand the changes in the patients' mental states according to their thinking and which medicine the patient needs using the methods of cognitive science. Therefore, they can help patients in critical situations as smart robots.

Artificial intelligence can play an effective role in designing human interaction systems [11]. Machine learning algorithms can play a prominent role in system design. Predicting the patient's condition by artificial intelligence algorithms helps the medical diagnosis system to predict the patient's condition according to the patient's position. In case of illness, necessary warnings are given through alarms. Disease records, age conditions, and geographic location that cause certain diseases in people can be given as primary information to the medical diagnosis system. Then the system predicts the physical and mental state of the patient using deep learning algorithms. This forecast makes the medical equipment needed for the patient be prepared faster by the treatment staff. And the equipment, used for the treatment of the patient, is under control. Real-time algorithms in predicting the patient's condition can reduce the delay time in the patient's treatment. Informing the treatment staff in the shortest possible time increases hope and motivation and increases the patient's life expectancy.

Using the experience of users in the use of medical devices can help to determine the level of need for devices, and then services are provided in medical centers based on the need for medical devices. Each patient can declare his needs according to his need for medical supplies [12]. Then, based on the age, gender, and the needs chosen by each patient, it is concluded that there are different needs in each center based on the conditions of the patients. Designing this HMI system based on the needs of each patient can help medical centers to provide better services. Artificial intelligence patterns and clustering based on the needs of each patient help to design a human-machine system to meet the needs of patients.

Maintaining the security of patient information in human–computer systems is also very important and increases patients' trust in intelligent service delivery [13]. If patients feel that the information related to their mental and physical conditions is not safe, they do not use smart systems, and smart medical devices that can record their information. Refusing to use smart tools causes errors in clustering algorithms. Therefore, it causes the quality of medical systems in providing services to decrease.

The cognitive Internet of Things can cause a big transformation in human-based systems for medical equipment [14]. The use of the Internet of Things in medical equipment makes patients for using the tools intelligently whenever they need them. The movement of the eyes of the patients, the movement of their hands, and the recognition of the patients' voices when needed make the medical devices turn on and meet the needs of the patients. Making decisions about the needs of patients and analyzing their opinions using cognitive science makes a system based on cognitive science based on human–computer interaction to be designed to make important decisions for them together with humans. These decisions make humans feel sympathy and intimacy with human-based robot-like intelligent tools. Along with all the benefits that these systems have in providing services, they can help for improving their physical and mental conditions by establishing a friendly relationship with patients. In fact, these systems in the role of a helping robot can strengthen the feeling of sympathy in patients.

According to the studies, it can be concluded that the implementation of cognitive science concepts can play a significant role in increasing the quality of systems designed based on human–computer interaction for medical services. These concepts make it possible to design a system that can help patients to improve their illness and treatment by understanding the conditions of patients at the time of illness and discharge, as well as by analyzing their behaviors.

## 7.5 HCI System Based on Image Processing

Today, the use of image processing patterns can identify the purpose of each users by looking them to the things. Designing a human-based system that can record the movement of each user's eyes using a camera can be a good choice for medical systems. Patients can use the human-based system without physical movement by eye movement and looking. In Tan *et al.* [15], an algorithm has been introduced to detect image processing for human-based systems. This method is a suitable option for disabled people who do not have the strength to move their hands to use computer programs without changing the mouse by looking at the desktop screen. This method can be useful for patients to use medical equipment. Patients with different age groups and different abilities (physically disabled, mentally disabled, etc.) can use this system in using medical services. Also, by looking at the monitor screen and moving their eyes, they can understand what they mean by needing medicine or needing help.

Face analysis can help in providing services to patients. Analyzing their eye and lip movements makes it possible to identify patients' need for help. Human-based systems use facial analysis patterns to accurately diagnose patients' behaviors [16]. Recognizing their behavior can lead to the recognition of their decisions in their minds. Designing a camera that analyzes patients' images in real-time and recognizes their needs can play an effective role in creating a proper relationship with patients. Studies can be done in this field that patients when their lips are down or up indicate happiness or sadness, or when they raise their eyebrows, it indicates that they need help when the distance between their eyebrows is reduced and confused. They are suffering from pain and discomfort and need help. The analysis of these cases makes a human-based system detect human behavior and decisions using image processing patterns. Such systems create a strong user relationship and play an effective role in providing services to patients in hospitals and medical centers.

In the study by Biele [17], the various models of human movement in a machine-based system have been investigated. Eye movement, face movement, hand movement, whole body movement, and movement of body parts in different positions can indicate symptoms of users. The detection and analysis of human movements in the machine-based system designed for the design of medical equipment can increase the quality of the systems. The processing of human movement images in machine-based systems in the medical system is a supporter of patients during the treatment period or vacation time, which makes it possible to recognize their need for help by analyzing human movement in different situations. To increase the accuracy in the design of based systems on humans, based on image processing, clustering algorithms can be used to analyze patients based on age, gender, medical records, and their need for help. The clustering methods in the designed system can lead to the design of an intelligent system that can detect the age of the patients based on the face and detect the youthfulness of the face, and provide medical services to the patients based on their age and gender.

According to the review of ideas in the design of human-based systems based on image processing, it can be concluded that the design of a human-based system using a camera to detect the need of patients for medical services can record the movements of the patient's body by analyzing the images which are recorded to recognize the gender and age of the patients. Also, recognizing the facial expression of the patients at different times can indicate that the patients need services. Such a system can establish a user interface between patients, nurses, and doctors. Creating a user interface will increase the quality of treatment, and then increase their life expectancy.

### 7.5.1    Patient's Facial Expression

Recognition of facial expressions is one of the most important parts of identifying expressions in patients, which should be investigated. Emotional states, shame, embarrassment, sadness, happiness, etc. are identified on the face. A face image processing system can check different states of the patient in different conditions. Based on the recognition of the patient's facial expression, the need for help is done more accurately. Of course, facial expression recognition in a human-based system may encounter errors. Because some patients declare the need for help by changing different positions in their body according to their age and disease conditions. Therefore, a strong intelligent system should be able to process all the patient's organs in general and by examining different states in the movement of the organs and the face, have a correct understanding of the pain intensity in patients. Since all the pain states of the patients and their need for help are determined by the facial nerves, it is more important to check the facial expressions of the patients. Examining different facial recognition patterns can create a human-based system with high accuracy. A sense of security helps patients to more accurately express their emotions when their faces are recognized using a machine-based system. Therefore, the intelligent system can provide more accurate services in diagnosing the condition of patients, and the quality of treatment of patients' increases.

## 7.5.2   Gender and Age

Based on the studies and our own experience throughout life, human decision-making and thinking power can be changed according to age. Young age is the best time to learn. Of course, this does not mean that older people do not have the power to learn. Maybe there were people who used their ability and their thinking by doing a new job in their middle age. The meaning of learning at a young age is that people at a younger age have fewer worries and preoccupations and can do something with more concentration. Aging causes other problems such as Alzheimer's, cardiovascular problems, etc. That is why most of the patients in the hospital wards are middle-aged people. On the other hand, middle-aged people use fewer smart tools than young people and due to diseases such as Alzheimer's their learning rate is less. Therefore, in the design of human-based systems, the age of the patients should be taken into account. Factors such as the age and gender of patients play an important role in designing a user-friendly system. In Hall et al. [18], cognitive aging is discussed as an important factor in human performance. Determining the age of people using facial image processing, the level of learning of people in using the system, etc. can help to design a system based on intelligent humans for communication between patients and doctors. Human-based system for medical diagnosis should be used intelligently based on people's age and learning level. If the age of users is detected, the access level will be different and users can easily use smart tools.

Also, age can play an effective role in people's cognitive performance [19]. As people age, the risk of diabetes increases. On the other hand, diabetes causes various changes in the level of hormones in the body and thus causes problems such as learning disorders and dementia. For this reason, to design a human-based system in medical diagnosis, people's diseases should be recorded as a factor. After registering various factors, the intelligent system should be able to create a user-friendly access level suitable for each patient. This system has different levels of access based on people's cognitive performance. The spread of different diseases in any country can cause other different disorders. Therefore, the intelligent diagnosis system works intelligently according to different times and conditions and helps patients to use medical devices and necessary services by detecting the age of people.

In Huq et al. [20], the main challenges in using smart systems for the elderly have been studied and investigated. Communication systems are different for people in different age groups. The learning rate of people using smart systems is different based on their age. Therefore, old people should use different chat applications compared to young people. In this article, the challenges in the design of conversational systems are presented, which can be used for the design of computer-based systems in medical diagnosis. Patients in special situations who need to consult a doctor can use this conversation system. This system can work with a user-friendly design for disabled people. Due to their movement and mental disorders, the elderly can communicate with doctors through voice and video. An intelligent system that can activate access tools by detecting the type of disorders in people and according to their age conditions can be a very good option in medical systems.

The Internet of things on medical systems can make machine-based medical devices intelligent [21]. The combination of Internet of Things technology and patients' conditions makes it easier to diagnose their diseases. Therefore, the length of each patient's treatment period is reduced. Patients can easily use medical services using medical systems consisting of the Internet of Things. Every patient according to their age, gender and conditions can use the Internet of Things applications and send signals to the device whenever they need by eye movement or voice recording. The processing of medical signals makes the devices recognize the needs of the patients and provide more quality services.

The machine-based system, which operates based on tongue and eye movements, has a positive effect in diagnosing the needs of people with disorders [22]. This system can help disabled patients or elderly people by analyzing facial muscles, tongue, and eye movements. Patients in different age groups may have physical injuries and movement disorders. Therefore, this machine-based system can help people of different age groups according to their movement disorder by examining the type of movement of eyes, hands, tongue, and other main body organs.

The issue of gender is one of the important issues that are discussed and challenged in various topics. Looking at people based on gender causes discrimination in service delivery. This discrimination causes discomfort and discomfort that must be carefully investigated. Providing services to people in the field of health and health is also one of the issues that should be far from a gender perspective [23]. So far, according to the reports obtained from the World Health Organization, services have been provided to people in medical centers and hospitals for all people of any gender. But the issue that seems to be considered is the difference in providing services to people of different genders due to their different mentalities. Men and women have equal rights in terms of the ability to think and make decisions in life, but having a different spirits and physical strengths in them makes them make different decisions [24].

Investigating this issue and the existing challenge in the difference between men and women will lead to the implementation of an intelligent system based on the different abilities and attitudes of people. Because women are more emotional than men, their learning level is different when they are sick. Hormonal changes in men and women cause changes in their mood and decision-making. Therefore, the design of intelligent systems suitable to people's moods can help the user-friendliness of systems according to people's moods in different time frames. An intelligent medical system by recognizing people's gender using image processing can change according to people's moods. For example, a computer-based medical system for women can choose a different color and model online, or use words with more emotional lexical meaning. This issue strengthens the morale of patients when using smart medical devices and reduces the length of the treatment period. Increasing life expectancy is another benefit of increasing the morale of patients of different genders during their treatment and discharge period.

The difference between gender and sex is also influential in the design of medical systems for people. According to the study, accurate diagnosis of people in terms of sex or gender causes the use of medical systems to change for people based on their different moods. Human-based medical systems can provide different medical services by examining the mental and physiological conditions of patients. As mentioned in the previous explanations, medical services based on the conditions of each patient create a friendly relationship between the patient and smart medical services. This communication can create a sense of sympathy for patients and strengthen the patient's mental condition. As a result, the patient recovers in a shorter period of time.

Gender bias in medical diagnosis may cause doctors not to treat patients because of their gender. It is important that patients are treated equally in the hospital. Skin color, race, gender, etc. are issues that should not be the criteria for treating patients in the field of medicine [25]. So far, during the survey conducted in the following article, women have more pain tolerance due to their different gender. This has caused doctors to pay more attention to men during treatment. This should not cause discrimination in treatment. Of course, as mentioned, this gender difference does not mean that women are weaker than men, but the difference in physiological structure has caused women to have different physical and mental changes than men and tolerate pain more during illness. An intelligent human-based medical system should be able to completely eliminate this discrimination and help the patient by diagnosing the type of disease and the gender of the person according to the physical and mental conditions of each patient.

This intelligent system should be able to provide the ability to communicate with patients. In this case, it can be useful for patients.

Figure 7.2 shows that an HCI system must be able to recognize the gender, age, and people's ability level, and then use medical equipment for treatment according to the results obtained.

Actually, the design of HCI systems without prejudice can help in fair treatment. Unfortunately, gender discrimination can endangers the physical and mental health of people. The issue that should be culturalized is the same view of people with race, skin color, gender, etc.

The interesting thing mentioned in Ghassemi and Nsoesie [27] is that the existence of discrimination in healthcare has a long history, which should be done by raising awareness about this issue to eliminate this disgusting act. When these biases are caused by people's thinking, it makes intelligent algorithms such as machine learning techniques use this bias. Analyzing the data using a pattern that is caused by gender and racial discrimination causes the application space of the algorithm to become discriminatory automatically. Therefore, it cannot be claimed that medical services and the use of medical equipment can be error-free only through intelligent systems. These systems can be discriminating intelligent systems because the thinking of humans and data analysts is behind them. The use of clustering algorithms in the direction of clustering people's gender and age should not be aimed at creating discrimination. Rather, this clustering should be aimed at providing medical services to people according to their needs in terms of gender and age. Defining a positive view on the design of artificial intelligence algorithms will lead to

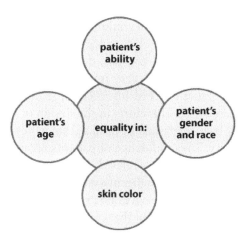

**Figure 7.2** Treatment of patients based on the equality in HMI system.

positive decision-making in algorithm design. This positivist thinking makes the level of user-friendliness of programs high and the level of satisfaction of patients in receiving services from medical centers during treatment and after discharge is positive.

An important point that can be mentioned in this section is the attitude of intelligent system designers toward gender and racial discrimination. The attitude of data analysis in the design of practical applications for the design of medical systems can lead to the design of a widely used medical service delivery system without bias. In other words, if the system designer examines the issue with a discriminatory point of view during the analysis of the available data, it will cause the clustering of medical data, which includes the analysis of the opinions of patients in providing services, the need of patients for services during the treatment period, etc., in a discriminatory manner. be done. This clustering with the wrong criteria causes an intelligent system to provide intelligent services incorrectly. More precisely, it can be said that the medical diagnosis system indirectly provides discriminatory services.

Investigating and analyzing huge data requires intelligent techniques in order to determine the result in real-time and without error according to the required parameters. Healthcare systems and diagnosis of medical equipment on a larger scale require the use of human-based systems to analyze huge data. The parameters in the diagnosis of patients' conditions according to the patient's records may require a large database to store a lot of data. Various challenges arise in huge data, which should be investigated according to the level of importance of the data. In Manogaran *et al.* [30], various algorithms for analyzing huge data are examined. Considering the importance of medical and healthcare discussion and the necessity of using medical equipment, smart techniques should be used in examining huge data.

In the discussion of big data analysis, data security techniques should also be used. Patient privacy is a very important issue in healthcare and health. Maintaining patient record information is important when using human-based systems [31]. Therefore, in the design of human-based systems, user-friendly features should be used so that patients can understand the feeling of security. The confidence of patients regarding the preservation of their privacy and the data related to their conditions makes them have a good interaction with intelligent systems in providing medical services. This interaction makes services be provided at a higher speed for a large number of patients. The point that can be taken from this issue is that providing services to patients in healthcare and health issues and the use of medical equipment is done intelligently if patients have good cooperation with intelligent systems. This good partnership also results from the discussion of trust building and privacy protection for patients. Therefore, human-based systems that can maintain data security using encryption algorithms can be a reliable option for patients, and intelligent interaction is taken in the direction of patients' health.

### 7.5.3    Emotional Intelligence

In the design of computer-based systems that are used for medical diagnostic equipment, the factor of emotional intelligence should be considered. Emotional intelligence in patients causes it to have different effects on their mental states. It also affects the decision-making of patients. In Shahraki and Nafchi [26], the impact of emotional intelligence on the elderly is discussed. Due to their age conditions, the elderly are more likely to suffer from various diseases and therefore need more medical services. Computer-based systems can examine and diagnose patients' mental states according to their age. Medical services for patients are different according to their age and level of emotional intelligence.

Computer-based systems can use machine learning algorithms to diagnose different conditions of patients and their condition. Since this emotional intelligence affects the mental state and conditions of patients, intelligent systems based on machine learning can diagnose medical equipment according to the needs of patients. Accurate decision-making regarding the diagnosis of medical equipment makes patients of different age groups feel empathy. Therefore, it strengthens their morale and cures them faster. By using user analysis techniques by machine learning, the effect of using medical services is realized. If patients do not have a positive feeling about using certain medical services in medical centers, the conditions are changed to improve service delivery. Deep learning models can analyze the age of users and examine their conditions based on the analysis of their messages and patient surveys, and measure the level of patient satisfaction based on different age groups.

The recognition of people's emotions is discussed using the analysis of video frames [28]. Recognizing people's emotions such as anger, irritability, sadness, fear, etc. from their faces is one of the complex processes that is also mentioned in Shahraki and Nafchi [26]. This issue becomes more important in a situation where people with different emotional states have different needs for treatment. Recognizing people's feelings can determine their level of feeling toward pain and their need for medicine.

Body language and changing body posture when feeling uncomfortable are things that can play a role in analyzing the condition of patients.

Accurate detection of body posture by using image processing algorithms makes it possible to identify patients' feelings more accurately. By accurately identifying the conditions of patients, services can be provided well. Computer-based systems can intelligently prescribe drugs by detecting the level of the disease from the processing of facial images and gestures of patients. Using data mining algorithms, a set of facial expressions of patients should be analyzed and stored in a database. This database can be divided into different parts related to the different emotions of patients using a clustering algorithm. The design of these databases helps to provide services and prescribe medicine to patients in the shortest possible time.

Recognition and analysis of facial and tongue movements can play a positive role in controlling smart mobile devices such as wheelchairs [22]. Using human-based systems, these devices can control the conditions of patients who have disabilities. Disabled patients who have physical and movement disabilities can use computer-based systems that are activated on a wheelchair or a smart cane [29]. In this case, using image processing algorithms, their facial gestures and tongue movements are analyzed and their need for medical equipment is solved. The design of computer-based systems for patients with disabilities should be user-friendly for these people. Disabled people should be able to communicate with these intelligent systems and easily express their needs by moving their tongues and facial expressions. The intelligent recognition system recognizes the emotions of these people based on the specific changes in their faces and acts to serve them.

Image processing algorithms can help recognize facial muscle states so that patients' emotions can be correctly recognized in different situations. For example, changing the angle of the cheeks, changing the movement of the lips upwards or downwards, the eyebrows falling together, etc. can determine the amount of pain or discomfort that the patient feels. Medical signal processing helps to identify the feelings of patients in different situations. At this time, a human-computer interface system can analyze the patient's condition by processing medical signals. Medical equipment can be used to serve patients with these conditions. The use of brain signal detection algorithms can measure the patient's condition more accurately. Designing a user interface system for patients can determine the patient's feelings by examining the nerves of the brain. This system, which also operates based on the analysis of brain signals, is more accurate than systems that only rely on facial image processing.

# 7.6   Blockchain

Maintaining data related to patients' information makes patients feel safe during their care and treatment. Protected data must be stored in a secure environment to prevent hacking and disclosure. The blockchain system can be useful for maintaining data security. In health and treatment centers where the number of data related to the characteristics of patients and their disease records must be kept accurately without any changes, a blockchain system can undertake this task. There are various challenges in the design of blockchain systems that must be considered according to the need to use blockchain. Cryptographic algorithms in blockchain systems should be designed based on the need to store information. In other words, the design of different parts of the blockchain system should be designed according to the importance of the stored data. In Attaran [32], it examines the challenges in designing a blockchain system in order to preserve data in health and care centers. The challenges that need to be addressed in data sharing are important points that need to be addressed. When sharing data in healthcare centers, a safe space should be used for sharing. The data can be shared with other systems without change. In data transfer, having a high-security network is necessary for transferring the data without delay and at high speed [33]. 6th generation technology policy ensures security in sending data. Maintaining the privacy of data related to patients' records in medical centers using 6th-generation technology increases patients' trust in the government for their treatment. Building trust in medical centers and any other center that is related to people's health and health creates security for people and therefore, through indirect intermediaries, it leads to the development of society in terms of technological, political, social, and cultural progress.

Remote monitoring of patients by blockchain systems can play a vital role in patient care. The elderly, the disabled, and any person who needs special care and is unable to attend medical centers for care due to physical conditions can be monitored using the designed blockchain systems [34]. Designing human-based systems based on the blockchain can increase data security in these systems. The diagnosis of medical equipment based on the blockchain increases the efficiency of systems in healthcare. The architecture of medical equipment detection systems based on the blockchain system helps to design a strong system with high security that prevents hacking.

The design of the blockchain system helps to manage medical data to be stored securely. In the design of human-based systems, blockchain architecture can be used to manage medical data [35]. Based on the structure of this system, information about patients is given as input to the system. This information is stored in a blockchain system and then information is sent to the doctor from the stored data. The blockchain system is placed as an intermediary between the input of information and the display of information in the output. Various methods can be implemented in this intermediary system. These methods with encryption algorithms and data security can help medical data, which have a large volume, to be processed more quickly. By using optimization methods, it is possible to help improve the performance of data processing algorithms to transfer the required data from the blockchain system to the output with more accuracy and less error. The implementation of encryption algorithms and information security together with optimization algorithms and algorithms for finding the shortest path can help transfer medical data from the blockchain system to design and implement a high-quality system.

Also, blockchain makes a large volume of medical data remain anti-manipulation, and if needed, the data can be tracked to provide better services [36]. Blockchain can categorize the data that exists in a decentralized mode in different parts of health and care centers and analyze the required data using data management algorithms. In this case, a blockchain system with a high ability to track and be impenetrable can be very good benefits for treatment systems.

On the other hand, dividing the cloud blockchain into small blocks can increase data security [36]. In such a way that encryption algorithms are implemented in each block separately so that they can manage and secure smaller data. Cloud blockchain design in human-based systems can save information on a large scale. Health and care systems can use blockchain design to store a lot of data related to patients. The security of data in the cloud blockchain is more than the storage space in physical servers and prevents data manipulation by hackers. Of course, it should be mentioned that the methods of hacking data in online systems are becoming more complex day by day. Therefore, data security methods should be strengthened to prevent hacking or loss of huge data in the cloud.

In Lee *et al.* [37], the proposed model for medical blockchain is simulated. This model prevents patient data from internet attacks. The advantage of this model is that there is no need to modify medical equipment in the hospital. This system can also be implemented on medical devices that are not smart and updated. In fact, a smart contract is created between the medical blockchain and medical equipment, and the blockchain system intelligently performs data security and privacy protection for patients.

According to the studies conducted on blockchain, we can hope for a positive trend in the development of blockchain-based systems in medical services. Today, blockchain can play a prominent role in maintaining the security of patients' data and their privacy. In the future, a new technology may be offered for the security of big data. In any case, it is necessary to use new technologies to update smart systems. Service delivery in the age of technology requires conditions that can maintain data security in any situation. Undoubtedly, it is necessary to use the latest methods to protect people's privacy in any situation. This action creates a positive and empathetic feeling with intelligent methods and people are encouraged to trust intelligent systems in different situations. This trust-building will reduce human errors and human-based intelligent systems will meet human needs with high accuracy and speed.

## 7.7   Virtual Reality

Today, we believe that the age of technology can bring great changes in various industries. The medical industry has faced many developments. With the use of artificial intelligence, intelligent medical tools and equipment have been designed that have made the treatment and care of patients easier and also made the treatment process easier for doctors. The practical meaning of virtual reality, which has been presented since 1999, can make great changes [38]. The idea of not being physically present in a situation but being able to do something may not have been in the human mind decades ago. But today, it is possible that we can feel our physical presence in a place or a situation, while we are geographically far away from the desired situation. Virtual reality has been able to provide the possibility for anyone to use the facilities of virtual reality according to their purpose and to do something in another geographical location. Games, travel, warfare, the medical industry, etc. have all been able to use virtual reality. Doctors treat patients remotely using smart virtual reality equipment. Even patients can use the medical services of hospitals using virtual reality. Applications that are based on virtual reality can meet the needs of people in using virtual reality to do something. The direct conversation between the patient and the doctor in virtual reality makes the patients feel relaxed and comfortable about their treatment. Doctors observe the physical conditions of patients in virtual reality and treat them more accurately. Virtual reality technology can be launched on a human-based system and provide a strong intelligent system for the treatment and diagnosis of medical equipment.

Thinking about the world of virtual reality is very fascinating and amazing. But the challenges that we may face in creating a virtual reality world should also be reviewed. The mental challenges that patients face when faced with virtual reality tools should be investigated and the situation should be managed by using intelligent models of cognitive science and control of emotions and feelings. This virtual reality device must have the ability to manage the emotions of patients, which include feelings of fear, joy, worry, anxiety, etc. when using virtual reality technology, and in conditions where patients experience severe emotional changes that lead to harm to them, the reality tool Virtual can change physical and emotional conditions for patients. Patients' use of virtual reality should be examined from different dimensions. Due to the conditions they have and are being treated for, patients are psychologically more vulnerable and are at greater risk. Therefore, psychological models should be able to influence the design of virtual reality tools for the medical industry as a strong user interface. The user-friendliness of tools based on virtual reality can increase the effectiveness of using virtual reality. The services provided in virtual reality imaging should be able to increase the positive feeling in users. In any case, the design of human-based systems in the diagnosis of medical equipment using virtual reality services can create a positive role in providing services to patients.

To design systems based on virtual reality, hardware devices that can implement virtual reality must be used. Cameras are designed to view virtual reality images that every person can use and imagine himself in a specific physical position by observing the conditions and space seen in the camera. Using virtual space cameras, doctors observe their own presence in the office to visit patients, the operation of patients in the operating room, etc. and can communicate with patients virtually. According to the purpose of using virtual reality in life, different equipment is also needed. For example, when using virtual reality in online games, there is a need for users to use safe covers as a result of being injured due to high excitement. By designing hardware gloves, hand movements and hand tremors can be simulated so that the user can experience the feeling of touch. By using special glasses in virtual reality, it is possible to help stimulate the eye nerves so that the user can find more vision when viewing images and enjoy being in the existing space. However, virtual reality helps users who use this technology to meet their needs and virtual reality gives a positive feeling to their needs. The software tools that are used to implement virtual reality are smart applications for target recognition. Using machine learning algorithms, an intelligent program can be designed to identify users' conditions and meet their needs based on their criteria.

In Samadbeik *et al.* [39], the importance of virtual reality in the field of surgery is discussed. Using virtual reality, doctors can identify the level of disease in a patient and perform surgery in case of an emergency. This issue can reduce the costs of surgery. By examining the conditions of the patient's organs, virtual devices show whether surgery is the answer to the disease or not. In this case, use other solutions without surgery. Virtual reality can deal with the effect of different drugs on the patient's body and observe the side effects of drugs and chemical reactions that occur. Also, virtual reality technology can check the effect of using health services on the patient's body on his mental health. This technology can prevent dangerous or costly complications in the field of health.

Virtual reality can help patients in neurosurgery [43]. Also, because patients need special care after neurosurgery, the use of virtual reality can help to closely examine their brain nerves during the care period. Virtual reality hardware is used to take pictures of the patient's brain. Surgeons can check the conditions instantly and treat the patient immediately in case of unpleasant changes in the brain nerves such as bleeding or rupture of brain vessels. Virtual reality increases the speed of diagnosis and the treatment of the patient is carried out in the shortest possible time. In this case, the patient gets a better understanding of the treatment and the patient's recovery process is better. In any case, the use of virtual reality in medical equipment will increase the quality of treatment and improve the conditions of patients.

Recognition of people's finger movements when using virtual reality-based tools can be implemented using machine learning algorithms. The speed of the fingers can also be detected [40]. In fact, if virtual reality can be used to detect sensors, we can command virtual reality what to do without the intervention of hand and foot movements. Imaging using sensors or stimulating the body's nerves without physical movement of the body makes it possible to design a strong intelligent virtual reality system. Human-based systems can be effective for improving the quality of using virtual reality. Human-based systems can create a better connection between a person and virtual reality. The design of human-based systems using the level of user-friendliness makes it possible to provide a unique. If this system is used for patients in the direction of communication between doctors and patients, it will reduce treatment costs and also create a positive feeling in the treatment environment.

Li *et al.* [41] introduced a smart robot that can activate visual, auditory, and touch sensors by interacting with the skin. Based on this, it seems that this design can be used to use medical equipment to diagnose patients' conditions. In this way, by using activated sensors and stimulation of signals due to touching the skin, the reactions obtained from the patients due to the stimulation of the sensory and motor nerves are analyzed and the conditions of the patients and their needs are determined instantly. This robot can be used in different conditions according to the needs of patients.

Incorporating new technologies into medical devices requires exploring the full potential and benefits of integration. So using 5G technology can also be effective in strengthening the communication network between data in order to prevent delays in data transmission and maintain privacy, among other things [42].

## 7.8   The Challenges in Designing HCI Systems for Medical Devices

The point that needs to be mentioned in this section is that we must pay attention to the fact that a widely used system is a system that is updated based on the needs of the day. Considering that daily social and geographical conditions and unknown symptoms cause new diseases, therefore, the systems used in the treatment and care of patients should be updated based on the needs of the patients. The smart system that is designed and presented today and can keep patients away from the risk of disease cannot be practical in the coming decades. Therefore, all countries should be able to communicate with each other in the discussion of designing and building intelligent systems for treatment.

To design a human-based system in the medical industry, the conditions of the patients should also be considered geographically. People in different countries get diseases related to that geographical area according to the climate and specific geographical conditions they have. Therefore, it seems that if human-based systems can measure the conditions of the region, heat degree, etc. based on the geographical location (by GPS) and intelligently use predictive algorithms to predict the diseases that may occur, they can transform and create greatness in the medical industry. According to the conditions of each geographical region, these systems will be able to detect the level of the immune system of people, and based on that, they will check the required drugs and medical equipment needed in the specific geographical region. Such a system can be an intelligent super system in medical science.

Unfortunately, the geographical, social, cultural, and political conditions of the countries have caused the health of people in the society to be affected. Most of the different societies, due to their political differences, prevent the purchase of the latest medical tools from other countries, and therefore the health of the people in the society is endangered due to the lack of modern treatment methods. We hope that peace and tranquility will be established in all countries and poverty and lack of basic living conditions will not prevent human deaths. The whole purpose of science should be to grow and raise the welfare conditions for humanity, not to show power to eliminate people.

## 7.9    Conclusion

In this chapter, the design of human-based systems for use in the field of medicine and health is challenged. Human-based systems are a new generation of intelligent systems to establish communication between humans and computers, which are designed in line with different goals to meet the needs of humans. In the medical industry and patient care, it should be noted that patients are also mentally vulnerable due to their physical discomfort. Therefore, establishing a feeling of sympathy and safety in medical centers for patients can help to increase their morale. Preservation of patients' privacy is an important point that should be considered in the design of human-based systems. By using human-based systems, doctors can remotely monitor the conditions of their patients who are admitted to the hospital and provide medical services remotely if needed. On the other hand, doctors can communicate with their patients remotely. This communication with the doctor while the patient is being treated increases their confidence and morale and improves the patient's immune system. Human-based systems can be effective in establishing doctor-patient communication and controlling patient conditions. In this chapter, various methods to design and implement an optimal human-based system were examined. Various technologies that can have a positive impact on human-based system design in an intelligent way have been presented. In this chapter, we tried to review the latest methods that were presented for applications of human interaction systems in the medical industry. The comments given about each reference can help to improve the medical industry in the future. We hope that this chapter has helped to get to know more about new technologies and that the comments given can help in the development of technology to improve the health of patients physically and mentally.

# References

1. Carlisle, J.H., Evaluating the impact of office automation on top management communication. *AFIPS '76*, 1976.
2. Wang, Y., Research on the construction of human-computer interaction system based on a machine learning algorithm. *J. Sens.*, 2022, 1–11, 2022.
3. Li, X. and Xu., Y., Role of human-computer interaction healthcare system in the teaching of physiology and medicine. *Comput. Intell. Neurosci.*, 2022, 5849736, 2022.
4. Acharya, C., Thimbleby, H., Oladimeji, P., Human computer interaction and medical devices. *Proceedings of HCI 2010*, vol. 24, pp. 168–176, 2010.
5. Lilleheie, I., Debesay, J., Bye, A., Bergland, A., A qualitative study of old patients' experiences of the quality of the health services in hospital and 30 days after hospitalization. *BMC Health Serv. Res.*, 20, 1, 1–14, 2020.
6. Hartgerink, J.M., Cramm, J.M., Bakker, T.J., Mackenbach, J.P., Nieboer, A.P., The importance of older patients' experiences with care delivery for their quality of life after hospitalization. *BMC Health Serv. Res.*, 15, 1, 1–7, 2015.
7. Lilleheie, I., Debesay, J., Bye, A., Bergland, A., Experiences of elderly patients regarding participation in their hospital discharge: A qualitative metasummary. *BMJ Open*, 9, 11, e025789, 2019.
8. Mahmud, M., Zannat, N., Nowshin, N., An elderly-centered design approach for mobile chat application. *J. Inf. Syst. Digital Technol.*, 4, 1, 147–172, 2022.
9. Wei, X., Dong, C., Xu, Y., The mechanical and system design of finger training rehabilitation device based on speech recognition. *J. Appl. Data Sci.*, 3, 2, 60–65, 2022.
10. Datwani, K., Ogawa, M.C., Crosby, M.E., Understanding humans' cognitive processes during computational thinking through cognitive science, in: *International Conference on Human-Computer Interaction*, Springer, Cham, pp. 242–260, 2022.
11. Alkatheiri, M.S., Artificial intelligence assisted improved human-computer interactions for computer systems. *Comput. Electr. Eng.*, 101, 107950, 2022.
12. Raviselvam, S., Subburaj, K., Höltta-Otto, K., Wood, K.L., Systematic application of extreme-user experiences: Impact on the outcomes of an undergraduate medical device design module. *Biomed. Eng. Educ.*, 2, 233–252, 2022.
13. Sreedevi, A.G., Nitya Harshitha, T., Sugumaran, V., Shankar, P., Application of cognitive computing in healthcare, cybersecurity, big data and IoT: A literature review. *Inf. Process. Manage.*, 59, 2, 102888, 2022.
14. Anand, R., Sindhwani, N., Juneja, S., Cognitive Internet of Things, its applications, and its challenges: A survey, in: *Harnessing the Internet of Things (IoT) for a Hyper-Connected Smart World*, pp. 91–113, Apple Academic Press, 2022. https://www.google.com/books/edition/Harnessing_the_Internet_of_Things_IoT_fo/azWAEAAAQBAJ?hl=en&gbpv=1&dq=A+survey,+in:+Har

nessing+the+Internet+of+Things+(IoT)+for+a+Hyper-Connected+Smart+ World&pg=PA91&printsec=frontcover.

15. Tan, J.K., Chew, W.J., Phang, S.K., The application of image processing for human-computer interface (HCI) using the eye. *J. Phys.: Conf. Ser.*, 2120, 1, 012030, IOP Publishing, 2021.

16. Liao, Z., Samuel, R., Krishnamoorthy, S., Computer vision for facial analysis using human–computer interaction models. *Int. J. Speech Technol.*, 25, 2, 379–389, 2022.

17. Biele, C., *Human movements in human-computer interaction (HCI)*, vol. 996, Springer, 2022. https://link.springer.com/book/10.1007/978-3-030-90004-5.

18. Hall, A., Boring, R.L., Miyake, T.M., Cognitive aging as a human factor: Effects of age on human performance. *Nucl. Technol.*, 209, 3, 261–275, 2022.

19. Messier, C., Tsiakas, M., Gagnon, M., Desrochers, A., Effect of age and glucoregulation on cognitive performance. *J. Clin. Exp. Neuropsychol.*, 32, 8, 809–821, 2010.

20. Huq, S.M., Maskeliūnas, R., Damaševičius, R., Dialogue agents for artificial intelligence-based conversational systems for cognitively disabled: A systematic review. *Disabil. Rehabil.: Assist. Technol.*, 1–20, 2022.

21. Banyal, S., Mehra, D., Banyal, S., Sharma, D.K., Ghosh, U., Computational intelligence in healthcare with special emphasis on bioinformatics and internet of medical things, in: *Intelligent Internet of Things for Healthcare and Industry*, pp. 145–170, Springer, Cham, 2022.

22. Bouyam, C. and Punsawad, Y., Human-machine interface-based wheelchair control using piezoelectric sensors based on face and tongue movements. *Heliyon*, 8, 11, e11679, 2022.

23. Hay, K., McDougal, L., Percival, V., Henry, S., Klugman, J., Wurie, H., Raven, J. *et al.*, Disrupting gender norms in health systems: Making the case for change. *Lancet*, 393, 10190, 2535–2549, 2019.

24. World Health Organization, Integrating gender data in health information systems: Challenges, opportunities and good practices, 2021.

25. Medicine:Gender-bias in medical diagnosis, HandWiki, 2021, December 30, Retrieved 09:42, November 27, 2022 from https://handwiki.org/wiki/index. php?title=Medicine:Gender-bias_in_medical_diagnosis&oldid=890711.

26. Shahraki, Z.A. and Nafchi, M.A., The effect of emotional intelligence applications on the lifestyle of the elderly, in: *Multidisciplinary Applications of Deep Learning-Based Artificial Emotional Intelligence*, pp. 216–233, IGI Global, 2023. https://www.igi-global.com/chapter/the-effect-of-emotional-intelligence-applications-on-the-lifestyle-of-the-elderly/313353

27. Ghassemi, M. and Nsoesie, E.O., In medicine, how do we machine learn anything real? *Patterns*, 3, 1, 100392, 2022.

28. Rai, M., Maity, T., Yadav, R.K., Yadav, S., A review on detection of human emotions using colored and infrared images, 2022, Available at SSRN 4161798.

29. McGunnigle, C. (Ed.), *Disability and the academic job market*, Vernon Press, 2022.

30. Manogaran, G., Thota, C., Lopez, D., Human-computer interaction with big data analytics, in: *Research Anthology on Big Data Analytics, Architectures, and Applications*, pp. 1578–1596, IGI global, 2022. https://www.igi-global.com/chapter/human-computer-interaction-with-big-data-analytics/291053

31. Varshney, M., Bhushan, B., Haque, A.K.M., Big data analytics and data mining for healthcare informatics (HCI), in: *Multimedia Technologies in the Internet of Things Environment*, vol. 3, pp. 167–195, Springer, Singapore, 2022. https://link.springer.com/chapter/10.1007/978-981-19-0924-5_11.

32. Attaran, M., Blockchain technology in healthcare: Challenges and opportunities. *Int. J. Healthc. Manag.*, 15, 1, 70–83, 2022.

33. Nafchi, M.A. and Shahraki, Z.A., IT governance and enterprise security policy in the 6G era, in: *Next-Generation Enterprise Security and Governance*, pp. 227–245, CRC Press, 2022.

34. Ramzan, S., Aqdus, A., Ravi, V., Koundal, D., Amin, R., Al Ghamdi, M.A., Healthcare applications using blockchain technology: Motivations and challenges. *IEEE Trans. Eng. Manage.*, 1–17, IEEE, 2022. https://ieeexplore.ieee.org/abstract/document/9839538.

35. Hovorushchenko, T., Moskalenko, A., Osyadlyi, V., Methods of medical data management based on blockchain technologies. *J. Reliab. Intell. Environ.*, 8, 11, 5–16 2022.

36. Xi, P., Zhang, X., Wang, L., Liu, W., Peng, S., A review of blockchain-based secure sharing of healthcare data. *Appl. Sci.*, 12, 15, 7912, 2022.

37. Lee, J.-S., Chew, C.-J., Liu, J.-Y., Chen, Y.-C., Tsai, K.-Y., Medical blockchain: Data sharing and privacy preserving of EHR based on smart contract. *J. Inf. Secur. Appl.*, 65, 103117, 2022.

38. Székely, G. and Satava, R.M., Virtual reality in medicine. Interview by Judy Jones. *BMJ (Clinical Res. Ed.)*, 319, 7220, 1305–1305, 1999.

39. Samadbeik, M., Yaaghobi, D., Bastani, P., Abhari, S., Rezaee, R., Garavand, A., The applications of virtual reality technology in medical groups teaching. *J. Adv. Med. Educ. Prof.*, 6, 3, 123, 2018.

40. Zhu, J., Ji, S., Yu, J., Shao, H., Wen, H., Zhang, H., Xia, Z., Zhang, Z., Lee, C., Machine learning-augmented wearable triboelectric human-machine interface in motion identification and virtual reality. *Nano Energy*, 103, 107766, 2022.

41. Li, F. and Hu, R., Intelligent robotic virtual reality. *Matter*, 5, 6, 1642–1644, 2022.

42. Sahija, D., Critical review of mixed reality integration with medical devices for patientcare. *International Journal for Innovative Research in Multidisciplinary Field (IJRMF)*, 10, 100–105, 2455–0620, 2022.

43. Vayssiere, P., Constanthin, P.E., Herbelin, B., Blanke, O., Schaller, K., Bijlenga, P., Application of virtual reality in neurosurgery: Patient missing. A systematic review. *J. Clin. Neurosci.*, 95, 55–62, 2022.

# 8

# Human-Machine Interaction in Leveraging the Concept of Telemedicine

**Dipa K. Israni[1*] and Nandita S. Chawla[2]**

*[1]Dept. of Pharmacology, L.J. Institute of Pharmacy, LJ University,
Ahmedabad, Gujarat, India
[2]L.J. Institute of Pharmacy, L.J. University, Ahmedabad, Gujarat, India*

## Abstract

Since the invention of the computer, several investigations and research projects in the area of human-machine interaction (HMI) have been carried out to continuously enhance the communication between human operators and automated systems. HMI has gained popularity in a variety of industries one of them being healthcare. The concept of "anywhere, anytime healthcare" is changing client attitudes and fostering a new wave of Telemedicine. Telemedicine is the practice of providing therapeutic services remotely via two-way, real-time audio and video communication between a patient and a medical specialist. There are various technological advances in human-machine interactions like artificial intelligence (AI), machine learning (ML), Blockchain, Big Data, and The Internet of medical things (IoMT) that can be utilized in telemedicine. Presently portable telemedicine monitoring devices and Telerobots collect vital life physiological signs; Ambient Assisted Living (AAL), a new development in technology that allows remote patient monitoring; the latest sensor technologies, where a person's vital data can be collected, and bio-information can be wirelessly or online transmitted to medical databases and healthcare specialists are being used in many countries. This review focuses on the human-machine interaction in leveraging the concept of telemedicine that provide a smart triage of patients and remote monitoring.

*Keywords*: Human-machine interaction, telemedicine, artificial intelligence, machine learning, big data, Internet of medical things

*Corresponding author*: dipaisrani@gmail.com
Dipa K. Israni: ORCID: 0000-0002-5382-9352
Nandita S. Chawla: ORCID: 0000-0003-4990-9269

Rishabha Malviya, Sonali Sundram, Bhupendra Prajapati and Sudarshan Kumar Singh (eds.)
Human-Machine Interface: Making Healthcare Digital, (211–246) © 2024 Scrivener Publishing LLC

## 8.1    Introduction

The use of telecommunications technology to enable the provision of healthcare remotely is known as telemedicine [1]. Before COVID, telemedicine was a concept, but it was constrained and sometimes hampered by physician reimbursement difficulties. The COVID-19 crisis hastened the spread of virtual medicine. Currently, telemedicine is delivered through commercial apps using telephones, encrypted texting, and audio-video conference calls [2]. Telemedicine enables remote patient care and medical interaction. It comes in a variety of forms, including those that assist in delivering advice, reminding people about their health, educating them, and integrating healthcare systems. Even in situations when the patient and the essential expert are separated by great distances, telemedicine should make learning, monitoring, and health data management easier. The patient and the expert can communicate clinically through video conference thanks to telemedicine. Additionally, telemedicine systems are used to give better outcomes in urgent and critical care [3].

These technologies support reliable data and picture transmission of health-related information from one location to another and enable contact among individuals and medical personnel. Telemedicine was originally implemented using straightforward telephone lines. Later, client-server programs supporting more telemedicine equipment and improved medical diagnostic procedures were developed to facilitate in-home medical exams. Patient remote or home monitoring is the most significant telemedicine or telehealth function. The expert can track the patient's health-related measurement readings thanks to this capability. Real-time health monitoring requires software to analyze the measurement data, trustworthy wearable healthcare equipment or devices, and a dependable, unbroken internet connection for both the expert and the patient. The patient's wearable device(s) may capture data that the health monitoring system reads while they are being used by the patient [4].

Various technologies in human-machine interactions are being utilized in healthcare sectors. AI and ML are here to optimize the doctor's time, support the patient before the doctor comes in by providing guidance to the user while collecting the data, and enable healthcare providers to make the right judgments more quickly. Blockchain technologies can be applied to telemedicine to guarantee extremely secure data transport and archiving. Big data technologies assist healthcare professionals in achieving the objective of converting massive amounts of information into knowledge that can be used to customize healthcare within the context of precision medicine. The IoMT sector is being driven by a rise in the quantity of practical connected medical devices that are patient-centric and gather, analyze, and transfer data to healthcare IT systems. The development of sensors, WSN, and other more recent technologies like WBAN and Internet of things have made remote health monitoring practical.

Different physiological data is sensed by health monitors positioned on the body and inside it, includes temperature of the body, heartbeat, glucose level, neuronal activity, and other vital signs, among other things [5]. The relevant medical specialists get these data and analyze them to determine the patient's health state, diagnosis, and course of therapy. If a preventative medical approach or a modification in the patient's prescription is necessary, it may be determined after data analysis. Doctors can keep an eye on individuals in real time if the monitoring equipment have direct internet connections. Additionally, combining the remote surveillance system with advanced analytical tools gives doctors additional visibility and understanding of a patient's health state. Remote health monitoring is becoming increasingly popular due to the increasing use of biosensors and wearable technology. This has encouraged the development of several healthcare applications for conditions including diabetes, heart disease, cancer detection, Parkinson's, asthma, Alzheimer's, etc [5].

There are now more applications for telemedicine due to the quick development of communication, robot, and virtual reality technologies. The range of telemedicine applications demonstrates a broad development [6]. There are several application forms available overseas, including those for monitoring systems, surgical minimally invasive workstations, electronic medical records (EMR), etc.

The third stage of development is the twenty years of widespread use of the Internet. Since Internet services have become more widely used in recent years, several international hospitals have developed its unique telehealth content and services [1].

## 8.2  Innovative Development in HMI Technologies and Its Use in Telemedicine

Blockchain, robots, big data, IoT, AI, and cloud computing are some of the developing HMI technologies that can be used in telemedicine in the healthcare industry. Figure 8.1 shows the emerging technologies of human-machine interface used in Telemedicine.

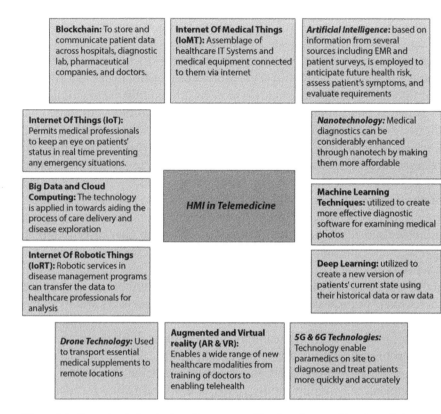

**Figure 8.1** Emerging technologies of human-machine interface used in telemedicine.

## 8.2.1   Nanotechnology

Nanotechnology-related applications will significantly advance healthcare 5.0. Nanotechnology offers unprecedented opportunities to change healthcare services. Rapid diagnoses, surveillance, and monitoring, as well as the development of novel vaccinations and personal protective equipment, all largely rely on nanotechnology. The manipulation, production, materials, processes, and applications of nanodevices are all included in nanotechnology. With this technique, nonviral nanostructures have been widely used in gene therapy, sickness prevention, disease treatment, and target-specific medication delivery. This is shown by the advancement of healthcare utilizing nanotechnology, which has led to substantial improvements in the spotting, diagnosing, and treating disease by the creation of nanomaterials, nanodevices, nanomedicine, nano implants, and Nano biosensors as well as the internet of nano things (IoNT).

The application of the IoNT idea in healthcare has enabled more customized, rapid, and practical patient monitoring and treatment. Examples of nano goods in the healthcare industry include smart medical implants that use nanoscale biosensors and nanosensors and biosensors that have been downsized to the nanoscale. The application of this healthcare technology is for smart medication delivery and nanoscale treatments. Nano biosensors employ a biochemical and biophysical message to detect illnesses at the molecular or single-cell level as well as in their early stages. For instance, COVID-19 has been discovered using nano-based optical/colorimetric, electrochemical, and chiral sensors. Therefore, the IoNT and nanosensors will assist in the development of nano-based health monitoring applications for a number of reasons, including sugar, lipid, and salt monitoring [7].

## 8.2.2   The Internet of Things (IoT)

The quantity of mobile devices has overtaken the number of people on the planet during the previous ten years [8]. As a result, computers and other objects are becoming increasingly interconnected, maintaining connections even in the absence of intentional human contact. The "Internet of Things" is the name given to this network to distinguish it from the conventional internet, which connects people. It is a network of actual physical objects that can exchange and understand data, have sensors, and interact often and automatically with other objects or people. The current networks are used to connect people, but as more people begin to utilize wireless metering, mobile payments, linked refrigerators and heating systems, and autonomous automobiles to commute in smart cities, the network's capacity requirements will increase quickly [9].

IoT has been extensively utilized in the medical industry to link medical equipment and share online patient data. In the medical industry, there are a number of recent sensor-based IoT applications, each with unique characteristics. IoT makes it easier to introduce the internet of things, such as the wearable internet of things (IoMT), cognitive internet of medical things (IoNT), and internet of mobile health things (IoMT). Nanoscale devices require a connection to the existing communication networks in order to carry out functions including electromagnetic radiation detection, actuation, and transmission is referred as Internet of Nanotechnology (IoNT). In an effort to promote the widespread use of advanced medical technology and the thorough transfer of health data, these IoT versions offer networked healthcare. Smart devices, for instance, transform the idea of traditional healthcare into smart healthcare by enabling remote monitoring of healthcare services.

As a consequence, medical professionals may use IoT innovations to remotely access, assess, and analyze health data in order to improve the delivery of healthcare services as identified by biosensors and intelligent wearable technology. Additionally, omnipresent healthcare is now possible because to the internet of things for health, wearable internet of things, cognitive internet of medical things, and internet of mobile health things. These developments enable personalized treatment, compliance, continuous monitoring, early sickness detection accuracy, effective diagnosis, omnipresent care, and intelligent rehabilitation [7].

### 8.2.3   Internet of Medical Things (IoMT)

The term "IoMT" refers to a network of physical connections between sensors, worn healthcare products, and software developers that enables communication between items and numerous medical and information technology systems. IoMT devices can store and analyze the collected data since they are linked to cloud systems. In sensor's industry, novel ideas are ubiquitous. The utilization of WBSN (Wireless Body Sensor Network) technologies for remote patient monitoring has lately grown significantly. WBSN, a group of wearable sensor devices, allows for the real-time recording of data and the monitoring of a person's mobility patterns and physiological status. Worn sensors that are positioned strategically, such as on the chest, within socks, the skin, or even wearable UV sensors that provide signals when UV levels are extremely high, allow the wearer to go about his daily activities.

Sensors can be implanted into a tissue or placed close to the patient's skin to continuously monitor their health. This allows for the collection of critical data about their health no matter where they are. In order to save healthcare expenses, intellectual nodes, which are sensors made expressly for medical exams, may evaluate critical physiological indications for early risk detection and sickness prevention. Numerous chronic medical conditions are difficult to monitor and manage, including diabetes, coronary heart failure, bronchitis, and loss of memory in Alzheimer's, dementia, Autism, or other cognitive impairments. Intelligent wireless networked sensors can monitor people remotely by collecting behavioral, bodily, and physiological information about them and analyzing patterns in real-time. Commercial wearable sensor systems have gained a lot of interest recently and are widely accessible for remote monitoring of numerous physiological indicators [10].

### 8.2.3.1    Motion Detection Sensors

Accelerometers are used by wearable motion detection sensors to identify physical activity, and real-time sensor data is gathered and transferred through the GSM or ZigBee protocol [11].

### 8.2.3.2    Pressure Sensors

A widespread medical issue called hypertension, sometimes known as high blood pressure, frequently goes undiagnosed or untreated. Low, normal, and high values for both systolic and diastolic blood pressure are provided via wearable pressure sensors. They are employed to keep tabs on a person's heart rate and blood pressure [11].

### 8.2.3.3    Temperature Sensors

Body temperature is one of the most essential variables for pathological symptoms linked to human health. Temperature sensors track variations in body temperature in real-time, allowing for subsequent analysis to determine whether they are signs of infection, heat, inflammation, or hypothermia [12].

### 8.2.3.4    Monitoring Cardiovascular Disease

A chest strap and ePatch Sensors that detect physical exertion and record electrocardiogram (ECG) heart signals can be worn [10].

### 8.2.3.5    Glucose Level Monitoring

Diabetes patients can use Google smart contact lenses and insulin pumps to continually monitor changes in their blood glucose levels. Wireless transmission of data gathered from the Smart Contact Lenses to the gateway servers for additional analysis is possible.

### 8.2.3.6    Asthma Monitoring

The amounts of ozone, nitrogen dioxide, and carbon monoxide may all be observed via a wristband. The sensor can track heart rate variability as well.

### 8.2.3.7   GPS Smart Soles and Motion Detection Sensors

It is possible to identify cognitive illnesses like Alzheimer's, autism, dementia, and other types, as well as unusual scenarios like patient roaming. The sensor data is wirelessly transferred for processing and analysis. In case of an emergency, caregivers are texted with alerts.

### 8.2.3.8   Wireless Fetal Monitoring

Cardiotocography measures uterine contractions as well as the mother's and fetus's heart rates using sensors and doppler-based technologies. On a smartphone or tablet connected wirelessly through Bluetooth and acting as a data gateway, the initial fetal cardiotocography may be watched. A cloud-based server receives data from the gateway device and forwards it for extra storage and analysis. In times of crisis, experts are consulted for recommendations on therapy [13].

### 8.2.3.9   Smart Clothing

Sensors are incorporated into textile clothes to detect heart rate and evaluate vital signals like emotions [11].

Researchers in Japan have developed a gel-based adhesive sensor that sticks to the organ and collects data. Researchers from Korea have created electrical skin sensors that are a blessing for those with Parkinson's disease since they allow for the monitoring of the responses of the muscle. Driver Drowsiness Sensor Wearable EEG System Based on Wristwatch. The Sensory Input Unit (SIU) and Sensory Processing Unit (SPU) of a wireless EEG device is designed to prevent serious accidents on national roads caused by sleepy drivers (SPU). The detected data is transformed into digital data and Bluetooth-transmitted to a wristwatch. The vibrating sensor is part of the wristwatch. If the driver became sleepy before, it will offer an early warning; if the driver does not respond, it will vibrate to awaken him or her. Data streams from wearable Internet of Things devices can be tracked inside a distributed health information system. In a diverse context, this technology is utilized to map device data to consumers a posttraumatic stress disorder wearable health monitoring device. Veterans are frequently afflicted by posttraumatic stress disorder (PTSD), which is caused by a sudden, traumatic incident. Patients can monitor dreadful situations with the use of wearable sensors. Through the use of ML approaches, the already-collected data will be trained to provide an optimum patient monitoring and decision-making solution. Virtual-Blind-Road-based following wearable navigational aid for the blind [10, 14].

### 8.2.4   AI

Healthcare 5.0 will be the consequence of automation and AI's transformation of the delivery of healthcare services. Smart wearables and other highly integrated sensor-based AI-embedded devices are used to collect, monitor, and diagnose illnesses using the symptoms obtained from the sensory information. Sensors are used by intelligent systems to recognize their environment and take the required action [15]. A wide range of concepts are covered by AI in the field of medicine, including automated and precise disease prediction, detection, and diagnosis, the development of smart drugs, effective patient surveillance systems, effective use of surgical robotic systems, and the development of emotional sensor-based AI smart products [16, 17].

Notably, medical smart sensors are no longer intellectually capable of monitoring patients' emotions, particularly those of persons with post-traumatic stress disorder. Telemedicine will make use of sensor-based AI systems with cognitive skills to gather information, sensors to communicate with people, get information from the outside world, think, and respond to cogent human-like behavior. These AI-based expression systems will be created as highly adaptable, bio-inspired hybrid systems that can express emotions and engage in complex reasoning. There are several ways that sensor-based cognitive AI systems could alter how healthcare is delivered. In the creation of mental health monitoring applications that listen to people's mobile conversations and analyze the speaker's speech to detect symptoms of worry and mood swings, for instance, healthcare might be enhanced by utilizing sensor-based cognitive AI systems.

The use of emotional AI in healthcare 5.0 may potentially lead to the creation of intelligent wearables that assess the levels of sadness, stress, anxiety, and pain in patients with chronic diseases by analyzing their behavior Additionally, this can help forecast the risky behavior of patients with chronic illnesses so that individualized care can be given and readmissions can be decreased. It enhances medical imaging diagnostics, medication discovery, and production, supporting research and clinical trials, and effectively implementing autonomous robotic surgery, AI along with other new technologies that might be used. AI and telemedicine, in that order, offer robust patient monitoring, medical information technology, intelligent diagnosis aids, and medical data analysis. AI is utilized in many different applications, including picture identification and interpretation, diagnostic support, creating alerts and reminders, arranging therapy, etc. AI offers cost savings, cost reduction, virtual presence, and telemedicine in addition to quick and precise diagnosis to lessen human mistakes [14].

### 8.2.5 Machine Learning Techniques

Machine learning is simply an application of artificial intelligence where knowledge is acquired via comparison and correlation of multiple comparable patterns in the obtained data to generate patterns that may potentially forecast things [18]. Using previous data, machine learning is used to train computers to predict the future. Well-known applications for ML techniques include the fields of biology, finance, social networks, healthcare, and finance. ML algorithms can forecast patient diagnoses for clinicians to assess in healthcare applications. In Social Networks, a dating website's ML-enabled model may anticipate specific match preferences to increase compatibility. ML algorithms are additionally utilized in the finance sector to foresee credit card fraud. Customer turnover may also be anticipated in e-commerce, and it is crucial for identifying trends in DNA changes that could indicate cancer in biology.

The three primary types of machine learning are supervised, unsupervised, and reinforcement learning. supervised learning Instead of the usual human-labeled data, machine learning employs data that has been tagged. Regression or classification issues are solved with it. Continuous values, which can be any number without restrictions and include things like a property's price or the outside temperature, are projected in the first. The second option includes categorizing the response into two or more groups. instruction without supervision. Robots cannot learn from labelled data in unsupervised learning. There is no one "right" approach to educate a machine since it learns on its own from unlabeled data to find patterns in the data and arrange them. To provide an answer or result, a machine is meant to discover patterns on its own from the data [10].

Depending on what the user wishes to group, it can cluster or associated data. When solving a subjective problem like clustering, unsupervised learning is used to group people into groups based on things like their hobbies or gender. From huge datasets, association aids in revealing hidden and intriguing links. Frequently occurring item sets and association rules are common ways to represent it. Frequent item sets are a grouping of things that frequently appear together, whereas association rules suggest a strong link between two or more items. Association rules are frequently used in the retail business, but other possible applications include the monitoring of website traffic and data relating to healthcare.

It is a subset of AI that uses a mechanism that awards the machine for learning successfully and penalized if it learns badly to help the machine learn continually and iteratively from the input. Some well-known applications of reinforcement learning include self-driving automobiles and teaching a computer to play games [10].

### 8.2.6  Deep Learning

A branch of machine learning called "Deep Learning" (DL) has ushered in new developments in information technology. DL may use neural networks that are analogous to the human brain to investigate the underlying characteristics in data from various processing layers [19]. In medical practice, DL is useful in image-centric specialties, demonstrating its effectiveness by identifying malignant melanoma from digital skin pictures and pulmonary TB from chest radiographs [20]. Traditional eye illness diagnosis techniques rely on clinical evaluation and, increasingly, image-capture technologies of various modalities.

Ophthalmology is one of the specialties that are particularly well-suited to DL methods and their practical use, although the procedure is time-consuming and expensive. The automated screening and detection of common disorders that affect eyesight, such as diabetic retinopathy, has been claimed to be achieved by applying DL to ophthalmic pictures, such as digital fundus photos and visual fields (DR), glaucoma, age-related macular degeneration (AMD) and retinopathy of prematurity (ROP) [21] with high accuracy. As a result, DL may show to be a useful and practical addition to the current diagnostic procedures and may even have a place in place of ophthalmologists and qualified human image graders [22].

Recently, it has been more common to apply innovative DL algorithms to optical coherence tomography (OCT) pictures, which may improve the sensitivity of early disorder diagnosis, particularly in AMD and DR with the detection of diabetic macular edema [23]. Although the cost-effectiveness of these systems is still unknown, it is anticipated that the integration of DL into ophthalmic practice will change the present disease management process, may increase early identification, and eventually improve outcomes. Given the potential for AI and DL to advance ophthalmic delivery services, it is the clinician's obligation to critically assess how these technologies work and decide if they may be safely incorporated into clinical practice [22].

### 8.2.7    Home Monitoring Devices, Augmented and Virtual

The healthcare industry may be significantly impacted by augmented reality, which generates and visually augments information on the fly. In the last ten years, people with visual impairment have benefited from the usage of VR technologies like IrisVision™ and NuEyes™ [24]. The IrisVision™ VR headgear is attached to a smartphone that captures a picture of the patient's surroundings, displays it in peripheral vision, and can enlarge the image. The VR immersive device utilized by NuEyes™ to enlarge visuals is no longer in development. The headsets' occlusive and digitally immersive design is the biggest drawback of VR for medical use. It is unsafe to use a VR headset while walking or moving since the user cannot see the surrounding area well.

For the goal of visual rehabilitation, AR has a considerable benefit over VR since it enables patients to keep their peripheral vision and engage with the actual world while using digital augmentation. Using an image remapping method, the Oculenz™ AR headset allows patients to view the picture that is often obscured by each eye's scotoma and can only be seen by the neighboring functioning retina. Remapping may aid to enhance eyesight, particularly for reading, according to studies [25]. Oculenz™ AR platform features 4K cameras and algorithms built in that can identify scotomas in each eye and remap lost images onto healthy nearby retinas. As the illness progresses, the mapping algorithm adapts the picture positioning. The display picture must be stabilized on the neighboring retina independent of gaze direction for remapping to function properly [24].

Oculenz uses unique eye-tracking technology keep the projected picture and the user's gaze in alignment. Early patient testing can enhance 4-5 lines on a Snellen chart with just one use, while still being under development. Using AR technology to monitor AMD is an innovative approach. A key element of the Oculenz system is in-home monitoring of the scotoma or visual impairment. Its AI system monitors the development of scotomas. AI quantifies any changes in the scotoma and notifies the doctor's office if they are found. It is critical to have the capacity to monitor a patient's illness precisely and continually. Macular disease patients typically are not aware of slow, subtle changes in their vision. Therefore, by the time a patient notices a change, it could be too late for a doctor to act to prevent vision loss [22].

Applications for AR technology in ocular surgery have recently surfaced. In particular, AR headsets have been created to increase vision and improve ergonomics in operating rooms. Due to the ergonomic restrictions of prolonged staring at a microscope, ophthalmic surgeons historically worked while looking through the operating microscope's oculars, which limited surgeon mobility during surgery and caused spine issues. To solve these problems, Alcon (Ngenuity™) and Zeiss (Artevo™) developed digital head-up displays for ocular surgery [26, 27]. With the use of these digital viewing devices, the surgeon may see surgery on a sizable monitor placed next to the patient's operating table more comfortably while doing surgery and donning 3D glasses [22].

## 8.2.8   Drone Technology

Drones and other autonomous technologies are continuing to transform the global health industry. Their increased use during the COVID-19 epidemic serves as proof of this. In order to execute COVID-19 measures, such as lockdowns and mobility restrictions, for example, regulatory agencies have begun using drones. 53 Drones may transport blood samples, food, and medical supplies in the future. They may also be used to conduct surveillance, identify signs of illness, and raise public awareness. In COVID-19 high-risk regions, drones are already being deployed to clean polluted surfaces [7].

## 8.2.9    Robotics

The development of telerobots, collaborative robots, [28] autonomous robots, social robots [29] and wearable robots [30] is being driven by recent developments in digital automation and robotics technology. These robots performed surgical procedures, identified and diagnosed ailments, and created vaccinations, all of which significantly enhanced the delivery of healthcare services. Personalized care, ubiquitous health applications, a lack of emotional smart gadgets, and the lack of emotive emotion detection, however, necessitate considerable advancements in robotics, particularly in healthcare 5.0.

To improve coordination, information sharing, security, configuration, and protection, the most recent Internet of Robotic things (IoRT) initiative has brought new convergence challenges including programmability and communication across diverse mobile/robotic things into the picture. The most prominent IoRT subtypes are as follows: (1) Telesurgery: assistance for surgery given via video, i.e., ROBOTIC arms are used to carry out remote surgical stages with good accuracy. (2) Tele-consultation: between multiple carers in a real-time or store-and-forward mode without patient involvement. (3) Tele-education: between non-expert patient and Internet expert. (4) Telemonitoring: transfer clinical information [14].

### 8.2.9.1 Robotics in Healthcare

Numerous health difficulties are being resolved through the use of robotic technology in healthcare. In terms of surgery, this technique is far better than all others. The following are some of the key characteristics of robotic technology: programmability, sensor systems, portability, and adaptability, which may work with various programs and manipulate and move things in several ways.

### 8.2.9.2 History of Robotics

The best machine equipment used to reduce risks, and burdens, and provide superior surgical results at a cheap cost is the robot. Effective patient-doctor communication depends on the usage of robotic technology in the medical industry. It offers a special symbiosis between medicine, health science, and numerous engineering subdisciplines. Robotic technology offers accurate diagnosis, and keeps up with digital imaging technologies, electronic medical records (EMRs), and disease history preservation. Understanding the present level of robots in healthcare and the need for more dependable security while switching between electronic records are the key goals of this part. Over real-time access to massive amounts of processing of data through a dependable transmission line, such as patient X-rays, robotic technology improves the healthcare systems.

LIE *et al.*, [31] created the Sister Kenny Home Therapy system (SKOTEE), a low-cost robotic device that helps patients stay on track with their medications, home activities, alerts, and doctor communications.

Several wearables and wireless body area network sensors for health monitoring assist the domestic robotic tool function more effectively. Multiple concurrently monitored and prescribed patients from various geographic regions can be managed by clinicians with ease. Sealand *et al.*, [32] more accurate movement forecasts from brain activity measures, such as electroencephalograms (EEG), utilizing robotic technology that promotes more spontaneous human-machine interaction [14].

### 8.2.9.3 Tele-Surgery/Remote Surgery

Robotic surgery was used to do the procedure, with a human surgeon controlling it from a distance. The surgeon explains surgical techniques and therapy options to the distant patient. The Da-Vinci robotic platform was created to enable surgery away from the patient and the robot in the operating room. It enables medical professionals to perform surgery in another room or building and offers professional guidance through tele-conferences, teleradiology, and telepathology. There are the following five crucial new dimensions for robotic surgery: The following factors must be taken into consideration: (1) technology, which enhances surgical precision and yields positive results; (2) cost; (3) evidence, which supports the best robotic operation; (4) training, which increases system accuracy; and (5) awareness, which is necessary for both patients and society [33].

Robotics can be used in a variety of professions, such as (1) surgery for robotic treatments, (2) physical therapy for range of motion and flexibility, (3) care provider interaction, (4) bionic prosthetics (replacement limbs, organs), (5) simulation software (procedure planning, education), (7) logistics for material handling and transportation, and (6) pharmacy for compounding and dispensing [14].

### 8.2.10    5G Technology

To enable successful electronic management of intelligent devices in healthcare 5.0, there is a need for emerging global wireless standards that provide a high rate of data transmission and bandwidth in a multiple-in-multiple-out architecture. Digital automation of emerging technologies like as robots, AI, smart devices, nanotechnology, and cloud computing needs fast and smooth data rates in order to collect, store, format, and trace health data for quicker and more dependable access. 5 G technology has become a key and essential technology due to its capacity to handle 1000 times more data in the transmission channel, as well as its higher usage data rate and network signal coverage.

Extremely low latency, limited feasible communication, and strong data security are all attributes of this technology. The technology of 5G represents a paradigm shift from the present mobile networks in terms of delivering ubiquitous high-rate connectivity and a smooth user experience. High-speed remote clinical services, such as healthcare delivery and diagnostics, can be provided using sensor-based intelligent systems [34].

### 8.2.11    6G

The 6G programme has already started, and the launch is expected to happen within the next 10 years. With 6G, both humans and machines will be able to use growing mobile holograms and augmented reality (XR), which might have a big influence on healthcare. The limitations of mobile devices' computational power will be solved by 6G through the flexible integration of entities inside networks. Additionally, it will address many of the security and privacy concerns resulting from the increasing data collecting and sharing [22].

## 8.2.12   Big Data

The volume of health data will eventually increase due to the future connectivity of smart sensors, smart devices, and other virtual care technologies, leading to big data in healthcare 5.0. In addition to providing tailored treatment, this data will eventually be utilized for illness surveillance, diagnosis, and control. Big data is expected to have an unprecedented influence on health systems and put patients and healthcare professionals in a terrific position. For instance, AI models analyzed large data in the form of health data (such as symptoms, patient outcomes data, X-ray findings, clinical history, close connections, and proximity data) to diagnose COVID-19 from X-ray chest photos and to efficiently locate suspects using intelligent mobile applications [34].

It is the best big data processing method and technique for analyzing medical images. The workflow includes the following steps: obtaining healthcare data (images from various diagnostic systems), inspecting, storing, processing, querying, classifying, and [7] programming healthcare picture identification. The significance of leveraging compressed healthcare data is discussed while contrasting two key big data architectures based on (1) MapReduce in Hadoop and (2) Spark.

They have suggested using Spark architecture, which enables the creation of appropriate, well-organized methods that can manage the enormous number of datasets (such as healthcare photographs) utilized for indexing for individualized reference to one another It offers a well-organized framework for the analysis of healthcare datasets and is comprehensive, simpler to use, and customizable. Its integrated libraries also make it easier to create algorithms. The suggested workflow can handle gathered information for distributing and archiving of pictures and facilitates the interchange of datasets, i.e., photos, much as traditional systems [14].

## 8.2.13   Cloud Computing

Cloud computing includes sending computer system resources, including data, over the Internet by using remote servers to host programs and store data. It contributes to the efficient management and storage of patient health data at lower data storage costs. This technology offers quick, flexible, and cutting-edge ways to access cloud resources. Cloud service providers make use of the Internet's infrastructure by creating cloud-based health apps to facilitate communication between patients and healthcare professionals. We developed a smart helmet for miners that is cloud-based and has sensors to measure their levels of stress, fatigue, and attention.

The delivery of such therapies can be enhanced to offer individualized healthcare. Additionally, cloud computing may enable online health data storage, patient monitoring from a distance, health data exchange and modification, and, most crucially, online therapy and diagnosis. This is crucial because smart apps and smart devices will be coordinated and integrated. To connect with other digital health devices, however, necessitates a significant shift in communication protocols and the creation of powerful application programming interfaces [14].

### 8.2.14    Blockchain

Blockchain makes use of the blocks that openly and chronologically store the required data [35]. An ever-expanding list of transactions is stored in this append-only data structure. Immutability and non-reputability are two crucial characteristics of blockchain. Because it is computationally impossible to change or manipulate any executed transactions on the blockchain, immutability is achieved. Since a blockchain's transactions are copied by several entities, they cannot be undone. As a result, healthcare institutions are implementing blockchain to provide efficient and safe health information transmission.

For instance, [36] advised implementing blockchain technology in the healthcare sector to augment virtual access regulations, boost data accumulation and liquidity, protect patient distinctiveness and confidentiality, and guarantee data integrity (safe transfer of health data between different entities). Blockchain has been broadly utilized in EMR, among other applications, [37] prescription supply chain, medical insurance claims, and telemedicine monitoring. But by creating strong API links across various digital health systems, the deployment of blockchain in telemedicine might promote interoperability driven by patients and manageability [7].

Blockchain frameworks have been effectively supplied by a number of medical service providers and blockchain-focused firms to enhance this medical assistance medical assistance for both doctors and patients. Blockchain is quickly evolving into an indispensable tool for the medical business, revolutionizing the sector by decentralizing patient health records, monitoring drugs, and expanding possibilities. There are a number of operational and research issues when attempting to combine blockchain technology with current EHR systems. Blockchain applications in healthcare have received very little research so far, despite new research fields regularly emerging. It is designed to carry out a variety of duties, such as managing epidemics and securely encrypting patient data. Clinical studies, patient records, drug monitoring, and device tracking may all use blockchain [38].

### 8.2.14.1  Clinical Trials

It maintains an unalterable record of patient permission and makes sure the experiment conforms with informed consent laws, regulators may easily keep an eye on clinical trial standards. This is crucial since among the most prevalent kinds of healthcare fraud are falsified informed consent forms, data manipulation, and false patient agreements. To stop this fraud, a high degree of trial subject authentication would be necessary. By creating a smart contract system that prevents physicians from accessing patient data until a key is released at the conclusion of an auditable smart contract procedure that needs consent from the patient at each stage of the trial, this system might be improved even further. Using a blockchain-based clinical trial consent ledger gives trial participants control of their data and gives healthcare personnel, researchers, and regulators access to an audit trail.

### 8.2.14.2  Patient Records

By giving individuals access to data, blockchain has the power to change the medical industry. MedRec maintains a permanent record of patient and provider medical information. Its tactic is to compensate miners by providing them with access to anonymous healthcare data in return for maintaining the network [39]. MedRec employs smart contracts, where the contract displays a list of references describing the linkages between blockchain nodes, to map patient-provider relationships (PPR). Additionally, it provides patients authority over PPRs by enabling them to approve, reject, or alter collaborations with healthcare organizations including hospitals, insurers, and clinics [40].

### 8.2.14.3  Drug Tracking

A digital start-up offering a solution that creates a chain that identifies the location of a drug's creation, its current location, and the time it was given to patients is one example of how to avoid pharmaceutical scam and stealing. This makes it possible for healthcare providers to adhere to current healthcare standards for pharmaceutical supply security, with a focus on provider interoperability. The Counterfeit Medicines Project was started by the open-source blockchain working group Hyperledger to solve the problem of fake medicines. Blockchain technology may be used to identify the sources of fake pharmaceuticals and remove them from the supply chain [40].

### 8.2.14.4   Device Tracking

Another way blockchain can revolutionize healthcare is by monitoring medical devices from their production through their decommissioning. To help with regulatory compliance, this technology uses blockchain to create an immutable record that reveals the device's location, where it has been during its history, as well as its creator, distributor, and registration number. Medical equipment integration and capital management are the sectors of the healthcare business that government players in the sector believe to be the most disruptive, according to a poll by IBM. A blockchain approach provides a number of benefits over conventional location monitoring solutions.

The most noticeable features of blockchain are its immutability and tamper-proof nature. This prevents a rogue person from changing or deleting a device's location history. Stealing of medical instruments has grown to be a major issue in the USA and the UK, this is especially pertinent. This immutability also avoids equipment from being lost and having to be ordered again, which is expensive in n terms of supplies and maintenance expenses. Given that it just involves a quick tap of the device with a smartphone or reader, then enter the gadget's current position, this technique should not dramatically increase the workload of nurses, porters, or support staff.

Blockchain provides the opportunity to develop a centralized system for the timely and secure storage and retrieval of health information by authorized users. By reducing communication barriers between various healthcare professionals and the patient, many errors can be prevented. It is now feasible to diagnose and treat patients more quickly, and even from a distance, treatment may be tailored to each patient's needs. The personal health record (PHR) is made up of medical data that patients themselves have access to and control via wearables like smartwatches. Patients may provide healthcare professionals access to the data gathered by PHRs [40].

## 8.3    Advantages of Utilizing HMI in Healthcare for Telemedicine

Several emerging technologies must be integrated in order to provide universal and customized treatment, -centralized patient care, intelligent sickness identification, forecasting, and remote monitoring. Remote patient nursing and following refers to the delivery of medical services to patients via various communication platforms and virtual care technologies. This may be accomplished through intelligent wearable technology, sensor-based intelligence technologies, and smart health applications [41]. As a result, remote medical monitoring is now used to track a variety of patient parameters, such as heartbeat, blood oxygen saturation, warmth, inhalation, sleep quality, and movement levels. When a patient's physiological factors become worrisome, they can be warned, which typically avoids the need for hospital admission. Through the cellphone, a video link, or other internet platforms, virtual clinics offer digital engagement between medical specialists and patients for distant clinical consultations. Virtual clinics can help reduce the transmission of extremely infectious illnesses, cut down on patient wait times, and improve healthcare by reducing direct patient contact [42, 43].

### 8.3.1    Emotive Telemedicine

Numerous technology toolkits are available in telemedicine that can bring innovative approaches to the provision of healthcare services. Telemedicine offers a wide range of services, as shown in Table 8.1. Telerehabilitation

**Table 8.1** Telemedicine services and its applications.

| Sr. no. | Telemedicine categories | Applications |
|---------|------------------------|--------------|
| 1 | Tele-Radiology | Transmission of radiographic pictures or films across locations for the purpose of interpretation and consultation |
| 2 | Tele-Dermatology | Employing audio, visual, and data connectivity to conduct remote consultations for diagnosis, consultation, and treatment as well as ongoing education. Information sharing on tumours and skin disorders. |

*(Continued)*

**Table 8.1** Telemedicine services and its applications. (*Continued*)

| Sr. no. | Telemedicine categories | Applications |
|---|---|---|
| 3 | Tele-Cardiology | Arrhythmias, congestive heart failure, sudden cardiac arrest, chronic and acute coronary heart disease, etc. are all treated and diagnosed for heart conditions remotely. |
| 4 | Tele-Home Healthcare | One of the healthcare professions that is growing the fastest is the monitoring of the health of elderly people who are bedridden at home. This tele-care focuses on the quickly evolving disciplines of remote nursing and community support. |
| 5 | Tele-Monitoring | A subject's vital signs can be remotely monitored by gathering and communicating vital physiological parameters to a monitoring facility or a doctor. |
| 6 | Tele-Ophthalmology | Telemedicine-based eye care delivery employing digital medical equipment. |
| 7 | Tele-Psychiatry | Complex emotional data from patients in psychiatric facilities is transmitted and received for consultation. |
| 8 | Tele-Pathology | Image transfer for research, training, and diagnosis in the field of pathology. In kinetic telepathology, a distant location controls the microscope to choose and gather pictures of the material; still images can be transmitted for evaluation. |
| 9 | Tele-Surgery | Applications of virtual reality in healthcare. virtual prototypes of surgical tools and operating rooms, virtual reality simulators, and 3D anatomy visualisation for medical education. |

may be offered as a service provided to patients after their diagnosis or after their admission if they need rehabilitation as part of their care or for their overall health [44]. Patients who have had physical damage and injuries frequently adopt smart virtual therapy. Audiology, neurobiology, and speech-language pathology are examples of non-physical services. It cannot be stressed how important it is for those participating in this new type of intervention to have the right training and instruction, and technology-based therapies for older users need to be available, inexpensive, and simple to use. Telemedicine has been used to treat a variety of infectious and illnesses that are not contagious, lessen the burden on medical systems, and improve access to care.

## 8.3.2 Ambient Assisted Living

Identifying and treating ailments, as well as maintaining surveillance on patients, have grown more sophisticated with the application of technologies like artificial intelligence (AI), surgical robots, and nanotechnology. With ambient assisted living (AAL), individuals of all ages may live independently despite their medical issues by using technology to monitor their health and help them with everyday tasks. For instance, a smart home support system has been effectively used in AAL to monitor patients' health state and get prescriptions from doctors remotely [45]. [46] successfully installed a embedded digital home system designed for ambient supported living for persons with loss of memory. For patients who are elderly, autistic, in recovery, or have difficulties, AAL systems are widely employed. Wire-free body area networks, wireless sensor networks, monitoring sensors, and wearable technology that may connect to pertinent medical information systems for efficient monitoring are among the technologies used in AAL.

### 8.3.2.1 Wearable Sensors for AAL

There are reports of textile-based sensors in wearable platforms combined with different communication technologies and wire free monitoring systems. Where a thorough evaluation of a number of current, inexpensive, non-invasive wearable activity monitoring technologies is done. The wearable sensor extracts patient diagnostic data, which includes cardiac parameters like hypertension, temperature, and heartbeats of numerous patients at once, and sends it over Bluetooth to an Android tablet. The information is then transmitted over Wi-Fi/3G from the smartphone to the web application, which processes the data and displays the patient's health condition and personal data on the online interface. If a patient requires further attention or an investigation, the designed system notifies the clinician via emergency alerts based on specified threshold levels. The objective of ambient aided living has been greatly advanced by recent developments in AAL technology, including e-textile, smart homes, assistive robots, and mobile, and wearable sensors [10].

### 8.3.3 Monitoring and Controlling Intelligent Self-Management and Wellbeing

Focusing on self-identified criteria that call for routine monitoring, self-management is a continual, perhaps lifelong effort [47]. The basic elements of healthcare 5.0 include actual patient self-monitoring, prompt feedback on health data, and prompt regulation of medical behavior. However, smart solutions have been created, including wristbands, smart activity trackers, smart homes, intelligent implantable devices, and smart health data systems connected to IoT, wifi, and Bluetooth, to answer the need for intelligent health monitoring. The effects of self-management or self-treatment techniques based on inaccurate or faulty data generated by invalidated apps must be carefully considered [7].

### 8.3.4 Intelligent Reminders for Treatment, Compliance, and Adherence

Online prescription and medicine delivery are both considered forms of smart therapy. Utilizing smart wearables and smart health applications, compliance and adherence to treatment may be tracked with the use of smart technology [48]. Healthcare providers will be informed whenever the patient opens the remainder, including the time, the number of tablets, and the date. A warning email will be issued to patients and healthcare providers if the patient misses their dose [49].

### 8.3.5 Personalized and Connected Healthcare

Healthcare practitioners may remotely access, interpret, and analyze health data to deliver individualized and linked healthcare utilizing bio-sensors and smart wearable devices. By utilizing cutting-edge technology to specifically meet the healthcare requirements of patients, smart digital healthcare will significantly enhance healthcare. This is accomplished by bringing together patients, medical service providers, and healthcare workers through the prompt exchange and display of relevant and accurate patient health data. The deployment of a more proactive, episodic healthcare model—completely distinct from the more reactive approach of conventional healthcare—will thus be driven by developing technologies in healthcare 5.0 [7].

## 8.4   Obstacles to the Utilize, Accept, and Implement HMI in Telemedicine

### 8.4.1   Data Inconsistency and Disintegration

Data accessibility is essential to the intelligence of digital health systems. The use of various database types and heterogeneous data formats by healthcare institutions makes it challenging to harmonize and make them interoperable, which has an impact on data collection and analysis as well as the use of modeling and optimization computer models. Heterogeneity influences the availability of data, which has an impact on the datasets needed to train healthcare AI models [7].

### 8.4.2   Standards and Interoperability are Lacking

Interoperability is hampered by the absence of standards in the creation of digital healthcare technologies [50]. Even after IoT has gathered the health data, analysis will be challenging without data format standardization. This has an impact on how patient data is shared among healthcare organizations and how smart healthcare solutions are adopted since they might not be compatible with an organization's present digital healthcare systems. Additionally, the absence of semantic compatibility in electronic medical records necessitates manual review and ontology mapping by human specialists.

### 8.4.3   Intermittent or Non-Existent Network Connectivity

Intermittent or nonexistent Internet connectivity is one of the ongoing issues with the adoption and use of digital technology in underdeveloped nations. Even if there is Internet access, connections can occasionally be unreliable [51]. However, network connections are necessary for smart healthcare [52]. Making the use of healthcare 5.0 difficult due to unstable network connectivity. The effective implementation of healthcare 5.0 may also be hampered by bandwidth problems in underdeveloped nations, unexpected communication mediums caused by biological noise in sensors, and communication range for Bluetooth technologies, sensors, and nanodevices [52].

### 8.4.4    Sensor Data Unreliability and Invalidity

If healthcare choices are made without consulting medical specialists and are based only on sensor data, this might put human lives in jeopardy. Health choices in healthcare 5.0 are based on information gathered from sensors and other nanodevices. Such sensor data must be trustworthy, genuine, and accurate to avoid serious consequences like misdiagnosis [53]. It is crucial to have validation processes in place for data gathered by sensors. However, there are not any systems in place to validate sensor data, which can prevent people from using and implementing healthcare 5.0 [7].

### 8.4.5    Privacy, Confidentiality, and Data Consistency

When working with patient data, confidentiality and privacy are essential factors to take into account. Even if technology improves healthcare, if it undermines privacy and confidentiality, it could still be avoided. Patients remain worried about privacy, quantum, and collusion assaults on their data while utilizing digital health, despite the safer blockchain employed in healthcare 4.0. Utilizing cloud-based health services presents the greatest hurdles due to security, privacy, and data leak issues. Since the communication routes used to transmit patient information may be vulnerable to hacking, smart health systems must guarantee data protection both at rest and while in transit [52].

### 8.4.6    Scalability Issues

Healthcare 5.0 solutions must be easily scalable because of the growing amount of health data being acquired through IoT and IoMT. However, because it is impractical to store enormous amounts of healthcare data on-chain due to substantial performance deterioration, blockchain-based healthcare applications have scaling problems [50].

### 8.4.7    Health Consequences

One typical component of healthcare 5.0 is sensors. However, as most sensor systems employ electrical or electromechanical sensors, they are often calibrated because of their susceptibility due to alignment issues, magnetic waves, and less dense packing [54]. Such electrical and electromechanical sensor flaws are often undesired in soft wearable robots. Because of these disadvantages, the adoption and efficient use of healthcare 5.0 systems may be impeded by the use of traditional sensors that utilize electromechanical or electrical sensors.

### 8.4.8   Clinical Challenges

Even though there are several current studies on biosensors, their practical use faces a number of difficulties. How and when to utilize biosensors in therapeutic settings, as well as where to put them on or within the human body, are some issues that need to be addressed. In contrast to deeper bodily sections, such as the heart, aorta, or other circulatory systems, where biosensors must be implanted via invasive procedures, the optimal site for a biosensor is subcutaneous tissue or superficial mucosa. Although the optimal place to implant a biosensor is in the subcutaneous tissue, the sensor's sensing capability may affect the formation of fibrous tissue between the sensor and the body, which might result in device failure [55].

### 8.4.9   Nanosensors and Biosensors Offer Health Risks

Despite the potential advantages of nanomaterials for healthcare, such as diagnosis of diseases and timely delivery of medications to the body, health professionals and researchers are concerned about inserting nanodevices with emanating signals in the human because there is a risk that such devices will endanger the human body, with such effects lasting a long time. Furthermore, prolonged interaction with silicon or silver-based nanomaterials and biosensors may cause particular body components to malfunction, gather inside organs, and restrict blood and oxygen flow. This harm to the human body is a health danger that may dissuade individuals from embracing and using biosensors and Nanosensors, thus affecting how people utilize healthcare 5.0. Furthermore, wearable sensors and nanodevices may be detected by the body as alien objects, causing it to create pathogen cells to attack them. However, the body's ongoing creation of pathogen cells may compromise the immune system [55].

### 8.4.10   Limited Computing Capability and Inefficient Energy Use

Mobile gadgets and nanodevices both have short battery lives and need to be recharged often. Additionally, the computational power of digital healthcare systems that employ nano processors with tiny transistors is constrained. Though the size of the gadget will increase, adding more nano processors can boost computing capability [55]. When the size becomes too enormous, it may not be safe to implant it within the human body.

### 8.4.11   Memory Space is Limited

The data must first be momentarily buffered by nanodevices and sensors before being sent. However, as these gadgets and sensors have limited memory and can only store one data packet at a time, it becomes difficult for them to temporarily retain all biological data. This is especially true given that additional data would be created in real time [55].

### 8.4.12   Models of Digital Technology are Rigid and Sophisticated

Static models are difficult to modify as demands change, whereas complicated models risk overfitting. Furthermore, due to their complexity, models may be difficult to employ. Overfitting is bad since it affects the accuracy of the model.

### 8.4.13   Regulatory Frameworks

Public policy, scientific knowledge, and clinical practice are never ahead of technological advancements. It is difficult for policymakers to keep up with the rate of innovation [56]. Regulations for digital technology must safeguard users' security and privacy. However, there are not any regional or global frameworks for integrating digital technologies that have been authorized by the WHO. Additionally, it is critical to have regulatory frameworks in place to guarantee the reliability and security of digital technology, products, and apps. Lack of regulatory frameworks slows down the adoption and use of digital advances, which has an impact on smart healthcare [57, 58].

### 8.4.14   Incorporated IT Infrastructure

Not simply for healthcare use, the availability of information and communications technology (ICT) infrastructure is frequently a problem in developing and low-resource nations [51]. ICT infrastructure is necessary for the acceptance and successful use of healthcare 5.0. However, in some regions of poor nations, supporting ICT infrastructure is sometimes weak or nonexistent [59]. The ICT infrastructure is crucial, particularly for the analysis of the data that has been gathered.

### 8.4.15  Misalignment with Nations' e-Health Policies

Adoption and utilization of such healthcare-related technologies may be limited by a misalignment between digital health advancements and national e-health ambitions. Innovations must be consistent with national e-health plans. Because governmental online health goals are established in e-health strategy papers, it is critical to align digital health developments with e-health plans.

### 8.4.16  Implementing Costs

The implementation of such technologies is hampered by the significant capital expenditure and specialized labor required to implement healthcare 5.0, particularly in poor nations where resources are typically scarce. For instance, running AI models demands a lot of computing power, and teaching users on how to use the new systems costs a lot of money. Although there is a case to be made that smart health will ultimately be less expensive, there are significant upfront expenses [7].

### 8.4.17  Operational and Systems Challenges

Similar to electronic medical records, telehealth platforms have associated hardware and software expenditures, and major funding is presently going toward enhancing their "quality of experience." In addition, the pressure to maintain clinical productivity through telemedicine is mounting on healthcare systems and providers. There is a concern that some of these additional expenses may be passed on to vulnerable groups like people with disabilities who would not be able to purchase them because it is uncertain how they will be commoditized. Additionally, telemedicine has not been as easily incorporated into everyday healthcare delivery in many healthcare organizations as it has in certain private practices, especially academic institutions and facilities that heavily rely on graduate medical trainees. This has had a substantial influence on groups' access to telemedicine, such as those with impairments who frequently rely on healthcare provided by trainees [60].

### 8.4.18    Logistical Challenges

Traditional in-person healthcare is frequently seamlessly linked with auxiliary medical services like diagnostic tests and lab work, which frequently need to be scheduled before such appointments. Navigating and planning such arrangements can be particularly difficult because these supplementary services still need people with disabilities to physically visit a testing location [60].

### 8.4.19    Communication Barriers

Most telemedicine platforms lack specialized capabilities to facilitate healthcare conversations for those who are blind, deaf, or have cognitive impairments. Additionally, there is a lack of patient education resources for people who have literacy and language barriers. Even if the system is properly established, telemedicine providers might not be aware of and unable to resolve accessibility concerns with their patients. Telemedicine platforms must uphold web accessibility guidelines that cater to people with impairments [60].

### 8.4.20    Unique Challenges

When utilizing telemedicine to obtain healthcare, people with disabilities could furthermore have difficulties unique to their particular impairment type. For those with intellectual disabilities, effective communication could be difficult. People with mobility or motor dexterity disabilities may have trouble engaging with the virtual interface or bio peripheral device, making tele physical evaluation problematic. For telemedicine to be effective with people who have communication disabilities, such as those who have neurological or speech issues, special solutions may be required. Similar modifications must be made to the virtual interfaces to account for the limitations of people who have mental illnesses or autism spectrum disorders. These specific challenges call for specialized solutions if disabled individuals are not to be left behind in this telemedical era [60].

## 8.5    Conclusions

The healthcare industry is using HMI innovations to more effectively offer cutting-edge medical services. Since this pandemic has revealed the potential of new digital health advances and an adaptive digital health environment, we as a discipline are now confronted with the issue of continuing to nurture and include this part of medicine. HMI in telemedicine improves patient quality of life, lessens the need for hospitalization and readmission, and thereby lowers medical costs. The medical personnel may keep an ongoing eye on patients from any location. Patients and family members can immediately get in touch with emergency medical assistance. As it incorporates cutting-edge communication technologies, protocols, and encrypted medical servers, HMI in telemedicine has the ability to completely transform the medical field. The effort and error involved in diagnosis and prescription are considerably reduced. Different physiological data are scanned by the high-end health sensors and communicated to medical experts, who make a judgement based on those results. The Internet of nano things (IoNT), for example, is being used in healthcare more and more, therefore it is anticipated that this industry will continue to expand. It is suggested to develop an intelligent medical system for ambient assisted living that takes use of big data analytics, machine learning, and the Internet of medical things. Patients, medical practitioners, and caretakers all use wearable sensors that will all be connected via software and communication technologies as part of IoMT, the future evolution of technology. While it has made access easier for some, there are still a number of obstacles that need to be thoroughly evaluated. In order to remove these obstacles moving forward, improve healthcare access, and improve results for persons with disabilities, significant, long-term changes in the technical, governmental, and legal framework are needed. Individualized solutions to particular patient and healthcare system demands must also be part of these reforms.

# References

1. Zhang, J., Lu, Q., Shi, L., The influence of telemedicine on capacity development in public primary hospitals in China: A scoping review. *Clin. eHealth* [Internet], 5, 91–9, 2022, https://doi.org/10.1016/j.ceh.2022.10.001.
2. Ahmed, A., Charate, R., Pothineni, N.V.K., Aedma, S.K., Gopinathannair, R., Lakkireddy, D., Role of digital health during coronavirus disease 2019 pandemic and future perspectives. *Card. Electrophysiol. Clin.*, 14, 1, 115–23, 2022.
3. Matusitz, J. and Breen, G.M., Telemedicine: Its effects on health communication. *Health Commun.*, 21, 1, 73–83, 2007.

4. Garai, Á., Péntek, I., Adamkó, A., Revolutionizing healthcare with IoT and cognitive, cloud-based telemedicine. *Acta Polytech. Hungarica*, 16, 2, 163–81, 2019.

5. Pramanik, P.K.D., Nayyar, A., Pareek, G., WBAN: Driving e-healthcare beyond telemedicine to remote health monitoring: Architecture and protocols [Internet], in: *Telemedicine Technologies: Big Data, Deep Learning, Robotics, Mobile and Remote Applications for Global Healthcare*, pp. 89–119, Academic Press, Cambridge, Massachusetts, Elsevier Inc., 2019. http://dx.doi.org/10.1016/B978-0-12-816948-3.00007-6.

6. Marcin, J.P., Ellis, J., Mawis, R., Nagrampa, E., Nesbitt, T.S., Dimand, R.J., Using telemedicine to provide pediatric subspecialty care to children with special healthcare needs in an underserved rural community. *Pediatrics*, 113, 1 I, 1–6, 2004.

7. Mbunge, E., Muchemwa, B., Jiyane, S., Batani, J., Sensors and healthcare 5.0: Transformative shift in virtual care through emerging digital health technologies. *Glob. Health J.* [Internet], 5, 4, 169–77, 2021, https://doi.org/10.1016/j.glohj.2021.11.008.

8. Simkó, M. and Mattsson, M.O., 5G wireless communication and health effects—A pragmatic review based on available studies regarding 6 to 100 GHz. *Int. J. Environ. Res. Public Health*, 16, 18, 1–23, 2019.

9. Li, J.P.O., Liu, H., Ting, D.S.J., Jeon, S., Chan, R.V.P., Kim, J.E. *et al.*, Digital technology, tele-medicine and artificial intelligence in ophthalmology: A global perspective. *Prog. Retin. Eye Res.* [Internet], 82, September 2020, 100900, 2021, https://doi.org/10.1016/j.preteyeres.2020.100900.

10. Syed, L., Jabeen S, S.M., Alsaeedi, A., Smart healthcare framework for ambient assisted living using IoMT and big data analytics techniques. *Future Gener. Comput. Syst.* [Internet], 101, 136–51, 2019, https://doi.org/10.1016/j.future.2019.06.004.

11. Freitas, E. and Azevedo, A., Wireless biomedical sensor networks: The technology. *Proc. 2nd World Congr. Electr. Eng. Comput. Syst. Sci.*, pp. 1–8, 2016.

12. An, B.W., Shin, J.H., Kim, S.Y., Kim, J., Ji, S., Park, J. *et al.*, Smart sensor systems for wearable electronic devices. *Polym. (Basel)*, 9, 8, 303, 2017.

13. Boatin, A.A., Wylie, B., Goldfarb, I., Azevedo, R., Pittel, E., Ng, C. *et al.*, Wireless fetal heart rate monitoring in inpatient full-term pregnant women: Testing functionality and acceptability. *PLoS One*, 10, 1, 1–12, 2015.

14. Banerjee, A., Chakraborty, C., Kumar, A., Biswas, D., Emerging trends in IoT and big data analytics for biomedical and healthcare technologies [Internet], in: *Handbook of Data Science Approaches for Biomedical Engineering*, pp. 121–152, Academic Press, Cambridge, Massachusetts, Elsevier Inc., 2019, http://dx.doi.org/10.1016/B978-0-12-818318-2.00005-2.

15. Pasluosta, C.F., Gassner, H., Winkler, J., Klucken, J., Eskofier, B.M., An emerging era in the management of Parkinson's disease: Wearable technologies and the internet of things. *IEEE J. Biomed. Health Inform.*, 19, 6, 1873–81, 2015.

16. Alexandru, A., Adriana Alexandru, C., Coardos, D., Tudora, E., Healthcare, big data and cloud computing. *WSEAS Trans. Comput. Res.* [Internet], 4, October, 123–31, 2016, https://www.researchgate.net/profile/Adriana_Alexandru/publication/310416741_Big_Data_and_Cloud_Computing/links/58836436aca272b7b443d59e/Big-Data-and-Cloud-Computing.pdf.

17. Raghupathi, W. and Raghupathi, V., Big data analytics in healthcare: Promise and potential. *Health Inf. Sci. Syst.*, 2, 1, 1–10, 2014.

18. Maini, V. and Sabri, S., Machine learning for humans. *Medium* [Internet], 1–97, 2017, https://www.dropbox.com/s/e38nil1dnl7481q/machine_learning.pdf?dl=0.

19. Lecun, Y., Bengio, Y., Hinton, G., Deep learning. *Nature*, 521, 7553, 436–44, 2015.

20. Lakhani, P. and Sundaram, B., Deep learning at chest radiography: Automated classification of pulmonary tuberculosis by using convolutional neural networks. *Radiol.* [Internet], 284, 2, 574–582, 2017, http://dx.doi.org/10.1007/978-1-4612-4700-5_3.

21. Brown, J.M., Campbell, J.P., Beers, A., Chang, K., Ostmo, S., Chan, R.V.P. *et al.*, Automated diagnosis of plus disease in retinopathy of prematurity using deep convolutional neural networks. *JAMA Ophthalmol.*, 136, 7, 803–10, 2018.

22. Li, Y., Zheng, L., Wang, X., Flexible and wearable healthcare sensors for visual reality health-monitoring. *Virtual Real. Intell. Hardw.*, [Internet], 1, 4, 411–27, 2019, http://dx.doi.org/10.1016/j.vrih.2019.08.001.

23. Bogunović, H., Montuoro, A., Baratsits, M., Karantonis, M.G., Waldstein, S.M., Schlanitz, F. *et al.*, Machine learning of the progression of intermediate age-related macular degeneration based on OCT imaging. *Investig. Ophthalmol. Vis. Sci.*, 58, 6, BIO141–50, 2017.

24. Deemer, A.D., Bradley, C.K., Ross, N.C., Natale, D.M., Itthipanichpong, R., Werblin, F.S. *et al.*, Low vision enhancement with head-mounted video display systems: Are we there yet? *Optom. Vis. Sci.*, 95, 9, 694–703, 2018.

25. Xu, K., Gupta, V., Bae, S., Sharma, S., Metamorphopsia and vision-related quality of life among patients with age-related macular degeneration. *Can. J. Ophthalmol.*, [Internet], 53, 2, 168–72, 2018, http://dx.doi.org/10.1016/j.jcjo.2017.08.006.

26. Eckardt, C. and Paulo, E.B., Heads-up surgery for vitreoretinal procedures: An experimental and clinical study. *Retina*, 36, 1, 137–47, 2016.

27. Palácios, R.M., Kayat, K.V., Morel, C., Conrath, J., Matonti, F., Morin, B. *et al.*, Clinical study on the initial experiences of french vitreoretinal surgeons with heads-up surgery. *Curr. Eye Res.* [Internet], 45, 10, 1265–72, 2020, http://dx.doi.org/10.1080/02713683.2020.1737136.

28. Naldini, L., Gene therapy returns to centre stage. *Nature*, 526, 7573, 351–60, 2015.

29. Miller, A.D., Retroviral vectors: From cancer viruses to therapeutic tools. *Hum. Gene Ther.*, 25, 12, 989–94, 2014.

30. Rogers, G.L., Martino, A.T., Zolotukhin, I., Ertl, H.C.J., Herzog, R.W., Role of the vector genome and underlying factor IX mutation in immune responses to AAV gene therapy for hemophilia B. *J. Transl. Med.*, 12, 1, 1–10, 2014.

31. Oddsson, L.I.E., Radomski, M.V., White, M., Nilsson, D., A robotic home telehealth platform system for treatment adherence, social assistance and companionship - An overview. *Proc. 31st Annu. Int. Conf. IEEE Eng. Med. Biol. Soc. Eng. Futur. Biomed EMBC 2009*, pp. 6437–40, 2009.

32. Seeland, A., Woehrle, H., Straube, S., Kirchner, E.A., Online movement prediction in a robotic application scenario. *Int. IEEE/EMBS Conf. Neural Eng. NER*, pp. 41–4, 2013.

33. Ashrafian, H., Clancy, O., Grover, V., Darzi, A., The evolution of robotic surgery: Surgical and anaesthetic aspects. *Br. J. Anaesth.* [Internet], 119, i72–84, 2017, http://dx.doi.org/10.1093/bja/aex383.

34. Sejnowski, T.J., Churchland, P.S., Movshon, J.A., Putting big data to good use in neuroscience. *Nat. Neurosci.* [Internet], 17, 11, 1440–1, 2014, http://dx.doi.org/10.1038/nn.3839.

35. Ahir, S., Telavane, D., Thomas, R., The impact of artificial intelligence, blockchain, big data and evolving technologies in coronavirus disease-2019 (COVID-19) curtailment. *Proc. - Int. Conf. Smart Electron. Commun. ICOSEC 2020*, pp. 113–20, 2019(Icosec.

36. Gordon, W.J. and Catalini, C., Blockchain technology for healthcare: Facilitating the transition to patient-driven interoperability. *Comput. Struct. Biotechnol. J.* [Internet], 16, 224–30, 2018, http://dx.doi.org/10.1016/j.csbj.2018.06.003.

37. Kunchur, P.N., Pujar, P., Hiremath, K., Budnimath, A., Bangarashetti, S., Pandurangi, V., Blockchain technology in healthcare. *JNNCE J. Eng. Manage.*, 5, 1, 15, 2021.

38. Bell, L., Buchanan, W.J., Cameron, J., Lo, O., Applications of blockchain within healthcare. *Blockchain Healthc. Today*, 1, 1–7, 2018.

39. Azaria, A., Ekblaw, A., Vieira, T., Lippman, A., MedRec: Using blockchain for medical data access and permission management. *Proc. - 2016 2nd Int. Conf. Open Big Data, OBD*, pp. 25–30, 2016.

40. Jafri, R. and Singh, S., Blockchain applications for the healthcare sector: Uses beyond Bitcoin [Internet], in: *Blockchain Applications for Healthcare Informatics: Beyond 5G*, pp. 71–92, Academic Press, Cambridge, Massachusetts, Elsevier Inc., 2022, http://dx.doi.org/10.1016/B978-0-323-90615-9.00022-0.

41. Seshadri, D.R., Davies, E.V., Harlow, E.R., Hsu, J.J., Knighton, S.C., Walker, T.A. *et al.*, Wearable sensors for COVID-19: A call to action to harness our digital infrastructure for remote patient monitoring and virtual assessments. *Front. Digit. Health*, 2, June, 1–11, 2020.

42. Gilbert, A.W., Billany, J.C.T., Adam, R., Martin, L., Tobin, R., Bagdai, S. *et al.*, Rapid implementation of virtual clinics due to COVID-19: Report and early

evaluation of a quality improvement initiative. *BMJ Open Quality,* 9, 2, 1–8, 2020.

43. Gordon, W.J., Henderson, D., Desharone, A., Fisher, H.N., Levine, D.M., Maclean, L. *et al.,* Remote patient monitoring program for hospital discharged COVID-19 patients. *Applied Clinical Informatics,* 11, 5, 792–801, 2020.

44. Peretti, A., Amenta, F., Med, P., Tayebati, S.K., Nittari, G., Telerehabilitation: Review of the state-of-the-art and areas of application corresponding author. *JMIR Rehabil. Assist. Technol.,* 4, 1–9, 2017.

45. Taiwo, O. and Ezugwu, A.E., Since January 2020 Elsevier has created a COVID-19 resource centre with free information in English and Mandarin on the novel coronavirus COVID-19. *Inform. Med. Unlocked.,* 20, 100428, 2020.

46. Demir, E., Demir, E., Köseoğlu, E., Sokullu, R., Şeker, B., ScienceDirect smart home assistant for ambient assisted living of elderly smart home assistant for ambient assisted living of elderly people with dementia people with dementia. *Proc. Comput. Sci.,* [Internet], 113, 609–14, 2017, http://dx.doi.org/10.1016/j.procs.2017.08.302.

47. Choi, Y.K., Demiris, G., Lin, S., Iribarren, S.J., Landis, C.A., Smartphone applications to support sleep self-management: Review and evaluation, *Journal of Clinical Sleep Medicine (JCSM),* 14, 10, 1783–1790, 2018.

48. Frangou, S., Sachpazidis, I., Stassinakis, A., Sakas, G., Telemonitoring of medication adherence in patients with schizophrenia. *Telemedicine Journal and e-Health,* 11, 6, 675-83, 2005.

49. Van Der Krieke, L. and Wunderink, L., E – Mental health self-management for psychotic disorders: State of the art and future perspectives. *Psychiatr. Serv.,* 65, 1, 33–49, 2014.

50. Fekih, R.B. and Lahami, M., Application of blockchain technology in healthcare: A comprehensive study [Internet], vol. 2, pp. 268–276, Springer International Publishing, Newyork, USA, Springer International Publishing, 2020, http://dx.doi.org/10.1007/978-3-030-51517-1_23.

51. Batani, J., Musungwini, S., Rebanowako, T.G., An assessment of the use of mobile phones as sources of agricultural information by tobacco smallholder farmers in Zimbabwe an assessment of the use of mobile phones as sources of Agricultural information by tobacco Smallholder farmers in Zimbabwe, *Journal of Systems Integration,* 10, 3, 1–22, 2019.

52. Pramanik, P.K.D., Upadhyaya, B.K., Pal, S., Pal, T., Internet of Things, smart sensors, and pervasive systems: Enabling connected and pervasive healthcare [Internet], in: *Healthcare Data Analytics and Management,* pp. 1–58, Academic Press, Cambridge, Massachusetts, Elsevier Inc., 2019, http://dx.doi.org/10.1016/B978-0-12-815368-0.00001-4.

53. Haleem, A., Javaid, M., Pratap, R., Suman, R., Telemedicine for healthcare: Capabilities, features, barriers, and applications. *Sens. Int.* [Internet], 100117, 2021, https://doi.org/10.1016/j.sintl.2021.100117.

54. Leal-junior, A.G., Diaz, C.A.R., Avellar, M., Jos, M., Polymer optical fiber sensors in healthcare applications: A comprehensive review, *Sensors*, 1–30, 2019.
55. Kanti, P., Pramanik, D., Solanki, A., Debnath, A., Nayyar, A., El-sappagh, S. *et al.*, Advancing modern healthcare with nanotechnology, nanobiosensors, and Internet of Nano Things: Taxonomies, applications, architecture, and challenges. *IEEE Access*, 8, 65230–66, 2020.
56. Meskó, B., Drobni, Z., Bényei, É., Gergely, B., Győrffy, Z., Digital health is a cultural transformation of traditional healthcare. *mHealth*, 3, 38–38, 2017.
57. Mahomed, S., Healthcare, artificial intelligence and the Fourth Industrial Revolution: Ethical, social and legal considerations. *S. Afr. J. Bioethics Law*, 11, 2, 93, 2018.
58. World Health Organisation, Digital technologies: Shaping the future of primary healthcare, pp. 1–12, 2018, https://www.who.int/docs/default-source/primary-health-care-conference/digital-technologies.pdf?sfvrsn=3efc47e0_2.
59. Coleman, A., Factors influencing e-health implementation by medical doctors in public hospitals in Zimbabwe, 1–9, 2016.
60. Annaswamy, T.M., Verduzco-Gutierrez, M., Frieden, L., Telemedicine barriers and challenges for persons with disabilities: COVID-19 and beyond. *Disabil. Health J.* [Internet], 13, 4, 100973, 2020, https://doi.org/10.1016/j.dhjo.2020.100973.

# 9

# Making Hospital Environment Friendly for People: A Concept of HMI

**Rihana Begum P.[1], Badrud Duza Mohammad[2]\*,
Saravana Kumar A.[3] and Muhasina K.M.[4]**

[1]*Department of Pharmacy Practice, JSS College of Pharmacy, JSS Academy of
Higher Education & Research, Ooty, The Nilgiris, Tamil Nadu, India*
[2]*Department of Pharmaceutical Chemistry, GRT Institute of Pharmaceutical
Education and Research, GRT Mahalakshmi Nagar, Tirutanni, Tamil Nadu, India*
[3]*Department of Pharmacology, GRT Institute of Pharmaceutical Education and
Research, GRT Mahalakshmi Nagar, Tirutanni, Tamil Nadu, India*
[4]*Department of Pharmacognosy, JSS College of Pharmacy, JSS Academy of Higher
Education & Research, Ooty, The Nilgiris, Tamil Nadu, India*

## Abstract

Human-machine interfaces (HMIs) are fully on-board software and hardware that enable control and communication with medical devices and processes, including cardiac defibrillators, hospital beds, infusion pumps, kidney dialysis machines, diabetes monitoring equipment, staff communication devices, ambulance switch panel, etc. The use of artificial intelligence and human-machine interference to assist medical personnel in monitoring and treating vulnerable patients in ways that enhance results while protecting privacy might help avoid many of the fatalities that occur each year because of medical mistakes. As crucial as any other element of providing effective medical treatment, maintaining a safe atmosphere shows a degree of compassion and attention to patient welfare. HMI will increase efficiency for professionals using medical products with more user-friendly operating systems. The development of an automated, adaptive system that ensures human integration into the environment and achieves mutual tune with it is made possible by HMI. This chapter primarily focuses on how the human-machine interface is making hospitals more patient-friendly in various healthcare systems. HMI systems may significantly enhance communication in medical settings using a variety of techniques. Medical staff can interact more quickly and effectively to

\**Corresponding author*: grtiperpchem3@grt.edu.in

Rishabha Malviya, Sonali Sundram, Bhupendra Prajapati and Sudarshan Kumar Singh (eds.)
*Human-Machine Interface: Making Healthcare Digital*, (247–278) © 2024 Scrivener Publishing LLC

make sure patients receive care. Additionally, HMI assists minimize clutter and concentrating on what matters most: the well-being and health of patients.

*Keywords*: Health, hospital environment, brain, ambient intelligence

## 9.1   Introduction

There are many people who were affected by the hospital environment in the U.S., including patients, their families, and hospital staff [1]. It has been shown that patients' psychological state affects healing. Stressed patients' wounds were found to heal 24% more slowly than unstressed patients' wounds, resulting in longer hospital stays [2]. In addition to increasing patient satisfaction, short hospital stays decrease healthcare costs. Patients' environments greatly influence their health outcomes, according to several scholars. There are several theoretical frameworks, including restoration theory [3], positive distraction [4], and supportive design. Supportive environments can enhance healing processes and decrease patients' stress, according to supportive design theory. An empirical review of environmental factors and patient outcomes was presented [5]. The rapid modernization of the world has resulted in a rapid evolution of intelligent systems with neural interfaces in the twenty-first century. Medical engineering and technology are especially affected by this. The availability of newer HMI interface systems has enabled real-time control of a variety of machine functions with high levels of accuracy, but simultaneous control of a machine has improved significantly in recent years [6, 7]. Human performance and nuclear safety are dependent on HMI in terms of advanced instrumentation and control systems, which contribute to human safety [7]. Using bioelectric signals produced by biochemical reactions within living cells, computers and machines can be controlled explicitly [8]. Biochemical reactions take place in thousands of cells throughout the body, resulting in ionic currents and bioelectrical signals. BCI (brain-computer interface) controls external elements using bioelectrical signals generated by the brain [9]. In recent years, wearable sensors have become increasingly popular, and touch control strategies have become more widespread. These include tapping, sliding, and combining mechanical contacts. Such devices are mostly controlled by touching the sensor's surface with the fingers, which makes HMI systems easy to use [10, 11]. It is common for most applications to utilize piezoelectric or triboelectric effects of the material in response to mechanical stimulation, which results in generating an electrical current that can be used as an input to speech commands or virtual reality glasses to control the devices [12, 13].

## 9.2   A Scenario for Ubiquitous Computing and Ambient Intelligence

In computing, the term "ambient intelligence" refers to a design that fosters and supports the Involvement and interactions of its users in an intelligent, pervasive, and unobtrusive manner. The computation must be brought into the real world so that people can interact with it just as they interact with their friends and family. Mind and computation are both psychologically and computationally impacted by this interaction. It is not possible to separate the effort involved in adapting the functionalities from those involved in adapting the subjects. Human-machine interfaces (HMIs) should be nested cognitive systems that must be capable of adapting to the individual's needs, as well as being embedded within the ambient environment. It takes a considerable amount of embedded infrastructure to interface with and participate in the real world with such a complex system. There are many possible practical solutions that can be adapted to fit different applications and users, depending on their needs.

People need to be able to directly interact with any kind of computational device in any kind of architecture by using a general architecture with computation everywhere in the environment, including clothes. A sensor network results when the environment is embedded with sensors and transducers and centralized processing and control are provided by the central unit. When you hear those words, you are still in that place, but you are in a totally different state of being than before [14, 15]. The old stadium was able to hold 50,000 people and was used for many different events, there were wild animal hunts, gladiator fights, and sea battles. On your left-hand side of vision when you turn your head, you will see a virtual reality kiosk. In order to see through the glass, you have to approach it and put on the special glasses. In just a few seconds, a 3D animation is superimposed over the scene: in no time at all, a 3D replica of the original Colosseum replaces the old stadium. Inside the stadium, there are two gladiators that fight against wild animals in front of crowds of shouting spectators. In this example, such as "immersion" or "being in" are unable to explain the technologies such as realities. In light of Slater's observation, the traditional notion of presence is no longer accepted as an adequate description of what it is to be present.

As a first sign of change, completely new interactive communication environments have emerged, including CMC and CSCW. The following three steps are:

- A greater focus on person-machine interaction and immersive virtual telepresence (IVT) may be achieved through the development of multimedia technologies.
- A new generation of mobile communications, "Beyond 3rd Generation" (B3G), has emerged beyond the Universal Mobile Telecommunications System (UMTS).
- Technology that facilitates the diffusion of intelligence around us as a result of the development of networks.

A new vision emerges when these trends are integrated within the paradigm of "being aware there." Ambient Intelligence helps users interact with their surroundings in a pervasive and unobtrusive manner.

## 9.3   Emergence of Ambient Intelligence

An Ambient Intelligence (AmI) vision has been presented to the European Commission by the Information Society Technologies Advisory Group. The vision envisions a pervasive network of intelligent devices that will provide information collection, processing, and transport. To the European Commission, the Information Society Technologies Advisory Group presented AmI's vision. A fundamental role for virtual reality technologies, in particular immersive Virtual Telepresence (IVT) and wireless technologies, in enabling AmI to meet its needs for natural user interfaces, as well as ubiquitous communication, will be played by VR technologies. The AmI is expected to be able to be controlled naturally and in a personalized way through voice interactions and gesture inputs in the future [16]. Additionally, it will facilitate communication between electronic devices and users while providing the network's backbone. Besides technology, AmI requirements encompass a wide range of other factors. There are several characteristics that will make AmI an acceptable technology to society at some point in the future as identified by ISTAG.

## 9.4   Framework for Advanced Human-Machine Interfaces

Human-machine interfaces (HMIs), such as mice and keyboards, are systems that allow low-level interaction between man and machine. While advanced HMIs move toward a new concept of the interface, they offer a high level of interaction. In addition to the introduction of new topics pertaining to the optimization of communication processes, the report introduces a series of new items related to (Ambient Intelligence) applications. A human-machine interface combined with AHMI can be used to develop a systematic, automated, and adaptive system aimed at ensuring that human beings are integrated into their surrounding environments, resulting in attunement (mutual tuning) between the individuals and their surroundings. It is through attuning that the system is capable of both inducing, acquiring, and processing sensitive signals and adapting its actions based to improve the effectiveness or comfort of the services provided [17].

A speech recognition system can help illustrate this concept, but it can also enhance it in order to identify frustrations or fatigue in different tasks through the understanding of voice modifications. Videoconferencing can be used to improve communication with other people by using facial expressions collected during the conversation, for example, to identify the needs of the other person. A HMI's greatest asset, according to the authors, is the capability of observing and identifying people's psychophysiological states to improve communication and the execution of tasks. As a rule, we believe that such a highest-range interaction is essential to achieving a real-time adaptation to human needs by identifying the patient's condition as well as the important role that biosignal monitoring plays in the realization of such a highest-range interaction in order to establish the high-level interaction. A new scenario describes the possibilities of exploiting AHMI when the human is aware that the machine is able to comprehend what he is saying and can work with him in achieving a common goal.

New interfaces with ambient intelligence can be viewed in this context as autonomously negotiating between user needs and interface capabilities. A useful interface could, for example, include the following distinguishing features, among others:

- Interactivity can be achieved in two ways
- Physiological and nonverbal communication signals are processed and interpreted.

This context makes it particularly important for the user to need the interface configuration, which includes two types of channels. Input/Output architectures are strictly determined by context and application: stretching biosignals monitoring can provide enough information in a simple AmI environment; however, to integrate an artificial cognitive system into an AmI environment requires recording voice, analyzing facial expressions, and analysing biosignals, among other channels.

## 9.5    Brain Computer Interface (BCI)

### 9.5.1    The BCI System: An Introduction

It is important to note that the Brain Computer Interface (BCI) is one of the newer forms of human-machine communication that is utilizing the channel between the brain and the outside world, as opposed to relying on the normal output pathways of the central nervous system, such as peripheral nerves and muscles. This creates an active communication path center of the brain detect the outside world. This activity in various parts of the brain has been shown to be correlated with the subject's intention or his or her interactions with the out of the world: for example, when attention is caught, the P300 importance occurs, then it is associated with an event triggered by a cognitive stimulus.

This phenomenon is thought to be exploited by BCI equipment to detect brain activity changes. There are two types of patterns: exogenous and endogenous. Exogenous patterns can be induced by a specific external stimulus, and endogenous patterns can be induced by autonomic processes, such as concentration or imagination. In essence, there is a fundamental principle whereby those variations are associated with commands that can be executed by computers or similar devices that interact with the outside world. There has been a growing interest in BCIs for defence purposes since the 1970s. In terms of gathering throughput and reliability, the organization was unable to drive an aircraft or activate a weapon system. Researchers are investigating the newest messages of brain-computer interfaces in other areas, and they are connecting the brain directly to the outside environment via a direct physical connection, and a brain-computer interface allows the brain to communicate directly with the outside environment. A BCI, however, has the most intriguing and important application for persons with disabilities right now. Since there are many other technologies that can increase the residual abilities of humans with severe disorders, in this BCI was developed as a tool to assist people with such disabilities. In spite of the fact that there are many current research projects in the field of behavioural computer interaction aimed at probing or exploring brain functions from an interaction perspective, Specifically, the interaction between different brain areas and their dynamic mechanics, there are several potential applications in the realm of advanced communication that could be explored using BCI.

### 9.5.2   The Characteristics of a BCI

#### 9.5.2.1   Dependent and Independent BCIs

Brain-computer Interface (BCI) is a type of communication system that avoids the normal output pathways of the CNS, such as peripheral nerves and muscular tissue, for sending messages. BCIs based on EEG activity, for instance, encode messages in EEG activity. BCIs provide their users with alternative methods of interacting with the world. There are two types of BCIs: dependent and independent. BCIs that are dependent on brain activity do not utilize brain's usual external message to transmit messages. By looking directly at a letter, the user can select a letter through one dependent BCI. A particular letter flashes higher visual evoked potentials (VEP) than other letters do when the scalp over visual cortex is stimulated. Here, the brain's output channel is the EEG signal, but the signal is generated based on the gaze direction, and therefore depends on the extraocular muscles and the cranial nerves that activate them.

In essence, dependent BCIs work by detecting messages through alternative routes other than the brain's natural output channels. For example, eye position is monitored rather than gaze direction, which is detected through measuring the EEG of the subject. In some cases, a dependent BCI can be valuable even if it does not create an independent communication channel for the brain.

#### 9.5.2.2   Motor Disabilities: Options for Restoring Function

Neuromuscular channels that connect the brain to the outside world can be disrupted by a variety of disorders. Many diseases impair the neural pathways that control muscles or the muscles themselves, including Amyotrophic lateral sclerosis (ALS), brainstem strokes, spinal cord injuries, cerebral palsy, muscular dystrophy, multiple sclerosis, and numerous others. There are nearly two million people suffering from these diseases in the United States alone, and there are many more in other countries as well. The ability to move their eyes and breathe may be completely lost to some people, and they may be totally unable to communicate with each other. Individuals who are locked in can benefit from modern life-support systems, even if they are unable to move, extending and escalating their disabilities' social, economic, and personal burdens. Currently, there are three options for restoring function when there are no methods to repair the damage caused by these disorders. Firstly, the remaining pathways must be made more capable. Paralyzed muscles may be replaced by muscles that are under voluntary control. Hand movements and eye movements can also be used to make a synthetic speech by patients largely paralyzed by massive brain lesions. Restoring function to muscles is achieved by detour around broken neural pathways.

By controlling direct electrical stimulation, electromyographic (EMG) activity can restore useful movement to patients with spinal cord injuries. A direct brain–computer interface (BCI) for transmitting messages and commands to the external world is the final option for restoring function to those with motor impairments. Various methods for monitoring brain activity could be used as BCIs. A number of other methods are available, including electroencephalography (EEG), positron emission tomography (PET), magnetic resonance imaging (MRI), and optical imaging. The technical challenges and high costs associated with MEG, PET, fMRI, and optical imaging remain despite these advancements. Due to their reliance on blood flow for their time constants, PET, fMRI, and optical imaging are not appropriate for rapid communication because they are dependent on blood flow. Communication and control by non-muscular means are generally accomplished using electroencephalograms and related techniques, which have relatively short time constants, are adaptable to most environments, and require relatively cheap and simple equipment, enabling us to develop a practical non-muscular control and communication device.

### 9.5.3   Components of BCI

The BCI functions in the same way as any other type of communication or control system, with inputs (e.g. electrophysiological activity from the user), outputs (e.g. device commands), components that translate the inputs into outputs, and a protocol that determines the onset, offset, and timing of the operation.

### 9.5.4   Structure of the Human Brain and Its Signals

There are about 100 billion neurons in the human brain, which is the most complex of all the body's organs [18]. Using our five senses, we are able to find information about the outside world by evaluating information that comes into our brains. In different situations, the body obeys instructions to take the appropriate action. With the help of our speech and facial expressions, the brain is able to react to the surroundings and control the emotions, thoughts, and behavior of our bodies. It also controls the movements of our limbs and other voluntary and involuntary movements that occur within our bodies. In addition to speech, perception, and motor control, active in the brain, different parts of the body perform different functions [19]. Changing the connections in the brain is possible if it has been injured or has any problems so that signals can be routed along other neural pathways. In order to understand what this means, we must first understand the concept of neuroplasticity. There is no doubt that brain plasticity is one of the most crucial components of the recovery of normal brain function. The definition explains that it is the ability of the central nervous system to adapt its own organization and function based on its own requirements [20, 21]. In order to recover a particular brain function, a variety of mechanisms are employed, including unmasking, sprouting, super-sensitive denervation, and denervation [22–25]. Figure 9.1 illustrates the architecture of brain.

There are several working mechanisms of brain plasticity, including changes in neurochemical function, receptor function, and neurostructural function of different areas of the brain which are characterized by distinctive functional characteristics [26–28]. As a result of this, the brain generates multiple types of signals, each of which has a unique set of properties. Different types of applications can be made use of these signals in

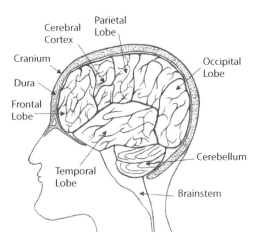

**Figure 9.1** Brain architecture.

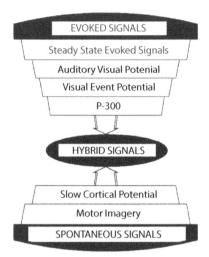

**Figure 9.2** Signals in the brain.

different ways. In addition to evoked signals and spontaneous signals, there are other types of control signals that exist as well: hybrid signals. Figure 9.2 shows the pathway of signals in the brain

### 9.5.4.1   A Signal That is Evoked

During the process of responding to an external stimulus, certain parts of the nervous system, including the brain, produce electrical signals. One of the signals that are evoked is P300, a steady-state evoked potential called, a visual events potential called [29]. After an ensuing visual or auditory stimulus, the peak of P300 occurs approximately 300 ms later. In response to the effects of sound frequencies impinging on the cortex, AVP signals are emitted from the cortex portion. This produces the same frequency potential difference. During visual stimulation, an evoked potential is generated in the cerebral cortex, which can be detected by visually evoked potentials (VEPs) and side-evoked potentials (SSVEPs) [30].

### 9.5.4.2   Spontaneous Signals

A spontaneous signal is generated without any external stimulation by the subject [31]. Our brain produces two types of spontaneous signals: Slow cortical potential, and motor imagery. EEG signals are generated by motor imagery in a specific area of the motor cortex as a result of the subject's motor intentions. These SCPs are recorded in several seconds using an event-relate design and have a frequency of less than 1 Hz. 0.05 seconds to 10 seconds later, a SCP appeared in response to voltage changes in the cerebral cortex [32, 33].

### 9.5.4.3 Hybrid Signals

Hybrid signals are generally understood to comprise a combination of spontaneous and evoked signals. They are used in order to overcome some of the disadvantages associated with the use of either signal alone [34–36].

## 9.6 Development in HMI Technologies and Their Applications

A more complex HMI enables more interaction, advancing the concept of an interface into a new field. A human-machine interface (HMI) is entered to improve low-level interaction between humans and machines, including the use of a mouse and keyboard. There were numerous new topics introduced related to enhancing the communication process and developing applications in order to make it more effective and efficient. According to this viewpoint, new interfaces with ambient intelligence must behave as an expert autonomous negotiation between the requirements and potential of the user. Both electromyography and electroencephalography were important techniques for seeing and capturing bioelectrical signals [37].

A process of recording and analysing electromyographic impulses that cause body movement during muscle contractions is called electromyography (EMG). Electrooculography, which analyses the corner-retinal static potential between the front back of the human eye, is another essential technique for signal recording. These signals can be used to control motorized wheelchairs by a paralyzed person [37]. A machine could get numerous instructions from these signals when they are combined [38]. Acquisition of signals and technical processes in HMI. The many signal acquisition techniques used in HMI technology were used to record the various physiological signals [39]. Invasive procedures implant electrodes in the brain's cerebral cortex through a craniotomy. A semi-invasive procedure was used to implant the devices beneath the scalp's skin on the exterior of the Gray matter. ECoG helps detect neurophysiological illness in persistent epilepsy patients. Non-invasively measuring brain activity through intact skulls was achieved using near-infrared light, which penetrates biological tissue. Optimal spectroscopy describes this. The active electrode was a better non-invasive solution for capturing high-quality bio-signals due to their analog front-end power amplifier. The EEG signals were feeble; thus 50,000 cortical neurons must activate synchronously to produce measurable signals.

## 9.7   Techniques of Signal Acquisition and Processing Applied to HMI

A variety of physiological signals can be captured using different acquisition techniques in HMI technology, which allows the technology to display them in real-time. In the main, these techniques can be classified as invasive, semi-invasive, and non-invasive in terms of their methods [40]. A craniotomy is a surgical procedure that involves inserting electrodes in an opening of a small size in the skull to stimulate the brain. Using electrodes implanted in the brain, signals from the cerebral cortex are recorded. A small portion of grey matter does not need to be implanted in immense techniques. Necessary placed underneath the scalp skin [41–46]. A minimally invasive surgery known as transgeival implant therapy involves inserting an implant into the brain tissue. Due to the innovative design of the mucoperiosteal flap, there is no need to reflect it from its place, and the blood supply is not halted to the tissues, which enables a faster and less painful surgical procedure. A non-BCI surgical implant technique, this technique assesses memory dysfunctions in patients using three types of electrodes, namely electrodes Subdural strip electrodes are implanted into the foramen ovale, and depth electrodes are stereotactically implanted. To determine whether there are memory issues, electrodes are located in the cerebral cortex [47, 48]. Electroencephalography (ECoG) can be used for certain purposes, such as evaluating the brain and determining whether related brain disorders are present. Neurophysiological disorders, such as chronic epilepsy, can be detected through electrocardiograms, which are well-known in the field [49–51]. A non-invasive method of placing electrodes on the scalp or skeletal muscles increases contact area and conductivity between them and the skin. In order to increase their skin, contact area, electrodes are often coated with conductive gel. Human brain activity can be assessed non-invasively with near-infrared light, a wavelength that is relatively good at penetrating biological tissue. It is known as optical spectroscopy, and it involves measuring the wavelengths of light [52]. Because active electrodes are equipped with an analogue front-end amplifier circuit, they are a more non-invasive option for capturing high-quality biosignals because the signals can be recorded without causing any damage to the patient [53–55]. In terms of temporal and microscopic spatial resolution, this method is more effective than the invasive technique. Non-invasive techniques, however, are much easier to perform and less complex than invasive techniques, which are more complex, expensive, and take longer to perform. The amplitude and frequency of almost all bioelectrical signals are low, regardless of the technique used to acquire the signal. As such, in order to make use of bioelectrical signals in a variety of applications, it is necessary to amplify their data and extract their features.

Eye movements in various directions can be detected using EOG signals in different directions. Eye problems are caused by the different electrical potentials between the cornea and retina a very low voltage is used to generate EOG signals (+0.40 mV to +1.00 mV). Consequently, most EOG signals have a very low voltage. EOG signals are generally recorded using patch electrodes and then amplification of the signals is carried out in stages such as pre-amplification and post-amplification after the signals have been recorded. There is a filtering process applied to the signals to remove the noise present in them that is designed specifically for electronic circuit boards. The filtered signals are then fed to the Arduino board that matches their impedance. The encoder converts analog signals to digital and sends them to the transmitter. Once it has been converted to digital form, it is sent to the receiver for actuating the motor on the device. EOG signals have a definite pattern despite the fact that their use is still in its infancy. They can readily be incorporated into a variety of HMI-based system management applications [56, 57].

Heartbeats are recorded using electrocardiograms (ECGs) for diagnosing heart problems. ECG data can be collected using a non-invasive electrode that is commonly made of silver chloride. During electrochemical reactions between the electrode material and the skin, the electrochemical reaction causes the electrode material to osmate from the skin and monitor the heart's electrical activity. In the case of positive ions drawn by electrodes, negative ions drawn by electrolytes are repelled by negative ions drawn by electrodes, and vice versa. When an electrode and an electrolyte exchange ion, the electrolyte functions as a gel or skin. The exchange rate of ions between electrodes and electrolytes depends on their chemical equilibrium [58].

It is important to note that the output of the ECG is in mV. Maximum noises accompany this that may be attributed to a variety of factors, including unwanted electrode movements, a variation in the moisture content of the skin, a variation in the temperature, and a condition in which gel leaks [59]. Analytical filtering and then amplification of the signals are always necessary to remove these noises from the system. There are usually two stages involved in the amplification of signals. The signal-to-noise ratio can be adversely affected if amplification is performed in just one stage, as the amplitude of unwanted noises can increase. Consequently, analogue to digital converters is capable of producing high signal-to-noise ratios (SNR) and signal amplitudes required by analogue to digital converters [60].

## 9.8    Hospital-Friendly Environment for Patients

### 9.8.1    Physiological Study State

Patients' physiological states were examined in three level 2 studies.

#### 9.8.1.1    Nature

One level 2 study found that 85 surgery patients' physiological conditions were improved by indoor plants. temperature, respiration rate, diastolic blood pressure, and heart rate. Researchers also investigated the effects of a ceiling fixture with a picture of the sky on patients in a level 2 experiment. Given that patients spend the majority of their time in bed, it would make sense to hang a natural image from the ceiling. The researchers discovered that the experimental group's systolic blood pressure was greater than the control groups.

#### 9.8.1.2    Music

According to another level 2 study, music can help lower diastolic blood pressure.

### 9.8.2    Pain State

Some environment's factors interrupt patient comfort were given below.

#### 9.8.2.1    Nature

An indoor plant study at level 2 looked at how indoor plants affect patient outcomes. There was a reduction in analgesic use among patients exposed to plants compared to the control group. It has also been demonstrated that even images of nature can had a positive impact on patient outcomes in several other studies. Unexpectedly, the experimental group used analgesics more frequently than the control group did. Although the experimental group reported less pain, the other group reported more pain. There may had differences in the subject's acuity levels that caused this inconsistency. A study identified image types that most affect pain based on behavioral and physiological indicators.

### 9.8.2.2    Natural Light

Two ICUs with varied degrees of natural light were examined for pain levels using a level 2 study; there was no statistically significant difference between the two for pain perception [61].

### 9.8.3    Sleep

#### 9.8.3.1    Nature Images

Nature images were examined at level 2 for their effect on sleep. Experimentally, the sky was pictured on the ceiling and exposed to patients. There was lower quality of sleep and greater use of sleep medication in the experimental group than standard. As per hypothesis, this finding was not consistent. Additional studies need to be conducted to minimize the acuity level since the level was not measured.

### 9.8.4    Patient Experience

There are two categories of patient experience: patient satisfaction and interaction.

#### 9.8.4.1    Patient's Satisfaction

Understanding the importance of three forms of patient satisfaction, i.e., nature, music and artificial ambient light.

##### 9.8.4.1.1    Nature

A level 2 study found that patients who stayed in rooms with houseplants expressed greater satisfaction than those who did not. In one level 2 investigation, patients who remained in rooms with ceiling murals of nature expressed 15 % higher levels of satisfaction with their circumstances than those who slept in rooms without any murals.

### 9.8.4.1.2    Music

In such a level 2 investigation, music was demonstrated to improve patient happiness. A subset of surgery patients received twenty minutes of music therapy twice daily. Patients who have been exposed to music reported feeling more satisfied than those who were not. However, there was no statistically significant change.

### 9.8.4.1.3    Artificial Ambient Light

Patient's satisfaction can be increased by artificial light. Level 3a study examined patient's satisfaction with a new paediatric emergency room equipped with a color-changing overhead light, LED screens, and ambient light to patient's satisfaction in an older ED without these features. Several measures of satisfaction with care were higher in the new ED than in the other group [62, 63].

### *9.8.4.2    Interaction*

Studying three forms of interaction, two level 2 studies and two level 3 studies investigated doctor-patient; family-patient also staff-family interactions [62, 63].

### 9.8.4.2.1    Room Brightness and Doctor–Patient Interaction

At level 2, researchers discovered that room illumination could affect patients' intentions to disclose themselves. Eighty-five participants were given either a low-threat or a high threat version of each scenario. The participants were then shown one of two images of an examination room, one being more lit up than the other. To gauge the participants' intentions to self-disclose, a survey was created.

### 9.8.4.2.2    Patients' Room and Family–Patient Interactions

It has been established that patient-family interaction and social support are impacted by hospital environment design [64]. In an advanced study, an Intensive facility with various designs was contrasted. Patients spend more time with the family in the patient-centred ward than in other group. In Intensive care unit with patient-centric architecture, patients and family can interact in a variety of ways.

### 9.8.4.2.3 Interactions of Family-Staff and Layouts

Family involvement in the treatment process can be advantageous, but interruption caregivers can make them more stressed. Large interaction between the families and staff were noticed during a level 3a study that was conducted in a setting that was intended to encourage family involvement [65]. Families' interruptions of caregiving might cause therapy delays and lower efficacy, according to nurses.

## 9.9 Applications of HMI for Patient-Friendly Hospital Environment

### 9.9.1 Healthcare and Engineering

HMI technology is impacting neuroscience, neurosurgeon, psychiatry, clinical applications, and rehabilitation engineering. Sensor-based HMI technology saves lives in life-supporting systems as well as during haemodialysis for renal patients. HMI-based home measurements that reliably track chronic pressure, systolic rate, plus systolic hypertension can assess cardiovascular prognosis. The existing HMI technology might be combined with the EMG and EEG bio-signals a complex mechanical drive contains several degrees of freedom that can be used to control prosthetic devices. In order to provide separate controls for any manipulations that were theoretically possible based on the user's preferences, these prosthetics either use neural signals produced by muscular contractions and relaxations. A new developing system is developed with the specific purpose of providing care and support to the patients after joint replacement surgeries during a critical period after the operation, and after surgery, it provides support and assistance in daily living activities by monitoring the home environment using sensor technology [66].

A prosthetic device controlled by the HMI technology that is currently available for controlling prosthetic devices can consist of an intricate mechanical system drive with multiple degrees of freedom. EEGs and EMGs generated are used to control these prosthetic devices independent of the user's intentions [67, 68]. As an additional tool for diagnosing and treating various diseases of the intracranial and extracranial vascular systems, electromagnetic, metabolic, and electrical neuroimaging techniques based on BCI are applied during motor, perceptual, and cognitive tasks by imaging their structural and functional elements. By utilizing BCI in the creation of sensory substitution systems, it is now possible to impart hearing, sight, and touch senses that are lost to people with impairments to the senses of hearing, seeing, and touching. Assistive devices such as wheelchairs controlled by EEG and autonomous humanoid robots such as the ARMAR, which consists of the end effectors and arms are identical, each possessing a range of motion of 20 degrees of freedom and capable of performing tasks in sync with humans, are other examples of HMIs [69–72]. Functional magnetic resonance imaging, also known as fMRI, is a type of magnetic resonance imaging scanning technique that detects changes in blood flow in order to determine how the brain responds to changes in hemodynamic conditions, thereby measuring the metabolic activity of the brain. Aside from this, it is also used for detecting and treating various disorders of the brain, as well as other MRI techniques cannot detect these types of diseases [73]. In radiology, PET is a procedure that is used for the examination of body tissues under specific conditions. Currently, PET is commonly used in the fields of neurology, cardiology, and oncology, and these are three of the most common applications for it. In the PET examination process, a radioactive substance called radionuclide is injected into the patient's bloodstream, emitted by the radionuclide, which then emits positrons and gamma rays. The radionuclides are monitored using special apparatus which analyzes the gamma rays as they emerge [74].

This phenomenon is known as biomagnetism, where the magnetic fields generated through the action of diverse organs produce various electrical currents in the body and are combined with the magnetic property of the human body constituent in order to produce magnetic fields. A magnetic cardiogram (MCG) is a type of biomagnetic signal that is generated by magnetic field activity in the heart and a magnetoencephalogram (MEG) is a type of biomagnetic signal that is generated in the brain according to the activity of the heart [75]. It has become a common practice to evaluate bio-impedance signals in order to monitor and analyze Bio-impedance signals are used to assess the electrical properties of biological tissues in order to determine a person's health status. Bio-impedance signals are being used as one of the methods to assess the composition and prognosis of the human body in clinical diagnostics of the body based on equations commonly used in predicting the outcomes of the clinical trial [76].

Surgeons use three-dimensional models based on HMI software as well as two-dimensional displays to evaluate the various anatomical studies. The use of virtual reality and augmented reality has enabled surgeons to diagnose and treat patients' anatomical conditions in a more precise manner [77, 78]. Modern healthcare and rehabilitation engineering are making use of human-machine interfaces as a way to interface humans and medical devices.

### 9.9.2    Controls for Robotic Surgery and Human Prosthetics

Through a combination of tactile and 3D acceleration sensors and contemporary brain control technology-based BCI systems, which use EEG patterns and features to create a real-time communication system, it controlled the motion of prosthetic hands. For improved control with prosthetic hands, the implanted electrode method produces greater results. The technique was first applied to animals then to humans using minimally invasive surgery. A surface EMG control was unable to allow the volunteer to manipulate two degrees of freedom simultaneously and intuitively using this technique. Using a sequence of data frames containing sets of varied postures by a real hand, as well as EMG data, was another cutting-edge technique for controlling prosthetic hands. It has been discovered that researchers have developed a new method to control highly dexterous prosthetic hands by employing functional control techniques and tactics.

There are certain surgical procedures that can be used to provide inherent control to an advanced prosthetic hand, such as targeted muscle reinnervation (TMR). An enhance-repair technique is one in which the residual nerves that remain from the amputated limb are used to re-enervate new muscle targets that had previously been deactivated [79]. Normally, tactile feedback is provided to the advanced prosthetic hands in order to aid in the recovery of the senses of force, temperature, vibration, etc., which are normally lost in the absence of such feedback [80]. Among the advanced prosthetic hands currently being developed, the most advanced ones have high functionality as well as better control systems that have distinct mechanical characteristics [81]. It has been found that anthropomorphic prosthetic hands can be developed in many ways, including Bebionic hands, Bebionic hands v2, iLimb pulses, Southampton hands, Michelangelo hands, Mero hands, and Vincent's hands [82–84].

Functional control strategies and techniques have been developed for highly dextrous prosthetic hands. Patients have to endure cumbersome exercise procedures before they can learn how to use a dextrous prosthetic hand, which leads to the need for new and better training/learning strategies based on HMIs in order to overcome the disadvantage of cumbersome exercises. As a result, training amputees through the use of virtual reality simulators is a recently emerging technique [85, 86]. As for the success rate of pattern recognition based on EMG data (more than 90%), it is consistent across multiple modes of motion. By using this type of control, a prosthetic hand can be controlled with a greater degree of freedom, providing better control [87]. Surface EMG has the disadvantage of being noisy and subject to other conditions such as wrong electrode displacement, fatigue, sweating, and a decrease in gel effectiveness due to the presence of these factors, among others [88, 89]. A combination of surface EMG measurements and inertial measurements for developing prosthetic hands enables multi-DOF functionality to be achieved and improved performance characteristics substantially without requiring excessive amounts of sensors in the hands. There is a task load index that has been developed by NASA's human performance research group, which measures workload after a task has been completed. In this questionnaire, the surgeons' subjective cognitive load is assessed by comparing baseline, mono and dual tasks they encounter during surgical procedures. A six-part index, based on six subscales, gives information about mental demands, time demands, physical demands, individual performance, frustration, and effort. HMI technology will enhance prosthetic devices' freedom and control, enabling them to have greater degrees of freedom and greater control over their movements. In human-machine interfaces, current technology does not allow us to replicate the exact function and working characteristics of human limbs.

### 9.9.3   Sensory Substitution System

A biosensor, an electronic coupling, as well as an activator are the three components that make up a perceptual replacement's technology. An electronic coupler system is in charge of organizing the activation of a stimulator, and a sensor facilitates the conversion of a specific type of radiation into impulses that can be interpreted by that system. By using the TVSS system, blind participants were able to recognise simple objects, including moving ones, and had other perceptions like depth estimations, magnification, viewpoint parallax, etc. The prototype is made up of a progressive set-up that connects a computer to a head-fixed camera and headphones while simultaneously recording and translating a visual scene into audio signals. Users of perceptual substitute devices had three main requirements: portable, flexibility, and lightness. Tiny size, low energy consumption, and convenience of use are other considerations.

By using auditory substitution devices, people who have impaired hearing can be able to hear effectively for the first time in their lives. Using the conceptual model of the retina and the inverse linear model of the cochlea, a rough model of auditory substitution has been developed. Using headphones, a camera mounted on a head and a computer are arranged in progressive arrangements to capture, convert, and hear visual images [90]. As a result of postural wobbling and an unstable gait, individuals with bilateral vestibular hypofunction have difficulties walking in dim light and on uneven terrain because they have an inability to maintain their balance.

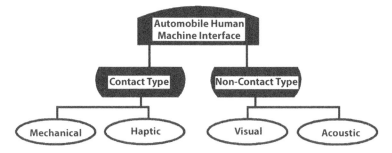

**Figure 9.3** Human-machine interface system.

In addition to enhancing the brain and body coordination, vestibular sensory substitution gives high levels of stability and efficiency. By combining visual, tactile, and proprioceptive systems, a bilateral substitution system identifies unique motion features on the body and reduces or eliminates defects in these motion features in order to eliminate or reduce deficiencies [91]. Figure 9.3 illustrates the detailed Human-Machine interface system.

The use of tactile pin arrays in advanced virtual reality sensory devices facilitates physical contact with the virtual environment in a non-visual manner. In this manner, tactile pin arrays allow the virtual environment to appear as though it is physically touching the user [92]. The HMI technology allows blind, deaf, and mute people whose vision, hearing, or speaking abilities have been significantly impaired due to birth injuries or diseases access to sensory substitute devices, which can help them partially or completely regain sight, hearing, and speaking abilities.

### 9.9.4 Mobile Robots and Wheelchairs With Neural Interfaces

EOG-driven wheelchairs, which use eye movements as steering and control signals, are becoming more and more common in society, particularly among those who are physically challenged. To execute the commands in an autonomous wheelchair, an interface between a bio-signal amplifier and SIMULINK software processes. Injured or physically disabled individuals can use the mobile exoskeleton device to stand up, walk, and engage in other bodily functions after being injured or suffering from various physical conditions. Additionally, it is used in military contexts or during relief efforts for natural disasters to increase the wearer's capacity to lift heavier loads and lower their level of fatigue.

A portable medical exoskeleton device allows people with various physical disabilities to stand up, walk, and perform a variety of movements in any direction with HMI [93]. These mobile robots and exoskeleton systems may enable individuals who are physically disabled or suffer from congenital diseases, such as Down syndrome, to improve their bodily function. An exoskeleton and a mobile robot equipped with a human-machine interface have been suggested as a way to enhance an individual's safety in difficult situations, such as explosive detection and disposal, in order to improve their overall safety level. Military and disaster management organizations also employ this product for the purpose of increasing load-carrying capacity and reducing fatigue levels among individuals who are wearing these devices.

### 9.9.5    Technology on Biometric System

Automated devices can be used to identify individuals by registering several physiological or behavioral characteristics of a person. Among them are the fingerprint, the iris, the voice, the facial, the retina, the handwriting, the vein pattern in the hand, the palm print, DNA, the signature, etc [94–96]. Biometric data recognition systems are designed to prevent multiple users from using the same application and to maintain the confidentiality of the application [97]. Ideally, the characteristics of a biometric should be universality, distinctiveness, attributability, performance, acceptability, dodging and permanence. A person's distinctiveness resides in the distinguishing biometrics characteristics that make them unique among all human beings, whereas universality refers to the biometrics characteristics that all humans have in common, which make identification and enrolment of every individual possible. It is usually more convenient and easier to accurately scan fingerprints by scanning the pupil or retina as opposed to scanning the iris or retina in most cases. The fingerprints can, however, be inaccurately scanned if dirty hands are used or if fingers are improperly positioned on the sensor. It is also possible for fingerprints to become dull over time as a result of wear out caused by age, working conditions, or injury [98, 99].

Electrocardiograms (ECGs), also known as heart rate variability signals (ECGs), are emerging biometric signals that are derived from an individual's unique physical characteristics, such as chest geometry, chest size, and electrolyte concentrations, which impart distinct rhythms between individuals [100]. The various bioelectrical signals, including the EEG, the EOG, the MMG and the GSR, are able to be used as biometric traits because it has unique identification attributes [101]. Hence, there is still a long way to go before biometric devices will be able to perform more effectively. There is a great deal of concern about the errors that can occur during the scanning of the different biometrics, as well as the reduction of delay time.

## 9.9.6    Enhancement of Cognition Level

This is a measure of a person's cognitive ability. This is their ability to assess, compute, and complete any task that requires the use of brain and motor skills using their mental and physical capabilities. The use of both medication and meditation is currently able to enhance a person's cognitive abilities in a number of ways as of right now. In order to elevate the brain functions, it is necessary to promote cognitive processing and to improve the structure of the brain through mindfulness meditation [102]. There are a number of substances and drugs that can boost cognitive function, and nootropics are one of them. Generally speaking, these drugs can be categorized into three types, which are methylphenidate, modafinil, and piracetam [103].

Usually, Modafinil is prescribed to patients who suffer from chronic sleepiness or narcolepsy. Furthermore, it can also aid in increasing alertness levels and reducing fatigue [104]. Memory, attention, and other functions of the brain are improved when humans use piracetam. Piracetam is a chemical drug. It is also used to treat diseases such as vertigo, epilepsy, dyslexia and sickle cell anaemia, in addition to treating vertigo, epilepsy, dyslexia and sickle cell anaemia. A legal status as a dietary supplement for the drug has not yet been issued by the Food and Drug Administration of the United States [105]. Additionally, to these three types of cognitive enhancement drugs, there are some other types of drugs that are currently being used to treat various disorders caused by various types of brain disorders, including oxiracetam, acetylcholine precursors, choline alfoscerate, citicoline, acetyl-carnitine, lecithin, phospholipase A2, docosahexaenoic acid, choline alfoscerate, citicoline, acetyl-carnitine, phospholipase A2, choline alfoscerate, citicoline, acetyl carnitine, acetylcarnitine, lecithin, citosahexa [106].

Thousands of cognitive enhancements and stimulations can be made possible using microelectromechanical systems on chip combined with brain chip interfaces [107, 108]. The brain can be stimulated with cranial chips that are surgically implanted for various purposes, including the cure of several diseases and illnesses [109]. Field-effect transistors made of electrolyte-oxide-metal-oxide-semiconductor can be used to investigate many aspects of brain functioning [110]. A new generation of HMI technology may transform everything when nanotechnology and microtechnology are used directly with the human body. It is estimated that HMI technology will enhance the cognitive abilities of anyone to an extremely high level in the next few years by enhancing their cognitive abilities to an extremely high level.

### 9.9.7   fNIRS-EEG Multimodal BCI as a Future Perspective

During the fundamental research on detecting subject intentions and recovering communication, researchers have found that functional near-infrared spectroscopy (fNIRS) EEG-based BCI systems represent the majority of the actual generations. In other words, electroencephalography or electrocorticography is the base technology used, but several criticisms exist both on the hardware and software side of these systems. Actual BCI systems have the following problems:

1. It costs more to produce a device (today, they require an "open" EEGraph).
2. Measurement and classification of specific cortical events in real-time.
3. Communication rates are low.
4. An assessment of the classification's accuracy.

In noninvasive functional brain mapping, for example, near-infrared light is used to measure changes in parameters associated with brain activity. In order to improve the reliability and efficiency of BCIs, it could be applied to reinforce EEG-BCIs. This approach could contribute to developing a next-generation BCI platform, as well as enhancing an understanding of brain physiology.

## 9.10   Conclusion

The most widely studied impacts are those brought about by nature, and many ideas exist to explain them. The findings of multiple studies suggest that various representations of nature, including pictures of nature, indoor plants, and views of nature from windows, might significantly improve patients' outcomes, including reduced pain, anxiety, and sadness in patients, as well as their durations of stay. Sadly, not enough research has looked at these essential architectural elements. It is recommended to use objective measures and approaches instead of subjective ones because they may produce more reliable results. Furthermore, studies with genuine patients are advised due to the use of volunteers in some studies who were not actual patients, which can alter outcomes. To function like a real human hand, it still needs to be much improved. More study is being done in this area. HMI technology would be crucial in creating better and safer working environments for people to collaborate with machines in nearly every aspect of life.

# References

1. McDermott, K., Elixhauser, A., Sun, R., Trends in hospital inpatient stays in the United States, 2005-2014, Agency for Healthcare Research and Quality, Rockville, MD, 2017.
2. Kiecolt-Glaser, J.K., Marucha, P.T., Mercado, A.M., Malarkey, W.B., Glaser, R., Slowing of wound healing by psychological stress. *Lancet*, 346, 1194–1196, 1995.
3. Kaplan, R. and Kaplan, S., *The experience of nature: A psychological perspective*, Cambridge University Press, Cambridge, New York, 1989.
4. Ulrich, R.S., Effects of healthcare environmental design on medical outcomes, in: *Design and Health: Proceedings of the Second International Conference on Health and Design*, Svensk Byggtjanst, Stockholm, Sweden, pp. 49–59, 2001.
5. Wanluk, N., Visitsattapongse, S., Juhong, A. *et al.*, Smart wheelchair based on eye tracking. *9th Biomedical Engineering International Conference (BMEiCON)*, Laung Prabang, Laos, pp. 1–4, 2016.
6. M.M. Lech, T.D. Hill, A.L. Arvidson *et al.*, Quality management system with human-machine interface for industrial automation. United States Patent US 6,539,271 B2, 2003 March 25.
7. Kim, I.S., Human reliability analysis in the man machine interface design review. *Ann. Nucl. Energy*, 28, 11, 1069–1081, 2001.
8. Varela, D.T., Penaloza, F.G., Rodelas, C.J.V., Characterized bioelectric signals by means of neural networks and wavelets to remotely control a human-machine interface. *Sensors*, 19, 8, 1923, 2019.
9. Moore, M.M., Real-world applications for brain-computer interface technology. *IEEE Trans. Neural Syst. Rehabil. Eng.*, 11, 2, 162–165, 2003.
10. Shahin, M.K., Tharwat, A., Gaber, T. *et al.*, A wheelchair control system using human-machine interaction: Single-modal and multimodal approaches. *J. Intell. Syst.*, 28, 1, 115–132, 2019.
11. Lee, Y., Kim, J., Jang, B. *et al.*, Graphene-based stretchable/wearable self-powered touch sensor. *Nano Energy*, 62, 259–267, 2019.
12. Shi, Q., Zhang, Z., Chen, T. *et al.*, Minimalist and multifunctional human-machine interface (HMI) using a flexible wearable triboelectric patch. *Nano Energy*, 62, 355–366, 2019.

13. Ferreira, A., Celeste, W.C., Cheein, F.A. *et al.*, Humanmachine interfaces based on EMG and EEG applied to robotic systems. *J. Neuroeng. Rehabil.*, 5, 10, 2008.

14. Buzsaki, G., Anastassiou, C.A., Koch, C., The origin of extracellular fields and currents–EEG, ECoG, LFP and spikes. *Nat. Rev. Neurosci.*, 13, 6, 407–420, 2012.

15. Clark, J.W., The origin of biopotentials, in: *Medical Instrumentation: Application and Design*, 4th edition, J.G. Webster (Ed.), John Wiley & Sons, New Jersey, US, 1998.

16. Vasileios, C.P., Themis, P.E., Dimitrios, I.F., Chapter 2 – Types and sources of medical and other related data, in: *Medical Data Sharing, Harmonization and Analytics*, V.C. Pezoulas, T.P. Exarchos, D.I. Fotiadis (Eds.), pp. 19–65, Academic Press, Cambridge (MA), 2020.

17. Atwood, H.L. and Mackay, W.A., *In essentials of neurophysiology*, B.C. Decker, Hamilton, 1989.

18. Guyton, A.C. and Hall, J.E., *Textbook of medical physiology*, vol. 548, Saunders, Philadelphia, 1986.

19. Papanicolaou, A.C., Moore, B.D., Del'Tsch, G., Reorganization of cerebral function following lesions in the left hemisphere, in: *Traumatic Brain Injury*, P. Bach-y-Rita (Ed.), pp. 105–119, Demos, New York, 1989.

20. Bach-y-Rita, P., Brain plasticity as a basis for recovery of functions in humans: Recovery function: Theoretical considerations for brain injury rehabilitation. *Neuropsychologia*, 28, 6, 547–554, 1990.

21. Bach-y-Rita, P., *Recovery of function: Theoretical considerations for brain injury rehabilitation*, Hans Huber, Bern, SW, 1980.

22. Bach, Y., Brain plasticity, in: *Rehabilitation Medicine*, J. Goodgold (Ed.), pp. 113–118, CV Mosby Co, St. Louis (MO), 1988.

23. Cotman, C.W. and Sampedro, M.N., Progress in facilitating the recovery of function after central nervous system trauma. *Ann. N.Y. Acad. Sci.*, 457, 1 Hope for a Ne, 83–104, 1985.

24. Finger, S., LeVere, T.E., Almli, C.R. *et al.*, Recovery of function, in: *Brain Injury and Recovery*, S. Finger, T.E. Levere, C.R. Almli, D.G. Stein (Eds.), pp. 351–361, Springer, Boston. MA, 1988.

25. Stein, D.G., Rosen, J.J., Butters, N., *Plasticity and recovery of function in the central nervous system*, Academic Press, New York, 1974.

26. Sale, A., Berardi, N., Maffei, L. *et al.*, Environment and brain plasticity: Towards an endogenous pharmacotherapy. *Physiol. Rev.*, 94, 1, 189–234, 2014.

27. Kornorski, J., The physiological approach to the problem of recent memory, in: *Brain Mechanisms Learning*, A. Fessard (Ed.), pp. 115–132, Blackwell, Oxford, 1961.

28. Monday, H.R., Younts, T.J., Castillo, P.E., Long-term plasticity of neurotransmitter release: Emerging mechanisms and contributions to brain function and disease. *Annu. Rev. Neurosci.*, 41, 299–322, 2018.

29. Chumerin, N., Manyakov, N.V., Vliet, M.V. *et al.*, Pre-processing and decoding steady-state visual evoked potentials for brain-computer interfaces, in: *Digital Image and Signal Processing for Measurement Systems*, pp. 1–33, River Publishers, Denmark, 2012.

30. Nakanishi, M., Wang, Y., Wang, Y.-T. *et al.*, A high-speed brain speller using steady-state visual evoked potentials. *Int. J. Neural Syst.*, 24, 6, 1450019, 2014.

31. K€ubler, A., Neumann, N., Kaiser, J. *et al.*, Brain-computer communication: Self-regulation of slow cortical potentials for verbal communication. *Arch. Phys. Med. Rehabil.*, 82, 1533–1539, 2001.

32. Padfield, N., Zabalza, J., Zhao, H. *et al.*, EEG-based brain-computer interfaces using motor-imagery: Techniques and challenges. *Sensors*, 19, 6, 1423, 2019.

33. Zhang, W., Tan, C., Sun, F. *et al.*, A review of EEG-based brain-computer interface systems design. *Brain Sci. Adv.*, 4, 2, 156–167, 2018.

34. Li, Z., Yuan, Y., Luo, L. *et al.*, Hybrid brain/muscle signals powered wearable walking exoskeleton enhancing motor ability in climbing stairs activity. *IEEE Trans. Med. Robot. Bionics*, 1, 4, 218–227, 2019.

35. Choi, I., Rhiu, I., Lee, Y. *et al.*, A systematic review of hybrid brain-computer interfaces: Taxonomy and usability perspectives. *PLoS One*, 12, 4, e0176674, 2017.

36. Jiang, J., Zhou, Z., Yin, E. *et al.*, Hybrid brain-computer interface (BCI) based on the EEG and EOG signals. *Biomed. Mater. Eng.*, 24, 6, 2919–2925, 2014.

37. Huang, Q., He, S., Wang, Q. *et al.*, An EOG-based human-machine interface for wheelchair control. *IEEE Trans. Biomed. Eng.*, 65, 9, 2023–2032, 2018.

38. Zhang, J., Wang, B., Zhang, C. *et al.*, An EEG/EMG/EOGbased multimodal human-machine interface to realtime control of a soft robot hand. *Front. Neurorob.*, 13, 7, 2019.

39. Prashant, P., Joshi, A., Gandhi, V., Brain computer interface: A review. *5th Nirma University International Conference on Engineering (NUiCONE)*, Ahmedabad, pp. 1–6, 2015.

40. Yin, R., Wang, D., Zhao, S., Lou, Z., Shen, G., Wearable sensors-enabled human-machine interaction systems: from design to application. *Advanced Functional Materials*, 31, 11, 2008936, 2021.

41. Cauvery, N.K., Lingaraju, G., Anupama, H., Brain-computer interface and its types-a study. *Int. J. Adv. Eng. Technol.*, 3, 739–745, 2012.

42. Millan Jose del, R. and Carmena, J.M., Invasive or non-invasive: Understanding brain-machine interface technology. *IEEE Eng. Med. Biol. Mag.*, 29, 6–22, 2010.

43. Velliste, M., Perel, S., Spalding, M.C. *et al.*, Cortical control of a prosthetic arm for self-feeding. *Nature*, 453, 7198, 1098–1101, 2008.

44. Ganguly, K. and Carmena, J.M., Emergence of a stable cortical map for neuroprosthetic control. *PLoS Biol.*, 7, 1–3, 2009.

45. Behrens, E., Zentner, J., van Roost, D. *et al.*, Subdural and depth electrodes in the presurgical evaluation of epilepsy. *Acta Neurochir.*, 128, 84–87, 1994.

46. Yadav, M.K., Verma, U., Parikh, H. *et al.*, Minimally invasive transgingival implant therapy: A literature review. *Natl. J. Maxillofac. Surg.*, 9, 2, 117, 2018.

47. Kassiri, J.J., Pugh, J., Carline, S., Depth electrodes in pediatric epilepsy surgery. *Can. J. Neurol. Sci., Le Journal Canadien des Sciences Neurologiques*, 40, 48–55, 2013.

48. Shah, A.K. and Mittal, S., Invasive electroencephalography monitoring: Indications and presurgical planning. *Ann. Indian Acad. Neurol.*, 17, Suppl 1, S89–S94, 2014.

49. Schalk, G. and Leuthardt, E.C., Brain-computer interfaces using electrocorticographic signals. *IEEE Rev. Biomed. Eng.*, 4, 140–154, 2011.

50. Amanpour, B. and Erfanian, A., Classification of brain signals associated with imagination of hand grasping, opening and reaching by means of wavelet-based common spatial pattern and mutual information. *Conference Proceedings: Annual International Conference of the IEEE Engineering in Medicine and Biology Society.* Conference, 2013 Jul 3–7, IEEE Engineering in Medicine and Biology Society, Osaka, Japan, pp. 2224–2227.

51. Pistohl, T., Ball, T., Schulze-Bonhage, A. *et al.*, Prediction of arm movement trajectories from ECoG-recordings in humans. *J. Neurosci. Methods*, 167, 1, 105–114, 2008.

52. Villringer, A. and Chance, B., Non-invasive optical spectroscopy and imaging of human brain function. *Trends Neurosci.*, 20, 435–442, 1997.

53. Chi, Y.M., Deiss, S.R., Cauwenberghs, G., Non-contact low power EEG/ECG electrode for high density wearable biopotential sensor networks. *Sixth International Workshop on Wearable and Implantable Body Sensor Networks*, Berkeley, CA, pp. 246–250, 2009.

54. Xu, J., Yazicioglu, R.F., Van Hoof, C. *et al.*, An active electrode read out circuit, in: *Low Power Active Electrode ICs for Wearable EEG Acquisition. Analog Circuits and Signal Processing*, p. 125, Springer, Cham, 2018.

55. Gargiulo, G., Bifulco, P., Cesarelli, M. *et al.*, Problems in assessment of novel bio-potential front-end with dry electrode: A brief review. *Machines*, 2, 87–98, 2014.

56. Kavitha, C. and Nagappan, G., Sensing and processing of EOG signals to control human-machine interface system. *Int. J. Sci. Eng. Technol. Res.*, 4, 5, 1330–1336, 2015.

57. Guo, X., Pei, W., Wang, Y. *et al.*, A human-machine interface based on single channel EOG and patchable sensor. *Biomed. Signal Process. Control*, 30, 98–105, 2016.

58. Salinet, J.L. and Silva, O.L., Chapter 2 – ECG signal acquisition systems, in: *Developments and Applications for ECG Signal Processing*, J.P.V. Madeiro, P.C. Cortez, J.M.S.M. Filho, A.R.A. Brayner (Eds.), pp. 29–51, Elsevier, Academic Press, Cambridge, Massachusetts, 2019.

59. Macfarlane, P.W., Oosterom, A.V., Pahlm, O. *et al.*, *Comprehensive electrocardiology*, vol. 1, Springer Science & Business Media, Verlag, London, 2010.

60. Gao, Z., Wu, J., Zhou, J. *et al.*, Design of ECG signal acquisition and processing system. *International Conference on Biomedical Engineering and Biotechnology*, Macau, Macao, pp. 762–764, May 28–30 2012.

61. Ulrich, R.S. and Gilpin, L., Healing arts: Nutrition for the soul, in: *Putting Patients First: Designing and Practicing Patient-Centered Care*, S.B. Frampton, L. Gilpin, P.A. Charmel, (Eds.), pp. 117–146, John Wiley & Sons, San Francisco, 2003.

62. Park, S.-H. and Mattson, R.H., Ornamental indoor plants in hospital rooms enhanced health outcomes of patients recovering from surgery. *J. Altern. Complement. Med.*, 15, 975–980, 2009.

63. Pati, D., Freier, P., O'Boyle, M., Amor, C., Valipoor, S., The impact of simulated nature on patient outcomes: A study of photographic sky compositions. *HERD Health Environ. Res. Des. J.*, 9, 36–51, 2016a.

64. Shepley, M.M., Gerbi, R.P., Watson, A.E., Imgrund, S., Sagha-Zadeh, R., The impact of daylight and views on ICU patients and staff. *HERD Health Environ. Res. Des. J.*, 5, 46e–60, 2012.

65. Okken, V., van Rompay, T., Pruyn, A., When the world is closing in: Effects of perceived room brightness and communicated threat during patient-physician interaction. *HERD Health Environ. Res. Des. J.*, 7, 37–53, 2013.

66. Grant, S., Blom, A.W., Craddock, I. *et al.*, Home health monitoring around the time of surgery: Qualitative study of patients' experiences before and after joint replacement. *BMJ Open*, 9, 12, e032205, 2019.

67. Ruhunage, I., Perera, C.J., Nisal, K. *et al.*, EMG signal controlled transhumerai prosthetic with EEG-SSVEP based approach for hand open/close. *2017 IEEE International Conference on Systems, Man, and Cybernetics (SMC)*, Banff, AB, Canada, pp. 3169–3174, 2017.

68. Zhang, X., Li, R., Li, II. *et al.*, Novel approach for electromyography-controlled prostheses based on facial action. *Med. Biol. Eng. Comput.*, 58, 2685–2698, 2020.

69. Brammer, M., The role of neuroimaging in diagnosis and personalized medicine-current position and likely future directions. *Dialogues Clin. Neurosci.*, 11, 389–396, 2009.

70. Fukaya, N., Toyama, S., Asfour, T. *et al.*, Design of the TUAT/Karlsruhe hand. *Proceedings of the 2000 IEEE/ RS. International Conference on Intelligent Robots and Systems*, vol. 3, pp. 1754–1759, February 2000.

71. Asfour, T., Berns, K., Schelling, J. *et al.*, Programming of manipulation tasks of the humanoid robot ARMAR. *The 9th International Conference on Advanced Robotics (ICAR'99)*, Tokyo, Japan, pp. 25–27 October, 1999.

72. Wei, L., Hu, H., Yuan, K., Use of forehead bio-signals for controlling an intelligent wheelchair. Use of forehead bio-signals for controlling an intelligent wheelchair. *2008 IEEE International Conference on Robotics and Biomimetics*, Bangkok, pp. 108–113, 2009.

73. Xue, G., Chen, C., Lu, Z., Brain imaging techniques and their applications in decision-making research. Xin lixue bao. *Acta Psychol. Sin.*, 42, 120–137, 2010.

74. Piston emission tomography, [Online] Available from: https://www.hopkinsmedicine.org/healthlibrary/test_procedures/neurological/positron_emission_tomography_pet_92. p. 07654.

75. Malmivuo, J., Biomagnetism, in: *Wiley Encyclopedia of Electrical and Electronics Engineering*, pp. 1–25, 2017.

76. Khalil, S.F., Mohktar, M.S., Ibrahim, F., The theory and fundamentals of bioimpedance analysis in clinical status monitoring and diagnosis of diseases. *Sensors*, 14, 6, 10895–10928, 2014.

77. Wang, G., Li, L., Xing, S. *et al.*, Intelligent HMI in orthopaedic navigation, in: *Intelligent Orthopaedics. Advances in Experimental Medicine and Biology*, vol. 1093, G. Zheng, W. Tian, X. Zhuang (Eds.), pp. 207–224, Springer, Singapore, 2018.

78. Zhang, X., Chen, G., Liao, H., High-quality see-through surgical guidance system using enhanced 3-D autostereoscopic augmented reality. *IEEE Trans. Biomed. Eng.*, 64, 8, 1815–1825, 2017.

79. Cheesborough, J.E., Smith, L.H., Kuiken, T.A. *et al.*, Targeted muscle reinnervation and advanced prosthetic arms. *Semin. Plast. Surg.*, 29, 1, 62–72, 2015.

80. Osborn, L.E., Iskarous, M.M., Thakor, N.V. *et al.*, Chapter 22 – sensing and control for prosthetic hands in clinical and research applications, in: *Wearable Robotics*, J. Rosen and P.W. Ferguson (Eds.), pp. 445–468, Elsevier, Amsterdam, Netherlands, 2020.

81. Belter, J.T., Segil, J.L., Dollar, A.M. *et al.*, Mechanical design and performance specifications of anthropomorphic prosthetic hands: A review. *J. Rehab. Res. Dev.*, 50, 5, 599–618, 2013.

82. Kyberd, P.J. and Chappell, P.H., The Southampton hand: An intelligent myoelectric prosthesis. *J. Rehab. Res. Dev.*, 31, 4, 326–334, 1994.

83. Liu, H., Xu, K., Siciliano, B. *et al.*, The MERO hand: A mechanically robust anthropomorphic prosthetic hand using novel compliant rolling contact joint. *IEEE/ASME International Conference on Advanced Intelligent Mechatronics (AIM)*, Hong Kong, China, pp. 126–132, 2019.

84. Ting, Z., Wang, X.Q., Jiang, L. *et al.*, Biomechatronic design and control of an anthropomorphic artificial hand for prosthetic applications. *Robotica*, 34, 10, 2291–2308, 2015.

85. Brunner, I., Skouen, J.S., Hofstad, H., Virtual reality training for upper extremity in subacute stroke (VIRTUES): A multicenter RCT. *Neurology*, 89, 24, 2413–2421, 2017.

86. Perry, B.N., Armiger, R.S., Yu, K.E. *et al.*, Virtual integration environment as an advanced prosthetic limb training platform. *Front. Neurol.*, 9, 785, 2018.

87. Wang, Y., Liu, H., Leng, D. *et al.*, New advances in EMG control methods of anthropomorphic prosthetic hand. *Sci. China Technol. Sci.*, 60, 12, 1978–1979, 2017.

88. Reaz, M., Hussain, M., Mohd-Yasin, F., Techniques of EMG signal analysis: Detection, processing, classification and application. *Biol. Proc.*, 8, 11–35, 2006.

89. Jiang, N., Dosen, S., Muller, K. *et al.*, Myoelectric control of artificial limbs—Is there a need to change focus [In the Spotlight]. *IEEE Signal Process. Mag.*, 29, 152, Sep. 2012.

90. Capelle, C., Trullemans, C., Arno, P. *et al.*, A real-time experimental prototype for enhancement of vision rehabilitation using auditory substitution. *IEEE Trans. Biomed. Eng.*, 45, 1279–1293, 1998.

91. Tyler, M., Danilov, Y., Bach-y-Rita, P. *et al.*, Closing an open-loop control system: Vestibular substitution through the tongue. *J. Integr. Neurosci.*, 2, 159–164, 2003.

92. Steven, A.W. and Stephen, B., Sensory substitution using tactile pin arrays: Human factors, technology and applications. *Signal Process.*, 86, 12, 3674–3695, 2006.

93. Strausser, K.A. and Kazerooni, H., The development and testing of a human-machine interface for a mobile medical exoskeleton. *IEEE/RSJ International Conference on Intelligent Robots and Systems*, San Francisco, CA, pp. 4911–4916, 2011.

94. Li, S.Z. (Ed.), *Encyclopedia of biometrics*, Springer, US, 2009.

95. Ratha, N.K., Senior, A., Bolle, R.M., Automated biometrics, in: *Advances in Pattern Recognition – ICAPR 2001.* Lecture Notes in Computer Science, vol. 2013, S. Singh, N. Murshed, W. Kropatsch (Eds.), pp. 447–455, Springer, Heidelberg, Berlin, 2001.

96. Jain, A.K., Flynn, P., Ross, A.A., *Handbook of biometrics*, p. 556, Springer Nature, Switzerland, 2007.

97. Jain, A.K., Ross, A., Prabhakar, S., An introduction to biometric recognition. *IEEE Trans. Circuits Syst. Video Technol.*, 14, 1, 4–20, 2004.

98. Uludag, U., Pankanti, S., Prabhakar, S. *et al.*, Biometric cryptosystems: Issues and challenges. *Proc. IEEE*, 92, 6, 948–960, 2004.

99. Lanitis, A., A survey of the effects of aging on biometric identity verification. *IJBM*, 2, 1, 34, 2010.

100. Singh, Y.N., Singh, S.K., Ray, A.K., Bioelectrical signals as emerging biometrics: Issues and challenges. *Int. Sch. Res. Notices*, 2012, 1–13, 2012.

101. Pal, A., Gautam, A.K., Singh, Y.N., Evaluation of bioelectric signals for human recognition. *Proc. Comput. Sci.*, 48, 746–752, 2015.

102. Crescentini, C., Fabbro, F., Tomasino, B., Editorial special topic: Enhancing brain and cognition through meditation. *J. Cogn. Enhanc.*, 1, 2, 81–83, 2017.

103. Wilms, W., Wozniak-Karczewska, M., Corvini, P.F.-X. *et al.*, Nootropic drugs: Methylphenidate, modafinil and piracetam – Population use trends,

occurrence in the environment, ecotoxicity and removal methods – A review. *Chemosphere*, 233, 771–785, 2019.

104. Kim, D., Practical use and risk of modafinil, a novel waking drug. *Environ. Health Toxicol.*, 27, e2012007, 2012.

105. Malykh, A.G. and Sadaie, M.R., Piracetam and piracetam-like drugs. *Drugs.*, 70, 287–312, 2010.

106. Colucci, L., Bosco, M., Rosario Ziello, A. *et al.*, Effectiveness of nootropic drugs with cholinergic activity in treatment of cognitive deficit: A review. *J. Exp. Pharmacol.*, 4, 163–172, 2012.

107. Vassanelli, S., Brain-chip interfaces: The present and the future. *Proc. Comput. Sci.*, 7, 61–64, 2011.

108. Indiveri, G., Barranco, B.L., Legenstein, R. *et al.*, Integration of nanoscale memristor synapses in neuromorphic computing architectures. *Nanotechnology*, 24, 38, 1–13, 2013.

109. V. John and D.S. Kondziolka, Device for multicentric brain modulation, repair and interface. U.S. Patent No. 2008/0154331 A1, June 26, 2008.

110. Vassanelli, S., Mahmud, M., Girardi, S. *et al.*, On the way to large-scale and high-resolution brain-chip interfacing. *Cogn. Comput.*, 4, 1, 71–81, 2012.

# Part II

# EMERGING APPLICATION AND REGULATORY PROSPECTS OF HMI IN HEALTHCARE

# 10

# HMI: Disruption in the Neural Healthcare Industry

**Preetam L. Nikam[1]\*, Amol U. Gayke[1], Pavan S. Avhad[1], Rahul B. Bhabad[1] and Rishabha Malviya[2]**

*[1]SND College of Pharmacy, Yeola, Nasik, India*
*[2]Department of Pharmacy, School of Medical and Allied Sciences, Galgotias University, Greater Noida, India*

## Abstract

An area of growing interest and investigation is how technology might improve healing from central nervous system damage. Till today, communication and motor recovery or augmentation have received the most attention. To explain how cutting-edge technology might be included in subacute rehabilitation, this chapter provides details of the study experiments. The first study examines whether patients in a spinal cord injury hospital could use a brain–computer interface. In the second study, two virtual environments that are used in a rigorous outpatient neurorehabilitation program are examined for their validity with acquired brain damage. These pilot investigations confirm that the subacute stage of neurorehabilitation can use cutting-edge technologies. Participants said that these techniques were highly received, and both inpatient and outpatient rehabilitation could easily include them, programs for patients. The annual incidence of spinal cord injuries (12,000), acquired brain injuries (900,000), and traumatic brain injuries (1.7 million) in the US may not accurately reflect the long-term effects and annual societal costs, which may surpass $100 billion annually (1–5). The requirement for a multidisciplinary strategy emphasizing long-term outcomes, secondary problems, and quality of life is increased as medical care improvements increase survival rates in these populations. The fundamental health conditions must be conceived in connection to environmental and contextual factors with an emphasis on improvement. According to the health organization, function, health types, modes of action, and disabilities

---

*\*Corresponding author*: preetamnikam25@gmail.com

---

Rishabha Malviya, Sonali Sundram, Bhupendra Prajapati and Sudarshan Kumar Singh (eds.)
*Human-Machine Interface: Making Healthcare Digital*, (281–294) © 2024 Scrivener Publishing LLC

are international. Models and modern innovations like brain–computer interface. BCIs offer a risk-free, evidence-based strategy that has been shown to improve performance in all areas for business people, athletes, celebrities, students, and just about everyone else. The Department of Defense, NASA, and Darpa (Defence Advanced Research Projects Agency) collaborate to develop the most cutting-edge ones in the US.

*Keywords*: Brain–computer interface, neurorehabilitation, brain injuries

## 10.1   Introduction

Patients with neurologic impairment have found that applying bioelectric stimulation to their nervous systems is a useful way to improve or restore part of their function. Particularly important and promising from a clinical research standpoint, functional stimulation of paretic neurons merits thorough examination. Currently, several implantable nerve stimulators, including stimulation of cutaneous in trans form of the fifth nerve in migraine sufferers, hypoglossal a type of nerve stimulated in affected people with dangerous short sleep and chronic spinal cord stimulation in patients with severe neuropathic pain, have been clinically used and proven to be effective [1]. Brain deep stimulation (DBS), which is frequently utilized in therapeutic settings, is without a doubt the use of bioelectric technology in many conditions to treat a variety of neurological problems.

This article summarizes the most recent developments in bioelectric therapies that aim to influence or regulate brain function. We start by talking about the three possible locations for bioelectric technology to integrate with peripheral and central nerve systems while also examining clinical and useful issues [2]. There are three locations: the last organ, the peripheral form of the neural system, the CNS, or all three at one time, ordered from distal to peripheral. We also talk about how different disease processes are affected by intraneural multichannel microelectrodes. We discuss novel technologies that could considerably enhance the path of nerves and different forms of tissues involved in electric engineering comprised of biological conditions as well as their potential applications in the clinic for various conditions of clinical diseases. Finally, we talk about the biological, engineering, and legal barriers that prevent problems [3].

## 10.2    Stimulation of Muscles

Transcutaneous electrical stimulation, which is non-invasive, can be used to electrically stimulate end organs such as muscles. On the other hand, implantable electrodes are invasive. For example, an expert named McDonnall employed cutaneous condition in trans form and percutaneous electric form in terms of the rod to activate the muscle of oculi and helps in getting back the blinking functioning in affected patients having paralytic symptoms of the face in parallel form reducing the unpleasant effects of the stimulation [4]. They transcutaneously activated the nerves of facial form having branches to induce blinking of the eye. To enhance swallowing and breathing without impairing vocalization, Inwards has two form paralytic vocal forms, using a pacemaker in the larynx which is inserted into the muscles of the larynx. Electrodes inserted inside a mouse model's gastrocnemius muscle reduced using a pacemaker of larynx device placed into muscles of the larynx to provide a good fresh condition for breathing and feeding not involving or affecting vocal condition in individuals with bilateral vocal fold paralysis. In a mouse model following transection and regeneration of the tibial nerve, electrodes placed in the gastro muscle reduced muscular cramps not involving any nerve of motor innervation. The motions brought on by limb tremors may be recorded by muscle-specific electrodes, which would then activate the muscles to decrease the tremors [5, 6]. Despite the enormous promise of end-organ stimulation, many of the most recent advancements in the field are still only sporadically used in clinical settings. On the other hand, end-organ bioelectric interfaces for the auditory system are already being employed in common clinical settings [7].

## 10.3    Cochlear Implants

### 10.3.1    Implants for Cochlear

End organ stimulating devices have been used for many years to help individuals with severe sensorineural hearing loss, which is often brought on by irreparable harm to the nerve of the auditory and Sensory epithelium [8]. Cochlear implants (CI) are made up of a parallel channel charge arrangement which is inserted by doing the mechanism of surgery into the tympanic membrane in the cochlea part and a –stimulator which receives that is placed under tissue that is soft in the postauricular part [9]. Rosenthal's canal's spiral ganglion neurons receive electric current from chosen and preprogrammed platinum electrode connections causing these cells to become depolarized, creating a signal in the neural part at the proper range, and sending it up the path of the auditory form to the cortex of the auditory part. There are about 500,000 people who are not able to hear properly or are fully impaired by ear [10].

### 10.3.2   Prosthetics for Ears

An incapacitating disorder known as bilateral vestibulopathy, often known as Dandy's syndrome, is marked by oscillopsia and unsteadiness while moving. Both oscillopsia (due to bilaterally reduced vestibulo-ocular reflexes, or VOR) and unsteadiness (induced by a weak vestibulo-spinal reflex) severely impair while head and body movement, postural control, and image stability are necessary to improve the inner ear's ability to balance in animal models, cochlear implants have been adapted and employed as vestibular prosthesis recently. Many of these experimental gadgets track head accelerations using inertial sensors and then use that data to send electrical impulses and different types of signs to the system in the vestibular par, as a form of compensation [11].

Recently, Researcher converted their research to human tests in the hope to revive VOR. Based on head acceleration forces detected by a gyroscope inside a modified cochlear implant with a good intra-cochlear arrangement and the presence of electrodes in three parts which are to be placed inside the semicircular canals. Electrical stimulation with the prosthesis at 1 Hz resulted in a high VOR profit in implanted patients and impairment of the vestibular part to approximately 95% to 97% of the total gain in VOR found in healthy patients. Johns Hopkins University is conducting a comparable clinical study [12].

## 10.4   Peripheral Nervous System Interaction

In clinical practice, stimulation to the nerve of the periphery and even direct stimulation of the spinal nerve are frequently used. Direct the epidural implantation of leads in the back root ganglion (BRG) to treat the pain of the neural part and stimulation of the anterior root of the sacral nerve to upgrade the good bowel movement demonstrate that stimulation in terms of the electric form of nerves or their roots is a good, protective and effective clinical intervention in patients with spinal cord injuries.

The principal drawbacks of implantable devices are around the after-implant fibrotic foreign body reaction, especially after-implant within the peripheral or central nervous system [13]. The long-term effects of implantable neurostimulators are still not fully understood. Restricting the use of electrodes can lessen the gliotic reaction to electrode implantation.

## 10.5    Sleeve Electrodes

The most fundamental kind is a cuff electrode is a recording device in the epineural part. The coiling, the layer of cuff plated with silicon of the

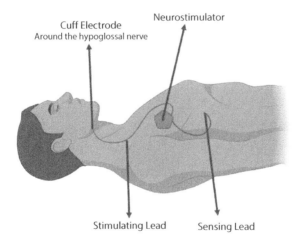

**Figure 10.1** A system diagram for Inspire Upper Airway Stimulation. To treat obstructive sleep apnea, an implantable technology stimulates the hypoglossal nerve (OSA). An implanted generation of pulse that is typically positioned in the body, especially the chest, and is coupled leads consist of two forms, is one of the system's components. The fourth intercostal gap is where the first lead, which is a sensing lead, is positioned. This detects the contraction of the intercostal muscles and turns on the lead which is to be stimulated, which is connected to the nerve of hypoglossal. The system also consists of external parts, such as the doctor and patient programmers (sleep remotes).

traditional electrode having cuff is bound to the nerve's surface & inserted into the nerve, with one to three strips of a platinum foil. This creates direct access to an electrical stimulation interface. Because the electrode may function at low stimulation thresholds, there is less chance of damaging nerves. Unfortunately, the cuff electrode only partially targets specific fascicles inside the nerve fiber and typically evokes all-or-nothing neuronal activity [14]. Despite research in rabbits finding that electrodes having cuffs have been used successfully for a long time, anyway, long-term cuff implantation will injure axons having a myelinated sheath, and axons are protected and recovered quickly [15].

In the treatment of epilepsy, the tenth nerve named the vagus stimulates the nerve (VSN) has been effective and depression having resistance, is frequently performed in the clinical context using the cuff electrode. According to certain theories, the VNS implant emits breaks the faulty sign that causes epileptic attack by dispersing energy centrally into the brain [16]. Additionally, in the administration (FDA)-has allowed Inspire® hypoglossal nerve stimulator for problems causing incomplete sleep commonly known as apnea, an electrode having cuff is bound or

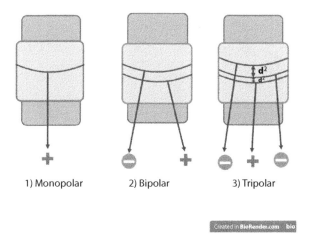

1) Monopolar    2) Bipolar    3) Tripolar

**Figure 10.2** 1) Due to depolarization of the point of contact, monopolar arrangement produces bidirectional action potential propagation. 2) A bipolar electrode arrangement tries to hyperpolarize the site of the nerve at the site of the anode to impede one route of action potential propagation. Such anodic current magnitudes, however, create a cathode having the virtual form and neutralize the cancellation effect, producing a bipolar action potential. 3) Platinum placements are a crucial component of tripolar electrodes (d2> d1). Virtual cathode formation beyond the closer anode (d1) is prevented by hyperpolarization which is time-changing the anode (d2). But the additional anode, a virtual cathode forms, producing a one-directional action capacity.

circled the nerve of hypoglossal (Figure 10.1). The motor nerve is stimulated, causing the tongue to descend in synchrony with the breathing cycle, this implant is being tested in clinical settings to improve the oropharyngeal airway [17].

A modified monopolar or bipolar electrode, or a tripolar electrode, would probably be needed for motor neuron stimulation. Although this has been challenging to reliably generate in reality, such designs that reduce unwanted signals can aid in unidirectional action potential propagation, the other direction. In contrast, traditionally to supply current to a single area, monopolar or bipolar electrodes are ineffective (Figure 10.2). However, the two-way directional potential to perform an action and propagate in efferent neurons which are stimulated as opposed to sensory nerve stimulation is less problematic and can consistently cause muscle activation [18–20].

## 10.6    Flat-Interfaced Nerve Electrodes

An electrode made of a cuff has a flat contact nerve electrode that has been modified (FINE). The central fascicles of the nerve can be brought closer to the surface thanks to FINE's ability to compress and restructure the nerves in flat conditions with changes in structure. Additionally, FINE can be built with several channels. A FINE device can autonomously select muscle activation. According to intraoperative investigations, the femoral nerve innervates the femoral nerve in humans [21]. Patients now that they can stand up from a lower trunk paralysis seated posture thanks to the surgical implantation of FINE, which specifically activates the leg muscles around the femoral trunk.

## 10.7    Transverse and Longitudinal Intrafascicular Electrode (LIFE and TIME)

Intrafascicular electrodes, as opposed to FINE, pierce the nerves protecting the epineurium and have a better sensitivity for stimulating or recording from peripheral nerves. Notably, a thin-film, longitudinal intrafascicular electrode made of polymers with improved recording selectivity than conventional metal LIFE exhibited no negative impact on the number, size, or thickness of nerve fibers after implantation in rabbit sciatic nerves for six months [22]. LIFE has also been utilized to control a robotic hand in a human patient by detecting brain impulses from the median and ulnar nerves in an amputee. By avoiding the dispersion of spatial selection outside of one fascicle the spatial selectivity of LIFE is inferior to transverse intrafascicular multichannel electrodes, especially time [23].

## 10.8   Multi-Channel Arrays That Penetrate

### 10.8.1   Numerous-Channel Arrays That Penetrate

Thanks to neural activity in intra form which is penetrated multi-channel arrays, Expertise has comprehensive access to a variety of brain circuitry. Array (USEA) and Array (UEA) are noteworthy.) multi-array electrodes that were created by the University of Utah researchers. Each can accommodate microneedles of around 90-100, which are placed into the neural tissue [24]. Among other achievements, earlier UEA studies have successfully recorded central nervous system-derived volitional motor commands. However, because of how intrusive this method is, there is a chance of long-term brain damage. The degree of nerve fiber activation selectivity generally increases with the degree of invasiveness of the neuroprosthetic interface at the expense of potential harm to invented the (UEA) and, two different forms of multi-array electrodes (USEA) [25]. Each is built to hold up to 100 tiny needles put into the neural tissue. Among other achievements, earlier UEA studies have successfully recorded central nervous system-derived volitional motor commands. However, because of how intrusive this method is, there is a chance of long-term brain damage. The activation of neural activity in fiber form and its selectivity at the risk of probable nerve damage is typically inversely correlated with the invasiveness of the neuroprosthetic interface. Intraneural multichannel Microelectrode arrays infringe on the perineurium and might result in glial scarring, but they also enable finely targeted activation of neuronal fibers. The nerve is normally only somewhat selectively activated when cuff electrodes, which gently encircle it, are used. Researchers studied intraneural cochlear nerve stimulation while utilizing a penetrating multi-electrode array created at the University of Michigan. Capturing the output of the downstream auditory route at the inferior colliculus of the brainstem. [26–29]. The penetrating intraneural array from NeuroNexus (Ann Arbor, MI) consistently outperformed a traditional intracochlear array in every significant cat anesthetized auditory electrophysiological measurement. Intraneural stimulation has also recently been discussed by our team about the feline model's facial nerve reanimation. In short-term trials, we were

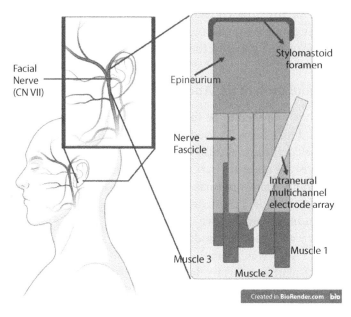

**Figure 10.3** An illustration of stimulation form in the intraneural case of the face using a multichannel path to selectively engage nerve fiber form or gathered together and stimulate particular muscle groups of the face.

able to selectively stimulate face muscles thanks to the facial nerve's primary trunk being implanted with the NeuroNexus multi-electrode array (Figure 10.3). Following stimulation, the EMG responses of four face muscles were recorded [30–33].

## 10.9 Spinal Cord Stimulation and Central Nervous System Interaction

### 10.9.1 Cortical Connections

Novel brain-machine interfaces called intracranial brain-computer interfaces (iBMI) record and interpret cerebral activity to understand motor intent and trigger a response (such as the movement of an artificial limb, for example, IBM's use electrocorticographic (ECoG) grids or microelectrodes implanted into the cortex to either directly trigger the muscles or nerves or to directly bypass damaged neural pathways operate mechanical limbs. Tetraplegic patients, for instance, have demonstrated the ability to voluntarily manipulate robotic arms, while other Patients have demonstrated the ability to employ iBMI-based techniques, to control their limbs. In addition to restoring motor function, iBMI can also improve communication, like in the case of ALS patients, for instance [34–36].

### 10.9.2    Stimulation of the Auditory Nucleus and Ganglions

The CI, which is intended to be implanted in the cochlea and electrically activate the auditory nerve, is used by patients who have damage or deformations of the cochlea or auditory nerve., is not a practical substitute for rehabilitation of the auditory part. Particularly in patients who experience bilateral vestibular Schwannomas due to neurofibromatosis type 2 (NF2) is seen, which calls for a brainstem's cochlear nucleus that activates the path of the auditory canal more centrally [37]. Patients with NF2 experience auditory and another modified cochlear implant called the brainstem implant (ABI) was created. A Dacron mesh support, it contains a flat array of 21 platinum electrodes. However, to yet, individuals without NF2 and kids with cochlear abnormalities have shown that ABIs are most helpful [38].

### 10.9.3    Stimulation of the Deep Brain

DBS is inserting tiny electrodes into certain several brain areas. The numerous microelectrodes are linked to an electrical pulse generator, through wires which are micro in form sends biphasic current pulses to the globus pallidus interna or subthalamic nuclei (up to 30 micro C/cm2). to treat Parkinson's disease [39]. Depending on where the electrodes are implanted, this device has also proved effective in treating tinnitus, melancholy, anxiety, obsessive-compulsive disorder, and other diseases.

## 10.10    Computer–Brain Interfaces

Additionally, it has been suggested that stimulating and recording different brain regions has enormous therapeutic potential. Intraparenchymal or subdural cortical electrodes are to relieve persistent discomfort and long-term seizure diagnosis A brain-computer interface (BCI) has shown to be a useful tool for a durable and dependable implant.

Stimulation of the cortex [40]. Additionally, MCS is a successful remedy for facial long-term neuropathic problems or has the potential to enable facial muscle activation in the context of facial reanimation and neuroprosthetic limbs.

## 10.11    Conclusion

Restoring paretic function using neuroprosthetics nerve function has the potential to significantly improve the path of neuron bioelectric tissue engineering, to improve patient health, even if today's surgical and physiotherapeutic procedures aim to get back to comfort, model, or function, have severe limits when it comes to facilitating cosmetic or functional rehabilitation. Instead, patients with motor nerve deficiencies may benefit from the restoration of volitional function thanks to the development of bioelectric technology. Bioelectric technology advancements are enabling a higher degree of selectivity when stimulating different populations of nerve fibers to activate certain muscles. Enhancing the functionality of implantable neuroprosthetics through boosting selectivity, stability, and electrode array design are significant advancements.

## References

1. Bayazit, Y., Kosaner, J., Celenk, F., Somdas, M., Yilmaz, I., Altin, G., Cevizci, R., Yavuz, H., Ozluoglu, L., Auditory brainstem implant in postlingual post-meningitic patients. *Laryngoscope*, *126*, 1889–1892, 2016.

2. Benfield, J., Maknojia, A., Epstein, F., Progressive paraplegia from spinal cord stimulator lead fibrotic encapsulation: A case report. *Am. J. Phys. Med. Rehabil.*, *95*, e30–33, 2016.

3. Boretius, T., Badia, J., Pascual-Font, A., Schuettler, M., Navarro, X., Yoshida, K., Stieglitz, T., A transverse intrafascicular multichannel electrode (TIME) to interface with the peripheral nerve. *Biosens. Bioelectron.*, *26*, 62–69, 2010.

4. Bouchard, K.E., Mesgarani, N., Johnson, K., Chang, E.F., Functional organization of human sensorimotor cortex for speech articulation. *Nature*, *95*, 327–332, 2013.

5. Carey, J., Multichannel vestibular implant early feasibility study. *Clin. Trials*, *42*, 370–376, 2016, Available via Johns Hopkins University; ClinicalTrials. gov. https://clinicaltrials.gov/ct2/show/NCT02725463. Accessed 11 Jul 2017.

6. Chen, X.L., Xiong, Y.Y., Xu, G.L., Liu, X.F., Deep brain stimulation. *Interv. Neurol.*, *1*, 200–212, 2013.

7. Choi, J.Y., Song, M.H., Jeon, J.H., Lee, W.S., Chang, J.W., Early surgical results of auditory brainstem implantation in nontumor patients. *Laryngoscope*, *121*, 2610–2618, 2011.

8. Clark, G.A., Ledbetter, N.M., Warren, D.J., Harrison, R.R., Recording sensory and motor information from peripheral nerves with Utah Slanted Electrode Arrays. *Conf Proc IEEE Eng Med Biol Soc*, vol. 2011, pp. 4641–4644, 2011.

9. Clinkard, D., Barbic, S., Amoodi, H., Shipp, D., Lin, V., The economic and societal benefits of adult cochlear implant implantation: A pilot exploratory study. *Cochlear Implants Int.*, *16*, 181–185, 2015.

10. Colletti, V. and Shannon, R.V., Open set speech perception with auditory brainstem implant? *Laryngoscope*, *115*, 1974–1978, 2005.

11. Colletti, V., Shannon, R., Carner, M., Veronese, S., Colletti, L., Outcomes in nontumor adults fitted with the auditory brainstem implant: 10 years' experience. *Otol. Neurotol.*, *30*, 614–618, 2009.

12. Collinger, J.L., Wodlinger, B., Downey, J.E., Wang, W., Tyler-Kabara, E.C., Weber, D.J., McMorland, A.J., Velliste, M., Boninger, M.L., Schwartz, A.B., High-performance neuroprosthetic control by an individual with tetraplegia. *Lancet*, *381*, 557–564, 2013.

13. Creasey, G.H. and Craggs, M.D., Functional electrical stimulation for bladder, bowel, and sexual function. *Handb. Clin. Neurol.*, *109*, 247–257, 2012.

14. Cronin, J.A., Wu, J., Collins, K.L., Sarma, D., Rao, R.P., Ojemann, J.G., Olson, J.D., Task-specific somatosensory feedback via cortical stimulation in humans. *IEEE Trans. Haptics*, *9*, 515–522, 2016.

15. Della Santina, C.C., Migliaccio, A.A., Patel, A.H., A multichannel semicircular canal neural prosthesis using electrical stimulation to restore 3-d vestibular sensation. *IEEE Trans. Biomed. Eng.*, *54*, 1016–1030, 2007.

16. Ethier, C., Oby, E.R., Bauman, M.J., Miller, L.E., Restoration of grasp following paralysis through brain-controlled stimulation of muscles. *Nature*, *485*, 368–371, 2012.

17. Fernandez, E., Greger, B., House, P.A., Aranda, I., Botella, C., Albisua, J., Soto-Sanchez, C., Alfaro, A., Normann, R.A., Acute human brain responses to intracortical microelectrode arrays: Challenges and future prospects. *Front. Neuroeng.*, *7*, 24, 2014.

18. Frigerio, A., Heaton, J.T., Cavallari, P., Knox, C., Hohman, M.H., Hadlock, T.A., Electrical stimulation of eye blink in individuals with acute facial palsy: Progress toward a bionic blink. *Plast. Reconstr. Surg.*, *136*, 515e–523e, 2015.

19. George, A.T., Dudding, T.C., Gurmany, S., Kamm, M.A., Nicholls, R.J., Vaizey, C.J., Pudendal nerve stimulation for bowel dysfunction in complete cauda equina syndrome. *Ann. Surg.*, *259*, 502–507, 2014.

20. Gilja, V., Pandarinath, C., Blabe, C.H., Nuyujukian, P., Simeral, J.D., Sarma, A.A., Sorice, B.L., Perge, J.A., Jarosiewicz, B., Hochberg, L.R., Shenoy, K.V., Henderson, J.M., Clinical translation of a high-performance neural prosthesis. *Nat. Med.*, *21*, 1142–1145, 2015.

21. Grill, W.M. and Mortimer, J.T., Stability of the input-output properties of chronically implanted multiple contact nerve cuff stimulating electrodes. *IEEE Trans. Rehabil. Eng.*, *6*, 364–373, 1998.

22. Hochberg, L.R., Bacher, D., Jarosiewicz, B., Masse, N.Y., Simeral, J.D., Vogel, J., Haddadin, S., Liu, J., Cash, S.S., van der Smagt, P., Donoghue, J.P., Reach and grasp by people with tetraplegia using a neurally controlled robotic arm. *Nature*, *485*, 372–375, 2012.

23. Hu, K., Bounni, F., Williams, Z., Advancement in brain-machine interfaces for patients with tetraplegia: Neurosurgical perspective. *Neurosurg. Focus*, *43*, E5, 2017, doi: 10.3171/2017.5.FOCUS17244.

24. IEEE Robotics and Automation Society, IEEE Engineering in Medicine and Biology Society. *Proceedings of the First IEEE/RAS-EMBS International Conference on Biomedical Robotics and Biomechatronics BioRob 2006 understanding how biological systems work, to guide the design of novel, high performance bio-inspired machines and to develop novel devices that can better act on, substitute parts of, and assist human beings*, Pisa, Italy, February 20–22, 2006.

25. Inspire Medical Systems, Inc., *Clinical trials*, Available via Inspire Medical Systems Stimulation Therapy for Apnea Reduction. ClinicalTrials.gov. https://clinicaltrials.gov/ct2/show/NCT02725463. Accessed 11 Jul 2017.

26. Jarosiewicz, B., Sarma, A.A., Bacher, D., Masse, N.Y., Simeral, J.D., Sorice, B., Oakley, E.M., Blabe, C., Pandarinath, C., Gilja, V., Cash, S.S., Eskandar, E.N., Friehs, G., Henderson, J.M., Shenoy, K.V., Donoghue, J.P., Hochberg, L.R., Virtual typing by people with tetraplegia using a self-calibrating intracortical brain-computer interface. *Sci. Transl. Med.*, *7*, 313ra179, 2015.

27. Jung, D. and Bhattacharyya, N., Association of hearing loss with decreased employment and income among adults in the United States. *Ann. Otol. Rhinol. Laryngol.*, *121*, 771–775, 2012.

28. Langhals, N.B., Urbanchek, M.G., Ray, A., Brenner, M.J., Update in facial nerve paralysis: Tissue engineering and new technologies. *Curr. Opin. Otolaryngol. Head Neck Surg.*, *22*, 291–299, 2014.

29. Larsen, J.O., Thomsen, M., Haugland, M., Sinkjaer, T., Degeneration and regeneration in rabbit peripheral nerve with long-term nerve cuff electrode implant: A stereological study of myelinated and unmyelinated axons. *Acta Neuropathol.*, *96*, 365–378, 1998.

30. Lawrence, S.M., Larsen, J.O., Horch, K.W., Riso, R., Sinkjaer, T., Long-term biocompatibility of implanted polymer-based intrafascicular electrodes. *J. Biomed. Mater. Res.*, *63*, 501–506, 2002.

31. Lertmanorat, Z., Montague, F.W., Durand, D.M., A flat interface nerve electrode with integrated multiplexer. *IEEE Trans. Neural Syst. Rehabil. Eng.*, *17*, 176–182, 2009.

32. Leuthardt, E.C., Schalk, G., Moran, D., Ojemann, J.G., The emerging world of motor neuroprosthetics: A neurosurgical perspective. *Neurosurgery*, *59*, 1–14, 2006.

33. Liem, L., Russo, M., Huygen, F.J., Van Buyten, J.P., Smet, I., Verrills, P., Cousins, M., Brooker, C., Levy, R., Deer, T., Kramer, J., One-year outcomes of spinal cord stimulation of the dorsal root ganglion in the treatment of chronic neuropathic pain. *Neuromodulation*, *18*, 41–48, 2015.

34. Lim, H.H., Lenarz, M., Lenarz, T., Auditory midbrain implant: A review. *Trends Amplif.*, *13*, 149–180, 2009.

35. Lim, H.H. and Lenarz, T., Auditory midbrain implant: Research and development towards a second clinical trial. *Hear. Res., 322,* 212–223, 2015.

36. Loeb, G.E. and Peck, R.A., Cuff electrodes for chronic stimulation and recording of peripheral nerve activity. *J. Neurosci. Methods, 64,* 95–103, 1996.

37. Malhotra, A., Hypoglossal-nerve stimulation for obstructive sleep apnea. *N. Engl. J. Med., 370,* 170–171, 2014.

38. Matthies, C., Brill, S., Varallyay, C., Solymosi, L., Gelbrich, G., Roosen, K., Ernestus, R.I., Helms, J., Hagen, R., Mlynski, R., Shehata-Dieler, W., Muller, J., Auditory brainstem implants in neurofibromatosis Type 2: Is open speech perception feasible? *J. Neurosurg., 120,* 546–558, 2014.

39. McDonnall, D., Guillory, K.S., Gossman, M.D., Restoration of blink in facial paralysis patients using FES. *I IEEE EMBS Conf. Neural, 76,* 376–381, 2009.

40. McKinnon, B.J., Cost effectiveness of cochlear implants. *Curr. Opin. Otolaryngol. Head Neck Surg., 22,* 344–348, 2014.

# 11

# Dynamics of EHR in M-Healthcare Application

**Eva Kaushik[1]\* and Rohit Kaushik[2]**

*[1]Department of Engineering (Information Technology), Dr. Akhilesh Das Gupta Institute of Technology & Management, New Delhi, India*
*[2]Department of CS and Mathematics (Data Analytics), University of Illinois, Springfield, USA*

## Abstract

Health systems and policies play a critical role in defining how health services are provided, run, and impact health developments. The years 2020 and 2021 have led to a huge crisis during the pandemic and the most abundant reason is the lack of a proper healthcare system. Technology has become an imperative component of the services, but still, we are weakened resulting in deaths, the spread of ailments, a shortage of pharmaceuticals, and inferior services. A common database and record system are globally known as the EHR model with various mutations which can help India to constrain all the health-related issues and become the finest in healthcare. This technique will not only maintain records but will also foreshadow the chances of forthcoming diseases, the tendency of ongoing diseases, and the deficiency of medicines. The records analyzed will help pharmaceutical companies to produce medicines according to the demands, saving a great amount of economic or financial resources and serving the best of health and medicine all over the country.

*Keywords:* Blockchain, healthcare system, patients, pharmaceuticals, semantic, security, total quality management (TQM), and actualization

*\*Corresponding author*: kaushikeva0026@gmail.com

Rishabha Malviya, Sonali Sundram, Bhupendra Prajapati and Sudarshan Kumar Singh (eds.)
*Human-Machine Interface: Making Healthcare Digital*, (295–310) © 2024 Scrivener Publishing LLC

## 11.1    Introduction

EHR and electronic health records are in practice in many developed nations. This system was introduced as a billing platform for all the health services citizens utilized. In this system, every user has a unique identifier that provides all the details of the user's case history and billing details. Later this system was updated with records of medicines and tests. The phrase "electronic health record" (later abbreviated "EHR") has a sparse and varied definition and is frequently used as a synonym for the "electronic medical record" (later referred to as EMR). Although the equivalency of EHR and EMR has been contested, the names are still frequently used interchangeably. For instance, the International Organization for Standardization (ISO) describes an electronic health record (EHR) as a repository for digital patient data that can be accessed by numerous authorized individuals and is securely kept and exchanged.

### 11.1.1    Why EHR is Needed in the Nation?

A person's EHR should mention a particular medicine if he wants to buy it from a pharmacy. A medical store cannot provide a citizen with any medicine of the EHR [1]. India is a developing nation, where on average, 13 crore people in 50 cities and 250 nationalities visit doctors daily. That means every 8th person we meet has visited a doctor for some reason or another. The high number of medical visits results in a large amount of medical data collected or recorded. However, India as a country has no record of patients visiting a doctor. 85% of prescriptions are written manually and used for single use. Patients lose their previous prescription every time they visit the doctor next. Due to this, a significant communication gap between the doctor and the patient arises as one cannot remember every patient's history, leading to severe health issues. Although EHR systems have simplified how healthcare is provided, they have also led to unexpected usability problems. According to Stanford Medical School research, 90% of doctors want the EHR to be more responsive, intuitive, and user-friendly. Furthermore, 6 out of 10 physicians (59%) believe that EHRs require a thorough redesign, and 38% of doctors hoped for very accurate voice recording technology that serves as a scribe during patient appointments. The scribe profession could ease the load of data entry, but they end up being costly in the long run. Natural language processing and artificial intelligence are seen by David Blumenthal, M.D., M.P.P., president of The Commonwealth Fund, as a long-term solution to the crisis. It may not be designed as the EHR with an improved interface. In fact, fresh functionalities to reduce EHR-related errors and a "fundamental redesign" are required. Clinicians will have more influence over the customization of the system as a result of this improvement, which will better suit their needs, flexibility, and reasonable expectations.

It is also necessary to improve the EHR's endemic one-dimensional decision-making capability. Clinical data must be used to create more predictive models and a more effective clinical decision support system (CDSS) [2, 3]. Many Indians are changing doctors quickly, leading to a significant communication gap. Furthermore, Indians are in the habit of taking medicines independently, taking a significant toll on their health. Introducing the EHR system in India can bring a major revolution in medical history.

## 11.1.2    Empowering Patients in Healthcare Management

As they are both the targets and participants of the EHR, patients are significant stakeholders in EHR projects. They have a right to see their electronic health record as citizens in many nations. For instance, this right has been in place since 2015 in the nations of the European Union. Patients would be able to view their medical history and track changes in their health by accessing the information therein, which would allow them to make independent healthcare decisions and take part in the decision-making process about their medical treatment [4].

From an ethical standpoint, the necessity that patients be treated as key stakeholders in EHR projects can be justified based on, for instance, the following various ethical foundations. First, healthcare must address the individual needs of each patient in accordance with the phenomenological and hermeneutical approaches to health, healthcare, and healthcare information systems. Since those requirements are founded on the unique experiences of patients, patients must be heard and taken into consideration when designing EHRs, which are the essential components of contemporary healthcare. Second, the Four Principles of Medical Ethics-beneficence, non-maleficence, autonomy, and justice-can be used as a basis for justification, even though there are criticisms of them [5]. There are also various ethical codes for healthcare and medicine, such as the WMA Declaration The fact that the patient-who is the primary aim and the true reason for the existence of healthcare—is overlooked while building the tools for healthcare, however, is peculiar if autonomy and justice are considered to be fundamental ideals. As a result, it appears that paternalism and technical determinism have buried autonomy and justice.

### 11.1.3   Data Management in EHR

From maintaining health records to medical records, the data can be stored and used better. Machine learning and artificial intelligence can bring in the best insights from medical health records. This data can be used to predict the early eruption of any disease, which can be taken care of well before in time. Moreover, the records can be used to maintain the inventory of all the pharmaceutical companies. By bringing this into action, there can be no shortage of medicines, and companies can maintain the overproduction of medicine [5, 6].

The system will have an automatic analysis system, which will ensure the security of data and proper analysis and prediction. This prediction will help the government to predict the early outbreak of diseases and the shortage of medicines. Moreover, suicides due to medicines can also be controlled. Deaths due to communication gaps between doctors and patients can also be reduced. Patients do not need to protect or maintain a file of all medical documents. An EHR card alone can handle all the issues and bring in the revolution. The paper flows with all the literature survey and background-related work, followed by an in-depth methodology and technology. Finally, the paper is further concluded with future scope, conclusion, and references.

### 11.1.4   Long-Term Architectural Approach

Traditional administrative solutions are built on the processing of data with limited automated interpretation in a static environment, but advanced management systems and medical department systems are based on the flexible, context-related processing and provision of information. It is the responsibility of departmental systems to overlay the relevant concepts, contexts, and functionalities on the data based on the data in the shared comprehensive EHCR repository and data warehouse. The information should be handled and recorded at the point of origin in order to guarantee its quality and integrity. Avoiding redundancies is a good idea. EHCRs are hence virtual, intellectually centralized, but not physically, solutions. Developing information and communication technology (ICT) strategies for the healthcare industry requires improving integration and evolution of core applications [7]. The various EHCR techniques have been unified by merging current development paradigms with the vast domain expertise demonstrated by other models, standards, and R&D project outcomes. The Magdeburg Medical Informatics Department's generic component approach, established in the mid-1990s, has been used for this. The ISO

Reference Model–Open Distributed Processing (ISO RM-ODP), which was initially designed with only three views, serves as the approach's starting point.

## 11.2    Background Related Work

According to Hong Kong's EHRSS, an individual's EHR may be shared for healthcare purposes. Although high security is provided by the Personal Data (Privacy) Regulation (Cap 486) and Electronic Health Record Sharing System Regulation (Cap 625) (together, "EHRSSO" and "PD(P)O") [2].

The Internet of Things (IoT) makes use of fast networks, cloud-based analytics, storage, and computing, as well as the integration of real-time medical data and information with hospital records. Discusses how a patient's electronic personal health information can boost their health, the efficiency of their physicians, and the expense of their care. legislation that promotes the establishment of ePHI and levies fines on those who hinder the transmission of health data This request for norms to guide and oversee the advancement of electronic personal health information systems concludes the discussion [4]. In a setting of shared maternity care, the EHR intends to include clinical consideration amongst doctors of General practice. GPs, birthing assistants, united wellbeing experts, and the lady herself. A combination of these consideration areas is a huge factor needed for the compelling and safe administration of pregnant ladies, with numerous methodologies being recognized [5].

Using the world wide web is the e-health strategy. Furthermore, the EHR will propose different healthcare offerings that will please patients, enhance their healthcare, and streamline workflows. Some patient-related objectives, include giving patients access to key components of their EHR, offering a vast library of self-care knowledge, and providing a quick, safe, and accountable method [6]. More timely and thorough clinical communication was found to be one of the three most crucial factors in a poll of affiliated physicians conducted in 2000. This led us to consider how we could give them access to EHRs. The EHR and Web apps can provide patient information to linked providers more quickly, securely, reliably, and affordably than conventional communication routes (such as U.S. mail, fax, radio, and face-to-face interactions). Information has been developed using allied service providers. A Web gateway was first made with information particular to each episode. The full EHR was then made accessible to partners by the developers. The routing of digitized and transcribed patient encounter documentation was most recently automated [7, 8].

This case report portrays a drive carried out to improve doctors' involvement in EHRs and is of a few techniques inside the association which was created to decrease doctor burnout credit. The EHR SWAT Team-a 10-part group with interdisciplinary portrayal from clinical informatics, drug store informatics, wellbeing data the board, clinical applications, and task the executives, is an immediate input channel for all doctors to communicate their EHR drawbacks and have their solicitations explored, focused on, and fixed conveniently [9].

This training applies to the way toward characterizing and recording the capacities, intelligent information sources, and pathways of information trade in regard to pharmacotherapy data administrations inside a given organization design serving a bunch of medical care constituents. It's anything but a specialized execution standard at the same time, rather, depicts how the execution strategies and methods can be utilized to arrange pharmacotherapy benefits intelligently inside an electronic well-being record (EHR) framework's climate including taking interest associations and destinations associated with an organized correspondence framework [10].

## 11.3   Methodology

The EHR system in India is going to be very complex and one has to be very cautious about maintaining it and running it in the entire country as there are many variables such as large population, overburdened healthcare system, etc. to consider. The first and most important function is to collect health records for the patients visiting hospitals or clinics. A portal for the hospital will be functioning 24x7 for them to enter or retrieve the medical history of a patient just by swiping a unique EHR card given to everyone which has all the login information of the patient. After the card swipe, doctors have all the medical background random of the patient which they can evaluate for better treatment, and new information can be added.

### 11.3.1   Use-Cases on Ground Base Reality

If a patient consults a new doctor, they will have all the medical history of the patient, which in usual cases patients fail to describe correctly and the doctor can evaluate and give better treatment. Using the supervised machine learning algorithm, companies can train it to show the most relevant information to the doctor.

There are many cases in which people are away from home like migrant workers, and the problem of not having the EHR card in person can be bypassed by using the Aadhar card and fingerprint of the patient [11]. The portal will be very user-friendly and the training for it to be used will be provided in vocational courses and the MBBS. All information about the diagnosis has to be entered correctly in the database and that responsibility lies with the hospital or the clinic.

To start with, the patient will register on our dashboard, and they will enter the basic details such as name, age, etc. Then the patient dashboard will open and there will be an option to share the medical records with the doctor. After uploading the records, files will be stored in IPFS storage, and the patient will be able to share the files with the specific doctor. After this process, the patient can easily login into their dashboard using their Meta Mask Wallet. Similarly, the doctor can also sign up on our dashboard by entering the basic details such as name, and age. Then the doctor dashboard will open and there will be an option to view the medical records of the patients who have shared their details [12].

After going through the patient's reports, the doctor can easily recommend the exact diagnosis. After this process, the doctor can easily log in to their dashboard using their Meta Mask Wallet. The patient can easily view the diagnosis given by the doctor by login into their Dashboard. Also, after viewing the diagnosis, the patient can remove access to the records. A central database will be maintained by the Ministry of Health with the coalition of the Ministry of Electronics and Information.

## 11.3.2 Integration of Technology to Solve Healthcare Issues

Presently, there are many government agencies and organizations which collect different medical data across different parts of the country, each one having a different parameter of management and therefore no uniformity is observed in the data collected. Even the health ministry has no fixed guidelines to collect the data because of the many agencies involved, which results in difficulty in analyzing the data and appropriate healthcare policies are not made therefore the system becomes weak [13]. Using the legacy tech algorithm, this data can be retrieved, so that we don't start from the beginning line [14].

An EHR mobile application will also be available where a customer can see their medical history, but they can modify or enter the information. The mobile application will also have a medicine schedule so that they don't mess it up and the application can also give an automatic reminder for the doctor's appointment as many people tend to forget about it.

This mobile application must contain a chat box, which uses natural language processing, especially Lemmatization and stemming, as Indians are not usually fluent in English, and can solve patients' minimal doubts about doctors and medicine.

On this data collected, one can also predict the chances of patients being prone to a disease such as The Framingham Risk Score is used to calculate the chances of patients getting coronary heart disease depending on the dataset.

### 11.3.3   Workflow

Managing workflow and process modification is a crucial factor to take into account when purchasing and implementing an EHR system. The way doctors work will change. Being unaware of this leads to a lot of needless frustration and inefficiency. Building a careful and objective procedure for choosing an EHR system is the first and most important consideration in the workflow. Consider enlisting outside support from industry experts or Regional Extension Centers (RECs) in your area if no one in your organization has experience doing this. It should be noted that RECs are federally funded organizations established to act as a resource for providers in need of EHR deployment and healthcare IT [15]. Realize that procuring and putting in place an EHR system is more than just an IT or technology undertaking. It requires the involvement of those who will be most affected by it, including scientists, in a deliberate and active manner. They must be involved in the planning process, vendor

1.  The system's capacity to be customized to the workflows of the medical personnel that will be utilizing it, limiting the amount of disturbance it will cause, is referred to as adaptability to physician work. When handling this flexibility, exercise caution. Chaos will result in the management of the practice and the patient records if each provider is allowed to handle things in their own way.
2.  When switching to an EHR system, evaluate your present procedures and workflows to see how they should be modified. Find a shared understanding among the medical team regarding the new workflow. Determine the criteria for data and processes that should be adhered to by everyone and the extent to which you will accept customization.

## 11.4   Tools and Technologies

We will use the fundamental ideas of Solidity, NodeJs, Metamask, and IPFS to create this project.

**Solidity:** Smart contracts are programmed that regulate account behavior in the Ethereum state. Solidity is a curly-bracket programming language aimed at the Ethereum Virtual Machine (EVM). C++, Python, and JavaScript are all influences.

**Ganache:** It is a private blockchain for Ethereum development, and Cord is a platform for building distributed applications. You can create, deploy, and test your apps using Ganache at every stage of the development cycle in a controlled environment.

**Node.js:** It is a cross-platform, open-source, and runs the program outside the web browser.

**Meta mask:** It is a tool that allows you to hide your identity. This database, having a real-life update, will also read the medicine usage trends, and will help us predict the medicine shortages before stocks perish and give us ample time to plan.

One often hears about the complications happening because of wrong medicine intake because of self-medication, and that problem can be solved using AI and blockchain in the

EHR system. The EHR will calculate the diseases one has and match them with the medicines one should seek. The pharmacies should use this card to extract those medicine names and give the appropriate medicines to the patients. Thus, saving any mishap [15].

We utilized homomorphic encryption, which uses encryption techniques that enable one to do calculations on encrypted data without access to the raw data. The computed results are the same as they would have been if the procedures had been carried out on the unencrypted data after encryption. High Security is thus ensured.

Off-chain storage is the strategy utilized in the existing development to help with the network storage constraint. People can easily and securely access their medical records with a variety of users, including doctors, hospitals, and insurance companies, utilizing the existing Health EHR DApp, while still preserving access control and security over the records. The application of blockchain is shown in Table 11.1.

**Table 11.1** Blockchain in healthcare.

| Performance/purpose | Advantages in healthcare |
|---|---|
| Decentralization | Avoids the restriction of single-point failure |
| Network Scalability | The blockchain's decentralized framework makes it hard to append healthcare techniques to the existing blockchain. |
| NONCE | Chooses the transaction's validator as part of the authorization procedure. |
| Permissioned Transaction | The degree of interference with stored data is reduced since all parties must agree before any type of data manipulation may take place. |
| Dynamic Records | Healthcare information is always evolving. Data must be regularly saved in blockchain blocks since it changes every second. Because each participant must consent, the alteration process takes longer, adding to the time complexity. |

The widespread illnesses that will be covered and treated by this system are:

Allergy and fungal infection. Drug Sensitivity, Malignant Neoplastic Disease, AIDS, Diabetes, Gastroenteritis, Influenza, Asthma, Hypertension, Migraine, Chronic Cholestasis, c - spine disease, Jaundice, Zika, Chicken pox, Dengue, Typhoid, Hepatitis C, Hepatitis D, Ebola, Alcoholic hepatitis, Paralysis (brain hemorrhage), Tuberculosis, Mild Cold, Dimorphic hemorrhoids, pneumonia (piles), heart attack, venous dysfunction, hyperthyroidism, hypoglycemia, and hypothyroidism Osteoarthritis, Arthritis, acne, psoriasis, urinary tract infection, and paroxysmal positional vertigo.

## 11.5   Limitations

One of the most difficult difficulties in healthcare today is financing. Despite the significant advantages of quality and safety enhancements, the EHR alone could not ensure the anticipated efficacy and a favorable return on investment. Reengineering the EHR into a clinical workflow management system with an integrated decision support system is crucial. Implementing formal distributed process management, formal knowledge management, and a unified semantic model of the EHR and medical terminologies are necessary for this. Preparing the care delivery team to utilize the Electronic Health Record (EHR) safely and efficiently is one of the key challenges in the installation and optimum utilization of the EHR. It has been well-documented that doctors are reluctant to adopt and use electronic health records. Low computer literacy and insufficient EHR training are two key barriers to practitioners using an EHR system.

## 11.6    Future Scope

The EHR system is the revolution in the medical history of India and many other developing countries. By proper implementation of this system, a country can win over most of the challenges. As health is an important aspect of our lives, governments should aim at implementing this system. With the implementation, a country can win over a medicine shortage, a sudden outbreak of diseases, and formulations of vaccines in advance.

### 11.6.1    Personalized EHR Cards

The country will have enough time to plan for precautions and post-out-break measures. Initially, the service can be brought to practice using Aadhar cards. Later, every citizen can get a personalized EHR CARD, which can be accessed at every medical shop and hospital. Reward points and perks of using this system to the citizens and a health-related organization can help the country achieve success very soon.

EHR systems can be the dawn of India's ministry of health. With one new change, people can win various battles against diseases. The health system can be cheaper, and the loss of lives due to the communication gap between two doctors can be reduced. Frauds in healthcare and pharma can come to nearly zero. Payments for medical expenses and the use of medical insurance will be effortless, and everyone could afford good medical facilities.

One of the most important aspects of an EHR system is data privacy. Furthermore, we can try adding functionality where another doctor can also access the patient's history.
1. We can try storing the patient's records in decentralized Blockchain-based Protocols.
2. We can also try connecting the medical records of the patients with their Aadhaar cards. Later, every citizen can get a personalized EHR CARD, which can be accessed at every medical shop and hospital. EHR system is

the revolution in the medical history of India and many other developing countries [16]. By proper implementation of this system, a country can win over most of the challenges. As health is an important aspect of our lives, governments should aim at implementing this system. With the implementation, a country can win over a medicine shortage, a sudden outbreak of diseases, and formulations of vaccines in advance.

## 11.7  Discussion

High hopes were held for Electronic Patient Records' ability to improve healthcare delivery, however, computerizing any clinical procedure will not be accepted if it does not optimize the procedure. Task automation, task specialization, automated communication, and decision support are examples of information technology systems that improve clinical operations. These mechanisms must be understood from two perspectives: functionality and ergonomics, both of which are essential for the user acceptance of data-processing tools. This suggests a previously underutilized effort in "software engineering" and "knowledge engineering."

### 11.7.1  Electronic Health Records and Personal Health Records

Previous research indicates that there is still disagreement among academics over the definition of EHR. However, EHR is frequently described as an information system that contains patient health information and is mostly managed by staff members of the healthcare provider [17]. A personal health record (later referred to as PHR) is an information system that restores health information about the patient and is controlled by the patient. This definition distinguishes EHR from PHR.

The information system, which was created for cancer patients to self-report their symptoms, is one example of such a personal health record. A separate information system that is integrated with an electronic patient record used in hospitals is another illustration. Patients can use this information system to do things like make appointments with medical professionals, contact them, keep track of their diets, and examine their discharge paperwork. We have chosen to broaden our inclusion criteria for this study in light of these findings. We have chosen to accept papers that cover personal health records in addition to those that mention electronic health records (EHR), provided that the records are related to EHR.

## 11.7.2    Physicians' Review Toward EHR

In response to their studies finding that dissatisfaction with EHRs is taking a significant toll on physicians, the American Medical Association (AMA) issued a press statement calling for a "design redesign of electronic health records to improve usability."

Time-consuming data entry and user interfaces that don't follow clinical workflow were two of the most common issues with EHRs. These issues are not new. Early on, in the 1970s, when pioneers in the field first started providing clinical systems intended for use by doctors, it was understood that gaining their acceptance and satisfaction posed difficult problems. Despite significant advancements in technology and methodology, the fundamental problems stubbornly persist.

1. Over 2,600 physicians from six different nations, including 601 from the United States, were surveyed by Accenture. The poll found that 79% of doctors thought they were more adept at using EHRs in their practices than they were two years prior [18, 19]. It also found that the use of routine EHR functions had significantly increased since 2012.
2. 71 percent of respondents thought healthcare IT reduced the amount of time spent with patients, and 58 percent of respondents said their EHR was challenging to use.

## 11.7.3    Interoperability

The primary benefit of information systems for digitized clinical data is that health practitioners are more interested in learning from the data than they are in simply looking at it. Many systems on the market today only convert old paper records into new electronic records. The WHO states that "e-Health" is a new term used to describe the combined use of electronic communication and information technology in the health sector or is the use of digital data transmitted, stored, and retrieved electronically for clinical, educational, and administrative purposes, both at the local site and at a distance.

- Enhancing the management of current resources
- Supporting diagnosis and treatment through the availability of more information in databases
- Increasing access to clinical data
- Automating care processes
- Improving user/patient communication.

## 11.8   Conclusion

Initially, the electronic healthcare record system was introduced in developed nations as a billing system for health-related service providers. It became a common platform for all doctors to put in their prescriptions to avoid the black market of medicines and illegal drugs. EHR system model that may maintain the security and privacy of EHR data while enabling scalability and flexibility of EHR systems in remote environments. We looked into one approach to addressing the security and privacy concerns with distributed EHR systems that do not rely on a single trusted authority. Additionally, we can offer configurable policies and fine-grained access control for secure EHR system architectures. No EHR system uses its database for the prediction of outbreaks of diseases and the shortage of drugs. Our paper breaks all the barriers and suggests the best method to implement and further use EHR systems with extreme security making it a better idea.

## References

1. *Electronic Health Record (EHR)*, Springer Reference, New York, USA, 2020.
2. *Hong Kong EHR sharing system*. Electronic health record, pp. 229–237, 2012.
3. Strain, J.J. *et al.*, *An updated electronic health record (EHR) for depression management*, Oxford Medicine Online, England, United Kingdom, 2018.
4. The Internet of Things (IoT), electronic health record (EHR), and federal legislation: The case for a national electronic personal health information (Ephi) record system. *Issues In Inf. Syst.*, 21, 3, 41, 2020.
5. Hawley, G., *The use of an electronic health record (EHR) in a maternity shared-care environment*.
6. Topper, J.E. and Dean, K.M., *Extending HER access to external physicians*, pp. 165–169, Health Informatics Implementing an Electronic Health Record System.
7. Hamsagayathri, P. and Vigneshwaran, S., Symptoms based disease prediction using machine learning techniques. *2021 Third International Conference on Intelligent Communication Technologies and Virtual Mobile Networks (ICICV)*, 2021.
8. Pal, A.K. *et al.*, Generic disease prediction using symptoms with supervised machine learning. *Int. J. Sci. Res. Comput. Sci. Eng. Inf. Technol.*, 11, 1082–1086, 2019.
9. Inbavalli, M., Fuzzy inference model for computation and prediction of disease pattern. *J. Adv. Res. Dyn. Control Syst.*, 12, SP4, 672–679, 2020.

10. Ampavathi, A. and Vijaya Saradhi, T., Multi disease-prediction framework using hybrid deep learning: An optimal prediction model (preprint). *J. Med. Internet Res.*, 8, 110, 2020.

11. Sparrow, M.K., *Electronic claims processing*, pp. 122–140, License to Steal, Colorado, USA, 2019.

12. Gu, Y. *et al.*, EHR data analytics and predictions: Machine learning methods, in: *Statistics and Machine Learning Methods for EHR Data*, pp. 273–293, 2020.

13. Wu, H., Use of EHR data for research: Future, in: *Statistics and Machine Learning Methods for EHR Data*, pp. 295–301, 2020.

14. Wu, H., Introduction: Use of EHR data for scientific discoveries—Challenges and opportunities, in: *Statistics and Machine Learning Methods for EHR Data*, pp. 1–17, 2020.

15. Shabbeer, S., Healthcare analysis using machine learning for mortality risk and readmission risk prediction based on EHR data. *J. Adv. Res. Dyn. Control Syst.*, 12, 3, 295–303, 2020.

16. Shen, L. *et al.*, Abstract 34: Improve decision making in clinical trials through machine learning and EHR. *Poster Presentations - Proffered Abstracts*, 2020.

17. Hebda, T., Hunter, K.M., Czar, P., Handbook of informatics for nurses and healthcare professionals. *Pearson*, 2019.

18. Wiegard, R., Degirmenci, K., Breitner, M.H., What influences the adoption of electronic medical record systems? An empirical study with healthcare organizations executives, 2017.

19. Stair, R.M. and Reynolds, G.W., Fundamentals of information systems. *Cengage Learning*, 2016.

# 12

# Role of Human-Machine Interface in the Biomedical Device Development to Handle COVID-19 Pandemic Situation in an Efficient Way

Soma Datta[1*] and Nabendu Chaki[2]

[1]Sister Nivedita University, Department of Computer Science and Engineering, Newtown, New Town, Kolkata, West Bengal, India
[2]University of Calcutta, Department of Computer Science and Engineering, Kolkata, India

## Abstract

The history of human civilization is witness to multiple surges in a pandemic situation. We have experienced multiple surges of COVID-19 in different demographical areas over the last eighteen months. Contemporary facts show that; there is a high chance that this COVID-19 pandemic situation will stay for a long time with multiple surges. Research articles show different influencing factors of this pandemic situation. It is tough enough to locate the most influencing factors that need to be addressed for reducing the risks of the pandemic situation. In this book chapter, the entire methodology section is divided into three consecutive parts. In the first part, cybernetic influence diagram (CID) is used to determine the major influencing factors of this pandemic situation. Second, a specific influence factor is analyzed in more detail with empirical data. The third part describes an outline of the household system, which may reduce the probability of COVID-19 infection transmission from outdoors to indoors. On the basis of discovered facts, a hypothetical conclusion could be established. These surges have a relation with the environmental temperature. Hence, the threats of the pandemic will stay for a long time. This increases the difficulty levels of physical and mental struggle. In this chapter, the discussion is not restricted to the boundary of establishing this hypothetical conclusion. We also focus on the outline of future research and

*Corresponding author*: soma21dec@yahoo.co.in

Rishabha Malviya, Sonali Sundram, Bhupendra Prajapati and Sudarshan Kumar Singh (eds.)
Human-Machine Interface: Making Healthcare Digital, (311–328) © 2024 Scrivener Publishing LLC

development trends for household healthcare systems. To combat multiple surges, different types of household devices are required to reduce the effect of COVID-19 on society. Guidelines for future research on household systems are discussed to reduce the probability of COVID-19 infection transmission from outdoors to indoors.

*Keywords*: SARS-CoV2, cybernetic influence diagram, thermal comfort, disinfection equipment, respirator, omicron, household healthcare systems

## 12.1 Introduction: Background and Driving Forces

The severe acute respiratory syndrome was first reported officially for a particular demographic area on December 2019. Then this syndrome was reported throughout the world within a very short span of time [1]. It was caused by an RNA virus, called SARS-CoV2 or COVID-19. As per Wang *et al.* [2], the mutation rate of this virus is quite high, near about 30.53%. Ninety-five full-length genomic sequences of SARS-CoV2 have been identified at the beginning of the year 2020. More than 2785 different genomic sequences of this virus have been identified till the beginning of 2021 [3]. This increases the difficulty level of the SARS-CoV2 vaccine-related research. This virus spreads all over the world. World Health Organization (WHO) declared it a global pandemic [4] on March 11, 2020. The spreading rate of this virus is much higher than its ancestor SARS-CoV. Some of the strain (genomic variations) of this virus is more infectious than its earlier strain. So far (September 1, 2021), about 218.8 million population in the world are reported to be COVID-19 positive; out of which 4.6 million people were deceased [5]. As per WHO, till now there is no specific common antivirus agent available for the treatment of all SARS-CoV2 virus strains. Depending on the condition of the patient, the treatment procedure varies. Day by day the number of affected people increased. Even people are affected by a different variant of Covid-19 in two to three times according to the COVID-19 wave numbers. Now omicron, the new variant is more infectious than the previous variant like delta. Although the Omicron affection rate is higher than the delta; however, the mortality rate of omicron is quite lesser than the mortality rate of delta [6, 7]. Table 12.1 shows the worldwide current situation of COVID-19. This table has been prepared according to World Health Organization (WHO) corona virus (COVID-19) dashboard [8].

Figure 12.1 shows the positive cases from March 2021 to December 2021 globally. It is observed from Figure 12.1 that the spike grows abruptly

**Table 12.1** Worldwide COVID-19 situation up to June 2021.

| Confirmed cases of Europe | Confirmed cases of Americas | Confirmed cases of South-East Asia | Confirmed cases of Eastern Mediterranean | Confirmed cases of Western Pacific | Confirmed cases of Africa |
|---|---|---|---|---|---|
| 12,00,07,077 | 11,96,48,309 | 4,77,23,964 | 1,78,07,464 | 1,32,79,664 | 78,12,182 |

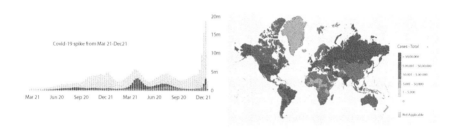

**Figure 12.1** Positive cases from March 2021 to December 2021 globally.

during the winter season. Worldwide 55,36,609 people died of these pandemic diseases! Situations are going worst day by day. It not only affects our economy, but it also badly influences our day-to-day life, especially for kids. In near future, our lifestyle would be changed. The following subsections show a few case studies along with some proposals for new engineering low-cost devices. Those devices also help us to fight against infectious diseases. The contributions of this research work are listed below-

1. Proposal of new engineering low-cost devices that help us to fight against infectious diseases.
2. Finding new research areas according to the technical competencies.
3. An overall situation comparison of COVID-19 using case studies.
4. Identification of influencing factors of COVID-19 using a Cybernetic Influence Diagram (CID).
5. A case study of COVID-19 that was observed in May 2021 in the Pacific region is also given.

### 12.1.1   Observed Scenario During May 2021

This section describes the facts that are associated with this COVID-19 pandemic.

#### 12.1.1.1   Transmission Medium

Some evidence has been found, which indicates that COVID-19 may be an air-born disease [9]. However, globally acceptable health organizations like WHO, CDC, etc. yet not declared that COVID-19 is an air-born disease (till 1st May 21).

### 12.1.2   Limitation of Vaccine Technology

Different genomic sequences of this SARS-CoV2 virus have been found in different demographic areas and the mutation rate of this virus is very high [2, 3]. So, it is very difficult to prepare a vaccine that will act on most of the different genomic sequences of this virus [10]. At present, almost all publicly available vaccine acts as an immunity buster but does not ensure that the virus will not attack [11]. This indicates that we have to face multiple waves (surge) of this SARS-CoV-2 virus attack [12, 13] in the near future. Wearing masks along with vaccination are the protective measures that we have to adapt.

### 12.1.3   Adverse Effect of Protective Measure

Wearing a face mask outdoors or even indoors is the most effective armor to protect from a COVID-19 virus attack. However, wearing an N95 respirator or surgical face mask for a long duration results in many adverse effects. The frequency of mouth breathing increases. This may alter the pattern of breathing and may change the respiratory milieu. Sometimes, airway symptoms are also been observed due to wearing an N95 respirator for a long duration (more than 3 hours a day) [14, 15].

In parallel with the COVID-19 pandemic, depression becomes another silent epidemic that is not in the limelight [16]. Children to adults, all age groups are victimized more or less. Increasing aggressiveness in the child age groups is the reflection of their insecurity feelings. They are addicted to computers or mobile games to get rid of this. The condition of the underprivileged children group is more miserable. They do not have the infrastructure to attend online classes and talk with friends and teachers [17].

Adults are also anxious about their future and family [18]. It is a matter of hope that a considerable number of European countries can reduce daily COVID-19–positive cases [5]. They have revoked some restrictions upon their citizens like night curfew, etc.

### 12.1.4 Revoking of Restrictions Causes Surges in Pandemic

In India, the second wave of this pandemic is devastating. In the first week of May 2021, the situation was almost out of control in the capital of India and other important cities. The situation was very chaotic. The physician community of India has warned regarding the second wave but the government has not taken enough precautionary steps to tackle the second wave. During this pandemic situation, the government conducts a lot of state-level elections. During the election different political parties made an uncountable number of public gatherings and rallies to establish their influence. Some of the public gatherings and rallies were crowded with more than 0.4 million people [19]. As a consequence, the pandemic situation becomes uncontrollable in some areas of India. International support is required to tackle this chaotic situation. Madras high court (in India) accuses the election commission (a government body that conducts elections in India), in this regard [20, 21].

Hence, it is a matter of a long time span when COVID-19 becomes an endemic disease from a pandemic disease. Hence, we have to deal with future surges of this pandemic. Research articles show different influencing factors of this pandemic situation [22, 23] and it is a multidimensional challenge. It is tough enough to locate the most influencing factors that need to address for reducing the vulnerability of the pandemic situation.

## 12.2 Methods

The entire methodology section is divided into three consecutive parts. In the first part, cybernetic influence diagram (CID) is used to determine the major influencing factors of this pandemic situation. In the second part, a specific influence factor (obtain from the first part) is analyzed in more detail with empirical data. The third part describes an outline of the household system which may reduce the probability of COVID-19 infection transmission from outdoors to indoors.

## 12.2.1   Determine Major Influencing Factors

At the time of analyzing a problem, our cognitive analytical skill becomes confused when the number of interlinked influencing parameters of the problem increases. In such a situation, system thinking tools are used to analyze the problem. The use of system thinking tools has started in 1956. A lot of revolutions have been observed in existing system thinking tools and in addition to this lots of new tools have been developed to strengthen the power of system thinking. The cybernetic influence diagram (CID) [24, 25] is one such tool. The crude form of this tool was developed by Tata Consultancy Service Ltd. in 2011. CID is a directed graph with nodes and edges. Each directed edge denotes the influences between two factors (node). Consider a CID with an edge and two nodes (influencing factors). If there is a proportional influence upon the destination node (factor) by the source node then the connected edge should show the positive symbol, it can be considered as the weight of the directed edge. If there is an inversely proportional influence by the source node on the destination node then there should be a negative symbol upon the directed edge. In the case of a circuit in the CID, all symbols of the directed edges in a circuit must not be the same. It indicates infinity gain; which indicates instability. CID assists to find all influencing factors (including missing factors) along with influence; this ultimately helps to model the problem. Figure 12.2 shows the major influencing factors associated with "new COVID-19 cases" using CID.

All influencing factors are not considered for the sake of simplicity; otherwise, it will be very complex to understand. It is clear from the CID that, "new COVID-19 cases" indirectly reduce economic growth as well as mental health. "New COVID-19 cases" are indirectly influenced by "tightening social gathering rules," "healthcare expenses for prevention," and "awareness and personal protection equipment." As per the CID, "Tightening social gathering rules" cannot be used for a long-term solution; it indicates instability as per CID rules. Consider the circuit "new COVID-19 cases," "probability of lockdown," "tightening social gathering rules," and back to "new COVID-19 cases"; apparently, it looks stable because the gain is not infinite. However, if we consider the adjoining circuit "new COVID-19 cases," "probability of lockdown," "tightening social gathering rules," "depression," "tendency to disobey social gathering rules," and finally, "new COVID-19 cases," the gain of this circuit is infinite as per CID rules. So, it indicates instability. All influences of the circuits are positive; so it indicates instability. Hence, we have to focus on other influences that reduce "new COVID-19 cases" from other directions. Those are "healthcare expenses for prevention" and "awareness and personal protection equipment."

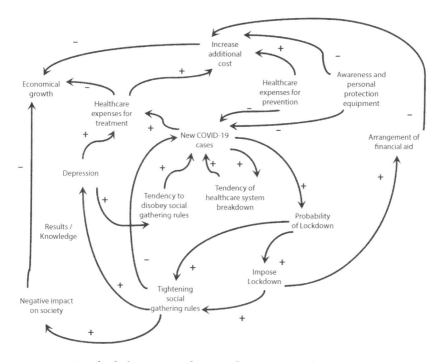

**Figure 12.2** CID for finding major influencing factors associated with "new COVID-19 cases."

## 12.2.2   Analyzed the Selected Influencing Factor

The "healthcare expenses for prevention" includes the discovery, manufacturing, and distribution of effective vaccine for COVID-19. At present, almost all publicly available vaccine acts as an immunity buster but does not ensure that the virus will not attack [11]. This indicates that we have to face multiple waves (surge) of this SARS-CoV-2 virus attack [12, 13] in the near future. A considerable number of European countries are able to reduce daily COVID-19-positive cases [5]. It could be assumed that the people of those countries are following the health guidelines provided by the respective government health agencies, these are part of "Awareness and personal protection equipment". The most common guidelines are as follows-

1. Wearing of mask and maintaining the mask related instructions properly.

2. Clean the exposed body part with soap and alcohol-based sanitizer for at least 20 seconds.
3. Maintain social distancing.
4. Ensure the safety of food items before eating.

In addition to these, some other hidden factors are there that assist to reduce the daily positive cases for those European countries. Table 12.2 shows a sample study for two European countries. This table shows daily new COVID-19-positive cases with respect to the temperature of the capital of those countries. The data are collected from the World-O-Meters [5] and AccuWeather website [26]. This data pattern gives a hazy idea, that when the "moving average" of environmental temperature is gradually increasing then the daily new COVID-19 positive cases are decreasing. It may be a combined effect of health guidelines and the rising environmental temperature. It could be argued that then why tropical regions (comparatively warm weather) have a considerably large number of COVID-19-positive cases. The lack of consciousness about the health guidelines and high population density are the reasons behind the new positive cases in tropical regions.

### 12.2.2.1   Evidence 1

As per the WHO document, SARS-CoV2 could not survive beyond 56°C [27]. That means rising environmental temperature creates an adverse condition for SARS-CoV2 [28].

### 12.2.2.2   Evidence 2

Table 12.3 shows a comparative study of the COVID-19 daily infection rate per million between India and Nepal. India and Nepal are two neighboring countries with a lot of cultural and behavioral similarities with each other. However, the main difference between these two countries is the climate. India is much warmer than Nepal. Table 12.2 shows the hike in the daily infection rate per million population (at the time of the second wave of COVID-19 in the Indian subcontinent) [5]. There are lots of political gatherings have been organized in India from March 21 to May 21 for state-level elections which influence the daily infection rate [20, 21]. In Nepal, the general election will be in next year (2022). So, the political gathering is not an issue for a hike in the daily infection rate for Nepal. At present, the daily infection rate per million population of Nepal exceeds the daily infection rate in India. There is a high chance that the change in daily infection rate is influenced by low temperature.

**Table 12.2** A sample study for those European countries with daily COVID-19 positive cases and temperature.

| Date | France | | Italy | | Germany | |
|------|--------|--|-------|--|---------|--|
| | New COVID-19 case/ day (3 days moving average) [5] | Temperature at capital city (Paris) [26] in degree Celsius | New COVID-19 case/ day (3 days moving average) [5] | Temperature at capital city (Rome) [26] in degree Celsius | New COVID-19 case/ day (3 days moving average) [5] | Temperature at capital city (Berlin) [26] in degree Celsius |
| 10-3-20 | 278 | 15 | 1423 | 16 | 255 | 11 |
| 15-3-20 | 849 | 17 | 3213 | 18 | 1023 | 12 |
| 20-3-20 | 1628 | 17 | 5172 | 18 | 3494 | 9 |
| 25-3-20 | 3071 | 13 | 5073 | 13 | 4150 | 10 |
| 30-3-20 | 3862 | 11 | 5078 | 18 | 5338 | 4 |
| 5-4-20 | 3791 | 23 | 4569 | 21 | 5109 | 16 |
| 10-4-20 | 4170 | 26 | 3996 | 22 | 4836 | 16 |
| 15-4-20 | 3601 | 21 | 2931 | 18 | 2300 | 16 |
| 20-4-20 | 1802 | 23 | 2930 | 20 | 1889 | 15 |
| 30-4-20 | 414 | 15 | 2017 | 22 | 1417 | 19 |
| 5-5-20 | 663 | 21 | 1229 | 24 | 682 | 12 |
| 10-5-20 | 428 | 23 | 1071 | 27 | 817 | 24 |
| 20-5-20 | 478 | 29 | 643 | 26 | 626 | 21 |
| 30-5-20 | 1916 | 26 | 510 | 20 | 467 | 18 |
| 10-6-20 | 386 | 21 | 255 | 22 | 213 | 22 |
| 30-6-20 | 448 | 22 | 147 | 30 | 381 | 24 |
| 10-7-20 | 647 | 25 | 228 | 33 | 411 | 25 |
| 30-7-20 | 1092 | 33 | 284 | 38 | 758 | 23 |
| 21-8-20 | 4108 | 23 | 810 | 36 | 1639 | 22 |
| 10-9-20 | 7810 | 21 | 1469 | 33 | 1494 | 18 |
| 30-9-20 | 7810 | 20 | 1670 | 23 | 2191 | 15 |
| 20-10-20 | 19879 | 15 | 10694 | 18 | 6388 | 12 |
| 10-11-20 | 27141 | 12 | 31203 | 16 | 15720 | 8 |
| 30-11-20 | 8244 | 11 | 21209 | 13 | 14146 | 2 |
| 20-12-20 | 14401 | 10 | 16508 | 15 | 25449 | 1 |
| 20-1-21 | 17497 | 5 | 18809 | 10 | 20009 | 3 |
| 31-1-21 | 20797 | 7 | 12512 | 15 | 10364 | -1 |

**Table 12.3** Comparative study of the COVID-19 daily infection rate per million between India and Nepal.

| Date | Daily infection rate per million in Nepal | Daily infection rate per million in India |
|---|---|---|
| 11-5-21 | 309 | 288 |
| 2-5-21 | 241 | 265 |
| 21-4-21 | 75 | 226 |
| 10-4-21 | 10 | 110 |
| 30-3-21 | 5 | 52 |

### 12.2.2.3   Evidence 3

As per earlier WHO guidelines, it was not an airborne disease. It spreads only through droplets [29]. However, this statement has been challenged by several groups of scientists. Thereafter, WHO changed its guideline partially [30]. It can be thought that the floating particles in the air may transport the virus to a long distance. If the virus survives in the floating particles of the air then the environmental temperature has an impact on the spreading of this virus. Hence, there is a chance of a COVID-19 surge after the end of the summer season.

### 12.2.3   Managing Mechanism to Reduce the Spreading Rate of COVID-19

The availability of a successful vaccine or the discovery of proper drugs that are dedicated to this disease could provide a permanent solution. However, the availability of these permanent solutions is uncertain. Hence, for this time being, we have to depend on the time being temporary safety solutions to reduce the danger of future surges of the pandemic. Some article shows that the SARS-CoV2 virus spreads through droplets and as well as aerosol emits from the nose and mouth of the infected person [31]. T. C. Bulfone *et al.* shows that in some situation, an outdoor environment is safer than an indoor environment with poor ventilation [32]. In the next subsequent sections, we will discuss the functionality and provide a guideline for the future household systems those are needed to be developed to reduce the spreading of the new strains of the SARS-CoV2 virus at the end of the summer season. Future household systems need to be developed to address the following matters.

1. Disinfect the personal belongings, necessary for outdoor, like winter clothing.
2. Modify the room air conditioning system to reduce the density of infectious aerosol particles.
3. Design the next-generation outdoor mask or respirator to reduce tresses on the lung.
4. Wearable smart device for health condition tracking for COVID-19 patients and estimating the risk factors.
5. Blending the real-time "Augmented Reality" features with modern home fitness equipment to reduce mental and physical tresses.

In this document, we are providing some hypothetical models for the selected systems mentioned above. Some technical details are also given These details are important for the physical implementation of these devices.

### 12.2.4    The Households Health Safety Systems to Disinfect Outdoor Cloths

Wearing a mask may protect us outdoors but clothes may carry this virus at home, where generally we are not using the mask. It is difficult to disinfect outdoor clothes (spatially winter clothes) on daily basis.

#### 12.2.4.1    *Present Households Disinfect Systems for Cloth and Personal Belonging*

Household disinfecting systems have a great impact in this regard. At present, a lot of standards and nonstandard household systems are available in the market to disinfect belongings. Most of them are UV based with poor safety measures. Only UV-C (100-280 nm) with proper intensity levels can kill this type of virus [33]. But this C-type UV is dangerous for the human eye. UV also acts as a stimulant for mutation [34], which may lead to skin carcinoma. WHO does not recommend UV for sanitization [35]. Moreover, UV-C based system can't disinfect the wrinkled and floppy fur portion of clothes. So, thermal-based systems are suitable to disinfect outdoor clothes (especially winter clothes). Samsung Air-Dresser is an expensive device that can disinfect clothes by using steam. It works like a "German steam iron" in a closed chamber. The main drawback of this system is that it uses steam; if steam is used on unclean cloths then it fixes the dust particles permanently on the outer surface of the cloths.

### 12.2.4.2  The Outline of Households Health Safety Systems to Disinfect Outdoor Clothes

At the time designing a household system to disinfect cloths using thermal energy should maintain the following factors.

1. The mode of transmission of heat should be convection; otherwise, un-uniform heating may damage the clothes.
2. The quantity of heat generation should be controlled in such a way that the surface temperature of the target object should be greater than 70°C and less than the tolerance temperature of the targeted material.
3. Disinfection process should be confined in a closed area with minimal air circulation. A thermal blower (like a hair dryer) can't be used for this purpose. It may blow the virus into the room air.

As an example, an outline of winter cloths disinfection system is discussed in this subsection. This system should be deployed within a small separate wardrobe, placed near the main door. The block diagram of the system is shown in Figure 12.3. In this figure, the dark-lined box denotes the periphery of the closed wardrobe. Inside this, a winter cloth is hanging upon a specially designed hollow hanger. The three red circles denote three low-speed air blowers. which are connected with a specialized hollow hanger. These three blowers receive hot air from the inlet (near the top of the hanger) portion and project the hot air into the inner side of the cloth. There are three temperature sensors marked with three different green shades. These are denoted by T1, T2, and T3. The blue solid arrows denote the direction of hot air flow. H1 is a heater to heat the air. The heating process is precisely controlled by the control unit via Triac. F1 denotes a fan. Its speed can be controlled by a separate speed controller. This F1 is used to control the volume of hot air within the closed wardrobe. The orange square near the H1 is an IR sensor. It is used to measure the heat radiation level of the heating coil. It acts as a sensor to take feedback at the time of generating a control signal for H1. In this method, the convection mode of heat transmission is used. The heating arrangement is placed at the bottom

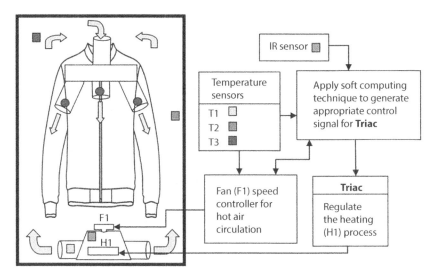

**Figure 12.3** Block diagram of the proposed conceptual system.

of the wardrobe for this mode of heat transmission. The operational workflow of the system would be as follows-

1. Place the winter clothes on the specialized hanger and close the wardrobe.
2. When the system starts up it sends a precise control signal to the Triac to start the heater (H1).
3. The T1 sensor, IR sensor, and speed of the F1 are organized in such a way that the emitting hot air temperature (t) from the heating module should lie between 700 < t < threshold.
4. By following the principle of convection, the hot air will be deposited in the top portion of the closed wardrobe.
5. When T3 senses the preferred ambient temperature then it starts the blowers. It is marked with the red circle in Figure 12.3.
6. When T2 sense the threshold temperature the heater (H1) and fan (F1) are controlled in such a way that the temperature sensed by all the sensors should not exceed the threshold.

The selection of threshold temperature depends on the material of the clothes. Cotton can tolerate 220°C whereas wool tolerance temperature is 150°C [36]. Hence, if the tolerance temperature is set to 800C then it is safe for all types of clothes and it also able to disinfect the cloths.

### 12.2.5   Upgradation of Individual Room Air Conditioning System

Nowadays, room air conditioning system becomes a part of the urban lifestyle [37]. In winter, room air heating and in summer room air cooling are desirable to maintain the comfort level. Both of these processes consume a considerable amount of energy. Energy optimization in individual air conditioning systems is becoming a major concern. These lead to poor ventilation in individual rooms. A study says that poor ventilation increases the spreading of the COVID-19 virus [9]. Hence, additional AI-controlled room ventilation systems need to be combined with the existing individual room air conditioning systems.

#### *12.2.5.1   The Outline of the AI-Based Room Ventilator System*

At the time designing an AI-based indoor room ventilation system to increase the quality of room air should have the following properties.

1. Inlet and outlet ventilators point should be placed far away from each other.
2. Inlet point should fetch fresh air from outdoors.
3. Outlet and inlet air should be treated by C-type UV.
4. The AI-based system would accelerate the air exchange process when the temperature difference between outdoor and preferred indoor air temperatures is minimum. This would optimize energy usage.
5. The air filter of the air conditioning system should be disinfected automatically at periodic intervals. Proper use of static electricity increases the performance of the air filter.
6. When the room is not in use, the air ventilator would work at full capacity.

### 12.2.6   Design of Next-Generation Mask

Mask with a higher filtration capacity (N95-N100) is essential for healthcare domain professionals. This type of mask uses different fiber layers for fencing tiny particles. This process creates resistance at the time of inhaling and exhaling. Wearing this type of mask, for a long time increases tresses upon the lungs and creates discomfort. The next-generation mask should be designed in such a way that it reduces the resistance at the time of inhaling and exhaling, without compromising safety. Mechanical arrangement with chemicals may be effective in this circumstance. Preliminary work has been stated to do this. However, acceleration of the progress to do these works on an urgent basis is required.

## 12.3    Results

On the basis of discovered facts, (section 12.2.2) a hypothetical conclusion could be established. This suggests that there is a high chance that this COVID-19 pandemic situation will stay for a long time with multiple surges. These surges have a relation with the environmental temperature. Hence, the threats of the pandemic will stay for a long time. This increases the difficulty levels of physical and mental struggle. Within this paper, the discussion is not restricted to the boundary of establishing this hypothetical conclusion. We also focus on the outline of future research and development trends (sections 12.2.4, 12.2.5, and 12.2.6) for household healthcare systems.

## 12.4    Conclusion

It is a matter of time before COVID-19 would become an endemic disease from a pandemic disease. During this period, we have to face multiple surges of this disease. If the situation becomes out of control, then "lockdown" like painful solution have to be adopted, which has an adverse effect on the economy. Hence, lots of research are required for different household systems to control the spreading of this disease in parallel with research in medical science. In this document, the outline of some conceptual models is discussed to combat with COVID-19 pandemic situation. Physical implementation requires lots of researches. As an example, in this outdoor winter clothing disinfecting system, the synchronization among different computing and control unit Petri Net model is useful [38]. This document gives a direction for product-based research to reduce the effect of COVID-19 surge in the upcoming days.

## Acknowledgment

The authors would like to thank Dr. Saumendu Datta for giving us relevant domain knowledge.

# References

1. Singhal, T., A review of coronavirus disease-2019 (COVID-19). *Indian J. Pediatr.*, 87, 4, 1–6, 2020.
2. Wang, C., Liu, Z., Chen, Z., Huang, X., Zhang, Z., The establishment of reference sequence for SARS-CoV-2 and variation analysis. *J. Med. Virol.*, 92, 6, 667, 2020.
3. Nakamichi, K., Shen, J.Z., Lee, C.S., Lee, A., Roberts, E.A., Simonson, P.D., Roychoudhury, P., Hospitalization and mortality associated with SARS-CoV-2 viral clades in COVID-19. *Sci. Rep.*, 11, 1, 1–11, 2021.
4. W. H. Organization *et al.*, Virtual press conference on COVID-19-11 March 2020, 2020, https://www.who.int/docs/default-source/coronaviruse/transcripts/who-audio-emergencies-coronavirus-press-conference-full-and-final-11mar2020.pdf.
5. Worldometer, COVID-19 coronavirus pandemic, 2021, URL: https://www.worldometers.info/coronavirus.
6. Cameroni, E., Bowen, J.E., Rosen, L.E., Saliba, C., Zepeda, S.K., Culap, K., Pinto, D., VanBlargan, L.A., Broadly neutralizing antibodies overcome sars-cov-2 omicron antigenic shift. *Nature*, 602, 7898, 1–9, 2021.
7. Nemet, I., Kliker, L., Lustig, Y., Zuckerman, N., Erster, O., Cohen, C., Regev-Yochay, G., Mendelson, E., Third bnt162b2 vaccination neutralization of SARS-CoV-2 omicron infection. *N. Engl. J. Med.*, 386, 5, 492–494, 2021.
8. WHO, WHO coronavirus (COVID-19) dashboard (Accessed Jan 18, 2022), 2022, URL: https://covid19.who.int/.
9. Greenhalgh, T., Jimenez, J.L., Prather, K.A., Tufekci, Z., Fisman, D., Schooley, R., Ten scientific reasons in support of airborne transmission of SARS-CoV-2. *Lancet*, 397, 10285, 1603, 2021.
10. W. H. Organization *et al.*, Evaluation of COVID-19 vaccine effectiveness: Interim guidance. Tech. Rep., World Health Organization, 2021.
11. WHO, Getting the COVID-19 vaccine, 2021, https://www.who.int/news-room/feature-stories/detail/getting-the-covid-19-vaccine.
12. Abdool Karim, S.S. and Oliveira, T., New SARS-CoV-2 variants clinical, public health, and vaccine implications. *N. Engl. J. Med.*, 384, 19, 1866–1868, 2021.
13. Pilz, S., Chakeri, A., Ioannidis, J.P., Richter, L., Theiler-Schwetz, V., Trummer, C., SARS-CoV-2 re-infection risk in Austria. *Eur. J. Clin. Invest.*, 51, 4, 201, 2021.
14. Zhu, J.H., Lee, S.J., Wang, D., Lee, H., Effects of long-duration wearing of n95 respirator and surgical facemask: A pilot study. *J. Lung Pulm. Respir. Res.*, 4, 97–100, 2014.
15. Radhakrishnan, N., Sudarsan, S.S., Raj, K.D., Krishnamoorthy, S., Clinical audit on symptomatology of COVID-19 healthcare workers and impact on quality-of-life (QOL) due to continuous facemask usage: A prospective study. *Indian J. Otolaryngol. Head Neck Surg.*, 10, 1, 1–8, 2021.

16. Ravens-Sieberer, U., Kaman, A., Erhart, M., Devine, J., Schlack, R., Otto, C., Impact of the COVID-19 pandemic on quality of life and mental health in children and adolescents in Germany. *Eur. Child Adolesc. Psychiatry*, 31, 6, 1–8, 2021.

17. Egan, S.M., Pope, J., Moloney, M., Hoyne, C., Beatty, C., Missing early education and care during the pandemic: The socio-emotional impact of the COVID-19 crisis on young children. *Early Child. Educ. J.*, 49, 5, 1–10, 2021.

18. Usher, K., Durkin, J., Bhullar, N., The COVID-19 pandemic and mental health impacts. *Int. J. Ment. Health Nurs.*, 29, 3, 315, 2020.

19. INDIA TODAY, Brigade face-off: The optics of mega rallies in Bengal, https://www.indiatoday.in/elections/west-bengal-assembly-polls-2021/story/bengal-election-kolkata-brigade-parade-ground-bjp-left-modi-mamata-rally-1776987-2021-03-08, 2021.

20. The Wire, Election commission should be charged with murder for allowing rallies: Madras HC, 2021, https://thewire.in/law/election-commission-should-be-charged-with-murder-for-allowing-rallies-/.

21. India Today, Madras HC holds election commission responsible for 2nd COVID wave, says officials should be booked for murder, 2021, https://www.indiatoday.in/india/story/madras-hc-election-commission-covid-wave-officials-booked.

22. Xie, Z., Qin, Y., Li, Y., Shen, W., Zheng, Z., Liu, S., Spatial and temporal differentiation of COVID-19 epidemic spread in mainland china and its influencing factors. *Sci. Total Environ.*, 744, 140929, 2020.

23. Karthik, R., Menaka, R., Hariharan, M., Kathiresan, G., AI for COVID-19 detection from radiographs: Incisive analysis of state of the art techniques, key challenges and future directions. *IRBM*, 43, 5, 486–510, 2021.

24. Kummamuru, S. and Mandaleeka, N., *Modeling the business system by applying cybernetic concepts*, pp. 1–6, IEEE, Melbourne, VIC, Australia, 2021.

25. Rai, V.K. and Mehta, S., Systems approach to as-is state formation of an engagement: A case study illustration, in: *2012 IEEE International Systems Conference SysCon 2012*, IEEE, pp. 1–6, 2012.

26. AccuWeather, weather-record, https://www.accuweather.com/en/in/new-delhi/187745/january-weather/187745?year=2020, 2020.

27. WHO, First data on stability and resistance of SARS coronavirus compiled by members of WHO laboratory network, 2020, https://www.who.int/csr/sars/survival_2003_05_04/en/.

28. Chan, K.J., Peiris, J.M., Lam, S., Poon, L., Yuen, K., Seto, W.H., The effects of temperature and relative humidity on the viability of the sars coronavirus. *Adv. Virol.*, 2011, 1, 1–7, 2011.

29. WHO, Modes of transmission of virus causing COVID-19: Implications for IPC precaution recommendations, 2021, https://www.who.int/news-room/commentaries/detail/modes-of-transmission-of-virus-causing-covid-19-implications-for-ipc-precaution-recommendations.

30. WHO, Transmission of SARS-CoV-2: Implications for infection prevention precautions, 2021, https://www.who.int/publications/i/item/modes-of-transmission-of-virus-causing-covid-19-implications-for-ipc-precaution-recommendations.

31. Chen, W., Zhang, N., Wei, J., Yen, H.L., Li, Y., Short-range airborne route dominates exposure of respiratory infection during close contact. *Build. Environ.*, 176, 106859, 2020.

32. Bulfone, T.C., Malekinejad, M., Rutherford, G.W., Razani, N., Outdoor transmission of SARS-CoV-2 and other respiratory viruses: A systematic review. *J. Infect. Dis.*, 223, 4, 550–561, 2021.

33. Gorvett, Z., BBC, Theres only one type of uv that can reliably inactivate COVID-19 and it's extremely dangerous, 2021, https://www.bbc.com/future/article/20200327-can-you-kill-coronavirus-with-uv-light.

34. Mackenzie, K. and Muller, H.J., Mutation effects of ultra-violet light in drosophila. *Proc. R. Soc. Lond. J. B-Biol. Sci.*, 129, 857, 491, 2020.

35. WHO, Raising awareness on ultraviolet radiation, 2020, https://www.who.int/activities/raising-awareness-on-ultraviolet-radiation.

36. Ironing Lab, The best steam iron advice and reviews, 2021, https://ironinglab.com/.

37. Ghosh, P., Bhattacharjee, D., Nasipuri, M., Dynamic diet planner: A personal diet recommender system based on daily activity and physical condition. *IRBM*, 42, 6, 442, 2021.

38. Ghosh, P., Bhattacharjee, D., Nasipuri, M., Intelligent toilet system for non-invasive estimation of blood sugar level from urine. *IRBM*, 41, 2, 94, 2020.

# 13

# Role of HMI in the Drug Manufacturing Process

**Biswajit Basu[1]\*, Kevinkumar Garala[2] and Bhupendra G. Prajapati[3]**

*[1]Department of Pharmaceutical Technology, School of Medical Sciences, ADAMAS University, Barasat, Kolkata, West Bengal, India*
*[2]School of Pharmaceutical Sciences, Atmiya University, Kalawad Road, Rajkot, Gujarat, India*
*[3]S K Patel College of Pharmaceutical Education and Research, Ganpat University, Mehsana, Gujarat, India*

## Abstract

The name "human-machine interface" (HMI) refers to a graphical user interface that enables human users to communicate with a system's machinery. HMIs are being used more frequently by consumers in regular chores as technology advances. Controls for using a machine, system, or instrument are provided by human-machine interface (HMI) systems. Every application of technology, including high-speed trains, CNC machining centers, semiconductor production machinery, and medical diagnostic and laboratory equipment, is made possible by sophisticated HMI systems. HMI systems include all the components a person will touch, see, hear, or employ to accomplish control functions and receive feedback on those actions. Today's HMI systems can transmit information to and receive information from other networked systems, such as materials handling or enterprise resource planning systems, as well as supervisory control and data acquisition (SCADA) and alarms (ERP). HMIs are used in self-service kiosks, ATMs, gas pumps, and checkout lanes to process user inputs, translate them into machine-readable code, and carry out activities without the assistance of an attendant, teller, or other staff members. An HMI offers a visual representation of the control system and real-time data acquisition in the context of industrial and process control systems. An HMI can boost productivity by offering a consolidated, exceptionally user-friendly representation of the control process. The use of HMIs in production lines allows users to update system processes without modifying

*\*Corresponding author*: bbasu.pharma@gmail.com

Rishabha Malviya, Sonali Sundram, Bhupendra Prajapati and Sudarshan Kumar Singh (eds.)
Human-Machine Interface: Making Healthcare Digital, (329–356) © 2024 Scrivener Publishing LLC

any hardware since they may monitor and control processes that are not controlled by a central processing unit (CPU) and may include data recipes, event logging, video feeds, and event triggering. In an automated system, HMIs are frequently used in conjunction with a programmable logic controller (PLC) to monitor and control processes. In general, the HMI gives the user a graphical interface through which to interact with the PLC (typically a touchscreen). In addition to allowing orders to be issued, this interface also collects and translates feedback data from the PLC, which is subsequently understandably displayed on the screen. This gives the operator crucial flexibility and command over a particular system. A tablet or smartphone with an integrated touchscreen that enables people to interact with the machine's programming is a great illustration of a typical HMI.

*Keywords*: Human-machine interface, materials handling, programmable logic controller

## 13.1    Introduction

A human-machine interface (HMI) is an effective tool that combines hardware and software to enable communication between systems and machines [1]. In the context of this chapter, we will refer to such systems as HMI even though they are also referred to as man–machine interfaces (MMIs), operator interface terminals (OITs), local operator interfaces (LOIs), and operator terminals (OTs) [2]. For information interchange and communication between systems/machines and a human operator, HMI includes hardware and software solutions. HMIs, which can range from straightforward inputs on a touch screen to control panels for extremely complicated industrial automation technologies, provide the control, management, and/or visualization of device operations. HMIs can be found in a variety of places, including on equipment, in centralized control rooms, and for machine and process control on factory floors. Appliances, digital signage, vending machines, medical, automotive, and smart buildings are just a few examples of applications.

A graphical interface that enables human users to communicate with a system's machinery is what is meant by the term "human-machine interface," or HMI. HMIs are being used more frequently by consumers in regular chores as technology advances. HMIs are used in self-service workstations, cash registers, ATMs, and petrol stations to process user inputs, translate them into computer codes, and execute tasks without the assistance of an attendant, banker, or other staff. An HMI offers a visual representation of the control system and real-time data capture in the context of industrial and process control systems. An HMI can

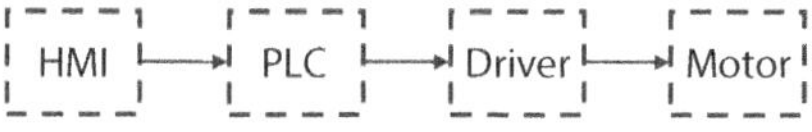

**Figure 13.1** HMI system diagram.

boost productivity by offering a consolidated, exceptionally manageable representation of the control process. The use of HMIs in production lines allows users to upgrade system functions without modifying any hardware since they may monitor and control processes that are not controlled by a central processing unit (CPU) and may include data recipes, event logging, video feeds, and event triggering. A manufacturing line must first be using a programmable logic controller (PLC), which serves as the CPU before it can be integrated with an HMI (Figure 13.1). The PLC translates the data from inputs (physical sensors or commands from the HMI) into production operations. The HMI displays the received inputs, control process outputs, and defined user variables being used to accomplish the tasks while these input data and operations are being carried out.

The pharmaceutical sector demands accuracy and efficiency, and the system must be able to automate manufacturing processes while maintaining compliance with data and user control. Pharmaceutical manufacturing achieves a new level of productivity and quality control with an HMI. Chemical-based pharmaceuticals come in a variety of forms, including sugar-coated pills, capsules, and powders. HMI plays a crucial role in the production of these medications. These interfaces are used to manually control procedural steps and see pertinent data during the procedure. These operating and monitoring systems must adhere to severe pharmaceutical standards, as well as criteria for explosions protection and the most cutting-edge production method.

### 13.1.1 Dialogue Systems

A conversation system is a computer program that interacts naturally with a human user. An interface between the user and a computer-based program is provided by the conversation System, allowing for a reasonably natural way with the application. The system can be used in telephones, PDA systems, cars, robot systems, and web browsers, among other devices. It can also be CUI, GUI, VUI, multi-model, etc. We communicate with the system using a text-based dialogue system. A spoken dialogue system is a type of computer system that allows for turn-by-turn conversation between humans and where spoken natural language interface is a key component of communication [3]. A multimodal dialogue system integrates the output of a multimedia system with the processing of two or more mixed user input types, such as speech, pen, touch, manual gestures, gaze, and head and body motions.

There are two types of dialogue systems, usually referred to as conversational agents, which employ text, speech, or both to interact with users in natural language. Conversation with users is used by task-oriented dialogue agents to aid in task completion. Give directions, operate appliances, find restaurants, or make calls using the digital assistants (Siri, Alexa, Google Now/Home, Cortana, etc.) that you can talk to. Conversational agents can respond to inquiries on business websites, communicate with robots, and even be employed for social good. For example, DoNotPay is a "robot lawyer" that assists clients in contesting unfair parking tickets, requesting emergency housing, or requesting asylum if they're refugees. Contrarily, chatbots are systems created for lengthy conversations that are meant to resemble the unstructured conversations or "chats" typical of human–human interaction. They are primarily used for entertainment but can also serve practical uses, such as trying to make task-oriented agents seem much more natural [4].

Conversational systems or chatbots, sometimes known as dialogue systems, are intelligent computer programs that simulate natural, interactive human communication [5]. The knowledge and retention of health education content can be enhanced via dialogue systems by making it more dynamic, engaging, and personal. For self-management of a variety of illnesses, such as cancer [6], mental health [7], hypertension [8], dementia [9], disabled people [10], and diabetes [11], numerous dialogue systems have been established.

The steps of input recognition, natural language understanding, dialogue management, task-oriented dialogue system (TOD) [12], response generation, and output rendering are the same for all conversation systems despite their varied architectural designs.

As seen in Figure 13.2, the whole dialogue solution uses an interpreter to translate text into useful features that the Dialogue State Tracker (DST) can process and use to update the dialogue state. The Dialogue Response Selection (DRS) module, which has been trained to output a response to user utterances, can provide a textual reply to the user by receiving the current dialogue state from DST. Later, a text-to-speech (TTS) synthesizer will turn this written response into speech. TTS and automatic speech recognition (ASR) [13] are complementary modules to a full conversation solution [14] because they are not directly related to dialogue management.

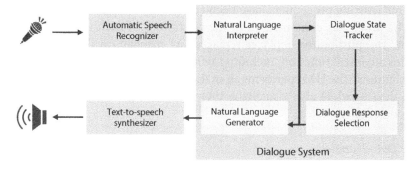

**Figure 13.2** Flowchart for the complete dialogue system.

An element of a dialogue system called a dialogue manager is in charge of distributing information among participants in human-machine interaction. Chatbots and frame-based dialogues are the two main categories of dialogue managers. In contrast to frame-based dialogues, where discussion frames are expertly constructed with slots and values that each slot can take, chatbot agents, are frequently trained to operate without any knowledge of the dialogue structure, which is most commonly referred to as open dialogue [15].

## 13.2    Types of HMI

HMI comes in a variety of different types, much like other electrical components. Push-button, Overseer, and Data Handling HMIs are the three basic categories of HMIs [16]. Depending on what the end-user wants to see/do from the HMI, a particular application will require a certain sort of HMI. We shall examine different kinds of HMI in greater detail below.

There are three primary categories of human-machine interfaces that you may encounter:

*The Pushbutton Replacer*
The replacement of all the machine's pushbuttons with these is rather self-explanatory. Without the need for numerous discrete physical pushbuttons, they concentrate total process/machine control from a single panel. The screen will show a graphical button that can be used for a variety of tasks, including start-stop, homing, screen navigation, and resets. Before the invention of the HMI, a control could have hundreds of push buttons and light-emitting diodes (LEDs) carrying out various functions.

Manufacturing procedures have been reduced by the pushbutton replacer HMI, which has combined all of the operations of each button into one spot. The pushbutton replacer replaces any mechanical device that performs a control function, including switches, On/Off buttons, LEDs, and/Off buttons. The HMI performs all of the same functions as these mechanical devices while also visualizing them on its LCD screen, making their deletion conceivable.

*The Data Handler*

This kind of HMI is utilized to display feedback from a machine's production report or performance report. Applications that need continuous feedback from the system or printouts of the production reports are ideal for the data handler. They can be used to set various recipes or view and accept machine-generated alarms. We must make sure the HMI screen is large enough to display information like graphs, visual representations of data, and production summaries with the help of the data handler. The database manager has features including recipes, data trending, data logging, and handling and reporting of alarms. Applications that need continuous feedback and tracking use the information handler. These data controllers frequently have huge capacity storage built in.

*The Overseer*

An overseer HMI is very helpful if an application uses SCADA (supervisory control and data acquisition) or MES (manufacturing execution systems). The overseer HMI has many Ethernet connectors and most likely needs Windows to function. The supervisor utilizes MES and SCADA. They can monitor and operate multiple machines and processes from a single location, rather than just one. These are centralized systems that keep an eye on and manage entire facilities or groups of sizable systems dispersed over sizable areas. To supply trends, diagnostic data, and management information, an HMI is typically connected to the SCADA system's databases and software programs.

## 13.3   Advantages and Disadvantages of HMI

Daily basis, technology improves while demand rises uniformly over the world. HMI technology is a vital component of any discussion of contemporary technology. The global HMI market was estimated to be worth $3.71 billion in 2020, and estimates indicate that by 2026, it will be worth

$7.24 billion [17]. Even though some people might not be familiar with it much, you can be sure that it's an important component of any industrial setup. Although implementing it into operations could be a bit pricey, it is worthwhile.

The dashboard (graphical interface) of an HMI is very user-friendly, which is its main benefit. The graphical interface includes color coding for quick identification (red for danger, for instance), as well as images and icons that enable quick recognition, lessening the difficulties caused by language barriers. HMIs can save production costs by improving system performance, which may result in higher profit margins. Modern HMI devices are very innovative, able to perform more complex, dynamic operations, and at larger capacities than they ever were. The HMI has several technological advantages, including the ability to transform hardware to software, do away with the mouse and keyboard, and enable multisensory computer/human communication.

### Convenience

The usefulness attained by digitizing a system with an HMI is unmatched, and the simplicity that an HMI offers is priceless. An HMI eliminates the need, for instance, to run to a red pushbutton to halt the production line in case of an emergency by combining all of the control elements generally present throughout the automated line and placing them in one centralized, remotely accessible area. With remote access, the operator can start, halt, or keep an eye on production without being physically close to the automated line. On a compact, centralized device, the operator has access to all of the identical settings. The usability of an HMI is significantly influenced by simplicity. The interfaces and features make it simple to control automation.

### Interface Flexibility

The ability to customize the interface of an HMI is of its most advantageous characteristics. The most sophisticated applications, with several screens and active processes, can be completely supported by an HMI. An HMI controller can be programmed directly in the HMI by the user if they want to do something more straightforward. Each HMI has a unique set of functionality; some can play audio or video, while others let you control it remotely. All of the usual user skills should be taken into account while designing the user interface, as well as environmental factors including noise, lighting, dust, vision, and technology advancements.

*Improved Productivity*

Although there are countless advantages to employing HMI systems, we cannot ignore the fact that output rises. Even though humans are capable of doing the majority of the tasks involved in this technology, manual operations typically take longer and are less efficient. HMI increases increasesvity through increased efficiency across a variety of manufacturing processes. High earnings are a given with more economic output and successful marketing. An HMI enhances the effectiveness of the assigned task. Even if a person could complete the task, this type of software or gadget vastly boosts productivity. Any industry may complete more work faster by using an HMI.

*Employee Satisfaction*

It has been demonstrated that using HMIs can significantly increase employee happiness in a given industry. It was observed that employees are more content to execute jobs that call for the usage of HMIs than tasks that do not. Consumers who shop online on touchscreen devices report feeling more satisfied than those who use standard monitors, according to some studies. This is so that they may easily access the websites of their choice thanks to touch-sensitive screens. HMI has the effect in that it lets workers communicate with the machine via an interface.

*Operation Management Becomes Versatile*

One can modify the interface using HMI technologies to meet certain needs or tastes. To track, monitor, and assist various systems, HMI systems are helpful. Although it takes a few steps to use either of the systems, the technique is effective for both simple and sophisticated systems. While a single employee can handle many displays at once, it is nearly difficult to operate multiple machines at once. The output rises as a result of making the HMI more user-friendly for different production steps. You can easily remote control particular processes when you use HMI technology in your sector. By doing this, you can easily track information for various procedures. On the other hand, because a worker can carry out numerous activities concurrently, this technology makes it simpler to manage operations.

*User Friendliness*

Although adopting human-machine interface technology has a few benefits, user-friendliness is the most alluring. This is because they provide basic graphical user interfaces that facilitate indentation and problem-solving through instantaneous recognition and automated color coding. The usage of a human interface avoids the need for some tools, which call for moving around to monitor different operations. It is possible to control numerous machines or devices in the manufacturing environment from one location using a single HMI. As a result, carrying out numerous activities becomes simpler and more affordable.

### Improve Data Capturing and Storing

Connect HMI to PLC for real-time information gathering to use it efficiently. Data is available through this link even when the HMI system is not active. It reduces the possibility that you will lose your data if your connection is lost. Even with inadequate internet connectivity, an HMI continues to function without data loss. When software is upgraded, data won't be lost. Some cutting-edge HMIs can retain unprocessed data for up to ten years with easy access. Due to easy and quick access to data, all procedures in companies that have implemented human-machine interface systems are successful.

### Benefits of an HMI Over a Standalone PLC

Without additional programming, a PLC cannot provide real-time feedback, trigger alarms, or make changes to the system. The main benefit of an HMI is its versatility; it may be used for straightforward tasks like a coffee maker controller or as the complicated control system for a nuclear power plant. With new HMI designs entering the market, operators can now access the terminal from a distance thanks to HMIs that support remote access. The flexibility to customize an HMI is another benefit. For best usability, the user can customize the user interface.

### Defend Against Workplace Accidents

Thousands of other workers also suffer serious injuries on the job each year in the United States, according to the Occupational Safety and Health Administration (OSHA) [18]. Human-machine interfaces, on the other hand, can lower these figures by shielding employees from frequent types of harm. Implementing an HMI solution, for example, will relieve employees of the strain of manually operating a machine. This will automate the process.

### Better Communications

The capacity of human-machine interfaces to improve communications between various technologies at work is one of their less well-known advantages. Remote I/Os, Ethernet ports, Dynamic Data Exchange, Data Highway Plus, Serial Port, and other features that allow for communication with external devices are frequently found on HMIs. A wide range of machines and gadgets can be linked together via human-machine interfaces, improving their ability to communicate and giving them new capabilities in the technique.

### Problem-Solving With Outdated Data

Based on a historical data feed, the HMI system recognizes and inspects the systems. Manually evaluating, isolating, and resolving the alarm took less time overall. HMI help with problem-solving at an early stage.

### Internet of Things

The phrase "internet of things" describes a group of gadgets that are all linked to the internet. Since HMIs are also devices, they can be connected to the internet. Applications like network monitoring and remote control access are made possible by this.

### Translation of Data

Certain HMIs convert the data from industrial control systems into human-readable visual representations. Thus, in an industrial plant, an operator may be able to operate the systems by, for instance, turning on and off pumps while seeing their diagrams.

### Reduce Hardware Prices

An HMI can lower a company's hardware costs, such as those for consoles, panels, and connections. A single HMI can save money by replacing hundreds of them. Organizations should purchase HMI solutions for this reason alone. The overall cost of hardware can be considerably decreased by utilizing human-machine interfaces. A single human-machine interface could take the place of dozens or even hundreds of different "indicator" lights, reducing the expense of extra hardware and making greater use of the space available.

### Asset Administration

Managers can be more effective and create precise maintenance plans for organizations thanks to accurate real-time data and reports. When it comes to maintaining and keeping track of numerous frequently moving assets, the drilling and fracking sectors face some of the most difficult challenges.

### Availability of Data

Data is a crucial component of decision-making. The value added to the process will be revealed by how users use these records. The strength is in the data's accessibility and relying on people's attitudes and skills to gain understanding and create improvements. Other analyses can also use this data.

*Messaging*
This feature is quite intriguing. When a specific event occurs, you can message, page, or fax the person concerned. Let's take the scenario where the hydraulic tank's oil level is getting low. When the oil level drops, a warning will sound, prompting the person in responsibility to top off the tank.

HMI essentially has no drawbacks. Their usefulness outweighs any minor faults. These days, people value and use them greatly. Any interface problem could arise as a result of the following.

*Security*
Although HMI application has long been thought to be protected from infection, they now offer a high risk of hacking due to their connectivity to the internet. A deficient HMI could serve as a point of entry for hackers to crash systems, potentially resulting in the loss of crucial security and confidential data.

*Poorly Designed Interface*
The majority of equipment and auto accidents are blamed on the human take, but when they are thoroughly investigated, it is frequently found that an HMI's poor design, which led to issues with the operator-machine interface, was actually to blame. A badly designed interface may have undesirable operational effects and mistakes that could have a serious negative effect on performance and safety.

## 13.4 Roles of HMI in the Pharmaceutical Manufacturing Process

Operator terminals for HMI are essential for managing processes in the pharmaceutical sector. A field that for many years was dominated by the herbal knowledge of the monks has developed into a high-tech industry that uses enormous amounts of data. Additionally, this data volume is still expanding: Industry 4.0 has also made it more crucial than ever to enable dispersed access to information and control functions. And manufacturing of pharmaceuticals is not an exception. Companies are increasingly depending on multipurpose plants that are created for the most effective manufacture of diverse pharmaceuticals. For the pharmaceutical business to achieve sustainable, effective manufacturing, HMI systems are crucial.

They must also adhere to GMP (Good Manufacturing Practices) guidelines and, in some cases, explosion protection guidelines, which are regulatory requirements for the production of pharmaceuticals.

Process and plant operators have three different needs in a pharmaceutical facility. Prioritizing cost-cutting, productivity optimization, and plant safety improvements while maintaining a high level of product quality assurance is the first goal. Cost-cutting measures include improving the purchasing of new goods and spare parts, promoting lean manufacturing practices, and lowering maintenance and upgrade expenses. Reducing downtime, improving output, and cutting waste can all help with productivity, and having simple, clear maintenance procedures and fewer installation mistakes can help with plant safety. Plant supervisors can accomplish all of this during the pharmaceutical manufacturing process thanks to the most recent HMIs. Pharmaceutical processing is often a batch process, in which the creation of the medicinal substance, or active pharmaceutical ingredient (API), requires numerous unit operations and is done so over several processes. The manufacture, extraction, processing, purification, and packaging of the finished product all involve the usage of HMIs, which are a crucial piece of piecesnery for controlling and monitoring these processes [19].

Generally, the earliest steps of pharmaceutical manufacturing consist of a series of reactions in which various functional groups are bonded to the initial raw material. The initial stage of ingredient manufacture involves adding raw or previously used material to a reactor along with heat and/or steam. To check that the conditions inside the reactor are right and to optimize the process, HMIs must give the operator clear data on a variety of factors, such as the amount of material fed to the reactor, the temperature, and the pressure. It is frequently necessary to provide additional information, such as a filling level, which notifies users via the Distributed Control System if the reactor is too full. Employees can securely terminate an operation using HMIs that can be modified and are equipped with stopping controls, which increases plant safety.

The upstream suppliers from fine chemistry, who give the basic materials to the pharmaceutical producers, are where the spectrum of operational sites starts. Every aspect must be perfect to obtain these compounds, including component purity, storage temperature, and pH level. They can only accomplish the required impact during the following production of active substances in this fashion. There is a reduction in the occurrence of highly combustible atmospheres as the pharmaceutical process progresses toward the manufacture of the active substance, or active pharmaceutical ingredient (API), along with an increase in vigilance over impurities.

This warning is necessary because, in the worst-case scenario, pollutants stuck to shoes, traces of a prior manufacturing procedure, or even a single human hair might render an entire batch useless. Operator workstations for interacting with the process or production control system in such environments, which frequently include pharmaceutical cleanrooms in compliance with GMP requirements, must be specially constructed for both chemical and mechanical resilience and be suitably cleanable.

To measure and regulate the quantity of coating solution applied to the tablets, HMIs are also employed in cleanroom applications for tablet coating. Here, stop buttons should be included on HMIs if a user has to halt the procedure, for instance, if the coating fluid is used more than what is necessary to coat the tablets, resulting in expensive wastage.

HMI must be utilized to monitor and regulate the transfer of liquids during the loading and unloading of liquids such as alcohol and chemicals into the plant. In this case, the fluids are injected into the storage space when they arrive, and HMIs can display information like the volume of liquid pumped and flow rate. The final area where monitoring and control are crucial is packing and dispatch. Pharmaceutical manufacturers may readily find the finished product with the use of HMIs that can be combined with barcode scanners and readers, which leads to higher production.

Pipelines and plant layout are major issues for pharmaceutical manufacturing facilities. HMI must be easily deployed and adapted inside an existing plant layout to save downtime and provide the operators with the functionality they need. Because it allows them to precisely operate and supervise their operation locally and on the outside, several companies opt to place their operator terminals on the plant floor near the operation. For conventional HMI systems, which are constructed as a single unit, this poses a problem since, to improve or maintain them, they must be taken apart off-site, which results in expensive downtime. In these dangerous environments, safety is also of utmost importance, and often cables between the HMI and processing sensors seek additional protection to ensure there is no possibility of a spark. HMI systems that are waterproof are required because pharmaceutical factories also need to be wiped down as part of a regular cleaning program to eliminate any leftover medicine particles and granules.

Furthermore, pharmaceutical industries employ some of the most cutting-edge packaging technology, constantly establishing trends that influence packaging norms in the food, beverage, and cosmetics industries. Human-machine interfaces are one such trend that has significantly impacted the entire packaging sector (HMI). Formerly a straightforward 1C CGA terminal, modern HMIs feature 16.7MC, HTML5 multimedia panels that give operators a visual representation of pertinent data to aid them in physically controlling stages [20]. In reality, HMI systems have developed to be a crucial component of the pharmaceutical production process, aiding in cost savings, productivity optimization, and plant safety while upholding a high level of quality assurance.

HMIs can reduce costs in a variety of ways, such as by enabling a lean production layout and ensuring that repair and upgrading expenditures are kept to a minimum. Lean production can boost output, decrease waste, and decrease downtime to maximize productivity. Easy and clear maintenance can also increase plant safety. HMI must, however, adhere to the essential regulatory standards for the manufacturing of pharmaceuticals. Because of these stringent safety and quality standards, the pharmaceutical industry has frequently taken the lead while other packaging businesses have lagged.

HMI design should prioritize severe pharmaceutical standards for explosion protection, Good Manufacturing Practices (GMPs), and other pertinent industry laws in addition to cutting-edge technology capabilities to ensure regulatory compliance. In their research on the machinery industry, the European Agency for Safety and Health at Work notes that a well-designed HMI is essential because of the high percentage of workers who interact with machines or other digital equipment [20]. In reality, a poorly designed HMI may raise workplace illnesses and may even result in workplace accidents, all of which can harm production, a professional brand, and user pleasure.

The following are a few advantages that HMI technologies in the health industry can provide:

*Simple to Clean*
Maintaining a clean, sterile atmosphere is crucial in medicine. HMI systems are frequently handled and touched, which makes them the ideal breeding ground for pathogens. Fortunately, HMIs are created with a surface that is simple to wipe and anti-microbial materials, removing the possibility of infection. The HMI technologies at e2ip technologies are created engineering expertise to safeguard against blood, gel, and other types of liquids and pathogens, keeping patients safe and extending the product's lifespan [21].

*High Chemical Tolerance*
Chemicals and strong solutions are frequently used to treat patients. Repeated exposure to such substances can cause many home systems to malfunction. Also, HMI provides, long-lasting HMI solutions made

especially for professionals that work with medical equipment. These HMI systems may be controlled with the touch of a finger, a pen, or a latex glove to increase efficiency.

*Transportable and Light*
Accessible medical gadgets are becoming more and more important as the market for home medical diagnostics expands. The mobility and simplicity of use of HMI systems are arguably some of their best qualities. The small, light, and ergo, nomic HMI created by e2ip are intended to improve user experience. Every system, regardless of function, is created using simple, universal, and understandable symbols for effective use. This helps medical professionals and increases the freedom of patients who utilize medical equipment at home.

*Enhancing Communication*
HMI systems may significantly enhance communications in hospital situations using a variety of techniques. Medical staff can interact more quickly and effectively to make sure patients receive the care they require. Additionally, HMI systems enable "paper-free workplaces," which assist minimize congestion and concentrate on what matters most: the health and wellbeing of sick people.

## 13.5    Common Applications for Human-Machine Interfaces

The need for human-machine interfaces (HMI) has skyrocketed in recent years. HMIs, which should not be confused with user interfaces (UIs), frequently concentrate on industrial applications and purposes. This does not imply that they aren't employed for other purposes, though. HMIs are used in both professional and domestic settings, as some people might already be aware [22]. The following is to find out more about HMIs and their applications [22].

### 13.5.1    Automotive Dashboards

The top manufacturers in the world are increasingly incorporating HMIs into their automobiles. A typical in-car HMI might have a touchscreen interface that allows the driver or passenger to operate various features including the radio, stereo, heating, air conditioning, and more. And this is a trend that won't be disappearing any time soon, as more automakers are expected to use HMI technology in the years to come, according to industry analysts.

### 13.5.2   Monitoring of Machinery and Equipment

The surveillance of machines or other pieces of equipment is another widely used technology for HMI. This is especially prevalent in industrial applications like factories where employees depend on HMIs to make sure their equipment is functioning properly. The HMI communicates with the relevant machinery and/or equipment, providing it with important information regarding its operations. Employees will observe a shift in the HMI if the machine starts to malfunction.

### 13.5.3   Digital Displays

In all addition, electronic or digital displays can also be employed with HMIs. In its simplest form, an HMI is nothing more than an interface that a human operator uses to operate a machine. As a result, an HMI might effectively be a touchscreen interface for e-ink text display. These HMI electronic screens are commonly used in offices and other business organizations.

### 13.5.4   Building Automation

Recent times have seen a rise in interest in the home and building automation. It entails tying together several interior technologies so that they may all be managed through a single user interface. Systems for lighting, security, humidity, heating and air-conditioning are just a few of the systems that might be integrated into a structure. Building automation commonly makes use of HMIs since they simplify the process and give the owner a practical control interface.

### 13.5.5   Video and Audio Production

The audio/video production industry is one of the less well-known HMI applications. HMIs can be used by A/V firms to operate their video cameras and microphones.

## 13.6    Healthcare System-Based Human–Computer Interaction

### 13.6.1    Healthcare System

(1) Current status of healthcare: The assurance of a better life for the public is healthcare. China has a sizable population, which results in high demand for medical treatment and more stringent specifications for the development of a healthcare system. According to pertinent public information, this chapter has sorted out the domestic health and medical demand market and the application market conditions of medical devices in recent years. This chapter also sorts out the domestic healthcare supply market [23]. In recent years, there has been an upsurge in the usage of medical rehabilitation equipment. The most popular of these is currently magnetic stimulation rehabilitation medical equipment, which is being used more and more. Medical robot use is gradually growing in the second category, which is electrical stimulation rehabilitation equipment. It is anticipated to surpass medical equipment for electrical stimulation rehabilitation based on this trend. Domestic health examinations' market size is expected to surpass 190 billion yuan by 2020, which also demonstrates how much care individuals are giving to their health [24].

(2) Domestic healthcare issues include the fact that China's society and economy are still undergoing a period of rapid change and development, that the distribution of social resources has not yet reached its ideal level, and that there are still some inconsistencies in the sector of healthcare, which is crucial to people's ability to support themselves. For instance, the availability and distribution of medical resources are inadequate, and the medical system is not ideal [25].

There are only about 2 professional doctors per 1,000 people in the country as a whole, whereas there are about 4 in wealthy nations like France and Switzerland, demonstrating the lack of adequate medical resources at home. In addition to being insufficient overall, domestic medical resources are not distributed fairly. The uneven distribution of resources has made some remote locations more in need of medical care due to the relatively limited domestic medical resources [26, 27]. Traditional medical care requires several steps, including scheduling appointments, waiting in a medical treatment line, treating symptoms, and reviewing results. The diagnosis method is only one, the procedure is labor-intensive and ineffective, and the medical treatment method is ineffective.

## 13.6.2   Teaching of Medicine and Physiology

(1) The current situation of physiology and medicine teaching

It is essential to use various physiological and medical education strategies to close the enormous domestic healthcare technician shortage and increase people's awareness of healthcare. Figure 13.3 illustrates how traditional physiology and medicine teaching courses are restricted to specific locations like schools and hospitals, and the teaching objects are typically the groups of teachers and students associated with majors. Everyone understands that everyone has a connection to healthcare, and everyone should be able to learn about healthcare at any time, anywhere, regardless of age, to better promote national healthcare. Online education has received a lot of support and use as a result of the growth of the Internet and domestic educational innovation. Network education has several benefits, including the ability to learn at any time and from any location, inexpensive teaching costs, a variety of course offerings, and retrospective teaching content, which can only partially address the issues associated with teaching physiology and medicine [28, 29].

(2) Physiological and medical teaching combined with the Internet

Teaching conventional medical information and theories is only one aspect of medical education; to stay current with modern medicine, medical educators must also keep up with it. Medical educators can acquire the most recent information online and share their knowledge, viewpoints, and accomplishments on relevant websites. Additionally, it is frequently challenging to directly exhibit educational content in medical education, such as human body structure, and disease progression, and it is challenging to show diverse organisms and operations for an extended period. But with the CAI demonstration, higher-quality, more logical, and longer-lasting educational outcomes can be made possible [30, 31].

Figure 13.3  Traditional medicine and physiology teaching.

**Figure 13.4** HMI interaction.

(1) Concept

Many of the tasks completed by computers involve a combination of humans and machines. Figure 13.4 illustrates the necessity for human–computer interaction in this situation where computers and people must interact.

(2) Origin and development

It is typically divided into four stages: the founding period, from 1969 to 1970, saw the publication of many monographs and the establishment of two research centers; the succession of many monographs from 1980 to 1995 saw the publication of numerous research centers; and the stage of the International Conference on Human-Machine Systems, in 1960, saw the concept of "close human-machine coexistence" proposed as the enlightenment point of view of human-machine interaction [32, 33].

(3) Human–computer interaction design

People, the activities that people do to provide commands, and machines, often referred to as human factors, activity factors, & object factors, are necessary components for human–computer interaction design. Realizing the user's mental model to accomplish the user's purpose is the aim of human–computer interaction design. The usefulness, dynamism, ease of use, diversity, and pleasure of human–computer interaction design should all be taken into consideration while realizing the user's mental model. Figure 13.5 illustrates the stark contrast between conventional interaction design concepts and contemporary interaction design principles [34].

(4) Classification of human–computer interaction

Functional, emotional, and environmental human-machine interfaces are three categories under which human-machine interaction can be classified. The relationships between these three categories are intricate and not entirely independent of one another. Functional human–computer

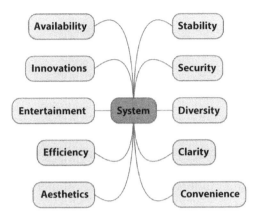

**Figure 13.5** Design of modern interaction principles.

interface refers to functional data on controls, objects, and controls used in human–computer interaction. It also includes docking with the manufacturing process or the use of materials and technology. An emotional human-machine interface is required for items to be able to express emotions through the interface, return to humans, and have an emotional resonance with people. A functional interface shows how to design and artificial objects work together. This type of perceptual information is transmitted in a way that combines predefined information with differences in person and environment, creating a seamless blend of known facts and unknowable feelings. The interaction between humans and machines in the environment is known as the environmental human-machine interface. The physical conditions and spiritual ambiance of the environment serve as crucial interface factors because products are inextricably linked to them [35, 36].

(5) Healthcare system based on human–computer interaction
The current domestic healthcare system is mostly composed of the components like medical security system, medical facility management system, medical institution service system, medication management system, and medical teaching system [37]. The primary components of the medical education system are the teaching of forensic medicine, emergency medicine, epidemiology, social medicine, medical ethics, sports medicine, psychological medicine, psychiatry, diving medicine, aerospace medicine, navigation medicine, ultrasound medicine, biomedical engineering, and so forth.

## 13.7   Performance Test of Healthcare System Based on HCI

### 13.7.1   HCI-Based Medical Teaching System

(1) Teaching system evaluation model.
The assessment indicators include teaching material, user-friendly human–computer interaction design, technical services, and subjective user satisfaction.

(2) Construction of teaching system.
An administrator module and a common user module are the two components of the system used to educate physiology and medicine in this study. User login, course study, forum question-answering, and evaluation feedback are just a few of the aspects found in the common user module. The administrator module has several important aspects, including administrator login, course management, and website management, while the course learning area has multiple components, including course search, browsing, and playback. In addition, course administration entails the distribution of instructional films and the assignment of homework [38].

Building a modern healthcare system, utilizing the aforementioned system and the primary components of the healthcare system allows for the creation of a library of teaching resources for physiology and medicine as well as the integration of human–computer interaction technology. This advances national healthcare by enabling everyone to study physiology and medicine teaching courses whenever and wherever they choose [39].

## 13.8   Human-Machine Interface for Healthcare and Rehabilitation

This strategy depends on the creation of new miniaturized systems for the discrete monitoring of biological signals using wearable or embedded sensors incorporated in Advanced HMI.

### 13.8.1   Ambient Intelligence and Ubiquitous Computing Scenario

Ambient Intelligence (AmI) is a term used to describe an intelligence that is pervasive and unobtrusive in the environment and supports the activities and interactions of the users [40] to bring computation into the actual, physical world and to enable people to interact with computational systems in the same way they would interact with other people. The computational and psychological underpinnings of this interaction touch on ideas from both the theory of computation and the philosophy of mind. The mechanisms involved in the adaptation of the functionality of the surrounding environment are not isolated from the subjects [41]. The human-machine interface (HMI) adapts to the needs of the user and becomes a nested component of an ambient cognitive system. Such complex systems need to be controlled by highly integrated acquisition and computational infrastructure, which implies that many connections to the real world are necessary to participate in it. Depending on the applications and the consumers, there are undoubtedly a variety of feasible practical solutions [42]. To enable and facilitate people's direct interaction with any type of computational device, a general architecture requires computation to be everywhere in the environment, including embedded in clothing. In contrast, another model can only be described with sensors and transducers that are embedded in the environment, realizing a wireless or wired sensor network with a centralized processing and control device [43].

### 13.8.2   The Advanced Human-Machine Interface Framework

To enable and facilitate people's direct interaction with any type of computational device, a general architecture requires computation to be everywhere in the environment, including embedded in clothing. In contrast, another model can only be described with sensors and transducers that are embedded in the environment, realizing a wireless or wired sensor network with a centralized processing and control device. To ensure that people are integrated into the environment they are in and achieve an attunement (mutual tuning) with it, AHMI can enable the pursuit of an automated, adaptable system. The system may induce, acquire, and process emotional signals through tuning, and it can then modify its behavior to the comfort or effectiveness of the services it provides. Consider a speech recognition system that is often used to issue instructions or compose sentences. This system can be improved to comprehend voice alterations to recognize exhaustion during various jobs [44]. In other instances, the computer can use the facial expressions of the individuals it is communicating with to better understand their needs, like in images captured during a videoconference. It is important to note that one of the most intriguing features of the AHMI is the ability to observe and characterize people's psychophysiological states, which enhances human-machine interaction and improves communication and task execution. We maintain that to accomplish a real-time adaptation to human demands, such a high-level interaction must be realized through the identification of subjects' conditions with the crucial role played by the biosignals monitoring. In new circumstances, AHMI is exploited when a person is aware that a computer might comprehend him and works with him to complete a task [45].

## 13.9   Human-Machine Interface for Research Reactor: Instrumentation and Control System

Based on cutting-edge human-machine interface design, a physical design for Research Triga PUSPATI's (RTP) New Instrumentation and Control System is suggested. Three key variables must be taken into account while building the human-machine interface for the research reactor: aesthetic, environmental, and human concerns. To meet safety requirements, a redundant and trustworthy system is required while proposing a new console reactor employing an HMI system. Instead of the aesthetic and operator interface geometry, physical parameters, experiences, trainability, and long-standing habit patterns are highly significant for the user interface to control and monitor the research reactor [46]. A physical design is suggested for Research Triga PUSPATI's (RTP) New Instrumentation and Control System based on cutting-edge human-machine interface design. When designing the human-machine interface for the research reactor, three important factors must be taken into account: aesthetic, environmental, and human issues. While proposing a new console reactor using an HMI system, a redundant and reliable system is necessary to meet safety criteria. To control and monitor the research reactor, physical parameters, experiences, trainability, and ingrained habit patterns are much more important for the user interface than aesthetics and operator interface geometry [47].

The human-machine interface (HMI) technology is advancing constantly, but it is new for use with Research Triga PUSPATI. As many users have pointed out, a subpar human-machine interface can be very annoying. On one end of the spectrum, a flawed or non-functional interface could make things difficult since it does not function as intended. On the opposite end of the spectrum, the interface is functional but has been created in a way that makes it difficult for people to understand and use since it is not intuitive. A thorough grasp of how people interact with their surroundings and a knowledge of human psychology is essential to building intuitive interfaces that will be used by a variety of people [47].

## 13.10   Future Scope of Human-Machine Interface (HMI)

HMI is now a part of our daily life and has many potential uses. The capacity to communicate with technology, from cell phones to robotic arms, is revolutionizing our way of life. The human–computer interaction will improve as more sensors become accessible. We will now be able to engage with computers and other things in ways we never imagined imaginable, which is fantastic news. We will also undoubtedly save time and money. By 2026, the HMI market is anticipated to have increased from USD 4.3 billion to USD 7.24 billion [17].

HMI devices' market growth is impacted by several important variables. For instance, the adoption of AI technology will be influenced by the market's expansion. Intelligent systems are used in manufacturing facilities for a variety of reasons, including more profitability and productivity as well as lower expenses.

The HMI not only improves communication but also eliminates or greatly reduces the number of push buttons, indicator lights, and other devices. Over the past few decades, machine-human interfaces have seen a significant transformation, moving from a push-button interface to the digital twin in manufacturing.

There will be more adjustments as a result of these. New HMI technologies will increase precision, safety, and problem-solving efficiency by enabling machine-to-human communication. To enhance the entire experience of employees in enterprises, industry 4.0 developers are combining new HMIs, such as enhanced touch-screen displays, voice interfaces, gesture detection, and AR/VR tools.

An entirely new form of the symbiotic relationship between humans and machines will soon be possible thanks to AI's ability to interact with human emotion. The distinctions between people and machines will practically disappear. Because humans are fundamentally social beings, AI will strengthen that bond. An intriguing technique to bring people and machines closer together is the most recent advancement in human-machine interface technology. The remote control is the means via which contemporary HMI will transform the world. Through the use of virtual, augmented, or mixed reality, we will be able to operate devices from a distance.

By enabling more widespread usage of these devices, technology will open up the globe to more individuals. The advantages of HMIs are therefore tremendous. By using these technologies, people will be able to converse with machines without using their minds. Additionally, it will make learning simpler and might improve human abilities. Thus, the world will undergo a revolution thanks to these instruments. Manufacturers anticipate that HMIs will link to more devices in the future and be capable of communicating with them from any place. The straightforward application-driven method for the creation of human–computer interfaces naturally extends to interconnecting Internet Internet-of-things.

Jennifer McLaughlin, a product designer, and futurist, has sketched out the future of human-machine interaction, including sensors, robotics, AI, and AR/VR [46]. HMI will become more complicated and dynamic as businesses continue to explore ways to boost productivity. HMI must be capable of keeping up with the quick changes as technological innovation continues to grow.

Manufacturers must invest in technological advancements that simplify interactions between people and computers. Efficiency requires a high degree of flexibility. The HMI is developing into a crucial component of the industrial process as technology progresses. HMI has a bright future ahead of it thanks to the constant addition of new possibilities. Wearable technology is another significant HMI trend. In the future, a smartwatch will serve as the user's assistant. The future of the human–computer interface is being set up by new technologies like speech, VR, and smart wearables, all generating novel interaction patterns.

## 13.11    Conclusion

How we connect with computers will significantly change over the next ten years. The way we interact with computers has been changed by smartphones and tablets. These new technologies have made it possible to create amazing new human-machine interfaces. We shall have the capacity to command things and people with our minds within the next 5 to 10 years.

## References

1. Stouffer, K., Pillitteri, V., Lightman, S., Abrams, M., Hahn, A., Guide to industrial control systems (ICS) security NIST special publication 800-82 revision 2. NIST Spec. Publ. 800-82 Rev 2, pp. 1–157, 2015, [Online]. Available: http://industryconsulting.org/pdfFiles/NIST Draft-SP800-82.pdf.
2. HMI guide, https://www.anaheimautomation.com/manuals/forms/hmi-guide.php (accessed Dec. 05, 2022).

3. Yamamoto, K., Inoue, K., Kawahara, T., Character expression for spoken dialogue systems with t-supervised learning using variational auto-encoder. *Comput. Speech Lang.*, 79, 101469, Dec. 2022.

4. Jurafsky, D. and Martin, J., Speech and language processing - dialogue systems and chatbots. *Speech Lang. Process.*, 2020, [Online]. Available: https://web.stanford.edu/~jurafsky/slp3/26.pdf.

5. Rose-Davis, B., Van Woensel, W., Raza Abidi, S., Stringer, E., Sibte Raza Abidi, S., Semantic knowledge modeling and evaluation of argument theory to develop dialogue based patient education systems for chronic disease self-management. *Int. J. Med. Inform.*, 160, 104693, Apr. 2022.

6. Car, L.T. *et al.*, Conversational agents in healthcare: Scoping review and conceptual analysis. *J. Med. Internet Res.*, 22, 8, e17158, Aug. 2020.

7. Fitzpatrick, K.K., Darcy, A., Vierhile, M., Delivering cognitive behavior therapy to young adults with symptoms of depression and anxiety using a fully automated conversational agent (Woebot): A randomized controlled trial. *JMIR Ment. Health*, 4, 2, e19, Apr. 2017.

8. Giorgino, T. *et al.*, Automated spoken dialogue system for hypertensive patient home management. *Int. J. Med. Inform.*, 74, 2–4, 159–167, Mar. 2005.

9. Russo, A. *et al.*, Dialogue systems and conversational agents for patients with dementia: The human-robot interaction. *Rejuvenation Res.*, 22, 2, 109–120, Apr. 2019.

10. Abma, T.A. and Broerse, J.E.W., Patient participation as dialogue: Setting research agendas. *Health Expect.*, 13, 2, 160, Jun. 2010.

11. Reid, M. *et al.*, Development of a health dialogue model for patients with diabetes: A complex intervention in a low-/middle income country. *Int. J. Afr. Nurs. Sci.*, 8, 122–131, Jan. 2018.

12. Zhao, M., Wang, L., Jiang, Z., Li, R., Lu, X., Hu, Z., Multi-task learning with graph attention networks for multi-domain task-oriented dialogue systems. *Knowl.-Based Syst.*, 259, 110069, Jan. 2023.

13. Chen, Y. and Celikyilmaz, A., Deep learning for dialogue systems_tutorial, vol. 1, no. Dm, pp. 25–31, 2011, [Online]. Available: http://deepdialogue.miulab.tw.

14. Serban, I.V. *et al.*, A survey of available corpora for building data-driven dialogue systems: The journal version. *Dialogue Discourse*, 9, 1, 1–49, 2018.

15. Merdivan, E., Singh, D., Hanke, S., Holzinger, A., Dialogue systems for intelligent human computer interactions. *Electron. Notes Theor. Comput. Sci.*, 343, May, 57–71, 2019.

16. Kadam, M.S., Ovhal, M.A., Kajulkar, M.K., Lad, M.R., Importance of human-machine interface in artificial intelligence and data science. *Int. J. Eng. Res. Technol.*, 8, 5, 1–3, Mar. 2020.

17. Global human-machine interface market size 2026, Statista, https://www.statista.com/statistics/1120222/global-human-machine-interface-market-size/ (accessed Dec. 21, 2022).

18. Commonly used statistics, Occupational Safety and Health Administration, https://www.osha.gov/data/commonstats (accessed Dec. 21, 2022).

19. A. Note, Innovative HMI and visualization systems for pharmaceutical processing, no. October, 2016, Accessed: Dec. 21, 2022. [Online]. Available: www.mtl-inst.com.

20. How HMI create leaner, more flexible pharmaceutical print processes, Pharmaceutical Technology, https://www.pharmaceutical-technology.com/sponsored/how-hmi-create-leaner-more-flexible-pharmaceutical-print-processes/ (accessed Dec. 21, 2022).

21. Human-machine interfaces in the medical industry, e2ip, https://e2ip.com/the-benefits-of-human-machine-interfaces-systems-in-the-medical-industry/ (accessed Dec. 05, 2022).

22. Common applications for human-machine interfaces, Nelson Miller, https://nelson-miller.com/common-applications-for-human-machine-interfaces/ (accessed Dec. 21, 2022).

23. Gutsalyuk, O.M. and Navolokina, A.S., Research on the economic interaction of the labor market and human resources IN the healthcare sector IN Ukraine. *Econ. Innov.*, 22, 74, 37–51, 2020.

24. Suresh, K. and Chellappan, C., Robust spontaneous human behaviour prediction system IN healthcare. *Int. Res. J. Pharm.*, 8, 11, 172–178, 2017.

25. Kwon, O., Kim, J., Jin, Y. *et al.*, Impact of human-robot interaction on user satisfaction with humanoid-based healthcare. *Int. J. Eng. Technol.*, 7, 2, 68–75, 2018.

26. Cernasev, A., Hillman, L., Okoro, O., Kamau, N., "I'm human. Listen to me.." African-American women's perspectives on interaction with the US healthcare system. *Res. Soc. Adm. Pharm.*, 14, 8, e46–e47, 2018.

27. Kimberly, S. and Mustapha, M., Human-computer interaction trends in healthcare: An update. *Proc. Int. Symp. Hum. Factors Ergon. Healthcare*, 7, 1, 88–91, 2018.

28. Olaronke, I., Oluwaseun, O., Oluwaseun, O., Rhoda, I., State of the art: A study of human-robot interaction in healthcare. *Int. J. Inf. Eng. Electron. Bus.*, 9, 3, 43–55, 2017.

29. Su, H., Di Lallo, A., Murphy, R.R., Taylor, R.H., Garibaldi, B.T., Krieger, A., Physical human-robot interaction for clinical care in infectious environments. *Nat. Mach. Intell.*, 3, 3, 184–186, 2021.

30. Abdullahi, I.N., Intestinal amebiasis and associated risk factors among pregnant women attending university of maiduguri teaching hospital, Nigeria. *Tanzan. Med. J.*, 31, 1, 31–47, 2020.

31. Nadin, M., Smart watches for physiological monitoring: A case study on blood pressure measurement, in: *Anticipation and Medicine*, pp. 231–252, 2017.

32. Van Sint Jan, S. and Geris, L., Modelling towards a more holistic medicine: The virtual physiological human (VPH). *Morphologie*, 103, 343, 127–130, 2019.

33. Friedl, K.E., Military applications of soldier physiological monitoring. *J. Sci. Med. Sport*, 21, 11, 1147–1153, 2018.

34. Douglas, J., Pearson, S., Ross, A., McGuigan, M., Ec-centric exercise: Physiological characteristics and acute responses. *Sports Med.*, 47, 4, 663–675, 2017.

35. Busso, D.S., Mclaughlin, K.A., Sheridan, M.A., Dimensions of adversity, physiological reactivity, and externalizing psychopathology in adolescence: Deprivation and threat. *Psychosom. Med.*, 79, 2, 162–171, 2017.

36. Lekli, I., Haines, D.D., Balla, G., Tosaki, A., Autophagy: An adaptive physiological countermeasure to cellular senescence and ischaemia/reperfusion-associated cardiac arrhythmias. *J. Cell. Mol. Med.*, 21, 6, 1058–1072, 2017.

37. Hammers, D.W., Merscham-Banda, M., Hsiao, J.Y., Engst, S., Hartman, J.J., Sweeney, H.L., Supraphysiological levels of GDF 11 induce striated muscle atrophy. *EMBO Mol. Med.*, 9, 4, 531–544, 2017.

38. Adler, M., Ivic, S., Bodmer, N.S. *et al.*, Thromboelastometry and t analysis under normal physiological conditions - systematic review. *Transfus. Med. Hemother.*, 44, 2, 78–83, 2017.

39. Dubray, S., Gérard, M., Beaulieu-Prévost, D., Courtois, F., Validation of a self-report questionnaire assessing the bodily and physiological sensations of orgasm. *J. Sex Med.*, 14, 4, 255–263, Apr. 2017.

40. Rouse, W.B., *Design for success: A human-centered approach to successful products and systems*, Wiley, New York, 1991.

41. Sheridan, T.B., *Telerobotics, automation, and human supervisory control*, The MIT Press, Cambridge, MA, 1992.

42. Sheridan, T.B., *Humans and automation: System design and research issues*, Wiley, New York, 2002.

43. Sundström, G.A. and Salvador, A.C., Integrating field work in system design: A methodology and two case studies. *IEEE Trans. Syst. Man Cybern.*, 25, 385–399, 1995.

44. Fejes, L., Johannsen, G., Strätz, G., A graphical editor and process visualisation system for man-machine interfaces of dynamic systems. *Vis. Comput.*, 10, 1, 1–18, 1993.

45. Johannsen, G., Towards a new quality of automation in complex man-machine systems. *Automatica*, 28, 355–373, 1992.

46. Future of human-machine interface (HMI) in the world we are building, https://futurside.com/future-of-human-machine-interface-hmi-in-the-world-we-are-building/ (accessed Dec. 21, 2022).

47. Ibrahim, M. M., Mutalib, R. A., Minhat, M. S., Manan, M. K., Farid, M. F. A., Ligam, A. S., Joha, N. A., Design and implementation of digital instrumentation and control system for PUSPATI TRIGA Mark II Reactor, Malaysia, in: *International Atomic Energy Agency (IAEA)*, IAEA, 2021, https://inis.iaea.org/search/search.aspx?orig_q=RN:52073132.

# 14

# Breaking the Silence: Brain–Computer Interface for Communication

**Preetam L. Nikam[1]\*, Sheetal Wagh[1], Sarika Shinde[1], Abhishek Mokal[1], Smita Andhale[1], Prathmesh Wagh[1], Vivek Bhosale[1] and Rishabha Malviya[2]**

*[1]SND College of Pharmacy, Yeole, India*
*[2]Department of Pharmacy, School of Medical and Allied Sciences, Galgotias University, Greater Noida, India*

## Abstract

A hardware and software communications system called a "brain activity" is used in brain–computer interfaces (BCI). To command computers or other external devices. BCI assists in providing communication ability to severely disabled people, whether they are completely disabled or "trapped" by neurological disabilities or certain musculoskeletal diseases. A BCI system functions by capturing brain signals, classifying the signals using machine learning methods, and executing an action that is computer-controlled. ECoG stands for "electrocorticography," which is providing an increase in interest as a recording method for BCI use since it is more suitable for fundamental neuroscience studies and the subsequent prospects for translation. Electron encephalographic signals are contrasted with those obtained from the scalp (EEG). The signal acquisition stage of a generic BCI system record includes processing artefacts and noise reduction for brain signals. The pre-processing stage gets the signals ready for further processing by putting them in the right format. The signals from the brain that have been recorded serve as discriminatory data during the step of feature extraction. The signal is measured and then converted into a vector that contains useful and discriminative characteristics from the observed signals. This information must be extracted, which is an extremely difficult task. Brain signals from a limited number of brain activities are combined with other signals, and things cross over in time and space. One of the biggest issues with BCI high-dimensional feature vectors are used in the design to enhance the classification of the signals, pertinent characteristics, and feature-based classification. This research aims to make a better suggestion.

*\*Corresponding author*: preetamnikam25@gmail.com

Rishabha Malviya, Sonali Sundram, Bhupendra Prajapati and Sudarshan Kumar Singh (eds.)
Human-Machine Interface: Making Healthcare Digital, (357–374) © 2024 Scrivener Publishing LLC

BCIs based on electroencephalographic potentials or oscillations are ready to undergo large clinical studies and commercial production as an adjunct or a major assisted communication device for paralysed and locked-in patient. A series of studies using BOLD response regulation with functional magnetic resonance imaging (fMRI) and near infrared spectroscopy demonstrated a tight correlation between voluntary changes in brain metabolism and behaviour.

*Keywords*: Brain–computer interface, neurorehabilitation, brain injuries, brain signals, vestibular cochlear reflexes, electron encephalographic, hardware and software communication, muscle stimulation

## 14.1   Introduction

In today's world, the prospectus of interfaces includes the interface between people and computers. Various forms have been present in different structures, like the typical keyboard, mouse, pen, and touchscreen technology. Human interaction with cutting-edge technology has increased as a result of this. Apart from those other ways that had been developed to establish connections, there is now a connection between a human and a computer without physical contact. which came into existence under the name of a natural interface [1]. A human-computer touchless interface with facial, voice, and motion capture capabilities However, patients who are physically disabled or have other syndromes and are unable to interact with or communicate with a computer using no words or gestures [2]. Locked in syndrome, sometimes known as "false coma," describes the condition in which a patient is unable to speak or move verbally due to paralysis of voluntary muscles. One of the most well-liked methods for enabling communication between people with locked-in syndrome is brain-computer interface (BCI), also referred to as BCI. and computers. Computer-brain interface (BMI). There are numerous methods to define BCI. A BCI, in its broadest sense, is a technology that uses computers to monitor and analyse brain signals. A direct link between a computer and the brain is the conventional definition of a BCI, using control signals produced by electroencephalographic activity instead of peripheral nerves and muscles. Using a hardware and software communication device known as a BCI, users can communicate with their environment. acts with the ability to command a computer or other external devices. Another application for a BCI is the recovery of cognitive and sensory-motor abilities in people. It allows users to converse with one another and gives those with motor limitations the ability to mentally operate wheelchairs, prosthetic limbs, or mouse cursors. But it's crucial to understand that a The BCI does not read minds. It is crucial to use BCI in the healthcare industry. For instance, it was applied when creating a drowsiness detection system. Additionally, it has been applied to assist patients with partial or total disabilities in moving around using robotic arms and legs. It makes it possible for those with paralysis to engage in mental games. Patients with BCI can use their brains to navigate the internet. by coupling an outside camera. As a result, BCI can be viewed as a significant technological advance for those with physical disabilities [3]. Despite having many advantages, BCI systems have a number of drawbacks. The ethical concerns surrounding the risk of infection or hemorrhage, the psychological harm brought on by a patient's unsuccessful attempt to operate an external device, the frequent typing errors from a BCI, the unintended movement of a robot arm or a wheel chair, and the privacy and confidentiality of patient information are just a few of the BCI in healthcare's major challenges. Additionally, a significant barrier to the effective use of BCI devices in the healthcare system is their lack of reliability. This is brought on by the BCI technology's high mistake rate. This is frequently caused by a weak brain signal that was retrieved. Legal problems are another difficulty that BCI technologies encounter. The obstacles to BCI deployment in healthcare, however, have received little attention. As a result, this paper explores the overall structure and fundamental elements of a typical BCI. This study also examines the various methods for obtaining brain signals.

## 14.2    Survey of BCI

In 1973, the phrase "brain–computer interface" (BCI) was first used. According to reports, Dr. Grey Walter was the first to implant electrodes into a surgery patient's brain using BCI technology. BCI is an interdisciplinary field with links to clinical rehabilitation, engineering, applied mathematics, psychology, computer science, and clinical neurology. It is a field of computer science that emerged from the engineering of robots and the interface of humans and computers, two subfields of artificial intelligence. BCI, on the other hand, represents the most recent innovation in the field of computer-human interaction. The brain and computer's direct connection and communication, as well as that of other external devices such as intelligent wheelchairs, is known as a computer-brain interface

(BCI) [4]. A BCI can be viewed as a tool that modifies the brain, converting impulses into activities that a computer is capable of carrying out. Alternatively, a BCI can only be used with systems that rely on brain signals, such as nerves, muscles, or voice. BCIs aren't regarded as activated. The nature of the brain impulses may be electrical, metabolic, or magnetic. In BCI systems, these signals are often used to deduce human intentions. These impulses are converted by converting user intents into digital commands that are used to execute them, such as operating a wheelchair or computer cursor. Usually, sophisticated algorithms are used to complete this task. BCI, however, is not just used with human brains. Several scholars have now divided the BCI into different groups. Venthur stressed, for instance, that there are two categories of BCI. These include BCIs based on motor imagery and attentiveness. When using attention-based BCI, the user is exposed to a variety of stimulation, like visual, haptic, or auditory stimuli, to develop the brain patterns needed to carry out particular activities. BCI has been divided into a number of categories by different authors. Examples include visually evoked potentials and event-related potentials in steady state (ERP) (SSVEP). The ERP and SSVEP are different in that the ERP normally presents the stimuli sequentially, whereas the SSVEP typically presents the stimuli constantly. As implied by its name, it is based on motor imagery. A system that performs a task is known as a BCI. Active, reactive, and passive (or emotional) BCI are a few examples of BCI. A user directly and consciously controls an application in an active BCI, utilising outputs derived from brain activity that is unrelated to an outside event. In a reactive BCI, a user's brain activity in reaction to an external event indirectly controls an application, whereas in a passive or affective BCI, the output for controlling an application is derived from idling mental activity without the user's conscious involvement. Asynchronous BCI, also referred to as self-paced BCI, enables the user to perform motor imagery at their own rate. BCIs fall into one of two categories: independent or dependent. A dependent BCI depends on muscles or peripheral nerves to produce the brain activity required to complete a task, whereas an independent BCI does not. This contrasts with the dependent BCI research conducted by scientists [5]. Endogenous and exogenous BCI are two other types of BCI. Despite the fact that exogenous BCI does not need much training to achieve the precise brain patterns needed to execute a task, endogenous BCI must.

## 14.3    Techniques of BCI

### 14.3.1    Potentials Associated With an Event

Activity takes place in a time-locked event after a stimulus is presented, before a movement is carried out, or following the identification of a new stimulus. An electrophysiological reaction to an internal or external stimulus is known as an ERP. A typical An ERP is exemplified by the P300 spellchecker. Users of the P300 communication device can spell letters and numbers. It was first proposed by scientists in 1988 [6].

### 14.3.2    Cortical Gradual Potentials

Electroencephalography (EEG) voltage shifts slower than 1 Hz are known as gradual cortical potentials (SCP). SCPs are frequently linked to modifications in brain cortical activity. As an illustration, a positive SCP value denotes a reduction in individual cell activity, whereas a negative SCP denotes an increase in neuronal activity [7]. The SCP's ability to be used to control external equipment by both healthy and paralysed users is a key benefit. On the other hand, SCP calls for thorough training methods.

### 14.3.3    Evoked Visual Possibilities

A visual evoked potential (VEP) is created by the brain's visual cortex in response to a stimulus. with a visual cue, traditional VEPs are therefore ineffective for paralysed patients with oculomotor deficits. The steady state visual evoked potential (SSVEP) is a form of VEP. Visual stimuli like SSVEP are typically measured using light-emitting diodes (LEDs), cathode-ray tube (CRT) monitors, or liquid crystal displays (LCDs) [8]. LED displays, on the other hand, outperform LCD and CRT displays because they provide more visual cues. An action, such as the movement of a prosthesis, the choice of icons, or the choice of alphabet letters, is represented by the visual stimuli. Users of SSVEP can choose targets using eye gaze while the brain handles the rest. The frequency of visual stimuli causes a pattern to be perceived by the user's brain, which is subsequently translated and carried out in accordance with the user's wishes. SSVEP should not be performed on people who have severe ALS, also known as amyotrophic lateral sclerosis, or intractable neck or eye movements. Contrarily, only those with typical vision and eye movements should use SSVEP [9]. A strong signal-to-noise ratio and a short learning curve are advantages of the SSVEP. A reliable paradigm for non-invasive BCI communication. There are also spellers that use sensorimotor rhythms.

### 14.3.4    Sensorimotor Rhythms

Because they are composed of beta waves, they are often referred to as beta and mu rhythms. Beta rhythms are oscillations in the mu or Rolandic band and the beta band (13–30 Hz). (7–13 Hz) of brain activity. According to researchers, motor imagery is tied to sensory-motor rhythms in the absence of actual movement [10]. SSVEP spellers outperform and are more reliable than P300 spellers. The Bremen-BCI speller is a speller.

### 14.3.5    Motor Imagery

The left or right foot's creative ability is often the foundation of motor imagery. Movement that causes the synchronisation or desynchroniza-tion of sensorimotor cortex events. When visualising motion, BCIs are more accurate than ERP, but they also require more training. It's cru-cial to understand that some spellers use motor imagery. The Artificial Intelligence and Robotics Laboratory (AIRLab), Department of Electronics and Information, Politecnico di Milano, the Technical University of Milan, Italy, published a sample example of a motor imagery-based speller. AIRLab's spellchecker offers 27 characters, word recommendations, dis-abled implausible symbols, and other features. It shows the user interface for the AIRLab speller. According to physicists, the speller is in two states of mind. Right foot and hand motions are envisioned [11]. A circle sur-rounds the speller.

## 14.4    BCI Components

BCI generally consists of four crucial parts:

1. Signal capturing
2. Processing of signals
3. Theft of data
4. Feedback

### 14.4.1    Signal Acquisition

Signal acquisition, according to this definition, is the assessment of the brain's neurophysiological condition. It involves getting electrical impulses from the brain as well. Electrodes can be used to collect electrical impulses either from the scalp, the brain's surface, or mental activity. The indicators are typically magnified according to the strength of the brain's signal, which is typically low [12].

### 14.4.2    Signal Processing

To get control signals, this includes analyzing the obtained signals. The three fundamental techniques for signal processing are signal translation, feature extraction from the signals, and signal categorization [13].

### 14.4.3    Extraction of Features

The technique of removing a specific form from brain signals is known as extraction of the main content. Feature extraction is frequently used to remove electrical hum and unwanted signals from obtained signals. There are many techniques for taking features out of BCI. These techniques include both parametric and non-parametric techniques. Some of the autoregressive (AR) and adaptive autoregressive (AAR) methods are parametric methodologies. Scientists claim that the AR model is more appealing than AAR techniques because it can effectively summarise data and convert it to feature vectors [14]. However, whereas AAR approaches are successful for detecting non-stationary time fluctuations in brain signals.

### 14.4.4    Signal Categorization

Signal classification entails converting signal processing to device commands. They are in charge of executing the intentions of the users [15]. Linear discriminant analysis is an example of a signal classification method (LDA). A simple classified form like LDA that divides patterns into two or more categories. A hyperplane is a representation of a linear discrimination function in the feature space according to LDA, whereas several hyperplanes are used for multi-class pattern classification.

## 14.5   BCI Signal Acquisition Methods

From the mind, signal acquisition can be accomplished in three ways. Both fully and partially invasive BCIs fall within this category [16].

## 14.6   BCI Invasion

These technologies make use of chemical compounds, electrodes, or sensors that are directly inserted into the body. In neurosurgery, the brain's grey matter is used. to record brain impulses. When doing invasive BCI, the electrode signals that are received are referred to as the ECG [17]. The ECoG comes in two different forms. Both epidural and subdural electrocorticograms fall under this category. Subdural electrocorticograms are signals acquired beneath the brain's dura mater, whereas electrodes are positioned on the cortex's surface outside of it. BCI is the most precise and least noisy, and it has the strongest signal. On the other hand, invasive BCIs are exceedingly harmful since they are susceptible to the development of scar tissue. BCI research has thus far only been carried out using animal models. There are, however, two varieties of invasive BCI. Both single- and multi-unit BCIs are among them. invasive method using only one unit. While several units use invasive ways to get data from various regions of the mind, single-unit invasive techniques only catch signals from a single location of brain cells. The image shows an intrusive BCI electrode [18].

## 14.7   BCI With Limited Invasion

Electrodes used in partially invasive BCI are frequently encased in a thin plastic pad that is applied to the skin on top of the cortex. As a result, electrodes are placed outside the brain but inside the skull. in semi-invasive BCI. However, compared to fully invasive BCI, the signal strength is weaker, and there is a decreased chance of developing scar tissue [19].

## 14.8   BCI Not Invasive

Medical scanning apparatus or sensors are frequently worn on a cap or headgear during non-invasive BCI. Brain signals can be read with a headband. Because of this, non-invasive BCI does not require a device implanted in the brain or brain surgery. This type of catheter poses no risk of infection or bleeding and is completely safe to use. Additionally, they cost less than fully and partially invasive BCIs. In comparison to non-invasive BCI, invasive and partially invasive BCI produce a lesser signal. Signal attenuation as it travels via the scalp, dura, and skull is the main drawback of non-invasive BCI [20].

## 14.9    BCI Applications

BCI has been used in a variety of ways to help those who are afflicted with depression, disabilities, and other ailments. Communication problems and disorders of consciousness (DOC) people that fit this description frequently include those with Amyotrophic Lateral Sclerosis (ALS), cerebral palsy, brainstem strokes, spinal cord injuries, muscle dystrophies, and persistent peripheral neuropathies. These illnesses often result in impaired muscle function, leaving patients fully locked into their bodies even when their cognitive abilities are still intact. Contrarily, BCI systems allow people who suffer from locked-in syndrome to convey using a computer interface, you can provide words, letters, and commands that are then translated into a user-controllable computational output [21].

### 14.9.1    Movement

The ability to move from one location to another is referred to as loco-motion. It is challenging for patients with motor disorders like ALS, poly-neuropathy, amputees, and paraplegia to move around. In order to assist patients with mobility challenges, BCI technology, such as robotic arms and legs, voice-activated wheelchairs, joystick- and remote-controlled wheelchairs, BCI-driven wheelchairs, and prosthetic knees and hands, has been created. As a result, their level of autonomy increases [22].

### 14.9.2    Recreation

Those who have severe motor disabilities can play video games with BCI to sharpen their motor skills. It satisfies their psychological needs. BCI also enables patients with disabilities to unwind. In Mind Balance, EEG, cerebral data nodes, and Bluetooth are utilized. The brain ball game, which was also developed by researchers, aids patients in managing stress [23].

### 14.9.3   Reconstruction

BCI technologies are also employed to aid the recovery of sensory and motor functioning in people with impairments. neurological conditions to lessen their emotional and social suffering. For instance, it has been claimed that bionic eyes can help those who have lost their sight. A prosthesis can be used to restore locomotion. Accordingly, researchers developed a neuromotor tool to aid those who have had spinal cord injuries in regaining grasp function [24]. According to one scientist, a two-way directional response between the user and a type of BCI results in physical adjustments that allow neurologically impaired people to regain control over their motor and communicative abilities [25].

### 14.9.4   Interaction

BCI technologies are used to aid communication between locked-in patients. Examples of communication devices include applications for BCI speech devices and management of the environment. Electric Stimulation Function (ESF) or any other devices [26]. The use of basic word processing functions and icon selection on computer screens are also permitted by BCI devices [27]. BCI programmes also make it possible for people with neurological conditions to access the Internet by using their brains [28].

### 14.9.5   Interaction With Others

BCI technologies are being employed increasingly frequently as a result of recent improvements in their portability and simplicity. They are currently employed in mobile applications to gather user emotional data for inclusion in posts on social media. As a result, the patient's emotional state becomes more conscious [29].

### 14.9.6   Diagnosis and Treatment of Depression

On the basis of clinical observations and patient self-reports, depression is routinely measured. BCI methods, on the other hand, are used to collect any type of emotional data from a specific user. As a result, BCI can be used to quickly identify depression in patients using the emotional data collected from them. As a result, these wards can receive appropriate care in a timely manner [30].

### 14.9.7    Reduces Healthcare Costs

By lowering the need for ongoing supervision, BCIs cut healthcare costs. For rehabilitation, therapists the morality of medical protocol, as a collective form of people, is founded on the condition of a set of moral standards that are close to medicine practice. Healthcare is one of the cornerstones of medical ethics. Basic medical ethics are covered in this part, along with the moral issues utilised for effective use in the healthcare system with the help of BCI.

## 14.10    BCI Healthcare Challenges

Applications of CI in healthcare include services like movement control, social interaction, rehabilitation, pain management, and communication supports. However, it is not a frequently used technology in healthcare due to the multiple difficulties it faces. These challenges include moral and legal dilemmas, as well as problems with usage, acceptance, safety, and design. As a result, this section looks at the things that prevent BCI from being used effectively in healthcare. attention given to the moral dilemmas surrounding the application of BCI in medicine [31].

### 14.10.1    Ethical Difficulties

The word "ethics," which is related to "systems, habits, and practices," is where the word comes from. People's morals, a study of a person's most essential values and virtues, is the focus of the philosophical subfield of ethics. Society. Medical morals are stabilised by a set of moral precepts that are mainly pertinent to the practice of medicine, customer service. Medical ethics primarily serves as a framework for decisions about patient care and interactions between healthcare professionals, the person in pain, and members of his or her family.

### 14.10.2    Goodwill

The capacity of healthcare professionals to assist others is known as beneficence, according to researchers. They follow what's best for the patient. On the other hand, they stressed that beneficence encompasses more than merely avoiding harm. In this regard, researchers define the capability of healthcare providers to avoid and eliminate patient problems. In order to provide beneficence in healthcare, healthcare practitioners must maintain an upgrade of expertise and good knowledge in the application of today's best medical practices. However, one of the major barriers to BCI adoption in healthcare is the prohibitively expensive cost [32].

### 14.10.3    Legality

The ability of healthcare resources to be disbursed equitably among society's members is referred to as the justice principle. BCI technologies, however, are not frequently accessible to people in need. This results from the customised nature of the technology.

### 14.10.4    Freedom of Privacy

It is related to an individual's desire to protect their personal data from being exposed to others, as well as their claim to be free from outside scrutiny or government interference. Contrarily, BCI techniques require the gathering and formulation of private data from people who are hampered while keeping an eye on brain activity. BCI systems are therefore susceptible to assaults like active interception and passive eavesdropping [33].

### 14.10.5    Issues With Standardization

Standards are predetermined requirements that permit independent product manufacturing. Whether it be digital or physical, there is no condition or particular file for sharing BCI data between patients and healthcare professionals. BCI applications are therefore incompatible.

### 14.10.6    Problems With Reliability

Most BCI systems are unreliable. One factor that contributes the low signal intensity normally taken from the brain contributes to the unreliability of BCI systems. Signal amplification is therefore frequently needed in BCI applications. The majority of BCI systems use amplifiers; however, many of them are of poor quality.

### 14.10.7   Prolonged Training Process

The acquisition of skills that must be properly used and maintained is necessary for the successful use of BCI applications. Patients with severe paralysis must therefore receive effective training in using BCI to carry out a motor task. However, training normally takes a lot of time.

### 14.10.8   Expensive Acquisition and Control

The cost of buying numerous BCI systems is expensive. Furthermore, the cost of establishing BCI applications is prohibitively expensive [34]. Therefore, it provides advice for their successful use in healthcare. BCIs are typically used to enhance the communication and mobility of individuals who are severely paralysed in order to improve their quality of life. Patients who are severely paralysed can restore motor function with the aid of BCI technologies. It encourages social connection between people with disabilities and their families. It can be used to reduce discomfort as well. However, a number of obstacles prevent the efficient application of BCI technology in healthcare.

These concerns vary from moral and legal considerations to those relating to accuracy, usability, and uniformity. As a result, BCI technologies often receive little social acceptance. This paper provides guidance to BCI stakeholders, including patients, healthcare professionals, the government, decision-makers, and device manufacturers, to do the following: Medications are generally out of reach for people with motor deficiencies. Some of the following are possible:

1. After getting complete, up-to-date, and accurate information about BCI from healthcare professionals, patients must be made to comply.
2. Decide to hire BCI voluntarily without being coerced or subjected to unfair pressure. As a result, informed consent is required for the use of BCI devices on patients with the current syndrome.
3. All the affected individuals need to be informed about the advantages and disadvantages of BCI. This helps prevent patients from becoming disappointed if a BCI system doesn't work as intended.

4. Patients and healthcare professionals should receive thorough instruction on how to use BCI tools like spell checkers.
5. The government and politicians ought to pass suitable legislation for research.

## 14.11    Conclusion

Simply described, a BCI involves a straight-forward relationship providing communication between the neural part and the hardware, as well as other external devices like intellectual wheelchairs. BCI is used in a number of industries, including healthcare, entertainment, and education. However, the application of BCI in healthcare is crucial. This is due to the fact that BCI systems lower healthcare expenses while also enhancing the health of those who suffer from severe motor disabilities. Accordingly, the overall idea of BCI, BCI methodologies, BCI acquired signal methods, and the advantages and difficulties of using BCI in health systems are the main topics of this study. A comprehensive examination of the literature served as the study's foundation. BCI can be employed, the review found. The study also showed that BCI can assist patients in controlling home ambient elements, including thermostats, lighting, and televisions, as well as monitor patients' emotions and sleep habits. However, the study found that accuracy, dependability, standardization difficulties, confidentiality, and neurological crime are the drawbacks of BCI in the healthcare system. The survey does, however, recommend that healthcare professionals and affected individuals be properly trained in the applications implied by BCI, as well as that appropriate legislation be enacted to protect the information collected about patients.

## References

1. Nijboer, F., Furdea, A., Gunst, I., Mellinger, J., McFarland, D.J., Birbaumer, N., Kübler, A., An auditory brain–computer interface (BCI). *J. Neurosci. Methods*, 167, 1, 43–50, 2008 Jan 15.
2. Nicolas-Alonso, L.F. and Gomez-Gil, J., Brain computer interfaces, a review. *Sensors*, 12, 2, 1211–79, 2012 Jan 31.
3. Jung, T.P., *Principles and applications of brain-computer interfaces*, Center for Advanced Neurological Engineering and Swartz Center for Computational Neuroscience and University of California San Diego, USA, 2010, URL: https://cfmriweb.ucsd.edu/ttliu/be280a_12/BE280A12_BCI1.pdf.

4. Mak, J.N. and Wolpaw, J.R., Clinical applications of brain-computer inter-faces: Current state and future prospects. *IEEE Rev. Biomed. Eng.*, 2, 187–99, 2009 Dec 1.

5. Chan, A.T., Quiroz, J.C., Dascalu, S., Harris, F.C., An overview of brain com-puter interfaces, in: *Proc. 30th Int. Conf. on Computers and Their Applications*, 2015 Jan 1, p. 22.

6. Farwell, L.A. and Donchin, E., Talking off the top of your head: Toward a mental prosthesis utilizing event-related brain potentials. *Electroencephalogr. Clin. Neurophysiol.*, 70, 6, 510–23, 1988 Dec 1.

7. Wolpaw, J.R., Birbaumer, N., McFarland, D.J., Pfurtscheller, G., Vaughan, T.M., Brain-computer interfaces for communication and control. *Clin. Neurophysiol.*, 113, 767–791, 2002.

8. Wolpaw, J.R., Brain–computer interfaces, in: *Handbook of Clinical Neurology*, vol. 110, pp. 67–74, Elsevier, Albany, NY, US, 2013 Jan 1.

9. Lin, C.T., Chen, Y.C., Huang, T.Y., Chiu, T.T., Ko, L.W., Liang, S.F., Hsieh, H.Y., Hsu, S.H., Duann, J.R., Development of wireless brain computer inter-face with embedded multitask scheduling and its application on real-time driver's drowsiness detection and warning. *IEEE Trans. Biomed. Eng.*, 55, 5, 1582–91, 2008 Apr 15.

10. Yger, F., Berar, M., Lotte, F., Riemannian approaches in brain-computer interfaces: A review. *IEEE Trans. Neural Syst. Rehabil. Eng.*, 25, 10, 1753–62, 2016 Nov 9.

11. Cecotti, H., Spelling with brain-computer interface-current trends and prospects, in: *Neurocomp 2010-Cinquième Conférence Plénière Française de Neurosciences Computationnelles*, 2010 Aug 6, pp. 215–220.

12. Moore, M.M., Real-world applications for brain-computer interface technol-ogy. *IEEE Trans. Neural Syst. Rehabil. Eng.*, 11, 2, 162–5, 2003 Jun.

13. Ramadan, R.A., AbdElGawad, A.E., Alaa, M., JustThink: Smart BCI appli-cations, in: *Proceedings of Seventh International Conference on Bio-Inspired Computing: Theories and Applications (BIC-TA 2012)*, vol. 1, Springer India, pp. 461–472, 2013.

14. Jeyabalan, V., Samraj, A., Kiong, L.C., Motor imaginary signal classification using adaptive recursive bandpass filter and adaptive autoregressive models for brain machine interface designs. *Int. J. Bioeng. Life Sci.*, 1, 5, 242–9, 2007 May 22.

15. Krishnaveni, C.V., Lakkakula, R.B., Manasa, S., Artificial vision-A bionic eye. *Int. J. Comput. Sci. Technol.*, 3, 400–6, 2012 Jan.

16. Vidal, J.J., Toward direct brain-computer communication. *Annu. Rev. Biophys. Bioeng.*, 2, 1, 157–80, 1973 Jun.

17. Niedermeyer, E. and da Silva, F.L. (Eds.), *Electroencephalography: Basic prin-ciples, clinical applications, and related fields*, Lippincott Williams & Wilkins, Albany, NY, US, 2005.

18. Krausová, A., Legal aspects of brain-computer interfaces. *Masaryk Univ. J. Law Technol.*, 8, 2, 199–208, 2014.

19. McFarland, D.J., Krusienski, D.J., Sarnacki, W.A., Wolpaw, J.R., Emulation of computer mouse control with a noninvasive brain–computer interface. *J. Neural Eng.*, 5, 2, 101, 2008 Mar 5.

20. Ramadan, R.A., Refat, S., Elshahed, M.A., Ali, R.A., Basics of brain computer interface, in: *Brain-Computer Interfaces: Current Trends and Applications*, pp. 31–50, 2015.

21. Daly, J.J. and Wolpaw, J.R., Brain–computer interfaces in neurological rehabilitation. *Lancet Neurol.*, 7, 11, 1032–43, 2008 Nov 1.

22. Shih, J.J., Krusienski, D.J., Wolpaw, J.R., Brain-computer interfaces in medicine. *Mayo Clin. Proc.*, 87, 3, 268–279, 2012 Mar 1, Elsevier.

23. Wang, W., Sudre, G.P., Xu, Y., Kass, R.E., Collinger, J.L., Degenhart, A.D., Bagic, A.I., Weber, D.J., Decoding and cortical source localization for intended movement direction with MEG. *J. Neurophysiol.*, 104, 5, 2451–61, 2010 Nov.

24. Iqbal, K., Brain-computer interfaces in neurological rehabilitation. *British Society of Rehabilitation Medicine*, pp. 1–4, 2013.

25. Hochberg, L.R., Serruya, M.D., Friehs, G.M., Mukand, J.A., Saleh, M., Caplan, A.H., Branner, A., Chen, D., Penn, R.D., Donoghue, J.P., Neuronal ensemble control of prosthetic devices by a human with tetraplegia. *Nature*, 442, 7099, 164–71, 2006 Jul 13.

26. Hoffmann, U., Vesin, J.M., Ebrahimi, T., Recent advances in brain-computer interfaces, in: *IEEE International Workshop on Multimedia Signal Processing (MMSP07)*, no. CONF, pp. 17–17, 2007.

27. Fazel-Rezai, R., Allison, B.Z., Guger, C., Sellers, E.W., Kleih, S.C., Kübler, A., P300 brain computer interface: Current challenges and emerging trends. *Front. Neuroeng.*, 14, 5, 2012.

28. Anupama, H.S., Cauvery, N.K., Lingaraju, G.M., Brain computer interface and its types-a study. *Int. J. Adv. Eng. Technol.*, 3, 2, 739, 2012 May 1.

29. Friman, O., Volosyak, I., Graser, A., Multiple channel detection of steady-state visual evoked potentials for brain-computer interfaces. *IEEE Trans. Biomed. Eng.*, 54, 4, 742–50, 2007 Mar 19.

30. Pfurtscheller, G. and Neuper, C., Motor imagery and direct brain-computer communication. *Proc. IEEE*, 89, 7, 1123–34, 2001 Jul.

31. Vialatte, F.B., Maurice, M., Dauwels, J., Cichocki, A., Steady-state visually evoked potentials: Focus on essential paradigms and future perspectives. *Prog. Neurobiol.*, 90, 4, 418–38, 2010 Apr 1.

32. Guger, C., Daban, S., Sellers, E., Holzner, C., Krausz, G., Carabalona, R., Gramatica, F., Edlinger, G., How many people are able to control a P300-based brain–computer interface (BCI)? *Neurosci. Lett.*, 462, 1, 94–8, 2009 Sep 18.

33. Li, Q., Ding, D., Conti, M., Brain-computer interface applications: Security and privacy challenges, in: *2015 IEEE Conference on Communications and Network Security (CNS)*, IEEE, pp. 663–666, 2015 Sep 28.

34. Hassib, M. and Schneegass, S., Brain computer interfaces for mobile interaction: Opportunities and challenges, in: *Proceedings of the 17th International Conference on Human-Computer Interaction with Mobile Devices and Services Adjunct*, pp. 959–962, 2015 Aug 24.

.

# 15

# Regulatory Perspective: Human-Machine Interfaces

**Artiben Patel[1]\*, Ravi Patel[2], Rakesh Patel[3], Bhupendra Prajapati[4] and Shivani Jani[5]**

*[1]Department of Regulatory Affairs, Cosette Pharmaceuticals Inc., New Jersey, United States*
*[2]Department of Research and Development, Cosette Pharmaceuticals Inc., New Jersey, United States*
*[3]Department of Research, University of Iowa, Iowa City, IA, United States*
*[4]Department of Pharmaceutics and Pharmaceutical Technology, Shree S.K. Patel College of Pharmaceutical Education and Research, Ganpat University, Mehsana, Gujarat, India*
*[5]Smt. S. M. Shah Pharmacy College, Gujarat Technological University, Amsaran, Gujarat, India*

## Abstract

By drawing novel and significant ideas from the enormous quantity of data created during the daily provision of healthcare, human-machine interfaces (HMI) possess the capacity to revolutionize the way that healthcare is provided. But because of their intricacy and the continuous statistics nature of their creation, they also raise certain issues that should be taken into account. Traditionally, the FDA evaluates medical devices using a premarket process that is appropriate but not intended for adaptive HMI systems. The extremely repetitive, autonomous, and adaptable character of these tools necessitates a novel, total product lifecycle (TPLC) regulation strategy that supports a quick loop of product innovation and permits these instruments to advance continuously while offering reliable protection.

This chapter describes the regulatory perspective and potential approach to developing safe and quality HMI technologies for patients. It describes current regulations, standards for categorizing risks, a framework for weighing benefits and risks, rules for managing risks, and product life cycle approaches. Further, a description of guiding principles for the creation of good machine learning

*\*Corresponding author*: artikpatel25@yahoo.com

Rishabha Malviya, Sonali Sundram, Bhupendra Prajapati and Sudarshan Kumar Singh (eds.)
*Human-Machine Interface: Making Healthcare Digital*, (375–410) © 2024 Scrivener Publishing LLC

practice (GMLP) would aid in promoting high, secure, and reliable medical equipment using HMI technologies. It details the kind of adjustment that is envisaged as well as the approach used to accomplish such modifications in a regulated way that minimizes hazards to individuals.

*Keywords*: HMI technologies, regulatory approaches, good machine learning practice, medical devices, device user interface, pre-market approval, specifications

## Abbreviations

| | |
|---|---|
| GMLP | Good machine learning practice |
| HMI | Human-Machine Interfaces |
| TPLC | Total Product Lifecycle |
| GUI | Graphical user interfaces |
| CDRH | The Centre for Medical Devices and Radiological Health |
| MDUFA | Medical Device User Fee Amendments |
| IRB | Institutional Review Board |
| IDE | Investigational Device Exemption |
| HDE | Humanitarian Device Exemption |
| QSR | Quality System Regulations |

## 15.1    Introduction

An interface called a human-machine interface (HMI) enables users to operate devices, computers, or sensors. Some HMI systems transform data into understandable visuals. The automobile, pharmaceutical, and clinical industries are just a few that utilize human-machine interfaces. HMI is particularly crucial in a hospital context because it helps give devices functionality that enhances the experiences of both the administrator and the patient. HMI systems are crucial in the medical sector and can hasten to heal, enhance medical surveillance, and potentially protect lives [1].

Considering the history of the HMI in healthcare, HMI first entered the medical industry back in the 1950s. Integrate health data, it was done mostly through a procedure termed batch processing. This task needed the operator to define the steps and specifics in order to be completed correctly. Usually, a punch card was used for this, which was then fed into a device that would output the data. However, because each piece of data needed to be put in order and with all the necessary details, user error was frequently a possibility. Following batch processing, graphical user interfaces (GUIs) became also a typical HMI system. Users might interact with machines using these interfaces by clicking on displays, images, or icons. They may communicate using the interface through a mouse or keyboard during this time period, known as the WIMP-Phase. New technologies would emerge each ten to fifteen years, furthering the development of human-machine interfaces like people understand them nowadays. The earliest clear multitouch display wasn't developed until 1984. This invention featured a cathode ray tube (CRT) screen with a grid of touchscreens set on it and a metallic layer with voltage supplied over it.

Advancement in medical devices with human-machine interface helps to establish chemical resistance, easy to sterilize, Portable, and innovative technological medical system to improve the health of patients. Hence, regulations of medical devices apply to such technology to provide safe and effective use of the technology [1].

## 15.2    Why are Regulations Needed?

Human-machine interfaces in medical equipment aid in the diagnosis, treatment, or monitoring of patients with suspected disease conditions. They must be reliable, serve the medical function for whom they were intended, and prevent injury to the patient and user in order to do this. According to several studies, the international sourcing of medical devices has led to an increase in the reporting of adverse events, including serious and fatal ones. In reality, there have been considerably above 1.5 million injuries and around 80,000 fatalities in the USA in only the past ten years despite its strict as well as vast regulatory structure. The aggressive advertising of vaginal mesh, which resulted in extreme discomfort, bleeding, as well as other terrible side effects after its use in vaginopexy, is one stark illustration of medical products that are not adequately regulated. In the last ten years, medical devices reportedly were blamed for over 80,000 fatalities and 1.7 million injuries, as per statistics published by the U.S. Food & Drug Administration (FDA). The goal of regulation is to make medical equipment safer, higher quality, and more aesthetically pleasing. In addition, additional expenses for development, production, and services are associated with regulation for manufacturers [2]. Costs for individuals and healthcare professionals will rise as a result, limiting the sale of devices and impeding innovation.

The following information explains why medical device regulation is necessary:

### 15.2.1   Safety

People that utilize or operate medical equipment must not be harmed by the devices. Instead, they ought to improve the patient's health. To demonstrate to the patient whether this is genuine, adherence to medical device regulations is crucial. Pacemakers and implants are more strictly controlled than contact lenses and sticky plasters because they are more likely to present a safety issue.

### 15.2.2   Uniform Requirements

It is possible to make sure that all items sold for a therapeutic purpose comply with these requirements by unifying the fundamental design and specifications. Other aspects may have their own standards, but they are voluntary. Any technique may be employed as long as the procedure and the finished product meet the fundamental specifications [2].

The milestone framework, as well as the quality control and manufacturing processes, include the research, development, and clinical testing of devices. Users are urged to report adverse reactions after the product has been marketed, and the producer is mandatory to notify of any major adverse events. This makes it possible to spot safety problems and take appropriate action.

### 15.2.3   Promote Innovation

Regulatory supervision can redirect the focus to genuinely useful innovation in the guise of safer, more efficient, or less priced gadgets - any or all of such, in any ratio. This is in addition to taking non-compliant products off the market. If the regulations in the manufacturing nation are aligned with those in the exporting nations, domestic as well as international product innovation will be promoted.

### 15.2.4   Free Movement of Goods

The import and export of goods are made possible by uniform standards, which eliminate the need for independent research between nations. The provision of equitable market accessibility, clinical security, and transparency regarding device compatibility with regulatory requirements and pricing control all contribute to improving the product selection process.

### 15.2.5 Compensation

Patients can receive compensation for damages brought on by defective devices because of strict regulation [3].

### 15.2.6 Fostering Innovation

Customized or unique medical devices are frequently created based on ones that have already received approval; hence, in principle, the modern device is a variant of the previous one. The more recent ones can leave the approved area and turn into uncontrolled products. The ongoing struggle involving innovation and regulation is crucial for the protection and welfare of patients. Regulations can often inhibit innovation since it would be too expensive and time-consuming to comply with them. Standards, on the other hand, are occasionally insufficient to provide suitable evaluation criteria. When open-source blueprints for frequently used medical devices are made available, for example, others are free to make improvements, discuss their ideas with others, and give quick end-user comments. However, this also obstructs regulation and quality control. Evidence for regulatory clearance may be excessively costly for small quantities of units. On the contrary hand, non-traditional technologies like 3D printing may dispense with the required procedures for testing and development. Regulations must be strict enough to protect patients while remaining adaptable sufficiently to enable cutting-edge methods that encourage innovation. One such necessity is the need for common and up-to-date documentation, which helps to avoid duplicating development and testing activities for a single section and tracks the initial design as well as subsequent revisions.

## 15.3 US Regulatory Perspective

As per the literature, the US holds a 48.1% share of the global market using medical devices. As a result, the FDA controls the safety and efficacy of medical devices marketed in the US. From basic tongue depressors and medical gowns to sophisticated programmed artificial hearts and robotic surgical systems, medical equipment comes in all shapes and sizes. The Centre for Medical Devices and Radiological Health (CDRH) of the FDA has developed a Medical Device Product Classification database that covers more than 6,000 different types of medical equipment and the classification given to each type. Federal rules like the Code of Federal Regulations, Title 21 specify conditions that must be met in order for CDRH to authorize or certify devices sold in the United States, based on the device classes and other elements.

### 15.3.1    History of Medical Device Regulation and Its Supervision in the United States

The earliest thorough consumer rights organization in the US is the Food and Drug Administration (FDA). The Pure Food and Drugs Act, which President Theodore Roosevelt approved in 1906, marked the beginning of the FDA's regulation of foods and medications. Ever since, the FDA's involvement in defending and advancing the production of pharmaceuticals for humans and animals, biologics, medical equipment, radiation-emitting goods, food for humans and animals, and cosmetics has been increased by Congress [3].

The timeline that follows illustrates significant turning points in American medical device law history.

**1906: Pure Food and Drugs Act (also known as Federal Food and Drugs Act)**

- Established the foundation for the current FDA
- Interstate trade in contaminated and misbranded food and medications is forbidden

**1938: Federal Food, Drug, and Cosmetic Act (FD&C Act)**

- Extends the ban of inter - state trade to misbranded and contaminated cosmetics and curative medical devices;
- Is the primary act that enables the FDA to regulate and supervise medical products;
- Power to conduct plant inspections.

**1944: Public Health Service Act**

- Increased monitoring of biologics
- Formalized licensing for laboratories

**1968: Radiation Control for Health and Safety Act**

- Designed to reduce exposure to strong magnetic fields and radiation from electrical products

- Developed performance criteria for radiation-emitting items, such as microwaves, MRIs, diathermy equipment, ultrasound, UV equipment, and laser equipment

**1970: President Nixon established the Cooper Committee**

- The committee was formed to examine the necessity of medical device regulations. It made the recommendation that any future legislation is focused on devices because they pose different problems than drugs.
- Developed the idea of risk-based medical device categorization.

**1976: Medical Device Amendments to the FD&C Act**

- Aimed at offering a fair level of assurance regarding the efficacy and safety of medical equipment.
- Developed a risk-based, three-class classification scheme for all medical equipment.
- Developed the regulatory framework (Investigational Device Exemption (IDE)) for novel investigational medical equipment to be tested on people.
- Establishing GMPs, monitoring of adverse incidents concerning medical devices, initial registration with the FDA, and marketing of devices among other important post market regulations.

**1977: The Bureau of Medical Devices and Diagnostic Products was renamed as the Bureau of Medical Devices**

**1990: Safe Medical Devices Act (SMDA)**

- Obliging user facilities, including nursing homes and hospitals to identify adverse reactions involving medical devices, will improve post-marketing supervision of devices.
- Permitting the FDA to order manufacturers to conduct post-marketing surveillance on devices that are implanted continuously in the event that they fail and cause irreversible injury or death.
- Defined significant equivalence (the requirement for selling a product through the 510(k) program), which gives the

FDA the authority to mandate device recalls and levy civil fines for FD&C Act violations.

- Modified processes for setting up, changing, or removing performance standards.

## 1992: Mammography Quality Standards Act (MQSA)

- Mandatory accreditation and government certification of mammography facilities as adhering to quality requirement.
- Facilities must pass yearly assessments by federal or state auditors after receiving initial accreditation.

## 1997: Food and Drug Administration Modernization Act (FDAMA)

- Made the "least onerous" pre-market review requirements.
- Added the choice for initial premarket evaluations of some devices to be carried out by certified third parties.
- Allowed the use of information from studies conducted on prior iterations of such a technology in premarket applications for new iterations of the device.
- Offered easier access to experimental devices.

## 2002: Medical Device User Fee and Modernization Act (MDUFMA)

- Authorized the FDA to levy user fees on a limited number of medical device marketing authorisation submissions, which will aid the FDA in enhancing the effectiveness, consistency, and reliability of medical device proposal evaluations.
- Implemented the Office of Combination Products.
- The Small Business Determination (SBD) programme was designed to allow eligible small enterprises to pay lower pre-market clearance fees.
- FDA established performance targets for handling particular premarket application determinations.
- New regulatory standards have been established for "reprocessed" equipment.
- Approved medical device companies' electronic certification.

## 2007: Food and Drug Administration Amendments Act (FDAAA)

- Improved premarket assessment timeframes and re- registered the medical equipment user charge (MDUFA II).

- Mandated that the FDA create a system for distinctive device identification for medical devices and mandated that almost all licensing and listing processes be carried out electronically.

## 2012: Food and Drug Administration Safety and Innovation Act (FDASIA)

- Added shared result targets with industry and improved pre-market review periods within medical device user charges programme (MDUFA III).
- Modified the requirements for rejecting an IDE.
- When the proprietor of the application requests one, the FDA must produce a Substantive Synopsis. This has allowed the FDA to collaborate with international governments to unify regulatory standards.
- Extensive premarket review use of the "lowest burdensome" criteria [4].

## 2016: 21st Century Cures Act

- Mandated the development or amendment of procedures and guidelines aimed at facilitating consumer accessibility to innovative medical devices, such as: Enacting legislation to codify the FDA's enhanced review procedure for ground-breaking devices, Extending the use of "lowest burdensome" standards in marketing authorization evaluations, Requesting the FDA to update the licensing of pharmaceutical formulations, Allowing the utilization of central Institutional Review Board (IRB) supervision instead of mandating solely local IRBs for IDE and HDE operations, Writing a procedure for presenting applications for the acceptance or rejection of a norm into law.
- Defining the types of medical technology which can and aren't controlled as devices explained what certain digital healthcare goods can be controlled.

## 2017: Food and Drug Administration Reauthorization Act (FDARA)

- Recommended further process changes for device installation inspections, including the authorization of risk-based

examination scheduling; separated peripheral categorization from parental device categorization; and mandated that
at minimum one pilot study be carried out by the FDA to
examine how actual data might enhance post marketing
surveillance [4].

### 15.3.2   Classification of Medical Devices

About 1,700 distinct generic varieties of devices have been categorized
by the FDA and placed in 16 panels of medical specializations. Based on
the degree of regulation required to ensure the device's safety and efficacy,
every generic category of devices is categorized into any of the three regulatory classes. The three classifications and the criteria that pertain to them
are as follows:

Class of Device and Regulatory Controls: General Class I Controls,
With and Without Exemptions, General and Special Controls of Class II,
With and Without Exemptions, Premarket Approval, and Class III General
Controls. The device's class governs, amongst other factors, the kind of pre-
marketing filing or application needed to obtain FDA approval for marketing. If your device falls under Class I or II classification and is otherwise
exempted, a 510k would be needed before it may be marketed. The restrictions on exemptions apply to all devices that are categorized as exempt.
Device exclusion limitations are handled by 21 CFR xxx.9, wherein xxx is
a designation for Parts 862–892. A premarket approval request will be necessary for Class III products unless yours is a pre-amendment device (on
the marketplace before the medical equipment amendments were passed
in 1976, or practices similar to a similar device), in which case premarket
clearance requests are not required. A 510k will serve as the path to market
in that situation.

Device categorization is based on both the intended application and
the use-indicating characteristics of the device. For instance, a scalpel
is designed to dissect tissue. When an additional specialized purpose is
appended to the device's labelling, such as "for producing cuts in the cornea," a subcategory of intended usage results. The labelling of the gadget
contains instructions for operation, but they can alternatively be verbally
explained while the product is being sold. Additionally, categorization
is risk-based, meaning that a key component in determining the class to
which a device is placed is the danger that it presents to the user or patient.
Instruments with the least danger are classified as Class I, while ones
with the highest risk are classified as Class III [5]. All device classes are

subjected to general controls, as was already mentioned. The Food, Drug, and Cosmetic (FD&C) Act's fundamental standards, known as general controls, are applicable to all Class I, II, and III medical devices.

### 15.3.3    Reclassification

The FDA categorizes medical devices in general according to the risks involved by using the equipment and by assessing the level of control that offers a fair guarantee of the device's efficacy and safety. Reclassification is the process of altering the regulatory category of a specific device. Reclassification is primarily used to apply the proper amount of regulatory oversight for a particular device category depending on the latest recent data regarding that device type's safety and efficacy. Reclassification affects a device type rather than a specific device.

### 15.3.4    How to Determine if the Product is a Medical Device or How to Classify the Medical Device

When attempting to assess if a product is subject to FDA regulation as a medical device, the steps listed below may be useful. Step 1: Examine your product to see if it satisfies the requirements of the FDA. Step 2: Check to see if your product falls under a suitable product category.

▪ **Step 1: Check to see if the product satisfies the requirements for a medical device.**
If a product satisfies Section 201(h) of the Food, Drug, and Cosmetic Act's description of a medical product, the FDA deems the such item to be a device and subjected to FDA supervision. According to Section 201(h)(1) of the Food, Drug, and Cosmetic Act, a device is defined as (A) Listed in the USP or the official NF, or any supplements to it, (B) Designed to be used in the detection of illness or any other situations, in the therapy or management of disease in humans or animals, or for the healing or abatement of disease, (C) Aimed to impact the framework or any feature of a human or kind of animal's body, and that does not accomplish its main goals by acting chemically within or upon a human or other animal's body, and that also does not accomplish its main goals by acting chemically inside of or on a human or other animal, and that is not reliant on metabolism to accomplish its main goals. Software features banned under section 520 are not considered devices [6].

**Intended use:** The equipment's function or overall goal. The instructions for use are also part of this.

**Indications for use:** Includes information about the patient group for whom the device is designed as well as a summary of the ailment or problem the technology will detect, cure, avoid, heal, or ameliorate.

### Step 2: Determine if an appropriate product classification exists for the product.

Searching for current product categories that might relate to the product can be beneficial in evaluating whether your item is governed like a medical device. A solid indication that your item may represent a medical device is discovering an established category that matches the intended application or design of the product. The following sections detail three ways to check if the item has a product categorization. The pages that follow provide more details on ways to categorize a medical device:

### Method 1: Search the Product Classification Database

To find out if the product already has a categorization that fits, one can check the FDA Product Categorization Database: [7] Utilize the Quick Search function to conduct a keyword search(s). Always be aware that we might need to run several searches utilizing different phrases to characterize the item (for example, singular and plural forms of the words can be used). To locate via item id, regulation type, or device category, the Advanced Search tool can be used.

### Method 2: Search for Similar Devices

One can look into an FDA document or order authorizing the market if we find a comparable device that is lawfully marketed in the US. It might be able to ascertain the categorization of the device using the details in the correspondence or directive for a comparable device type.

The below databases can be searched using the Quick Research or Detailed Search option to find the FDA judgments that allow marketing approval: a) Premarket Approval (PMA) – It is necessary for the majority of Class III (greater risk) products prior it may be sold lawfully. This collection comprises premarket-approved devices and contains information on their labelling, assessment of security and efficacy, and approval sequence. b) Premarket Notification 510(k) – The FDA must first provide 510(k) approval for the majority of Class II (medium danger) devices prior to they can be lawfully commercialized. This database contains information that is 510(k) releasable. c) De Novo- De Novo offers one method for identifying innovative gadgets that provide a minimal to high hazard. De Novo categorization rulings and disclosure reports are included in this collection. d) The Humanitarian Device Exemption (HDE) offers a potential pathway for the marketing of medical products that could benefit individuals with uncommon illnesses or conditions. Devices having HDE clearance are listed in this database, together with the clearance order, the Statement of Security and Likely Benefits, and the authorized device's labelling [8].

**Method 3: Search for Similar Devices by Device Listing**
One can check the device registration data for a lawfully marketed device to see what product category it falls under. Searching the Establishment licensing and device filing system of the FDA using the Rapid or Detailed Search tool will yield information about device listings.

**Additional Considerations**
**Is the product a Device Software Function?**
Device software operations are what the FDA describes to as programming operations that are part of a device. The "mobile medical app" seems to be a programming feature that is used on a digital application and complies with the description of a gadget.

According to the FDA, software that is designed to be utilized for several medical purposes and accomplishes these objectives independently of a physical hospital equipment qualifies as a medical product.

**Further Assistance**
If a company is unsure to determine a device for the product after the above-mentioned steps, they can contact the DICE.

In the Device Determination email inquiry, please provide the necessary details: a) Targeted Use (for instance, what condition or diagnosis is the product intended to treat? b) Your contact details; c) A description of the product's physical characteristics and its mode of action;

## 15.3.5   Device Development Process

As per the US FDA database, medical devices are developed in accordance with well-established procedures to guarantee their effectiveness and safety before being released to the general public. FDA evaluates research evidence and statistics regarding pharmaceuticals and devices prior to being made accessible to the general public, from conception to approval and thereafter [9] a) Keeps an eye out for drug abuse issues as medications and equipment become widely available. b) Keeps an eye on drug-related data and marketing. c) Maintains medicine quality. Both the development of pharmaceuticals and devices follows a similar five-step approach. The procedures vary, nevertheless, within various stages. The following write up describes the process of Device Development: There are following five main steps for the development processes of device: First stage: Device Conception and Research, Second stage: Replica for Preclinical investigation, Third stage: The Approval process, Fourth stage: FDA Review, Fifth stage: FDA post-market safety inspection.

A detailed description of each step is provided herewith:

**Step 1: Concept and Device Discovery**
Because the development procedure varies based on the classification of the device, it is crucial to comprehend how devices are categorized.

**A. Classifications [10]**
Depending on the risk a device poses, the FDA categorises medical devices. Depending on the findings of scientific research, classification schemes for medical devices may vary.

- Class 1: General Controls: The least dangerous devices are those in class 1. "General controls" are applied to these reduced risks devices, like oxygen masks and surgical instruments. Once a device is created, general controls guarantee its effectiveness and safety. General controls take into account the following elements: a) Strict production standards b) Requirements for general documentation, registration, and notifying adverse events the FDA
- Class 2: General Controls with Special Controls: Consumers are more in danger from Class 2 devices than they are from Class 1 devices. As a result, in addition to standard controls, Class 2 devices also are subjected to additional controls.
- Class 3: General Controls and Premarket Approval: Class 3 devices typically promote or support life, have an implant in the body, as well as pose an undue risk of disease or harm. Breast implants, pacemakers, and HIV diagnostic tools are a few examples. Therefore, Class 3 devices need premarket authorization. Manufacturers who can demonstrate that a product is reliable and secure will be granted this. General controls also apply to Class 3 devices.

## B. Development/Concept

The process for developing medical devices is well known. As researchers create, hone, and test the devices, a lot of these phases cross over. The development procedure often starts when researchers identify an unfulfilled medical necessity. Following that, they develop a notion or proposal for a novel device. The next step is for researchers to create a "proof of concept," which is a paper outlining the procedures required to ascertain if the concept is practicable or not.  Concepts are frequently impractical. The ideas that do have potential advance to other stages of creation.

## Step 2: Preclinical Research—Prototype

A prototype, or initial form, of a medical device, is created by researchers. The prototype of the device is not yet fit for human usage. The prototypes are put through supervised laboratory testing by researchers. Researchers can learn crucial details regarding the product's prospective uses for humans by improving the prototype. The prototype method aims to lower the danger to individuals. Risk cannot be completely eliminated, though.

## Step 3: Pathway to Approval [11]

The classification of a medical device's risk determines its process for approval.

## A. Device Application Process

Developers have a wide range of possibilities due to the wide difference in how devices are categorised. Section 513 of the FDA created the hazard dependent medical device classification scheme. Every device is categorised into any of 3 regulatory categories - Class I, Class II, or Class III dependent on the degree of regulation required to reasonably ensure its effectiveness and security. Class, I devices are subjected to the lowest amount of regulation, while Class III devices are subjected to the highest regulation, as the device classes go from Class I-Class III. Pathways of the device to the market: a) Most exempt from premarket submission (Class I) b) Premarket Notification [510(k) (Class II) c) Premarket Application [PMA] (Class III): d) "De Novo": Device "types" that have never been marketed in the U.S., but whose safety profile and technology are now reasonably well understood. e) Humanitarian Device Exemption (HDE): Devices for orphan diseases, intended to benefit patients in diagnosis and/or treatment of disease or condition affecting or manifested in fewer than 4,000 patients per year in the United States.

## B. Premarket Approval (PMA)

PMA relates to the technical and regulatory examination required to assess the following: the security and efficacy of Class III devices; devices that have been determined via the 510(k) procedure to be not significantly similar to a Class I or Class II comparator. The PMA process is the utmost complex and to logically conclude whether a device is reliable and secure, the PMA mandates: Scientific proof that the potential health benefits of a device's proposed use exceed the potential dangers; indicates that a significant section of the target audience will benefit considerably from the item. A key idea for PMAs is independence, which states that information regarding a device should not be utilized to justify second and thus every PMA should prove the efficacy and safety of the device undergoing examination. Digital mammography, non-invasive and minimally intrusive glucose monitoring devices, implantable middle ear devices, and implanted defibrillators are a few examples of PMAs [12].

## Step 4: FDA Review

Developers of medical devices may submit a request to market their products to the general public if they have sufficient knowledge of the safety and efficacy of their products. The class of the device determines the kind of application they submit. a) Humanitarian Device Exemption: By treating or detecting a sickness or disease that impacts less than 4,000 people, humanitarian use devices aid patients. Manufacturers need to file a human device exception and show there are no comparable, legally accepted devices in the marketplace and that there seem to be no alternative ways to sell a Humanitarian Use Device before they may put one on the market. b) Premarket Notification or 510(k)–Class 1, 2, and 3 Devices: A 510(k), commonly referred to as a premarket notification, certifies that a class 2 medical device seems comparable to other products already on the market. The creator makes a comparison between the new product and one or more analogous, legally advertised products to back up the assertion. c) Premarket Approval Application–Class 3 Devices: Applications for premarket authorization should be completed for Class 3 devices that should contain information from both nonclinical and clinical research. The FDA will examine the production facilities and labs in which the device would be created throughout the approval procedure to look for acceptable manufacturing standards. At a public discussion, the FDA may, if necessary, contact an advisory committee. Groups of professionals make up FDA Advisory Boards, which offer FDA unbiased advice on a subject. If a device should be authorized or not is suggested by the panels. Following the meeting of the advisory committee, the FDA chooses whether to approve the device or not, or whether to ask for more details. FDA is required by law to publish its judgement along with all accompanying documentation in the Federal Record.

**Step 5: FDA Post-Market Safety Monitoring**
Even while premarket clinical studies are crucial for learning about a device's performance and safety, it's likely that once the product is available in the market, additional safety issues will arise. As a consequence, even once a device has received approval, the FDA still keeps an eye on its performance. a) Manufacturer Inspections: Inspections of American medical device factories are routinely carried out by FDA personnel. Inspections may be disclosed in advance to manufacturers or they may occur without warning. Inspections could be necessary as a rule or because of a specific issue. These checks are done to ensure that developers are adhering to good manufacturing procedures. If criteria are not fulfilled, FDA has the authority to close a manufacturing plant [13]. b) Reporting Problems: Producers, medical professionals, and patients can report issues involving authorized medical devices through a number of FDA initiatives. MedWatch, the FDA's adverse incident reporting program, serves as a hub for discovering new health data and reporting issues with health products (drugs and devices). MedWatch safety notifications are regularly available for subscription. Medical Product Safety Network (MedSun), which is an adverse event reporting program, checks the efficacy and safety of medical devices. c) Active Surveillance: The FDA is creating a new nationwide system as part of the Sentinel Initiative to identify potential safety risks more rapidly. To monitor the safety of authorized medicinal items in real time, the system will employ very large current electronic health databases, including registries, bureaucratic and insurance claims datasets, and electronic medical record platforms. This technology will supplement the FDA's current post-market safety evaluation methods, not replace them [24].

## 15.3.6    Overview of Device Regulations

Companies that produce, repurpose, rebrand, and/or trade medical devices marketed in America are subject to regulation by the FDA's Centre for Devices and Radiological Health (CDRH).

### A. Basic Regulatory Requirements
The following is a list of the fundamental legal standards that producers of medical devices sold in the US must follow: A) Establishment Registration - 21 CFR Part 807: The FDA requires all domestic and international medical

device manufacturers and first distributors (importers) to register their businesses. Unless FDA has approved a waiver, all site applications must be filed electronically. Between October 1 and December 31 of every year, all registration data must be validated. Foreign manufacturers are required to appoint an American agent in addition to registration. Most businesses must submit an entity registration charge starting on October 1, 2007.

B) Medical Device Listing - 21CFR Part 807: Devices must be registered with the FDA by manufacturers. Manufacturers, contractual manufacturers, contractual sterilisers, repackagers and relabelers, protocol developers, reprocessors of single-use devices, and remanufacturers are among the businesses that must list their products [25].

C) Premarket Notification 510(k) - 21 CFR Part 807 Subpart E [14]: A person cannot commercially sell a device if it requires the filing of a 510(k) Premarket Notification until there is a letter from the FDA stating that the person is permitted to do so. A 510(k) must show that the device is approximately similar to one that was lawfully available for commercial sale in the US: (1) prior to May 28, 1976; or (2) to a device which the FDA has deemed to be essentially equivalent. It permits the FDA to impose a charge for Premarket Notification 510(k) reviews of medical devices. A start-up company could have to pay less. For Traditional, Abbreviated, and Special 510(k)s, there is also an application cost. Premarket review fees are not in any way connected to how FDA will ultimately decide on a submission.

D) Premarket Approval (PMA) - 21 CFR Part 814: Products that need PMA are Class III types, which are high-risk products that carry a high risk of disease or injury, or products that the 510(k)-process determined were not fairly comparable to Class I and II antecedent products. The PMA procedure entails several steps and calls for the provision of clinical evidence to back up device claims. Medical device fees are applicable to initial PMAs and specific types of PMA amendments beginning with the financial year 2003 (October 1, 2002, to September 30, 2003). Small companies are entitled to fee reductions or waivers.

E) Investigational Device Exemption (IDE) - 21CFR Part 812: Before clinical research with a device carrying a high level of risk may start, the Institutional Review Board (IRB) and FDA must both provide their approval. Only the IRB must approve studies using low-risk devices before the trial can start [26].

F) Quality System Regulation (QS regulation) - 21 CFR Part 820: The quality system guideline comprises rules for the procedures used in developing, purchasing, producing, packaging, labelling, storing, fitting, and maintaining medical equipment, as well as the equipment and controls used in doing so. FDA inspections of manufacturing sites ensure adherence to QS standards.

G) Medical Device Reporting - 21 CFR Part 803: Under the Medical Device Monitoring programme, incidents where a device may have led to a fatality or severe injury must be notified to FDA. Additionally, several issues need to be reported. The FDA and companies can track and identify major adverse occurrences entailing medical devices through the MDR regulation. The regulation's objectives are to quickly identify and address issues [15].

### B. General Controls

Under sections 501, 502, 510, 516, 518, 519, and 520 of the FD&C Act, general measures are regulatory obligations. Unless specifically exempted by laws, all medical devices are subject to general oversight [27]. If a device is excluded from any of the general regulations, the categorization rule for that device specifies this exemption. For instance, the manual tooth brush classification regulation, 21 CFR 872.6855, outlines the general standards through which tooth brushes can be excluded.

## 15.3.7 Quality and Compliance of Medical Devices

Increased quality medical device development and manufacturing are encouraged by the FDA. The FDA also acknowledges the importance of performing routine medical device management, maintenance, and servicing in order to preserve the devices' reliable, safe, and efficient operation. The FDA has developed Quality System Regulations (QSR) that cover acceptable manufacturing practises as well as device development and validation. Investigations into complaints and other methods of monitoring device functioning are covered by FDA regulations. The FDA assists manufacturers in achieving regulatory conformance and, when necessary, conducts enforcement action. When manufacturers might not be adhering to medical device regulations, the FDA initiates administrative action to force manufacturers into conformity [28]. However, depending solely on disciplinary measures does not always result in or contribute to manufacturers concentrating on raising the caliber of their goods. The FDA has put in place programmes like the Case for Quality to encourage good design and production processes and to offer choices for proving compliance. Through such efforts, the FDA collaborates with businesses and other partners to pinpoint obstacles to the quality of medical devices and develop creative solutions to get rid of them, giving users exposure to great-quality medical equipment.

From 01 January 2014 to 31 December 2016, FDA, alongside its international partners, took part in a pilot programme for medical device single audits. On June 29, 2017, a report outlining the findings of potential "proof-of-concept" standards created to verify the feasibility of a Medical Device Single Audit Process was generated. Based on the information gathered throughout the course of the three (3) year pilot, the results are described in the Final MDSAP Pilot Report. The MDSAP Regulatory Authority Council (the international MDSAP regulatory body) concluded that the MDSAP Pilot has successfully established the feasibility of the Medical Device Single Audit Program based on its assessment of the MDSAP Final Pilot Report [29]. FDA will keep accepting MDSAP audit reports in place of typical Agency examinations. The FDA will continue to inspect businesses for their compliance with the Electronic Product Radiation Control (EPRC) requirements of the Act.

With the goal of maximizing medical device excellence and patient protection, this guideline clarifies for FDA employees and business the benefits and risks that FDA may take into account when allocating funds for conformity and regulatory actions [16]. FDA acknowledges that decisions about these measures should be taken with consideration for the effects on patients in order to fulfil the agency's aim of safeguarding and improving the human safety. Taking into account the device's benefit-risk profile could help avoid regulatory actions that have unanticipated negative effects on individuals (e.g., shortage of medically necessary devices).

Guidance has described following factors for the assessment of Medical Device benefits: type of benefits, magnitude of benefit, likelihood of patients experiencing one or more benefits, duration of effects, patient perspective on benefit, benefit factors for healthcare professionals or caregivers, medical necessity. Guidance has described following factors for the assessment of Medical Device risks: a) Risk concerns for healthcare workers or guardians. b) Patient endurance of risk c) Dispersion of nonconforming devices d) Period of exposure to population e) Totally incorrect or factually inaccurate results f) Patient intensity of harm g) Probability of risk. Further benefit-risk considerations to take into account when deciding on Product Offerings, Conformity, and Enforcement have also been outlined in guidance. The points to be noted are: Uncertainty, Mitigations, Detectability, Failure mode, Scope of the device issue, Patient impact, Preference for availability, Nature of violations/Nonconforming product, Firm compliance history.

• List of Device Recalls

The FDA publishes informational summaries on the most significant medical device recalls. Such items are included in the listing since there is a plausible possibility that they could result in severe health issues or perhaps death. To learn regarding Class I medical device recalls as well as certain Class II and III recalls of relevance to patients, the annual lists should be checked [17]. What should be done if the company owns or use one of such products is explained in the links. A search can be done in the Medical Device Recalls Index to learn more about a recall, a rectification, or a deletion activity that has still not been assigned a classification. The FDA includes medical device recall alerts according to the date on which the recall was posted, not the date the recall was first issued. The content of the recall notification contains the date on which a company began the recall.

• Centre for Devices and Radiological Health (CDRH) Compliance Programs

The Federal Food, Drug, and Cosmetic Act as well as other regulations that are governed by FDA are evaluated for industry conformity using the methods outlined in the FDA's Compliance Programs. The Freedom of Information Act allows for the public to access Compliance Programs. Compliance initiatives do not obligate the FDA or the general public and do not grant anyone any new rights. As far as the method complies with the criteria of the relevant laws and regulations, an alternate approach may be employed [18].

## 15.3.8    Human Factors and Medical Devices

The focus of human factors and usability design is on how people and technology interact. A representation of the exchanges between a person and a technology, the functions carried out by both, and the user functionality between them are shown in Figure 15.1. The device user experience, shown as the red zone, is the crucial component in these interactions [19].

Understanding how humans receive data from a device, interpret that data to decide what to do with it, and interact with the device, its parts, and/or its controls is crucial to comprehending the user-device system. (For instance, change a setting, swap out a part, or turn off the device). It's also crucial to comprehend how gadgets take user input, react to it, and let the user know the results of their actions through feedback. Designing the user interface makes use of human factors and usability design [32]. The components that consumers engage with when unpacking, setting

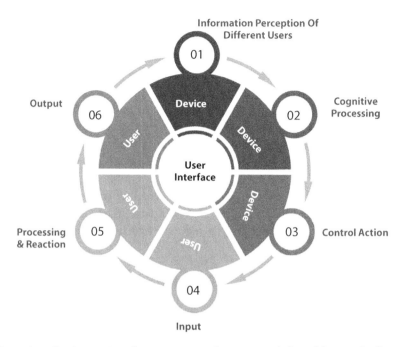

**Figure 15.1** Device user interface in operational perspective (adapted from Redmill, F., & Rajan, J. (1997). The causes of human error. Human factors in safety critical systems).

up, calibrating, using, or maintaining a device are all included in the user interface (e.g., making repairs, replacing a battery, and cleaning).

## A. Why is Human Factor Engineering important to medical devices?

The reduction of usage-related risks and hazards is the primary objective of the human considerations/engineering process for medical devices. Once this objective has been achieved, it is crucial to ensure that users can utilize the device securely and efficiently. Safer links with both medical device parts and accoutrements (such as power cables, leads, tubing, and cartridges), enhanced safeguards and displays interaction, improved user comprehension of the device's situation and function, superior user comprehension of a patient's overall health condition, more proper management of alarm transmissions, easier device service and repair, and reduced device downtime are some of the specific positive results of integrating human considerations/engineering to medical devices [19].

## B. Human Factors Engineering

Human factors engineering (HFE) and usability engineering are disciplines that focus on comprehending how people engage with technologies

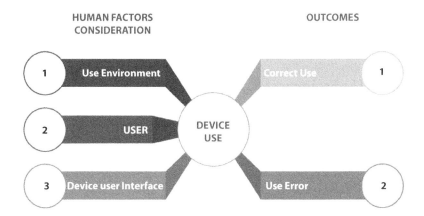

**Figure 15.2** Interactions among HFE/UE considerations result in either safe and effective use or unsafe or ineffective use (adapted from https://www.fda.gov/medical-devices/human-factors-and-medical-devices/human-factors-considerations).

and whether user interface design influences those interactions. The three main elements of the setup: device users, device use settings, and device user interactions, are taken into account while developing medical devices from an HFE/UE perspective. Figure 15.2 illustrates graphically how the three components interact with one another and the potential outcomes.

### C. Device Users

A medical device's intended users shall be able to operate it without creating mistakes that could endanger customer or user safety or medical care. Device users may only be qualified caretakers, such as doctors, pharmacists, registered nurses, occupational and physical therapists, counsellors, and home health aides, depending on the particular device and its intended purpose. Medical technicians, radiology practitioners, and laboratory experts could all be additional user populations. Professionals who setup, configure, and cleanse, manage, fix, or repurpose the devices are examples of other device user groups. Instead of professionals, some devices may be used by non-professionals, such as patients who use them on themselves for self-care and relatives or friends that act as lay caretakers for patients getting treatment in their homes, such as parents who use them on their kids or watch them use them [20]. A user's capacity to use a medical device relies on his or her individual traits, including: Dimension, power, and endurance, Fine motor skills, flexibility, and synchronization, Sensory skills (such as hearing, vision, and tactile awareness), Medical issue regarding which the device is used, Comorbidities, or having numerous illnesses or disorders, literacy and linguistic proficiency, general health, emotional and mental well-being, Education level and literacy levels in relation to the underlying medical condition [33].

### D. Device Use Environment

A great user interface layout may be influenced by a range of factors that may be present in the places where medical devices are utilized. Medical equipment may be employed in moving cars, community settings, or clinical or non-clinical settings. The following are some instances of environmental use circumstances: Depending on the illumination, it may be difficult to view gadget displays or controls [34]. It may be difficult to hear device operating feedback, auditory notifications, and alarms, much alone tell one alarm from another, due to a high noise level. The same gadget, component, or accessory could be found in many models throughout the space, making it challenging to recognize and choose the right one. The space may be crowded with furniture, clutter, or individuals and activities, rendering it complicated for individuals to move around and creating distractions that could befuddle or overload the device user. The gadget may be utilized in a speeding vehicle, which could cause vibration and jolting that might make it challenging to the person to comprehend a screen or use their fine motor skills.

### E. Device User Interface

All points of contact between a user and a device, including all aspects of the device that the user can interact with, are considered to be part of the user interface. When setting up, using, or maintaining a device, a user interface may be employed, such as when unpacking, setting up, calibrating, or cleaning the device. It encompasses the device's size and shape (especially for wearable and hand-held devices), information-delivery components including led light, displays, and audible and visual alerts, graphic user experiences of device software products, and the logic of the user's overall engagement with the system, including when, how, and how information (such as feedback) is presented to the user, hardware elements the user controls to regulate device functioning, such as valves, buttons, and dials; parts or accessories attached to or coupled to the patient; labeling and packaging, which includes operating directions, training resources, and other items.

### F. Human Factors Team

Human Factors at Centre for Devices and Radiological Health (CDRH)
The Human Factors Team at OPEQ is there to make certain any new medical devices are created with the intended user groups in mind, and that

they are safe and efficient when used by them. Evaluating new device filings and fostering efficient and targeted human factors analysis as well as excellent design principles for medical devices are the main objectives of the initiative. The team collaborates with scientists from all over OPEQ to assess application risk assessments, human elements data, and validation study statistics forwarded as part of different premarket submission types [35]. According to the FDA's Quality System Regulation, the team makes suggestions on human aspects elements of producers' design validation documentation. The team offers consultations on human aspects reviews to colleagues at other FDA Centers as well [30].

The team also: a) Creates information for FDA guidance publications to assist manufacturers in comprehending and using human factors engineering. b) Presents in conferences and open forums in order to reach out to business and academia. c) Offers instruction and direction to other FDA employees regarding human aspects, usage safety, and medical device design. d) Assists in the creation of Human Factors-related Guidelines alongside National and International Standards bodies. e) Promotes the use of the FDA's Medical Device Reporting (MDR) program for consumers and producers to report severe adverse events concerning medical devices. f) Assists in the examination of post-market complaints and returns of medical devices that entail usage mistake. Table 15.1 describes the details on international and national standards recognized by FDA for HFE/UE [31].

**Table 15.1** International and national standards recognized by FDA (adapted from https://www.mauricenavarro.com/ressources/applying-human-factors-and-usability-engineering-to-medical-devices/).

| Standard | Title | Principal goal |
|---|---|---|
| AAMI/ANSI HE75:2009 | Human Factors Engineering – Design of Medical Devices | A thorough reference that covers general principles, application error risk management, design aspects, and integrated alternatives. |
| ANSI/AAMI/ IEC 62366-1:2015 | Medical devices – Part 1: Application of usability engineering to medical devices | Every application of HF/ usability to medical device development underwent the HFE/UE process, which took risk management into account. |

*(Continued)*

**Table 15.1** International and national standards recognized by FDA (adapted from https://www.mauricenavarro.com/ressources/applying-human-factors-and-usability-engineering-to-medical-devices/). (*Continued*)

| Standard | Title | Principal goal |
|---|---|---|
| ANSI/AAMI/ ISO 14971:2007/ (R)2010 | Medical Devices – Application of risk management to medical devices | Process for managing risk for medical devices. |
| IEC 60601-1-6:2010 | Medical electrical equipment – Part 1-6: General requirements for basic safety and essential performance – Collateral standard: Usability | Enables communication between ANSI/AAMI/IEC 62366 and IEC 60601-1. |
| IEC 60601-1-8 Edition 2.1 2012-11 | Medical electrical equipment — Part 1-8: General requirements for basic safety and essential performance — Collateral Standard: General requirements, tests and guidance for alarm systems in medical electrical equipment and medical electrical systems | Medical electrical systems and device alarm design standards. |
| IEC 60601-1-11:2010 | Medical electrical equipment – Part 1-11: General requirements for basic safety and essential performance – Collateral Standard: Requirements for medical electrical equipment and medical electrical systems used in the home healthcare environment | Standards for non-clinical uses of medical electrical equipment, including concerns about the use of medical devices by laypeople. |

### G. FDA-Recognized Standards on Human Factors

Device-specific and generalized agreement standards established by national and international regulatory groups have received formal FDA recognition. The following is a list of FDA-recognized standards for human factors and the implementation of HFE/UE in medical devices:

## H. FDA-Guidance Documents Related to Human Factors

To assist device manufacturers in using proper human factors techniques in the creation of their products, FDA has created a number of guidance guidelines [21] a) Integrating Human Aspects and Usability Engineering to Medical Devices is one of them. b) Priority List of Equipment for Human Factor Assessment (draft guidance). c) Premarket Applications for Software in Medical Devices: Content Recommendations. d) Premarket Notification for an Infusion Pump: Guidance for Industry and FDA Staff [510(k)] Submissions. e) Validation Techniques and Marking for the Remanufacturing of Medical Devices in Healthcare Environments.

## I. Use Error Reporting

A usage error is when a device is used in a way that results in something other than what was intended—and not because the device itself is broken. The mistake can have resulted from a technology that was improperly designed or from its use in a circumstance that encouraged improper usage. Similar or worse repercussions may result from other users making the same use fault. By documenting the actual incidents and near-misses that happen at the institution, the company may assist regulatory authority in locating these mistakes. Reporters frequently omit information from an unfortunate incident that can be used to pinpoint the circumstances or events that contributed to it. Reports are more beneficial if companies can be as specific as possible while describing the situation [36].

*An effective problem explanation example:*
"A nurse was adjusting the dosage of a drug that was being administered through a pump. She misinterpreted the default settings while programming a bolus prior to the concentration shift and took the bolus concentration as the prescribed dose. The patient consequently received a triple dosage."

Along with a thorough explanation, the report should also contain the following significant data: a) The kind of device, the maker, the brand, and, if relevant, the lot number b) The event's precise location c) Was there injury to the patient or the device operator? d) Was there a flaw, failure, break, etc., in the product? e) Was the device being used at the time the incident occurred? Who, if so? f) Were the patient receiving any other treatments just at point of the incident that might have related to or caused it?

**J. Post-Market Reporting of Adverse Events, Use Errors and Product Problems**

- Medical Device Reporting (MDR) [21]: Producers, distributors, and user facilities are included in this. Demands the notification of all major adverse medical device incidents
- MedWatch: Includes both patients and healthcare workers. Takes voluntarily submitted reports of serious adverse events or issues with medical items. Requirement to Report Adverse Occurrence (Form 3500A)
- eMDR - Electronic Medical Device Reporting
- MedSun: Through a programme called MedSun, the FDA has also created a pilot programme to facilitate monitoring and follow-up on harmful occurrences. The FDA collaborates with more than 300 hospitals and care homes on MedSun. To find issues and collaborate with the producer to create a safer product, the MedSun method is employed [37].
- Internet Reporting of Illegal Medical Product Sales

### 15.3.9   Continuous Improvement of Regulations

The FDA envisions that AI/ML-based Software as a Medical Device (SaMD) would bring safe and efficient software capability that raises the standard of care for patients with appropriately customised complete product entire life cycle regulatory supervision. As part of its ongoing efforts to create and implement cutting-edge strategies to the regulatory oversight of medical device software as well as other digital health innovations, the FDA authored a discussion paper and request for feedback in April 2019 titled "Proposed Regulatory Framework for Modifications to Artificial Intelligence/Machine Learning (AI/ML)-Based Software as a Medical Device (SaMD)." This article outlined the theoretical underpinnings of the FDA's proposed premarket review strategy for software updates powered by AI and machine learning. The fundamentals of risk classification from the International Medical Device Regulators Forum, the benefit-risk structure from the FDA etc. were all taken into consideration when formulating the ideas outlined in the discussion paper. The Agency is providing its AI/ML-Based Software as a Medical Device Action Plan in reaction to stakeholder's comments on the discussion document and in line with the goals of the recently established Digital Health Centre of Excellence. Agency has succinctly outlined a five-part Plan of action to promote this work, as well as briefly summarizing the comments it has obtained from partners in this area.

## A. Tailored Regulatory Framework for AI/ML-Based SaMD [22]

What the Agency received Stakeholders made a lot of recommendations for improving the Predetermined Change Control Plan that is outlined in the discussion paper as well as the suggested regulatory framework for AI/ML-based SaMD. Agency's plans include: In order to revise the conceptual methodology for AI/ML-based SaMD, draught guidelines on the planned change control plan were released. A framework for modifying AI/ML-based SaMD that is based on the idea of a "Predetermined Change Control Plan" was proposed in the discussion paper. As was said above, the Algorithm Change Protocol (ACP) describes "how" the algorithm will adapt and modify while staying safe and effective. The SaMD Pre-Specifications (SPS) specify "what" features the manufacturer plans to change through learning.

Stakeholders approved of the Agency's facilitation of evolving and bettering algorithms, and many developers welcomed the opportunity to proactively collaborate with the Agency on ideas for potential changes to their products. The aspects that could be incorporated in the SPS/ACP to promote safety and efficacy as the SaMD and its related algorithm(s) change over time were specifically mentioned by stakeholders. In addition to feedback regarding the SPS and ACP, other sectors also received feedback. The types of changes to AI/ML software devices suggested in the discussion paper were generally agreed to be pertinent and suitable, however there were proposals for further changes to be specifically mentioned as types of changes that should come within this framework. The agency also received comments and queries regarding the scope, format, and timing of a "Focused Review" of a Predetermined Change Control Program. FDA is dedicated to making more advancements in the creation of the framework outlined in the consultation document. The Predetermined Change Control Plan has garnered considerable community attention, so the Agency plans to release a draught guidance for feedback. The proposed content for an SPS and ACP to enhance the security and efficacy of AI/ML SaMD algorithms is part of this draught guidance. The Agency will make use of recent submission experience as well as the comments obtained on the AI/ML-based SaMD discussion paper. Improvements to the framework's identification of the types of alterations that are appropriate will be made in addition to details on the targeted review, such as the submission/review procedure and submission content [38]. Community feedback will be needed to build these improvements on a continuing basis.

## B. Good Machine Learning Practice (GMLP)

What the Agency Heard: There was a request for the FDA to promote harmonisation of the creation of GMLP via collaborative standards initiatives as well as other community activities. Stakeholders strongly supported the concept and significance of Good Machine Learning Practice (GMLP).

What the agency will do: Promote the development of Good Machine Learning Practices. A set of AI/ML quality standards that are comparable to good software engineering practises or quality system practises were referred to in the discussion paper as excellent machine learning practises, or GMLPs. By encouraging manufacturers to follow well-established best practises and/or standards, the creation and acceptance of these practises is crucial for both directing the business and process design and simplifying monitoring of these complex products. To date, various efforts have been made, including those listed below, to specify the standards and best practises that potentially make up GMLP. Stakeholders generally expressed a significant appreciation for the GMLP concept and its significance [22]. There was also a request for the FDA to support the harmonisation of the multiple GMLP development projects, including through the development of consensus standards, the utilisation of pre-existing workstreams, and participation from other AI/ML organisations. The Agency has actively participated in a number of GMLP development-related initiatives due to the necessity for them, including standards and protocols and cooperative communities. For instance, FDA keeps in touch with various agencies. FDA formally joined the Xavier AI World Consortium Collaborative Community in 2021, as well as the Pathology Innovation Collaborative Community. The FDA is committed to intensifying its involvement with these communities as parts of such an Action Plan in order to promote consensus results that are most beneficial for the advancement and regulation of AI/ML-based technology. These GMLP initiatives will be conducted in close cooperation with the Agency's Medical Device Cybersecurity Initiative, in line with FDA's hard dedication to a strong approach to medical device cybersecurity [23].

## C. Patient-Centred Approach Incorporating Transparency into Users

What the Agency Heard: Stakeholders urged FDA to continue the conversation about how AI/ML-based systems engage with humans, including their openness to users and patients in general.

Agency's plans include: We will organize a public session about how device labelling improves user transparency and increases trust in AI/ML-based devices as a follow-up to the agency's previous Patient Engagement Advisory Committee session on the topic. The agency understands that

AI/ML-based technologies have special considerations that call for a proactive, patient-centred strategy to its design and use that takes into consideration issues like accessibility, fairness, confidence, and accountability. The FDA is tackling these challenges in part by promoting the openness of such devices to users and patients more generally regarding their operation. Promoting transparency is a crucial component of a patient-centered strategy, and in our opinion, it is crucial for AI/ML-based medical devices since they may integrate algorithms that are somewhat opaque and may learn and evolve over time. Numerous stakeholders have discussed the particular difficulties in labelling AI/ML-based devices and the requirement for producers to provide precise information about the data utilised to educate the algorithm, the applicability of its inputs, the logic it uses (when possible), the purpose of the output, and the proof of the device's effectiveness. The agency is dedicated to promoting a patient-centred approach, which calls for manufacturers to be transparent with users about how AI/ML-based devices work in order to guarantee that users are aware of the advantages, dangers, and restrictions of these devices. To this purpose, the Agency hosted a Patient Engagement Advisory Committee (PEAC) conference in October 2020 specifically focused on AI/ML-based devices to get feedback from patients on the variables that influence their trust in these technologies. The Agency is now collating the feedback obtained throughout this PEAC conference; the planned next action is to organise an open workshop to discuss lessons learned and to solicit feedback from the broader group on how device labelling improves clarity to users. We plan to take into account this feedback when selecting the categories of data that the FDA would advise a manufacturer to include in the labelling of AI/ML-based medical devices to promote user transparency. The FDA's involvement in community initiatives, such as standards creation and patient-focused programmes, will inform these efforts to encourage the openness of it and confidence in AI/ML-based technology. They will be a part of a larger initiative to support a patient-centred strategy for AI/ML-based solutions built on user transparency [39].

### D. Regulatory Science Methods Related to Algorithm Bias & Robustness

What the Agency heard: Stakeholders discussed the need for better approaches to assess algorithmic bias, deal with it, and enhance algorithm resilience.

Agency's plans include: Support the efforts being made by regulatory scientists to create a methodology for assessing and enhancing machine-learning algorithms, including the detection and eradication of bias and the assessment and development of algorithm resilience. The problem of prejudice and generalisation is not limited to AI/ML-based technology. It is crucial to consider carefully these challenges for AI/ML-based products because to the opaque nature of the workings of many AI/ML algorithms and the disproportionate position Agency anticipate such devices to have in healthcare [40]. Due to the fact that AI/ML systems are created and taught using historic data, they are subject to bias and are likely to replicate it. Because the provision of healthcare is known to differ depending on criteria like race, nationality, and socioeconomic background, it is likely that algorithms could unintentionally introduce biases present in the healthcare system. The Agency is aware of the critical need for enhanced approaches for the discovery and enhancement of algorithms for machine learning as well as the critical significance for medical devices must be properly adapted for an ethnically and racially diverse intended population of patients. This covers techniques for spotting and getting rid of bias as well as the durability and durability of such algorithms to handle shifting clinical inputs and circumstances. The FDA is funding a wide range of regulatory scientific research initiatives to create these techniques for assessing AI/ML-based medical software. As they continue to work together on initiatives to improve the assessment and commercialization of these new goods, regulatory science activities will be built and expanded.

**E. Real-World Performance (RWP)**
What the Agency heard: - The need for clarification on RWP tracking for software was mentioned by stakeholders.

Agency's plans include: Work with the piloting RWP process. Manufacturers may be able to comprehend where their products are used, find areas for improvement, and proactively address security or usage concerns by collecting effectiveness data on the actual use of the SaMD. Manufacturers can use real-world data collecting and monitoring as a key tool to reduce the risk associated with AI/ML-based SaMD adjustments and to support the benefit-risk profile when evaluating a specific marketing submission. Stakeholders expressed a number of queries, such as: What kind of reference data are suitable to use in assessing the performance on the field of AI/ML software devices? Which stakeholders should be responsible for what proportion of the oversight? How frequently and what amount of data should the Agency receive? How can the assertions, models, and algorithms be verified and put to the test? How may end-user feedback be included in the development and testing of AI/ML-based SaMD? Stakeholder responses indicated a general need for direction and clarity in this area. By cooperating on a voluntary basis with stakeholders, the Administration will assist the testing of true measuring performance as component of this Action Plan. Collaboration with some other current FDA programmes that emphasise the utilisation of real-world data will be employed to achieve this goal. The goal of this effort is to assist FDA in creating a framework [40].

## 15.4   Conclusion

Bioelectrical signals are used in human-machine interface (HMI) approaches to achieve real-time coordinated interaction across the human body and machine operation. With less human input and greater efficiency, HMI technology not only offers real-time management accessibility but also the capacity to manage several processes simultaneously. Health monitoring, medical diagnosis, the creation of prosthetic and assistive devices, the automobile and aerospace industries, robotic controls, and many more disciplines can all benefit from increased control access provided by HMI technology. The medical device legislation is very necessary due to the safety and user requirements. The development of medical equipment with human-machine interfaces contributes to the creation of a portable, cutting-edge, technological medical system that is chemically resistant and easy to sterilise. As a result, laws governing medical devices are applicable to such technology to ensure its safe and efficient usage. The regulatory viewpoint and prospective strategy for creating secure, high-quality HMI systems for patients are discussed in this chapter. It outlines current laws, criteria for classifying hazards, a framework for balancing benefits and risks, guidelines for managing risks, and strategies for the product life cycle. A description of the principles that should be followed while developing Good Machine Learning Practice (GMLP) would also help to promote high-quality, secure, and dependable medical equipment that uses HMI technologies.

## References

1. Medical devices, USFDA, Division of Industry and Consumer Education Center for Devices and Radiological Health, Food and Drug Administration, 10903 New Hampshire Ave, Silver Spring, MD 20993, 2022, https://www.fda.gov/medical-devices.
2. EU medical device development, 2022, https://www.propharmagroup.com/regulatory-affairs/eu-medical-device-development/.

3. FDA medical device development and regulation consulting services, 2022, https://www.propharmagroup.com/regulatory-affairs/fda-medical-device-development/.

4. Al-Achi, A., Gupta, M.R., Stagner, W.C., *Integrated pharmaceutics: Applied preformulation, product design, and regulatory science*, John Wiley & Sons, Inc., Hoboken, NJ, 2022.

5. Banks, T.J. and Ahluwalia, G.S., FDA regulations for investigation and approval of medical devices: Laser and light-based systems, in: *Cosmetics Applications of Laser & Light-Based Systems*, pp. 417–472, William Andrew Publishing, Norwich, NY, US, 2009.

6. Lo, A.W., Siah, K.W., Wong, C.H., Machine learning with statistical imputation for predicting drug approvals, 2018.

7. DeMasi, O., Kording, K., Recht, B., Meaningless comparisons lead to false optimism in medical machine learning. *PLoS One*, 12, 9, 2017.

8. Nicora, G., Rios, M., Abu-Hanna, A., Bellazzi, R., Evaluating pointwise reliability of machine learning prediction. *J. Biomed. Inform.*, 1, 127, 103996, 2022.

9. Ciarkowski, A., *Risk management for medical devices*, Wiley Encyclopedia of Biomedical Engineering, John Wiley & Sons, Inc., Hoboken, NJ, 2006.

10. Osborn, D.G. and Jaffe, M.B., Standards and regulatory considerations, in: *Anesthesia Equipment*, pp. 593–613, WB Saunders, Elsevier B.V. Amsterdam, The Netherlands, 2021.

11. Gad, S.C., *Integrated safety and risk assessment for medical devices and combination products*, Springer Nature, USA, New York Plaza, NY, 2020.

12. Daizadeh, I., Why did the number of US FDA medical device guidelines begin to rise in the mid-2010s? A perspective. *Expert Rev. Med. Devices*, 19, 12, 921–939, 2022.

13. Maresova, P., Hajek, L., Krejcar, O., Storek, M., Kuca, K., New regulations on medical devices in Europe: Are they an opportunity for growth? *Adm. Sci.*, 12, 10, 16, 2020.

14. Campillo-Artero, C., A full-fledged overhaul is needed for a risk and value-based regulation of medical devices in Europe. *Health Policy*, 113, 38–44, 2013.

15. Altenstetter, C. and Permanand, G., EU regulation of medical devices and pharmaceuticals in comparative perspective. *Rev. Policy Res.*, 24, 5, 385–405, 2007.

16. Dey, D., Habibovic, A., Löcken, A., Wintersberger, P., Pfleging, B., Riener, A., Martens, M., Terken, J., Taming the eHMI jungle: A classification taxonomy to guide, compare, and assess the design principles of automated vehicles' external human-machine interfaces. *TRIP*, 7, 100174, 2020.

17. Silva, C., Masci, P., Zhang, Y., Jones, P., Campos, J.C., A use error taxonomy for improving human-machine interface design in medical devices. *ACM SIGBED Rev.*, 16, 24–30, 2019.

18. Jacob, R.J.K., Human-computer interaction: Input devices. *ACM Comput. Surv. (CSUR)*, 28, 177–179, 1996.

19. Herbert, R., Kim, J.-H., Kim, Y.S., Lee, H.M., Yeo, W.-H., Soft material-enabled, flexible hybrid electronics for medicine, healthcare, and human-machine interfaces. *Materials*, 11, 187, 2018.

20. Wang, H., Ma, X., Hao, Y., Electronic devices for human-machine interfaces. *Adv. Mater. Interfaces*, 4, 4, 1600709, 2017.

21. Halt, G.B., Donch, J.C., Stiles, A.R., VanLuvanee, L.J., Theiss, B.R., Blue, D.L., *FDA and intellectual property strategies for medical device technologies*, Springer International Publishing, New York, NY, 2019.

22. Eidenberger, R., Medical device registration, agreements on mutual recognition—A step forward to global harmonization? *Radiat. Phys. Chem.*, 57, 539–542, 2000.

23. Bach-y-Rita, P. and Kercel, S.W., Sensory substitution and the human-machine interface. *Trends Cognit. Sci., TiCS*, 7, 12, 541–546, 2003.

24. Ross, C.F., Sensory science at the human-machine interface. *Trends Food Sci. Technol.*, 20, 2, 63–72, 2009.

25. Papcun, P., Kajáti, E., Koziorek, J., Human-machine interface in concept of Industry 4.0, in: *2018 World Symposium on Digital Intelligence for Systems and Machines (DISA)*, IEEE, pp. 289–296, 2018.

26. Gong, C., Human-machine interface: Design principles of visual information in human-machine interface design, in: *2009 International Conference on Intelligent Human-Machine Systems and Cybernetics*, vol. 2, pp. 262–265, IEEE, 2009.

27. De Visser, E.J., Pak, R., Shaw, T.H., From automation to autonomy: The importance of trust repair in human-machine interaction. *Ergonomics*, 61, 10, 1409–1427, 2018.

28. Wright, P.C., Fields, R.E., Harrison, M.D., Analyzing human-computer interaction as distributed cognition: The resources model. *Hum.-Comput. Interact.*, 15, 1, 1–41, 2000.

29. Sainfort, F., Jacko, J.A., Edwards, P.J., Booske, B.C., Human–computer interaction in healthcare, in: *Human-Computer Interaction*, pp. 155–172, CRC Press, Taylor & Francis Group, Abingdon, OX, 2009.

30. Chan, E., The food and drug administration and the future of brain-computer interface: Adapting FDA device law to the challenges of human-machine enhancement. *J. Marshall J. Computer & Info. L.*, 25, 117, 2007.

31. 49 CFR Appendix E to part 236 - human-machine interface (HMI) design, 2022, https://www.govinfo.gov/app/details/CFR-2014-title49-vol4/CFR-2014-title49-vol4-part236-appE.

32. Human-system interface design review guidelines (NUREG-0700), 2022, https://www.nrc.gov/reading-rm/doc-collections/nuregs/staff/sr0700/index.html.

33. Human-system interface design review guidelines, 2022, https://www.osti.gov/servlets/purl/1644018.

34. Design considerations for effective, human-machine interface systems, 2022, https://eao.com/fileadmin/documents/PDFs/en/08_whitepapers/EAO_WP_HMI-Systems_EN.pdf.

35. Human-machine interface, 2022, https://www.sciencedirect.com/topics/computer-science/human-machine-interface.

36. Human-machine interface, 2022, https://oshwiki.eu/wiki/Human_machine_interface.

37. Human-machine interface systems for medical, diagnostic and treatment equipment, 2022, https://www.mouser.com/pdfDocs/eao-ta-hmi-medical-applications-en.pdf.

38. Greer, A.D., Human-machine interface for robotic surgery and stereotaxy. *Int. J. Comput. Assist. Radiol. Surg.*, 1, 295–297, 2006.

39. Gupta, I., Dangi, S., Sharma, S., Augmented reality based human-machine interfaces in healthcare environment: Benefits, challenges, and future trends, in: *2022 International Conference on Wireless Communications Signal Processing and Networking (WiSPNET)*, IEEE, pp. 251–257, 2022.

40. Derylo, I., Analyst insights–recent trends in human-machine interfaces. *Adv. Manuf. Technol.*, *31*, 8, 1–3, 2010.

# 16

# Towards the Digitization of Healthcare Record Management

Shivani Patel, Bhavinkumar Gayakvad, Ravisinh Solanki*,
Ravi Patel and Dignesh Khunt

*Graduate School of Pharmacy, Gujarat Technological University, Gandhinagar,
Gujarat, India*

## Abstract

In the age of information technology (IT), digital health records are essential for improving patient care. IT provides numerous opportunities to create and manage an efficient digital healthcare record management system in order to further improve care coordination. The current medical system's expanded reach and scope have made this practice necessary. Different types of health problems are treated with a wide range of drugs, which increases the risk of drug compatibility, drug resistance, and patient-specific allergies, among other things. Many times, patients are prescribed medications to which they are resistant or allergic, which does not help to improve the patient's condition but worsens it. Medical professionals perform and prefer their own medication schemes, which vary from person to person and can have a significant impact on patient treatment. Accurate reporting and documentation of a patient's condition reduces the possibility of error when designing treatment strategies and selecting medications. As digitization of health records can reflect all of the patients' medical history as well as diagnostic history, which can be used as reference by other medical professionals while dealing with the patient, it can reduce the scope of error. To eliminate the possibility of data duplication and fragmentation, server or cloud-based well-regulated data networks can be developed for each and every person with a single identity. Although there are certain worries about the safety and security of the data, patient consent and the ethical consent of the data users might be suggested as a solution to handle these concerns about patient personal information. The greatest way to create patient-focused healthcare advantages in the future will be

*Corresponding author*: 11mph307@gmail.com; ORCID ID: 0000-0003-2977-554X

Rishabha Malviya, Sonali Sundram, Bhupendra Prajapati and Sudarshan Kumar Singh (eds.)
*Human-Machine Interface: Making Healthcare Digital*, (411–448) © 2024 Scrivener Publishing LLC

through the implementation of these accurate and open digital healthcare data management infrastructure.

*Keywords*: Digital health records, electronic health records, health data management, digital health, digitization, medical IT infrastructure, data exchange, DHR practices

## 16.1   Introduction

Human minds are a miracle. They are capable of creating and making things that no one would have ever imagined was feasible. They have the potential to lead the globe in better paths that would be productive for society. One such idea created by human mind is Information Technology (IT). Since the early Sumerians in ancient Mesopotamia invented writing, around 3000 BC, humanity has been manipulating, storing, and exchanging knowledge. However, it wasn't until the middle of the 20th century, with the advent of early office technology, that the word IT became widely used and digitization was applied to every possible field. In a 1958 issue of the Harvard Business Review, Harold J. Leavitt and Thomas C. Whisler wrote, "the new technology does not yet have a single accepted name." We will refer to it as information technology [1].

Across the past few years, every field has progressed in the terms of digitization including the healthcare sector more specifically healthcare record management. Earlier was the era when records simply mean writing with pen on paper and now it is being transformed into a digital form. Digital record keeping helps to keep the records in an electronic media rather than a bunch of files which are tough to maintain, share and analyze. Recent developments in the Information Technology sector, in particular, are helping to handle medical appointments and records more effectively. Data has emerged as an increasingly important factor in the delivery, diagnosis, and management of healthcare services as a result of the proliferation of IT and management. Large-scale medical data gathered by hospitals and other providers may now be mined and analyzed due to the developments in data processing to help with planning and making the right decisions [2].

Similar to other industries like Agriculture, Electrical, Civil, and Mechanical which have evolved over the years, the Healthcare industry also progressed through various phases, from 1.0 to 4.0 as shown in Figure 16.1. The healthcare industry should be more administratively accessible than other industries in order to create a more ecological and user-friendly

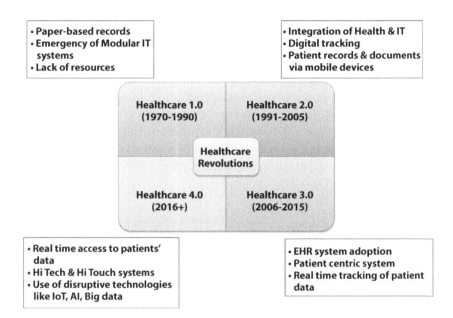

**Figure 16.1** Revolution in healthcare industry.

environment for everyone. Since the healthcare sector only officially began in 1970, it is still in its infancy. Healthcare 1.0 refers to that period since the efforts done at that time were essential and resources were limited. It was the phase of the emergence of modular IT systems while paper-based records still hold the power in the healthcare industry. The concept of healthcare 2.0 was introduced by later developments in the information technology sector and the creation of medical technologies like tracking and imaging systems. Computational intelligence tools and data processing systems have been the foundation for the development of novel and compelling therapeutic options. Healthcare 3.0 is moving in this direction, and it has gained traction between 2006 and 2015 as a result of the widespread adoption of digital health records. The EHR has been adopted in this phase to assist specialists in receiving important data promptly. The use of advanced communication systems and AI in the medical field allows for more precise and useful analysis for healthcare professionals. These value-based systems give the healthcare industry the tools it needs to make credentialed decisions about the care it provides (QoS) [3].

Then emerged the healthcare 4.0 phase which refers to the application of digital technologies to the provision of healthcare. The Internet of Things (IoT), Big Data (including mHealth), 5G (including mHealth), artificial intelligence (AI), computing (cloud, fog, and edge), and Blockchain are all part of the emerging "Healthcare 4.0" paradigm. The World Health Organization (WHO) defines healthcare 4.0 as a systemic capability of digital technology used to achieve health objectives and deployed within digital health apps and ICT systems, including communication channels like text messages [4]. Some of the examples of IoT along with its class are given in Table 16.1 [5].

In Healthcare Phase 3.0, hospitals started using information technology, and only in the last 10 years did most of them start using electronic health records. The digitization of patient records offers many advantages

**Table 16.1** Internet of things examples.

| Sr. no. | Class | Name | Examples |
|---|---|---|---|
| 1. | Wearable IoT | Smart watches | Pebble, Samsung gear, Apple watch |
| | | Wristband sensors | Fitbit, Metawear, Garmin Vivosmart |
| | | Smart glasses | Microsoft HoloLens, Google glass |
| | | e-textile and Health monitors | Heart rate, Electrocardiogram [ECG], Blood pressure monitors |
| 2. | Fabric and flexible sensors | Blood chemistry monitoring patches | Sano Intelligence's biochemistry patches |
| | | Stretchable digital tattoos | mc10's BioStamp |
| | | Cardiac rhythm monitoring patches | Zio Patch from iRhythm |
| | | Blood pressure monitoring patches | Sense A/S's blood pressure monitoring patches |
| | | Glucose monitoring patches | Continuous glucose monitor |
| | | UV sense patches | La Roche-Posay, ultra voilet sense |

to medical professionals, such as electronic notifications to prevent medication-related errors, improved information exchange among the healthcare staff, and enhanced accountability through the examination of meticulous and clear records of clinical history [6]. A greater number of people are using electronic medical record systems, which has made it much easier to use clinical data for research. Big data analysis is now widely acknowledged to have a significant impact on enhancing healthcare by assisting clinical decision-making, preventing unwanted negative clinical outcomes, identifying high-risk patients, automatic assigning of diagnosis codes, early detection of diseases, and improving statistics on clinical outcomes, naming a few encouraging examples. Despite certain concerns regarding the security and safety of the data, patient consent and the ethical consent of the data users may be offered as a way to address these problems about patient personal information. By putting in place this precise and transparent digital healthcare data management infrastructure, it will be possible to significantly improve patient-focused healthcare in the future [7].

The amount and variety of personal health information (PHI) being digitally collected and stored by organisations, including non-health organisations like Google and Microsoft, as well as healthcare institutions like hospitals, is growing daily and hence emphasizing the necessity of developing suitable policies to safeguard consumer privacy while enjoying the advantages of digitization. New models are required to provide comprehensive guidance while keeping the reality of a dynamic science in mind because technology, public knowledge and concern, and policy are largely co-evolving, as significant study notes. One such fundamental tenet to safeguard privacy is that the patient should retain control over the use of his or her personal information. Therefore, it is crucial to consider a future in which the customer is more empowered, a direction in which present policy is evolving, to the extent that privacy rules evolve in reaction to technology developments and consumer expectations [6].

This chapter provides a brief background about the actual concept and organization of electronic health records, the mechanism & operation lying behind it, and the advantages of using this format of health records. The risk and problems concerned with the use of this system are outlined along with the policies governing health data exchange. Data analysis which is an essential part of any digital system has been described separately. Future benefits of this record system are described keeping in consideration the success of applying it to healthcare systems across the world including the benefits to the various stakeholders in the system.

## 16.2   Digital Health Records: Concept and Organization

Digitization of healthcare records is termed as Electronic Healthcare Records or simply Electronic Health Records. It has long been a significant area of research in medical informatics. EHR as defined by Lakovidis is "lifelong records of a person's medical care that have been digitally archived for the benefit of education, research, and continuity of care while always maintaining confidentiality" [8].

Electronic health records are electronic versions of traditional paper medical charts. EHRs are a patient-focused system that provides authorized users with instant, secure access to data in real time. It contains a patient's medical history. Moreover, it goes beyond gathering clinical data to provide a more comprehensive understanding of a patient's care by making precise and accurate decisions through access to evidence based tools. Medical professionals working in EHRs document patient information in a variety of electronic formats, including charts, graphs, text, symbols, and more. It is easy to work with, transport, store, duplicate and replicate these digital data objects [3].

EHR includes various information like laboratory tests, observations, treatments, diagnostic imaging reports, therapies, demographic data, drug administration, allergies, and legal consent as shown in Figure 16.2. Multiple medical records systems exist today, each with its own method of storing this data. Files can be stored in a variety of different formats, including relational database tables, organized and unorganized document-based storage, and computerized hardcopies kept using the conventional data management approach [8].

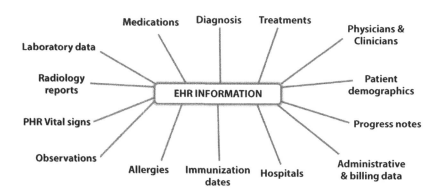

**Figure 16.2** Information included in EHR.

Electronic health records allow for the sharing of patient information with other healthcare organizations and communities, including but not limited to specialists' offices, dispensaries, diagnostic imaging centers, laboratory facilities, emergency departments, and primary care clinics. Therefore, all clinicians' input is sought in order to provide the best possible care for a patient. The data stored here should be protected from unauthorized access and use by law.

In an EHR system, patient's information is shared among the clinicians. Patients who want to recover from illness need to provide their personal data to doctors, including height, weight, blood pressure and past medical histories, in order for the doctors to diagnose the illness and prescribe the proper course of treatment. In some conditions like when a patient is suffering from HIV, he/she might feel uncomfortable to share their information because of social fear and prejudice. Sometimes patients are reluctant to disclose health information because they do not trust the EHRs system. Information about the patient may only be disclosed in accordance with the law or with the patient's consent. Therefore, privacy and security are the foremost concerns for maintaining data integration & an individual's trust. If in any cases the data gets leaked, it may lead to severe life-threatening consequences. Hence, the health information shared should be private and secure between the healthcare providers and the patient in order to obtain a more efficient outcome in the system.

The flow of information is shown in Figure 16.3. An EHR collects information from a wide variety of medical sources, including smart watches, wearable's, healthcare providers, primary healthcare records system, in-patient monitoring, and so on. The information is stored in a local database via a local gateway and later in a cloud server via a remote gateway after it has been generated. Attack and privacy concerns may arise as when the information is collected, stored, and shared.

To reduce this risk, a variety of privacy preservation strategies or mitigation techniques must be used. Some of the examples of former strategies are access control model, grant access, and pseudonymity and of the later are authentication and authorization. By assigning the appropriate level of access to each user, "Grant Access" ensures that only authorized individuals have access to sensitive data. For example, a physician and a nurse have different responsibilities and therefore should not have a copy of the same information. The most difficult approach is implementing an access control structure and authorization, as this requires a custom identity management system that comprises three key components: users, software, and regulations. The user access strategy verifies user activity within the system in accordance with the user's granted permissions or rights as specified by

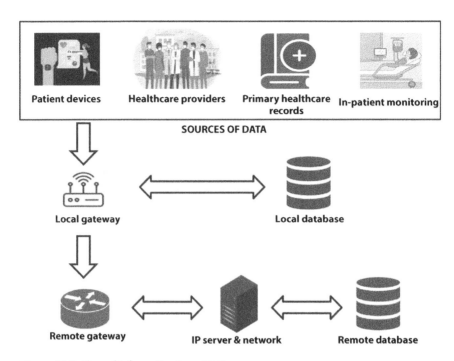

**Figure 16.3** Flow of information in an EHR.

the patient or other authorized parties. First, the data are kept safe in a centralized system. Then, access methodological approaches are used to make sure that only the right people can see the data. This method stores health data in a way that doesn't encrypt it. It also protects against unauthorized access by acting as a firewall and integrates data at the same time. Hence, it provides privacy and security of the health data. Another method is Pseudonymity in which the user has pseudonym identity i.e. unreal name so they can communicate in an anonymous way without being worried for securities. Only the system administrators have the access to real identity in this method [3].

Digitization of healthcare records has been studied in depth. Various case studies are carried out to understand the concept of electronic health records, the benefits of using this system, security and privacy in this system, comparison of it with paper records and so more. One of such study was carried out by Dell *et al.* by developing an android phone application in which he successfully tracked immunisation statistics of vaccines using bubble forms in the form of optical mark recognition (OMR) in rural Mozambique health institutions (leveraging in-built camera). There have been many studies conducted in this area because automated handwriting recognition is so much more difficult than bubble identification.

In a study conducted by Chrons *et al.* optical character recognition was found to have an accuracy of 85%, while human visual information processing abilities were found to have an accuracy of 99%. Research along these lines has shown that there is a void between what is possible at the present moment with the state of the art and what can be achieved by involving people in the process.

"Crowdsourcing" term was coined out to explain a decentralized method of hiring workers who are located all over the world in massively parallel settings. An internet service called Captricity employs crowdsourcing to enter data. Captricity users upload digital documents with predefined templates, and the service then shreds the files and sends them to Amazon's Mechanical Turk for transcription. And the workflow that emerged was significantly cheaper and required much less time to enter data than traditional service models.

Ratan *et al.* came up with the idea of capturing digital records at the same time as the original paper forms were being recorded, and they introduced a prototype for a portable electronic slate that verifies and records whatever is written on it digitally while simultaneously creating paper records. This shows benefits like reduced time, improved accuracy and record completeness. It costs approx. $100 and 5-6 hours of battery run.

Even in regions where few people are comfortable using computers, creating automated systems to enter data is a realistic option. In order to digitize paper forms, Parikh *et al.* created CAM, which makes use of the widespread availability of mobile phones equipped with cameras to scan barcodes that define each entry. The app on the mobile device can read the code and then request that the necessary data be entered via the keypad.

DeRenzi *et al.* introduced "e-IMCI," an electronic version of diagnostic processes based on personal digital assistants (PDAs) that aids healthcare professionals with procedural chores while gathering health information, in a manner analogous to that of assisted technology for data collection. Errors such as missed steps, incorrect computations, and faulty branching logic have been shown to be significantly reduced using this method [9].

## 16.3 Mechanism and Operation of Digital Health Record

The transition from a paper-based to an electronic health record system is labor-intensive and time-consuming. Before implementing an EHR system, it's crucial to comprehend the advantages an EHR offers to your practice. There are certain roadblocks to the successful adoption of an EHR which includes uncertain costs, difficulty in understanding your organization's need, and the extensive efforts required to implement a system. These roadblocks can be overcome by various factors like teamwork, readiness to perform any task, someone taking the responsibility to overcome the cause, EHR supporters among stakeholders, and a team of eager personnel. After applying this to practice, one must select an EHR system they will follow which may be a physician hosted EHR or a remotely hosted EHR [10].

### 16.3.1    Physician-Hosted EHR

Under this system, the health data is stored on the physician's own server. In this approach, the doctor is the only accountable party who must buy hardware and software and who is also in charge of data backup, maintenance, and security. A physician hosted EHR will cost less money to upgrade your internet connection if your practise doesn't currently have dependable, fast internet connectivity. While the data is under the control of physician, vendors may include a disabling code in the software which will help the vendor to be data hostage in case of any dispute.

### 16.3.2    Remotely-Hosted EHR

Under this system, the health data is stored on another entity's software rather than a physician's server. This separate entity owns the server that contains the information. When it comes to data storage, maintenance, backup, and security, all of that falls under the purview of the external party. There are three types of this system:

#### 16.3.2.1    Subsidized System

In this method, the finance for the EHR is subsidized by a third party that the doctor has a relationship with, such as a hospital. Usually, the sponsoring entity's servers are used and not the doctor's, therefore the doctor has no control over the data. Important factors to take into account include ownership of the data in the event that the relationship changes, such as when the doctor moves or ceases to be a part of the health insurance plan, as well as legal issues (such as antitrust/anti-kickback issues), particularly when hospital subsidies are involved.

## 16.3.2.2    Dedicated Hosted System

In this method, the doctor does not keep the EHR data on his or her personal servers. Instead, the vendor's dedicated servers are used to store the data. Data about patients is stored on servers in specific, well-known locations, but the doctor has no say over where this happens.

## 16.3.2.3    Cloud-Based or Internet-Based Computing

The data are stored by the provider in the "clouds," or online. Software as a service vendor were formerly known as application service providers (ASPs), but the term "SaaS" was coined to better reflect the nature of their business model. The EHR software is not installed on the computers of doctors; instead, the vendor's website is used to access the software. The data is frequently moved by the vendors who provide the online software, so the doctor might not be aware of its location beyond "somewhere in the clouds." The physicians neither have the control over the data, nor over the data's destination or timing of its transfer.

This system provides several benefits including reduced upfront hardware and software costs, reduced run time failures, reduced maintenance costs and more availability of IT services. Regarding professional liability, there are a number of reasons to be concerned about cloud systems. Firstly, vendors have control over the data during the contract period as well as after the period too, a circumstance that might make it more difficult for doctors to obtain the data. Secondly, "click and agree" internet contracts might not allow for term negotiation, which means they might not genuinely suit the needs of doctors' clinical practises. The last, and possibly most expensive, disadvantage of online contracts is that indemnity and other clauses may contractually bind doctors to obligations that go beyond those covered by medical professional liability insurance. Therefore, doctors should carefully read what they are signing and seek legal counsel if any clauses are unclear [11].

After selecting an appropriate EHR, next step is to implement the EHR to your system. Setting up the new EHR system, ensuring privacy and security compliance, establishing practice workflows, educating the care team, and monitoring the adoption process all require a multidisciplinary approach. Patients, doctors, and staff can all benefit from a more seamless transition to the new EHR system if it is implemented with care. To implement an EHR successfully, nine steps are involved:

**STEP 1: Establish an implementation team**

This team often consists of medical physicians, receptionists, nurses, medical assistants, office personnel in charge of compliance, and administrative personnel. Clinical members have dual roles to play. In addition to educating their peers on EHR usage, clinical team members often report back clinical issues to the implementation team. The roles of the lead doctor, the project manager, and the lead super user are all crucial ones.

- The chief doctor oversees all aspects of the operation and acts as a liaison between the business's back-office workers and its customers.
- The project manager maintains stakeholder focus on their timeframes, monitors project progress, and manages day-to-day challenges in close collaboration with the vendor and all practise staff.
- The lead super user will serve as the internal expert in the new EHR.

**STEP 2: Set up the software**

Begin by configuring your EHR to comply with the necessary security standards in conjunction with your health IT vendor. You might need to undertake a risk assessment for this purpose. Practices may also think about customizing software to enhance workflow. Create a list of everything that needs to be done outside of the EHR, including importing patient demographics from the PMS, setting up the COE, managing medications, configuring the default patient history, creating standing orders, developing treatment plans and protocols, and updating the billing/charge master with new consents and codes. Documentation is made easier with the help of EHR software, which can be customized to generate templates tailored to a doctor's area of expertise or specialty. Make sure you discuss pricing and personalization options with your EHR provider.

**STEP 3: Identify hardware requirements**

A right hardware can save a company's money and time. In certain clinics, having a printer in every room and a huge monitor each day help doctors save 20 and 30 minutes, respectively. Another way to reduce the time spent each day logging in and out of the system is to provide each employee with their own portable computer. The type of EHR purchased determines the system hardware (i.e., server and network) requirements. If you choose a cloud-based EHR, you need to have an excellent internet connection for all the devices. A network update or safe wireless routers may be needed in order to connect to the internet. If you choose dedicated hosted system, you need to purchase and install vendor-specific hardware.

## STEP 4: Transfer of data

- Identify the method for transferring data from the old recordkeeping system or other PMS modules to the new EHR. A practice can designate current employees to help with this process or by hiring temporary or additional staff to upload the patient's demographic details, immunization histories, list of allergies, recent visit notes and past social, medical, medication and family histories prior to the patient's next appointment.
- Make a list of the things that need to go into the EHR. By doing this, it will be made sure that no important information is lost in the transmission.
- Identify the time needed to transfer the patient's information. This can assist the practise in effectively allocating workload among staff members involved in uploading data and also help in setting realistic completion dates.

## STEP 5: Improve pre-launch processes

Prior to implementation of an EHR, workflows should ideally be optimised. Some businesses put off workflow optimization because they believe that once they have their new EHR, everything will be better. Due to this, the problems resulting from insufficient support staff or inefficient workflows will be increased as a result of implementation of an EHR.

As you go along, enquire:

- Is it required?
- Will it be to the patient's advantage?
- Is everything being carried out in the right sequence?
- Is the appropriate individual responsible for carrying it out?

For any action currently done by the physician, ask:

- Is a physician's skill and training needed for this?
- Can this task be delegated to another team member?

**STEP 6: Determine the room layout**
Location of the computer in the examination room has implications for patient care. Patient care could suffer if doctors and nurses are always looking at their screens during conversations with patients. Several groups have discovered the benefits of using a "triangle of trust" to facilitate communication between patients, doctors, and computers. One way to set up this triangle is with a semicircular desk, which allows the doctor and patient to sit facing each other while still being able to turn their bodies slightly to talk about the electronic knowledge source. The computer could also be installed on a mobile cart that the doctor could roll to any part of the examination room where eye contact was needed.

**STEP 7: Choose a launch approach: "big bang" vs. Incremental**
The "big bang" method is used by some facilities; all staff members are switched to using the EHR for all procedures and patients within a single day. This has the benefit of reducing the time needed to manage both the new electronic system and a paper record at the same time. Additionally, it can be quite disruptive and amplify minor errors but on the other hand requires a lot of resources and personnel support.

In other practices, the EHR is implemented gradually, with certain features being turned on one at a time i.e., starting with e-prescribing and adding visit note documentation features a few months later. Another incremental strategy is to roll out the EHR gradually throughout the organisation, starting with a small number of sites or departments and learning from and improving the process as you go further. This strategy allows medical professionals and personnel to gradually become proficient with the system's features and minimises productivity loss caused by operational and workflow modifications brought on by the deployment of EHR. However, this necessitates strict adherence to a work plan to keep implementation phases on schedule, close monitoring of hybrid processes because not all tasks can be completed electronically, and knowledge of the various functions that are being launched on different dates.

**STEP 8: Establish protocols for situation when your EHR is down**
In the event of a catastrophic system failure or power outage, what measures will you take to ensure the continuity of operations? To ensure that doctors and other staff members have clear instructions in the event that EHR is unavailable, it is necessary to create procedures for when it is. Patient care, such as check-in and visit documentation, may still need to be carried out during this downtime, so it is important to have a plan in place for how this will be communicated to doctors, employees, and patients. Electronic

and paper versions of downtime procedures and supplies should be made available for easier access. Some companies even go so far as to put their policies and procedures in a three-ring binder and store backup copies in a secure location.

**STEP 9: Start the training**
Training staff and physicians are essential for the successful implementation of EHR. Make sure everyone can use the EHR effectively before it's released by developing a training plan. A few guiding ideas can be helpful:

➢ **Proceed slowly-** It is necessary to provide basic skills to users which are needed for the launch. There is no need to teach them everything at a time and more than their capacity to absorb. It may be difficult for them to understand more than the basic skills because they haven't used the software in practice. Later when they get the chance to use the EHR for a week or so, conduct an additional training to refine their skills and discover further time-saving techniques, such as creating smart sets and other preferences. This is an excellent chance to create smart sets and review downtime protocols.

➢ **Make plans for your co-workers to mentor one another-** When feasible, prepare super users for each sort of role and specialisation. The best way for paediatricians to learn is from other paediatricians, neurologist from other neurologist, surgeons from other surgeons, and nurses from other nurses. These super users can eventually serve as an ongoing resource for their colleagues as their comfort level with the EHR increases.

➢ **Prepare for continual training requirements-** Practices should include a continuing improvement plan in addition to pre-implementation training. Many users will discover new functions or build shortcuts after a few months that they can share with co-workers. As EHR gets updated with new and/or better features, additional training will be required. Some chances to deal with these circumstances well include:

- Develop a means by which suggestions for enhancing EHRs can be submitted and followed up on, allowing the change team to proactively decide which ones to prioritize. You can improve the EHR by working together with the people who use it the most, the people who are already actively contributing to it through their frequent use. They have complete leeway in providing feedback and making suggestions to enhance the user experience.

- Develop a process to allow for ongoing EHR adaptation. Once the doctor and staff have adjusted to the new EHR, they may find that tweaks to the system in general can have a positive effect on efficiency.
- Whenever new clinical decision support rules become available, enable them. Keep in touch with the EHR vendor and employ ongoing IT support to create new or further customize existing templates for data entry, revise or reformat letters and forms produced by the EHR, and update order sets in response to new medical discoveries or changes in the services provided by other healthcare organizations.
- Determine potential for system integration.
- Plan ahead for any necessary group training on system updates and new features. Some patient appointments may have to be rescheduled because doctors need to attend training. Patients at the clinic will experience less downtime if necessary preparations are made in advance [12].

## 16.4   Benefits of Digital Health Records

Electronic health records are a fantastic tool for efficiently managing large amounts of paperwork, which can be time-consuming and costly when manually transcribed, refilled, and stored. Better and more accurate reimbursement coding for patient management is made possible by EHR systems. The software's ability to centralize patient data greatly reduces the possibility of medical mistakes and helps improve health by facilitating more effective disease management. Benefits of digital health records are best understandable when compared to the earlier paper record system. So here, we compare five key advantages of electronic health records to paper-based records.

### 16.4.1   Security

Security worries are a big problem for both paper and digital storage systems; therefore, security is a major concern for both. If a facility saves records electronically without sufficient and effective security procedures, unauthorized individuals may be able to access the data and misuse it. Paper records are prone to be misplaced, damaged, or stolen if they are kept in that format. Hence, when security system is properly put into place, electronic records are very secure and cannot be accessed by unauthorized individuals. This will help to gain patients' trust in the system and they would feel comfortable to freely share their data to the healthcare providers.

## 16.4.2   Costs

Due to the size and digitalization of the IT network, the costs to launch the EHR are initially very high, but it decreases over time. While physically storing paper records necessitates more staff to handle and preserve paper files, access and arrange a vast amount of papers, which considerably increases cost over time while on the other hand EHR can decrease cost in long run by saving man power, physical storage space and time.

## 16.4.3   Access

Electronic health records have a definite benefit over paper health records in terms of accessibility. Healthcare personnel are more productive because they can rapidly access information from digital health records whenever and wherever they need it whereas in case of paper records, these needs to be physically given to the healthcare professionals or by scanning or through email which is a time-consuming process.

## 16.4.4   Storage

Paper medical data needed enormous warehouses to keep them, but electronic health records can be kept in a secure cloud, making accessing them easier for those who need it. Paper records not only take up space but also cost more to store because they degrade over time when handled by numerous people and are not ecologically friendly.

## 16.4.5   Accuracy and Readability

EHRs are often written by the use of standard abbreviations which are accepted formats across the globe and hence are readable and accurate and reduces the chances of confusion. However, paper records which are handwritten are poorly legible in certain cases and can lead to medical errors. The limited space in paper medical records is the restricting factor which makes it impossible for healthcare practitioners to record all relevant information.

### 16.4.6   Practice Management

In case of appointment management, EHR improves medical practise management by integrating scheduling programmes that automatically code, manage claims, and link appointments to progress notes. This platform efficiently manages graphs that are unique to each patient and answers questions regarding the patient's status. A national conference on health statistics found that 79% of EHR users do their jobs better, 82% of EHR users say that giving prescriptions electronically (e-prescribing) saves them time, and 75% of EHR users get test results faster than usual.

### 16.4.7   Quality of Care

Since it is a digital platform that is connected to the internet, doctors can get information about their patients at any time and from anywhere. They can also give jobs to people who help them, like labs and other doctors. The best thing about these electronic records is that they can be linked to national and international health databases and registries. So, it helps doctors keep track of the spread of the disease they are treating and get ready for emergencies. This can greatly improve the effectiveness of primary care and the way care is coordinated [13].

## 16.5   Limitations of Digital Health Records

Moving the whole healthcare system from a paper-based system to one that uses real-time, information-ready media at the point of care is a big job that is still going on. Large organizations like private hospitals, hospitals run by universities, multi-specialty groups, and integrated healthcare delivery systems are more likely to have these systems set up and running. Small organizations, solo practitioners, and rural and small hospitals are less likely to switch to computerized systems because it costs a lot to set them up and use them. There are certain factors limiting the use of digital healthcare records [14].

### 16.5.1   Completeness

This means that not every piece of information that is available about a patient is always fully shown in the EHR database. EHRs still suffer from underreporting even with a consistent user interface collecting patient data in a methodical manner. Various reasons for this are:

- Patient data are not meticulously recorded in EHRs
- Medical professionals' failure to recognise particular diseases, such as adverse medication occurrences
- Inadequate doctor-to-doctor communication when multiple doctors are involved in the same patient record
- As patients switch hospitals, a significant portion of their medical history is lost due to integration issues between the various EHR systems utilized by different institutions.

### 16.5.2    Correctness

This concerns whether specific patient information reported in EHRs is accurate. Inaccurate information frequently takes the form of information that is not sufficiently explicit rather than, more rarely, information that is entirely incorrect. For instance, a patient's record can list a diagnosis of a generic skin illness when the true underlying condition is a skin disorder induced by medication. According to an assessment of 4200 medical records by the Swedish National Board of Health and Welfare, 20% of primary diagnosis codes assigned in EHRs were found to have significant mistakes.

### 16.5.3    Complexity

The intricacy of the data in EHRs is primarily discussed here. The varied forms of data present in EHRs bring to light the challenges associated with their analysis. Not only is it difficult to combine the many forms of data, but it is also difficult to analyze each type separately. Natural language processing is required to process the clinical notes in free text, and the duties are made difficult by the poor quality of the texts, which contain a large number of medical acronyms, typographical errors, and incomplete phrases. The clinical events that are documented in EHRs, such as diagnoses, treatments, and lab tests, are frequently temporal in character. Depending on how frequently a patient visits the hospital, each clinical event is frequently noted in the patient record in more than one category and more than once. The interval between two hospital visits frequently fluctuates, with the exception of a few patients who are periodically hospitalised. Therefore it is extremely challenging to capture the temporal information because each patient record really comprises of many time series with irregular intervals and varying lengths [7].

### 16.5.4 Acceptability

Despite the great hopes and interest in EMRs around the world, their adoption rates are generally low and they have a number of issues. These barriers are associated with different resources:

#### 16.5.4.1 People

Sometimes people that includes both- healthcare providers as well as patients, resist the use of EHR due to certain reasons:

- Lack of computer skills
- Lack of education and practical training
- Increased workload of physicians and nurses
- Change in traditional paper-based record culture to embrace technology
- Limited access to users
- Affects the interaction between patient and physician
- Affects productivity and disturbs workflow
- Lack of involvement of physician in design and implementation of EHR
- The patients' lack of literacy
- Lack of understanding of the value of EHR/EMR
- Lack of personnel

#### 16.5.4.2 Hardware, Software and Network

- Lack of IT facilities, equipment's and hardware functionality issues
- Lack of integration of EHR with the existing system
- Lack of network infrastructure for communications
- Lack of maintenance of system
- Issues of system configuration
- Lack of internet connectivity or network speed
- Applications and features for EHRs are not standardised

#### 16.5.4.3 Procedure

- Lack of project planning
- Cost associated with implementation, equipment purchase, maintenance and training
- Lack of policy and administrative support
- Worry about physicians' potential legal exposure

- Lack of ability to choose, procure, and use an EHR
- Issues with implementation
- Competitiveness among healthcare institution
- Risk of additional legal requirements
- Lack of future system maintenance and upgrade support from vendors [15].

## 16.6    Risk & Problems Associated With the System

Despite the high hopes and financial commitment, it appears that the EHR did not completely address the issues it was intended to address. The underlying issue arose during the earliest stages of execution. As computers became more common, problems arose with feeding and protecting clinical information about patients, hospital inventories, staffing, and resources.

### 16.6.1    Lack of Concord

Numerous vendors have supplied their services to the healthcare professionals and organisations over the years as the technology and operating systems have advanced. These suppliers have added new features and functions throughout time. Inconsistencies arise on many levels with the variety of software functions. In 2018, Black Book Market Research performed a survey and found that 18% of patient records in organisations have duplicates. Additionally, match rates between organisations, such as a hospital and a medical practise, might be very low. Due to different data entry processes, the match rates could drop as low as 50%, even when using the same EHR vendor.

### 16.6.2    Privacy and Data Security Issues

In Australia, more than 2.5 million people had chosen not to use My Health Record as of February 2019 due to privacy and cyber security concerns. Some medical professionals have refrained from adding patient data to the system due to privacy and cyber security concerns. Only 12.9 million of the 22.65 million entries, which account for roughly 90% of the population, include any data which furthered showed increase. Only 33% of private healthcare systems, 3% of systems that provide care for the elderly, and 41% of pathology and diagnostic imaging services have registered to use the records. These outcomes are definitely not in line with the project's initial goals and expectations despite having cost $2 billion.

### 16.6.3   Problems in Patient Matching

It is crucial to appropriately match patients with their medical records. Any discrepancy could perhaps endanger patient safety and waste money on pointless procedures or testing. When two patients have similar names, their records may be mixed, leading to wasteful organ removal or unjustified treatment. The duplication of patient records is another frequent issue. For example, Emma Peter Jones is identified as Emma P. Jones in her primary care provider's EHR; as Peter Jones in her ophthalmologist's record, as Emma P Jones at the endocrinologist's office, and as Emma Jones at the laboratory.

### 16.6.4   Alteration of Algorithms in Decision-Support Models

In the event that cyber security is breached, the programme is vulnerable to hacking. With malicious intent, it is feasible to change the algorithms for illicit benefits. A US-based EHR provider was fined $145 million because it changed medical tools for decision support at the point of care to help an opioid prescription company in exchange for kickbacks. This broke the professionals' trust in the program in a big way and put the security of the patients at risk.

### 16.6.5   Increased Workload of Clinicians

There are signs that EHRs may be making clinicians tired by being more harmful than helpful during and after the clinical interaction. On behalf of Stanford Medicine, Harris Poll asked more than 500 primary care physicians (PCPs) a lot of questions about EHRs. According to this, EHRs are taking up valuable time during clinical visits that could be used to talk to patients. Almost 62% of interactions with patients were done through the EHR. For example, during a 20-minute primary care visit, the doctor spoke with the patient for about 12 minutes, entered information into the electronic health record for 8 minutes, and recorded the visit for another 11 minutes after the patient left the office. According to another survey conducted in US, over the course of a 24-hour period, EHR usage accounted for more than 43% of the time spent by an average intern [16].

## 16.7   Future Benefits

One may envision future being entirely a technology driven era. The scope of EHR technology in future is bright and is already adopted by developed countries like China (96%), Brazil (92%), France (85%), and Russia (93%), with the highest adoption rate. Some countries are still in the process for implementing this system, for instance, in India; this adoption is very slow as EHR is not mandated [17]. When all healthcare providers eventually have installed, are using, and are exchanging data using EHR technologies, the opportunities for greater data collection and analysis to improve care will grow. According to some healthcare professionals, health data mining will be utilized to identify probable patients who may develop chronic conditions. The health data generated will then be able to be mined and this will open up greater opportunities for improving healthcare management. The data collected in this system can then be compared to the available best treatment options so that the best practices can be developed in the effective treatment and conditions. This data collection is termed as comparative effectiveness and according to the government; the use of data mining and analysis will lower healthcare expenditures [18].

EHR is a platform that is always changing; therefore making future predictions is not entirely definite. However, there are a few hypothesis for the future of EHR. Use of GPS technology through the EHR's practice for the real time personalized alerts and reminders to the patients will provide better care to them. Interactions via online video live streaming have become popular in recent years because of the global pandemic of COVID-19 virus. Technology advancements have been already put forward during this period. Future predictions indicate that many EHR platforms will incorporate this trend, enabling patients to consult with their doctors face-to-face while remaining in the comfort of their own homes. Interoperability is one of the loophole in the current EHR. One should anticipate this problem to be resolved in the upcoming years allowing you to seamlessly exchange patient data and other crucial information with the appropriate healthcare professionals through your EHR.

Although there have been recent advances, physician workflows should eventually become more efficient. In addition to enhancing patient care, this will free up more time and reduce stress for doctors. Many healthcare facilities currently employ a general EHR that is not suited to their practice. "ONE SIZE FITS ALL" is a unique EHR system which was introduced as a requirement when the Affordable Care Act was implemented. According to this regulation, every physician was required to convert to electronic medical record to compile the patient's whole medical history in one location. It was found that 70% physicians were unhappy with this system. No matter it was totally a new approach but didn't got any success in medical industry. Sooner than later, we anticipate that more practitioners will soon adapt more practice customizing their EHR to function better for their team and practice. Finally, we anticipate that more clinics will start outsourcing their medical transcribing services in order to free up doctors' time, cut costs, and improve EHR performance. The healthcare sector is seeing an increase in the use of outsourcing, and we anticipate that in the years to come, more people will be aware of the advantages of outsourcing medical transcriptions [19, 20].

## 16.8   Miscellaneous

### 16.8.1   Policies Regarding Data Exchange

Health Information Technology is the name for the electronic systems that doctors and patients use to analyze, store, and share information about health. It covers wide areas such as electronic health records, electronic pre-scribing (e-prescribing), personal health records (PHRs) and privacy and security. The Office of the National Coordinator for Health Information Technology (ONC) is a division of the United States Department of Health and Human Services responsible for managing the official Health IT web-site, HealthIT.gov. In order to achieve high-quality treatment, lower costs, a healthier population, and engaged individuals, ONC works with the pub-lic and commercial sectors to create and implement strategies to promote health IT and information utilisation [21]. It covers the health information exchange (HIE) basics. Electronic HIEs allows patients, physicians, nurses, pharmacists and other healthcare providers for the appropriate access and sharing patient's vital information securely via electronic mode and hence improving the quality, safety, speed and expense of patient care [22].

Digital record management includes data exchange among various healthcare providers. The system must provide the assurance that the indi-viduals' data would be protected and kept confidential. Individuals must have faith in an organization that their health information is private and secure for digital health information to deliver on its promise of health-ier, more cost-effective, and better health outcomes. Patients may be hes-itant to share their health information with you if they are wary of the security and reliability of electronic health records and health information exchanges. Avoiding disclosure of their medical condition could prove fatal. If a patient has confidence in you and health IT enough to share their information, you will both benefit from a more complete picture of the patient's health and the patient's ability to make informed decisions [23].

There are currently three different forms of HIEs available:

### 16.8.1.1    Directed Exchange

This type of exchange is used by one healthcare provider to directly exchange patient data such as laboratory tests and results, discharge summaries to another healthcare provider in an easy and secure way. This data is shared in a secure, unencrypted and reliable way over the internet among the healthcare provides who trust each other. This is similar to sending a secured email. Directed exchange HIEs are also used to send immunization data to public health organizations or to share quality attributes to The Centres for Medicare & Medicaid Services (CMS). This type of HIEs provides coordinated care, for instance, a primary care provider can directly share patients' information electronically to the specialist who is referring the patient. This will help to prevent unwanted and repeated data collections from patients, duplication of tests, medication errors and repeated visits.

### 16.8.1.2    Query-Based Exchange

Query-based exchange is used by the healthcare providers to conduct a search for and find available clinical sources about a patient. This form of exchange is used when unplanned care has to be delivered to the patients. For instance, in the event that a pregnant patient visits a hospital, query-based exchange can help a provider get the patient's pregnancy care record, enabling them to take safer care of the woman and her unborn child or emergency room doctors may modify treatment plans to prevent adverse drug reactions or redundant testing if they have access to patient information through query-based exchange, such as recent radiology images, medications and problem lists.

### 16.8.1.3    Consumer-Mediated Exchange

A patient's ability to take charge of his or her healthcare in an electronic setting is greatly facilitated by this type of data exchange. Patients can play an active role in care coordination when they have access to their own health information by:

- finding and correcting inaccurate or lacking health information
- sharing their health information with other physicians
- keeping track of and observing their own health
- recognizing and fixing inaccurate billing information [20]

Health IT has a certain sets of laws, policies and regulation electronic healthcare data and its exchange. Health IT legislation includes:

## a. 21ˢᵗ Century Cures Act

On December 13, 2016, President Obama signed into law the 21st Century Cures Act. Its goal is to speed up the process of creating new medical products and getting them to people who could benefit from them more quickly [21]. The free exchange of digital health records is promoted by a number of provisions in this act. The Office of the National Coordinator for Health Information Technology (ONC) is responsible for carrying out the Title IV provisions pertaining to delivery, including those that seek to improve the usability, accessibility, privacy, and security of health IT; foster interoperability; and prohibit information blocking. The Office of the National Coordinator for Health Information Technology (ONC) is committed to expanding access to electronic health information for all individuals, families, and medical professionals in order to improve the nation's health. According to the Cures Act, interoperability is the ability to share and use electronic health information without special user effort and without information blocking. When implementing the Cures Act, ONC concentrates on the following provisions:

- Section 4001: Health IT Usability
- Section 4002(a): Conditions of Certification
- Section 4003(b): Trusted Exchange Framework and Common Agreement
- Section 4003(e): Health Information Technology Advisory Committee
- Section 4004: Determining what actions are reasonable and necessary but do not constitute to information blockage

## b. The US Health Information Technology for Economic and Clinical Health (HITECH) Act

This legislation was passed as a section of ARRA, the American Recovery and Reinvestment Act of 2009. The law went into effect to promote efficient healthcare IT utilization Promoting health IT like electronic health records and private and secure electronic health information sharing is one of ONC's main initiatives because it has the potential to improve healthcare delivery in terms of quality, safety, and efficiency. The Health IT Advisory Committee (HITAC) was set up by the 21st Century Cures Act to ensure the smooth operation of these programs. The Federal Advisory Committee Act sets the rules of procedure for this group (FACA).

Advancing electronic access, exchange, and use of health information is a top priority for the HITAC, so it will be making recommendations to the National Coordinator for Health Information Technology on how to best achieve this goal. These recommendations will include policies, standards, implementation specifications, and certification criteria. HITAC is a new organization that combines the Health Information Technology Standards Committee and the Health Information Technology Policy Committee from before the passage of the 21st Century Cures Act [24].

### c. The Health Insurance Portability and Accountability Act (HIPAA) Security Rule

The Secretary of the United States Department of Health and Human Services (HHS) is tasked with drafting regulations to ensure the confidentiality of certain patient records in accordance with the Health Insurance Portability and Accountability Act of 1996. HHS published the HIPAA Privacy Rule and the HIPAA Security Rule to fulfill this mandate. Standardizing the protection of certain types of health information at the national level is the goal of the Privacy Rule, also known as the Standards for Privacy of Individually Identifiable Health Information. The federal government has issued a set of security guidelines known as the Security Rule or Security Standards for the Protection of Electronic Protected Health Information to protect specific types of electronic health data during storage or transmission. Implementing the safeguards outlined in the Privacy Rule, the Security Rule details the technical and non-technical security measures that organization known as "covered entities" must implement to protect individuals' "electronic protected health information" (e-PHI). Civil monetary penalties and voluntary compliance programs are the tools the HHS Office for Civil Rights (OCR) uses to ensure adherence to the Privacy and Security Rules. The Security Rule's primary goal is to protect individuals' health data privacy while allowing covered entities to take advantage of cutting-edge technology to improve care delivery [25].

### d. Electronic Health Record Standards for India, 2016

In September 2013, India's Ministry of Health and Family Welfare (MoH&FW) formally notified the country's Electronic Health Record (EHR) Standards. EHR/EMR and other similar clinical information systems can benefit from the guidelines provided by these standards. Following extensive consultation with relevant parties, these standards have been updated to reflect developments in the field. As a result, healthcare providers across the country have been notified of the 2016 EHR Standards and prepared to implement them in their information technology systems.

Interoperability, Health Information Technology, Health Data Ownership, and Data Privacy and Security Standards are all addressed. For the Data Exchange, various standards covered are:

   i.  ANSI/HL7 V2.8.2-2015, HL7 Standard Version 2.8.2 - An Application Protocol for Electronic Data Exchange in Healthcare Environments for event or message exchange
   ii. ASTM/HL7 CCD Release 1 (basis standard ISO/HL7 27932:2009) for Summary Records exchange
   iii. ISO 13606-5:2010 Health informatics - Electronic Health Record Communication - Part 5: Interface Specification for EHR archetypes exchange [Also, refer to as open EHR Service Model specification]
   iv. DICOM PS3.0-2015 (using DIMSE services & Part-10 media/files) for Imaging/Waveform Exchange [26].

## 16.8.2   Current Practices of Digital Health Records

### 16.8.2.1   India

The Ministry of Health and Family Welfare issued the first nationwide electronic health record (EHR) standard that same year (2013). Subsequently, a committee comprised of industry experts was formed to push for widespread EHR adoption and implementation. However, as of 2016, survey results suggested that adoption of the system was low compared to both middle- and high-income countries. Then, the National Health Protection Scheme provided a fresh chance to use technology to improve the standard of care and root out instances of fraud. The software is deployed on a cutting-edge infrastructure equipped with advanced computational capabilities. The purpose of this system is to provide an electronic tracking system for dealing with complaints and grievances as well as to detect fraud and misuse. The new National Health Authority has already established IT systems for beneficiary identification, hospital empanelment, and transaction management, including the PM-JAY Dashboard. There will also be a comprehensive PM-JAY portal to house all data pertaining to the scheme [27].

The Ayushman Bharat Digital Mission (ABDM) also plays a role in digital health records. It aims to develop the framework required to sustain the nation's integrated digital health infrastructure. Through digital highways, it would close the gaps between the various healthcare ecosystem stakeholders [28]. As part of this initiative, they've introduced the Ayushman Bharat Health Account (ABHA) number, a 14-digit identifier that will be used to verify your identity across India's electronic healthcare network. A person's ABHA number will serve as a secure and reliable identifier that is recognized by insurance companies and medical facilities all over the country. All of a participant's healthcare benefits can be linked to a single ABHA number, making it easier to sign up for personal health records, and it also serves as a unique and trustworthy identifier. In addition, each participant is assigned an ABHA address, a unique identifier that serves as a self-declared username for the purpose of accessing and sharing electronic health records [29].

### 16.8.2.2    Australia

In charge of Australia's overall digital health strategy is the Australian Digital Health Agency, which was established in July 2016. A national e-health program that is interoperable and built on patient-controlled UUIDs is already live. Unless they opted out of the system, every Australian had a My Health Record created for them by February 2019, but they could delete their record at any time. These files are used to back up clinical notes, prescription data, imaging results, and patient referrals. In the event that the patient is no longer able to make decisions about their own healthcare, they still have the option of reviewing and revising their medical records [27]. As of September 2022, 22.8 million My Health Records were already registered and over 757 million documents have been uploaded by the healthcare providers or consumers in the system [30].

### 16.8.2.3    Canada

Slowly but surely, the number of Canadians who use health IT has been growing over the past few years. The federal government is helping the provinces and territories create their own e-health records by funding Canada Health Infoway. Unfortunately, neither a national patient identification system nor a national strategy for establishing electronic health records exists at the present time. Canada Health Infoway reports that electronic data collection systems now cover the majority of populations in the provinces, though interoperability remains limited [27]. As per their annual report of 2021-2022, an estimated $50 billion benefit has been seen since its inception. About 93% of primary care physicians were using electronic medical records, 33% of patient- reported visits were virtual between January 2021 and March 2022 and 90% of patients were satisfied with their experience in virtual care. According to the Canadian digital health survey 2021, 82% of Canadians want their doctor to send their prescription electronically to their pharmacist, 75% of Canadians prefer computerized prescription renewal requests and for a prescription renewal, 65% of Canadians would prefer a virtual appointment than an in-person one [31].

### 16.8.2.4   USA

As the primary federal agency responsible for coordinating national initiatives to implement and increase the use of health information technology and the electronic exchange of health data, the Office of the National Coordinator for Health Information Technology was established in 2004. To promote the widespread adoption of EHRs, the 21st Century Cures Act of 2016 required that all healthcare providers provide patients with access to electronic versions of their medical records in a machine-readable format upon request [27]. Survey results from Health IT indicate that by 2021, 86% of non-Federal general acute care hospitals will have implemented an electronic health record that is compatible with the 2015 Edition. While 60% of general hospitals had adopted an EHR that was certified for the 2015 Edition, only 40% of rehabilitation hospitals and 23% of specialty hospitals had done so [32]. As of 2021, nearly 8 out of 10 (88%) U.S. doctors with an office practice used an EHR, and nearly 4 out of 5 (78%) had a certified EHR. From 42% in 2008 to 88% in 2018, the percentage of physicians using some form of electronic health records in their offices more than doubled. Since ONC and the CDC began tracking it in 2014, the percentage of office-based physicians who adopted a certified EHR has increased from 74% to 78% [33].

### 16.8.2.5   China

Virtually every hospital and clinic in China has developed its own electronic health records system. Electronic health records at hospitals are linked to health insurance systems to facilitate the payment of claims using unique patient identifiers (insurance ID or citizenship ID). Electronic health record systems, however, vary widely between hospitals and are rarely interoperable or integrated. Having a printed copy of one's health record is often required when seeing a doctor at a different hospital. There may be multiple EHR systems in use even among hospitals that are part of the same regional health authority or share academic ties. Patients rarely use EHR systems for tasks such as scheduling, communicating securely with their doctors, refilling prescriptions, or viewing their medical records. Despite the lack of a national plan, some areas are making plans to develop regional EHRs [27]. As per the GlobalData's recent Physician survey based report, 95% of physicians in China agreed that the implementation of EHR can improve the quality of care and 77% of them are already using EHR system [34].

**Table 16.2** Best smart watches to monitor health and fitness in 2022.

| Sr. no. | Name of smartwatch | Best monitoring feature | Price |
|---------|--------------------|--------------------------|-------|
| 1. | Fitbit Versa 2 Health and Fitness Smartwatch | Heart rate | $149.95 |
| 2. | Amazfit T-Rex Smartwatch | Fitness monitoring | $99.99 |
| 3. | Fossil Gen 5 Carlyle Stainless Steel Touchscreen | Heart rate & activity tracking | $174.47 |
| 4. | Garmin 010-01769-01 Vivoactive 3 | Built-in sports apps | $129.99 |
| 5. | Apple Watch Series 5 | Swim tracking and being waterproof | $399.00 |
| 6. | AGPTEK Smart Watch for Women | Waterproof activity tracking | $45.99 (On Amazon) |
| 7. | YAMAY Smart Watch | Sleep monitoring | $43.99 (On Amazon) |
| 8. | Willful Smart Watch | Mountaineering, dynamic cycling | $39.99 (On Amazon) |
| 9. | Donerton Smart Watch | IP67 waterproof pedometer | $37.99 (On Amazon) |
| 10. | Samsung Galaxy Watch | Best for an accurate accelerometer | $89.99 (On Amazon) |
| 11. | Tinwoo Smart Watch for Men | All-day activity tracking | $55.99 (On Amazon) |
| 12. | Ticwatch Pro 3 GPS Smart Watch Men's Wear | Heart rate monitoring | $299.99 (On Amazon) |

Despite the country specific scenarios for digital health records, it has a wide scale global acceptance. Internet of Things like Smart watches are now used by people in their normal day-to-day lives for heart rate, pulse rate and blood pressure monitoring, and for other functions like step counts, activity tracking, etc. Some of the smart watches considered best for health and fitness monitoring in 2022 are given in Table 16.2 [35].

### 16.8.3   Data Analysis

With the widespread adoption of EHRs, a structure has been set up for the collection and analysis of health data. In order to improve outcomes, data analysis is a crucial tool. These tools provide a framework for data analytics, which may eventually lead to more cost-effective and better-quality healthcare. It's possible that, as with other forms of platform technology, the real advantages won't show up right away. As machine learning and AI continue to advance, it is more important than ever to make use of the digital infrastructure and data that EHRs collect. When compared to more conventional decision-making aids, artificial intelligence and machine learning are in a league of their own. Traditional decision support algorithms are based on the explicit encoding of expert knowledge. With the proliferation of data, analytical tools like machine learning and artificial intelligence are now able to spot trends and uncover previously hidden insights.

Additionally, these statistical tools can be used to address a wide range of issues as a result of their adaptability. Commercial applications of machine-learning technologies initially focused on more traditional prediction tasks, such as calculating insurance risks and financial forecasts, but are now used in a wide range of tasks that aren't typically thought of as predictive. Driving, image recognition, language translation, etc., are just a few examples. Healthcare applications are equally varied. New studies show that machine learning can be used to address problems that were once viewed as statistical prediction issues, such as risk adjustment and severity evaluation.

Data from electronic health records (EHRs) and machine learning tools may soon make widespread adoption of individualized, evidence-based care feasible. Although randomized controlled trials (RCTs) provide compelling evidence with high levels of internal validity, it is essential to be aware of the limitations of such methods as they are considered the gold standard for causality. Randomized controlled trials are rarely scaled or designed to account for the variability seen in patients and providers. In order to address this issue, the US Food and Drug Administration emphasizes the importance of real-world evidence in guiding the approval and use of medicines. Electronic health record (EHR) data and machine learning techniques could be used to better understand the outcomes of medical decisions. This makes the application of such technologies in medicine a difficult empirical problem, as naive machine learning implementations may result in inaccurate diagnoses and inappropriate therapies. However, there is a growing body of literature on causality for machine learning; while these techniques cannot replace clinical trials, they may provide valuable supplementary data.

We may see significant shifts in the ways in which new information is discovered and created as a result of the new opportunities presented by unsupervised machine learning. The development of unsupervised learning has the potential to address two major issues: the inability to generalize beyond the typical patient who participates in an RCT and the inability to extract information from larger sets of findings across several RCTs. There are persistent worries about generalizability because the typical patient in most RCTs is an elderly white male from the United States. There are significant chances to combine data from existing research and understand how different impacts may appear among overrepresented and underrepresented groups, as treatment outcomes may vary according to comorbidities, race, gender, and other factors. These algorithms may be able to rapidly synthesize data from thousands of patients and studies, allowing them to mine new medical data without the need for potentially expensive RCTs [6].

### 16.8.4    Role and Benefits to the Stakeholders

We looked at least one of the ancillary benefits whether the healthcare provider is just thinking about making the switch from paper records to EHRs or is already using EHRs in the workplace. Depending on who you ask, these benefits fall into one of three buckets. There are both medical and non-medical stakeholders in an EHR system. The former group includes doctors and other medical professionals such as technicians and paramedics, while the latter group includes patients, office workers, and insurance providers [36]. Benefits of EHR system to these stakeholders are:

#### 16.8.4.1    Advantages to the Patient

- Improved standard of treatment:
  It makes it simpler for everyone to collaborate in order to ensure that the patients are receiving the right care. For

instance, the EHR keeps track of each patient's prescriptions so that doctors may avoid prescribing drugs to patients that could interact negatively with those already being taken.

- More convenient medical care:
  The use of EHRs can notify medical professionals when it is time to follow up with patients, monitor test results, or give patients a progress report on their health. Multiple clinicians can view the information concurrently with an EHR, eliminating the need for additional testing.

- Save time and efforts:
  EHR helps patients and caregivers save a lot of time and effort. It gives the caregiver the ability to treat the patient swiftly.

### 16.8.4.2    Advantages to the Healthcare Providers

- Encourage effective and reliable medical practises
- Remote patient information access
- Reduce time-consuming and repetitive work
- Enhanced billing financial system
- Increased internal contact between the offices of various healthcare providers
- Decrease in errors such as paper-based faults and human errors cost
- Reduce chart tugs
- Reduce chemist callbacks and boost prescription compliance with the formulary
- Quick handling of telephone calls for appointments and prescription refills as well as email, text messages, chats, and other electronic messaging

### 16.8.4.3    Advantages to the Society

- Aids in acquiring comprehensive statistical information for the framing of public health policy
- Increases the monitoring of disease research and public health
- Efficiency needs to be added to the overall health expenditure [3].

## 16.9 Conclusion

Healthcare systems are responsible for promoting the physical, mental, and social well-being of people all around the world. With the digitization of this system, it has become easier and more convenient to enhance patient care. Healthcare is one of the most crucial and zestful growth sectors in the economy. So, a strong healthcare system means a strong economy in a country. This chapter addresses the concept of digitization of healthcare record management describing how the implementation of EHRs has eased up the record keeping process in turn decreasing the work load of healthcare professionals. Smart watches, wristband sensors, smart glasses are some of the classic examples of wearable Internet of Things to monitor health and fitness in the current Healthcare 4.0 era. Current EHR systems are beneficial in terms of security, access, privacy, costs, accuracy & readability, practice management, and quality of care over conventional paper-based records. EHRs allow organized medical data of patients to be shared among authorized caregivers or healthcare professionals so as to boost the standard of healthcare delivery. With adequate Health IT policies like the 21st Century Cures Act, HITECH Act, HIPA Act & Security Rule, and Electronic Health Record Standards for India, 2016 safeguarding the health information exchange in EHR systems, security, and privacy are the foremost concerns of patient data are concisely addressed. Across the past few years, rates of EHR adoption and implementation have increased worldwide due to the introduction of ABHA number in India, My Health Record in Australia, and other country specific digital record systems. With this widespread adoption of EHR systems, Data Analysis is a crucial tool for the analysis of the collected data which may eventually lead to cost-effective and enhanced quality of healthcare. Completeness, correctness, acceptability, and complexity which are the limiting factors in the use of digital health records should be properly dealt with while implementing the EHR system to ensure the efficient working of system. EHR is an ever changing platform and hence we will explore more future applications of it like different storage techniques for efficient data retrieval from different sources across the globe to help a reader to apply one of the techniques by comparing the merits of it over the other available techniques.

# References

1. History of IT, https://www.complete-it.co.uk/the-history-of-information-technology/.
2. Yamin, M., IT applications in healthcare management: A survey. *Int. J. Inf. Technol.*, 10, 4, 503–509, 2018.
3. Tanwar, S., Tyagi, S., Kumar, N., Security and privacy of electronic healthcare records: Concepts, paradigms and solutions, in: *Institution of Engineering & Technology: Security and Privacy of Electronic Healthcare Records*. Institution of Engineering and Technology, March 2020.
4. Bongomin, O., Yemane, A., Kembabazi, B., Malanda, C., The hype and disruptive technologies of Industry 4.0 in major industrial sectors: A state of the art. *Preprints*, 1, June, 1–68, 2020.
5. Jayaraman, P.P., Forkan, A.R.M., Morshed, A., Haghighi, P.D., Bin Kang, Y., Healthcare 4.0: A review of frontiers in digital health. *Wiley Interdiscip. Rev. Data Min. Knowl. Discovery*, 10, 2, 1–23, 2020.
6. Atasoy, H., Greenwood, B.N., McCullough, J.S., The digitization of patient care: A review of the effects of electronic health records on healthcare quality and utilization. *Annu. Rev. Public Health*, 40, 487–500, 2019.
7. Zhao, J., Learning predictive models from electronic health records, March. 2017, [Online]. Available: http://urn.kb.se/resolve?urn=urn:nbn:se:su:diva-137936%0Ahttp://su.diva-portal.org/smash/get/diva2:1067764/FULLTEXT01.pdf%0Ahttps://www.diva-portal.org/smash/get/diva2:1067764/FULLTEXT01.pdf.
8. Eichelberg, M., Aden, T., Riesmeier, J., Dogac, A., Laleci, G.B., A survey and analysis of electronic healthcare record standards. *ACM Comput. Surv.*, 37, 4, 277–315, 2005.
9. Vaish, R., Ishikawa, S.T., Liu, J., Berkey, S.C., Strong, P., Davis, J., Digitization of health records in rural villages. *Proc. 3rd IEEE Glob. Humanit. Technol. Conf. GHTC 2013*, pp. 209–214, 2013.
10. Health IT, https://www.healthit.gov/playbook/electronic-health-records/#section-1-3.
11. Neal, D., Choosing an electronic health records system. *Innov. Clin. Neurosci.*, 8, 6, 43–46, 2011.
12. Hodgkins, M., Medical, C., Officer, I., P. Sustainability, Electronic health record (EHR) implementation, pp. 1–12, 2018.
13. Sahney, R. and Sharma, M., Electronic health records: A general overview. *Curr. Med. Res. Pract.*, 8, 2, 67–70, 2018.
14. Bottinger, E. P, Foundations, promises and uncertainties of personalized medicine. *Mt. Sinai J. Med.: J. Transl. Pers. Med.*, 74, 1, 15–21, 2007.
15. Gesulga, J.M., Berjame, A., Moquiala, K.S., Galido, A., Barriers to electronic health record system implementation and information systems resources: A structured review. *Proc. Comput. Sci.*, 124, January, 544–551, 2017.

16. Kataria, S. and Ravindran, V., Electronic health records: A critical appraisal of strengths and limitations. *J. R. Coll. Physicians Edinb.*, 50, 3, 262–268, 2020.

17. Sharma, M. and Aggarwal, H., EHR adoption in India: Potential and the challenges. *Indian J. Sci. Technol.*, 9, 34, 1–7, 2016.

18. Bej, M.D., Electronic health records. *Clevel. Clin. J. Med.*, 80, 12, 754, 2013.

19. Approaches of EHR, https://www.nethealth.com/why-one-size-fits-all-emrs-arent-the-right-fit-for-everyone/.

20. Future of EHR, https://datamatrixmedical.com/future-electronic-health-records/.

21. Health IT fact sheet, https://www.healthit.gov/sites/default/files/pdf/health-information-technology-fact-sheet.pdf.

22. Health information exchange, https://www.healthit.gov/topic/health-it-and-health-information-exchange-basics/what-hie.

23. HealthIT.gov, Guide to privacy and security of health information, no. April, pp. 27–40, 2013.

24. Health IT legislation, https://www.healthit.gov/topic/laws-regulation-and-policy/health-it-legislation.

25. HIPAA security rule, https://www.hhs.gov/hipaa/for-professionals/security/laws-regulations/index.html.

26. Ministry of Health & Family Welfare, EHR standards for India, M. H. F. W. G. eHealth Sect. Electron. Heal. Rec. Stand., India, pp. 1–48, 2016, [Online]. Available: http://www.mohfw.nic.in/showfile.php?lid=4138.

27. Commonwealth fund, https://www.commonwealthfund.org/international-health-policy-center/system-features/what-status-electronic-health-records.

28. Ayushman Bharat digital mission, https://abdm.gov.in/abdm.

29. ABHA number, https://healthid.ndhm.gov.in/.

30. Health record statistics, https://www.digitalhealth.gov.au/initiatives-and-programs/my-health-record/statistics.

31. Annual report, https://www.infoway-inforoute.ca/en/about-us/our-vision-mission/annual-report-2021-2022.

32. Adoption of EHR, https://www.healthit.gov/data/quickstats/adoption-electronic-health-records-hospital-service-type-2019-2021.

33. Adoption of EHR by physicians, https://www.healthit.gov/data/quickstats/office-based-physician-electronic-health-record-adoption.

34. Implementation of EHR, https://www.pharmaceutical-technology.com/comment/electronic-health-records/.

35. Smartwatches, https://www.softwaretestinghelp.com/best-smartwatch/.

36. Stakeholders in EHR system, https://www.researchgate.net/figure/Stakeholders-of-Electronic-Health-Records_fig1_269708552%0A%0A.

# 17

# Intelligent Healthcare Supply Chain

**Chirag Kalaria[1], Shambhavi Singh[2] and Bhupendra G. Prajapati[3]***

*[1]Dabur International Limited, Dubai, United Arab Emirates*
*[2]NMIMS's School of Pharmacy and Technology Management Shirpur,*
*Maharashtra, Shirpur, India*
*[3]Shree S.K. Patel College of Pharmaceutical Education & Research, Faculty of*
*Pharmacy, Ganpat University, Mahesana, India*

## Abstract

The healthcare sector remains actively focused on innovative medicines and treatments to improve the quality and longevity of human lives. Merely, the development of such innovations is not enough but making them available to the end consumer is imperative and that's where the HSC comes into the picture. As per the report, global medicine consumption crossed 4.5 trillion doses a year, with over 50% of people take more than at least one daily dose of medicines, HSC management is vital for human lives.

The Healthcare Supply Chain (HSC) is the most critical operation as it demands integrity, agility, resilience and cost-effectiveness. The legacy supply chain is not capable to handle the challenges of counterfeiting, geopolitical issues, disruptions due to pandemics and scarcity of skilled manpower to deliver products and services to the end consumers. Worldwide Covid-19 pandemic disruption has further strengthened the quest to revamp the HSC by making it more resilient and intelligent. Technologies like deep learning (DL) human-machine interface (HMI), machine learning (ML), blockchain, robotics, cloud computing, AI, big data analytics (BDA), Digital Twins, Industry 4.0, IoT and control towers aid for developing end-to-end intelligent, integrated and data-driven supply chain.

*Keywords*: Intelligent healthcare, supply chain, blockchain, robotics, Internet of Things, big data analytics, industry 4.0., RxAll, cloud computing, digital twins, artificial intelligence, human-machine interface

*\*Corresponding author*: bhupen27@gmail.com; bhupendra.prajapati@guni.ac.in

Rishabha Malviya, Sonali Sundram, Bhupendra Prajapati and Sudarshan Kumar Singh (eds.)
*Human-Machine Interface: Making Healthcare Digital*, (449–482) © 2024 Scrivener Publishing LLC

## 17.1   Introduction

The healthcare industry is constantly seeking new and innovative ways to improve the quality and longevity of human lives through the development of new medicines and treatments. However, it is not enough to simply create these innovations; they must also be made available to the end consumer.

This is where the HSC comes into play. With global medicine consumption surpassing 4.5 trillion doses per year and over 50% of people taking multiple daily doses of medicine, the management of the HSC is vital for human well-being. The HSC must be agile, resilient, cost-effective, and maintain integrity to effectively deliver products and services to end consumers. The importance of HSC to be more resilient and have intuitive intelligence from the wake of COVID-19 pandemic [1].

The intelligent supply chain assures end-to-end visibility; demand forecasting/sensing; planning and inventory management; intelligent automation and timely information sharing by Industry 4.0/IoT; predictive maintenance to avoid breakdown of machines/fleets as well as provide resilient alternatives to any possible disruptions by analyzing thousands of permutation combinations. A digital transformation roadmap includes various steps like starting small, scaling fast and thinking big; identifying internal cost and value drivers; building a blueprint of data architecture; learning and collaborating with other industries.

Human-Machine Interface (HMI) has led the way in the retail and service industry to provide multiple choice to customers and enable them to place orders remotely without the help of humans. It is an intelligent way of two-way communication, and it helps to develop agile supply chains by providing timely alerts, temperature control, and end-to-end integrity by deploying AI and blockchain technology beneath the HMI control station. HMI will be the face of the supply chain control tower that runs millions of permutation combinations of disruption events and provide alerts as well as a possible solution for the disruption. In this chapter, we provide the aspects, structure and futuristic development of the intelligent and rationale HSC [2].

In this chapter, we will explore the role of various technologies, including AI and the IoT, in the development of an intelligent and integrated HSC. We will also discuss the steps involved in digitally transforming the supply chain, including building a blueprint of data architecture and collaborating with other industries. Finally, we will examine the future of the intelligent HSC and the role of the Human-Machine Interface as a control tower for supply chain management.

## 17.2 Supply Chain – Method Networking?

A supply chain is a network of organizations, human resource, miscellaneous resources, as well as information intricated in production, handling, and distribution of various goods as well as services. It includes the processes and infrastructure that are needed to get products or services from the supplier to the customer [1].

The supply chain begins with raw materials procurement and continues through the stages of production, testing, distribution, and delivery. It may also include the disposal or recycling of products after they have been used.

Effective supply chain management is essential for businesses to operate in proficient manner. To make sure that the appropriate goods are delivered to the correct place at the correct time, it includes coordinating actions of several parties [1].

## 17.3 Healthcare Supply Chain and Steps Involved

The HSC exemplify to the flow of services and goods that are necessary for the delivery of healthcare services. It includes the procurement, distribution, and management of medical supplies, equipment, and pharmaceuticals, as well as the delivery of healthcare services to patients.

The following steps are indulged in the HSC:

- **Procurement:** This process of acquiring services and goods that are needed to deliver healthcare. It includes identifying the necessary items, selecting suppliers, negotiating prices, and placing orders.
- **Distribution:** This involves getting the goods and services from the supplier to the healthcare facility or the patient. This may include the use of warehouses, transportation companies, and logistics providers.
- **Inventory management:** This involves tracking the inventory of healthcare supplies and ensuring that there are sufficient quantities on hand to meet the needs of patients.

- **Quality control:** This involves ensuring that the goods and services provided meet the necessary standards of quality and safety.
- **Waste management:** This involves the proper disposal of waste materials, such as expired or unused medications, to ensure that they do not pose a risk to public health.
- **Patient care:** This is the final step in the HSC, in which healthcare provider delivers medical services and treatments to patients using the supplies and equipment procured through the supply chain.

## 17.4   Importance of HSC

Effective and efficient supply chain management is the key to success for any organization in the current disruptive scenario due to a series of events like Covid19, the Roose-Ukraine war, looming recession fear and very high inflation in all segments. But, when it comes to healthcare, it becomes rather imperative to maintain the preparedness of the supply chain as it will impact human lives [1].

A recent example is the pandemic outbreak has put the entire world on halt and horror. Millions of people were impacted either by Covid19 or the consequences of its impacts on the economy. The entire hysteria came under control when the healthcare industry developed the vaccines for the same. Further, developing a vaccine for Covid19 was only half-work done and the major challenge was producing and distributing vaccines to 7.8 billion people in the world [1].

This event itself is the biggest evidence of the emphasis of HSC Management.

Further, healthcare is flourishing so rapidly in developed as well developing countries. It can be understood from the following figure shows the rising per capita use of medications in pharma emerging markets.

In 2020, when the global population will have surpassed 7.5 billion, there will be 1.6 Standard Units (Sus) of medication used per person per day. The majority of affluent nations use more than two SUs per person per day, and by 2020, China, India, Brazil, and Indonesia will have seen significant rises in moderate pharmaceutical volume utilisation [2].

Effective HSC management can have a positive impact on global human health in several ways:

- **Access to essential healthcare supplies:** A well-functioning HSC ensures that healthcare providers have access to the medical supplies and equipment they need to deliver care to patients. This is particularly important in low-income countries, where access to essential healthcare supplies can be limited.
- **Quality of care:** The quality of care that patients receive depends in part on the availability of high-quality supplies and equipment. A well-managed HSC helps to ensure that healthcare providers have access to the supplies and equipment they need to deliver the best possible care to patients.
- **Efficiency:** A well-functioning HSC can help to cut costs and enhance the ability of healthcare delivery. Optimizing the flow of goods and services, healthcare providers can reduce waste and minimize unnecessary expenses.
- **Disease prevention and control:** The HSC is also important for the prevention and control of diseases. For example, the distribution of vaccines and other preventive measures can help to reduce the spread of infectious diseases.

Overall, the HSC plays a crucial role in ensuring that healthcare providers have the necessary resources to deliver high-quality care to patients for their health and well-being.

## 17.5    Risks and Complexities Affecting the Globally Distributed HSC

The HSC is critical for ensuring that healthcare providers have the necessary supplies and contrivances to deliver high-quality care to patients (Figure 17.1). As it permits the flow of commodities and services required for the provision of healthcare services, it plays a crucial part in the global healthcare system.

### 17.5.1    Legacy HSC

A legacy HSC system refers to an older, established system for procuring, distributing and managing the flow of services and goods that are fundamental for the delivery of healthcare. These systems may have been in place for many years and are based on traditional methods of procurement and distribution, such as manual processes and paper-based systems.

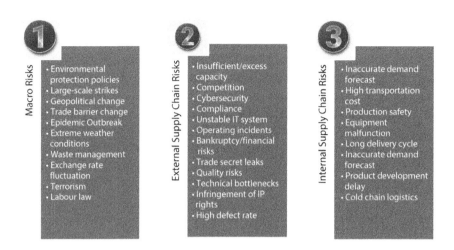

**Figure 17.1**  Risks affecting globally distributed (HSCs).

Legacy HSC systems can be inefficient and may not be well-suited to the needs of modern healthcare systems. They may be prone to errors and delays and may not be able to keep up with the demands of a rapidly changing healthcare environment.

In contrast, modern HSC systems are often more automated and may make use of advanced technologies, such as electronic health records (EHRs) and supply chain management software, to improve efficiency and accuracy. These technologies could be more suited to the requirements of today's healthcare professionals and patients, and they could also help to lower costs and raise the standard of care.

### 17.5.1.1   SWOT Analysis of Legacy HSC

A SWOT (Strengths, Weaknesses, Opportunities, Threats) analysis is an engine used to evaluate the internal and external factors that can impact an organization (Table 17.1). Here is a SWOT analysis of a legacy HSC system.

### 17.5.2   What is an Intelligent Supply Chain?

An intelligent supply chain uses cutting-edge technology to optimise and automate the movement of goods and services in a supply chain, including AI, IoT and BDA.

**Table 17.1** SWOT analysis of legacy HSC.

| Strengths | Weaknesses |
|---|---|
| **Established system:** A legacy HSC system may have been in place for many years, which can give it a sense of stability and reliability.<br>**Familiarity:** The staff of a healthcare organization may be familiar with a legacy supply chain system, which can make it easier to use and maintain. | **Inefficiency:** Legacy HSC systems may be prone to errors and delays and may not be able to keep up with the demands of a rapidly changing healthcare environment.<br>**Limited technology:** Legacy systems may not make use of advanced technologies, such as electronic health records (EHRs) and supply chain management software, which can limit their capabilities and efficiency. |
| **Opportunities** | **Threats** |
| **Modernization:** A legacy HSC system may present an opportunity to modernize and improve efficiency by incorporating advanced technologies and processes.<br>**Cost savings:** Modernizing a legacy HSC system may help to reduce costs and improve the efficiency of healthcare delivery. | **Competition:** A legacy HSC system may be at a competitive disadvantage compared to more modern systems that can take advantage of advanced technologies and processes.<br>**Changes in regulations:** Changes in regulations, such as new requirements for electronic health records (EHRs) or supply chain transparency, may require a legacy HSC system to be updated or replaced. |

An intelligent supply chain aims to proceed towards a proficient, reduction in costs, and escalate the speed and accuracy of all the workings inclusive to supply chain. It can also lend a hand to improve visibility and traceability throughout the supply chain, which can be valuable for quality control and risk management.

Some of the principal features of an intelligent supply chain include:

- **Real-time data:** An intelligent supply chain relies on real-time data to make informed decisions about the flow of goods and services. This may include data on inventory levels, demand patterns, and supply chain disruptions.
- **Predictive analytics:** By analysing data on past trends and patterns, an intelligent supply chain can make more accurate

predictions about future demand and supply. This can help to optimize inventory levels and reduce the risk of shortages or excesses.

- **Automation:** An intelligent supply chain may use automation to streamline and optimize various supply chain processes, such as order processing, warehousing, and transportation.
- **Collaboration:** An intelligent supply chain may involve collaboration and communication among multiple parties, including suppliers, manufacturers, distributors, and logistics providers, to assure that goods and services are being delivered to the designated person/organization at the set place and time.

### 17.5.3   Difference Between Legacy HSC and Intelligent HSC

Legacy supply chains are traditional systems for procuring, distributing and managing the flow of goods and services. These systems may have been in place for many years and may be based on manual processes and paper-based systems.

Intelligent supply chains, on the other hand, are more modern systems that make use of advanced technologies, such as the IoT, AI, and BDA, to optimize as well as automate the flow of goods and services.

Following are the key differences between legacy and intelligent supply chains:

- **Efficiency:** Intelligent supply chains are designed to be more efficient than legacy supply chains, as they make use of advanced technologies to optimize and automate various processes.
- **Accuracy:** Intelligent supply chains can make use of actual-time data and predictive analytics to make more accurate decisions about the flow of goods and services. This can help to reduce errors and enhance the accuracy of supply chain operations.
- **Visibility:** Intelligent supply chains may provide greater visibility and transparency through traceability in the due course the supply chain, which can be valuable for quality control and risk management.
- **Speed:** Intelligent supply chains may be able to operate more quickly than legacy supply chains, as they can take advantage

of automation and real-time data to make more informed decisions.

- **Cost:** Intelligent supply chains may be able to reduce costs by optimizing and automating various processes and by minimizing errors and waste.

## 17.6    Technologies Come to Aid to Build an Intelligent HSC

### 17.6.1    HMI

The channel between a controller and operator, either physical or digital. An HMI can be a physical control panel with buttons and indicator lights, or it can run on an industrial PC with a colour graphics display and specialised HMI software.

Human-machine interface (HMI) refers to the interface between humans and machines, such as computers or other automated systems. It typically includes input devices, such as keyboards and touchscreens, and output devices, such as displays and speakers.

In an intelligent supply chain, HMI can be used to improve efficiency, accuracy, and traceability by allowing humans and machines to communicate and collaborate more effectively.

Following are examples of how HMI can be used in an HSC:

- Order processing: An HMI system can be used to streamline the process of placing orders for healthcare supplies and equipment. For example, a healthcare provider may use an HMI system to place orders with a supplier, track the status of the order, and receive alerts when the order has been shipped or received.
- Inventory management: An HMI system can be used to track inventory levels and manage the reordering of healthcare supplies. For example, an HMI system may be used to supervise inventory levels in actual time and automatically generate orders for additional supplies when inventory reaches a certain level.
- Quality control: An HMI system can be used to improve the accuracy and traceability of quality control processes in the HSC. For example, an HMI system may be used to record and track the testing and certification of healthcare

supplies and equipment, and to alert staff if any problems are identified.

- Waste management: An HMI system can be used to track the disposal of waste materials, such as expired or unused medications, to establish that they are disposed of in a safe and environmentally friendly manner.

Overall, HMI can be a valuable tool for building an intelligent supply chain in the healthcare industry by improving efficiency, accuracy, and traceability, and by enabling humans and machines to communicate and collaborate more effectively.

## 17.6.2   AI

The development of computer systems capable of decision-making, problem-solving, and learning—tasks that frequently require human intelligence—is known as AI.

In an intelligent supply chain, AI can be used to improve efficiency, accuracy, and traceability by analyzing large amounts of data and making informed decisions about the flow of goods and services.

Following are examples of how AI can be used in an HSC:

> **Predictive analytics:** AI can be used to analyze data on past trends and patterns to make more accurate predictions about future demand for healthcare supplies and equipment. This can help to optimize inventory levels and curtail the risk of shortages or excesses.
>
> **Supply chain optimization:** AI can be used to optimize the passage of goods and services in the HSC by analyzing data on factors such as demand patterns, transportation routes, and supplier performance.
>
> **Quality control:** AI can be used to improve the accuracy and traceability of quality control processes in the HSC. For example, AI algorithms may be used to analyze data on the performance of healthcare supplies and equipment, and to alert staff if any problems are identified.
>
> **Waste management:** AI can be used to analyze data on the disposal of waste materials, such as expired or unused medications, to identify patterns and identify opportunities to reduce waste and improve efficiency.

Overall, AI can be a valuable tool for building an intelligent supply chain in the healthcare industry by improving efficiency, accuracy, and traceability, and by enabling the analysis of large amounts of data to inform decision-making.

### Case Study 1 – Merck Kgaa uses Machine Learning to optimize Demand Forecasting

Merck KGaA, A significant German multinational pharmaceutical, chemical, and life sciences corporation with its headquarters in Darmstadt, commonly known as the Merck Group, has started a data-driven supply chain operation to improve demand forecasting [3].

Merck is using Aera Technology, formerly FusionOps, an ML and cloud-based software solution that enables a holistic and actionable view of a company's supply network to increase efficiency across its supply chain, including demand forecasting. Aera continuously combs through enterprise systems to collect, harmonise and refine data, and to consequently provide real-time analytics and end-to-end visibility of the company's supply chain operation and performance [4].

With the use of this technology, Merck was able to increase the forecast accuracy of 90% of its goods. Aera's AI algorithms employ information gathered from Merck's enterprise resource planning software to swiftly and precisely estimate the location and volume of the company's product demand [5].

### 17.6.3   ML/DL

Machine learning (ML) is a type of AI that allows computated systems to learn and improve their performance without being explicitly programmed. ML algorithms are trained using large amounts of data and can make predictions or decisions based on patterns and trends that they learn from this data.

Deep learning (DL) is a type of machine learning that uses artificial neural networks to learn and make decisions based on patterns and trends in data. DL algorithms are trained using large amounts of data and can learn to recognize complex patterns and relationships in the data.

In an intelligent supply chain, ML/DL can be used to improve efficiency, accuracy, and traceability by analyzing large amounts of data and making informed decisions about the flow of goods and services.

Following are the examples of how ML can be used in an HSC:

- **Predictive analytics:** ML can be used to analyze data on past trends and patterns to make more accurate predictions about future demand for healthcare supplies and equipment. This can help to optimize inventory levels and cut down the risk of shortages or excesses.
- **Supply chain optimization:** ML can be used to optimize the passage of goods and services in the HSC by analyzing data on factors such as demand patterns, transportation routes, and supplier performance. As the system learns from new data, it can continually improve its performance and decision-making.
- **Quality control:** ML can be used to improve the accuracy and traceability of quality control processes in the HSC. For example, ML algorithms may be used to analyze data on the performance of healthcare supplies and equipment, and to alert staff if any problems are identified.
- **Waste management:** ML can be used to analyze data on the disposal of waste materials, such as expired or unused medications, to identify patterns and identify opportunities to reduce waste and improve efficiency.

Overall, ML can be a valuable tool for building an intelligent supply chain in the healthcare industry by improving efficiency, accuracy, and traceability, and by enabling the analysis of large amounts of data to inform decision-making and improve performance over time.

## 17.7   Blockchain

Blockchain is an apportioned ledger technology that grants multiple parties to securely record and track transactions and other data without the need for a central authority. In a supply chain, blockchain can be used to improve transparency, traceability, and security by providing a secure, decentralized record of transactions and data.

Following are the examples of how blockchain can be used in an HSC:

- **Supply chain transparency:** Blockchain can be used to provide a secure, decentralized record of the flow of goods and services in the HSC. This can help to increase transparency and traceability and to reduce the risk of fraud or errors.

- **Quality control:** Blockchain can be used to track the quality and safety of healthcare supplies and equipment. For example, it can be used to record and track the testing and certification of these products, and to provide a secure record of their history and usage.
- **Clinical trials:** Blockchain can be used to record and track data from clinical trials, such as patient data and results. This can help to improve the transparency and integrity of clinical trials and to reduce the risk of fraud or errors.
- **Medical records:** Blockchain can be used to securely store and manage electronic health records (EHRs). This can help to improve the accuracy and security of patient records and to reduce the risk of errors or unauthorized access.

Overall, blockchain can be a valuable tool for building a secure, transparent, and traceable supply chain in the healthcare industry by providing a decentralized record of transactions and data that can be accessed and verified by multiple parties.

### Case Study 2 – FarmaTrust is using AI tools and Blockchain to provide a secure platform for decision making

FarmaTrust is a startup that provides blockchain and AI-powered digital solutions to build an immutable, secure, and transparent system for making data-driven judgements [6].

FarmaTrust's solution provides end-to-end traceability of biopharma products to safeguard the supply chain from being corrupted with falsified or substandard medicines. In addition, their clients can use their Consumer Confidence App for authentication of medicinal products.

The FarmaTrust platform can automate procedures including purchase orders, automatic payments, and regulatory compliance while ensuring the accuracy of the data. Its solutions are implemented and working for a range of clients.

## 17.8   Robotics

Robotics refers to the use of robots or automated systems to perform tasks that are typically carried out by humans. In a supply chain, robotics can be used to improve efficiency, accuracy, and speed by automating various processes, such as material handling, transportation, and quality control.

Following are the examples of how robotics can be used in an HSC:

- **Material handling:** Robotics can be used to handle and move materials, such as healthcare supplies and equipment, within a warehouse or distribution centre. This can help to improve efficiency and reduce the risk of errors or accidents.
- **Transportation:** Robotics can be used to transport materials within a healthcare facility, such as a hospital or clinic. For example, robots may be used to deliver medications or other supplies to patient rooms or to transport waste materials to disposal areas.
- **Quality control:** Robotics can be used to perform quality control tasks, such as inspecting and testing healthcare supplies and equipment. For example, robots may be used to inspect medical devices for defects or to test the purity of medications.
- **Surgical assistance:** Robotics can be used to assist with surgical procedures. For example, robots may be used to perform precise movements or to provide additional support during surgery.

Overall, robotics can be a valuable tool for building an efficient and accurate supply chain in the healthcare industry by automating various processes and tasks, and by improving the speed and precision of these processes.

## Case Study 3 – Cobots being used to cope with staff shortage in the Nursing field

Healthcare staff shortages are becoming a global problem, particularly since Covid came to light. More and more healthcare administrators are seeking for solutions that increase employee potential to meet this rising problem. Cobots are among the most prominent examples of this.

**Cobots:** Collaborative healthcare robots are automated devices used in the medical field to carry out various duties and free up professionals. This can range from office work to patient care to lab work to surgical instruments. At Tsinghua University [7] this technology has already been put to the test with researchers designing a cobot to help healthcare staff test for the virus.

To meet global health goals, 6 million more nurses are required in the globe today [8]. In addition, there have been more general staff absences due to illness. Cobots and the new interactions they offer will enter the healthcare mix constantly in order to combat this.

## 17.9   Cloud Computing

Cloud computing is the distribution of computing services, such as software, networking, storage, and processing, through the internet as opposed to local servers or individual devices.

In an intelligent supply chain, cloud computing can be used to improve efficiency, scalability, and accessibility by providing a flexible and secure platform for storing and accessing data and applications.

Following are the examples of how cloud computing can be used in an HSC:

- **Data storage and analysis:** Cloud computing can be utilized to store and analyze enormous load of data from various sources, such as electronic health records (EHRs), supply chain data, and quality control data. This can help to improve the accuracy and efficiency of decision-making in the HSC.
- **Supply chain management:** Cloud computing can be used to manage and optimize the flow of goods and services in the HSC. For example, cloud-based supply chain management software may be used to track inventory levels, place orders with suppliers, and coordinate transportation.
- **Collaboration:** Cloud computing can be used to enable collaboration among multiple parties in the HSC, such as manufacturers, suppliers, logistics providers and distributors. Example in place, cloud-based collaboration tools may be used to share documents, track progress, and communicate in real time.
- **Disaster recovery:** Cloud computing can be used to ensure the availability of critical data and systems in the event of a disaster, such as a power outage or natural disaster. For example, cloud-based data backup and recovery systems can help to protect against data loss and ensure the continuity of healthcare delivery.

Overall, cloud computing can be a valuable tool for building an intelligent supply chain in the healthcare industry by providing a flexible and secure platform for storing and accessing data and applications, and by enabling collaboration and data analysis to inform decision-making.

## Case Study 4 – RxAll is using Deep Learning to fight fake medicines around the world

RxAll, a US-based start-up, has developed an AI-based technology to assure that patients across the world have access to authentic, high-quality drugs. Their platform combines a proprietary molecular sensor (a spectrometer) and a cloud-based DL algorithm, which uses a database of spectral signatures of drugs, to perform non-destructive verification of drug authenticity.

Their newest device, the RxScanner II, can identify the authenticity and quality of prescription drugs – in tablet, powder or liquid forms – in 20 seconds and with an accuracy of 99.9 per cent.

On the RxScanner platform, a customised database of drug spectral signatures is developed, and real-time data on drug quality and locations where brand counterfeiting is occurring may be examined. Various parties, including hospitals, pharmaceutical firms, pharmacies, and regulatory authorities worldwide, can use this technology. Their AI technology can quickly alert pharmaceutical makers to counterfeiting and continuously learns from spectral reads.

In 2017, RxAll was selected to participate in the Merck Accelerator Program in Nairobi, Kenya, and, in 2018, was selected to join the Norwegian Katapult Accelerator to help expand its operations [9]. They are currently operating in Canada, China, Ethiopia, Gambia, Ghana, Kenya, Myanmar, Nigeria, Uganda and the US, and plan to expand in Africa, the Americas and Southeast Asia.

More recently, RxAll began collaborating with a top pharmaceutical business with sales activities in 120 nations to enable quicker brand counterfeit detection in troublesome regions of the world. RxAll created a spectral library for the client's important brand, and the client's drug security team deployed the RxScanner to instantly test knockoffs of that brand in high-risk areas. Importantly, they enabled real-time connections between test results and the drug security control centres in the US and UK. The introduction of RxScanner and real-time test reports to the two control centres decreased the reaction time for taking this brand's counterfeit copies off the market from six weeks to two weeks over the course of six months. In order to cover new brands with significant issues with counterfeiting, RxAll is currently extending its library.

## 17.10    Big Data Analytics (BDA)

Big data analytics is the process of examining enormous and intricate databases in order to uncover patterns, trends, and insights that can guide decision-making. BDA often entails the processing and analysis of substantial volumes of data using cutting-edge analytical methods like machine learning and AI.

In a supply chain, BDA can be used to improve efficiency, accuracy, and traceability by analyzing data from various sources, such as customer data, supply chain data, and quality control data.

Following are the examples of how BDA can be used in a supply chain:

- **Predictive analytics:** BDA can be used to analyze data on past trends and patterns to make more accurate predictions about future demand for goods and services. This can help to optimize inventory levels and taper the risk of shortages or excesses.
- **Supply chain optimization:** BDA can be used to optimize the passage of goods and services in the supply chain by analyzing data on factors such as demand patterns, transportation routes, and supplier performance.
- **Quality control:** BDA can be used to improve the accuracy and traceability of quality control processes in the supply chain. For example, BDA may be used to analyze data on the performance of goods and services, and to alert staff if any problems are identified.
- **Customer analytics:** BDA can be used to analyze customer data, such as purchase history and preferences, to inform the design and delivery of goods and services. This can help to improve customer satisfaction and loyalty.

Overall, BDA can be a valuable tool for building an efficient and accurate supply chain by enabling the analysis of bulk data to inform decision-making and improve performance over time.

## 17.11    Industry 4.0

The fourth industrial revolution, commonly referred to as "industry 4.0," is the incorporation of cutting-edge technologies, such as the IoT, AI, and

BDA, into manufacturing and other industries. The goal of Industry 4.0 is to improve efficiency, accuracy, and productivity by enabling the automation and optimization of various processes and tasks.

In the healthcare industry, Industry 4.0 can be used to improve the efficiency and accuracy of various processes and tasks, such as patient care, quality control, and supply chain management.

Following are the examples of how Industry 4.0 can be used in the healthcare industry:

- **Patient care:** Industry 4.0 technologies, such as IoT sensors and AI algorithms, can be used to monitor and track patient data, such as vital signs and medical history, in real time. This can help to boost the accuracy and competency of patient care and to reduce the risk of errors or delays.
- **Quality control:** Industry 4.0 technologies, such as IoT sensors and robotics, can be used to automate and improve the accuracy of quality control processes in the healthcare industry. For example, sensors may be used to monitor the temperature and humidity of medications, and robots may be used to perform inspections or testing.
- **Supply chain management:** Industry 4.0 technologies, such as IoT sensors and BDA, can be used to optimize and automate the flow of goods and services in the HSC. This can lower the chance of errors or delays while also increasing the supply chain's efficiency and accuracy.
- **Clinical trials:** Industry 4.0 technologies, such as blockchain and BDA, can be used to improve the transparency, traceability, and accuracy of clinical trials. For example, blockchain can be used to securely store and manage data from clinical trials, and BDA can be used to analyze data from many sources to identify trends and patterns.
- **Connected Health Devices:** These gadgets gather data on a patient's health indicators and send it back to medical professionals for analysis. Consider Fitbits, continuous glucose monitoring devices, or wearable cardiac monitors.
- **Remote Patient Monitoring (RPM):** RPM technology resembles connected health equipment but is more in line with telemedicine services. They continuously monitor and report on patients, many of whom have chronic conditions. Digital blood pressure monitors, Hinge Health initiatives, or Philips tools for care teams are a few examples of them [10].

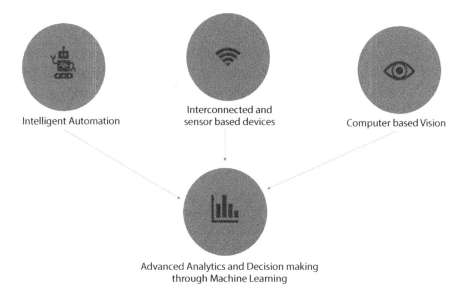

**Figure 17.2** Benefits from intelligent automation, industry 4.0 and IoT.

Overall, Industry 4.0 technologies can be a valuable tool for improving the efficiency and accuracy of various processes and tasks in the healthcare industry, such as patient care, quality control, and supply chain management (Figure 17.2).

## 17.12    Internet of Things (IoT)

The IoT deals with the interconnected physical devices, such as sensors, actuators, and other smart devices, that are connected to the internet and can communicate with each other and with other systems.

In a supply chain, IoT can be used to improve efficiency, accuracy, and traceability by providing real-time data and enabling the automation of various processes.

Following are the examples of how IoT can be used in an HSC:

- **Inventory management:** IoT sensors and devices can be used to track inventory levels in real time and to automatically generate orders for additional supplies when inventory reaches a certain level. This can help to optimize inventory levels and reduce the risk of shortages or excesses.

- **Quality control:** IoT sensors and devices can be used to monitor the quality and safety of healthcare supplies and equipment. For example, IoT devices may be used to track the temperature of medications or to alert staff if any problems are identified with medical devices.
- **Supply chain visibility:** IoT sensors and devices can be used to provide visibility and traceability throughout the HSC. For example, IoT devices may be used to track the location and condition of shipments in transit, and to alert staff if any problems are identified.
- **Environmental monitoring:** IoT sensors and devices can be used to monitor environmental conditions in healthcare facilities, such as temperature and humidity, to ensure the safety and quality of healthcare supplies and equipment.

Overall, IoT can be a valuable tool for building a supply chain in the healthcare industry by providing real-time data and enabling the automation of various processes, and by improving visibility and traceability throughout the supply chain.

## Case Study 5 – Smarter devices create new healthcare applications

Accenture's global lead for connected health Ronan Wisdom discussed new forms of human-machine collaboration and their potential impact on healthcare and clinical development at the recent Medidata NEXT conference in New York.

In addition to being worn on the wrist, connected health gadgets are increasingly becoming accurate and therapeutically relevant. This enables new types of health monitoring, such as tracking the development of diseases by using smart clothes to track behaviour and cognitive performance. Digital tablets and injectable nanodevices that serve as biomarkers are two more recent examples. But beyond that, everyday objects are also becoming smarter and more connected, which Wisdom argues, gives them a new potential for healthcare applications.

"The mirror we use in the morning can detect changes in skin condition and eye health. The bed we sleep in at night can detect sleep patterns, interruptions and body temperature" [11].

## 17.13   Digital Twins

A digital twin is a virtual representation of a real-world system, process, or product that may be used to replicate and assess its behaviour and functionality. Digital twins can be used to improve the efficiency and accuracy of various processes and tasks by providing a virtual representation of the system that can be tested and analyzed without the need for physical experimentation.

In a supply chain, a digital twin can be used to optimize and automate various processes, such as inventory management, quality control, and transportation.

Following are the examples of how a digital twin can be used in an HSC:

- **Inventory management:** A digital twin of the HSC can be used to simulate and analyze different scenarios for managing inventory levels. For example, the digital twin can be used to predict demand for different products and to optimize inventory levels based on this demand. This can help to reduce the risk of shortages or excesses and to improve the resourcefulness of the supply chain.
- **Quality control:** A digital twin of the HSC can be used to simulate and analyze different scenarios for quality control processes. For example, the digital twin can be used to identify potential problems or defects in products or processes and to suggest solutions to these problems. This can help to enhance the accuracy and efficiency of quality control in the supply chain.
- **Transportation:** A digital twin of the HSC can be used to simulate and analyze different scenarios for transportation processes. For example, the digital twin can be used to optimize routes and schedules for transporting goods and to identify potential problems or delays. This can help to improve the productivity and accuracy of the supply chain.

Overall, a digital twin can be a valuable tool for building an efficient and accurate supply chain in the healthcare industry by providing a virtual representation of the system that can be tested and analyzed to inform decision-making and optimize processes.

### Case Study 6 – Supplycycle – Using Digital Twins to drive efficiencies and reduce costs for manufacturers

A simulation and optimization engine from Deloitte called SupplyCycle aids manufacturers in finding better ways to balance their output and inventory. SupplyCycle analyses whole product portfolios and constructs digital twins of production lines to discover the best approach to meet demand and develop a model that minimises the amount of time needed to switch between items. To find the best production frequency for each commodity, it then optimises the expenses associated with production and storage [12].

The periodicity and sequencing recommendations are combined by SupplyCycle to provide the ideal production pattern. Additionally, by specifying precisely how much stock should be kept in each warehouse, it statistically optimises inventory [13].

In the final step of the simulation, SupplyCycle tests models against millions of possible permutations to validate findings and arrive at a new operational model. SupplyCycle has shown the potential to cut manufacturers' changeover times by up to 20 per cent and reduce inventories by up to 30 percent [13].

One of the biggest spirits firms in the world was the first to adopt SupplyCycle to streamline their intricate production processes. It was implemented across five production lines and in under, a year realised a working capital reduction of €1.81 million and additional savings of €210,000. More recent pilot projects involved a producer of home care items and a worldwide brewer. The formerly identified savings of €2.9 million and a working capital reduction opportunity of €700,000 across 10 production lines; the latter identified €1.1 million savings and a working capital reduction opportunity of €1.4 million across seven production lines [13].

## 17.14    Supply Chain Control Tower

The movement of goods and services in a supply chain is managed and optimised using a supply chain control tower, which is a central monitoring and control system. The control tower typically uses advanced technologies, such as the IoT, AI, and BDA, to collect and analyze data from various sources, such as inventory levels, transportation data, and customer data.

By giving real-time visibility and control over multiple processes and tasks, a supply chain control tower can significantly improve the efficiency and accuracy of the supply chain in the healthcare industry.

Following are examples of the role of a supply chain control tower in the healthcare sector:

- **Inventory management:** A supply chain control tower can be used to supervise and optimize inventory levels in real-time, based on data from various sources, such as demand patterns, supplier performance, and transportation data. This can help to reduce the risk of shortages or excesses and to improve the efficiency of the supply chain.
- **Quality control:** A supply chain control tower can be used to monitor and optimize the accuracy and traceability of quality control processes in the HSC. For instance, the control tower might be used to monitor how well products and services are performing and notify workers if any issues are found.
- **Transportation:** A supply chain control tower can be used to optimize and audit the transportation of goods in the HSC. For example, the control tower may be used to track the location and condition of shipments in transit, and to alert staff if any problems are identified.
- **Collaboration:** A supply chain control tower can be used to enable collaboration among multiple parties in the HSC, such as suppliers, manufacturers, distributors, and logistics providers. To explain with example, the control tower may be used to share documents, track progress, and communicate in real time.

Overall, by supplying actual visibility and control over numerous processes and tasks, a supply chain control tower can be a useful instrument for enhancing the effectiveness and accuracy of the HSC.

### Case Study 7 – IBM Sterling wants to untangle complexity with smarter supply chains

To assist businesses in achieving end-to-end visibility, tech giant IBM developed Sterling Supply Chain Insights with Watson, a control tower that uses AI to link data from disparate platforms. In order to analyse 80%

of unstructured data, including digital media and weather reports, Watson AI correlates data from both internal and external sources. Companies are now better able to comprehend and evaluate how these data affect their whole supply chain thanks to these capabilities. When disruptions happen, Sterling Supply Chain Insights supports quicker decision-making to link issue resolution with business objectives, optimising management while addressing unforeseen events. The IBM Sterling Supply Chain Suite, an integrated suite that enables businesses to connect vital data and supply chain operations while utilising AI, blockchain, and IoT, includes Sterling Supply Chain Insights as a key component. Intelligence Services and Control Tower capabilities of the IBM Sterling Supply Chain Suite are powered by Sterling Supply Chain Insights [14].

In order to reduce disruptions and enhance customer order management, Lenovo, a multinational technology and manufacturing firm, sought to gain greater visibility across its complex supply chain systems and data sources. Lenovo used IBM Watson Supply Chain Insights to optimise supply chain orchestration and achieve complete supply chain visibility. With the use of this technology, Lenovo adopted an AI-powered risk management strategy, cutting down on the average amount of time it took to respond to supply chain interruptions from days to minutes (up to 90% faster than previously). This gave Lenovo the chance to save expenses and increase revenue. Ultimately, these innovations could enable Lenovo to generate more precise delivery estimates for its clients in real-time, adding value to its offering [15].

## 17.15   Predictive Maintenance

Utilizing data and analytics to forecast when equipment or systems are likely to fail allows for the scheduling of preventative maintenance before a failure takes place. Predictive maintenance is a proactive approach to maintenance. By lowering the chance of unplanned downtime and increasing the dependability of equipment and systems, predictive maintenance can help to increase the efficiency and accuracy of maintenance processes.

In the healthcare industry, predictive maintenance can be particularly important for ensuring the availability and performance of critical equipment and systems, such as medical devices and hospital infrastructure.

Following are examples of how predictive maintenance can be used in an HSC:

- **Medical devices:** Predictive maintenance can be used to monitor the performance and condition of medical devices, such as imaging equipment, ventilators, and monitoring systems, and to predict when maintenance is required. This can help to assure the availability and authenticity of these devices and to cut-down the risk of unplanned downtime.
- **Hospital infrastructure:** Predictive maintenance can be used to monitor the performance and condition of hospital infrastructures, such as electrical systems, heating and cooling systems, and elevators, and to predict when maintenance is required. This can help to enforce the safety and authenticity of these systems and to assure the risk of unplanned downtime.
- **Supply chain management:** Predictive maintenance can be used to optimize the passage of services and goods in the HSC by predicting when maintenance is required for equipment and systems used in the supply chain. For instance, predictive maintenance may be used to optimize the maintenance of transportation equipment, such as trucks and planes, to reduce the risk of unplanned downtime.

Overall, predictive maintenance can be a valuable tool for re-modelling the competence and reliability of the HSC by reducing risk of unplanned downtime and optimizing maintenance

## 17.16   A Digital Transformation Roadmap

Implementing technology and procedures into a supply chain can increase responsiveness to client requests, cut costs, and improve efficiency. Here are some steps you can follow to create a roadmap for converting your legacy supply chain to an intelligent supply chain:

- **Assess the current state of your supply chain:** Identify the key bottlenecks, inefficiencies, and pain points in your current supply chain. This will help you determine the areas that need the most improvement.
- **Define your goals and objectives:** Clearly define what you hope to achieve with your digital transformation. This could

include improving efficiency, reducing costs, increasing flexibility, or enhancing customer satisfaction.

- **Identify opportunities for improvement:** Look for opportunities to use technology and data to enhance the efficiency and results of your supply chain. This could include automating processes, using analytics to optimize demand forecasting and inventory management, or implementing digital tools for communication and collaboration.
- **Choose the right technology:** Select the technology and tools that will help you achieve your goals and objectives. This could involve advanced analytics tools, transportation management systems, or enterprise resource planning (ERP) systems.
- **Develop a roadmap:** Create a roadmap that outlines the steps you will take to implement your digital transformation. This should include a timeline, budget, and resources needed to complete each step.
- **Implement and test:** Begin implementing the technology and processes you have chosen. Test and iterate as needed to ensure that everything is working as intended.
- **Monitor and optimize:** Continuously monitor and optimize your supply chain to ensure that it is meeting your goals and objectives. Use data and analytics to identify areas for improvement and make adjustments as needed.

By following these steps, you can create a roadmap for converting your legacy supply chain to an intelligent supply chain that is more efficient, cost-effective, and responsive to customer needs (Figure 17.3).

A plan to help HSCs evolve into digital organisations - Start small, grow quickly, and think broadly (Pilot projects, agile methodologies, value-driven approach, digital foundry); Identify internal cost and value drivers (value leakages like 30% logistics loss, 25% quality degrade in vaccines due to incorrect shipping, 20% temp sensitive deterioration); Build a blueprint of your data architecture (Landing AI accelerating quality of data management in manufacturing – AI Saas Solutions, AI transformation and Visual inspection system) ( Layers of Data Architecture – Data source, data collection, data storage, Data processing and insights generations and decision making); Collaboration and learn from other industries – industry 4.0 GSK is accelerating technology adoption in manufacturing – Siemens and GSK collaboration to develop state-of-the-art 'smart space').

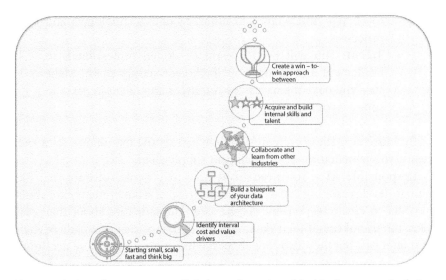

**Figure 17.3** A roadmap to support digital transformation of the biopharma supply chain.

## 17.17    Prerequisite for Designing Intelligent HSC

There are several prerequisites for implementing an intelligent supply chain. Here are some key factors to consider:

- **Data:** An intelligent supply chain relies on data to make informed decisions. Make sure you have the data infrastructure and systems in place to collect, store and analyze data from all areas of your supply chain.
- **Technology:** Implementing an intelligent supply chain requires the use of advanced technology, such as enterprise resource planning (ERP) systems, transportation management systems (TMS), and analytics tools. Make sure you have the necessary hardware and software in place to support these technologies.
- **Processes:** Review and optimize your current processes to ensure that they are efficient and aligned with your goals and objectives. Consider automating processes wherever possible to improve efficiency and reduce errors.
- **Culture:** Implementing an intelligent supply chain requires a shift in culture and mindset. Make sure you have buy-in from all stakeholders and that your organization is open

to change and willing to embrace new technologies and processes.

- **Talent:** You will need a team of skilled professionals to implement and manage an intelligent supply chain. Make sure you have the necessary resources and talent in place to support your transformation.

By addressing these prerequisites, you can set the foundation for a successful implementation of an intelligent supply chain.

**Responsible AI** - You need to be able to provide software that has human-level reasoning capabilities some grasp of what humans care about in order to create responsible AI,' he said. Humans care about their privacy, the useful use of their data, and the decisions that are made in their best interests, but they also care about having control over these decisions. Therefore, you must take into account these issues when designing AI that is moral and responsible [16].

## 17.18   HMI—Usage in HSC Management

Human-machine interface (HMI) refers to the interface through which humans and machines communicate and interact. In the HSC, HMI technologies can be used to improve efficiency and accuracy in a variety of ways. Some examples include:

**Automating tasks:** HMI technologies can be used to automate tasks such as inventory management and order processing, reducing the need for manual labour and increasing accuracy.

**Providing real-time data:** HMI technologies can provide real-time data on inventory levels, order status, and other key metrics, allowing healthcare organizations to make informed decisions and respond to changes in demand.

**Enhancing communication:** HMI technologies can be used to improve communication and collaboration among supply chain partners, allowing them to share information and coordinate activities more effectively.

**Improving accuracy:** HMI technologies can help reduce errors by automating tasks and providing real-time data, improving the accuracy and reliability of the HSC.

By using HMI technologies in the HSC, organizations can enhance the efficiency, decrease costs, and enhance quality of care they provide to patients.

## 17.19    HMI—A Face of the Supply Chain Control Tower

A centralised platform known as a supply chain control tower offers visibility and control over the whole supply chain. It gives businesses the ability to keep an eye on, evaluate, and optimise every part of their supply chain, including demand, inventory, and logistics.

Human-machine interface (HMI) technologies can be an important part of a supply chain control tower by providing a user-friendly interface through which humans can interact with the control tower system. HMI technologies can include graphical user interfaces (GUIs), touchscreens, and other types of interfaces that allow users to input data, view real-time data and perform other tasks.

By using HMI technologies, organizations can make their supply chain control tower more user-friendly and intuitive, making it easier for supply chain professionals to use and access the information and insights provided by the control tower (Figure 17.4). The supply chain control tower and the entire supply chain may benefit from this, increasing their efficacy and efficiency.

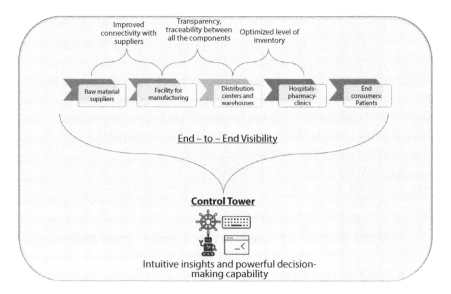

**Figure 17.4** End-to-end visibility of the supply chain.

## 17.20   The Intelligent Future of the Healthcare Industry

The future of intelligent supply chains is likely be driven by a combination of advances in technology and changes in customer expectations and behaviours. Some key trends and developments to watch include:

- **Greater use of automation and AI:** As technology continues to advance, we can expect to see greater use of automation and AI in supply chain. This could include the use of robotics and autonomous vehicles for handling and transportation, as well as the use of AI for tasks such as demand forecasting and optimization.
- **Increased focus on sustainability:** As consumers become more aware of environmental issues, there will be increasing pressure on organizations to adopt more sustainable practices in their supply chain. This could include the use of renewable energy, the adoption of circular economy principles, and the implementation of eco-friendly logistics solutions.
- **Increased adoption of blockchain:** Blockchain technology has the potential to revolutionize supply chain management by providing a secure, decentralized platform for tracking and verifying the movement of goods. We can expect to see increased adoption of blockchain in the supply chain as organizations look to improve transparency and reduce the risk of fraud and errors.
- **Greater use of real-time data:** As technology continues to improve, we can expect to see greater use of real-time data and analytics in the supply chain. This will enable organizations to make faster, more informed decisions and respond more quickly to changes in demand.
- **Increased use of technology:** We can expect to see continued advances in healthcare technology, including the development of new medical devices, diagnostic tools, and treatments. This could include the use of AI for tasks such as diagnosis and treatment planning, as well as the adoption of telemedicine and other digital health solutions.
- **Ageing population:** As the global population continues to age, there will be an increasing demand for healthcare

services, particularly in areas such as geriatric care and chronic disease management.

- **Changes in healthcare financing:** There is likely to be an ongoing debate about the best ways to finance healthcare, with some advocating for a shift towards universal healthcare systems and others supporting more market-based approaches.

- **Greater focus on preventative care:** There is likely to be a greater emphasis on preventative care as a way to reduce the burden of chronic diseases and reduce healthcare costs. This could include initiatives such as wellness programs and population health management.

- **Increased use of data and analytics:** The healthcare industry is likely to continue to adopt data analytics and other advanced technologies to enhance the efficiency and validity of care delivery. This could include the use of actual-time data to inform treatment decisions and the adoption of population health management approaches to identify and address the needs of at-risk populations.

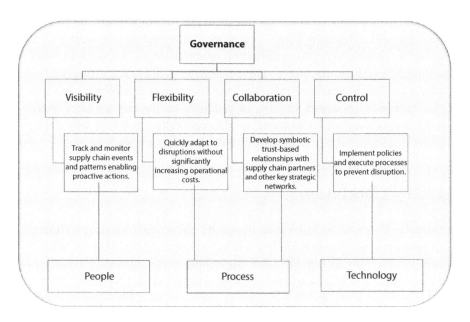

**Figure 17.5** Risk management and four pillars of a resilient supply chain.

Overall, the future of intelligent supply chains is likely to be characterized by a continued focus on improving efficiency, reducing costs, and enhancing customer satisfaction through the use of advanced technology and data-driven decision-making (Figure 17.5).

## Case Study 8 – GSK is accelerating technology adoption in manufacturing

GSK has created a "pharmaceutical factory of the future" as part of its embrace of the fourth industrial revolution. In 2016, GSK created the IIM Digitization Lab in Stevenage, UK, using the expertise other companies had obtained from utilising Industry 4.0 technologies. The "world of digital" offers enormous prospects, and GSK created this facility to serve as a proof-of-concept facility to show what a "data-based strategy" for manufacturing within the corporation could entail [17].

As advanced models are still being developed for pharma, GSK contacted numerous partners, including Siemens, to build the IIM Digitization Lab. It is essential to have a method for quickly evaluating how pertinent emerging technologies can help the pharma business model as game-changing technology advancements alter other industries. In this collaboration, Siemens played a crucial role in integrating data collection, utilisation, and workflow execution, including the abolition of paper records [18].

This cutting-edge facility with integrated technology can be utilised for training with a "learn by doing" philosophy, allowing various workers and operators to imitate regular production processes in an "artificial and safe" setting. 124 GSK thinks this is a quicker and more efficient training method to reduce the possibility of mistakes, and that it may completely alter how the business approaches learning in production. The current work being done in this "smart environment" could eventually result in a fully digital and virtual approach to designing and developing new medications.

# 17.21   Conclusion

The role of various technologies, like as AI and the IoT, in the creation of an intelligent and integrated HSC will be examined in this chapter. We will also go over how to digitally alter the supply chain, including creating a data architecture blueprint and working with other sectors. The future of the intelligent HSC and its function as a supply chain management command centre will be discussed in the last section.

# References

1. Aitken, M., Find out more, www.theimsinstitute.org.
2. Aitken, M., Find out more www.theimsinstitute.org.
3. Aera brings AI decision-making to Merck supply chain, IT Pro Today: IT News, How-Tos, Trends, Case Studies, Career Tips, More https://www.itprotoday.com/artificial-intelligence/aera-brings-ai-decision-making-merck-supply-chain.
4. Aera Technology, About us. https://www.aeratechnology.com/about-us.
5. Jakovljevic, P.J. and Com, W.T., Striving toward self-driving supply chains contents, Aera Technology, 2018.
6. FarmaTrust, Pharmaceutical blockchain and AI solutions, London. https://www.farmatrust.com/.
7. Tsinghua robot responds rapidly to COVID-19, Tsinghua University. https://www.tsinghua.edu.cn/en/info/1399/9814.htm.
8. Collaborative robots: A helping hand in healthcare. https://roboticsand automationnews.com/2020/05/11/collaborative-robots-a-helping-hand-in-healthcare/32189/.
9. Accelerator, Accelerating impact tech, Katapult. https://katapult.vc/startups/accelerators/.
10. Exploring human-machine collaboration in healthcare, GDS Group. https://gdsgroup.com/insights/article/exploring-human-machine-collaboration-in-healthcare/.
11. Human + machine: Accenture on the future of digital healthcare, Medical Device Network. https://www.medicaldevice-network.com/analysis/human-machine-accenture-future-digital-healthcare/.
12. Pioneering a better future, McLaren Applied. https://www.mclarenapplied.com/.
13. How Formula 1 technology is shaking up manufacturing sector | Impact report, Deloitte UK. https://www2.deloitte.com/uk/en/pages/impact-report-2019/stories/supplycycle.html, 2019.
14. IBM sterling solution brief.
15. Case studies corporate landing page, IBM. https://www.ibm.com/case-studies/search.
16. A journey into human/machine interactions in healthcare • healthcare-in-europe.com. https://healthcare-in-europe.com/en/news/a-journey-into-human-machine-interactions-in-healthcare.html.
17. Home, GSK. https://www.gsk.com/en-gb/.
18. (12) Digitalisation - the art of the possible at GSK, LinkedIn. https://www.linkedin.com/pulse/digitalisation-art-possible-gsk-mark-higham/.

# Index

.

Printed and bound by CPI Group (UK) Ltd, Croydon, CR0 4YY

27/10/2024

14580177-0005